Prominent Murder Victims of the Pre- and Early Islamic Periods
Including the Names of Murdered Poets

I0592998

Prominent Murder Victims of the Pre- and Early Islamic Periods Including the Names of Murdered Poets

أسماء المغتالين من الأشراف في الجاهلية والإسلام

وَأَسماءُ مَنْ قُتِلَ مِنَ الشُّعَراء

By

Muḥammad Ibn Ḥabīb (d. AH 245/AD 860)

تأليف

أبي جعفر محمد بن حبيب

المتوفى سنة ٢٤٥هـ/٨٦٠م

Introduced, Edited, Translated from the Arabic, and Annotated by

Geert Jan van Gelder

TUTA SUB AEGIDE PALLAS · 1683 ·

BRILL

LEIDEN | BOSTON

Originally published in hardback in 2021 as Volume 150 in the series Handbook of Oriental Studies – Handbuch der Orientalistik Section, Section 1, The Near and Middle East.

Cover illustration: Calligraphy by Nihad Nadam, 2025.

The Library of Congress has cataloged the hardcover edition as follows:

Names: Muḥammad ibn Ḥabīb, -860, author. | Gelder, G. J. H. van, editor. | Muḥammad ibn Ḥabīb, -860. Asmāʾ al-mughtālīn.
Title: Prominent murder victims of the pre- and early Islamic periods including the names of murdered poets / by Muḥammad Ibn Ḥabīb (d. AH 245/AD 860) ; introduced, edited, translated from the Arabic, and annotated by Geert Jan van Gelder.
Description: Leiden ; Boston : Brill, 2021. | Series: Handbook of Oriental studies. Section one, The Near and Middle East, 0169-9423 ; 150 | Includes bibliographical references and indexes. | Bilingual Arabic edition of Asmāʾ al-mughtālīn with English translation.
Identifiers: LCCN 2020052769 (print) | LCCN 2020052770 (ebook) | ISBN 9789004446342 (hardback) | ISBN 9789004446359 (ebook)
Subjects: LCSH: Islamic Empire–Biography–Early works to 1800. | Murder victims–Islamic Empire–Biography–Early works to 1800. | Poets, Arab–Islamic Empire–Biography–Early works to 1800.
Classification: LCC DS38.4.A2 M83513 2021 (print) | LCC DS38.4.A2 (ebook) | DDC 362.88/293092256–dc23
LC record available at https:///lccn.loc.gov/2020052769
LC ebook record available at https:///lccn.loc.gov/2020052770

Typeface for the Latin, Greek, and Cyrillic scripts: "Brill". See and download: brill.com/brill-typeface.

ISBN 978-90-04-75904-6 (paperback, 2026)
ISBN 978-90-04-44634-2 (hardback)
ISBN 978-90-04-44635-9 (e-book)

Copyright 2021 by Koninklijke Brill NV, Leiden, The Netherlands.
Koninklijke Brill NV incorporates the imprints Brill, Brill Hes & De Graaf, Brill Nijhoff, Brill Rodopi, Brill Sense, Hotei Publishing, mentis Verlag, Verlag Ferdinand Schöningh and Wilhelm Fink Verlag.
All rights reserved. No part of this publication may be reproduced, translated, stored in a retrieval system, or transmitted in any form or by any means, electronic, mechanical, photocopying, recording or otherwise, without prior written permission from the publisher. Requests for re-use and/or translations must be addressed to Koninklijke Brill NV via brill.com or copyright.com.

This book is printed on acid-free paper and produced in a sustainable manner.

Contents

Preface VII

Introduction 1

1 The Author 1
2 Sources on Ibn Ḥabīb 5
3 Works 6
4 The Book on Prominent Murder Victims and Poets Who Were Killed 9
5 Editions 21
6 The Translation 25
7 Transliteration 26
8 Abbreviations in the English 27
9 Abbreviations in the Notes to the Arabic Text 27

Text and Translation 29

Bibliography 347
List of Sections 362
Index of Persons, Tribes, Nations, Groups 366
Geographical Index 378
Index of Rhymes فهرست القوافي 381

Preface

Having collaborated happily and fruitfully with others for many years—with Gregor Schoeler and the editors of the Library of Arabic Literature on Abū l-ʿAlāʾ al-Maʿarrī's *Risālat al-ghufran* (*The Epistle of Forgiveness*), with Emily Selove on Abū l-Muṭahhar al-Azdī's *Ḥikāyat Abī l-Qāsim al-Baghdādī* (*The Portrait of Abū l-Qāsim al-Baghdādī*), with Emilie Savage-Smith and some six others on Ibn Abī Uṣaybiʿah's *ʿUyūn al-anbāʾ* (*A Literary History of Medicine*)—I deemed the time had come to work on some other text wholly, or almost wholly, by myself. This has obvious advantages and equally obvious disadvantages that need not be spelled out. Where some scholars (notably American ones) profusely thank scores of individuals (including extended family and sometimes pets) by name in their prefaces, forewords, and acknowledgements (once I counted 99 persons), I name only a handful. My wife, Sheila Ottway, read and corrected my English; Anna Livia Beelaert (Leiden), very helpfully tried to make sense of an obscure, garbled verse in some kind of Persian. During a brief visiting professsorship at Leiden University I had the privilege and pleasure to contribute to a course for MA students designed and taught by Peter Webb, whose work on brigand poets (*ṣaʿālīk*, *futtāk*) naturally overlapped with mine on murderers and their victims.

It should not be necessary to justify the choice of Muḥammad ibn Ḥabīb's book, written at some time in the middle of the ninth century. Murder is a perpetually fascinating subject. Ibn Ḥabīb's entertaining book, although occasionally used by historians, is not very well known, even though it is among the earliest Arabic sources, and it has never been translated. It is full of interesting, often lively stories, replete with incident, oddities, pithy sayings, and poetry. Unencumbered by long, scholarly chains of authority, free of over-ornate language or tedious and tendentious moralising, it is a work of literature as well as of history.

I thank Kathy van Vliet-Leigh (Brill) for her encouragement since the moment I told her about my work on the book; Abdurraouf Oueslati (Brill) for pleasant and effective email contact; an anonymous reader for some useful suggestions; and Cas Van den Hof (TAT Zetwerk) for his expert and meticulous typesetting.

Geert Jan van Gelder
Haren, the Netherlands, December 2020

Introduction

1 The Author

Abū Jaʿfar Muḥammad ibn Ḥabīb was born at an unknown date probably in Baghdad and he died in Samarra (on the Tigris some 125 km north of Baghdad), for a while the residence of the Abbasid caliphs during the third/ninth century, on 23 Dhū l-Ḥijjah of the year 245 of the Hijra, corresponding with 21 March 860.[1] Some sources have a slightly longer lineage for him: Muḥammad ibn Ḥabīb ibn Umayyah ibn ʿUmar (or ʿAmr),[2] but others say that Ḥabīb was not his father but his mother.[3] Being called after one's mother is somewhat unusual, in Arabic or English (there are Johnsons and Harrisons but no Janesons or Harrietsons), but in Arabic, though uncommon, it is not exactly rare.[4] It could mean that his father was unknown or a nobody. Ibn Ḥabīb was a *muʾaddib* (tutor) and an expert in genealogy (*ansāb*), historical accounts (*akhbār*), lexicography (*lughah*), poetry, and tribal history. A much earlier Ibn Ḥabīb, a prominent grammarian and philologist from Basra, Yūnus ibn Ḥabīb, who died at an advanced age c. 182/798, is also said to have been called Ibn Ḥabīb after his mother.[5]

Although he obviously knew a lot about Arab tribes, we do not know if he himself belonged to one; he is called a *mawlā*, client or freedman, attached to a branch of the Abbasid dynasty, the family of al-ʿAbbās ibn Muḥammad ibn ʿAlī,[6] so it is possible that he was not ethnically an Arab. Ḥabīb (which means "Beloved", male or female) can be a woman's name as well as a man's

1 The year AH 245 is given by all sources that give a death date, except Ibn Shākir, *ʿUyūn al-tawārīkh*, 405 who gives 250 (AD 864–865).

2 Ibn al-Nadīm, *Fihrist* (Sayyid), i, 327–329; Yāqūt, *Muʿjam al-udabāʾ*, xviii, 113; al-Suyūṭī, *Bughyah*, i, 73.

3 Abū l-Ṭayyib al-Lughawī, *Marātib*, 152; Ibn al-Nadīm, *Fihrist* (Sayyid), i, 328; Yāqūt, *Muʿjam al-udabāʾ*, xviii, 112 and other sources. Abū l-Ṭayyib adds that Ḥabīb, being a feminine name, is of the so-called diptote declination (*lā yuṣrafu*, implying that the fully inflected form would be *Ibnu Ḥabība* rather than *Ibnu Ḥabībin* if Ḥabīb had been the father).

4 See Levi Della Vida, "Muḥammad Ibn Ḥabīb's 'Matronymics of Poets'".

5 Ibn Khallikān, *Wafayāt*, vii, 248, al-Ṣafadī, *Wāfī*, xxix, 382. On Yūnus ibn Ḥabīb (a *mawlā*, like Muḥammad ibn Ḥabīb) see *EI2*, s.v. (R. Talmon), Sezgin, *Geschichte*, viii, 57–58, ix, 49–51, xvi, 271–272.

6 Ibn al-Nadīm, *Fihrist* (Sayyid), i, 328 mentions the Banū l-ʿAbbās ibn Muḥammad (i.e., the sons of al-ʿAbbās ibn Muḥammad ibn ʿAlī ibn ʿAbd Allāh ibn al-ʿAbbās, the last one being the eponymous ancestor of the dynasty); on this al-ʿAbbās ibn Muḥammad, who died in 185/801 or 186/802, see al-Ṣafadī, *Wāfī*, xvi, 638.

© KONINKLIJKE BRILL NV, LEIDEN, 2021 | DOI:10.1163/9789004446359_002 name (as, for instance, in the case of his contemporary, the Andalusian scholar ʿAbd al-Malik ibn Ḥabīb, who died in Cordova in 253/853), but one is tempted to believe the view that Ḥabīb was Muḥammad's mother and not his father. This would go some way towards explaining his extraordinary interest in mothers. Among his shorter works are *Man nusiba ilā ummihī min al-shuʿarāʾ* ("Poets Who are Traced to their Mother"); *Alqāb al-shuʿarāʾ wa-man yuʿrafu minhum bi-ummih* ("Nicknames of Poets and Those of them who are Known by their Mother's Name"); *Ummahāt al-Nabī* ("The Prophet's Female Ancestors"); *Ummahāt aʿyān Banī ʿAbd al-Muṭṭalib* ("The Female Ancestors of the Leading Members of the Banū ʿAbd al-Muṭṭalib"); *Ummahāt al-sabʿah min Quraysh* ("The Female Ancestors of the Seven of Quraysh"). His book *al-Muḥabbar* also has many sections on women, such as wives, mothers, and female relatives of famous men.[7]

Generally, a *muʾaddib* or tutor had a higher status than a *muʿallim*, a schoolteacher. In an anecdote about Ibn Ḥabīb, however, it seems that he equates himself, self-deprecatingly, with the despised *muʿallim*:[8]

> Ibn Ḥabīb said, "If you ask a man, 'What's your job?' and he answers, 'Schoolteacher (*muʿallim*)', then box his ears!"; and he quoted:
> A schoolteacher always remains a schoolteacher
> even if "he taught Adam all the names".[9]
> Whoever teaches infants is made infantile by them,
> even sons of caliphs and princes.

In al-Qifṭī's *al-Inbāh* this anecdote is told by a certain Abū Ru'bah, who says, "I went over to Ibn Ḥabīb in Mecca, while he was teaching the children of al-ʿAbbās ibn Muḥammad. He said 'If you ask a man …'" There are, however, no indications that Ibn Ḥabīb ever taught in Mecca and it appears that *fī Makkah* is a copyist's or editor's error for *fī maktabihī*, "in his school", or "classroom", as in the versions of Yāqūt's *Muʿjam al-udabāʾ*, Ibn Shākir's *ʿUyūn al-tawārīkh*, and al-Ṣafadī's *Wāfī*.

---

7 See Lichtenstädter, "Muḥammad Ibn Ḥabîb and his Kitâb al-Muḥabbar", 13–14.

8 Al-Marzubānī, *Nūr al-qabas*, 321; the anecdote is also in Yāqūt, *Muʿjam al-udabāʾ*, xviii, 112; Ibn al-Qifṭī, *Inbāh*, iii, 121; Ibn Shākir, *ʿUyūn al-tawārīkh*, 405; al-Ṣafadī *Wāfī*, ii, 326. The verb *anshada* ("he recited" or "he quoted") leaves it undecided whether he quoted someone else or was himself the poet. The former is perhaps more likely, since no other poetry by Ibn Ḥabīb is known, despite his great knowledge of poetry. A different version of the two lines is quoted, also anonymously, at the court of caliph al-Wāthiq (r. 227–232/842–847), see al-Iṣfahānī, *Aghānī*, ix, 236, al-Marzubānī, *Nūr al-qabas*, 223.

9 cf. Q al-Baqarah 2:31.

Perhaps his works, including his book on murder victims, *Asmāʾ al-mughtālīn*, were commissioned by his Abbasid patrons, as education for their sons. The books on horses (*al-Khayl*) and plants (*al-Nabāt*) are lost but it is likely that they were lexicographical, as was his work on obscure words in the Hadith (*Gharīb al-Ḥadīth*), also lost. His short lexicographical monograph *Khalq al-insān* (*Human Anatomy*), however, is extant and has been published; it is a pioneering work in its use, apparently for the first or almost the first time, of an alphabetical arrangement.[10]

Apart from being a private tutor, he also taught larger circles. Thaʿlab, a famous grammarian who died in 291/904 at the age of almost 90, relates that he attended a session (*majlis*) of Ibn Ḥabīb and was surprised that he did not dictate his material:[11]

> I said, "Come on, dictate! Why don't you?" But he didn't, and in the end I left. By God, he was someone who had memorized a great deal and he was trustworthy. Yaʿqūb [Ibn al-Sikkīt] was more knowledgeable than Ibn Ḥabīb, but the latter knew more about genealogy and historical accounts.

A different account of the same is related by Abū l-Ṭayyib al-Lughawī (d. 351/962):[12]

> Muḥammad ibn ʿAbd al-Wāḥid told us: Thaʿlab told us: Once I came past a session of Ibn Ḥabīb in the Friday Mosque. I went to join it and sat down, while he was dictating. But when I was seated he stopped dictating. "Go on," I said, "with what you were doing!" But he replied, "With you present? By God, I shall not!"

A yet fuller version is offered by al-Zubaydī (d. 379/989):[13]

> Abū l-ʿAbbās Aḥmad ibn Yaḥyā [Thaʿlab] said, I went to Muḥammad ibn Ḥabīb, for I had heard that he was dictating the poetry of Ḥassān ibn

---

10 Baalbaki, *The Arabic Lexicographical Tradition*, 151, 155–156, 330–331.

11 Thaʿlab, *Majālis*, 131; also quoted in al-Baghdādī, *Tārīkh Madīnat al-Salām*, iii, 88–89, Ibn al-Qifṭī, *Inbāh*, iii, 120.

12 Abū l-Ṭayyib al-Lughawī, *Marātib*, 153.

13 Al-Zubaydī, *Ṭabaqāt*, 139–140, also in Yāqūt, *Muʿjam al-udabāʾ*, xviii, 114–115, al-Qifṭī, *Inbāh*, iii, 120. The anecdote continues with Ibn Ḥabīb being asked a question about an expression in a line of poetry, which he was unable to answer properly, unlike Thaʿlab who proffered an explanation. After this, Ibn Ḥabīb gave up his sessions.

> Thābit.[14] But when he became aware I was present he stopped dictating. I left and then returned; I was friendly to him and he dictated. He used not to sit in the Friday Mosque and I reproached him for that, but he refused. It was only after my persisting that he had sessions in the Friday Mosque, where people gathered.

His reputation is generally high, yet there is at least one report of his unscrupulous attitude as a scholar. Although Muḥammad ibn ʿImrān al-Marzubānī (d. 394/993), quoted by Yāqūt, calls Ibn Ḥabīb's books "sound" (*ṣaḥīḥah*),[15] he also relates: "It is said that Ibn Ḥabīb raided other people's books and claimed them as his, omitting their names".[16] A gross example of such plagiarism is given, involving the wholesale copying and appropriating of a work by the obscure Ismāʿīl ibn Abī ʿUbayd Allāh. Al-Marzubānī continues:

> I do not know of any scholar who did such a thing, or who would deem it right to lower himself to this ugly level. I think that what brought him to this was the fact that the book by Ismāʿīl was not often transmitted and not widely in the possession of literate people, so that Ibn Ḥabīb guessed that his doing would not be revealed and his plagiarism would obliterate his colleague's name.[17]

Very little about his personal life is known. That he is called Abū Jaʿfar shows that he had at least one son.[18]

14 Ḥassān ibn Thābit was the first major poet who supported the prophet Muḥammad.

15 Yāqūt, *Muʿjam al-udabāʾ*, xviii, 112.

16 Yāqūt, *Muʿjam al-udabāʾ*, xviii, 113; Ibn al-Qifṭī, *Inbāh*, iii, 121; al-Ṣafadī, *Wāfī*, ii, 326; al-Suyūṭī, *Bughyah*, i, 73.

17 Yāqūt, *Muʿjam al-udabāʾ*, xviii, 113.

18 Ḥājjī Khalīfah, *Kashf al-ẓunūn*, col. 167–168 mentions "Abū Muḥammad Jaʿfar ibn Muḥammad ibn Ḥabīb al-Baghdādī, who died in AH 245" as the author of a work on proverbial sayings on the pattern *afʿal*. But this work is ascribed to Muḥammad ibn Ḥabīb in other, older sources such as Ibn al-Nadīm's *Fihrist* (see below), and this Jaʿfar ibn Muḥammad ibn Ḥabīb may be spurious.

2 Sources on Ibn Ḥabīb[19]

The following is a list, arranged chronologically, of the main sources about Ibn Ḥabīb and his works, indicating whether or not his book on murder victims (here abbreviated as AM) is mentioned.

Abū l-ʿAbbās Aḥmad ibn Yaḥyā Thaʿlab (d. 291/904), al-*Majālis* [*The Sessions*], 131.

ʿAbd Allāh ibn al-Muʿtazz (d. 296/908), *Ṭabaqāt al-shuʿarāʾ* [*The Classes of Poets*], mentions him as a source on Abbasid poets, 341, 359, 417.

Abū l-Ṭayyib al-Lughawī (d. 351/962), *Marātib al-naḥwiyyīn* [*The Ranks of Grammarians*], 152–153 (no mention of AM).

Abū l-Faraj al-Iṣfahānī (d. c. 363/972), *al-Aghānī* [(*The Book of*) *Songs*], quotes Ibn Ḥabīb many times as a source.

Abū Bakr al-Zubaydī (d. 379/989), *Ṭabaqāt al-naḥwiyyīn* [*The Classes of Grammarians*], 139–140 (no mention of AM).

Ibn al-Nadīm (d. c. 380/990), *al-Fihrist* [*The Catalogue*] (ed. Flügel) 106–107, (ed. Sayyid) i, 327–329, in the chapter on historians (*akhbāriyyūn*) and genealogists (*nassābūn*); see below for the book list given for Ibn Ḥabīb. AM is listed as *Maqātil al-fursān.*

al-Khaṭīb al-Baghdādī (d. 463/1071), *Tārīkh Madīnat al-Salām* [*The History of Baghdad*], iii, 87–88 (no mention of AM).

Yāqūt (d. 626/1229), *Muʿjam al-udabāʾ* [*Dictionary of Literary Men*], xviii, 112–117, quoting al-Marzubānī,[20] al-Zubaydī, and Ibn al-Nadīm (lists AM as *Maqātil al-fursān*).

Ibn al-Qifṭī (d. 646/1248), *Inbāh al-ruwāh ʿalā anbāʾ al-nuḥāh* [*Informing Transmitters about the Accounts of Grammarians*], iii, 119–121 (no mention of AM).

Ibn Shākir al-Kutubī (d. 764/1364), *ʿUyūn al-tawārīkh* (AH *219–250*) [*Highlights of Histories*], 405–406 (lists AM as *Maqātil al-fursān*).

---

19 Modern sources on Ibn Ḥabīb include: *EI2*, vii, 401–402 (Ilse Lichtenstädter); Brockelmann, *Geschichte*, i, 106, Supplement, i, 165–166; Sezgin, *Geschichte*, i (mentioning him as source of *Aghānī*: 80, 250, 179, 180n; 310); idem, *Geschichte*, ii (see index); idem, *Geschichte*, vii, 347; idem, *Geschichte*, viii, 90–92; idem, *Geschichte*, xvi, 154–158 (158 on AM), 280–281; Lichtenstädter, "Muḥammad Ibn Ḥabîb and his Kitâb al-Muḥabbar"; Levi Della Vida, "Muḥammad Ibn Ḥabīb's 'Matronymics of Poets'"; Bray, "Lists and Memory: Ibn Qutayba and Muḥammad b. Ḥabīb" (see pp. 221–226 on Ibn Ḥabīb's *al-Muḥabbar*; she mentions AM, calling it a "booklet", in a note, 230–231); Tayyara, "Ibn Ḥabīb's *Kitāb al-Muḥabbar* and its Place in Early Islamic Historical Writing" (it does not mention AM).

20 Yāqūt is quoting no doubt from al-Marzubānī's *al-Muqtabas*, which is preserved only in its abridged form entitled *Nūr al-qabas*, in which Ibn Ḥabīb does not have an entry.

al-Ṣafadī (d. 764/1363), *al-Wāfī bi-l-wafayāt* [*The Completion of the Obituaries*], ii, 325–327 (lists *AM* as *Maqātil al-fursān*).
al-Suyūṭī (d. 911/1505), *Bughyat al-wuʿāh fī ṭabaqāt al-lughawiyyīn wa-l-nuḥāh* [*The Desire of the Attentive: On the Classes of Lexicographers and Grammarians*], i, 73–74 (lists *AM* as *Maqātil al-fursān*).
Ḥājjī Khalīfah (d. 1068/1657), *Kashf al-ẓunūn ʿan asāmī l-kutub wa-l-funūn* [*Dispelling Doubts about the Names of Books and Disciplines*], col. 1778–1779 (*Maqātil al-fursān*).
ʿAbd al-Qādir al-Baghdādī (d. 1093/1682), *Khizānat al-adab wa-lubb lubāb lisān al-ʿArab* [*The Treasury of Erudition and the Prime of the Pith of the Arabic Language*], mentions and quotes from *K. al-Maqtūlīn ghīlatan* i, 24, 53 (on ʿĀmir ibn Juwayn, *AM* § 79), ii, 271–272 (on Ṭasm and Jadīs, *AM* § 3), xi, 270–271 (on ʿAmr ibn Masʿūd and Khālid ibn Naḍlah, *AM* § 13), and from *K. Man qutila min al-shuʿarāʾ* ii, 104 (on Suḥaym ʿAbd Banī l-Ḥasḥās, *AM* § 118), 217 (on ʿAbīd ibn al-Abraṣ, *AM* § 81), iv, 441 (on Bishr ibn Abī Khāzim, *AM* § 83).

3 Works

Among Muḥammad ibn Ḥabīb's books are several important historical sources, notably his *al-Muḥabbar* and *al-Munammaq*, both of which have been preserved and have been published. The latter is devoted to the members of Quraysh, the tribe of the Prophet. *Al-Muḥabbar* is essentially a book of lists, of genealogy and categories of people, with sections on the most diverse pre-Islamic and early Islamic topics. Ibn Ḥabīb is not afraid to include lists that contain only one member, as was observed by Albrecht Noth and Julia Bray:[21] an extreme case that does not apply to the present book about murderers. Ibn al-Nadīm's *al-Fihrist* (*The Catalogue*) lists the following titles by Ibn Ḥabīb:

al-Amthāl ʿalā afʿal wa-yusammā l-Munammaq [on proverbial expressions of the form "more so-and-so than …"; obviously not the work published as *al-Munammaq*. Partly published in *Majallat al-Majmaʿ al-ʿIlmī al-ʿIrāqī* 4 (1956) by Muḥammad Ḥamīd Allāh (not seen)]
al-Nasab [on genealogy]
al-Suʿūd wa-l-ʿUmūr ["Saʿds and ʿAmrs". The editions by Flügel and Sayyid have *al-Suʿūd wa-l-ʿumūd*, of uncertain meaning, which is copied by Yāqūt and

21 Noth, *The Early Arabic Historical Tradition* (tr. Michael Bonner), 97, mentioned in Bray, "Lists and Memory", 227 note 4.

al-Ṣafadī. I follow Sezgin, *Geschichte*, xvi, 157 in taking it to be about tribal names involving the two very common names Saʿd and ʿAmr.[22]]

al-ʿAmāʾir wa-l-Rabāʾiʿ[23] [*fī l-nasab*] [on genealogy; it may be a similar work on two common names. The singular of ʿAmāʾir could be ʿAmīrah or ʿUmārah, that of Rabāʿiʾ is Rabīʿah]

al-Muwashshaḥ [subject unknown]

al-Muʾtalif wa-l-mukhtalif [*fī l-nasab*] [On genealogy; probably an excerpt of *K. al-Qabāʾil al-kabīr*. Published by F. Wüstenfeld in 1850 and by Ibrāhīm al-Abyārī in 1980]

al-Muḥabbar [published by Ilse Lichtenstädter]

al-Muqtanā [subject unknown]

Gharīb al-Ḥadīth [on strange words in the Hadith]

al-Anwāʾ [on the "rain stars" and traditional Arab meteorology]

al-Mushajjar [subject unknown][24]

al-Muwashshā [subject unknown]

Man ustujībat daʿwatuh [on those whose prayers (or summons?) were answered]

al-Mudhahhab fī akhbār al-shuʿarāʾ wa-ṭabaqātihim [on the lives of poets]

Naqāʾiḍ Jarīr wa-ʿUmar ibn Lajaʾ [the flytings of Jarīr and ʿUmar ibn Lajaʾ]

Naqāʾiḍ Jarīr wa-l-Farazdaq [the flytings of Jarīr and al-Farazdaq, transmitted from Abū ʿUbaydah; published by A.A. Bevan]

al-Mufawwaf [subject unknown]

Tārīkh al-khulafāʾ [history of the caliphs]

Man summiya bi-bayt qālahū [on those called after a verse they composed]

Maqātil al-fursān [on the killings of heroes]. This is clearly the book presented here, which is in fact a combination of two works: *Asmāʾ al-mughtālīn min al-ashrāf fī l-Jāhiliyyah wa-l-Islām* [*The Names of Prominent Murder Victims of the Pre- and (Early) Islamic Periods*] and *Asmāʾ man qutila min al-shuʿarāʾ* [*The Names of those Poets who were Killed*].

Alqāb al-shuʿarāʾ [*wa-man yuʿrafu minhum bi-ummih*] [on the nicknames of poets and those called after their mother; published by ʿAbd al-Salām Hārūn]

---

22 On ʿUmūr and Suʿūd as possible plurals of ʿAmr and Saʿd, both extremely common personal names, see Sībawayh, *Kitāb*, ii, 96–97. Compare e.g. Ibn Ḥabīb, *Munammaq*, 148, where someone asks, "Who are the Saʿds (*al-Suʿūd*)? Saʿd of Tamīm, Saʿd of Hawāzin, Saʿd of Hudhaym, Saʿd of Bakr?"

23 Thus ed. Flügel and Yāqūt; Sayyid's edition of *al-Fihrist* has *al-rawābil*, in al-Ṣafadī, *Wāfī* it is *al-r.bāʿ*, and in Ibn Shākir, *ʿUyūn* it is *al-riyāḥ*.

24 The term *mushajjar*, derived from *shajarah*, "tree", is sometimes used for works written in tree format. Rosenthal, *History of Muslim Historiography*, 97, thinks Ibn Ḥabīb's work could have been an early example of a genealogical book in tree format.

Kunā l-shuʿarāʾ [*wa-man ghalabat kunyatuhū ʿalā ismih*] [on the paedonymics (names beginning with Abū) of poets and those whose paedonymic prevailed over their given name; published by ʿAbd al-Salām Hārūn]
al-ʿAql [The usual sense of *ʿaql* is "intelligence, reason", but in view of Ibn Ḥabīb's interests a less common meaning, "bloodwit", seems more likely.]
al-Simāt [on brand marks[25]]
Ummahāt al-Nabī [on the female ancestors of the Prophet; facsim. of MS published by Ḥasan ʿAlī Maḥfūẓ]
Ayyām Jarīr allatī dhakarahā fī shiʿrih [on the tribal "battle days" mentioned by Jarīr in his poetry]
Ummahāt aʿyān Banī ʿAbd al-Muṭṭalib [on the female ancestors of the prominent offspring of ʿAbd al-Muṭṭalib, the Prophet's grandfather]
al-Muqtabas [subject unknown]
Ummahāt al-Sabʿah min Quraysh [on the female ancestors of the "Seven of Quraysh" (it is not clear who these seven are)]
al-Khayl [on horses]
al-Nabāt [on plants]
al-Arḥām allatī bayn Rasūl Allāh wa-bayn aṣḥābihī siwā l-ʿaṣabah [on the Prophet's kinship with his Companions, other than those in the male line]
Alqāb al-Yaman wa-Rabīʿāh wa-Muḍar [on the nicknames among the tribes of al-Yaman (South Arabs) and Rabīʿah and Muḍar (North Arabs)]
al-Alqāb wa-yashtamilu ʿalā alqāb al-qabāʾil [on nicknames, including tribal ones]
Kitāb al-Qabāʾil al-kabīr wa-l-ayyām [the great book of tribes and battle days]

To these can be added:

al-Munammaq fī akhbār Quraysh [on the tribe of Quraysh; published by Khūrshīd Aḥmad Fāriq]
Man nusiba ilā ummihi min al-shuʿarāʾ [on poets called after their mother, published by G. Levi Della Vida in *Journal of the American Oriental Society*, 65 (1942), 156–171, and by ʿAbd al-Salām Hārūn]
Khalq al-insān [a lexicographical work on human anatomy; published by Khalīl Ibrāhīm al-ʿAṭiyyah]
Several redactions of and commentaries on *Dīwān*s, such as those of Jarīr [published by Nuʿmān Muḥammad Amīn Ṭāhā]; Ibn al-Dumaynah [published by

25 On the importance of brand marks, *simāt*, of camels and other livestock see e.g. al-Jāḥiẓ, *Ḥayawān*, i, 161.

Aḥmad Rātib al-Naffākh]; and Ru'bah ibn al-ʿAjjāj [preserved in MS]. Yāqūt mentions among Ibn Ḥabīb's works *Kitāb dīwān Zufar ibn al-Ḥārith*; *Kitāb shiʿr al-Shammākh*; *Kitāb shiʿr al-Uqayshir*; *Kitāb shiʿr al-Ṣimmah*; and *Kitāb shiʿr Labīd al-ʿĀmirī*.[26]

4 The Book on Prominent Murder Victims and Poets Who Were Killed

Several of Ibn Ḥabīb's books have florid titles, such as were becoming frequent in his time. They include the two major works that have been published: *al-Munammaq* could be translated as *The Adorned* (*Book*) and *al-Muḥabbar* as *The Variegated* (*Book*) or (*The Book*) *Woven with Stripes*. There are at least five more such titles ascribed to him,[27] but one should not conclude that these metaphors reflect the author's style in the works themselves. In none of his extant works does Ibn Ḥabīb use ornate language and he eschews any rhetorical display such as rhymed prose or striking figurative speech. This is also the case in *Asmāʾ al-mughtālīn*, his book on murder victims together with the second part, on poets who were killed: the style is straightforward and the only "literary" elements in it are the poetry that is quoted and the occasional utterances in rhymed prose (*sajʿ*). His great interest in poetry is evident from this book and from his many other works on poets and their works; yet he was not a poet himself.

His accounts are also markedly concise and one often finds longer and more detailed versions of the murder stories in other, multi-volume sources, such as al-Balādhurī's *Genealogies of Prominent People*, al-Ṭabarī's *History*, and al-Iṣfahānī's *Book of Songs*. But there are many details in some stories, some gruesome and some even funny, as when a Persian called Fayrūz sneaks into the bedroom of his victim, al-Aswad ibn Kaʿb, at night but cannot see him in the dark, and when the victim's colluding wife helpfully points out where her husband is sleeping, the murderer discovers he has left his sword outside (§ 28). Almost grotesque is the highly dramatic story of Hudbah and Ziyādah, which involves no fewer than three noses that are cut off (§ 110).

---

26 Yāqūt, *Muʿjam al-udabāʾ*, xviii, 116–117.

27 *Al-Muwashshaḥ, al-Muwashshā, al-Mushajjar, al-Mufawwaf, al-Mudhahhab fī akhbār al-shuʿarāʾ wa-ṭabaqātihim*. He seems to have been fond of the passive participle pattern *mufaʿʿal* for he titles of his major books (cf. Tayyara, "Ibn Ḥabīb's *Kitāb al-Muḥabbar*", 393 note 10).

As is shown in the list of sources given above, Ibn Ḥabīb's book is sometimes given a different title: *Maqātil al-fursān* ("Killings of Knights, or Heroes"),[28] perhaps in order to align it with a quite extensive literature on *maqātil* in Arabic,[29] a well-known example being *Maqātil al-Ṭālibiyyīn* by Abū l-Faraj al-Iṣfahānī, on Shi'ite and 'Alid martyrs. Works called *Maqātil al-fursān* (*Killings of Heroes*) are also attributed to Abū 'Ubaydah,[30] al-Qālī,[31] Ibn Abī Ṭāhir Ṭayfūr,[32] and al-Khaṭīb al-Tibrīzī.[33] Al-Mas'ūdī mentions Abū 'Ubaydah's *Maqātil fursān al-'Arab* (*Killings of Arab Heroes*) and a work by himself called *Maqātil fursān al-'Ajam* (*Killings of Non-Arab Heroes*).[34] A work entitled *Maqātil al-ashrāf* (*Killings of Nobles*) is attributed to Abū 'Ubaydah[35] and a book called *Maqātil al-shu'arā'* (*Killings of Poets*) is attributed to Ibn Abī Ṭāhir Ṭayfūr.[36]

The author could have called his book simply *Kitāb al-mughtālīn*, "the Book of Murder Victims". Instead, he chose to entitle it *Kitāb asmā' al-mughtālīn*, "the Book of the Names of Murder Victims". But although names, lineages, and tribal affiliations abound and are undoubtedly important to the author, they are not the main concern of the book. The general reader may be put off by the large number of Arabic names, some of which are inordinately long by modern standards, going back many generations (even as many as twelve). *Asmā' al-mughtālīn* is largely unencumbered, however, by *isnāds*, chains of authority at the beginning of each *khabar* or report.[37] Unlike many similar texts, including his other books *al-Muḥabbar* and *al-Munammaq*, the author does not mention his sources.[38] One can surmise that they were present in the original but were left out by a transmitter or copyist more interested in storytelling than in scholarly accuracy and reliability—not that an *isnād* guarantees historical truth, of

28 See the entries on Ibn Ḥabīb in Ibn al-Nadīm, *Fihrist* (Flügel) 106–107, (Sayyid) i, 327–329; Yāqūt, *Mu'jam al-udabā'*, xviii, 112–117; al-Ṣafadī, *Wāfī*, ii, 325–327; al-Suyūṭī, *Bughyat al-wu'āh*, i, 73–74.

29 On the genre see Günther, "*Maqātil* Literature in Medieval Islam"; it deals mostly with the deaths of members of the Prophet's family and does not mention Ibn Ḥabīb.

30 Yāqūt, *Mu'jam al-udabā'*, xix, 161, Ibn Khallikān, *Wafayāt*, v, 239.

31 Yāqūt, *Mu'jam al-udabā'*, vii, 29, Ibn Khallikān, *Wafayāt*, i, 226.

32 Ibn al-Nadīm, *Fihrist* (Sayyid), i, 452, Yāqūt, *Mu'jam al-udabā'*, iii, 91.

33 Yāqūt, *Mu'jam al-udabā'*, xx, 28, Ibn al-Anbārī, *Nuzhat al-alibbā'*, 271.

34 Al-Mas'ūdī, *Tanbīh*, 102.

35 Yāqūt, *Mu'jam al-udabā'*, xix, 161–162, Ibn Khallikān, *Wafayāt*, v, 239.

36 Ibn al-Nadīm, *Fihrist* (Sayyid), i, 452, Yāqūt, *Mu'jam al-udabā'*, iii, 91.

37 There are some exceptions: see e.g. §§ 37, 39, 51, 73.

38 In other works, where he does mention sources, he is not always careful (Lichtenstädter, "Muḥammad Ibn Ḥabîb", 27: "Ibn Ḥabîb's carelessness in quoting his sources is somewhat astonishing at a time when his contemporaries are very careful to quote their authorities in full ...").

course. That such chains of authority were part of the original text at least in some cases can be seen from quotations, as when Abū l-Faraj al-Iṣfahānī opens the story of al-Jassās ibn Murrah (*AM* § 11) as follows:[39]

> ʿAlī ibn Sulaymān al-Akhfash [d. 315/927] informed me: al-Ḥasan ibn al-Ḥusayn al-Sukkarī [d. 275/888 or 290/903] informed us: Muḥammad ibn Ḥabīb [d. 245/860] told us, on the authority of Ibn al-Aʿrābī [d. 231/846], on the authority of al-Mufaḍḍal [d. after 163/780], on the authority of Abū ʿUbaydah [d. 209/824–825], that the last person to be killed in the war of Bakr and Taghlib was Jassās ibn Murrah ibn Dhuhl ibn Shaybān. He is the one who killed Kulayb ibn Rabīʿah …

The chronology seems odd, in that al-Mufaḍḍal died long before Abū ʿUbaydah, but the latter is said to have been born in 110/728, so he could easily have been al-Mufaḍḍal's source.

The entry on ʿAbd Allāh ibn Mūsā al-Hādī (§ 71) has a parallel in *Aghānī*, x, 197 with the following *isnād*: *akhbaranī ʿAlī ibn Sulaymān al-Akhfash fī kitāb al-mughtālīn qāla ḥaddathanā Abū Saʿīd al-Sukkarī ʿan Muḥammad ibn Ḥabīb qāla …*; Sezgin remarks[40] that Abū l-Faraj al-Iṣfahānī used a book entitled *Asmāʾ al-mughtālīn* by ʿAlī ibn Sulaymān al-Akhfash (d. 315/927), which via al-Sukkarī goes back to a book by Ibn Ḥabīb, not identical with the printed text, because the fragments in *Aghānī*, ii, 97–105, 105–126, 133, 140–146 are much longer. A source of Ibn Ḥabīb's book is a work by Ibn al-Aʿrābī.[41] The absence of sources in *Asmāʾ al-mughtālīn* may therefore be attributed to copyists or an unknown redactor. One cannot, however, be wholly certain that this is always the case.

Many of the murders are part of the *ayyām al-ʿArab*, "the Battle Days of the Arabs", an extensive genre of stories with poetry about the pre-Islamic tribal feuds and wars.[42] These stories were avidly collected by historians, genealogists, and philologists. Among Ibn Ḥabīb's many lost works is *Kitāb al-qabāʾil al-kabīr wa-l-ayyām* ("The Great Book of Tribes and Battle Days"), apparently his *magnum opus*. Ibn al-Nadīm says that he compiled it for al-Fatḥ ibn Khāqān, a high

---

39 Al-Iṣfahānī, *Aghānī*, v, 60–61.

40 Sezgin, *Geschichte*, ii, 179, in the entry on ʿAdī ibn Zayd.

41 Al-Iṣfahānī, *Aghānī*, ii, 97, 133, 140.

42 On the *ayyām al-ʿArab* see e.g. Caskel, "*Aijām al-ʿArab*: Studien zur altarabischen Epik"; Meyer, *Der historische Gehalt der Aiyām al-ʿArab*; *EI2*, "Ayyām al-ʿArab" (E. Mittwoch); *EI3*, "Ayyām al-ʿArab" (Alan Jones); al-Qāḍī, "La composante narrative des «Journées des Arabes» (*Ayyām al-ʿArab*)".

official and close companion of caliph al-Mutawakkil; both were murdered together in 247/861. Ibn al-Nadīm continues:[43]

> I have seen, in the presence of al-Qāsim ibn Abī l-Khaṭṭāb ibn al-Furāt,[44] this selfsame copy, written on Ṭalḥī paper,[45] some twenty volumes but incomplete, indicating that it may have comprised some forty volumes, each volume containing two hundred folios or more. This copy had an index of tribes and battle days mentioned in the book in the handwriting of al-Sindī ibn ʿAlī, the bookseller, of some fifteen folios, in an inferior handwriting.

It is possible that the stories in *Asmāʾ al-mughtālīn* were taken, perhaps in shortened form, from this much larger work. Sayyid Kasrawī Ḥasan, in the introduction to his edition of the book, thinks that Ibn Ḥabīb may never have finished it and that what we have is a *musawwadah*, a draft.[46] The time of composition is unknown but it was written after his *al-Munammaq*, because on one occasion (§ 26) he refers to it, as *Akhbār Quraysh*, for more details.

The word *mughtāl* is ambiguous: it can be both an active and a passive participle of the verb *ightāla* ("to murder, assassinate"). One notices, incidentally, that many murderers were themselves murdered. Nevertheless, it is clear that in the title and elsewhere in the book *mughtāl* has a passive sense, "murdered". The words most often used for "killer" or "murderer" are *qātil* or *fātik*. There is a difference between the verbs *qatala* and *ightāla*, or between books on *maqātil* and on *mughtālūn*: the former is about any kind of killing, any violent death, the latter more precisely is about being murdered or assassinated, excluding being killed in battle or by execution; the victim is usually unaware until the last. *Ightiyāl* (the verbal noun) and its synonym *ghīlah* imply guile and cunning.[47]

---

43 Ibn al-Nadīm, *Fihrist* (ed. Sayyid), i, 329, (ed. Flügel), 107, quoted in Yāqūt, *Muʿjam al-udabāʾ*, xviii, 116.

44 The son of Abū l-Khaṭṭāb al-Faḍl ibn Jaʿfar ibn al-Furāt (d. 327/938), a high official and vizier.

45 Quality paper made of cotton, called after the Ṭāhirid ruler of Khorasan, Ṭalḥah ibn Ṭāhir, see Ibn al-Nadīm, *Fihrist*, i, 48, *EI2*, "Kāghad" (Cl. Huart & A. Grohmann).

46 SKḤ, 12–13.

47 Ibn Manẓūr, *Lisān al-ʿArab* (*GhWL*): *ightālahū: ahlakahū wa-akhadhahū min ḥaythu lam yadri; … qatala fulānun fulānan ghīlatan ay fī ghtiyāl wa-khufyah wa-qīla huwa an yakhdaʿa l-insān ḥattā yaṣīra ilā makān qad istakhfā lahū fīh man yaqtuluhū*. There is some uncertainty about the root of the verb, because there are similar definitions under *GhYL*: *al-ghīlah bi-l-kasr: al-khadīʿah wa-l-ightiyāl, wa-qutila fulān ghīlatan ay khudʿah wa-huwa an yakhdaʿahū fa-yadhhaba bihī ilā mawḍiʿ fa-idhā ṣāra ilayhi qatalahū … al-ghīlah fī kalām al-ʿArab īṣāl al-sharr wa-l-qatl ilayhi min ḥaythu lā yaʿlamu wa-lā yashʿuru … qatalahū ghīlatan*

Nevertheless, some deaths in the book are better described as executions than as murders; the dividing line between the two is often indistinct. Murders and assassinations are committed by proxy, ordered by those in power wishing to conceal their evil intentions. But such murders sometimes come out. The verb *dassa*, "to scheme, plot, to send someone secretly, to administer (a poison) surreptitiously, etc.", is used in twelve chapters by Ibn Ḥabīb in connection with such murders.[48] The story of Ṭarafah (§ 82) offers the Arabic equivalent of the motif of the letter that condemns the bearer, known from Hebrew (Uriah), Greek (Bellerophon), and English (Rosencrantz and Guildenstern).

The book is in fact two texts, perhaps originally separate but joined together, one on prominent murder victims (*al-mughtālīn min al-ashrāf*) and one on poets who were killed (*man qutila min al-shuʿarāʾ*). The former title uses the verb *ightāla*, "to murder, assassinate", the second uses the verb *qatala*, "to kill", which of course is not the same as "to murder". This is reflected in the text. As some poets were actually murdered (and poets often are prominent people), a number of them are found in the first part, with a cross-reference in the second: "He has already been mentioned among the murder victims" (§§ 84, 90, 92, 98, 111, 115).

Although the verb *ightāla* has a connotation of stealth, all murderers in the book are known by name and their identity is at most only temporarily hidden. In one case a revelation brought by the angel Gabriel to the Prophet Muḥammad was necessary to identify the killer (§ 27 note 324), but most perpetrators do not take much trouble to remain unknown after the act. The Jewish woman who prepared a shoulder of mutton for the Prophet and a companion even asked beforehand which part of the sheep the Prophet liked best before she put lots of poison in it.

Ibn Ḥabīb's interest in murder stories is also apparent in his *al-Muḥabbar*, which has sections on *futtāk al-jāhiliyyah* (*The Reckless Men* [or *Killers*] *of the Pre-Islamic Period*) (192–216), *futtāk al-Islām* (*The Reckless Men of Islam*) (212–232) and sundry shorter sections: *aʿraq al-ʿArab fī l-qatl* (*Those Arabs Most Rooted in Killing*)[49] (189); *tasmiyat alladhīna qatalū Kaʿb ibn al-Ashraf* (*Naming Those Who Killed Kaʿb ibn al-Ashraf*) (282); *alladhīna qatalū Ibn Abī l-Ḥuqayq* (*Those Who Killed Ibn Abī l-Ḥuqayq*) (282–283); *alladī qatala l-ʿAṣmāʾ bint Marwān* (*The Man Who Killed al-ʿAṣmāʾ bint Marwān*) (283). The word *fātik* (pl.

---

idhā qatalahū min ḥaythu lā yaʿlamu, wa-fataka bihī idhā qatalahū min ḥaythu yarāhu. The frightening shape-shifting demon called *ghūl* (which is found in English as ghoul and in the name of the eclipsing binary star Algol) likewise moves between the same two roots.

48 §§ 36, 42, 48, 51, 52, 54, 56, 67, 68, 69, 71, 74.

49 This is about sequential killings: A kills B, C kills A, D kills C …

futtāk) is often used for "murderer" but it does not always involve killing: the verb also means "to act boldly or recklessly" and may even have positive connotations: "courageous".[50]

One notes that "assassination", common in English and other European languages especially for murders driven by politics or religion, has an Arabic etymology going back to the sect of the "Assassins", the "Hashish-eaters", a derogatory name allegedly given to a Shi'ite movement called the Nizārīs. In fact, one does not find the word (al-Ḥashshāshiyyah or al-Ḥashshāshiyyūn) in classical Arabic texts about the Nizārīs.

A fascination with murder and killing is, one supposes, found in any culture, language, or civilisation, and I do not wish to convey the impression that the Arabs are more prone to writing or reading about murder than others, or indeed more prone to commit murder. In the West we seem not just fascinated but positively obsessed with murder and we watch and read detective stories and thrillers in large quantities. Bookshops will have a usually quite large "crime section" and when zapping on TV one regularly comes across channels that seem to specialise in "real crime", usually involving murder, preferably of the more spectacular or gruesome kind. Judith Flanders writes on 19th-century fiction in her *The Invention of Murder*,[51] and one thinks of Thomas De Quincey's satirical essay "On murder Considered as One of the Fine Arts", of 1827.

But fascination with murder and killing is of course not a 19th-century invention. For centuries readers have relished the accounts of the horrible deaths of Christian martyrs, whether under the Romans, the Catholics, or the Protestants. The classics of western literature abound with killings: the Old Testament, the *Iliad*, Roman history, and dramatic works by Shakespeare and contemporaries spring to mind. The western world has often credited "Oriental" nations—Arabs, Turks, Chinese, Japanese—with more than ordinary cruelty and bloodthirst. A perhaps trivial matter may be remotely related to this attitude. When I studied Semitic Languages in Amsterdam in the 1960s the standard grammar books for Arabic (by Carl Brockelmann in German, William Wright in English) and Hebrew (Lettinga in Dutch, Bauer—Leander in German) all used the verb *qatala* (Arabic) or *qāṭal* (Hebrew), both meaning "to kill" for paradigms illustrating the standard regular verb. This was not a reflection of Mediaeval Arabic or Hebrew scholarship, because the old grammarians writing in Arabic or Hebrew used the perfectly neutral "dummy" verb "to do",

50 See e.g. the often-quoted line by Bashshār ibn Burd: *Man rāqaba l-nāsa lam yaẓfar bi-ḥājatihī | wa-fāza bil-ṭayyibāti l-fātiku l-lahijū* (Bashshār, *Dīwān*, ii, 56). On the word *fātik* see Webb, *Arab Thieves*, 27–29.

51 Flanders, *The Invention of Murder*.

faʿala/paʿal for their conjugation paradigms. One can understand why this verb, with its laryngeal consonant, was deemed unsuitable for beginning non-Arab learners but I have never understood why *qāṭal/qatala* was chosen by western Hebraists and Arabists in its stead.[52]

Most works on categories, *ṭabaqāt*, such as works on poets, Companions of the Prophet, jurists, Hadith scholars, grammarians, robbers, Sufis, physicians, etc., are about groups of people who have a characteristic in common. The murder victims in Ibn Ḥabīb's book, however, do not share any specific traits apart from meeting a violent end. Yet one can say that they all were prominent in some way, either as leaders, poets, or both: they count as *ashrāf*, as the title indicates. Some are better known than others, but no one is an obscure nobody. If there is a moral, it is that being prominent goes with risks to one's life. *Ashrāf* is one of the plural forms of *sharīf*, literally "exalted", also "noble, eminent". I have not translated *ashrāf* as "noble men" or "noblemen", for by no means all victims belong to the "nobility" in the sense of people of rank and birth, the aristocracy. It is true that *sharīf* often refers, as a technical term, to descendants of the Prophet, especially those of his daughter Fāṭimah and her husband ʿAlī, but it also has a much broader meaning, such as head of a prominent clan or family, a person of importance and distinction. It is this sense that it has in Ibn Ḥabīb's work. I thought about "eminent" instead of "prominent" but chose the latter because "eminent" often implies excellence, distinction, and being outstanding in something, which cannot be said of all our murder victims.

Some prominent murder victims are absent. One may wonder why the third caliph, ʿUthmān, is not given a section. He was killed by rebels in his own house while he was reading the Qur'an and one could easily describe his death as murder. Of the four first, "rightly guided" caliphs only one, Abū Bakr, died a natural death, and even he is said to have been killed by the Jews with a slow poison (*summ sanah*) in some sources;[53] but this is not in Ibn Ḥabīb's book. It is likely to be an invention of anti-Jewish sentiments.

Among poets who were killed one misses, for instance, Bashshār ibn Burd, "father of the modern poets", and the first non-Arab who was a major poet. He was beaten to death on the orders of the caliph al-Mahdī in 167/783, allegedly for heresy, as was Ṣāliḥ ibn ʿAbd al-Quddūs, executed either by al-Mahdī per-

---

52 The Latin grammar of Arabic by Thomas van Erpe, or Erpenius, in 1617 used *faʿala*, not *qatala*, and A.S. Tritton's *Teach Yourself Arabic* (from which I taught myself the basics of Arabic grammar before entering University) uses *kataba*, "to write".

53 e.g. al-Ṭabarī, *Tārīkh*, i, 2127–2128, tr. *The History*, xi, 129, Ibn ʿAbd Rabbih, *ʿIqd*, iv, 263, vi, 276.

sonally or somewhat later, under Hārūn al-Rashīd.[54] A violent death was also the fate of the Umayyad caliph al-Walīd ibn Yazīd (r. 125–126/743–744), who was a bad ruler but a talented poet. Among absent minor poets are Zayd ibn ʿAmr ibn Nufayl, murdered some five years before the Prophet began to preach;[55] Abū Jildah al-Yashkurī, said to have been executed by the governor al-Ḥajjāj;[56] Jaʿfar ibn ʿUlbah al-Ḥārithī, implicated in a murder case, executed in Mecca by the governor of al-Manṣūr[57]—not mentioning several who fell in battle on various occasions.

Not surprisingly, almost all murderers and murder victims in the book are men. There are nevertheless a few female murderers, or women who incited to murder: al-Zabbāʾ, the Arabic guise of the 3rd-century Palmyran queen Zenobia (§ 1), who avenged her father's death; Bilqīs, the Arabic name of the Queen of Sheba (§ 7), who had her tyrant predecessor killed; and Zaynab bint al-Ḥārith, the Jewish woman who poisoned the prophet Muḥammad if the story in § 23 is to be believed. An unnamed wife of al-Aswad "the Liar" al-ʿAnsī is an accomplice to his murder (§ 28). Ḥabbah, the wife of the caliph Marwān ibn al-Ḥakam, smothered her husband with a pillow after he had insulted her son and herself (§ 45). Women, by their behaviour (ʿUfayrah, § 3, the sister of Mālik ibn al-ʿAjlān, § 15) or with their poems calling for revenge (the daughter of Tamīm ibn al-Akhtham, § 112, the mother of Muzāḥim al-Salūlī, § 116), can effectively make sure a perpetrator is killed or executed. Female relatives lament their killed fathers or brothers in elegies (§§ 38, 85, 102) but elegies are by no means an exclusively female genre. Among the murder victims there is one woman, the poet Ghaḍūb (§ 121).

The sequence of stories is basically chronological, with some discrepancies. Ḥassān ibn Tubbaʿ's killing (§ 2) precedes the section in which he is alive to massacre Jadīs (§ 4). The section on poets (§§ 78–120) starts again the with pre-Islamic period, but the chronology is somewhat haphazard: the penultimate section (§ 120) is about Qays ibn al-Khaṭīm, who died shortly before the Hijra, while Sudayf ibn Maymūn (§ 117) died in early Abbasid times in 147/764. The most recent event described, in the section (§ 76) on those who killed their kinsfolk, between the two main parts, is the death in 223/838 of al-ʿAbbās, a son of caliph al-Maʾmūn, during the reign of al-Muʿtaṣim. This was in Ibn Ḥabīb's lifetime.

---

54 Sezgin, *Geschichte*, ii, 461.

55 Sezgin, *Geschichte*, ii, 271.

56 Sezgin, *Geschichte*, ii, 375: "soll von al-Ḥaǧǧāǧ hingerichtet worden sein".

57 Sezgin, *Geschichte*, ii, 451.

It is impossible to determine the extent to which the stories are fact or fiction. There are many studies on historicity and fictionality in Arabic literature[58] and I shall not contribute to the subject here. It is obvious that many of the murders and killings reported by Ibn Ḥabīb took place in reality, especially those in Islamic times, even though the details and the dialogues, given in direct speech, are clearly invented by the transmitters as plausible and necessary elements. It is equally obvious that stories from a nebulous past are mostly or wholly fictional, such as the stories about Jadhīmah and al-Zabbāʾ (§1) and Bilqīs (§7). Ibn Ḥabīb does not comment on the matter of fact vs. fiction, a dichotomy that he would not have acknowledged.

A book with stories about violence, bloodshed, cruelty, revenge, passion, betrayal: one would expect a Muslim author or compiler to use them to drum in a moral. The Qur'an is full of stories, mostly short, that have a clear and usually explicit point. Al-Muḥassin al-Tanūkhī (d. 384/994) wrote his entertaining book *al-Faraj baʿd al-shiddah* (*Relief after Distress*) to demonstrate God's providence, even though he often seems to let the entertainment factor prevail over the ethical. The prolific historian, theologian, and preacher Ibn al-Jawzī (d. 597/1201) wrote three slim volumes with tales about clever, stupid, and witty people. He never fails to point a moral. Ibn Ḥabīb's book could not be more different, for he refrains from explicit moral commentary. Lessons may be drawn but they are not drummed in. The book does not contain a study of murder, its forensic, technical or psychological aspects, a science one might jestingly call "phonology" (with short first o, from Greek *phŏnos*, "murder"). There is no introduction justifying the compilation, for instance by saying that he was asked to do so, or an exposition explaining the topic; the text begins starkly and drily with *Min al-mughtālīn Jadhīmah al-Abrash* ("One of those who were murdered is Jadhīmah al-Abrash"). He never condemns a murderer explicitly. And this while by any standards many of these murderers, from ordinary people to caliphs, could be called villains. He does not even curse Ibn Muljam, the murderer of the universally beloved caliph ʿAlī (§34), or Abū Luʾluʾah, the assassin of the great caliph ʿUmar ibn al-Khaṭṭāb (§30). In fact, the only person he wishes a descent into Hell is a victim, not a murderer: Abū Muslim, the great architect of the Abbasid revolt, who was killed by the caliph al-Manṣūr as soon as the dynasty's power

58 See, for instance, Bonebakker, "Nihil obstat"; Drory, "Three Attempts"; Vogt, *Figures de califes entre histoire et fiction*; Egbert Meyer, *Der historische Gehalt der Aiyām al-ʿArab*; several studies in Leder (ed.), *Story-telling in the Framework of Non-fictional Arabic Literature*, among them Leder, "Conventions of Fictional Narration" and Kilpatrick, "The Genuine Ashʿab"; and several studies in Kennedy (ed.), *On Fiction and* Adab *in Medieval Arabic Literature*, including Leder, "The Use of Composite Form".

was secured (§ 63). There are a few instances of very noble victims who, dying, say that their assassin should not be killed. The Prophet Muḥammad, said to have been poisoned, forgives the woman poisoner who did it, in one version (§ 24). ʿAlī's son al-Ḥasan refuses to divulge the name of the person who may or may not have poisoned him, because he does not want to be responsible for the death of an innocent man (§ 37). ʿUmar ibn al-ʿAzīz, the "good" Umayyad caliph, finds out that a slave has been given one thousand dinars, a very tempting sum, to poison him, but on his death-bed he lets the man escape after demanding back the dinars, which he puts into the treasury (§ 51). Again, although such noble behaviour is mentioned, Ibn Ḥabīb refrains from praising it explicitly. He is generally neutral, which no doubt is an admirable attitude for a historian.

It is sometimes said that Arab Muslim historiography is generally about salvation, imbued with religion, showing God's will and His favour to the community of Islam, and so on.[59] That is not my impression, certainly not in the case of Ibn Ḥabīb, who does not discuss religious ideas at all. If God is mentioned it is almost always in formulas, such as the opening *basmalah* formula ("In the name of God …"), pious expressions such as *raḥimahu llāh*, "God have mercy on him", for a deceased person, "God bless and preserve him" for the Prophet, or exclamations such as *wa-llāhi*, "By God!" On some two occasions, in accounts of the battles of the early Muslims, God is said to have routed the unbelievers. There are very few quotations from the Qur'an or pious quotations of Hadith. Quite often a short poem or a few lines from a poem commenting on the events is quoted. All in all, Ibn Ḥabīb does not seem to have had an obvious agenda. His book is refreshingly free from it. He differs in this from, for example, his great contemporary al-Jāḥiẓ, whose works almost invariably have an agenda or several agendas. His entertaining book on misers, *al-Bukhalāʾ*, condemns misers and miserliness and it also seems to condemn non-Arabs, especially Persians. In addition it has been argued there is an underlying theological debate, as there is in his great work on animals and living beings, *al-Ḥayawān*, and even his book on eloquence, or "Clarity and Clarification" (*al-Bayān wa-l-tabyīn*) is ultimately about religion and theology according to James Montgomery.

So why did Ibn Ḥabīb compose his book? Perhaps, being a tutor of his patrons' children, he was commissioned to do so, or he thought it would be a useful educational tool, combining information and entertainment. Or he just liked listing things. It is possible that his work began as merely a list of names, hence the title, that begins with *Asmāʾ*, "Names of". There is at least one

59 See e.g. Robinson, *Islamic Historiography*, Ch. 7 "God and models of history", 124–142.

such work that consists of names only: al-Haytham ibn ʿAdī (d. c. 821) made a list of people with physical defects (blind, one-eyed, squint-eyed, blue-eyed, and *afqam*, "having an underbite").[60] Ibn Ḥabīb's book *al-Muḥabbar* has many chapters that are merely lists of names, such as "Prominent Lepers" (*al-Burṣ al-ashrāf*) and "Prominent One-Eyed people" (*al-ʿŪrān al-ashrāf*) and many such chapters begin with *Asmāʾ*, "the names of" or *Tasmiyat*, "Giving the names of". But listing only the names of murder victims is unsatisfactory because they cry for the stories. His readers would no doubt have known many of these stories already, but there would be no harm in repeating them, even in shortened form, to remind the reader. As a proper historical source his book is not very useful; there is a striking absence of dates, for there is only one instance that mentions a year, in the section on Ḥumayd al-Ṭūsī who is said to have died in AH 220 (§ 70).[61] Striking, too, is the almost complete absence of that ubiquitous element of Arabic historical discourse, the *isnād*: as said before, *Asmāʾ al-mughtālīn* is not encumbered with those long chains of authorities that intend to authenticate a report.

All stories end in death, an unhappy ending, at least for the victim. The theme of the book contrasts with a genre on happy endings called in Arabic *al-faraj baʿd al-shiddah*, "Relief after Distress", or "All's Well that Ends Well", the most famous and most readable book in this category being *al-Faraj baʿd al-shiddah* by al-Muḥassin al-Tanūkhī, mentioned above. In modern crime fiction and detective stories the murder is often the beginning of the story, followed by detection and identification of the perpetrator, the chase to find him or her, and retribution. This provides a certain suspense followed by a sense of a happy ending or at least a feeling of justice having been done. All or most of this is lacking in Ibn Ḥabīb's stories, where the murder comes at the end (sometimes quite abruptly) and that is that. Retribution occasionally follows but it is not a fixed element. Detective stories are rare in Arabic (for a case of detection see the note at § 23).[62] There are, at least, many cases—too many to enumerate here—that offer a sense of justice being done, when murderers are themselves murdered or executed, even though their deaths may not be directly linked to the murder they committed.

Among the common motives for murder and killing in the book are vengeance or retaliation, for instance in a blood feud, or defending one's honour after an insult (§ 110 Ziyādah ibn Zayd, § 118 ʿAbd Banī l-Ḥasḥās, § 121 Ghaḍūb).

60 See the appendix to al-Jāḥiẓ, *Burṣān*, 564–570.

61 In § 76 he refers to "the year Amorium was captured" but he does not give the year.

62 See also Malti-Douglas, "The Classical Arabic Detective".

Political intrigue, eliminating potential rivals, often involving betrayal, is another motive. Passion and sexual jealousy are rare. A caliph kills his wife's lover (§ 119), but the motif is the noble avoidance of scandal rather than the revenge of an enraged cuckolded husband. Innocent people get killed in cold blood by raiding robbers such as the famous pre-Islamic brigand poet Ta'abbaṭa Sharrā, who is himself killed afterwards (§ 85). There are no random murders, by madmen or psychotics, no sexual murders. Some victims clearly deserve a sticky end, at least by the standards of popular and literary, even poetic, justice. Many others may not deserve being murdered perhaps, but at least provoked it by their too powerful and overbearing behaviour. Decidedly harsh and unjust, according to our modern views, is the murder of the only female, the poet Ghaḍūb, merely because of some invective verses she composed (§ 121), but the power of poetry in Arab culture and history is well known and a lampoon could destroy someone's honour, with dire consequences. A poet may be executed by a ruler for his invective, for instance Aʿshā Hamdān, executed by the Umayyad governor al-Ḥajjāj (§ 113). Rulers who execute opponents or have them murdered ("Will no one rid me of this turbulent …") are of all times. Readers may be reminded of a notorious case of a gruesome murder of an Arab journalist in 2018; to a large extent, modern journalists have taken over the role of poets in premodern times. It has already been mentioned that poems can kill, as when relatives of murder victims, often women, incite to vengeance (§§ 112, 116). The first Abbasid caliph, al-Saffāḥ, killed some members of the defeated Umayyad Dynasty after hearing incendiary poems by Sudayf ibn Maymūn (§ 117, the poems are not quoted by Ibn Ḥabīb). The book also mentions a bungled murder, when the wrong man was killed (§ 35).

The murder victims are said to be prominent, *min al-ashrāf*. In many cases they are certainly more prominent than their murderers. The caliphs ʿUmar and ʿAlī are more prominent, of course, than Abū Lu'lu'ah and Ibn Muljam. The tyrant ʿImlīq, in legendary pre-Islamic times, is killed by a subject, as is the ruler of the South-Arabian Sabeans, Zuhayr ibn ʿAbd Shams, another legendary tyrant. He is killed by a woman called Bilqīs, who becomes queen after him and who is better known to us as the Queen of Sheba. However, there are very many murder cases in which the murderer, or at least the one ultimately responsible for it, is more prominent than the victim. Muʿāwiyah, the founder of the Umayyad dynasty, a strong ruler known for his cunning but also for his *ḥilm* ("forbearance, self-control, wisdom"), has several rivals or opponents killed (§§ 33, 36, 38, 39). Another caliph, the Abbasid al-Ma'mūn, whom we know as being interested in Aristotle, philosophy, and theology, is said to have instigated several murders, too, those of two sons of the caliph al-Hādī (§§ 69, 71) and of his trusted general Ḥumayd al-Ṭūsī (§ 70). Possibly he was also responsible for the murder of his able vizier al-Faḍl ibn Sahl (§ 68), although, as is told in other sources, he displayed grief at al-Faḍl's death, had the four actual murderers executed, and their heads sent to al-al-Faḍl's brother al-Ḥasan, who succeeded him as vizier. Al-Ma'mūn's father, Hārūn al-Rashīd, is said to have been behind the death of an uncle of his (§ 74). No motive is given, and no other source seems to mention it. One wonders if Ibn Ḥabīb, who was a *mawlā* of the victim's sons, had picked up a family rumour.

The means of killing are many. Most often the deed is done with a sword or a knife, sometimes a lance or spear is used (§§ 35, 109). Several times the victim is shot with one or more arrows (§§ 4, 25, 70, 83, 87, 96, 97, 102, 109, 114). Bloodless killings come in many forms. Poison is often used: §§ 13, 24, 31, 33, 34 (a poisoned sword), 36, 37, 39, 51, 52, 65 (a poisoned dagger), 66, 67, 70, 71, 74. Other methods are smothering with a pillow or cloth (§§ 45, 56, 57, 116, and see § 19 note); twisting and breaking the neck (§ 52); putting into quicklime (§ 57); flogging or beating to death (§§ 69, 76c); pummelling with a sandbag (§ 116); deprivation of water (§ 78); choking to death in a hammam (§ 108); and burying alive (§ 119, and see § 117 note). In a few cases someone is killed because a building collapses, which does not sound like murder unless the collapse was intended, as is clearly implied (§§ 62, 110). Two deaths were possibly suicide (§§ 53, 54), but these may have been falsely reported by the real killers.

Parallel texts are numerous especially for the most famous victims; they are given in notes at the beginning of each section but not exhaustively, nor will there be a systematic discussion of the relationship and interdependency of these parallels. Major sources of such parallels are Ibn Hishām's *al-Sīrah al-nabawiyyah*; his *al-Tījān*; al-Balādhurī's *Ansāb al-ashrāf*, al-Wāqidī's *al-Maghāzī*; al-Ṭabarī's *Tārīkh*; Ibn Sa'd's *Kitāb al-Ṭabaqāt al-kabīr*; Abū l-Faraj al-Iṣfahānī's *al-Aghānī*; and Ibn Ḥabīb's own works, *al-Muḥabbar* and *al-Munammaq*. It is tempting to give translations of the fuller stories in notes or appendices, but it would swell the present volume inordinately. Only occasionally is an interesting detail or variant mentioned in the annotation. There are, however, several stories that are only found in the present book and for which no parallels have been found (see §§ 6, 17, 48, 54, 55, 70, 72, 96, 99, 103).

5 Editions

Ibn Ḥabīb's *Asmāʾ al-mughtālīn* has been edited twice. The text was first edited by the renowned scholar and editor of numerous classical Arabic texts, ʿAbd al-

Salām Hārūn (1909–1988) in his collection *Nawādir al-makhṭūṭāt* (*Rare Manuscripts*), 2 vols. Cairo: Maktabat Muṣṭafā al-Bābī al-Ḥalabī, 1972–1973, ii, 105–278 (text: 111–275). It was first published in 1954–1955.[63]

The editor explains in his introduction (pp. 110–111) that his edition is based on a unique manuscript of 140 folios preserved in Maktabat ʿĀshir in Istanbul, no. 873,[64] a photocopy of which is in Dār al-Kutub in Cairo (no. 2606 *tārīkh*). The copyist, Yūsuf ibn Muḥammad known as Ibn al-Wakīl al-Mallawī,[65] finished his copy on 18 Jumādā I 1114 (10 October 1702), adding that he copied from a manuscript written *bi-l-Kūfī bi-khaṭṭ muḥarraf*, i.e., in Kufic script, which suggests an old manuscript. I suspect *muḥarraf* means "slanting" here, which often applies to Kufic. Hārūn, however, seems to take it to mean "corrupt", since he speaks of the "bad corruption (*taḥrīf shadīd*) which the copyist attempted to correct" and it is indeed obvious that the original manuscript used by Ibn al-Wakīl contained many errors. In 1296/1879 the well-known scholar Muḥammad Maḥmūd al-Shinqīṭī (or al-Shanqīṭī, 1816–1904) made a copy of this manuscript, correcting some of its mistakes. The copy is preserved in Dār al-Kutub (57 *adab*). Hārūn used this copy and refers to its emendations in his critical apparatus.

The text as edited by ʿAbd al-Salām Hārūn in 1972–1973 has been used as basis (its pagination is added in the margins). It contains a few errors, which have been corrected with appropriate notes. On many occasions Hārūn emends an obviously faulty or incomprehensible reading by adopting a reading from a parallel text such as al-Iṣfahānī's *Aghānī*, explaining this in a note. In the present edition such notes have not been copied in every case. A curious feature of Hārūn's text is the occasional use of *anna* or *annahū*, "that (he)" without a preceding "*qīlā*" ("it is said"), *ḥaddathanī* ("I was told"), or *kāna sabab qatlihī*

63 See *Mélanges, Institut dominicain d'études orientales du Caire*, 2 (1955) 296–297 (G. Anawati).

64 Hārūn has "872"; it is in fact no. 873 in the catalogue of Maktabat ʿĀshir Afandi, p. 55 (Istanbul, n.d., accessible at https://ia800205.us.archive.org/35/items/defteriktooista/defteriktooista.pdf).

65 He is the Egyptian *adīb* Ibn al-Wakīl al-Mallawī (the *nisbah* is spelled variously), author of *Bughyat al-musāmir wa-ghinyat al-musāfir*, a collection of stories. He is also the copyist of al-Ṣūlī, *Adab al-kuttāb* (see the colophon, 259). Brockelmann, *Geschichte*, II, Suppl., 414 calls him Yūsuf ibn al-Wakīl al-Mīlawī; in al-Ziriklī, *Aʿlām*, viii, 252 he is called Yūsuf ibn Muḥammad al-Mīlawī (al-Mawlawī) Abū l-Ḥajjāj Ibn al-Wakīl, and in Winter, "Historiography in Arabic during the Ottoman Period", 175 he is called "Yūsuf al-Mallawānī, also called Ibn al-Wakīl", author of a chronicle, *Tuḥfat al-nuwwāb bi-man malaka Miṣr min al-mulūk wa-l-nuwwāb*. He died after 1114/1702 according to al-Ziriklī; c. 1719 according to El-Rouayheb, *Before Homosexuality*, 28, and in 1131/1719 according to Winter.

("the cause of his being murdered was"). In such cases I have changed *anna* to *inna*.[66] I have also replaced the "Egyptian" undotted final *yāʾ* with dotted *yāʾ* when standing for *-ī*.

A second edition by Sayyid Kasrawī (or Kisrawī)[67] Ḥasan was published in Beirut (Dār al-Kutub al-ʿIlmiyyah, 2001, 293 pp.). This edition is obviously based on the earlier one by Hārūn. Rather than correcting its errors it adds very many new errors (all recorded in notes to the Arabic text, below). Apparently in the belief that explicit sexual references are much worse than reporting murder most foul, he also bowdlerises some passages, for instance when he distorts a verse in the story of al-Sulayk (p. 227, § 93), by replacing *nīkat* with the unmetrical *nukiḥat*, adding in a patronising note that he thought it fit to change the word but has left the more obscure words that the common people would not understand. He omits a line by Muzāḥim al-Salūlī (p. 273, § 116) because, as he explains, "my pen was too chaste to quote it", and five obscene *rajaz* lines by Ziyādah ibn Mālik (p. 263, § 110) are expurgated without even an acknowledgment, making the text incoherent. The edition contains some useful notes, including many very lengthy quotations of parallel sources, often in footnotes of more than one page. It has an appropriately lurid cover with dripping blood and a brandished sword.

The Arabic text offered in the present volume may be considered a somewhat improved version of ʿAbd al-Salām Hārūn's edition. I did not make an effort to find the original manuscript and al-Shinqīṭī's copy, partly to save me trouble but also because al-Shinqīṭī and Hārūn, both excellent Arabists and the latter an experienced and very prolific editor, can be trusted to have done a good job with the text generally. They made many obviously correct emendations, carefully recorded in Hārūn's critical apparatus. Therefore I took Hārūn's edition as a good substitute for the manuscript. That I was able, nevertheless, to correct a good many errors is because I clearly had more time to spend on the text and I was greatly helped by modern search engines, enabling me to compare Ibn Ḥabīb's text with many parallel texts. The notes to the Arabic text mostly concern textual matters, including some emendations and discrepan-

66 § 5: *wa-annahū shariba …*; § 28 *wa-anna l-Aswad …*; § 50 *wa-annahū wafada …*; § 60 *wa-anna Dāwūd …*; § 72 *wa-anna Nafīs …*, *wa-anna Aḥmad amara …*, *wa-anna Aḥmad tanāwala …*; § 73 *wa-annahū saqaṭa …*; § 74 *wa-anna l-ʿAbbās …*; § 86 *wa-anna Abā Thawr …*; § 97 *wa-annahū qatala …*, *wa-anna Banī Salāmān …*, *wa-annahū marra …*, *wa-anna rajulan …*; § 99 *wa-anna l-Ḥārith …*; § 103 *wa-anna Ḥumrān …*

67 The former seems to be more common, even though Kisrawī is the standard "classical" form. At the end of his introduction (SKḤ, 25) he signs his name in classical style as Abū Islām Sayyid ibn Kasrawī ibn Ḥasan.

أسماء المغتالين من الأشراف
في الجاهلية والإسلام
ويليه
كنى الشعراء
ومن غلبت كنيته على اسمه
كلاهما من تأليف
الإمام العلامة أبي جعفر محمد ابن حبيب البغدادي
المتوفى سنة ٢٤٥هـ
تحقيق
سيد كسروي حسن
منشورات
محمد علي بيضون
لنشر كتب السنة والجماعة
دار الكتب العلمية

cies between the two earlier editions; for matters of interpretation and background information the reader is referred to the English translation. For the division into paragraphs, see below, on the English translation. I have followed ʿAbd al-Salām Hārun and Sayyid Kasrawī Ḥasan in not cluttering the Arabic text with editorial insertions indicating the metres of verse, as is done in many modern editions. For the metres the interested reader is referred to the Arabic rhyme index, *fihrist al-qawāfī*.

6 The Translation

The translation must be read in tandem with the annotation. The notes are indispensable to a non-specialist reader, who will not know many facts, persons, and backgrounds that were familiar to Ibn Ḥabīb and his mediaeval readers. Ibn Ḥabīb's stories are very concise compared with the often longer and more detailed parallels found in other sources written in his time or in the following centuries, such as al-Ṭabarī's *Tārīkh al-rusul wa-l-mulūk* (*History of Prophets and Kings*) or Abū l-Faraj al-Iṣfahānī's *Kitāb al-Aghānī* (*The Book of Songs*). Even specialists will not have all the necessary facts at their fingertips and may benefit from the notes, which provide explanations of what may not be readily known and give references to parallels in primary sources and to some modern secondary literature. Entries in the *Encyclopaedia of Islam*, both the second (*EI2*) and the still incomplete third edition (*EI3*), are often mentioned. Since tribal affiliations are so important in pre-Islamic and early Islamic Arab history, there are many references to Werner Caskel's arrangement, in tree format and in transliteration, of Ibn al-Kalbī's genealogical work, with an index volume (*ǦN*, for *Ǧamharat an-nasab*).

Readers not used to classical Arabic works may be put off by the bewildering abundance of names, often long ones, many of which are easily confused, especially because there are so many ʿAbd Allāhs, ʿAlīs, ʿAmrs, and Muḥammads. There is the additional difficulty in that a person could be mentioned by several different names. The second Abbasid caliph, who founded Baghdad, is usually called al-Manṣūr, which is his regnal name, but his given name was ʿAbd Allāh and in our text he is often called by his paedonymic (a name referring to one's child), Abū Jaʿfar. To mitigate possible confusion I could have decided to stick to one name, al-Manṣūr, but I have stayed true to the original Arabic and have occasionally added a clarifying note.

Conversely, premodern Arabic narrative texts often omit names where we would expect them. There is a profusion of "he", "him", and "his" and it is not always immediately clear who is who or whom is whom. In my translation I have made pronouns explicit where it seemed helpful, which unfortunately has added to the number of names but at least helps the understanding, one hopes.

Pious formulas are regularly found in the Arabic after the names of the Prophet and his family or other early Muslims. They are a hindrance to the non-Muslim reader of a translation because they interrupt the flow, but omitting them altogether seems wrong. In the translation they have been abbreviated as "(ṣ)", for *ṣallā llāhu ʿalayhi wa-sallam* ("God bless and preserve him", the standard formula referring to the Prophet Muḥammad) or "(*r*)", for *raḍiya llāhu ʿanhu/ʿanhā* ("God be pleased with him/her", etc., used for members of the Prophet's family or prominent early Muslims); they are often abbreviated in Arabic too, though they are written out in full in the present text.

Very often the Arabs in our text emphasise their words by using the expression *wa-llāhi* (just as they do today). One could argue that in ordinary English it is the equivalent of "really" or a similar emphatic term, but I decided to use the more literal "By God" or "I swear by God". I have not, however, rendered the common expressions *wayḥak* and *waylaka* with the customary but too archaic "Woe unto you!", but I have attempted to find utterances that suited the context. Arabists often seem to think that every word present in Arabic must be rendered with an English word, translating *Yā Aḥmad* as "O Aḥmad!" and *inna* (a fronting particle) as "Indeed" or "Verily". But in normal English, unlike modern or Classical Arabic, people are not addressed with "O", and *inna* does not normally have the force of "indeed", let alone "verily".

The division of the Arabic text and the English translation into numbered paragraphs is mine. It is not identical with the numbering used in the edition by Sayyid Kasrawī Ḥasan (hereafter SKḤ), who allots two numbers to a section involving two victims (e.g. §13 below, on ʿAmr ibn Masʿūd and Khālid ibn Naḍlah, numbered 13 and 14 respectively in SKḤ's edition, or §110 on Ziyādah and Hudbah, numbered 117 and 118 by SKḤ), whereas I have merely used a number whenever the text begins with *wa-minhum* ("and among them is/are …" or "and another is …"). As in the Arabic text, the pagination of Hārūn's edition is supplied in the margin in the translation.

7 Transliteration

For the transliteration of Arabic words and names the system of the third edition of the *Encyclopaedia of Islam* is used, with a few minor differences: the Arabic pausal feminine ending is *-ah* instead of *-a*; compound personal names with Allāh are not written as one word (ʿAbdallāh, ʿUbaydallāh) but as two (ʿAbd Allāh, ʿUbayd Allāh), as in Arabic orthography, just as all other compound names beginning with ʿAbd. An apostrophe is used to distinguish a combination of two consonants (e.g. *d'h* as in *ad'hān*, "oils") from a digraph (e.g. *dh* as in *adhān* "call to prayer"). In many standard works, including the *Encyclopaedia of Islam*, "ibn", "son (of)", especially when occurring between names, is often abbreviated to "b.". This is not done in the present translation, for it may encourage the common (and spreading) solecism of using "bin", which is found in modern names such as Bin Laden but must never be used for classical Arabic names. It is only in the index, to save space, that I have used "b." (and "bt" for *bint*, "daughter of") when occurring between two names.

8 Abbreviations in the English

AM	*Asmāʾ al-mughtālīn al-ashrāf*
ʿASH	ʿAbd al-Salām Hārūn's text of *AM* in *Nawādir al-makhṭūṭāt*
EAL	Julie Scott Meisami and Paul Starkey (eds), *Encyclopedia of Arabic Literature*
EI2	*Encyclopaedia of Islam, New [= Second] Edition*
EI3	*Encyclopaedia of Islam, Third Edition*
ĞN	Ibn al-Kalbī / Wernel Caskel, *Ğamharat an-nasab* (vol. i containing genealogical trees and vol. ii the index of tribal and personal names)
Q	Qur'an (Qur'anic quotations are given between guillemets). Qur'anic translations are by me unless indicated otherwise.
(*r*)	*raḍiya llāhu ʿanhu/ʿanhā/ʿanhum* ("God be pleased with him/her/them"), pious formula on mentioning members of the Prophet's family or his Companions
(*ṣ*)	*ṣallā llāhu ʿalayhi wa-sallam* ("God bless and preserve him"), pious formula on mentioning the Prophet Muḥammad
SKḤ	edition of *AM* by Sayyid Kasrawī (or Kisrawī) Ḥasan
WKAS	*Wörterbuch der klassischen arabischen Sprache*

9 Abbreviations in the Notes to the Arabic Text

ك	edition of *AM* by Sayyid Kasrawī (Kisrawī) Ḥasan
هـ	ʿAbd al-Salām Hārūn's text of *AM* in *Nawādir al-makhṭūṭāt*

Text and Translation

كتاب أسماء المغتالين من الأشراف في الجاهليّة والإسلام
وأسماء من قُتل من الشعراء
لأبي جعفر محمّد بن حبيب

بسم الله الرحمن الرحيم

[§ ١] **من المغتالين** جَذيمة الأبرش بن مالك بن فَهْم بن غَنْم بن دَوْس بن عُدْثان الأَزْديّ. ١١٢
وكان أفضلَ ملوك العرب رأياً، وأبعدَهم مُغاراً، وأشدَّهم نِكايةً وهو أوّل من استجمع له المُلك
بأرض العراق. وكانت منازله ما بين الأنبار وبَقّةَ وهِيت وعين التمْر وأطراف البرّ والقُطْقُطانة وخَفيّة
والحِيرة. وكان يُغير على الأمم الخالية من العرب العاربة الأُوَل. وكان مَلِكُ العرب بأرض الجزيرة
ومَشارف الشام عمرو بن الظَّرِب بن حسّان بن أُذَيْنة بن السَّمَيْدَع بن هَوْبَر العامليّ، من عاملة
العماليق. فجمع جذيمةُ جموعَه من العرب وسار إليه، فالْتقى هو وعمرو بن الظرب فقتل | ١١٣
جذيمةُ عَمْراً وفضّ جموعَه.

1 The story of Jadhīmah, al-Zabbāʾ, ʿAmr ibn ʿAdī, and the faithful counsellor Qaṣīr is found in many Arabic sources, Ibn Ḥabīb's version being among the oldest. Much older yet, if authentic, is the poem attributed to ʿAdī ibn Zayd (d. c. 600) (see Ibn Qutaybah, *Shiʿr*, 227–228, ʿAdī ibn Zayd, *Dīwān*, 180–184), whose own death is told below (§19). A prominent motif of the story is also found in Herodotus. See Muth, "Zopyros bei den Arabern", where many Arabic versions are given (but not *Kitāb al-Mughtālīn*). For Arabic parallels see, among many others, Abū ʿUbaydah, *Dībāj*, 109–112; al-Mufaḍḍal, *Amthāl*, 64–68; al-Akhfash al-Aṣghar, *al-Ikhtiyārayn*, 717–729; ps.-al-Jāḥiẓ, *Maḥāsin*, 257–262; al-Ṭabarī, *Tārīkh*, i, 750–769, tr. *The History*, iv, 129–149; al-Masʿūdī, *Murūj*, ii, 213–223; al-Maqdīsī, *al-Badʾ wa-l-tārīkh*, iii, 195–199; al-Iṣfahānī, *Aghānī*, xv, 315–320; Ibn Saʿīd, *Nashwat al-ṭarab*, 59–66; Ibn Nubātah, *Sarḥ al-ʿuyūn*, 77–81, 84–85. Jadhīmah, a legendary pre-Islamic king of the third century AD, was a leper, hence his nickname al-Abrash. He is mentioned in a 3rd-century inscription. A murder victim in the present story, he himself was suspected of having murdered his page ʿAdī ibn Naṣr when he found out that, when drunk, he had rashly allowed him to marry his sister (al-Masʿūdī, *Murūj*, ii, 214–215, al-Iṣfahānī, *Aghānī*, xv, 312–313).

2 On the tribe of Azd, see *EI2*, "Azd" (G. Streniok). The genealogy of Jadhīmah may be seen in *ĞN*, i, 211 and (going up the tree) 210.

3 i.e., the southern half of present-day Iraq.

4 An ancient town on the Euphrates, some 60 km east of where Baghdad was founded on the Tigris much later.

5 Yāqūt, *Muʿjam al-buldān*: "a place near al-Ḥirah; it is also said: a fortified place two parasangs (c. 12 km) from Hīt."

6 An ancient town on the Euphrates, some 100 km upstream from al-Anbār.

PROMINENT MURDER VICTIMS of the Pre- and Early Islamic Periods, Including the Names of Murdered Poets

In the Name of God, the Merciful, the Compassionate

[§ 1 Jadhīmah al-Abrash[1]]

Among the murder victims was Jadhīmah al-Abrash ("the Speckled") ibn Mālik 112
ibn Fahm ibn Ghanm ibn Daws ibn ʿUdthān of the tribe of Azd.[2] He was the
most astute of the kings of the Arabs, the one whose raids reached farthest
and whose power was most fearsome. He was the first to rule over the whole
of Iraq.[3] His home territories were between al-Anbār,[4] Baqqah,[5] Hīt,[6] ʿAyn al-
Tamr,[7] the extremities of the land,[8] Quṭquṭānah,[9] Khafiyyah,[10] and al-Ḥīrah.[11]
He carried out campaigns against the ancient Arab nations and the early pure
Arabs.[12] The king of the Arabs in al-Jazīrah[13] and the Syrian heights was ʿAmr
ibn al-Ẓarib ibn Ḥassān ibn Udhaynah ibn al-Samaydaʿ ibn Hawbar al-ʿĀmilī,
i.e., from the ʿĀmilat al-ʿAmālīq.[14] Jadhīmah gathered his troops of Arabs and
marched to him. He and ʿAmr met in battle, in which Jadhīmah | killed ʿAmr 113
and routed his troops.

---

7 A town in a fertile depression (the name means "Source of Dates") west of the Euphrates, between al-Anbār and Kufa (not far from present-day Najaf, south of present-day Baghdad).

8 Southern Iraq bordering on to the Gulf.

9 Yāqūt, *Muʿjam al-buldān*: "a place near Kufa, towards the desert".

10 Yāqūt, *Muʿjam al-buldān*: "a wooded place (*ajamah*) in the agricultural land (*sawād*) of Kufa".

11 The main town of the Lakhmid dynasty, not far from present-day Najaf.

12 *Al-ʿArab al-ʿāribah al-uwal*, according to traditional Arab genealogy the Arabs descended from Qaḥṭān, also called the "South Arabs", to be distinguished from *al-ʿArab al-mustaʿribah*, "the Arabicised Arabs", who are the descendants of ʿAdnān ("North Arabs").

13 Upper Mesopotamia, the regions between the Euphrates and the Tigris north of Hīt.

14 The ʿAmālīq or ʿAmāliqah (the Amalekites of the Old Testament), according to Arab genealogists, were an ancient Arabian people descended from ʿImlīq or ʿImlāq and among the earliest speakers of Arabic; see also the story of ʿImlīq, below (§ 30). They are usually described as oppressors (see e.g. Roberto Tottoli, "ʿAmālīq", in *EI3*). The ancient tribe of ʿĀmilah was apparently thought to incorporate the remnants of the ʿAmālīq. The name Udhaynah is found in Roman sources as Odenathus, the founder of the Palmyrene kingdom who reigned AD 263–267 and who was succeeded by his widow, the famous Zenobia (d. c. 273). A legendary version of her appears in the present story as al-Zabbāʾ. Zenobia's name also appears frequently in Arabic as Zaynab, still a popular name.

فملك من بعدِ عمرو ابنتُه الزَّبّاء، وكانت تخاف أن يغزُوَها ملوكُ العرب، فبَنَتْ لنفسها حِصْناً على شاطئ الفُرات، وسكرَتِ الفرات على قِلّة الماء، وبنتْ في بطنه أَزَجاً من الآجُرّ، وأجْرَتْ عليه الماء، فكانت إذا خافت عدوًّا دخلت النَّفَق، فخرجت إلى مدينةِ أختها الزُّبَيْبة. فلمّا اجتمع لها أمرها واستحكم مُلكها جمعت لتغزو جذيمةَ ثائرةً بأبيها. فقالت لها أختها زُبيبة، وكانت ذاتَ رأْي وحزم: إنّكِ إذا غزوْتِ جذيمة فإنّما هو يومٌ له ما بعده، وإن ظَفِرتِ أصبْتِ ثأرك، وإن قُتلتِ هلك مُلكك، والحرب سِجال، وعَثَراتها لا تُستقال، ولم يزلْ كعبُك سامياً على من ناواكِ، ولا تدرين لمن تكون العاقبة، وعلى من تكون الدائرة. والرأي أن تحتالي له وتَخْدَعيه وتمكُري به.

فكتبت الزبّاء إلى جذيمة تدعوه إلى نفسها ومُلكها، وأن تصل بلادَه ببلادها، وأنّها لم تجدْ مُلك النساء إلّا إلى قُبح في السماع، وضَعْف في السلطان، وقلّة في بسط المملكة، وأنّها لم تجدْ لها كُفؤاً غيرَك، فأقبِلْ إليَّ واجمعْ مُلكي بملكك، وصِلْ بلادي ببلادك، وتقلَّدْ أمري مع أمرك.

فلمّا قدِم عليه رُسُلها وكتابها استخفّه ذلك ورغِب فيما أطعمتْه فيه، فجمع أهلَ الحِجا من
ثِقات أصحابه وهو بالبقّة فاستشارهم، فأجمعوا على أن يسيرَ | إليها ويستوْليَ على مُلكها. ١١٤
وخالَفهم قَصير بن سعد بن عمرو بن جذيمة بن قيس بن هُلَيْل بن رَبِيّ[١] بن نَمارة بن لَخْم، فقال: هذا رأْي فاتر وغدْر حاضر. فإن كانت صادقةً فلْتُقْبِلْ إليك، وإلّا فلا تمكِّنْها من نفسك فتَقَعَ في حِبالها، وقد وترْتَها وقتلتَ أباها.

١ هـ، ك: (دمى)، والتصحيح من جمهرة النسب لابن الكلبيّ وتاريخ الطبريّ.

15 The name al-Zabbā' could be translated as "the hairy woman". Hair plays a role later in the story (see below, note 25); but in fact the name goes back to Aramaic Bath-Zabbay, "daughter of Zabbay or Zabday (Zebediah)".

16 The account in *al-Aghānī* (xv, 316) mentions two tunnels, one from the river to the fortress and another from the fortress towards the desert and her sister's town. Instead of al-Zubaybah (as vowelled in ʿASH and SKḤ) the name could also be read as al-Zabībah (like the mother of the poet al-Shanfarā, see *Aghānī*, viii, 237). In either case the name is inspired by al-Zabbā'.

After ʿAmr's death his daughter al-Zabbāʾ succeeded him.[15] She was afraid that the kings of the Arabs would raid her land, so she built a fortress on the bank of the Euphrates. She dammed the river when the water was scarce. Inside the fortress she built a vault made of brick and let the water flow in it. Whenever she feared an enemy she would enter the tunnel, and she would come out reaching the city of her sister al-Zubaybah.[16] Once she was in command and her rule was established she mustered troops to attack Jadhīmah and avenge her father. Her sister Zubaybah, who was astute and prudent, said to her, "If you attack Jadhīmah it will be a battle with consequences. If you win you will have your revenge but if you are killed your kingdom will be lost. War, like buckets, has ups and downs, and missteps in it cannot be undone.[17] Your glory is still rising over your adversaries, but you don't know how things will end and who shall be brought low by fortune's wheel. The right thing to do is to scheme, to deceive him and cheat him."

Al-Zabbāʾ wrote to Jadhīmah, inviting him to visit her and her realm, and to join his lands to hers. She wrote that she had found that the reigns of women always have a bad reputation, what with the weakness of their authority and the little extent of their rule. She had not found anyone worthy of her "except you,[18] so come to me, unite my kingdom with yours, join my lands to yours, and take over my command with yours!"

When her messengers arrived with her letter he was overjoyed and longed to have what she had enticed him with. He gathered his wise counsellors and trusted courtiers in al-Baqqah and asked their advice. They all agreed that he
should travel | to her and take possession of her kingdom. They were opposed, 114
however, by Qaṣīr ibn Saʿd ibn Jadhīmah ibn Qays ibn Hulayl ibn Rabī[19] ibn Numārah ibn Lakhm. "This is the wrong thing to do," he said, "and treachery will result. If she is sincere, let her come to you. In any case do not put yourself into her power or you will be caught in her snare. You have, after all, wronged her, killing her father."

17 This sentence uses rhymed prose (*sajʿ*) and especially the first part (*al-ḥarb sijāl*) is often found as a proverb. This is the first of many proverbs in the story, one of many stories that serve as aetiology giving the supposed origin of proverbs. The sayings may be found in many ancient collections of proverbial expressions.

18 Here the reported (written) speech shifts to direct speech.

19 Thus, following *ǦN*, i, 246 and al-Ṭabarī, *Tārīkh*, i, 619, instead of *D.m.y.* as in ʿASH and SKḤ.

فلم يوافق جذيمةَ ما أشار به قصير وقال: أنت امرؤٌ رأيك في الكِنّ لا في الضِّحّ. ومضى جذيمة في وجوه أصحابه فأخذ على شاطئ الفُرات الغربيّ، فلمّا نزل الفُرضة دعا قصيراً فقال: ما الرأي؟ فقال: ببقّةَ تركْت الرأي. قال: فما ظنُّك بالزبّاء؟ قال: القول رِداف، والحزم عَيْرانة[١] لا تخاف. واستقبله رُسُلها بالهدايا والألطاف فقال: يا قصير، كيف ترى؟ قال: خَطَر يسير في خَطْب كبير، وستلقاك الخيول، فإن سارت أمامَك فالمرأة صادقة، وإن أخذت [جَنْبَيْك وأحاطت بك][٢] فالقوم غادرون بك.

فلقِيَتْه الخيول فأحاطت به حتّى دخل على الزبّاء، فلمّا رأته كشفتْ عن فَرْجها فإذا هي مضفورة الإسْب، فقالت: يا جذيمة، أدأْبَ[٣] عَروس ترى؟ قال: بُلغ المَدى، وجفّ الثَّرى، وأمْرَ غَدْرٍ أَرى! فقالت: واللّٰهِ ما بنا من عَدَمِ مَواس، ولا قلّة أَواس، ولكنّها شِيمةُ ما أُناس. ثمّ أجلستْه على نِطْع، | وسَقَتْه الخمر، ثمّ أمرت بقَطْع رواهشه، فجعل دمُه يسيل في طَسْت من ذَهَب، فلمّا رأى دمه قال: لا يحزُنْك دمٌ أهراقَه أهلُه.

١ هـ، كـ: (عثراته)؛ والتصحيح من الأغاني.

٢ هامش هـ: التكملة من الأغاني وابن الأثير والطبريّ ومجمع الأمثال. وموضعها بياض في النسختين.

٣ هـ، كـ: (أذات)؛ وما أثبتّ هو من تاريخ اليعقوبيّ وتاريخ الطبريّ وغيرهما.

20 Another saying that became a proverb. According to al-Zamakhsharī (*Mustaqṣā*, ii, 380–381) it is said about someone who is pampered and weak.

21 Hārūn's edition offers two readings of the verb, *taraktu/tarakta*, "I/you have abandoned"; The more usual version, one found in the proverb collections, is "In Baqqah the affair was decided (*quḍiya*, or *ubrima*, *l-amr*)".

22 He uses rhymed prose.

23 Emending *ʿatharatuhū* (ʿASH, SKḤ) to *ʿayrānah*.

24 As is told in longer versions, Qaṣīr escapes at this stage, later becoming al-Zabbāʾ's nemesis as the hero of an extraordinary story of loyalty and revenge that is reminiscent of, and possibly related to, the story of the Persian called Zopyrus told in Herodotus' *Histories*, Bk III, 153–160; see Muth, "Zopyros bei den Arabern".

But Jadhīmah did not agree with Qaṣīr's advice. "You are a man who thinks of what is hidden out of sight, not what is broad daylight!"[20] Jadhīmah went out with his principal courtiers, travelling along the western bank of the river Euphrates. When he stopped at the ford he summoned Qaṣīr and asked, "What do you think?" He replied, "In Baqqah I have abandoned thought!"[21] Jadhīmah asked, "What do you think of al-Zabbā'?" Qaṣīr answered,[22] "Words are camels riding at the rear, prudence is a swift and hardy camel[23] that does not fear." Al-Zabbā''s messengers came to meet them, bringing presents and precious objects. "What do you think, Qaṣīr?" he asked. "A thing of trifling import, with a great danger. The cavalry will come to meet you; now if they ride in front of you the woman is sincere. But if they cover your flanks, surrounding you, then they mean treachery."[24]

The cavalry arrived and surrounded him all the way into al-Zabbā''s presence. When she saw him she bared her genitals; her pubic hair was plaited. "Do I look like a bride to you?" she asked.[25] He replied, "The end has been reached; the ground is parched. It is treachery I see!" She said, "It is not because we lack razors, or have few maids to shave us! It is a habit some people gave us."[26] She
sat him on a leather mat | and gave him wine to drink. Then she gave orders 115
for the arteries in his arms to be cut, letting the blood flow in a golden basin. When he saw his blood flow he said, "Do not grieve for blood that is shed by those entitled to it."[27]

---

25 Emending the reading *a-dhāt ʿarūs tarā*, found in several sources but syntactically strange, to *a-daʾb ʿarūs tarā* (al-Yaʿqūbī, *Tārīkh*, i, 237; al-Ṭabarī, *Tārīkh*, i, 621), The question (literally, "Do you see the custom of a bride?") is ironical. The sources do not explain the significance of the hair, but it may be assumed that a woman ready for marriage would have had her pubic hair shaved. The same words were said by the faithful wife of the murdered caliph ʿUthmān, who pulled out her two front teeth, addressing the future Umayyad caliph Muʿāwiyah who wanted to marry her (al-Washshā', *Muwashshā*, 84, where the woman is called Ḥubayshah; in Ibn Qayyim al-Jawziyyah, *Akhbār al-nisā'*, 128 it is the more famous Nā'ilah). That the word *zabbā'* may refer to pubic hair is clear from a bawdy joke quoted in al-Tawḥīdī, *Baṣā'ir*, ii, 84: "A hairy woman (*imra'ah zabbā'*) married a bald man. He saw her look at him and think. 'What is the matter?' he asked. 'I wish', she replied, 'that your baldness was on my cunt and the hair on my cunt on your bald pate, so that I would not have to pluck my hair and you would have a proper appearance.'"

26 She uses *sajʿ*, rhymed prose.

27 This, too, is found in books on proverbs such as al-Maydānī, *Majmaʿ*, ii, 273, al-Zamakhsharī, *Mustaqṣā*, ii, 268.

[§ ٢] **ومنهم** حسّان بن تُبَّع، وكان أعسرَ أحْول. وإنّه خرج من اليمن سائراً حتى وطئ أرض العجم، وقال: لأبلُغنّ من البلاد ما لم يبلغه أحد من التبابعة! فأوغل بهم في أرض خُراسان، ثمّ مضى إلى المغرب فبلغ رُومة وخلّف عليها ابن عمّ له، وأقبل إلى العراق حتّى إذا صار إلى فُرضة نُعْم بشاطئ الفرات قالت وجوه حِمْيَر: ما نُفني أعمارنا[١] إلّا مع هذا، يطوف في الأرض كلّها، نَغيب عن أولادنا وعِيالنا وبلادنا وأموالنا؛ وما ندري ما يخلّف عليهم بعدنا. فكلّموا أخاه عَمْراً وقالوا: كلِّمْ أخاك في الرجوع إلى بلده ومُلكه. فقال:[٢] هو أعسر من ذاك وأنكد. فقالوا: فاقتُلْه وتملَّكْ علينا فأنت أحقّ بالمُلك من أخيك، وأنت أعقل وأحسن نظراً لقومك. فقال: أخاف ألّا تفعلوا، وأكونَ قد قتلتُ أخي وخرج المُلك عن يدي. فواثقوه حتّى ثَلِجَ إلى قولهم، واجتمع الرؤساء كلّهم معه على قتل أخيه إلّا ذي رُعَيْن. فإنّه خالَفهم وقال: ليس هذا برأيي، يذهَب المُلك من حِمير! فشجّعه الباقون على قتل أخيه، فقال ذو رُعين: إن قتلتَه بادَ مُلكك. فلمّا رأى | ذو ١١٦
رُعين ما اجتمع عليه القوم أتاه بصحيفة مختومة فقال: يا عمرو، إنّي مستودِعك هذا الكتاب، فضَعْه عندك في مكان حريز. وكتب فيه:

١ هـ: (أعماوَنا)

٢ هـ: (فقالوا) والسياق يقتضي (فقال) كما في كـ

28 Longer or shorter versions of the story (which may be assigned to the fifth century AD) are also found in Ibn Hishām, *al-Sīrah al-nabawiyyah*, i, 28–29 (tr. Guillaume, 12–13); Ibn Hishām, *Tījān*, 308–310; Ibn Qutaybah, *Maʿārif*, 633–634; al-Yaʿqūbī, *Tārīkh*, i, 222–223, tr. *The Works*, 501; al-Iṣfahānī, *Aghānī*, xxi, 315–319; al-Ṭabarī, *Tārīkh*, i, 914–917, tr. *The History*, v, 183–188; Ibn Saʿīd, *Nashwat al-ṭarab*, 15–51; and several later sources.

29 The word that introduces this and all subsequent entries, *wa-minhum*, literally "and among them (is)" (in one case, *wa-minhum ayḍan*, "and also among them", §4), is consistently printed in a smaller font in ʿASH, but I have assumed it to be part of Ibn Ḥabīb's text, since normally any editorial additions are given within square brackets.

30 Tubbaʿ is a title, rather than a name, of the pre-Islamic rulers of Ḥimyar in Yemen. Ḥassān's name is given in other sources as Ḥassān ibn Tubān (or Tubbān, or Tibān) Asʿad Abū Karib.

[§ 2 Ḥassān ibn Tubbaʿ[28]]

Another is[29] Ḥassān ibn Tubbaʿ.[30] He was lefthanded and had a squint. He set out from Yemen, invading as far as the lands of the Persians.[31] "I shall reach lands", he said, "such as no one of the Tubbaʿs has ever reached!" He penetrated deeply with his men, reaching Khorasan.[32] Then he went west and reached Rūmah,[33] where he left a nephew of his as his deputy. He turned towards Iraq and when he arrived at Nuʿm's Ford,[34] on the bank of the Euphrates, the leading men of Ḥimyar said, "This man will be our death! He roams the whole earth while we are away from our children, our families, our lands, and our belongings. We don't know what he will compensate them with after our death." They spoke to his brother ʿAmr, saying, "You must speak to your brother about returning to his country and his kingdom." He replied,[35] "He is too difficult[36] and bad-tempered!" "Then kill him," they said, "and be our king, for you are more entitled to it than your brother. You are more intelligent and look after your people better." He answered, "I am afraid that you may not do as you say, and that I will have killed my brother with the kingship slipping from my hand." They assured him of their loyalty and in the end he trusted them. All the leading men agreed with him on killing his brother, except Dhū Ruʿayn,[37] who opposed them. "This is wrong!", he said, "It will be the end of the kingdom of Ḥimyar." But the others strongly encouraged him to support the killing of Ḥassān. Dhū Ruʿayn said, "If you kill him your rule will perish!" But when he saw | that they 116
were all agreed he gave ʿAmr a sealed document and said, "I am entrusting this writing to you, ʿAmr, so put it in a safe place." He had written in it:

31 Other versions say explicitly that he first invaded the lands of the Arabs. Needless to say, the grand conquests mentioned here are a complete fiction. Ḥassān's father, Abū Karib Asʿad, however, did invade Arabia towards the end of the fourth century.

32 Khorasan (Khurāsān) was a large region in parts of what are now Iran, Afghanistan, Turkmenistan, and Uzbekistan.

33 Either Rome (more usually Rūmiyah) or, more plausibly but still a fiction, the lands of the Byzantines (al-Rūm).

34 Furḍat Nuʿm, mentioned in Yāqūt, *Muʿjam al-buldān*, said to be named after a wife of Ḥassān ibn Tubbaʿ, who built a palace for her there.

35 ʿASH has "they said", which is probably an error.

36 The word *aʿsar*, translated above as "lefthanded", also means "more difficult".

37 Several persons from Ḥimyar called Dhū Ruʿayn are mentioned, see e.g. *ǦN*, i, 274, 276, ii, 237 (there were two, the older called Yarīm ibn Zayd and the younger ʿAbd Kulāl ibn Muthawwib, see al-Baghdādī, *Khizānah*, ii, 290). But the person in the present story is said to be from the branch Dhū l-Kalāʿ in Ibn Saʿid, *Nashwat al-ṭarab*, 150.

ألا من يشتري سَهَراً بنوْمٍ سعيدٌ مَن يَبيت قريرَ عيْنِ
فإن تكُ حِمْيرٌ غدرتْ وخانتْ فمَعْذِرة الإله لِذي رُعَيْنِ

وإنّ عَمراً أتى حسّان أخاه وهو نائم على فراشه، فقتله واستولى على ملكه فلم يبارَك له فيه، وسُلِّط عليه السهر، وامتنع منه النوم، فسأل الكُهّان والعُيّاف، فقال له كاهن منهم: إنّه ما قتل رجل أخاه قطّ بُغْياناً عليه إلّا امتنع نومه. فقال: هذا عمل رؤساء حمير، هم حملوني على قتله ليرجِعوا إلى بلادهم. لم ينظروا لي ولا لأخي.

فجعل يقتل من أشار بقتله رجلاً رجلاً، حتّى خلص الأمر إلى ذي رُعين، وأيقن بالشرّ، فقال له ذو رعين: أما تعلم أنّي أعلمتُك ما في قتله ونهيْتُك؟ قال: ما أذكُر هذا، ولئن كان ليس عندك إلّا ما تدّعي لقد طُلَّ دمك! قال: إنّ عندك لي براءةً وشاهدا. قال: وما هو؟ قال: الكتاب الذي استودعتُك. فدعا بالكتاب فلم يجدْه، فقال ذو رعين: ذهب دمي على أخْذي بالحزم فصرتُ كمن أشار بالخَطاء.[١] فقال الملك أن ينعم طلبه، فأُتي به فقرأه، فإذا فيه البيتان اللذان كتبناهما، فلمّا قرأهما قال: لقد أخذت بالحزم. قال: إنّي حسبتُ ما رأيتك صنعت بأصحابي.

١١٧ وتشعّث أمر حِمْيَر حين قُتل أشرافها، واختلفوا عليه، حتى وثب على عمرو لَخْنيعة يَنوف، ولم يكن من أهل المملكة، فقتله.

---

١ كـ: (بالخطأ).

Ah, who would buy sleeplessness for sleep![38]
Fortunate is he who spends the night happily.
Though Ḥimyar be treacherous and disloyal,
God will absolve Dhū Ruʿayn from guilt.[39]

ʿAmr went to his brother Ḥassān while he was asleep in bed and killed him. He took over the kingship from him, but he was not blessed in his undertaking. He fell victim to insomnia, unable to sleep. He consulted soothsayers and augurs. One soothsayer said to him, "No man has ever unjustly killed his brother but sleep was denied to him." He replied, "It is the work of the leaders of Ḥimyar: they have incited me to kill him, so that they could return home. They had no concern for either me or my brother."

He set out to kill all those who had counselled him to murder him, man for man. Finally he came to Dhū Ruʿayn, who feared the worst. He said, "Don't you remember what I told you would happen if you killed him, and that I spoke out against it?" "I do not remember that," replied ʿAmr, "but if what you claim is the only thing you can offer, your blood may be shed with impunity!" Dhū Ruʿayn said, "But I am innocent and you have proof!" "What is it"? "The document that I gave you for safekeeping." ʿAmr called for the document but it could not be found. Then Dhū Ruʿayn said, "My blood will be shed though I took a prudent course and now I have become like those who gave faulty counsel!" Thereupon the king said that a thorough search must be made, and it was brought to him. He read it and there were the two verses we have quoted above. When the king saw them he said, "You have indeed taken a prudent course." Dhū Ruʿayn said, "I took into account[40] what I saw you did to the others."

When its noblemen were killed the Ḥimyarite rule disintegrated, with differ- 117
ent claimants to it. Finally, Lakhnīʿah Yanūf, who did not belong to the dynasty, attacked ʿAmr and killed him.[41]

38 This hemistich made it into the collections of proverbs (e.g. al-Maydānī, *Majmaʿ al-amthāl*, i, 110–111).

39 For different English translations of these lines, see Guillaume, *The Life of Muhammad*, 12 and, rhymed, in Nicholson, *Literary History*, 26. Although the verses and all dialogue are in Arabic, it must be remembered that the language of the Ḥimyarites was a form of South Arabian, belonging to a different branch of the Semitic language family.

40 Instead of *ḥasabtu*, *Aghānī* has *khashītu*, "I feared".

41 He, too, was a murder victim, as related below, § 16.

[§٣] **ومنهم** عِمْليق ملك طَسْم بن لاوُذ بن إرَم بن سام بن نوح. وكان منازلهم عُذْرة في موضع
اليمامة. وكان سبب قتله أنّه تمادى في الظُّلم والغَشْم والسِّيرة بغير الحقّ، وأنّ امرأة من جَديس
كان يقال لها هُزَيلة ولها زوج يقال له قديس، فطلّقها وأراد أخْذ ولدِها منها، فخاصمتْه إلى
عمليق، فقالت: أيّها الملك، إنّي حملتُه تِسعاً، ووضعته دَفْعاً، وأرضعتُه شَفْعاً، حتّى إذا تمّت
أوصاله أراد أن يأخذه كَرْهاً، وأن يتركني بعده وَرْها.[١] فقال لزوجها: ما حُجّتك؟ قال: حُجّتي
أيّها الملك أنّها قد أُعْطِيَت المَهْرَ كاملاً، ولم أُصِبْ منها طائلا، إلّا وليداً خاملاً، فافعلْ | ما ١١٨
كنت فاعلاً. فأمر بالغلام أن يُنزع منهما جميعاً ويُجعل في غِلمانه، وقال لهُزيلة: أَبغيه ولدا، ولا
تنكِحي أحداً، وأجْزيه[٢] صَفَدا. فقالت هزيلة: أمّا النكاح فإنّما يكون بمهر، وأمّا السِّفاح فإنّما
يكون بلا مهر، وما لي فيهما من أمر! فلمّا سمع عمليق ذلك منهما أمر أن تُباع وزوجها، فيُعطَى
زوجُها خُمْسَها، وتُعْطى هُزيلة عُشْرَ ثمن زوجها، ويُسترقّا. فأنشأت تقول:

١ ك: (بعدع درها).

٢ هـ: (واجْزيه).

42 He is the ancestor of the ʿAmālīq or ʿAmāliqah (the Amalekites), on whom see above, note 14. Among the numerous parallel texts are al-Ṭabarī, *Tārīkh*, i, 771–772, tr. *The History*, iv, 151–152; Ibn Hishām, *Tījān*, 495–499; ps.-al-Jāḥiẓ, *Maḥāsin*, 280–282; al-Dīnawarī, *al-Akhbār al-ṭiwāl*, 17–18; al-Iṣfahānī, *Aghānī*, xi, 164–167; al-Masʿūdī, *Murūj al-dhahab*, ii, 264–269; Ibn Ḥamdūn, *Tadhkirah*, vii, 362–364; Ibn al-Athīr, *Kāmil*, i, 271–272; Ibn Badrūn, *Sharḥ Qaṣīdat Ibn Zaydūn*, 52–56; al-Nuwayrī, *Nihāyat al-arab*, xv, 339–340; al-Baghdādī, *Khizānat al-adab*, ii, 271–274; Abū ʿUbayd al-Bakrī, *Masālīk*, i, 100–102; idem, *Faṣl al-maqāl*, 116; Yāqūt, *Muʿjam al-buldān*, v, 442–444 (entry on al-Yamāmah). In some versions the king is called ʿUmlūq, to be distinguished from his ancestor ʿImlāq.

43 Ṭasm is a legendary Arabian tribe; see *EI2*, "Ṭasm" (W.P. Heinrichs). In traditional Arab genealogy they are traced back to the earliest times: ʿImlīq is the grandson of Sām (Shem) and great-grandson of Nūḥ (Noah). Instead of Lāwudh (or Lāwadh) one finds Lūdh (Lud in Genesis 10), Iram matches Aram (Genesis 10).

44 The word ʿUdhrah is not found in parallel versions; it is not known as a place name. The territory of the famous tribe of ʿUdhrah was the Hijaz in western Arabia, whereas al-Yamāmah is in central and eastern Arabia.

[§ 3 ʿImlīq[42]]

Another is ʿImlīq, King of Ṭasm, ibn Lāwudh ibn Iram ibn Sām ibn Nūḥ.[43] Their territories were ʿUdhrah, in al-Yamāmah.[44] The cause of his murder were his extreme injustice, tyranny, and bad conduct. There was a woman of Jadīs[45] called Huzaylah, who was married to a man called Qadīs.[46] He divorced her and wanted to take her son away from her. She litigated with him appealing to ʿImlīq.[47] "Sire," she said, "I have carried him for nine months; I delivered him, pushing; I suckled him for a couple of years. And now, when his limbs are full-grown, he wants to take him away forcibly, leaving me without him, distraught!"[48] The king asked her husband, "What is your argument?" He replied, "My argument, Sire, is that she has been given the bridal gift in full but I have
had nothing in return, except a weak young child. Do | what you must do." The 118
king then gave orders for the young boy to be taken from both of them and to be made one of his pages. He said to Huzaylah, "I desire him as a son. Do not get married to anyone. I shall bestow a gift upon him."[49] Huzaylah answered, "As for marriage, that should be with a bridal gift; cohabitation goes without a bridal gift.[50] I will not have to do with either."[51] When ʿImlīq heard what she said he gave orders for her and her husband to be sold, with her husband to be given one fifth of her price, and Huzaylah to be given one tenth of the husband's price, and both of them to be made slaves. Then Huzaylah said,

---

45 A tribe associated with Ṭasm.

46 The name could also be read as Qiddīs. Other sources have Q.rq.s (*Aghānī*, reading uncertain), Māsh (*Murūj al-dhahab*, *Nihāyat al-arab*), or Qāshir (*Tījān*).

47 The motif of the battle over the custody of a child is also found in other stories; see al-Jāḥiẓ, *Bayān*, i, 408 (on an unnamed Bedouin woman); Ibn Abī Ṭayfūr, *Balāghāt al-nisāʾ*, 70–72 (on Abū l-Aswad al-Duʾalī and his wife), also in Ibn Qutaybah, *ʿUyūn*, iv, 122; al-Qālī, *Amālī*, ii, 12; al-Marzubānī, *Nūr al-qabas*, 14–17; Ibn Ḥamdūn, *Tadhkirah*, vii, 222–223; al-Batlūnī, *Tasliyat al-khawāṭir*, 64–65, also quoted in Brünnow & Fischer, *Arabische Chrestomathie aus Prosaschriftstellern*, 6–7. The speeches of the wife and the husband are in rhymed prose in all versions.

48 Translation uncertain; *warhā* (for *warhāʾ*) normally means "clumsy, dumb". Other versions have "empty-handed (*ṣifrā*)" or "distraught (*walhā*)".

49 His words rhyme nicely but their sense is not clear if the verbs are read as imperatives, as in editions of parallels. Instead of *abghīhi* ("I want him"), *Murūj* and *Aghānī* have (*i*)*bghīhi* ("you must desire him"). Instead of *wa-jzīhi* as in ʿASH I have adopted the reading *wa-ajzīhi* (as e.g. in Yāqūt, *Muʿjam al-buldān*, v, 443).

50 Instead of the repetitive *bi-l-mahr*, *Murūj*, *Aghānī* and *Khizānah* have *bi-l-qahr*, "by force".

51 The two terms are *nikāḥ* and *sifāḥ*, the former regular "marriage" and the latter "cohabitation", to be distinguished from the more casual *zinā*, "fornication".

أتيْنا أخا طسمٍ ليحكُمَ بيننا فأنفذَ حُكْماً في هُزيلةَ ظالما
لَعَمْري لقد حَكَمْتَ لا متورِّعا ولا كنتَ فيما تُبْرِمِ الحُكمَ عالما
نَدِمتُ ولم أندَمْ وأُبْتُ بعَبْرتي وأصبح بَعْلي في الحكومة نادما

فلمّا سمع عمليق قولها أمر ألّا تُزوَّج بِكْرٌ من جديس فتُهْدى إلى زوجها إلّا يؤْتى بها عمليقُ فيفترعها هو قبل زوجها. فلَقُوا من ذلك جهداً وذُلًّا ولم يزل يفعل ذلك أربعين سنة فيهم، حتّى زُوّجت الشَّموس عفيرة بنت عَفار الجديسيّة، أخت الأَسْود الذي وقع إلى جَبَلَيْ طيّ‌ء وسكنوا الجَبَلين بعده، فلمّا أرادوا أن يُهْدوها إلى زوجها وانطلقوا[١] بها إلى عمليق ليَنالها قبله، ومعها الوليدات يتغنَّيْن ويقلْن:

ابْدَيْ بعمليقٍ وقُومي فارْكَبي وبادِري الصُّبح بأمرٍ مُعْجِبِ
فسوف تَلْقَيْن الذي لم تطلُبي وما لبِكرٍ عنده من مَهْرَبِ

فلما دخلت عليه افترعها، وخلّى سبيلها، فخرجت إلى قومها في دمائها، شاقّةً دِرْعَها عن قُبُلها ودُبُرها، وهي تقول:

---

١ كذا في هـ ولعلّ الصواب (انطلقوا) بدون واو العطف.

---

52 ʿASH and the editors of *Aghānī*, *Murūj*, *Masālik*, *Khizānah*, and *Nihāyah* read *ḥukkimta*, "you were made arbiter"; but the reading *ḥakamta* is metrically possible in older poetry and makes better sense.

53 This hemistich is obviously problematic. Instead of *ubtu bi-ʿabratī*, *Aghānī* and *Nihāyah* have *wa-annā bi-ʿathratī* (perhaps "how could I have stumbled?"); *Muʿjam al-buldān* has *wa-annā bi-ʿitratī* ("where can I get my family?"); *Tījān* reads *innī la-ghirratun* ("I am really naïve"); *Murūj* and *Masālik* have *nadimtu fa-lam aqdir ʿalā mutazaḥzaḥin* ("I regretted but I could not withstand …"—meaning of *mutazaḥziḥ* unclear; Ibn Badrūn, *Sharḥ* has *qadimtu fa-lam aqdir ʿalā mutaraḥraḥin*).

We came to our brother of Ṭasm to let him be judge between us,
but he passed a judgement wrongful to Huzaylah.
Upon my life, you passed judgement[52] irresponsibly,
you were ignorant about deciding the verdict.
I regret and I did not regret and I returned in tears,[53]
and my spouse now regrets the arbitration.

When ʿImlīq heard these words he decreed that no virgin of Jadīs would marry and be given to her husband before she would be taken to him, ʿImlīq, who would deflower her before her husband did.[54] This caused them distress and humiliation. He kept this practice for forty years, until the marriage of al-Shamūs ʿUfayrah,[55] daughter of ʿAfār[56] of Jadīs, sister of al-Aswad, who had arrived at the two mountains of the tribe of Ṭayyiʾ, where they dwelled after his death.[57] When they wanted to give her to her husband they took her to ʿImlīq, so that he could have her before her husband. With them were young girls, who sang:[58]

Begin with ʿImlīq! Then get up and ride
And in the morning do something amazing!
You will find something you did not seek
And no virgin that is with him will escape.

When she went in to him he deflowered her and let her go. She left and went to her people, bleeding, having torn her shift, front and behind, saying,[59]

54 For another instance of the motif of *ius primae noctis*, see below, §15.

55 Vowelled ʿAfīrah in *Aghānī*. *Masālik*: Ghufayrah; *Khizānah*: ʿUmayrah. *Murūj* offers both ʿUfayrah and Ghufayrah.

56 *Maḥāsin, Murūj, Masālik, Khizānah*: Ghafār; *al-Akhbār al-ṭiwāl*: Ghifār; *Aghānī*: ʿAbbād.

57 Ajaʾ and Salmā are the two mountains often associated with the large tribe of Ṭayyiʾ; see the long entry on Ajaʾ in Yāqūt, *Muʿjam al-buldān*, where it is said that al-Aswad ibn Ghifār (or Ghafār) al-Jadīsī fled to the region, having escaped from Ḥassān Tubbaʿ; see the following section on how he was murdered.

58 The metre is *rajaz*, the oldest and simplest metre, often used in extemporised verse.

59 In *rajaz muzdawij* (i.e., with paired rhyme, *aabbcc*).

١١٩ لا أحدٌ أذلُّ من جديسٍ   أهكذا يُفْعَل بالعَروسِ
يرضى بهذا يا لَقومِ حُرُّ   أُهدى وقد أعطى وسِيقَ المَهرُ
لَأَخْذةُ الموتِ كذا من نفسهِ   خيرٌ مِنَ أنْ يَفْعَلَ ذا بعِرْسِهِ

ثمّ قالت تحرّض قومَها فيما أتى عليها:

أيصلُح ما يؤتى إلى فتَياتكمْ   وأنتمْ رجالٌ فيكُمُ عَدَدُ النَّمْلِ
وتُصبح تمشى في الدماء صَبيحةٌ   عشيّةَ زُفَّت في النساء إلى بَعْلِ
فإنْ أنتُمُ لم تغضَبوا بعد هذه   فكونوا نساءً لا تَغِبُّ من الكُحْلِ
ودُونَكُمُ طِيبَ العَروس فإنَّما   خُلقْتُم لأثواب العَروس وللغِسْلِ
فلو أنَّنا كنّا رجالاً وأنتمُ   نساءٌ لكنّا لا نُقيم على الذُّلِّ
فبُعْداً وسُحْقاً للذي ليس دافعاً   ويختال يمشي بيننا مِشْيةَ الفَحْلِ
فموتوا كراماً أو أَميتوا عدوَّكمْ   ودِبُّوا لنار الحرب بالحَطَب الجَزْل

فلمّا سمع ذلك أخوها الأسْود، وكان سيّدا مُطاعاً، قال لقومه: يا معشرَ جديس، إنّ هؤلاء القوم ليسوا بأعزَّ منكم في داركم، إلّا بما كان من مُلك صاحبهم علينا وعليهم وأنتم أذلُّ من النِّيب، ولولا عجزُنا لما كان له فضل علينا، ولو امتنعنا كان له منه النَّصَف، فأَطيعوني فيما آمُرُكم به؛ فإنّه عزُّ الدهر وذَهاب ذُلّ العمر، واقبَلوا رأيي.

١٢٠ وقد أحمس جديساً قولُها، قالوا: نُطيعك، | ولكنّ القوم أكثر منّا عدداً وأقوى. قال: فإنّي أصنع للملك طعاماً، ثمّ أدعوهم إليه، فإذا جاءوا يرفُلون في حُلَلهم متفضّلين مشيْنا إليهم بالسيوف فقتلناهم، فأنفرد أنا بالعمليق، وينفرد كلُّ واحد بجليسه. فاجتمع رأيهم على ذلك.

60 The editions of several versions, including ʿASH and SKḤ, read the verb as a passive (*yufʿala*), "better than what is done to his bride", but the active *yafʿala* fits the context better, in laying the guilt of inaction on the cowardly husband.

No one is more despicable than Jadīs! 119
Is this what is done to a bride?
Would a noble man condone this, O men?
I am given as a bride, the bridal gift was given.
Truly, to kill himself
Were better than doing[60] thus to his bride.

Then she said, spurring on her menfolk because of what had happened to her:

Is it right what happens to your maidens,
while you are men numerous like ants?
A young woman[61] walks in her blood in the morning,
who the evening before was led to a master.
If after this you are not angry,
then be women and don't skip one day putting kohl on your eyes!
Put on perfume like a bride, for you are
created only for bride's clothes and lotion!
Now if we were men and you were women
we would not suffer this humiliation.
Down and away with him who does not defend us,
walking proudly in our midst like a stallion!
Die as noble men or kill your foe,
bring ample firewood to the fire of war!

When her brother al-Aswad heard his—he was a leader with authority—he said to his men, "Men of Jadīs! These people are not mightier than you where you live, except that this man of theirs rules over us and them. You are lowlier than old she-camels! If we were not so weak he would not prevail over us. But if we resist we would have justice from him! So obey me in what I tell you to do, for it will lead to lasting glory and the end of a lifelong humiliation. Accept my plan!"

Jadīs had been stirred by the woman's words. "We will obey you!", they said, | 120
"But those men are more numerous and stronger than we!" Al-Aswad replied, "I shall prepare a meal for the king and invite them to it. When they come, trailing their robes and having tied the ends of their garments around their necks, we shall come upon them with our swords and kill them. I myself will take care of ʿImlīq and each one of you will take care of the one sitting next to him." They all agreed to act accordingly.

---

61 *Aghānī*: ʿAfīrah (or ʿUfayrah).

وإنّ الأسود اتّخذ طعاماً كثيراً، وأمر القوم فاخترطوا سيوفهم، ودفنوها في الرمْل تحتهم، ودعا القومَ فجاءوا يرفُلون في الحُلَل، حتّى إذا أخذوا مَجالسهم ومدّوا أيدِيَهم إلى الطعام أخذوا سيوفهم من تحت أقدامهم، فشدّ الأسود على عمليق وكلُّ رجل على جليسه حتّى أناموهم، فلمّا فرغوا من الأشراف شدّوا على السِّفْلة فأفنَوْهم، فلم يَدَعوا منهم شطْراً، فقال الأسود:

ذُوقي ببَغْيِكِ يا طَسْمُ مجلَّلةً   فقد أتيتِ لَعَمري أعجبَ العَجَبِ
إنّا أتينا فلم ننفكَّ نقتُلهمْ   والبغْي هيَّجَ منّا سوْرَةَ الغَضَبِ
فلن يعودَ علينا بغْيُهمْ أبداً   ولن يكونوا لدى أنْفٍ ولا ذَنَبِ
ولو رعيْتم لنا قُربى مؤكَّدةً   كُنّا الأقاربَ في الأرحامِ والنَّسَبِ

[§ ٤] **ومنهم أيضاً** الأسود بن عَفار هذا، وكان هرب من حسّان بن تُبَّع، حين استغاثه
الطَّسْميّ، فغزا جديساً فقتلها، وأخرب جوًّا، فمضى الأسود فأقام بجَبَلَي طيّئ قبل نزول
طيّئ إيّاهما.[١] | وكان سبب قتله أن طيّئاً كانوا يسكنون الجوْف من أرض اليمن، وهو اليوم ١٢١
مَحَلّة مُراد وهَمْدان، وكان مَسْكنهم وادياً يُدعى ظَريباً، وكان سيّدهم يومئذ أُسامة بن لُؤَيّ
بن الغَوْث بن طيّئ. وكان الوادي مَسْبَعةً وهم قليل عديدُهم، وقد كان ينْتابهم بعيرٌ في أزمان
الخريف، فيضرِب في إبلهم، فإذا انقطع الخريف لم يُدْرَ أين يذهب، ولم يَرَوْه إلى قابل.
وكانت الأزْد قد خرجت من اليمن أيّامَ العَرِم فتفرّقتْ، فاستوحشوا لذلك، وقالوا: قد ظعن إخْوتُنا

١ كـ: (إياها).

62 Perhaps meaning they will never have high or even low positions. *Aghānī*: "they will not be like having nose or tail" (where *anf*, "nose", could also mean "pride").

63 His story is of course closely connected with those of Ḥassān ibn Tubbaʿ and ʿImlīq. See the sources mentioned above, the closest being al-Iṣfahānī, *Aghānī*, xi, 167–169; see also e.g. Yāqūt, *Muʿjam al-buldān*, entries "Ajaʾ" and "al-Yamāmah".

64 It is unclear who is meant.

65 Yāqūt, *Muʿjam al-buldān* mentions al-Jaww as a region in al-Yamāmah; Abū ʿUbayd al-Bakrī (*Masālik*, i, 40, 294) says that Jaww was the name of al-Yamāmah itself at the time. Al-Yamāmah (which means "dove"), it is said (e.g. al-Baghdādī, *Khizānah*, ii, 275), is named after the remarkable woman of Ṭasm called Zarqāʾ ("the blue-eyed woman") al-Yamāmah, who had married a man of Jadīs and with her miraculous eyesight was able to see the advancing army of Ḥassān Tubbaʿ, camouflaged with branches, Birnam-Wood-style. Like Cassandra she was not believed. Ḥassān massacred Jadīs, gouged out Zarqāʾ's eyes and crucified her on the gates of Jaww; see e.g. *EI2*, "Zarḳāʾ al-Yamāma" (Irfan Shahîd).

Al-Aswad had a copious meal prepared. He told his men to unsheathe their swords and bury them in the sand below their feet. He invited the men and they arrived, trailing their robes. When they were all seated and stretched their hands towards the food, they took the swords from beneath their feet. Al-Aswad attacked ʿImlīq and every man attacked the one sitting next to him, until they had felled them all. When they had finished off the nobles they attacked their minions and annihilated them, not leaving a single one. Then al-Aswad said,

Have a taste of your own tyranny, Ṭasm, coming to all of you!
You committed, upon my life, a truly strange thing.
We came to you and did not stop killing:
tyranny stirred in us the force of anger.
Their tyranny shall never return to us
and they shall no longer be with nose or tail.[62]
But if you observe the assured closeness between us
we shall be relatives with bonds of kinship and lineage.

[§ 4 al-Aswad ibn ʿAfār[63]]

Also among them is this al-Aswad ibn ʿAfār. He had fled from Ḥassān Tubbaʿ when the man from Ṭasm[64] asked the latter for help. Ḥassān attacked Jadīs and killed them, destroying Jaww.[65] Al-Aswad left and dwelled at the two mountains of Ṭayyiʾ[66] before the tribe of Ṭayyiʾ themselves settled there. | The cause 121
of his being murdered was as follows. The tribe of Ṭayyiʾ used to dwell in al-Jawf in Yemen,[67] which today is the area of the tribes of Murād and Hamdān. They used to live in a wadi called Ẓarīb[68] and their leader at the time was Usāmah ibn Luʾayy ibn al-Ghawth ibn Ṭayyiʾ. The wadi was abounding in predators;[69] they themselves were few in number. Every year in the autumn a camel stallion would come and mount their camels; at the end of autumn it went nobody knew where and they would not see it again until the following year. The tribe

66 See above, note 57. The importance of Ṭayyiʾ or Ṭayy (on whom see e.g. *EI2*, "Ṭayyiʾ" [Irfan Shahîd]) is illustrated in the Syriac word for Arabs in general, *Ṭayyāyē*.

67 Al-Jawf (which like al-Jaww means "hollow, depression") is the name of several places, see e.g. Yāqūt, *Muʿjam al-buldān*, *EI2*, "Djawf" (M. Quint). Instead of al-Jawf, *Aghānī* has al-Jurf.

68 In al-Sijistānī, *Muʿammarūn*, 80, Ẓarīb is called a *jabal* ("mountain" or "mountainous area").

69 *Masbaʿah*, derived from *sabʿ* which often means "lion" but can also refer to other animals of prey.

فصاروا إلى الأرياف. فلمّا همّوا بالظَّعْن قالوا: يا قوم، إنّ هذا البعير الذي يأتينا من بلدٍ ريفٍ وخِصْب، وإنّا لَنُصيب في بَعره النَّوى، ولو أنّا تعهّدْناه عند انصرافه فشخصْنا معه لعلّنا نصيب مكاناً خيراً من مكاننا هذا. فأجمعوا أمرهم على ذلك. فلمّا كان الخريفُ جاء الجمل فضرب في إبلهم، فلمّا انصرف احتملوا فتَبِعوه، فجعلوا يسيرون بسَيْره، ويَبيتون حيث يبيت، حتّى هبط بهم على الجبليْن، فقال أُسامة بن لُؤَيّ:

اجعَلْ ظَرِيباً كحبيبٍ يُنْسَى   لكلِّ قومٍ مُصْبَحٌ ومُمْسَى

فهجمت طيّئ على النخل في الشِّعاب، ومَواشٍ كثيرة وَحْشيّة كانت لقوم من جديس، وإذا هُمْ برجل في شِعب من تلك الشِّعاب، وهو الأسود بن عَفار، | فهالَهم ما رأوْه من عِظَمِ ١٢٢
خِلْقته وتخوَّفوه، فنزلوا ناحية من الأرض، [وسبروها هل يرَوْن بها أحداً غيره فلم يروْا، فقال][1] أسامة بن لؤيّ لابنٍ له يقال له الغوْث: أيْ بُنَيَّ، إنّ قومك قد عرفوا فضلَك عليهم في الجَلَد والبأس والرَّمْي، فإن كفَيْتَنا هذا الرجلَ سُدْتَ قومَك آخِرَ الدهر، وكنت أنت الذي أنزلْتَنا هذا البلد.

فانطلق الغوثُ حتّى أتى الرجل فكلّمه وساءله، فعجِب الأسود من صِغَر خَلْق الغوث، فقال له: من أين أقبلتم؟ قال: من اليمن. وأخبره خبر البعير، وأنّا رهبنا ما رأيْنا من عِظَم خلقك. فشغلوه بالكلام، وختله الغوث فرَماه بسهم فقتله، فأقامت طيّئ بالجبليْن.[2]

١ كما في هامش هـ، في النسختين بياض والتكملة من الأغاني.

٢ بعده في ك: (فأقامت طيئ بالجبلين).

of Azd had left Yemen in the days of the flood of ʿArim[70] and had dispersed. The Ṭayyiʾites felt abandoned as a result. "Our brothers have departed," they said, "and have moved to fertile lands". They made preparations to depart too and said, "Men, this camel stallion that visits us must come from a cultivated and fertile land, for one finds date stones in its dung. If we stay with it when it moves off and depart with it, it may take us to a better place than this!" They all agreed to do so. When autumn came, the camel returned, mating with their camels. At its leaving they loaded their belongings on their camels and followed it, travelling wherever it went and spending the night wherever it did. Finally it led them to the two mountains. Then Usāmah ibn Luʾayy said,[71]

> Make Ẓarīb like a loved one who is forgotten;
> Every people has a place in the morning and another in the evening.

Then Ṭayyiʾ took possession of the date palms in the valleys between the mountains, and of a lot of livestock roaming in the wild but belonging to Jadīs. In one of these valleys they came upon a man; this was al-Aswad ibn ʿAfār. | They were 122
in awe of his large body and were filled with fear. They settled some distance away, exploring the land to see if there was anyone else, but they saw nobody but him.[72] Usāmah ibn Luʾayy said to one of his sons, al-Ghawth, "Your people, my boy, know that you excel them in toughness, strength and shooting. If you protect us against this man you will be the leader of your tribe forever and you will be the one to make us settle in this land."

Al-Ghawth went up to the man and addressed him, asking him a question. Al-Aswad was struck by his small size. He asked him, "Where have you come from?" Al-Ghawth replied, "From Yemen", and he told him the story of the camel, adding, "We were scared when we saw how big you are!" They kept him engaged in conversation and then al-Ghawth shot him, unawares, with an arrow, killing him. Then Ṭayyiʾ remained at the Two Mountains.

---

70 A reference to the bursting of the dam in Maʾrib, an event mentioned briefly in the Qurʾan (Q Sabaʾ 34:15–16): «There was a sign for Sabaʾ (i.e., Sheba) in their dwelling-place (…) but they turned away, so We let loose on them the flood of ʿArim». The meaning of the word *ʿarim* is unclear and much disputed. The remnants of irrigation works at Maʾrib can still be seen. This event, which may not have been as cataclysmic as described in legend but may have been more gradual, was followed by widespread migrations of tribes.

71 In al-Sijistānī, *Muʿammarūn*, 80 these *rajaz* verses are said by the eponymous ancestor of the tribe, Ṭayyiʾ ibn Udad (who is said to have lived for five hundred years).

72 This sentence with the following "(he) said" is supplied by ʿASH from *Aghānī*, to replace a lacuna in the MSS.

[§ ٥] **ومنهم** عامر الضَّحْيان بن سعد بن الخَزْرَج بن تيْم اللّٰه بن النَّمِر بن قاسط، وكان صاحبَ مِرباعِ ربيعةَ بن نزار ومُنْزِلَها في نُجَعها وحَكَمَها في خصوماتها،[١] وكانت ربيعة تغزو المَغازِيَ وهو في مَنزله، فتبعث له نصيبه[٢] ولنسائه حِصّة إعظاماً له، فمكث بذلك حيناً. وفي ذلك قول بعضهم:

تُعْجِبني أُسُدٌ ضارياتٌ ويأكل مِرباعهنَّ الضَّبُعْ
تَمارس عَنّا بصُمِّ القَنا لشيخِ أُمامةَ[٣] أن يضْطجِعْ

وكان أعرج. وإنّه شرب الخمر فاشتهى لحماً، فذُكرت له نَعْجة غريبة | لكعب بن الحارث بن ١٢٣
عامر بن عبد القيس، كانت امرأته مَرِضت فخلّفها ظئراً لابنه، فبعث إليها الضحيان فذبحها وكعبٌ غائب، فرجع كعب فرأى ابنَه يضغو جُوعاً، فسأل عن النعجة فأخبروه أنّ الضحيان أكلها، فخرج بحَرْبته حتّى انتهى إلى منزله ليلاً فصرخ به فقالت له امرأته: الذي يدعوك يريد قتلك، فلا تخرج إليه! فقال: لو دُعي عامر لطعنةٍ أجاب![٤] وخرج فبدره كعب فأوجره الحربةَ فقتله.

١ ك: (خصومتها).
٢ ك: (نصيبه مما تصيبه).
٣ ك: (أمامه).
٤ ك: (لأجاب).

[§5 ʿĀmir al-Ḍaḥyān[73]]

Another is ʿĀmir al-Ḍaḥyān ibn Saʿd ibn al-Khazraj ibn Taym Allāh ibn al-Namir ibn Qāsiṭ.[74] He was the owner of the pasture grounds of Rabīʿah ibn Nizār[75] and the one who made them live on their foraging lands. He was the arbiter in their disputes.[76] He would stay at home while Rabīʿah carried out raids; they would send him his share of the spoils, and a portion to his wives, out of respect for him. This went on for some time. One of them said about this:

> I am amazed at those predatory lions,
> seeing that a hyena eats from their pasture grounds.
> They exert themselves with solid spears
> that Umāmah's old man may sleep.[77]

He was lame. Once he was drinking wine and craved for some meat. He was told about a wonderful ewe | belonging to Kaʿb ibn al-Ḥārith ibn ʿĀmir ibn ʿAbd 123
al-Qays.[78] Kaʿb's wife was ill; he had left her behind to nurse his son. Al-Ḍaḥyān sent for the ewe and slaughtered it, while Kaʿb was away. When Kaʿb returned he saw his son howling from hunger. He asked about the ewe and they told him that al-Ḍaḥyān had eaten it. He went out with his short spear and arrived at al-Ḍaḥyān's place in the evening. He called out to him. ʿĀmir's wife said, "That man who is calling you wants to kill you; don't go outside!" But ʿĀmir said, "If ʿĀmir is called for a stabbing he will respond!"[79] When he went outside Kaʿb sprang upon him, piercing him with his spear and killing him.

---

73 For a very short parallel of this murder story see Abū ʿUbayd al-Bakrī, *Muʿjam*, 80.

74 He was called al-Ḍaḥyān because he used to sit with his people in the forenoon (*ḍuḥā*), when making decisions, see Muḥammad ibn Ḥabīb, *Muḥabbar*, 135; Ibn Qutaybah, *Maʿārif*, 95; al-Iṣfahānī, *Aghānī*, xxi (ed. Brünnow), 186. For his lineage see ǦN, i, 167.

75 Rabīʿah ibn Nizār ibn Maʿadd ibn ʿAdnān and its brother group Muḍar together are the two main branches of the so-called "North Arabs". ʿĀmir al-Ḍaḥyān belonged to the tribe of al-Namir ibn Qāsiṭ, which is part of Rabīʿah.

76 He is listed by al-Yaʿqūbī (*Tārīkh*, i, 299, tr. *The Works*, 582) among "the arbiters (*ḥukkām*) of the Arabs".

77 Umāmah is presumably ʿĀmir's wife or daughter. The poem has not been found elsewhere.

78 Not found elsewhere.

79 For a similar response, see below, §22.

[§٦] **ومنهم** عَبْدة بن مُرارة بن سَوّار بن الحارث بن سعد بن مالك بن ثعلبة بن [...][١] وهِلال بن أُمَيّة الخُزاعيّ، فحبا الأسديَّ حِباءً كثيراً، ولم يَحْبُ هِلالا شيئاً. فأقفلا حتّى إذا كانا[٢] بِوادٍ يقال له وادي طُفيل مالا إليه، فنزلا[٣] فغدا الخزاعيّ على عبدة بن مرارة وهو راقد فقتله، وأخذ ما حُبي به. فلمّا قَدِم سئل عنه فقال: مات! فصدّقوه، واشترى بما أخذ منه إبلاً وخيلا.

فتغنّى يوماً الخزاعيّ وقد أخذ فيه الشراب:

أبلِغْ بني أَسَدٍ بأنَّ أخاهُمُ بِلِوَى طُفيلٍ عَبْدة بن مُرارَهْ
يؤْتي فقيرَهُمُ ويمنَعُ ضيْمَهمْ ويُريح بعد[٤] المُعْتِمين عِشارَهْ ١٢٤

فلمّا سمعت بذلك بنو أسد نهضوا إلى بني كِنانة فقالوا: حليفُكم هذا قتل أخانا، فإن تَدُوه دِيَةَ الملوك نَقْبَلْ، وإن تأْبَوْا نقتُلْ! فوَدَوْه دِيَةَ الملوك ألفَ بَعير.

١ بياض في الأصل.
٢ كـ: (كان).
٣ كـ: (فنزل).
٤ لعلّ الصواب (قبل) كما في معجم البلدان.

80 No parallels of this story have been found except a brief mention in Yāqūt, *Muʿjam al-buldān*, s.v. "Liwā Ṭufayl".

81 *ĞN*, i, 55 mentions one ʿAbd [thus] ibn Murārah ibn Suwāʾah ibn Saʿd ibn Mālik ibn Thaʿlabah (ibn Dūdān ibn Asad). There is a lacuna in the MSS of approximately six words.

82 Unidentified. He is not the Hilāl ibn Umayyah who was one of the Medinan Anṣār ("Supporters") of the prophet Muḥammad. On the tribe Khuzāʿah see *EI2*, s.v. (M.J. Kister), on Asad see *EI2*, s.v. (H. Kindermann).

83 Partly because of the lacuna it is not wholly clear what has happened. From the poem below it would appear that ʿAbdah is the giver, and the man from Asad (also ʿAbdah's tribe) the one who received. However, the murdered ʿAbdah is said to be robbed "of what he has been given".

[§ 6 ʿAbdah ibn Murārah[80]]

Another is ʿAbdah ibn Murārah ibn Sawwār ibn al-Ḥārith ibn Saʿd ibn Thaʿlabah ibn […][81] and Hilāl ibn Umayyah al-Khuzāʿī.[82] He gave the man from Asad[83] a lot but he gave Hilāl nothing. Both men[84] went back. When they came near a place called Wādī Ṭufayl[85] they went to it and made their camp. In the morning the man from Khuzāʿah attacked ʿAbdah ibn Murārah while he was asleep, killed him, and took what he had been given. When he arrived home they asked him about ʿAbdah. "He died", he replied, and they believed him. He bought camels and horses with what he had taken.

One day the Khuzāʿi, under the influence of wine, was singing:

> Tell the tribe of Asad that their brother
> lies in the twisting valley of Ṭufayl: ʿAbdah ibn Murārah!
> He gives to the poor and protects them from being wronged 124
> and makes his pregnant camels rest before those that travel at night.[86]

When the men of Asad heard this they went to the tribe of Kinānah[87] and said, "This man, who is allied with you, has killed our brother! If you pay the blood money[88] given for kings we will accept it, if you refuse we shall kill you." They paid the blood money for kings, one thousand camels.[89]

---

84 From the following it appears that ʿAbdah and Hilāl are meant.

85 Between Yemen and Mecca according to Yāqūt (entry "Liwā Ṭufayl").

86 ʿASH explains in a note: "The Bedouins rest their camels shortly after sunset, making them kneel for a while to let them recuperate (…); therefore the version in Yāqūt, *qabla* ("before") [instead of *baʿd* ("after"), as in AM] is to be preferred." I take *ʿishār* to be a plural of *ʿusharāʾ* ("a she-camel that has been ten months pregnant"); "it is said that camels are most precious to their owners when they are *ʿishār*" (Lane, *Lexicon*, s.v.).

87 On Kinānah see *EI2*, s.v. (W.M. Watt).

88 The pre-Islamic system of compensation for homicide and injuries, *diyah*, was adopted in Islamic law; see *EI2*, "diya" (E. Tyan). The normal tariff for homicide was one hundred camels of various categories; for deliberate homicide the camels would be of more valuable kinds. The *diyat al-mulūk* ("blood money for kings") was said in ancient times to be three hundred camels (al-Baghdādī, *Khizānah*, vii, 370–371, quoting a line by al-Farazdaq) or one thousand camels (ibid. 374 and Ibn ʿAbd Rabbih, *ʿIqd*, v, 148–149).

89 For the motif of the killer who betrays himself, see also below, the story of al-Ḥārith ibn Kaʿb (§ 8) and the story of Kuntus in al-Tawḥīdī, *Imtāʿ*, ii, 153–155, which goes back to the Greek story of Ibycus; see Van Gelder, "On Coincidence".

[§ ٧] **ومنهم** زُهير بن عبد شمس من بني صَيْفيّ بن سَبَأ الأصغر، وقتلتْه[١] بِلْقِيس بنت [اليشرَح بن ذي جَدَن بن يَشْرح بن الحارث بن قيس بن] صيفيّ.[٢] وكان سبب ذلك أنّه كان ملكاً، فعَلا في مملكته وتكبَّر، وجعل يعتذر النساء قبل أزواجهنّ، كما كان يفعل عِمليق، حتّى أدركت بلقيسُ فقالت لأبيها: إنّ هذا الرجل قد فضح نساءكم فائْتِهِ فقُل له: إنّ لي بنتاً قد أعصرتْ، وليس في قومها شبيهٌ لها حُسناً وجمالاً. فإنْ قال لك: فابعَثْ بها إليّ، فقل: إنّ مِثلي في شَرَفي ونَسَبي لا تُعتذَر ابنتُه إلّا في بيته! فأتاه فذكر ذلك له، فلمّا قال له: ابعثْ بها[٣] قال له ما علّمتْه ابنتُه، فقال له: كيف بنُزْلي | ونُزْلِ مَن معي من أصحابي؟ فقال: ما أَحْمَلَني لِنُزل الملك، وأشدَّ ١٢٥
سروري به، لأ[نّها] مَكْرُمة لي، ويَدٌ وضعها الملكُ عندي.

فأجابه إلى إتْيانه، ولم يُجِبْ إلى ذلك غيرَه. فأتي داره فزخرفها وزخرف أبياتاً ثلاثة بأحسنِ ما يكون من زينةِ ذلك الزمان، وحَشَد لنُزله، ثمّ أتاه فأعلمه بالفَراغ، فركب فأتاه وقد أدخلت بلقيس نَفَراً من أقاربها بأَسْلِحتهم. ولمّا دخل البيت الأوّل أعجبه ما رأى من هيْئته، ثمّ دخل البيت الثاني فكان أحسنَ، ثمّ دخل الثالث وفيه بلقيس في حَلْيها وحُلَلها مع جمالها، فلمّا استلقى على الفِراش، وأخرج حَرَسَه وأجناده، وأمر بالباب فأُغلق دونه وكان معه المَقاوِل قالت للنَّفَر: اخرُجوا. فخرجوا فقتلوه. ثمّ أرسلتْ إلى رجل آخَرَ من مَقاوِلته وخواصِّه تدعوهم فيقتلونهم[٤] ولا يظُنّ مَن يُرسَل إليه إلّا أنّ الملك يدعوه، حتّى أتت على آخِرهم. ثمّ أرسلت إلى أبيها وقومها فخرجت إليهم وقالت: هذا الخبيث قد فضح نساءكم وجعلكم شُهرةً في الناس قد أراحكم

١ كـ: (قتلته).

٢ هـ: (بِلْقِيس بنت [اليشرح بن ذي جدن بن يشرح بن الحارث بن قيس بن] صيفي)، والتكملة من المحبّر لابن حبيب.

٣ الكلمة ناقصة في كـ.

٤ كـ: (فيقتلوهم).

90 See also Van Gelder, *Classical Arabic Literature*, 117–118. Bilqīs, the name of the Queen of Sheba in Arabic, is very famous but the story of her murderous ascension to the throne is less often found. For a somewhat different version, see Ibn Hishām, *Tījān*, 157–169, where the murdered king is called ʿAmr Dhū l-Adhʿār.

91 A fuller genealogy is given e.g. in *ĞN*, i, 275, 274, 176: Yalammaqah (Bilqīs) bint Ilīsharaḥ ibn Dhī Jadan ibn Ilīsharaḥ ibn al-Ḥārith ibn Qays ibn Ṣayfī ibn Saba' (al-Aṣghar, "the younger") ibn Kaʿb ibn Zayd ibn Sahl, ultimately going back to Ḥimyar ibn Saba' (the Biblical Sheba)

[§ 7 Zuhayr ibn ʿAbd Shams[90]]

Another is Zuhayr ibn ʿAbd Shams, of the Banū Ṣayfī ibn Sabaʾ al-Aṣghar. He was killed by Bilqīs, daughter of Ṣayfī.[91] The cause of this was that he was a king who ruled despotically and overbearingly; he used to deflower women before their husbands, just as ʿImlīq had done.[92] But when Bilqīs reached adulthood, she said to her father, "This man has dishonoured your women! Go to him and say: 'I've got a daughter who has become nubile. There is nobody as beautiful and attractive as she!' Then, if he says to you, 'Send her to me!' you must say: 'The virginity of the daughter of a nobleman like myself is not taken except in his own house!' " The father went to him and said all this to him. When Zuhayr said, "Send her to me!" he said what his daughter had told him. Zuhayr replied,
"What about entertainment for me | and the followers I am bringing along?" He 125
replied, "I am very capable of entertaining the king and very pleased to do so; it will be an honour for me and a favour from the king towards me!"

Zuhayr agreed to come to him, something he had done for nobody else. The father went home and decorated his house; he decorated three rooms in the most ornate fashion of his day, and he made everything ready for the king's entertainment. Then he went to Zuhayr and told him that everything was ready. Zuhayr mounted and rode to him. Bilqīs had hidden a number of her kinsmen, with their weapons. When Zuhayr entered the first room he was amazed by what he saw. Then he entered the second room, which was even more beautiful. Then he entered the third room, where Bilqīs was, all decked out in her jewels and robes, in all her beauty. When he lay down on the bed, having sent his guard and his soldiers outside, and having ordered the door to be locked (he had some vassal princes with him), she said to her own men, "Come out!" They came out and killed him. Then she sent for one of his vassals and courtiers, calling all of them one after the other, upon which they killed them; whoever was summoned thought that it was the king who called him. This went on until she had them all killed. Then she called for her father and his people. She left the room and came to them, saying, "This evil man had dishonoured your women and made you infamous among the people: God has relieved you of him! Now

ibn Qaḥṭān (ancestor of the "South Arabs"). For a different genealogy, see e.g. Ibn Qutaybah, *al-Maʿārif*, 628. The name Bilqīs, by which the Queen of Sheba is known in Arabic lore, has been connected with the Greek *pallakis* (παλλακίς), "concubine". Her mother is said to have been a demon (*jinniyyah*, e.g. Ibn Hishām, *Tījān*, 171, al-Jāḥiẓ, *Bighāl*, 371).

92 See above, § 3.

اللّٰه منه، فدونَكم ملِّكوا مَن شئتم. فقالوا بأجمعهم: ما أحدٌ أوْلى بهذا منكِ! فملّكوها عليهم
فملكتْهم، حتّى كان من أمر الهُدْهُد وسُليْمان عليه السلام ما كان.

[§٨] **ومنهم** الحارث بن كعب وقتله ضَبّة بن أُدّ. وسبب ذلك أنّ ضبّةَ تفرّقتْ إبلُه تحت ١٢٦
الليل، وكان له ابنان:[١] سَعْد وسُعَيْد، فخرجا يطلُبانها، فتفرّقا في طَلَبها، فجاء بها[٢] سعد ولم
يرجع سُعيد، فأتى على ذلك ما شاء اللّٰه تعالى أن يأتي، لا يرى سُعيداً ولا يَعلم له خبراً.

ثمّ إنّ ضبّة بعد ذلك بَيْنا هو يَسيرُ والحارثَ بن كعب في الأشْهُر الحُرُم وهُما يتحدّثان،
إذ مرّا على سَرْحةٍ بمكان، فقال له الحارث: أَترى هذا المكان؟ فإنّي لقِيتُ به[٣] شابًّا من هَيْئته
كذا وكذا—فوصف له صِفةَ سُعيد—فقتلتُه وأخذتُ بُرْداً كان عليه، من صفة البُرد كذا وكذا!
فوصف له صفة البرد وسيفاً كان عليه. فقال ضبّة: فما صفة السيف؟ قال: ها هو ذا عليَّ. قال
ضبة: فأَرِني السيف. فأراه إيّاه، فعرفه فضربه حتّى قتله. ولام الناس ضبّةَ فقالوا: قتل رجلاً في
الأشهُر الحُرم! فقال ضبّة: سبق السَّيف العَذْل! فصارت مَثَلا.

١ ك: (ابنا:).

٢ الكلمة ناقصة في ك.

٣ ك: (فيه).

93 The story of the hoopoe, the Queen of Sheba, and Sulaymān/Solomon is briefly told in the Qur'an (Q Saba' 27:15–44). For an elaborated account see the annotated English translation from the encyclopaedia of animals by al-Damīrī (d. 808/1405), *Ḥayāt al-ḥayawān al-kubrā* (one of many versions) in Van Gelder, *Classical Arabic Literature*, 298–304.

94 For parallel versions see al-Balādhurī, *Ansāb*, xi, 316–362 and the proverb collections on the saying *al-ḥadīth shujūn* (al-Mufaḍḍal, *Amthāl*, 4–5; al-Maydānī, *Majmaʿ al-amthāl*, i, 258–259; al-ʿAskarī, *Jamharat al-amthāl*, i, 303–304; Abū ʿUbayd al-Bakrī, *Faṣl al-maqāl*, 67–68) or the saying *a-Saʿd am Suʿayd* (al-Zamakhsharī, *Mustaqṣā*, i, 168–169). Neither saying occurs in the present version.

choose yourself a king, anyone you wish." They all said, "No one is worthier of this than you!" So they made her their queen and she ruled over them, until the matter of the hoopoe and Solomon (peace be upon him).[93]

[§ 8 al-Ḥārith ibn Kaʿb[94]]

Another is al-Ḥārith ibn Kaʿb, who was killed by Ḍabbah ibn Udd.[95] The cause of this was that Ḍabbah's camels dispersed in the night. He had two sons, Saʿd and Suʿayd, who went out in different directions in search of them. Saʿd brought them back but Suʿayd did not return. Only God knows what happened to him, for Ḍabbah never saw Suʿayd again nor did he hear anything about him. 126

One day, when Ḍabbah was walking along with al-Ḥārith ibn Kaʿb—it was during the Sacred Months[96]—they came past a large tree[97] at some place. Al-Ḥārith remarked to Ḍabbah, "You see that tree? Once I met a young man there ..." He went on to describe his appearance, which turned out to be that of Suʿayd. "... And I killed him and took a robe he was wearing ..." He described the robe. "... and a sword he was carrying." Ḍabbah asked him, "What did the sword look like?" Al-Ḥārith replied, "I am carrying it, here it is!" "Show me the sword", said Ḍabbah. He showed it to him. Ḍabbah took it and recognised it. Then he struck al-Ḥārith with it and killed him.[98] People blamed him, saying that he had killed a man during the Sacred Months. But Ḍabbah said, "The sword was quicker than the blame", which became a proverb.[99]

---

95 Ḍabbah ibn Udd is the eponymous ancestor of a tribe. He is only seven generations after ʿAdnān, ancestor of the "North Arabs"; see *ǦN*, i, 59, 89. There are many persons called al-Ḥārith ibn Kaʿb (*ǦN*, ii, 308 lists twenty of that name). He is probably to be identified as al-Ḥārith ibn Kaʿb ibn ʿAmr, ancestor of the tribe of Balḥārith ibn Kaʿb, which is part of the larger tribe of Madhḥij (*ǦN*, i, 258 and ii, 308).

96 During the sacred months markets were held and pilgrimages were performed; fighting and shedding blood were taboo.

97 It is a *sarḥah*; described as a tree of great size, without thorns, with a yellow fruit resembling the olive (Lane, *Lexicon*, s.v.).

98 For another instance of a murderer using his victim's sword, see below, §17.

99 This saying, too, is found in the usual proverb collections. It is also found in al-Qālī, *Amālī*, i, 106, where the killer and coiner of the saying is wrongly said to have been al-Ḥārith ibn Ẓālim; he is corrected in Abū ʿUbayd al-Bakrī, *Simṭ al-laʾālī*, i, 324.

١٢٧ [§٩] **ومنهم** داود بن هُبالة بن عمرو بن [عوْف بن ضجْعم بن][١] سعد بن سَلِيح[٢] بن حُلوان بن عِمْران بن الحاف بن قُضاعة. وكان أوّلُ مُلكِ الروم بالشام على عهده. وذلك أنّه كان مَلكاً فغلبه ملك الروم على مُلكه، فصالحَه داودُ على أن يُقِرَّه في منازله ويَدَعَه فيكونَ تحت يده، ففعل فكان يُغير بمن معه، ثمّ تنصّر وكَرِهَ الدِّماء وبنى ديْراً، فكان ينقُل الطِّين على ظهره والماء، فسُمِّي اللَّثِق، فنُسب[٣] الدير إليه، وأنزله الرُّهْبانَ. فلمّا تعبّد اجتُرئ عليه فقال له ملك الروم: اغْزُ بِمَن معك من العرب. فلم يجِدْ بُدًّا من أن يفعل، فغزا فكان على خَيْله جعفر بن صُبْح التَّنوخيّ، وكان معه في جيشه زُهير بن جَناب بن هُبَل الكَلْبيّ، فغزا عبدَ القيْس، فقتل زهيرُ بن جناب هَدّاجَ بن مالك بن عامر بن الحارث بن أنمار بن عمرو بن وديعة بن لُكَيْز بن أَفْصى بن عبد القيس، وأغار في وجهه على [بَكْر][٤] بن وائل فقتل زهيرٌ أيضاً هَدّاجَ بن مالك بن تيْم اللّٰه بن ثَعْلَبة بن عُكابة، فقال حُداد[٥] بن ظالم بن ذُهل بن عِجْل العَبْديّ:

---

١ هـ: التكملة من حواشي الاشتقاق.

٢ ك: (سليم) كما في النسختين، والتصحيح في هـ من المحبّر لابن حبيب والاشتقاق لابن دريد.

٣ ك: (فسب).

٤ هـ: موضعها بياض في النسختين، والتكملة بقلم الشنقيطيّ.

٥ هـ، ك: (حُذار) والتصحيح من جمهرة النسب لابن الكلبيّ وغيرها من المراجع.

---

100 A brief parallel in Ibn al-Kalbī, *Nasab Maʿadd wa-l-Yaman*, 691–692. Dāwūd ibn Hubālah (or Habālah, or Habūlah as in *Nasab Maʿadd wa-l-Yaman*) is mentioned in Muḥammad ibn Ḥabīb, *Muḥabbar*, 250 as one of the *jarrārūn* ("leaders of a thousand men") of the tribe of Quḍāʿah.

101 The name can also be read as Ḍujʿum; it means "strong, sturdy". "The Ḍajʿams (*al-Ḍajāʿim*)", descendants of Dāwūd's ancestor, were kings of Syria before the Ghassānids (Ibn Ḥabīb, *Muḥabbar*, 370, Ibn Durayd, *Ishtiqāq*, 319). The Ghassānids, also called Jafnids after their leading clan Jafnah, were Byzantine vassals from the beginning of the sixth century. The bracketed words are added by Hārūn.

102 *ĞN*, i, 326 and 279: Dāwūd (al-Lathiq) ibn Habālah ibn ʿAmr ibn ʿAwf ibn Ḥamāṭah (Ḍujʿum) ibn Saʿd ibn ʿAmr (Salīḥ) ibn Ḥulwān ibn ʿImrān ibn al-Ḥāfī ibn Quḍāʿah. See also ii, 232. On the tribe (or rather group of tribes) Quḍāʿah, see *EI2*, "Ḳuḍāʿa" (M.J. Kister).

103 Al-Rūm, referring to Romans or Byzantines.

104 It was called Dayr Dāwūd (Ibn Durayd, *Ishtiqāq*, 319). It is not mentioned in al-Shābushtī's book on monasteries, *al-Diyārāt*, or in Yāqūt's *Muʿjam al-buldān*.

[§ 9 Dāwūd ibn Hubālah[100]]

Another is Dāwūd ibn Hubālah ibn ʿAmr ibn [ʿAwf ibn Ḍajʿam[101] ibn] Saʿd ibn 127
Salīḥ ibn Ḥulwān ibn ʿImrān ibn al-Ḥāf ibn Quḍāʿah.[102] The beginning of the rule of the Romans[103] in Syria was in his time. He was king but the emperor of the Romans conquered his kingdom. Dāwūd made peace with him on condition that he would be left to rule his lands as the Roman emperor's vassal. This was done and he went on to carry out raids with his men. Subsequently, he converted to Christianity. He became averse to shedding blood and built a monastery, carrying earth and water himself on his back. On account of this he was nicknamed al-Lathiq, "Muddy". The monastery was called after him[104] and he peopled it with monks. After he had become pious, however, others boldly took advantage of this. The Roman emperor told him, "Carry out raids with your Arabs!" He found himself compelled to comply and he went on campaign, with Jaʿfar ibn Ṣubḥ al-Tanūkhī[105] in charge of the cavalry. With him in his army was also Zuhayr ibn Janāb ibn Hubal al-Kalbī.[106] He attacked the tribe of ʿAbd al-Qays[107] and Zuhayr ibn Janāb killed Haddāj ibn Mālik ibn ʿĀmir ibn al-Ḥārith ibn Anmār ibn ʿAmr ibn Wadīʿah ibn Lukayz ibn Afṣā ibn ʿAbd al-Qays.[108] Likewise, he attacked Bakr ibn Wāʾil,[109] and Zuhayr ibn Janāb also killed Haddāj ibn Mālik ibn Taym Allāh ibn Thaʿlabah ibn ʿUkābah.[110] Then Ḥudād ibn Ẓālim in Dhuhl ibn ʿIjl, of ʿAbd al-Qays,[111] said:

---

105 Not found elsewhere, but his father is probably Ṣubḥ ibn al-Ḥārith ibn ʿAmr ibn Fahm (Tanūkh), see *ĞN*, i, 297.

106 Besides being a tribal leader and a famous warrior, he was also a poet; see Sezgin, *Geschichte*, ii, 146; *EI2*, "Zuhayr b. Dj̲anāb" (M. Lecker); al-Sijistānī, *Muʿammarūn*, 24–29; Ibn Sallām al-Jumaḥī, *Ṭabaqāt fuḥūl al-shuʿarāʾ*, 30–32; al-Iṣfahānī, *Aghānī*, xix, 14–29. He is said to have lived for 450 years (*Aghānī*, xix, 21), or 420 (*Muʿammarūn*, 25), or 400 (*Aghānī*, xix, 22), or a mere 250 years (*Aghānī*, xix, 21). He was a seer (*kāhin*), but in his dotage he would go out without knowing where to go (*Aghānī*, xix, 20–21). Tired of life, he drank unmixed wine and died (*Aghānī*, xix, 15, 24).

107 *EI2*, "ʿAbd al-Ḳays" (W. Caskel).

108 *ĞN*, i, 169, 168, ii, 276.

109 *EI2*, "Bakr b. Wāʾil", (W. Caskel); "The Bakr belonged to the same people—later known as Rabīʿa—as the ʿabd al-Qays".

110 There is some confusion here. For Mālik ibn Taym Allāh ibn Thaʿlabah, of Bakr, see *ĞN*, i, 151, 150, 141, but no Haddāj with this lineage is found. Ibn Mālik in the following poem, by a poet of ʿAbd al-Qays, is obviously from the same tribe, hence he must be the first-mentioned Haddāj.

111 *ĞN*, i, 169; ʿASH and SKḤ have Ḥudhār instead of Ḥudād.

لَعَمْري لقد أَرْدَتْ سيوفُ ابن ضجعمٍ   غداةَ الْـتَقَوْا مِنّا خطيباً وياسرا ١٢٨
أهانَ الرِّجال بعده فكأنّما   يَرى بالرِّجال الصالحين الأباعرا
فلا تَبْعَدَنْ إمّا لَقِيتَ ابنَ مالكٍ   سبيلَ التي فيها لقيتَ المعاذرا

وقال زهير بن جناب:

فجَّعتُ عبدَ القيس أمسِ بجَدِّها   وسقيْتُ هَدّاجاً بكأسِ الأوّلِ[1]

ثمّ أقبل داودُ حتّى إذا كان بناحية الرَّقَم تذاكر رجالٌ من قُضاعةَ ما دخلهم من الذُّلُ لصُنعه الذي صنعه بنفسه، فتواعد رجلانِ من قضاعة على قتل داود، أحدهما ثعلبة الفاتك[2] بن [عامر الأكبر بن عَوْف بن بكر بن عَوْف بن عُذْرة][3] زيد اللات بن رُفيدة بن ثوْر بن كلب، والآخر معاوية بن حُجَيْر[4] بن حُيَيّ[5] بن وائل بن أَمْر مَناة بن مَشْجَعة بن التَّيْم بن النَّمِر بن وَبَرة، أخو كلب بن وَبَرة. فأقبل داود يسير ليلاً وأمامه شَمَعة وهو منصرف إلى الشام، حتّى انتهى إلى موضع يقال له بُرْقة حارب، فتقدّما إلى الشمعة فأطفآها وشدّا عليه فقتلاه.

١ هـ، كـ: (الأفرل) كما في النسختين؛ ويظهر أن الصواب ما اقترحه هـ في الهامش: لعلّها (الأول)، أي التي شربها الأوّلون.

٢ هـ، كـ: (القايل).

٣ هـ: بعدها بياض لكلمتين؛ والتكملة من جمهرة النسب لابن الكلبيّ.

٤ هـ، كـ: (حجيو).

٥ هـ: (حى)، كـ: (حيّ).

112 Maysir was a gambling game, involved with dividing the portions of a slaughtered camel and associated with generosity, of great importance in pre-Islamic society but forbidden in Islam. See *EI2*, "Maysir" (T. Fahd); Jamil, "Playing for Time"; eadem, *Ethics and Poetry*, 266–276.

113 The sense is not wholly clear; perhaps he says that after Haddāj's death the relative lowliness of those who survived him became apparent. The meaning of the following (*fa-ka-annamā | yarā bi-l-rijāli l-ṣāliḥina l-abāʿirā*) also eludes me.

114 An ancient formula common in elegies.

115 Again, I do not understand *sabīla llatī fīha laqīta l-maʿādhirā*.

116 *Jadd* could also mean "ancestor" and "good fortune".

117 The text has *al-afral*, which has no meaning. ʿASH plausibly suggests reading *al-awwal*,

Upon my life, the swords of Ibn Ḍajʿam have killed, 128
the morning they met in battle, an orator of ours and a *maysir* player.[112]
He humbled the men after he had gone.[113] It was as if
he saw ... [?]
Do not go far![114] If you were to meet Ibn Mālik
... [?][115]

Zuhayr ibn Janāb said:

Yesterday I harrowed ʿAbd al-Qays, killing their grandfather[116]
and I gave Haddāj the cup of his ancestors[117] to drink.

Then Dāwūd went on with his raid. When he was near al-Raqam[118] some men of Quḍāʿah talked to one another about the humiliation they had had to suffer for what Dāwūd had done with himself. Two men of Quḍāʿah pledged to kill him. One of them was Thaʿlabah al-Fātik ("the killer") [ʿĀmir al-Akbar ibn ʿAwf ibn Bakr ibn ʿAwf ibn ʿUdhrah ibn][119] Zayd al-Lāt ibn Rufaydah ibn Thawr ibn Kalb and the other was Muʿāwiyah ibn Ḥujayr[120] ibn Ḥuyayy[121] ibn Wāʾil ibn Amr Manāh ibn Mashjaʿah ibn al-Taym ibn al-Namir ibn Wabarah, al-Namir being the brother of Kalb ibn Wabarah.[122] Dāwūd advanced at night, with a candle in front him, in the direction of Syria.[123] When he reached a place called Burqat Ḥārib[124] the two men went for the candle and extinguished it. They took hold of Dāwūd and killed him.

(coll.) "the ancestors". This is supported by a line by Jarīr: *aʿdadtu li-l-shuʿarāʾi summan nāqiʿān | fa-saqaytu ākhirahum bi-kaʾsi l-awwalī* (Abū ʿUbaydah, *Naqāʾiḍ Jarīr wa-l-Farazdaq*, 213, Jarīr, *Dīwān*, 940). The version in Zuhayr's *Dīwān*, 92: *al-aqzal*, looks implausible *pace* the editor's explanations.

118 Al-Raqam is a place in the Hijaz according to Abū ʿUbayd al-Bakrī, *Muʿjam mā staʿjam*, 666.

119 There is a lacuna of some two words in the MSS. Al-Qāyil, as in ʿASH and SKḤ, should be emended to al-Fātik. For the full name see *ĞN*, i, 288, 280. On the word *fātik*, see above, pp. 13–14.

120 Thus instead of *Ḥ.j.y.w.* as in ʿASH and SKḤ.

121 Thus instead of Ḥayy as in ʿASH and SKḤ.

122 For Muʿāwiyah's lineage see *ĞN*, i, 279.

123 Al-Shām could also refer to Damascus.

124 Yāqūt, *Muʿjam al-buldān* lists it, quoting the opening line of the following poem but without locating it; the same in al-Zabīdī, *Tāj al-ʿArūs* (*BRQ*). The poem by Thaʿlabah, below, has "between al-Burqatān ('the two Burqahs') and Ḥārib". Burqah is a very common topographical term (it means "rugged ground with sand and stones"). Ḥārib is said to be "in Ḥawrān near Marj al-Ṣuffar, in the lands of Quḍāʿah" (Yāqūt).

فقال عبد العاص بن ثعلبة التّنوخيّ يرثيه:

لَعَمْري لَنِعْمَ المرءُ من[1] آل ضجعمٍ ثَوى بين أحجار ببُرقةِ حاربِ
أصابتْك ذؤْبان الحليفَيْن عامرٍ ومَشْجعةَ الأوباشِ رهطِ ابن قاربِ
فتىً لم تلِدْه بنتُ[2] عمٍّ قريبةٌ فيَضْوى وقد يَضْوى وليدُ القرائبِ[3]
فتى ليسَ بالراضي بأدنى مَعيشةٍ وليس له ذو العجْز يوماً بصاحبِ

وقال ثعلبة الفاتك،[4] قاتله: ١٢٩

نحن الأُولى أرْدَتْ ظُباتُ سيوفنا داودَ بين البُرقتَيْنِ فحاربِ
خطرتْ عليه رِماحُنا فتركْنَه[5] لمّا شُرِعْنَ له كأمسِ الذّاهبِ
وكذاك إنّا لا تزالُ رِماحُنا تَنْفي العِدى وتفيد رُغْبَ الراغبِ[6]

كانت لداود ابنتان يقال لهما امْرَعَةُ واشْعَرَةُ، وكان خلّفهما بالشام، فقَدِم عبد العاص التنوخيّ الشام، فبعثت إليه امرعةُ تسأله عن أبيها، فعرّض لها فلم تفْهم، فقال:

١ الكلمة ناقصة في كـ.
٢ كـ: (ابن).
٣ كـ: (الغرائب).
٤ هـ، كـ: (القاتل).
٥ كـ: (فتَركْتُهُ).
٦ لعلّ الصواب (رعبَ الراعب) كما في معجم البلدان لياقوت.

125 Not identified. According to Ibn al-Kalbī, *Nasab Maʿadd wa-l-Yaman al-kabīr*, 692 it was Dāwūd's unnamed sister who made the lament; the second line is quoted.

126 This Ibn Qārib has not been identified.

127 On this line, often quoted and attributed to various poets including al-Nābighah al-Dhubyānī (*Dīwān* ed. Ahlwardt, 164), see also e.g. al-Jāḥiẓ, *Burṣān*, 24; Ibn Qutayba, *Maʿārif*, 503; al-Khālidiyyān, *Ashbāh*, i, 229; al-Tawḥīdī, *Imtāʿ*, i, 94; al-Maydānī, *Majmaʿ*, ii, 404: Abū ʿUbayd al-Bakrī, *Tanbīh*, 124; idem, *Simṭ al-laʾālī*, 871; al-Rāghib al-Iṣbahānī,

ʿAbd al-ʿĀṣ ibn Thaʿlabah, of Tanūkh,[125] said elegising him:

Upon my life, truly excellent was the man of the clan of Ḍajʿam
  whose resting place is between the stones of Burqat Ḥārib!
He was struck down by the wolves of the two allied clans, ʿĀmir
  and Mashjaʿah, that rabble, the men of Ibn Qārib.[126]
He was a man not born from a close paternal cousin
  and thus not stunted—for those born of close relatives are often stunted.[127]
A man not content with the lowest way of life,
  never associated with weaklings.

And Thaʿlabah al-Fātik, who killed him, said:[128] 129

We are those whose sword edges destroyed
  Dāwūd between al-Burqatayn and Ḥārib.[129]
Our quivering spears got him and left him,
  when they were pointed at him, like the day of yesterday, gone!
Likewise, our spears never fail
  to eliminate foes and to fulfil the wish of a wisher.[130]

Dāwūd had two daughters, called Imraʿah and Ishʿarah.[131] He had left them behind in Syria. When ʿAbd al-ʿĀṣ al-Tanūkhī came to Syria Imraʿah sent for him and asked about her father. He merely hinted at what had happened but she did not understand him. He said,

---

Muḥāḍarāt, i, 207; al-Zamakhsharī, *Asās* (ḌWY); Ibn Manẓūr, *Lisān al-ʿArab* (ḌWY). On the motif, see Van Gelder, *Close Relationships*, 11–35.

128 The lines are quoted anonymously in Ibn al-Kalbī, *Nasab Maʿadd wa-l-Yaman*, 604 and Yāqūt, *Muʿjam al-buldān*, s.v. al-Qurnatān.

129 See above, note 124; in Ibn al-Kalbī, *Nasab Maʿadd wa-l-Yaman* it is *bayna l-qaryatayni muḥāribī*, which appears to be a corruption. In Yāqūt it is *bayna l-Qurnatayni bi-Ḥāribī*.

130 The reading and translation of *tufīdu rughba l-rāghibī* is uncertain. Yāqūt has *wa-tufīdu ruʿba l-rāʿibī*, "to bring about the fright of the frightened", which may be better.

131 Both names, not found elsewhere, are given proper *hamzah*s in ʿASH and SKḤ, as if read Amraʾah and Ashʿarah. Since this pattern (*afʿalah*) is not a normal one as recognised in Arabic morphology, I prefer to read them with the pattern of (*i*)*mraʾah*, "woman". In the following poems the metre requires the absence of the *hamzah*s. Al-Zajjājī, *Ibdāl*, 32, quoting the first two lines of the following poem, actually thinks that *imraʿah* may be a phonetic variant of *imraʾah*.

حدِّثْ حديثَيْن ٱمْرعَهْ   فإنْ أبَتْ فأربعَهْ
ثمّ ٱدْعُها يا فَوْزَعَهْ   إلى الحديث والدَّعَهْ
ألا تراها مُقْنَعَهْ   وخَيْلَها[1] مسلَّعَهْ
في كلِّ عامٍ شَعْشَعَهْ   من عامرٍ ومَشْجَعهْ

ثمّ أرسلتْ إليه اشعرةُ فحكى لها فلم تفهم، فقال:

حدِّثْ حديثَيْنِ ٱشْعَرَهْ   فإنْ أبَتْ فعَشَرَهْ
يا رُبَّ خَيلٍ مُضْمَرَهْ   وغارةٍ مُحَذْفَرَهْ
وحُلّةٍ محبَّرَهْ   بين لِوى ...[2]

ففَهِمتا قوله فشقّتا جَيْبَيْهما وحلقتا رؤوسهما، فهُما أوّلُ مَن فعل ذلك من العرب. فَوْزعة الذي ذكر فوزعةُ[3] بن سلمة بن وَثاق بن عمرو بن عوْف | بن ذُهْل بن جُدَيّ[4] بن الدُّها بن عِشْم[5] بن حُلوان بن عِمران بن الحاف بن قضاعة، وكان رَسولاً لهما.[6]

---

١ ك: (وحيلها).

٢ بياض في النسختين.

٣ ك: (وزعة).

٤ هـ، ك: (جذي).

٥ هـ، ك: (غشم).

٦ ك: (لها).

Tell two stories to Imraʿah
Or if she rejects them, four![132]
Then call upon her, Fawzaʿah,
To talk and be calm.
Don't you see she will be convinced
When their horses are … (?)[133]
Every year … (?)
Of ʿĀmir and Mashjaʿah.

Then Ishʿarah sent for him. He told her but she did not understand either. He said,

Tell two stories to Ishʿarah
Or if she rejects them, ten!
Many a lean horse
And many a raid with a multitude
And a striped robe
Lies between the twisted sand dune of …[134]

Then the two women understood what he meant. They tore the collars of their dresses and shaved their heads. They were the first Arabs to do this. Fawzaʿah, mentioned in the poem, is Fawzaʿah ibn Salamah ibn Wathāq ibn ʿAmr ibn ʿAwf | ibn Dhuhl ibn Judayy[135] ibn al-Duhā ibn ʿIshm ibn Ḥulwān ibn ʿImrān 130
ibn al-Ḥāf ibn Quḍāʿah; he was the messenger of the two women.

---

132 A prose version of this is found in proverb collections as "Tell two stories to a woman (*imraʾah*), and if she does not understand then, four!" See Abū ʿUbayd al-Bakrī, *Faṣl al-maqāl*, 50–51; al-ʿAskarī, *Jamharah*, i, 305; al-Maydānī, *Majmaʿ*, i, 252.

133 *Musallaʿah* could mean "having bundles of *salaʿ* firewood attached to them", referring to a pre-Islamic custom of sacrificing animals to obtain rain. But this was done with bulls, not with horses (Lane, *Lexicon*, SLʿ). The words *ʿām shaʿshaʿah* in the following line are also obscure.

134 There is a lacuna in the MSS.

135 From here, see *ǦN*, i, 279. For al-Judayy, ʿASH and SKḤ have *Ḥ.dh.y*; for ʿIshm they have *Gh.sh.m*.

[§ ١٠] **ومنهم** هَمّام بن مُرّة بن ذُهْل بن شَيْبان، قتله ناشرة بن أغوات. وكانت أمّ ناشرةَ هذا هِنْد بنت معاوية بن الحارث بن بكر بن حُبَيْب، وكانت جارةً[١] لهمّام، فأرادت أن تَلِد، فاجتمع إليها النساء، فسمعهنّ همّام يقْبَلْنها يقُلن: قد جاء، قد جاء! يعْنِين الولد. فقالت أمّه: ادْقُقْن عُنقَه! فقال لها همّام: ويْحَكِ لا تفْعلي. قالت: وما يُعِيشه؟ قال همّام: أَمَة تُعيشه، ولِقْحة، وجَمَل ذَلول. قالت: بَلى. فأعطاها إيّاها.

فلمّا كان يومُ واردات وهو من أيّام حرب البَسوس خرج همّام يسقي النساء الماء واللَّبَن، فأبصره ناشرةُ فختله فطعنه فقتله، وهرب فلَحِق بقومه، فقالت أمّ ناشرة:

لقد عيَّلَ الأَيْتامَ طعنةُ ناشِرَهْ　　　أَناشرُ لا زالت يمينُك آشِرَهْ

١ ك: (جارية).

136 His story and that of his brother Jassās ibn Murrah (told hereafter) are part of the famous "War of Basūs" between the tribes of Bakr and Taghlib that is told in many sources and allegedly lasted forty years. See e.g. Abū ʿUbaydah, *Naqāʾiḍ Jarīr wa-l-Farazdaq*, 905–907; al-Mufaḍḍal, *Amthāl*, 55–56; idem, *Fākhir*, 124–127; al-Iṣfahānī, *Aghānī*, v, 34–64; Ibn ʿAbd Rabbih, *ʿIqd*, v, 213–223. For a short account in English, see Nicholson, *Literary History*, 55–61. On the genre of *Ayyām al-ʿArab* ("the battle days of the Arabs"), see *EI2*, "Ayyām al-ʿArab" (E. Mittwoch); *EI3*, "Ayyām al-ʿArab" (Alan Jones); Caskel, "*Aijām al-ʿArab*: Studien zur altarabischen Epik". Jones is rightly more sceptical than Mittwoch and many Arabs about their historical value. The war, especially the story of Kulayb, Jassās, and al-Hijris also became the subject of the even less historical popular epic *Qiṣṣat al-Zīr Salīm*, on which see Lyons, *The Arabian Epic*, ii, 651–660, iii, 272–276; idem, *The Man of Wiles*, 28–34; *EAL*, "Zīr Sālim, romance of" (G. Canova). On Hammām and his murderer, see al-Iṣfahānī, *Aghānī*, v, 45, Ibn al-Athīr, *Kāmil*, i, 418.

137 For the lineage of Hammām and Jassās ibn Murrah ibn Dhuhl ibn Shaybān, of the tribal group Bakr ibn Wāʾil, itself part of the larger group called Rabīʿah, see *ĞN*, i, 142. For Nashīrah ibn Aghwāth, of Taghlib ibn Wāʾil, see ibid., i, 165.

138 *ĞN*, i, 163.

139 *jāratan*; see *EI2*, "Idjāra" (W. Montgomery Watt). A single mother would be in need of protection. We are not told why she had left her son's father, Aghwāth, or he her.

[§ 10 Hammām ibn Murrah[136]]

Another is Hammām ibn Murrah ibn Dhuhl ibn Shaybān, who was killed by Nāshirah ibn Aghwāth.[137] Nāshirah's mother was Hind, daughter of Muʿāwiyah ibn al-Ḥārith ibn Bakr in Ḥubayb.[138] She lived in the protection[139] of Hammām. She was about[140] to give birth and the women came to her. Hammām heard them say, while they were assisting with the birth, "It has come! It has come!", meaning the child. Then the mother said, "Break its neck!" Hammām exclaimed, "O no! Don't!" "But how will it be able to live?" asked the woman. Hammām replied, "A slave-girl can take care of him, and a milch-camel and a meek stallion camel". "All right", she said, and he gave all this to her.

At the battle day of Wāridāt,[141] one of the battle days of the war of al-Basūs, Hammām went out doling out water and milk. Nāshirah saw him, crept up to him, stabbed him, and killed him. Then he fled and joined his own tribe. Nāshirah's mother said,

> Nāshirah's stab has left the orphans destitute:
> O Nāshirah, may your right hand be sawn off!

---

140 For this sense of *arāda*, normally "to wish, want", cf. Q al-Kahf 18:77.

141 See e.g. al-Iṣfahānī, *Aghānī*, v, 41–42, Ibn ʿAbd Rabbih, *ʿIqd*, v, 218. According to Yāqūt, *Muʿjam al-buldān*, Wāridāt is "on the left of the road to Mecca if you go in that direction". See also Abū ʿUbayd al-Bakrī, *Muʿjam*, 1362–1363. According to Muqātil (al-Aḥwal ibn Sinān ibn Marthad), an informant of Abū ʿUbaydah quoted in *Aghānī*, v, 45, Hammām was killed at the battle of al-Quṣaybāt. Muqātil's version differs from that of *AM*: "Hammām had found a young boy who had been abandoned. He took him up and brought him up as a foundling, calling him Nāshirah. When the boy grew up he became aware that he was of the Banū Taghlib. When the two tribes met in battle at al-Quṣaybāt, Hammām engaged in the fighting. When he got thirsty he went to his water-skin and drank from it, laying down his weapons. Nāshirah, finding that Hammām was not alert, attacked him with an iron-pointed stick and killed him. Then he joined his tribe, Taghlib." The lines quoted above follow anonymously and it is added that Nāshirah was subsequently killed by a man of the tribe of Yashkur; see also *Aghānī*, v, 55.

[§ ١١] **ومنهم** جسّاس بن مُرّة بن ذُهْل بن شَيْبان، وهو قاتلُ كُلَيْب بن ربيعة. وكانت أخته ١٣١
تحت كُليب، فقُتِل عنها وهي حامل، فرجعتْ إلى أهلها، ووقعت الحرب، حرب البَسوس،
فكان منها ما كان من القتل. ثمّ صاروا إلى المُوادَعة، بعدما كادت تتفانى القبيلتان، فولدتْ
أخت جسّاس غُلاماً فسمَّتْه الهِجْرِس، فرَبّاه جسّاس فلم يعرف أباً غيره، وزوَّجه[١] ابنتَه.

فوقع بين الهِجْرِس وبين رجل من بكر بن وائل كلام، فقال له البكريّ: ما أنت بمُنْتَهٍ حتّى نُلْحِقك بأبيك. فانصرف الهجرس حتّى دخل على امرأته بنت جسّاس مهموماً، فسألتْه عمّا به، فخبّرها الخبر. فلمّا أوى إلى فراشه ووضع أنفه بين ثَدْيَيْها وتنفّس الصُّعَداءَ تَنَفُّسةً تنفَّط منها ما بين ثَدْيَيْها، فقامت الجارية فَزِعةً قد أقلَّتْها رِعْدة حتّى دخلت على أبيها فحدّثته الحديث وقصّت عليه قِصّة الهجرس. فقال جسّاس: ثائرٌ وربِّ الكعبة! وبات على مِثْل الرَّضْف حتّى أصبح. فأرسل إلى الهجرس، فأتاه، فقال له: إنّما أنت ولدي وخَتَني، وبالمكان الذي قد عَلِمْتَ، وقد زوّجتُك ابنتي وأنت معي، وقد كانت الحربُ في أبيك زماناً طويلا حتّى كِدْنا نتفانى، وقد اصطلحْنا وتحاجزْنا، وقد رأيتُ أن تدخُل فيما دخل فيه الناس من الصُّلْح، وأن تنطلق معي حتّى آخُذ عليك مثلَ ما [أُخِذ][٢] علينا وعلى قومك. فقال الهجرس: أنا فاعل، ولكنّ مثلي لا يأتي قومه إلّا بلأْمته وفرسه.

فحمله جسّاس على فرس، وأعطاه لأمة ورُمْحاً، فخرجا حتّى أتيا جماعةً من قومهما، | ١٣٢
فقصّ عليهم جسّاس ما كانوا فيه من البَلاء وما صاروا إليه من العافية، ثمّ قال: وهذا ابن

١ ك: (وزوجته).

٢ هـ: التكملة من ابن الأثير والأغاني حيث نقل الخبر عن ابن حبيب.

142 Jassās is associated with the very beginning and also, as told here, the end of the War of al-Basūs. Ibn Ḥabīb's version is quoted, with *isnād*, in al-Iṣfahānī, *Aghānī*, v, 60–62 ("'Alī ibn Sulaymān al-Akhfash informed me: al-Ḥasan ibn al-Ḥusayn al-Sukkarī informed us: Muḥammad ibn Ḥabīb told us, on the authority of Ibn al-Aʿrābī, on the authority of al-Mufaḍḍal, on the authority of Abū ʿUbaydah, that the last person to be killed in the war of Bakr and Taghlib was Jassās ibn Murrah ibn Dhuhl ibn Shaybān. He is the one who killed Kulayb ibn Rabīʿah …"). Elsewhere in *Aghānī* (v, 52) one finds a surprising statement, attributed to "all transmitters" (*qālū jamīʿan*), that contradicts this version: "Jassās died a natural death (*ḥatf anfih*); he was not killed". On his death see also Ibn Nubātah, *Sarḥ al-ʿuyūn*, 95.

143 For his lineage, see that of his brother Hammām, above.

144 For his lineage, see *ĞN*, i, 164. Jassās killed Kulayb after the latter had killed a stray she-

[§ 11 Jassās ibn Murrah[142]]

Another is Jassās ibn Murrah ibn Dhuhl ibn Shaybān.[143] He is the one who killed Kulayb ibn Rabīʿah.[144] His sister was married to Kulayb and when he was killed she was pregnant. She returned to her own people. Then the war, the War of al-Basūs, broke out, with all the ensuing bloodshed. After the two tribes had mutually almost annihilated each other they made peace. Kulayb's sister gave birth to a son and called him al-Hijris. Jassās brought him up and the boy knew no father other than him. Jassās made him marry his daughter.[145] 131

One day al-Hijris had words with a man of Bakr ibn Wāʾil, who said to him, "Before you have done, we shall link you to your father!" Al-Hijris left and went to his wife, Jassās's daughter, troubled in mind. She asked him what the matter was and he told her what had happened. When he lay down on his bed he buried his face between her breasts, sighing so deeply that he almost blistered the skin between her breasts. The young woman got up, frightened; she shivered and went to her father, telling him the story and relating what al-Hijris had said. Jassās exclaimed, "By the Lord of the Kaaba, he will have his revenge!" He spent the night as if on red-hot stones until the morning. He sent for al-Hijris, who came. "You are my son and my son-in-law,"[146] said Jassās, "and you mean much to me as you know. I have married you to my daughter and you are living with me. The war about your father[147] lasted a long time, so that in the end we nearly annihilated one another. We have concluded a truce and abstained from fighting. I think you ought to be part of the truce people have made. You must come with me so that I can let you make the same pledge we and your people have made." Al-Hijris said, "I will, but someone like me cannot meet his people except with his armour[148] and horse."

Jassās gave him a horse to ride, armour, and a spear. They went on their way together. When they met some people belonging to both their tribes, | Jassās told them about the plight they had been in and the bliss they had now achieved. "This man", he said, "is the son of my sister. He has come to make the 132

---

camel belonging to an aunt of Jassās called al-Basūs. This caused the outbreak of the protracted war called after her.

145 It is odd that Jassās should have found this a normal thing to do and that al-Hijris should have consented, in the belief that he was marrying his sister or half-sister, but no one seems to have commented on this.

146 Instead of *waladī wa-khatanī* ("my son and my son-in-law") *Aghānī* has *waladī wa-minnī* ("my son and from me").

147 Speaking about "your father" he contradicts his preceding sentence and casually reveals the true state of affairs.

148 *Laʾmah*, referring to chain mail.

أختي قد جاء ليدخل فيما دخلتم فيه، ويَعْقِد ما عقدتم. فلمّا قرَّبوا الدم وقاموا إلى العقد أخذ الهجرس بوسط رمحه ثمّ قال: وفرسي وأُذُنيْه، ورُمْحي ونَصْلَيْه، وسيْفي وغَرْبَيْه، لا يترُك الرجلُ قاتلَ أبيه وهو ينظر إليه! ثمّ طعن جسّاساً فقتله ولَحِق بقومه. فكان آخِرَ قتيلٍ في بكر بن وائل.

[§١٢] **ومنهم** عَمْرو وإخوته، بنو الزَّبّان الذُّهْليّ. وكان سبب ذلك أن كثيف بن التَّغْلِبيّ انهزم في بعض أيّام بكر وتَغلِب، فأَلَظَّ به مالك بن كُومة الشَّيْبانيّ، وكان مالك رجلاً نحيفاً، وكان كثيف رجلاً أيِّداً، فلمّا لحقه ابن كومة اقتحم عن فرسه لينزل إليه مالكٌ فيقْهَره بفضل قُوّته وبَدَنه، فأوجره مالك الرمحَ وقال: واللّٰهِ لَتَستأسرنّ أو لَأُنْفِذنّك به! فاستأسر، ولحقه عمرو بن الزبّان فقال: أَسيري! وقال مالك: أسيري! فقالا لكثيف: لقد حكّمْناك في نفسك. فقال كثيف: لولا مالكٌ لأُلْفِيتُ في أهلي! فغَضِب عمرو بن الزبّان، فلطم خدّ كثيف، فقال مالك: تلطِمْ خدّ أسيري؟ يا كثيف فإنّي[١] قد جعلت فِداءك لك بلَطْمةِ عمرو خدَّك. وأطلقه.

فحرّم كثيف النساءَ والخمرَ حتّى يثأرَ من عمرو لطمتَه، فوضع عليه العيون، فأتاه رجل من غُفَيْلة بن قاسط، فقال: ألا أدُلّك على بني الزبّان، فقد نَتَجوا[٢] ناقةً حُواراً واشْتَوَوْه وهم يأكُلون، وكانت ندَّت لهم إبلٌ فخرجوا في طلبها فردُّوها.[٣] فقام كثيف | بضِعْف عِدّتهم، وقال: ١٣٣
مُرُّوا بجانبهم فإذا دُعِيتم إلى الطعام فلْيكتنفْ كلَّ رجل منهم رجلانِ منّا. فمرّوا بالقوم وهم

١ كذا في هـ، ک، والسياق يقتضي (إنّي).

٢ ک: (أنتجوا).

٣ ک: (فردُّها).

149 It is not clear if it is human or (presumably) animal blood that is used for the ceremony. Compare the *La'aqat al-dam* ("The Blood-lickers"), a federation of clans of Quraysh, who dipped their hands in camel blood to seal their covenant (*EI2*, "La'aḳat al-dam" [Ch. Pellat]).

150 He uses rhymed prose.

151 The main characters of this story cannot be found in *ĞN*. The story is found in al-Shimshāṭī, *Anwār*, i, 246–254, al-Zabīdī, *Tāj al-ʿarūs* (*KhT*ʿ), and in proverb collections: al-Mufaḍḍal, *Amthāl*, 58; al-Maydānī, *Majmaʿ*, i, 476–477 (under *ash'am min Khawtaʿah*); al-ʿAskarī, *Jamharah*, i, 111 (under *ākhir al-bazz ʿalā l-qalūṣ*); al-Zamakhsharī, *Mustaqṣā*, i, 2–3; briefly also Abū ʿUbayd al-Bakrī, *Faṣl al-maqāl*, 501 and al-Masʿūdī, *Murūj*, iii, 237.

152 In *Faṣl al-maqāl* it is al-Zabbān ibn Mujālid al-Dhuhlī.

153 In al-Mufaḍḍal, *Amthāl*, and al-ʿAskarī, *Jamharah*, he is called Kathīf (vowelled Kuthayf)

same pledge as you made, to fasten the knot as you did." When they brought the blood in order to make the covenant[149] and stood up to seal the covenant, al-Hijis grasped the middle of his spear and said, "By my horse and its ears, by my spear and its tip, by my sword and its edges: a man shall not leave the killer of his father when he sees him!"[150] Then he stabbed Jassās, killing him, and joined his own people. Jassās was the last man to be killed of Bakr ibn Wā'il.

[§ 12 ʿAmr and his brothers, sons of al-Zabbān al-Dhuhlī[151]]

Among them are also ʿAmr and his brothers, sons of al-Zabbān al-Dhuhlī.[152] The cause was as follows. Kathīf ibn al-Taghlibī[153] had fled at one of the battles between Bakr and Taghlib. Mālik ibn Kūmah al-Shaybānī[154] kept pursuing him. Mālik was a thin man, Kathīf was strong. When Ibn Kūmah overtook him, Kathīf jumped off his horse, expecting that Mālik would also dismount, so that he would be able to overcome Mālik with his strength and bulk. Mālik, however, stabbed him with his spear and said, "By God, you must ask to be my prisoner, or else I'll transfix you with it!" Then ʿAmr ibn al-Zabbān joined them and said, "My prisoner!" Mālik replied, "*My* prisoner!" Then they said to Kathīf, "We let you decide between us!" Kathīf said, "But for Mālik I would find myself to be with my people". ʿAmr ibn al-Zabbān became angry and slapped Kathīf's cheek. Mālik said, "You slap the cheek of my prisoner? Kathīf, I have hereby ransomed you with ʿAmr's slap and your cheek!" And he let him go.

Then Kathīf vowed he would not drink wine or have sex with women until he had his revenge from ʿAmr and his slap. He had people spying on him. A man of Ghufaylah ibn Qāsiṭ[155] came to him and said, "I can show you where the sons of al-Zabbān are. They have roasted a young she-camel and are eating it. Some camels of theirs have strayed, they went in pursuit of them and brought them back." Kathīf got up | with double their number and told his men, 133
"Go past them, and when they invite you to have some food, let each man of theirs be enclosed by two of ours." They passed along the men while they were

ibn Zuhayr al-Taghlibī; in al-Maydānī, *Amthāl*, it is Kathīf (vowelled Kuthayf and Kuthayyif) ibn ʿAmr al-Taghlibī.

154 Mālik ibn Kūmah has not been found except in versions of the present story. His full name is given in al-Shimshāṭī, *Anwār*, i, 246 as Mālik ibn al-Ṣāmit (or Zayd) ibn ʿAwf ibn ʿĀmir ibn Dhuhl ibn Thaʿlabah (see *ǦN*, i, 154): Kūmah is his mother's name.

155 See *ǦN*, I, 141 and ii, 275 (they were allied with Taghlib). The man is named as Khawtaʿah in other sources and in *Faṣl al-maqāl* it is said that Khawtaʿah's true name is ʿAbd Allāh ibn Ṣabirah, on whom see *ǦN*, i, 170, where Khawtaʿah is ʿAbd Allāh ibn Ṣabirah's son. But he is not of Ghufaylah ibn Qāsiṭ, so there must be some confusion.

على طعامهم فدعوْهم إلى الطعام فأقبلوا، ففعلوا ما أُمروا به، فلمّا حسر كثيف العِمامة عن وجهه قال له عمرو: يا كثيف، هذا خدّي فالْطِمْه ففيه وَفاءٌ من خَدّك، وما في بكر بن وائل أكرم منه. قال: لا، حتّى أقتلك. قال: فدَعْ هؤلاء الفِتيَة الذين لم يتلبّسوا من الحروب بشيء. قال: فأبى، فقتلهم أجمعِين، وبعث رءوسهم في غِرارة، وعلّقها في عنق الدُّهَيْم ناقة عمرو بن الزبّان.

[§١٣] **ومنهم** عمرو بن مسعود، وخالد بن نَضْلة الأَسَديّان. وكانا يَفِدان على المُنْذِر الأكبر اللَّخْميّ في كلّ سنة، فيقيمان عنده وينادمانه. وكانت أسد وغَطَفان حُلَفاءَ لا يَدينون للملوك، ويُغِيرون عليهم، فوفدا سنة من السنين ومعهما سَبْرة بن عُمَيْر[١] الشاعر الفَقْعَسيّ، وحبيب بن خالد.

فنادم المنذرَ عمرٌو وخالدُ بن نضلة، فقال المنذر يوماً لخالد، وهم على الشراب: يا خالد، مَن ربُّك؟ فقال خالد: عمرو بن مسعود ربّي وربّك. فأمسك عليهما،[٢] ثمّ قال لهما بعدُ: ما يمنعكما من الدخول في طاعتي، وأن تذُبّوا عنّي كما ذبّت تَميم وربيعة؟ فقالا: أَبَيْتَ اللَّعْن،

١ كذا في هـ، ك، ويظهر أنّ الصواب (عمرو).

٢ كذا في هـ، ك، وكما هي في خزانة الأدب؛ وفي الأصل (عليها). وجعلها الشنقيطيّ (عنهما).

156 In other sources they are said to be seven, all sons of al-Zabbān.

157 A rather gruesome sequel is given in al-ʿAskarī, *Jamharah*, al-Maydānī, *Majmaʿ*, and al-Zamakhsharī, *Mustaqṣā*. Al-Maydānī: "The camel returned while al-Zabbān was sitting in front of his tent. The camel kneeled down. 'That is ʿAmr's camel, girl,' he said, 'He and his brothers are late.' The girl got up and felt the sack. 'Your sons have found some ostrich eggs!', she said, bringing the sack. She put her hand into the sack and pulled out ʿAmr's head first and then the heads of his brothers. She washed them and placed them on a shield …" More bloodshed ensues.

158 Among the many parallels of this famous story see Ibn Qutaybah, *Shiʿr*, 268; al-Masʿūdī, *Murūj*, iv, 178; al-Iṣfahānī, *Aghānī*, xxii, 86–87; ʿAbīd ibn al-Abraṣ, *Dīwān*, 2–4 (and Lyall's Introduction, 8); al-Qālī, *Amālī*, iii, 195–196; Ibn al-Faqīh, *Mukhtaṣar kitāb al-buldān*, 179–180; al-Jarīrī, *Jalīs*, iv, 146–148; Ibn Badrūn, *Sharḥ Qaṣīdat Ibn ʿAbdūn*, 132–133; Yāqūt, *Muʿjam al-buldān*, iv, 197–199 (s.v. al-Ghariyyān); al-Baghdādī, *Khizānat al-adab*, xi, 270–273. The dual noun al-Ghariyyān refers to two posts or tower-like structures (standing for the two killed companions); *ghariyy* means "sticky", apparently with the blood of the victims.

159 ʿAmr ibn Masʿūd ibn Kaladah (ǦN, i, 55).

eating and they were invited to partake of the food. They came and did what they had been told to do. Then Kathīf took his turban off his face. ʿAmr said, "Kathīf! Here is my cheek, slap it! That will make up for your cheek!" There was no more generous man in Bakr ibn Wā'il than he. But Kathīf said, "No, I'll kill you". "But spare these young men," said ʿAmr. "They have not been involved in these wars at all" But Kathīf refused and had them all killed.[156] He put their heads in a sack and hung it on the neck of Duhaym, the she-camel of ʿAmr ibn al-Zabbān.[157]

[§13 ʿAmr ibn Masʿūd and Khālid ibn Naḍlah[158]]

Among them are ʿAmr ibn Masʿūd[159] and Khālid ibn Naḍlah,[160] of the tribe of Asad. They used to pay a visit to al-Mundhir the Great,[161] of Lakhm, every year. They would stay and be his drinking companions. Asad and Ghaṭafān[162] were allied tribes who did not submit to kings; they even carried out raids against them. One year, ʿAmr and Khālid visited the king in the company of Sabrah ibn ʿUmayr, the poet of the tribe of Faqʿas,[163] and Ḥabīb ibn Khālid.[164]

One day, al-Mundhir, having taken ʿAmr and Khālid ibn Naḍlah as drinking companions, asked Khālid while they were drinking, "Khālid, who is your lord?" Khālid replied, "ʿAmr ibn Masʿūd is my lord and yours!" The king held this against them.[165] Later, he asked them, "What stops you from being my vassals and from defending me,[166] as do the tribes of Tamīm and Rabīʿah?" "Sire,"[167]

---

160 He is called Khālid ibn Mālik al-Muḍallal ibn Munqidh in *Aghānī* and elsewhere (*ĞN*, i, 50 and ii, 342). There is one Khālid ibn Naḍlah, of Faqʿas (part of Asad), see *ĞN*, i, 50, but it seems that he is not the one meant here.

161 Al-Mundhir ibn al-Nuʿmān Mā' al-Samā', of the Lakhmid dynasty whose capital was al-Ḥīrah. He was killed in battle with his rival, al-Ḥārith of Ghassān, in AD 554. On the Lakhmids see *EI2*, "Lakhmids" (Irfan Shahîd) and *ĞN*, i, 246.

162 On this tribe, see *EI2*, "Ghaṭafān" (J.W. Fück).

163 Faqʿas is a branch of Asad. Sabrah ibn ʿUmayr is likely to be an error for Sabrah ibn ʿAmr al-Faqʿasī, a poet of Abū Tammām's *Ḥamāsah* (al-Marzūqī, *Sharḥ*, 237–239, al-Baghdādī, *Khizānah*, ix, 503–511).

164 The name can also be read as Ḥubayb. He is probably the son of Khālid ibn Naḍlah al-Faqʿasī (see e.g. al-Iṣfahānī, *Aghānī*, xvii, 247), but in the present story his rather unconcerned behaviour makes it unlikely that he is the son of the poisoned Khālid.

165 For the sense of *fa-amsaka ʿalayhimā* see al-Ṭabarī, *Tārīkh, Glossarium*, cdlxxxv.

166 Instead of *tadhubbū ʿannī*, *Khizānah* has *tadnuwā minnī*, "coming (to settle) near me".

167 They use a formula for addressing kings in pre-Islamic times: *abayta l-laʿnah*, "May you refuse being cursed!" (cf. Lane, *Lexicon*, *'BY*), or "Mayst thou avoid malediction!" (Nicholson, *Literary History*, 14), or "May you disdain to utter curses" (Stetkevych, *The Poetics of Islamic Legitimacy*, 333).

هذه البلاد لا تلائم مواشِيَنا، ونحن مع هذا قريب منك، نحن بهذا الرمل،[١] فإذا شئتَ أَجَبْناك. فعلم أنّهم لا يدينون له، وقد سمع من خالد الكلمة الأولى. فأومأ إلى الساقي فسقاهما سمًّا، فانصرفا من عنده من | السُّكْر على خلاف ما كنا ينصرفان، فلمّا كانا في بعض الليل أحسّ ١٣٤
حبيب بن خالد بالأمر لِما رأى من شِدّة سُكْرهما، فنادى خالداً فلم يُجِبْه، فقام إليه فحركّه فسقط بعضُ جَسَده، وفعل بعمرو مثلَ ذلك، وكان حاله كحال خالد.

فأصبح المنذر نادماً على قتلهما، فغدا عليه حبيب بن خالد فقال: أبيتَ اللعن، أسعدك الأهل، نديماك وخليلاك تتايعا[٢] في ساعة واحدة. فقال له: يا حبيب أَعَلى الموت تستعديني، وهل ترى إلّا أنّي ميِّتٌ وأخا ميّت وأبا ميّت؟[٣] ثمّ أمر فحُفر لهما قبْران ودُفنا فيهما، وبنى عليهما مَنارتَيْن، وهما الغَرِيّان، وعقر على كلّ قبر خمسين فرساً وخمسين بعيراً، وغَرّاهما بدِمائهما، وجعل يومَ نادَمَهما يومَ نَعيم، ويومَ دَفَنَهما يومَ بؤْس. وقال الشاعر فيهما:

ألا بكر النَّاعي بخَيْرَيْ بني أَسَدْ بعمرو بن مسعودٍ وبالسيِّد الصَّمَدْ
يُشَقّ بصحراء الحبيل له الثَّرى وما كنت أخشى أن يُزار به بَلَدْ

١ كـ: (بهذه الرسل).
٢ هذا ما رجّحه هـ، وفي الأصل وفي كـ: (تتابعا).
٣ كذا في النسختين، وفي هـ: (وهل تراني إلاّ ميّتاً وأخا ميت وأبا ميت؟)؛ وفي خزانة الأدب نقلاً عن أسماء المغتالين: (وهل ترى إلاّ ابنَ ميّت وأخا ميت؟).

168 Perhaps *saqaṭa baʿḍ jasadih* means "a part of his body fell off", but even a potent poison is unlikely to have such effect.

169 Following the suggestion of ʿASH, reading *tatāyaʿa* instead of *tatābaʿā* ("have followed each other").

170 The Arabic word here rendered as "two columns" is *manāratayn*, which could be "light-towers" (in Islamic times acquiring the sense of "minarets").

171 Ibn Ḥabīb omits the sequel, which is told in many other sources. The king would bestow, on the first person he met on a Day of Bliss, one hundred black camels, and on the first person he met on a Day of Woe the head of a black polecat, after which he would be slaughtered, and the pillars daubed with his blood (e.g. al-Iṣfahānī, *Aghānī*, xi, 86–87). The most prominent victim of this custom is the important early poet ʿAbīd ibn al-Abraṣ, whose story is told in § 81. The polecat (*ẓaribān*) is not mentioned in most sources; perhaps its presence is due to a confusion with *ṭirbālān* (possibly meaning "two prominent

they replied, "These lands do not agree with our cattle. Nevertheless, we are close to you, where we live in the sands. But if you wish, we will comply." But the king was aware that they did not want to submit to him, having heard what Khālid had said before. He signalled to the wine-pourer to poison their wine. When they left the presence of the king | they felt drunk as they had never felt 134
before. At some time during the night Ḥabīb ibn Khālid noticed that something was wrong when he saw how inebriated they were. He cried out to Khālid but he did not respond. He got up and shook him, but part of his body slumped down.[168] He did the same with ʿAmr but he was in a similar state as Khālid.

The following morning al-Mundhir regretted that he had killed them. Ḥabīb ibn Khālid came to him and said, "Sire! May your people make you happy! Your two drinking companions, your bosom friends, have collapsed[169] both in one hour!" The king replied, "Are you asking me protection against death? Don't you see that I too am mortal, or any brother, or any father?" Then he gave orders for two graves to be dug and to bury them in them. He built over them two columns: these are "the Two Daubed Pillars".[170] He slaughtered fifty horses and fifty camels on each grave and daubed them with their blood. He made the date on which he drank wine with them a Day of Bliss and the date he buried them a Day of Woe.[171] A poet said about the two:[172]

O! In the morning they announced the death of Asad's two best men:
ʿAmr ibn Masʿūd and the strong chief.
They dug the earth for him in the desert of al-Ḥabīl (?),[173]
though I did not know that a place would be visited with him.[174]

---

rocks"), another name of the two pillars (Ibn Qutaybah, *Maʿārif*, 649; idem, *Shiʿr*, 268; Yāqūt, *Muʿjam al-buldān*, iv, 196).

172 Anonymously in al-Qālī *Amālī*, iii, 195 (1st line) and Ibn Manẓūr, *Lisān al-ʿArab* (ṢMD); attributed to "a woman of Asad" in al-Jāḥiẓ, *Bayān*, i, 180 (3 lines); attributed to the daughter of Maʿbad ibn Naḍlah in al-Baghdādī, *Khizānah*, xi, 269 (1st line); called Hind bint Maʿbad ibn Naḍlah in Abū ʿUbayd al-Bakrī, *Muʿjam*, 996. No one knows the precise meaning of *ṣamad* (here rendered as "strong"), a word also applied to God in the Qur'an (Q al-Ikhlāṣ 112:2), where it is usually translated as "eternal" or "everlasting".

173 Al-Ḥabīl, or al-Ḥubayl, has not been identified. Perhaps one ought to read it as al-Jubayl ("little mountain"), the name of several places mentioned in Yāqūt's geographical dictionary.

174 A difficult line. I follow ʿASH in interpreting *akhshā* (literally, "I fear") as "I know"; the "place" (*balad*) is the grave. In al-Jāḥiẓ, *Bayān*, i, 180 this line is "They threw up (the earth) of his grave in al-Thuwayyah; I did not fear (or know) that his place would be distant". Al-Jāḥiẓ adds that al-Thuwayyah is a location near Kufa (the Islamic city built not far from al-Ḥīrah).

[§١٤] **ومنهم** خالد بن جعفر بن كِلاب. وكان وفد على الأَسْوَد بن المُنْذِر الأكبر، ووفد الحارث بن ظالم المُرّيّ. وقد كان خالد قتل زُهير بن جَذيمة بن رَواحة العَبْسيّ، وكان سيّد غَطَفان، | فقُدّم إليهما تمْر على نِطْع، فجعلا يأكُلان، فقال خالد للملك: أبيْتَ اللعْن، مَن هذا؟ قال له: هذا الحارث بن ظالم. فقال خالد للحارث: يا حارث، ما أحسبُني إلّا حَسَنَ البَلاء عندك فكيف شُكرك لي؟ فقال الحارث: وما بلاؤك عندي؟ قال: قتلتُ عمَّك فسُدْتَ قومَك. قال: سأجْزيك به.

وجعل الحارث ينبُث التمرَ بيده ولا يُبْصِر غَضَباً. فقال خالد: ما لك تنبث[١] التمر، أيّتهنّ تُريغ؟ فقال الحارث: على أيّتهنّ تَخافني؟ فأمر الملك برفْع التمر، وقام الحارث فانصرف إلى رَحْله، فقال الأسود: لِمَ تعرّضتَ لهذا الكلب وأنت جاري؟ فقال خالد: أبيت اللعن، هذا أحدُ عَبيدي.

فلمّا كان الليلُ بعث الأسود بجاريةٍ له، معها عُسٌّ ضَخْم مملوءاً خمراً إلى الحارث وقال له: يقول لك الملك: عزمتُ عليك لمّا شَرِبتَ هذا، يريد أن يُسْكِرَه فينامَ. فأخذه الحارث كأنّه

١ ك: (ينبث).

175 Among the parallels of this story (again merely an incident in a much longer chain of events), see Ibn Ḥabīb, *Muḥabbar*, 192–193; Abū ʿUbaydah, *Ayyām*, ii, 122–127; Ibn ʿAbd Rabbih, *ʿIqd*, v, 137–138; al-Iṣfahānī, *Aghānī*, xi, 96–98.

176 Khālid ibn Jaʿfar al-Aṣbagh ibn al-Aḍbaṭ ibn Kilāb ibn Rabīʿah, see *ĞN*, i, 93 and ii, 341; a chief of Kilāb.

177 Al-Mundhir al-Akbar is the Lakhmid king mentioned before (§13), i.e., al-Mundhir ibn al-Nuʿmān Māʾ al-Samāʾ; but elsewhere al-Aswad is said to have been his brother (e.g. Ibn ʿAbd Rabbih, *ʿIqd*, v, 137: al-ʿAskarī, *Jamharah*, ii, 287; al-Baghdādī, *Khizānah*, vii, 82, ix, 511).

178 Al-Ḥārith ibn Ẓālim ibn Jadhīmah ibn Yarbūʿ ibn Ghayẓ ibn Murrah, of Ghaṭafān, has his own entry in the present book, see below §94. On his genealogy, see *ĞN*, i, 127 and ii, 315. Books on proverbs often include the saying "more murderous (*aftak*) than al-Ḥārith ibn Ẓālim" (al-ʿAskarī, *Jamharah*, ii, 95; al-Maydānī, *Majmaʿ*, ii, 107; al-Zamakhsharī, *Mustaqṣā*, ii, 266); Ibn Ḥabīb lists him among the "killers" of the pre-Islamic period (*futtāk al-Jāhiliyyah*, *Muḥabbar*, 192). He also killed the young son of al-Samawʾal when the latter did not surrender the armour entrusted to him by the famous poet Imruʾ al-Qays (see e.g. Nicholson, *Literary History*, 84–85). He is, however, also proverbial for his loyalty (*Muḥabbar*, 192, 194, al-ʿAskarī, *Jamharah*, ii, 272, etc.). For two poems by him, see *al-Mufaḍḍaliyyāt*, 311–316, tr. Lyall, 250–256; see also Sezgin, *Geschichte*, ii, 139 and Oller, "Al-Ḥārith ibn Ẓālim".

[§ 14 Khālid ibn Jaʿfar ibn Kilāb[175]]

Another is Khālid ibn Jaʿfar ibn Kilāb.[176] He paid a visit to al-Aswad, son of al-
Mundhir the Great.[177] Al-Ḥārith ibn Ẓālim also visited the king.[178] Khālid had
killed Zuhayr ibn Jadhīmah ibn Rawāḥah al-ʿAbsī, who was the chief of Ghaṭa-
fān.[179] | The two men were offered some dates on a leather mat and they started 135
to eat. Khālid said to the king, "Sire, who is he?" "Al-Ḥārith ibn Ẓālim", replied
the king. Khālid said to al-Ḥārith, "Ḥārith, I should think I did well to you. Aren't
you thankful?" "How do you mean, did well to me?" asked al-Ḥārith. Khālid
explained, "I killed your kinsman[180] so you became the chief of your tribe." "I'll
repay you for that!", replied al-Ḥārith.

Al-Ḥārith was so angry that he began to grab dates without looking. Khālid asked him, "Why are you grabbing the dates? Which ones do you want?" Al-Ḥārith replied, "Which ones are you afraid I'll take?"[181] Then the king gave orders for the dates to be taken away. Al-Ḥārith stood up and left for his luggage. Al-Aswad asked Khālid, "Why did you provoke that dog? You are my guest." "Sire," answered Khālid, "He is one of my slaves!"

In the night al-Aswad sent a servant girl with a large bowl filled with wine to al-Ḥārith. She said, "The king says to you, 'I urge you to drink this!'" He intended to make him drunk and fall fast asleep. Al-Ḥārith took it as if he were going to

179 *ĞN*, i, 132, ii, 610.

180 The word *ʿamm* ("paternal uncle") is often used for more remote relatives; nevertheless, the lineages of the two men are so distant that the word is odd. Instead of *ʿammaka*, *ʿIqd*, v, 138 has *ʿanka*, approximately meaning "(I have killed) for you".

181 The passage is not wholly clear to me. Ibn Ḥabīb, *Muḥabbar*, 193: "Al-Ḥārith repeatedly stretched out his hand to the dates without thinking. Then Khālid asked him, 'Why do you grab dates (from the whole bowl)?'" A longer and different version is offered in al-Iṣfahānī, *Aghānī*, xi, 96: "Khālid ibn Jaʿfar began to eat and threw the stones of the dates he had eaten in front of al-Ḥārith. When the people had finished eating, Khālid ibn Jaʿfar said, 'Sire, look at all those stones in front of al-Ḥārith ibn Ẓālim! He has left nothing for me to eat!' Then al-Ḥārith said, 'I have eaten the dates and thrown the stones down, but you have eaten them with stones and all!' Khālid got angry; he was not one to pick a fight with. 'Do you want to pick a fight with me, Ḥārith?', he said, 'I have killed your kinsman and left you an orphan reared by women!' Al-Ḥārith replied, 'That was a battle where I was not present, but today I can defend my place.' 'Won't you be grateful to me', said Khālid, 'for I killed Zuhayr ibn Jadhīmah and made you chief of Ghaṭafān!' 'O yes, I'll thank you for that!' said al-Ḥārith." For another story with a close variant of the date-eating incident as given in *Aghānī*, see below, § 18.

يشربه، فسَفَحه بين ثَوْبَيْه وجَسَده. فلمّا مضى هُنَيٌّ من الليل قام إلى قُبّة خالد وقد أُشْرجتْ عليه، فهتك شَرْجها ودخل عليه فقتله[1] واغترز في رَحْله ومضى.

١٣٦ [§ ١٥] **ومنهم** الفِطْيَوْن وهو عامر بن عامر بن ثعلبة بن حارثة، وكان يهوديًّا، وكان عزيزاً بيَثْرِب ممتنِعاً، وكان يعتذر النساء قبل أزواجهنّ، وكانت يثربُ قد دانت له؛ فلم تزل تلك حالَه حتّى زُوّجت أخت مالك بن العَجْلان بن زيد الخَزْرَجيّ ثمّ القَوْقَليّ، وهو يومئذٍ شابٌّ، فلمّا كان يوم جِلائها وأُجلست على مِنَصّتها قامت على المنصّة، فخرجت على نادي قومِها كاشفةً عن ساقها. فلمّا رآها مالك وثب فقال: أيْ عَدُوّةَ اللّٰه، تخرُجين على قومك كاشفةً عن ساقَيْكِ، سَوْءةً لكِ! فقالت: سَوْءةً لكَ! فالذي يُراد بي[2] أقبحُ ممّا صنعتُ. إنّه يُذْهَب بي إلى غيرِ زوجي فيُصيبني! فارتاع مالك وقال: صدقْتِ واللّٰهِ فهل فيكِ خير؟ قالت: ينبغي أن يكون الخيرُ عندك.

فلمّا ذُهب بها لَبِس مالكٌ لِبْسةَ النساء واشتمل على سيف صارم، ودخل مع النساء فانكمى في داخل البيت، فلمّا خرج النساء وخلا الفِطْيَون مع المرأة خرج عليه مالك فضربه بالسيف حتّى بَرَد، وأخذ بيدِ أُختـه فخرج بها مع نسائها، وتصايحتْ يَهود، وطلبوا مالكاً، فامتنع بقومه، ثمّ خرج هارباً ومعه عِدّة من الأَوْس والخَزْرَج حتّى قَدِموا على أبي جُبَيْلة ملك غَسّان، فأعلموه

١ الكلمة ناقصة في ك

٢ ك: (به).

182 Parallels in ps.-al-Jāḥiẓ, *Maḥāsin*, 282–283; al-Dīnawarī, *Akhbār*, 43 (where al-Fiṭyawn appears as al-Qayṭūn); Yāqūt, *Muʿjam al-buldān*, v, 85 (entry "Madīnat Yathrib"), quoting Ibn al-Kalbī, with al-Fayṭuwān as alternative to al-Fiṭyawn; Abū ʿUbayd al-Bakrī, *Faṣl al-maqāl*, 360; al-Iṣfahānī, *Aghānī*, ii, 111–112 (in a longer section on the Jewish tribes in Yathrib, but not mentioning al-Fiṭyawn). The truth of the story is denied in the text that is attributed (spuriously) to ʿAbīd ibn Sharyah (quoted in Ibn Hishām, *Tījān*, 464): "Muʿāwiyah [the Umayyad caliph] said: 'I have heard, ʿAbīd, that the Jews were in it [viz., Yathrib/Medina] and al-Khazraj did not have any power, to the extent that a man who married a wife could not have her before a Jew had her first; they dominated them.' ʿAbīd replied, 'God forbid, O Commander of the Believers! What you have heard has never happened. The Jews there were submissive; al-Aws and al-Khazraj were too powerful and too strong to allow that …'" For invective lines mentioning al-Fiṭyawn and his *jus primae noctis*, see also al-Jāḥiẓ, *Bighāl*, in his *Rasāʾil*, ii, 359, also in al-Iṣfahānī, *Aghānī*, ix, 230–231. On the much-debated Jewish presence in pre-Islamic Medina, see e.g. *EI2*, "al-Madīna" (W.M. Watt, see 994–995); Lecker, "Were the Jewish Tribes in Arabia Clients of Arab Tribes?", 52–54, 57; Munt, "The Prophet's City before the Prophet" (who gives the story in the version of Ibn Zabālah, who died after 199/814, see pp. 113–116).

drink it; but he poured it between his clothes and his skin. After a short time he got up and went to the pavilion of Khālid, which had been closed with a tie. Al-Ḥārith ripped open the tie, went in, and killed him. Then he mounted into the saddle and left.

[§ 15 al-Fiṭyawn[182]]

Another was al-Fiṭyawn, i.e., ʿĀmir ibn ʿĀmir ibn Thaʿlabah ibn Ḥārithah.[183] He 136
was a Jew who was mighty and powerful in Yathrib,[184] and who used to deflower women before their husbands. Yathrib submitted to him. This went on until the marriage of the sister of Mālik ibn al-ʿAjlān ibn Zayd, of the tribe of al-Khazraj and the clan of Banū Qawqal.[185] He was a young man at the time. On the day of her wedding when she was sat on her bridal throne, she stood up from the throne and went to the congregated men of her tribe, baring her legs.[186] When Mālik saw this he jumped up and said, "Wicked woman![187] You come to your menfolk showing your legs! Shame on you!" "Shame on *you*!" she replied, "What is intended for me is worse than what I have done. They will take me to someone who is not my husband, and he will have me." Mālik was shocked and said, "You are right, by God! Have you any good idea?" "It is you who ought to have a good idea", she said.

When she was taken away Mālik dressed up as a woman, hiding a sharp sword under his clothes. He went in with the women and hid inside the house. When the women left and al-Fiṭyawn was alone with the woman, Mālik sprang upon him and struck him with the sword until he was stone dead.[188] He took his sister by the hand and went outside with her women. The Jews called out to one another and pursued Mālik, but he resisted with his kinsmen. Then he left, fleeing with a number of men from al-Aws and al-Khazraj. They went to Abū

---

183 One of the Jafnids of Ghassān; see *ĞN*, i, 195, ii, 157. Fiṭyawn, apparently a nickname, is said to be Hebrew (Ibn Durayd, *Ishtiqāq*, 259), but its meaning is unclear.

184 Yathrib is the name of Medina in pre-Islamic times.

185 See *ĞN*, i, 189 and ii, 385, where he is Mālik ibn al-ʿAjlān ibn Zayd ibn Ghanm ibn Sālim, but not a descendant of Qawqal, brother of Sālim. Al-Khazraj was one of the two main Arab tribes in Yathrib, the other being al-Aws; both were to play a very important role in the life of the prophet Muḥammad and in early Islam, see *EI2*, "al-Aws" and "al-Khazradj" (both by W. Montgomery Watt), *EI3*, "al-Aws" (Yaara Perlman).

186 Ps.-al-Jāḥiz, *Maḥāsin*, 283: "lifting her robe to her navel".

187 Literally, "Enemy of God!" (*ʿaduwwat Allāh*).

188 Literally, "struck him until he was cold".

١٣٧ غَلَبَةَ يهودَ عليهم وفعْلَهم، فقدِم أبو جُبيلة بيثرب واتّخذ | طعاماً ودعا إليه أشراف يهودَ والأوس والخزرج، فلمّا طَعِموا جعل يدفع إلى الرجل سيفاً فيضطربان به، حتّى قتل بهذا الفعل مائة من أشراف اليهود، فكان الرجل يقتل أخاه وابن عمّه، ثمّ انصرف راجعاً إلى الشام، فقَوِيَت الأوس والخزرج عليهم.

[§١٦] **ومنهم** لَخْنِيعة يَنُوف ذو شَناتر الحِمْيَريّ، وكان ملك اليمن، ولم يكن من أهل المملكة، وإنّما كان مَلَكهم حين قَتل مَوْثَبانُ أخاه، فاضطرب أمرُهم حتّى ملكهم لخنيعة، وكان فاسقاً يعمل عَمَلَ قومِ لُوط، وكان يبعث إلى أبناء الملوك فيَلُوط بهم، وكانت حِمْيَرُ إذا لِيطَ بالغُلام لم تملِّكْه ولا ترتفع[١] به. وكانت له مَشْرَبة فيها كُوّة تُشْرِف على حَرَسه، فإذا أتاه الغلام ينكحه قُطعت مَشافر ناقته وذَنَبها، ثمّ يطَّلِع لخنيعةُ من الكوّة وفي فيه مِسْواكُه فهي عَلامةُ نِكاحه إيّاه، فإذا نزل الغلام صاحوا به: أرَطْب أمْ يُباس؟

فمكث كذلك زماناً حتّى نشأ زُرْعةُ وهو ذو نُواس، وكانت له ذؤابة فبها[٢] سُمّي ذو نواس، وهو الذي تَهوَّد وتَسمّى يوسف، وهو صاحب الأُخْدود بنَجْران، وكانوا نصارى فحرّقهم

١ كذا في هـ، ک، كما في الأغاني، وفي الأصل (تنتفع).

٢ ک: (فيها).

189 Abū Jubaylah ibn ʿAbd Allāh (of al-Khazraj; see *ǦN*, i, 192) is oddly identified as the Ghassānid king in the story of al-Fiṭyawn (ibid., ii, 263). Several rulers of the Jafnids are called Jabalah; there is obviously some confusion with Jubaylah. Yāqūt (*Muʿjam al-buldān*, v, 85) adds: "In another version it is said that he (viz., Mālik ibn al-ʿAjlān) went to Yemen and complained to Tubbaʿ al-Aṣghar, son of Ḥassān, of al-Fiṭyawn and what he did to their women".

190 The passage is elliptic and cryptic, and the translation somewhat uncertain. I have taken the dual of the verb (*yaḍṭaribān*) to refer to the two tribes of al-Aws and al-Khazraj. It is not clear why brothers and cousins are killed. In other versions (*Aghānī*, *Muʿjam al-buldān*) the Jewish leaders are killed one by one as they arrive.

191 Parallels in Ibn Hishām, *Sīrah*, i, 29–31 (tr. Guillaume, 13–14, somewhat bowdlerised); Ibn Ḥabīb, *Muḥabbar*, 368; Ibn Hishām, *Tījān*, 311–312; Ibn Qutaybah, *Maʿārif*, 636; al-Yaʿqūbī, *Tārīkh*, i, 225 (tr. *The Works*, 504); al-Ṭabarī, *Tārīkh*, i, 917–919 (tr. *The History*, 189–190); al-Iṣfahānī, *Aghānī*, xxii, 318–319; al-Masʿūdī, *Murūj*, ii, 199; al-Maqdisī, *Badʾ*, iii, 181–182; al-Nuwayrī, *Nihāyat al-arab*, xv, 303–304.

192 Instead of Lakhnīʿah some sources have Lakhtīʿah; both are oddly formed by Classical Arabic standards and yet other sources have Lakhīʿah or Lukhayʿah. The name *Lḫyʿṯt* and its shorter form *Lḫyʿt* (Laḫīʿat) is attested in South Arabian inscriptions (see the note by Bosworth in his translation of al-Ṭabarī's version). Dhū Shanātir is said to mean "the one

Jubaylah, the king of Ghassān,[189] and told him how the Jews had subdued them and what they did. Then Abū Jubaylah went to Yathrib. He prepared | a meal and 137
invited the leaders of the Jews, of al-Aws, and al-Khazraj. When they were eating he gave each man a sword and the two tribes would strike with it,[190] until one hundred leaders of the Jews were killed; a man would kill his brother and his cousin. Then Abū Jubaylah returned to Syria; al-Aws and al-Khazraj then had the upper hand over the Jews.

[§16 Lakhnīʿah Yanūf Dhū l-Shanātir al-Ḥimyarī[191]]

Another was Lakhnīʿah Yanūf Dhū l-Shanātir al-Ḥimyarī, who was the king of Yemen,[192] though he did not belong to a royal dynasty. He only became their king when Mawthabān killed his brother.[193] Matters were in disarray until Lakhnīʿah took power. He was an evil man and a pederast. He used to send for young men of royal blood and sodomise them. The Ḥimyarites would not make a young man king if he had been sodomised and he would not be given a high status. He had an upper chamber[194] with a small window overlooking his guardsmen. Whenever a young man would come to him to be buggered, the lips and tail of his she-camel would be cut off. Then Lakhnīʿah would appear from the window with a toothpick in his mouth, as a sign that he had had sex with the lad. When the boy came down they would call at him, "Wet or dry?"

This went on for some time, until Zurʿah had grown up, also known as Dhū Nuwās ("He with the dangling lock"),[195] for he had a lock of hair and was therefore called Dhū Nuwās. He is the one who converted to Judaism, calling himself Yūsuf. He is also "the man of the Trench" in Najrān.[196] Its people were Christians; he burned them, he burned the Gospel, he destroyed the churches,

---

with fingers"; *shunturah* is said by the Arabic lexicographers to be a Ḥimyarite word for "finger".

193 ʿAmr ibn Tubbaʿ, called Mawthabān becaused he "sprang" (*wathaba*) upon his brother Ḥassān (al-Ṭabarī, *Tārīkh*, i, 917) or because he abstained from raiding, *withāb* meaning "bed" (Ibn Qutaybah, *Maʿārif*, 634). Ḥimyarite *WThB*, like Hebrew *YShB*, means "to sit" (Biella, *Dictionary of Old South Arabic, Sabaean Dialect*, 153).

194 *Mashrabah*, literally "place for drinking".

195 On him see *EI2*, "Dhū Nuwās" (M.R. Al-Assouad); *ĠN*, i, 275 and ii, 612.

196 Najrān is a town in northern Yemen. It was captured around AD 520 by Dhū Nuwās and the story of the martyrs who refused to convert and were burned in a trench (*ukhdūd*) is told in many sources, with its sequel of the invasion by the Christian Abyssinians (Ḥabash, Ethiopians) a few years later. See *EI2*, "Nadjrān" (Irfan Shahîd); Ibn Hishām, *Sīrah*, i, 31–37 (tr. Guillaume, 14–18), etc. The events are briefly alluded to in the Qur'an (Q al-Burūj 85:4–8: «The people of the trench were killed; the fire with fuel, while they [the perpetrators] were seated at it, as witnesses of what they were doing to the believers»).

وحرّق الإنجيل، وهدم الكنائس على أن يهوّدوا، فبسببه غَزَت الحَبَشةُ اليمنَ، وذلك لأنّ الحبشة نصارى، فلمّا عَلَت الحبشة على اليمن اعترض البحر فأقْحمه فَرَسه فغَرِق. فلمّا نشأ زُرعة هذا | قيل له: كأنّك بالملك قد دعاك فيلعَب بك كما لَعِب بغيرك! فاتّخذ سِكّيناً رقيقاً ١٣٨
فلمّا بعث إليه لخنيعة يدعوه عَرَف ما يريد، فجعل السكّين بين أخمصه ونَعْله، وأتاه على ناقة له يقال لها سَراب، فأناخها ثمّ صَعِد إليه، فلمّا صعد زرعة قام إليه كما كان يقوم لغيره، وذهب يعالجه، فانحنى زرعة وأخذ السكّين فوجأ به بطنه ......[١]

[§١٧] [**ومنهم** علقمة بن ذي قَيْفان][٢] ..... بجُرْأتهم عليه، فأقبل الحَيّانِ شاكرٌ ونِهْمٌ إلى زيد بن مَرِب[٣] فقالوا: أنت سيّدنا وأنت نديم الملك وجليسه، وقد آلى[٤] بما تعْلَم، وواللّٰهِ لا يصل إلى إخواننا ومنّا رجلٌ حيّ، فسَلْه فلْيَصْفَحْ. فقال: إنّه قد آلى، ولا يرجِع عن أَلِيَّته. قالوا: فإنْ أبى فاقْتُلْه ونحن نملّكك علينا. قال: لا تَعْجَلوا وأَمْهِلوا حتّى أرى لذلك موضعاً. فأمسكوا.

١ بقيّة القصّة ناقصة في الأصل، وتمامها كما في الأغاني:
... فقتله واحتزّ رأسَه فجعل السِّواكَ في فيه وأطلعه من الكوّة فرفع الحرسُ رءوسهم فرأوْه ونزل زرعةُ فصاحوا: زرعة يا ذا نواس! أرَطْب أم يُباس؟ وجاء إلى ناقته فركِبها، فلمّا رأى الحرس اطّلاع الرأس صعدوا إليه فإذا هو قد قُتل. فأتوْا زرعة فقالوا: ما ينبغي أن يملِكنا غيرُك بعد أن أرَحْتَنا من هذا الفاسق. واجتمعتْ حِمْير إليه.

٢ ما بين القوسين ناقص في الأصل وفي هـ، كـ

٣ هـ، كـ: (مرت)، والتصحيح من الإكليل للهمدانيّ.

٤ كـ: (أتى).

197 Sarāb means "mirage, fata morgana".

198 The story breaks off in the MS at the end of a folio. ʿASH and SKḤ supply the completion of the story as offered in *Aghānī* (with a chain of authorities including Ibn Ḥabīb): ... killing him. He cut off his head and stuck the toothpick in his mouth. He put it in the window. The guards raised their heads and saw it. Zurʿah went down and they called out to him, "Hey Zurʿah Dangling Lock! Is it wet or dry?" He answered, "The guards will know whether the arse of Dhū Nuwās is wet of dry!" [This exchange is in rhymed prose.] He walked to his camel and mounted it. When the guards saw the head looking out of the

unless they would convert to Judaism. This was why the Abyssinians invaded Yemen, because the Abyssinians are Christians. When the Abyssinians overran Yemen, Dhū Nuwās went as far as the sea; he made his horse plunge into it and drowned.

Now when he, this Zurʿah, had grown up, | people said to him, "It looks as if 138
the king will call for you; he'll have his sport with you like he sported with the others!" He took a thin knife and when Lakhnīʿah sent for him and summoned him, he was well aware of the king's intention. He hid the knife between his foot-sole and his sandal and arrived on a she-camel called Sarāb.[197] He made her kneel and went up. When Zurʿah was up the king turned to him as he used to do with the others and began to touch him. Zurʿah bent over, took the knife, and stabbed his in the belly, …[198]

[§ 17 ʿAlqamah ibn Dhī Qayfān[199]]

… with their recklessness. The two tribes, Shākir and Nihm,[200] turned to Zayd ibn Marib[201] and said, "You are our chief and you are a drinking companion of the king[202] and his friend. He has sworn an oath, as you know. I swear by God, it shall not happen to our brothers while there is any man of us alive. Ask him and let him forgive!" Zayd answered, "He has sworn an oath and he will not go back on his oath." They said, "If he refuses, kill him! We'll make you our king!" Zayd replied, "Don't be hasty! Give me some time to think of an occasion". The others stopped insisting.

---

window they went up and found the king dead. They went to Zurʿah and said, "No one but you ought to be king over us, for you have delivered us from that evil man." The Ḥimyarites all agreed.

199 For this incomplete tale, the beginning of which is missing, no parallels have been found except a few brief passages. See al-Hamdānī, *Iklīl*, x, 41 ("… Maʿdī Karib had a son, Marib; Marib had a son, Zayd, the king. He is the one who killed ʿAlqamah ibn Dhī Qayfān and who wrested his kingdom from him") and Ibn al-Kalbī, *Nasab Maʿadd wa-l-Yaman*, 545–546 ("ʿAlqamah ibn Sharāḥīl, who is Qayfān ibn ʿAlas Dhī Jadan, king of al-Bawn, the town of Hamdān in Yemen; he was killed by Zayd ibn Marib [thus instead of Murabb] ibn Maʿdī Karib al-Hamdānī … who became king after him").

200 Shākir and Nihm are brother tribes belonging to Bakīl, a subdivision of the South Arab tribe of Hamdān, see *ǦN*, i, 230, 227. On Hamdān, see *EI2*, "Hamdān" (J. Schleifer—W. Montgomery Watt).

201 ʿASH and SKḤ, incorrectly, *M.r.t.* For Zayd ibn Marib ibn Maʿdī Karib, of al-Sabīʿ, a subdivision of Hamdān, see *ǦN*, i, 228.

202 The Ḥimyarite king is ʿAlqamah ibn Sharāḥīl (or Mālik) Dhū Qayfān, see *ǦN*, i, 278, ii, 155.

قال:[١] فبيْنا زيدٌ جالسٌ مع عَلْقَمةَ إذ جرى ذكر السيوف، فقال علقمة: عندي سيف كان لأجدادي إليه المَيْل. فقال له زيد: أبيْتَ اللعْن، ادْعُ به لِأنظُرَ إليه. فدعا له، فنظر إليه علقمة ساعةً ثمّ ناولَه زيداً، فنظر إليه وإذا فيه مكتوب: ضِرْس العَيْر، سيف الجَبْر، بِاسْتِ امرئ وقع في يده لم | يغضَبْ لقومه. فهزَّه زيد ساعةً ثمّ ضربه به فقتله، ووثبتْ هَمْدان فألبسوه التاجَ وملّكوه ١٣٩
عليهم. وفي ذلك يقول شاعرهم:

فيمَّمَ[٢] ضِرْسَ العَيْر مَفْرِقَ رأسِهِ فخرَّ ولم يثبُتْ لحقِّك باطِلُهْ
فلم أرَ يوماً كان أكثرَ باكياً غَداةَ غَدا مِلْ بُونِ تُحْدى رواحِلُهْ
وغادره يكبو لحُرِّ جبينِهِ ووُرِّث زيداً تاجُه وحلائلُهْ

[§١٨] **ومنهم** الصِّمّة الأكبر وهو مالك بن بَكر بن عَلَقة[٣] بن جُداعة، أخو بني جُشَم بن معاوية بن بكر ابن هَوازِن، وكان غزا بني قيْس بن حَنْظَلة، من البَراجم، فأسره الجَعْد بن الشمّاخ

١ كذا في هـ؛ وفي كـ: (فقال) كما في النسختين.
٢ كـ: (فييمّم).
٣ هـ، كـ: (عُلّفة)، والتصحيح من الأغاني وغيره.

203 *Ḍirs al-ʿayr*, mentioned as the name of the sword of ʿAlqamah ibn Dhī Qayfān in the lexicons (al-Fīrūzābādī, *Qāmūs*, al-Zabīdī, *Tāj al-ʿarūs*, s.v. ḌRS). Ibn ʿAbd Rabbih (*ʿIqd*, iii, 370, cf. also Ibn Durayd, *Ishtiqāq*, 311) says that ʿAlqamah ibn Sharāḥīl Dhū Qayfān possessed the famous sword known as al-Ṣamṣāmah of the well-known warrior and poet ʿAmr ibn Maʿdī Karib (d. 9/631), quoting a line that shows, rather, that ʿAmr possessed ʿAlqamah's sword: "A sword of Ibn Dhī Qayfān I have, | its blade selected in the time of ʿĀd".

204 For this sense of *jabr*, see e.g. Lane, *Lexicon*.

205 The poet is unknown and the lines have not been found elsewhere except the first, which is quoted in al-Zabīdī, *Tāj al-ʿArūs* (ḌRS), beginning with "I struck (*ḍarabtu*) with the Onager Tooth …" and attributing it to Zayd himself.

206 The Arabic has *mil Bawn* (licence for *min al-Bawn*); Bawn (without article) is a town in Yemen according to Yāqūt, *Muʿjam al-buldān*; but he mentions a report that there are two places called al-Bawn (with article). Abū ʿUbayd al-Bakrī, *Muʿjam*, 285 mentions al-Bawn, in Yemen.

One day, when Zayd was sitting together with ʿAlqamah, they happened to talk about swords. ʿAlqamah said, "I have a sword that my ancestors were fond of." "Sire," said Zaid, "Have it brought here so that I can look at it!" ʿAlqamah asked for it to be brought and looked at it for a while; then he handed it to Zayd, who looked at it too. He found an inscription written on it: "Onager Tooth,[203] the King's[204] Sword in the arse of any man in whose hand it comes who does
not | defend his people!" Thereupon Zaid brandished the sword, struck the king 139
with it and killed him. All Hamdān rose up, crowned Zayd and made him their king. Their poet said on this:[205]

He aimed the Onager Tooth at the parting on his head
    and he fell down. His falsehood did not stand firm against your truth.
I have never seen a day on which more people wept,
    the morning he left al-Bawn[206] and his camels were led away.
He left it with his forehead on the earth,
    while Zayd was made to inherit his crown and his wives.

[§ 18 al-Ṣimmah al-Akbar[207]]

Another is al-Ṣimmah al-Akbar, who is Mālik ibn Bakr ibn ʿAlaqah[208] ibn Judāʿah, of the Banū Jusham ibn Muʿāwiyah ibn Bakr ibn Hawāzin.[209] He had raided the Banū Qays ibn Ḥanẓalah, one of al-Barājim,[210] and was taken pris-

---

207 For parallels see Abū ʿUbaydah, *Naqāʾiḍ*, 119–120; al-Balādhurī, *Ansāb*, xii, 113–114; Ibn Rashīq, *ʿUmdah*, ii, 207, in a section on the "battle-day (*yawm*) of ʿĀqil"; but Yawm ʿĀqil as described in al-Shimshāṭī, *Anwār*, i, 239–242 is another event not involving al-Ṣimmah or his tribe.

208 ʿASH and SKḤ have ʿUllafah.

209 There is some confusion about his lineage; see al-Āmidī, *Muʾtalif*, 144; al-Marzubānī, *Muʿjam al-shuʿarāʾ*, 257, 312–313; al-Iṣfahānī, *Aghānī*, x, 3. *ĞN*, i, 116 has Muʿāwiyah (al-Ṣimmah) ibn Bakrī ibn ʿAlaqah ibn Judāʿah ibn Ghaziyyah ibn Jusham; Abū ʿUbaydah, *Naqāʾiḍ*, 119 has Muʿāwiyah ibn Mālik ibn ʿAlaqah ibn Ghaziyyah. Al-Ṣimmah is apparently a nickname; *ṣimmah* may mean "stopper; male serpent; female hedgehog; courageous" according to the lexicographers. It is not known which sense is meant here. He is called al-Akbar (the Older) to distinguish him from his son Durayd ibn al-Ṣimmah, famous poet and tribal leader, who died 8/629 at the battle of Ḥunayn, fighting against the prophet Muḥammad and the Muslims; on him see below, § 91. Durayd is said to have had a brother called Mālik (*Aghānī*, x, 28), to be distinguished from his father, also a poet (*Aghānī*, x, 27); both were poets, too. On the large tribe of Hawāzin, see *EI2*, "Hawāzin" (W. Montgomery Watt).

210 On Qays ibn Ḥanẓalah, part of Tamīm, see *ĞN*, i, 59 and 73; al-Barājim (plural of al-Burjumī) refers to five branches of Ḥanẓalah (i, 59 and ii, 224).

البُرْجُميّ وفضّ أصحابه، فمكث عنده عاماً لا يُفْدى. فلمّا طال ذلك عليه جعل يأتيه في كل رأسِ شهر بأفعى فيقول: واللّٰهِ لَتُـفْدَيَنّ أو لَأُعِضَّنَّها بك! فلمّا طال ذلك عليه قال: يا هذا إنّ قوْمي لا أَراهم يَفْدونني، فجُزَّ ناصِيَتي على الثَّواب. ففعل وأطلقه.

ثمّ إنّ الجعد أتاه يستثيبه، [فقال له الصّمة ما لك عندي ثواب][1] فقدَّمه فضرب عنقه، فأتى
على ذلك ما شاء اللّٰه. ثمّ إنّ الصمّة حضر المَوْسِم، فاتّفق الصمّة وأبو مَرْحَب ثعلبة بن حَصَبة
بن أزنم بن ثعلبة بن يَرْبوع، عند حَرْب بن أُمَيّة، فقدّم إليهما سَوِيقاً وتمْراً، فجعل الصمّة يأكل
ويُلْقي النَّوى بين يديْ ثعلبة، فقال: ويْحَك يا ثعلبة، أكلتَ التمر كلَّه؛ أما ترى النوى بين يديْك؟
فقال له ثعلبة: إنّي[2] كنت أُلْقي النوى، وأنت تأكل التمر بنَواه، فلذلك عَظُم بطنُك. فقال الصمّة:
إنّما عظّم بطني | دِماءُ قومِك، أيْنَ[3] الجَعْدُ بن الشمّاخ؟ فقال أبو مَرْحَب: ما فَخْرُك برجلٍ أَسَرَك ١٤٠
ومَنَّ عليك ثمّ أتاك مستثيباً فقتلتَه؟ إنّ لِلّٰه عليَّ أن لا أراك في غير هذا الموضع إلّا قتلتُك أو متُّ
دونَك! فافترقا.

ثمّ إنّ الصمّة غزا بني تَميم فهُزم أصحابُه، وأُسر هو وابنُه معه وبعضُ أصحابه، أسره الحارثُ بن بَـيْبة المُجاشعيّ جَدُّ البَعيت الشاعر. فقال الصمّة للحارث بن بيْبة: سِرْ بي في

١ الزيادة من النقائض وليست في هـ، كـ.

٢ كـ: (إن).

٣ هـ، كـ: (ابن)، والتصحيح من النقائض.

211 Abū ʿUbaydah, *Naqāʾiḍ*, 119: al-Jaʿd ibn al-Shammākh, one of the Banū Ṣudayy ibn Mālik ibn Ḥanẓalah; al-Balādhurī, *Ansāb*, xii, 113, quoting Ibn al-Kalbī: al-Jaʿd ibn ʿĀmir ibn Mālik ibn Thaʿlabah ibn al-Ṣudayy.

212 Al-Jāḥiẓ, *Ḥayawān*, ii, 162: "The Arabs would cut off the forelock of captive knights, if they wanted to let them go and bestow a favour upon them." Al-Jāḥiẓ explains that this humiliation would prevent them from making scathing poetry on their captors. Ibn Qutaybah, *Maʿānī*, 1021: "In pre-Islamic times a man would cut off the forelock of a prisoner and let him go, putting the forelock in his quiver. At a boasting contest he would produce it and say, 'This is So-and-so's forelock!'". See also Ibn ʿAbd Rabbih, *ʿIqd*, v, 197–198.

213 The parenthesis, from *Naqāʾiḍ*, has been added to make the sudden turn of events slightly less abrupt.

214 *Mawsim*, a festival, often connected with market days. Abū ʿUbaydah and al-Balādhurī specifically mention ʿUkāẓ, the most famous pre-Islamic annual fair, not far from Mecca; see *EI2*, "ʿUkāẓ" (Irfan Shahîd).

oner by al-Jaʿd ibn al-Shammākh al-Burjumī,[211] who routed his men. Al-Ṣimmah spent a year with him without being ransomed. When al-Jaʿd thought it was taking too long, he began to show a viper to him at the beginning of every month, saying, "I swear by God, you shall be ransomed or else I'll let it bite you!" When this went on for a long time, however, al-Ṣimmah said, "I don't think my people will ransom me! Now cut off my forelock, as a token of your recompense in due course!"[212] Al-Jaʿd did so and he let him go.

Later, al-Jaʿd came to him asking for recompense, [but al-Ṣimmah said, "I don't think I owe you any recompense!"][213] and he sat al-Jaʿd down before him and struck off his head.

Some time went by. One day al-Ṣimmah attended a feast day.[214] He met with Abū Marḥab Thaʿlabah ibn Ḥaṣabah ibn Aznam ibn Thaʿlabah ibn Yarbūʿ,[215] and they visited Ḥarb ibn Umayyah,[216] who offered them *sawīq*[217] and dates. Al-Ṣimmah began to eat and threw the date stones in front of Thaʿlabah.[218] "I say, Thaʿlabah", he said, "You have eaten all the dates!" "I have thrown the stones down," replied Thaʿlabah, "but you have eaten the dates, stones and all. That's why you've got a fat belly!" Al-Ṣimmah said, "My belly is fat, rather, | 140
from the blood of your kinsmen! Tell me, where is[219] al-Jaʿd ibn al-Shammākh?" Then Abū Marḥab said, "Why are you boasting about killing a man who took you prisoner but granted you your freedom, who then came to you asking for recompense, and whom you killed? I swear to God, if I see you in some other place[220] I'll kill you, or die attempting!" They parted.

Subsequently al-Ṣimmah raided the Banū Tamīm but his men were routed and he and his son were taken prisoner, together with some of his men, by al-Ḥārith ibn Baybah al-Mujāshiʿī, the grandfather of al-Baʿīth, the poet.[221] Al-Ṣimmah said to al-Ḥārith ibn Baybah, "Take me to your lands until I get ransom

215 *ǦN*, i, 69 (without mentioning Abū Marḥab Thaʿlabah). Abū ʿUbaydah calls him Thaʿlabah ibn al-Ḥārith ibn Ḥaṣabah ibn Aznam.

216 The son of the eponymous ancestor of the Umayyad caliphs (and before them ʿUthmān ibn ʿAffān, the third caliph). He was "one of the leading figures of Mecca in his day" (*EI2*, "Ḥarb b. Umayyah b. ʿAbd Shams").

217 A broth of wheat or barley; for recipes (from a tenth-century cookbook and probably more luxurious than the pre-Islamic variety) see Ibn Sayyār, *Kitāb al-Ṭabīkh*, 37–38 (tr. *Annals of the Caliphs' Kitchens*, 126–127).

218 For this motif see also above, §14 note 181.

219 Reading, with *Naqāʾiḍ*, *ayna* instead of *ibn* (ʿASH, SKḤ); *Ansāb al-ashrāf* has "Do you know anything of (*hal laka ʿilm bi-*) al-Jaʿd ibn al-Shammākh?"

220 Shedding blood during a *mawsim* was taboo.

221 *ǦN*, i, 61 (where al-Baʿīth is the grandson of Baybah's brother Abū Khālid). On al-Baʿīth (Khidāsh ibn Bishr), who died probably in the first quarter of the 2nd/8th century, see Sezgin, *Geschichte*, ii, 363–364, *EI2*, "al-Baʿīth" (Ch. Pellat).

بلادك حتّى أفتدي أصحابي. وكانت الحجْرة[١] لبني رِياح بن يَرْبوع، إليها تجتمع بنو حنظلة في أمورها، فجاء الحارث مُرْدِفاً الصمّةَ حتّى إذا نزل رآه أبو مَرحب، فدخل بيته واشتمل على السيف، ثمّ خرج والناس غافلون، فضرب به بطن الصمّة فقتله، وصاح الحارث: يالَ دارم! قُتل أسيري في يدي![٢] فثارت يربوع ودارم، فكاد يقع القتال بينهم، فسَفَرت السُّفَراءُ بينهم، وأُرضي الحارثُ بن بيبة من الصمّة فسكنوا.

[§١٩] **ومنهم** عَدِيّ بن زيد بن أيّوب بن حِمار العِباديّ الشاعر، أحد بني امْرئ القيس بن
زيد مَناة بن تميم، وكان كاتباً لكِسْرى على ما يُجْتَبى من الغَوْر، وكان هو سبب مُلْك النُّعْمان
بن المُنْذِر اللَّخْميّ. وكان لعَديّ بن زيد عَدُوٌّ من أهل الحِيرة يقال له عَديّ بن مَرِينا. فلم يزل
يلاطف النعمانَ حتّى غلب على سَمَره ونزل منه[٣] أحسنَ منزلةً، فجعل يَبْغي عديَّ بن زيد
الغوائل، ويحمل النعمانَ عليه حتّى وغّر صدرَه، فكتب إلى | كسرى يستزيره متشوّقاً[٤] إليه، ١٤١

١ كـ: (الهجرة).

٢ (أسيري في يدي): ناقصة في كـ.

٣ الكلمة ناقصة في كـ.

٤ هـ: (متشوّفاً).

222 *Ḥajrah* or *ḥujrah*; see Lane, *Lexicon*.

223 Riyāḥ ibn Yarbūʿ ibn Ḥanẓalah, of Tamīm, see ĞN, i, 68. Instead, *Naqāʾiḍ* has Banū ʿĀṣim ibn ʿUbayd ibn Thaʿlabah ibn Yarbūʿ.

224 Dārim is the branch of Tamīm to which Mujāshiʿ and therefore al-Ḥārith ibn Baybah belong. Instead, *Naqāʾiḍ* has "Men of Mālik!", probably referring to the father of Dārim, Mālik ibn Ḥanẓalah (ĞN, i, 59).

225 ʿAdī ibn Zayd (d. c. 600) is an important poet with an interesting career, whose poetry is deemed to be somewhat tainted by his close contact with urban and courtly culture (he could read and write and knew Persian!). On him see EI2, "ʿAdī b. Zayd" (Ch. Pellat); EI3, "ʿAdī b. Zayd" (Tilman Seidensticker); EAL, "ʿAdī ibn Zayd al-ʿIbādī" (P.F. Kennedy); Sezgin, *Geschichte*, ii, 178–179. A long entry on him in al-Iṣfahānī, *Aghānī* (ii, 95–154) also provides versions of his murder in much greater detail than in the present book; see Sezgin, *Geschichte*, ii, 179. On ʿAdī's death, see also Ibn Qutaybah, *Shiʿr*, 228–229; al-Yaʿqūbī, *Tārīkh*, i, 243–244, tr. *The Works*, 523–525; al-Ṭabarī, *Tārīkh*, i, 1016–1024, tr. *The History*, v, 339–351.

226 For his lineage see ĞN, i, 80 and ii, 141. Instead of Ḥimār one also finds Ḥammād (Ibn Qutaybah, *Shiʿr*, 225, al-Iṣfahānī, *Aghānī*, ii, 97) and Ḥimāz (Ibn Qutaybah, *Shiʿr*, 229). Al-ʿIbādī,

for my men!" The adjacent country[222] belonged to the Banū Riyāḥ ibn Yarbūʿ,[223] where the Banū Thaʿlabah assembled for their affairs. Al-Ḥārith went there, seating al-Ṣimmah behind him on his camel. When he dismounted Abū Marḥab saw him. He entered his tent, hid a sword under his robe, came out again and before anyone noticed what was happening he struck al-Ṣimmah in the belly, killing him. Al-Ḥārith called out, "Men of Dārim![224] My prisoner has been killed!" All Yarbūʿ and Dārim were roused and they almost came to blows. Mediators went to and fro between the two sides; al-Ḥārith ibn Baybah was given satisfaction for the killing of al-Ṣimmah and peace was restored.

[§ 19 ʿAdī ibn Zayd[225]]

Another was ʿAdī ibn Zayd ibn Ayyūb ibn Ḥimār al-ʿIbādī, the poet, one of the Banū Imriʾ al-Qays ibn Zayd Manāh ibn Tamīm.[226] He served as secretary to Kisrā,[227] charged with the revenue of al-Ghawr.[228] He was instrumental in bringing al-Nuʿmān ibn al-Mundhir al-Lakhmī to power as king.[229] ʿAdī ibn Zayd had an enemy from among the people of al-Ḥīrah, called ʿAdī ibn Marīnā,[230] who fawned upon al-Nuʿmān until he became the king's main company in his conversations during evenings and he gained a high position with the king. He harboured evil intentions[231] towards ʿAdī ibn Zayd and he incited al-Nuʿmān against him, to the extent that he made the king's breast boil with rage. ʿAdī ibn Zayd wrote to | Kisrā, asking to be allowed to visit al-Nuʿmān[232] and 141

unlike most other adjectives ending in *-ī* in the book, does not indicate a tribal affiliation, for once: it refers to the ʿIbād ("slaves, or servants [of God]"), the sedentary Christians of al-Ḥīrah.

227 The Arabic form of Khusraw (Greek Chosroes), the name of the Persian Sassanid emperor; he was Khusraw Parwīz (or Khusrō Aparvēz), who reigned 590–628.

228 ʿASH reads al-Ghūr, as if referring to the region of that name in present-day Afghanistan. Rather, it is al-Ghawr ("the lowland"), which according to Abū ʿUbayd al-Bakrī (*Muʿjam*, 1008) is a place in Syria but which could also refer to the broad region of Tihāmah (the western coastal region of the Arabian Peninsula) and the lands adjacent to Yemen (Yāqūt, *Muʿjam al-buldān*, iv, 217). ʿAdī was "secretary for Arab affairs" (Seidensticker, in *EI3*).

229 He was the last king of the Lakhmids (r. 580–602), executed by his Sassanid overlord.

230 He is called ʿAdī ibn Aws ibn Marīnā in al-Yaʿqūbī, *Tārīkh*, i, 242; the "sons of Marīnā" are described as a noble family (*ashrāf*) in al-Ḥīrah, but no tribal affiliation is known.

231 The word *ghawāʾil* is cognate with *mughtāl* ("murder victim"), the word used in the title of the book.

232 The Arabic has "to visit him", but the context and other sources prove that the pronoun refers to al-Nuʿmān, not to Kisrā.

فأَذِن كِسْرى لعديّ في زيارته، فلمّا بلغ النعمانَ خروجُ عديّ إليه أجلس له قوماً فأخذوه قبل أن يَصِلَ إليه، فمضوْا به إلى الصِّنَّيْن فحبسه هناك، فقال عديّ بن زيد شِعْرَه كلَّه أو أكثرَه في الحبْس.

ثمّ إنّ أخاه كلّم كسرى، فوجّه رجلاً يُخرجه من السِّجْن. فلمّا أتاه الرجل بدأ بالسجن فدخله، ثمّ رجع إلى النعمان بكتاب كسرى في أمره، فوثب أعداؤه عليه فغَمُّوه حتّى مات، وكتب إلى كسرى إنّه مات قبل وصول كتاب الملك، وأوصى الرسولَ فستر أمرَ عديّ، ووافَق كتابَ النعمان.

[§ ٢٠] **ومنهم** عُرْوة الرَّحّال بن عُتْبة بن جعفر بن كِلاب. وسبب قتله أنّ النعمان بن المُنذر كان يوجّه في كلّ مَوْسِم بِعِيرٍ تحمل التِّجارات تُباع له في الموسم، فكان بَلْعاء بن قيس يَعْرِض لها، فكان يُجِيرها له بعضُ أشراف العرب الأَعِزّاء، فحضر عروةُ الرحال النعمانَ وقد جهَّز عِيرَه وجلس في فِنائه وعنده وُفودُ العرب، وحضر البَرّاض الكِنانيّ[١] وكان خليعاً فاتكاً، فقال النعمان: من يُجير هذه العير؟ فقال البرّاض: أنا أُجيرها. فقال له عروة: أنت تجيرها على أهل الشِّيح[٢]

١ ك: (الكتاني).

٢ ك: (الشيخ).

233 See also *Aghānī*, ii, 116; it is a place near Kufa (Yāqūt, *Muʿjam al-buldān*). It is a dual (meaning "Two Baskets") but Yāqūt specifies the oblique form rather than the expected nominative (al-Ṣinnān).

234 Several poems addressed to al-Nuʿmān are preserved in *al-Aghānī* and other sources. His poetry has been collected by Muḥammad Jabbār al-Muʿaybid (ʿAdī ibn Zayd, *Dīwān*).

235 He was called Ubayy according to al-Yaʿqūbī, *Tārīkh*, i, 243–244, *Aghānī*, ii, 105, 118–121.

236 Al-Yaʿqūbī specifies he was smothered with a pillow or cushion (*wisādah*).

237 Among the numerous parallels see Muḥammad ibn Ḥabīb, *Muḥabbar*, 195–196; idem, *Munammaq*, 164–168; Ibn Hishām, *Sīrah*, i, 184–186 (tr. Guillaume, 710); al-Balādhurī, *Ansāb*, i, 111–112; Ibn ʿAbd Rabbih, *ʿIqd*, v, 253–255; al-Iṣfahānī, *Aghānī*, xxii, 56–58; al-Maqdisī, *Badʾ*, iv, 134–136; al-ʿAskarī, *Jamharah*, ii, 94; al-Maydānī, *Majmaʿ*, ii, 105–106, Abū Tammām, *Dīwān*, ii, 312–313 (in the commentary by Abū l-ʿAlāʾ al-Maʿarrī), al-Thaʿālibī, *Thimār*, 128–130; Ibn Nubātah, *Sarḥ al-ʿuyūn*, 90–91; al-Nuwayrī, *Nihāyah*, xv, 425–427. The incident is part of what is known as "the second battle day (*yawm*) of al-Fijār", the "sacrilegious war"—because waged during holy months, see *EI2*, "Fidjār" (J.W. Fück). The prophet Muḥammad is said to have been present at some of the ensuing encounters as a boy of fourteen or fifteen years old.

saying that he was longing to see him. Kisrā sent his permission. But when al-Nuʿmān heard that ʿAdī was coming to visit him, he instructed some men who apprehended him before he arrived. They took him to al-Ṣinnayn,[233] where he was imprisoned. ʿAdī composed all or most of his poem while in prison.[234]

His brother[235] spoke to Kisrā and the latter sent a man to get ʿAdī out of prison. The man went to the prison first and entered it, then he turned to al-Nuʿmān with a letter from Kisrā about ʿAdī. But his enemies sprang upon him and smothered him until he died.[236] Al-Nuʿmān wrote to Kisrā informing him that ʿAdī had died before the arrival of the emperor's letter. He instructed the messenger to cover up the matter of ʿAdī and to make his story conform with al-Nuʿmān's letter.

[§ 20 ʿUrwah al-Raḥḥāl ibn ʿUtbah[237]]

Another is ʿUrwah al-Raḥḥāl ibn ʿUtbah ibn Jaʿfar ibn Kilāb.[238] The cause of his being killed was as follows. On every market festival[239] al-Nuʿmān ibn al-Mundhir used to send a caravan carrying goods to be sold at the market. The tribe of Balʿāʾ ibn Qays[240] stood in its way, so some powerful leaders of the Arabs provided protection.[241] Once ʿUrwah al-Raḥḥāl was in the presence of al-Nuʿmān, who had equipped his caravan and sat in his forecourt, together with Arab visitors. Al-Barrāḍ al-Kinānī also appeared; he was a dissolute and murderous character.[242] Al-Nuʿmān asked, "Who will protect this caravan?" Al-Barrāḍ answered, "I will!" Then ʿUrwah said, "You will protect it against 'the people of

---

238 *ǦN*, i, 93 and ii, 575; Sezgin, *Geschichte*, ii, 217–218 (on the confusion of ʿUrwah al-Raḥḥāl with al-Raḥḥāl ibn ʿAzrah ibn al-Mukhtār or al-Raḥḥāl ibn Majdūḥ al-Numayrī).

239 *Mawsim*, see above, note 214. Other sources (among them Ibn Ḥabīb in his al-*Muḥabbar*, 195) specify the market as ʿUkāẓ. Al-Raḥḥāl means "he who travels much"; "he was called al-Raḥḥāl because he often visited kings" (al-Maydānī, *Majmaʿ*, ii, 106).

240 *ǦN*, i, 36; they belong to Kinānah.

241 Instead of *yujīru* (from *ajāra*, "to provide protection, give safe conduct"), also found in many other parallels, it is *yujīzu* (from *ajāza*, "to let pass") in Ibn Ḥabīb, *Munammaq*; Abū Tammām, *Dīwān*; al-Iṣfahānī, *Aghānī*; al-Maydānī, *Majmaʿ*. Although both readings seem possible, the former is probably to be preferred.

242 He is al-Barrāḍ ibn Qays ibn Rāfiʿ ibn Qays, of Kinānah (*ǦN*, i, 42 and ii, 225); in Ibn Ḥabīb's *Munammaq* (164) and *Muḥabbar* (195) he is said to be al-Barrāḍ Rāfiʿ ibn Qays. He became proverbial: *aftak min al-Barrāḍ*, "more murderous than al-Barrāḍ", is found in several books on proverbs and Ibn Ḥabīb lists him among the *futtāk al-Jāhiliyyah* "the pre-Islamic killers" (*Muḥabbar*, 195). Abū Tammām (d. 232/845) mentions in a poem "a murder like that of al-Barrāḍ" (*Dīwān*, ii, 312); also al-Thaʿālibī, *Thimār*, 129, s.v. "*fatkat al-Barrāḍ*".

والقَيْصوم؟ إنّما أنت كالكلْب | الخليع—وكان البرّاضُ رَثَّ الهيئةِ ومعه سيف قد أُكِل غِمْدُه— ١٤٢
أنت أَضْيَقُ اسْتاً من ذلك، ولكنّي أيّها الملك أُجيرها من الحَيَّيْن، يريد قيْساً وخِنْدِف.[١] فقال
البرّاض: أنت تُجير على أهل تِهامة؟ فلم يلتفت النعمان إلى قوله وازدراه ودفعها إلى عروة. فخرج
بالعير وخرج البرّاض في أثره حتّى إذا كان ببعض الطريق أدركه البرّاض، فقدم أمام عيره وأخرج
الأزلامَ يستقسم بها، فمرّ به عروة فقال: ما تصنع؟ فقال: أستخيرُ في قتلك. فضَحِك ولم يره
شيئاً. ثمّ سار عروة حتّى انتهى إلى أهله دُوَيْنَ الجريب على ماء يقال له أُوارة، فأنزل اللطيمة
وسرّحوا الظَهْر. وقد كان البرّاض يبتغي منه غِرّة فلم يقدر عليها حتّى صادَفه نِصْفَ النهار في
ذلك اليوم وهو نائم وحْدَه في قُبّة من أَدَم، فدخل عليه فقتله ومضى.[٢]

[§ ٢١] **ومنهم** كَعْب بن عبد الله النَّمَريّ. وكان المنذر ذو القَرْنَيْن بن ماء السماء دعا ذاتَ
يومٍ الناسَ فقال: من يهجو الحارث بن جَبَلة الغَسّانيّ؟ فدعا حَرْمَلة بن عَسَلة الشَّيْبانيّ فيمن
دعا، | وأمّ حرملة من غسّان؛ فقال: اهْجُه. فقال: لا ينطلق لساني بشَتْمه. وأنشأ يقول: ١٤٣

١ ك: (وخندق).
٢ الكلمة ناقصة في ك.

243 "Someone who chews wormwood and southernwood (*al-shīḥ wa-l-qayṣūm*): said about someone of pure Bedouin stock" (al-Zamakhsharī, *Asās*, QṢM).

244 Qays probably refers to the large group Qays ibn ʿAylān (*ĞN*, i, 92, ii, 462). Khindif is a large tribal confederation including Tamīm as well as Kinānah (*ĞN*, i, 1, ii, 347).

245 Such arrow-shafts were used in the game called *maysir* (on which see *EI2*, "Maysir" [T. Fahd], Jamil, *Ethics and Poetry*, 239–276), which is usually connected with dividing a slaughtered camel. Here, they are used to seek an oracle.

246 Al-Jarīb is a large wadi in Nejd (Yāqūt, *Muʿjam al-buldān*; cf. Abū ʿUbayd al-Bakrī, *Muʿjam*, 378–380); on Uwārah, see Yāqūt, *Muʿjam al-buldān* and Abū ʿUbayd al-Bakrī, *Muʿjam*, 207.

247 The word used here, *laṭīmah*, also used in many parallel versions, refers to a caravan trading in perfumes and spices (*WKAS*, *Lām*, 755–757).

248 Incomplete in *AM*; parallels in Ibn Ḥabīb, *Man nusiba ilā ummih*, 94–95; al-Mufaḍḍal, *Amthāl*, 50–52; al-Āmidī, *Muʾtalif*, 157–158; al-ʿAskarī, *Jamharah*, i, 100–101; Ibn al-ʿAdīm,

wormwood and southernwood'?[243] But you're just like an impudent | dog! ..."— 142
al-Barrāḍ looked scruffy and he was carrying a sword in a shabby sheath—"... You are too tight-arsed for that! But, Sire, I will protect it against the two tribes!" He meant Qays and Khindif.[244] Al-Barrāḍ said, "You'll give protection against all the people of Tihāmah?!" But al-Nuʿmān did not pay attention to him and slighted him. He gave the job to ʿUrwah, who left with the caravan. Al-Barrāḍ followed him in his tracks and somewhere on the way overtook him. He stood in front of the caravan and got out his divining arrow-shafts in order to cast them.[245] ʿUrwah came past him and asked, "What are you doing?" "I am casting lots to find out how to kill you", replied al-Barrāḍ. ʿUrwah laughed, thinking nothing of it. He went on until he arrived at his people, a short distance before al-Jarīb, at a waterhole called Uwārah.[246] He unloaded the goods[247] and they sent the camels to pasture. Al-Barrāḍ attempted to get at ʿUrwah unawares but was unable to do so, until noon of that day. ʿUrwah was sleeping alone in a leather tent. Al-Barrāḍ went in, killed him, and left.

[§ 21 Kaʿb ibn ʿAbd Allāh al-Namarī[248]]

Another is Kaʿb ibn ʿAbd Allāh al-Namarī.[249] One day al-Mundhir Dhū l-Qarnayn ibn Māʾ al-Samāʾ[250] summoned the people and said, "Who will lampoon al-Ḥārith ibn Jabalah of Ghassān?"[251] Among those he had called for was
Ḥarmalah ibn ʿAsalah al-Shaybānī, | whose mother was of Ghassān.[252] "Lam- 143
poon him!", ordered the king; but Ḥarmalah said, "I can't bring my tongue to revile him." Then he recited,

---

Bughyah, 2186–2188; al-Baghdādī, *Khizānah*, x, 91–92 (quoting from Abū Muḥammad al-Aʿrābī, *Ḍāllat al-adīb* and Ibn Ḥabīb, *Kitāb al-maqtūlīn ghīlatan*).

249 He belongs to Namir (for this tribe, see *ǦN*, i, 167) but his lineage has not been found.

250 As Ibn Ḥabīb writes in his *Muḥabbar* (359), he is the Lakhmid king al-Mundhir ibn Imriʾ al-Qays (d. c. 554), Māʾ al-Samāʾ ("Heaven's Water") being his mother, whose real name was Māwiyyah bint ʿAwf. Dhū l-Qarnayn ("He with the two horns") is an epithet also given to Alexander the Great.

251 Ghassānid (Jafnid) king (d. 569 or 570), ruling in Syria at the eastern frontier of the Roman/Byzantine Empire; see *ǦN*, Tab 193 and ii, 305–306, *EI2*, "al-Ḥārith b. Djabala" (Irfan Shahîd). He was a vassal of the Romans and rival of the Lakhmids in Iraq, who were vassals of Persia.

252 He is Ḥarmalah ibn al-Ḥukaym ibn ʿUfayr, of Murrah—Dhuhl—Shaybān, see *ǦN*, i, 146 and ii, 318; ʿAsalah was his mother, which is why a parallel of the story is found in Ibn Ḥabīb's *Kitāb Man nusiba ilā ummih* ("The Book on Those Traced to their Mother"), 94.

ألم تَرَأَنِّي بلغْتُ المَشِيبا   وفي دارِ قومِيَ عَفًّا كَسوبا¹

وإنّ الإلهَ تنصَّفْتُـهُ   بأنْ لا أُعُقَّ وأنْ لا أَحُوبا

وأن لا أُكافرَ ذا نِعْمةٍ   وأن لا أخيِّـبَه مستثيبا

[وغَسّانُ قـومٌ هُـمُ والـدي   فهل يُنْسِيَنَّهُمُ أن أَغِيبا

فأُوْزِعْ بها بعضَ مَن يعْتريكَ   فإنّ لها من مَعَدٍّ كَليبا

وإنّ لِخـالِـيَ مَـنْـدوحةً   وإنّ علَيَّ بِغَيْبٍ رقيبا

فانبرى شِهاب بن العَيِّف أخو بني سُلَيمة من عبد القيس، فقال:

لاهُمَّ إنَ الحارثَ بن جَبَلَهْ   زَنّا على أبيه ثمّ قَتَلَهْ

وركِبَ الشادخة المحجَّلَهْ   وكان في جاراته لا عَهْدَ لَهْ

فأيَّ أمرٍ سيِّءٍ لا فَعَلَهْ

---

١   ك: (كوبا).

٢   بقيّة القصّة ناقصة في الأصل، وتمامها كما في كتاب من نُسب إلى أمّه لابن حبيب وخزانة
الأدب لعبد القادر البغداديّ.

Don't you see I've reached the age of grey hair
and that in the home of my people I'm chaste and a good breadwinner?
I have served God fairly
by being neither disobedient nor sinning,
By not being ungrateful to a Benefactor,
nor disappointing Him, asking for a reward.

[Ghassān[253] are people who are my ancestors:
should they be forgotten by my slandering them?
Charge someone else with it, of those who came to you;
some dogs of Maʿadd may do it![254]
My mother's brother is free to do as he likes[255]
and he keeps an eye on me though he is absent.

Then Shihāb ibn al-ʿAyyif, of the Banū Sulaymah of ʿAbd al-Qays,[256] cried out:

By God! Al-Ḥārith ibn Jabalah[257]
Oppressed[258] his father, then killed him.
He mounted a "horse with blaze and white fetlocks"[259]
And he did not keep his covenant with the women in his protection.
Is there any wicked thing he did not do?

---

253 Here, at the end of a folio, the story breaks off. Following ʿASH and SKḤ, the remainder is taken from al-Baghdādī, *Khizānat al-adab*, ix, 92–93.

254 Maʿadd ibn ʿAdnān is the ancestor of the "North Arabs" (*ĞN*, i, 1 and ii, 379). Maʿadd is often used in pre-Islamic poetry as "a salient label of collective identity" (Webb, *Imagining the Arabs*, 70). Maʿadd included the Lakhmids and Jafnids but not the Christian ʿIbād of al-Ḥirah (*ĞN*, ii, 379).

255 The sense of *wa-inna li-khāliya mandūḥatan* is not wholly clear to me.

256 For Sulaymah ibn Malik, of ʿAbd al-Qays, see *ĞN*, i, 169; Shihāb ibn al-ʿAyyif has not been found except in parallels to the present story. The following lines in *rajaz* metre are attributed to al-ʿAfīf al-ʿAbdī in Ibn Manẓūr, *Lisān al-ʿArab* (ZNʾ), and to Shihāb ibn al-ʿAyyif in al-Zabīdī, *Tāj al-ʿarūs* (ZNʾ).

257 The following four lines are taken from *Khizānah*, x, 89–90.

258 *Zannā*, poetic licence for *zannaʾa*.

259 This is explained as "he committed a blatantly ugly deed" (al-Baghdādī, *Khizānah*, x, 90–91, Ibn Manẓūr, *Lisān al-ʿArab* [*ShDKh*], etc.).

فأسرهما الحارث بن جبلة في هزيمة المنذر، فقال: يا حرملة، اختَرْ ما شئتَ في مُلْكي. فسأله جاريتَيْن ضرّابتيْن، فأعطاهما إيّاه، فنزل في النمر، فقعد يشرب هو ورجل من النَّمِر يقال له: كعب، فلمّا أخذ الشرابُ في النَّمَريّ، قال: يا حرملة، مَن هذه المرأة الحمراء؟ مُرْها فلْتَسْقِني. فغضب حرملة، ثمّ أعادها، فضربه حرملةُ بالسيف فقتله، وقال في ذلك:

يا كعبُ إنّك لو قَصرت على   حُسْنِ النِّدامِ وأنت ذو حِلْمِ
وسَماعِ مُسْمِعةٍ تُعَلِّلُنا   حتّى نؤوبَ تَناوُمَ العُجْمِ
لَوَجَدْتَ فينا ما تُحاوِل مِن   صافي الشراب ولَذّة الطَّعْمِ

مع أبيات خمسة أخرى، وقال لابن العيّف: اختَرْ منّي ثلاثَ خِلال: إمّا أن أطرَحك على أَسَدَيْن ضارِيَيْن في بئر، وإمّا أن أُلْقِيَك من سُورِ دمشق، وإمّا أن يقوم الدُّلامِص—سيّاف كان له—فيضربك بِعَصاه هذه ضربةً. فاختار ضربةِ الدُّلامص. فضربه زعموا على رأسه، فانكسرت فَخِذُه، فاحتمله راهب وداواه حتى برأ، وهو يَخْمَع منها، فكان هذا والحارث يومئذ بقِنَّسْرين.]

Subsequently al-Ḥārith ibn Jabalah took both of them prisoner when he defeated al-Mundhir.[260] He said to Ḥarmalah, "You may choose anything you wish in my kingdom." He asked for two slave girls who could play music and was given them. He settled among the tribe of al-Namir. One day he was sitting and drinking together with a man from al-Namir called Kaʿb. When the latter was under the influence of the wine, he said, "Ḥarmalah, who is that pretty[261] woman? Tell her to pour me some more." This angered Ḥarmalah. Kaʿb repeated his words, Ḥarmalah struck him with his sword and killed him. On this he composed the following lines:[262]

Kaʿb! If only you had restricted yourself
to good wine-companionship and self-control,
And to listening to a singing-girl pouring us wine
so that we could go home to sleep like Persians![263]
Then you would have found with us whatever you wished
of pure wine and tasty food!

There are five more lines. Al-Ḥārith said to Ibn al-ʿAyyif, "You may choose one of three things.[264] I'll throw you in front of two ravenous lions in their den; or I'll throw you down from the city wall of Damascus; or al-Dulāmiṣ ..."—an executioner of his—"... will come and hit you once with his cudgel." Ibn al-ʿAyyif chose the blow by al-Dulāmiṣ, who struck him, it is said, on the head so hard that his thigh-bone broke.[265] A monk carried him away and treated him until

---

260 Al-Hārith defeated his Lakhmid rival decisively in 554 at the battle of Ḥalīmah, see e.g. *EI2*, "Ḥalīma" (Irfan Shahîd).

261 Literally, "red", which here probably refers to the skin and can be the equivalent of "white", sometimes used for non-Arabs such as Greeks and Persians; see Lane, *Lexicon* (ḤMR).

262 Lines 1–2 are the opening lines of a poem of eight lines attributed to Ḥarmalah's brother ʿAbd al-Masīḥ ibn ʿAsalah (a Christian, his name meaning "Servant of Christ") in the famous early anthology *al-Mufaḍḍaliyyāt*, 556; cf. Lyall's translation, 220.

263 Al-Aṣmaʿī (d. c. 213/828), quoted in the commentary on *al-Mufaḍḍaliyyāt*, comments: "When Persians sleep nobody would dare to wake them". See also Lyall's commentary on his translation, 221.

264 On the motif of offering a choice of three, see Caskel, "*Aiyām al-ʿArab*", 49–52.

265 This seems improbable, especially seeing that the sufferer survived. ʿASH suggests that *fakhidhuh* ("his thigh") could be a corruption of *qamaḥduwatuh* ("the back of his skull"). Al-ʿAskarī, *Jamharah*, i, 101 has *fa-daqqa minkabahū*, "crushing his shoulder"; al-Mufaḍḍal, *Amthāl*, 52 has *fa-daqqa minkabahū wa-warikahū*, "crushing his shoulder and his hip".

[§ ٢٢] [**ومنهم** كعب بن الأشرف]

..... اللّه صلّى اللّه عليه وسلّم بقُرَيْش يومَ بَدْر خرج إلى مكّة، فجعل يرثي[١] أهل القَلِيب ١٤٤
ويحرِّض قُريشاً على الطَّلَب بثأرهم من رسول اللّه صلّى اللّه عليه وسلّم ويشبّب بنِساء المسلمين
حتّى آذاهم ذلك، فقال رسول اللّه صلّى اللّه عليه وسلّم: مَنْ لي بابن الأشرف؟ فقال محمّد
بن مَسْلَمَةَ، أخو بني عبد الأَشْهَل: أنا لك به يا رسول اللّه، أنا أقتُلُه[٢] إنْ شاء اللّه تعالى. فقال له
رسول اللّه صلّى اللّه عليه وسلّم: فافْعَلْ إنْ قدرتَ على ذلك. فمكث أيّاماً لا يأكُل من الطعام
إلّا ما[٣] يُعْلِق به نفسه. فذكروا ذلك لرسول اللّه صلّى اللّه عليه وسلّم، فدعاه فقال: لِمَ تركتَ
الطعام والشراب؟ فقال: يا رسول اللّه، قلتُ لك قولاً لا أدري أَفِي به أم لا. فقال صلّى اللّه عليه
وسلّم: إنّما عليك الجهْد. قال: فإنّه لا بدّ لنا أن نقول. فقال صلّى اللّه عليه وسلّم: قولوا ما بدا

١ هـ: (يرى).
٢ ك: (قاتله).
٣ الكلمة ناقصة في ك

266 Al-Mufaḍḍal, *Amthāl* adds that he remained *mukhabbal*, "mentally impaired".

267 An ancient town in Syria south of Aleppo; see *EI2*, "Ḳinnasrīn" (N. Elisséeff). It was near this town that al-Ḥārith defeated al-Mundhir.

268 The beginning of the story is missing from the manuscript. With it, one moves to the biography of the prophet Muḥammad, who himself, if not actually the murderer, gave orders for it, as he did for the assassination of Abū Rāfiʿ ibn Abī l-Ḥuqayq (see the following section, §23). Naturally, parallels of the story are innumerable; among them are Ibn Hishām, *Sīrah*, ii, 51–58 (tr. Guillaume, 364–369); Ibn Sallām al-Jumaḥī, *Ṭabaqāt*, 238–239; al-Wāqidī, *Maghāzī* (Calcutta), 184–189, (ed. Marsden Jones), 184–192; Ibn Saʿd, *Ṭabaqāt*, ii, 28–31; al-Bukhārī, *Ṣaḥīḥ* (*K. al-Maghāzī*), 990; ʿUmar ibn Shabbah, *Tārīkh al-Madīnah al-Munawwarah*, 454–462; al-Ṭabarī, *Tārīkh*, i, 1368–1372, tr. *The History*, vii, 94–97; al-Iṣfahānī, *Aghānī*, xxii, 132–133. Ibn Ḥabīb, *Muḥabbar*, 282 gives the names and lineages of the five murderers. See also Rubin, "The Assassination of Kaʿb. al-Ashraf"; *EI2*, "Kaʿb b. al-As̲h̲raf" (W. Montgomery Watt). Kaʿb ibn al-Ashraf had an Arab father of uncertain lineage, possibly from Ṭayyi', and a Jewish mother of the tribe of Naḍīr, one of the two main Jewish tribes of Medina (see *EI2*, "Naḍīr" [V. Vacca]), and he was considered to be part of his mother's tribe. This controversial episode in the Prophet's biography is still being hotly discussed, as a search on the Internet will show. As the present text shows, part of Kaʿb's offence leading to his murder were his inciting people against Muḥammad and the amatory and mildly erotic poems he composed on his opponents' wives, a common way of

he was cured, but he kept a limp from it.[266] This happened while al-Ḥārith was in Qinnasrīn.[267]]

[§ 22 Kaʿb ibn al-Ashraf[268]]

..... of God, God bless and preserve him,[269] with Quraysh[270] on the day of the battle of Badr,[271] Kaʿb ibn al-Ashraf went out to Mecca. He began to lament[272] the men who had been thrown into the pit[273] and incited Quraysh to seek vengeance for them on the Messenger of God (ṣ). He composed amatory verses on the women of the Muslims, hurting them with this. Then the Messenger of God (ṣ) said, "Who will rid me of Ibn al-Ashraf?" Muḥammad ibn Maslamah, of the Banū ʿAbd al-Ashhal,[274] said, "I'll do it, Messenger of God! I shall kill him if God wills!" "Do so, if you can!", said the Messenger of God (ṣ). For some days Muḥammad ibn Maslamah refrained from eating[275] anything except the barest food to sustain himself. They told this to the Messenger of God (ṣ), who called for him. "Why have you given up eating and drinking?", he asked him. "Messenger of God," he answered, "I told you I would do something but I don't know if I can fulfil it!" "You only have to do your best!", said Muḥammad (ṣ). "Then I must confer with others",[276] said Ibn Maslamah. "Consult as you think fit, you are free to do so", replied the Prophet (ṣ). 144

insult besides direct lampooning; some of these verses are preserved (al-Ṭabarī, *Tārīkh*, i, 1369). "He lampooned the Prophet (ṣ) and his men" (*Aghānī*, xxii, 132).

269 *Ṣallā llāhu ʿalayhi wa-sallam*, the standard formula used after mentioning the prophet Muḥammad, often translated less accurately as "peace be upon him" and abbreviated "p.b.u.h.". Hereafter it will be abbreviated as "(ṣ)".

270 The tribe of the prophet Muḥammad.

271 Badr is a location south of Medina where a small-scale but momentous battle took place in 2/624, in which the Muslims led by the Prophet defeated a Meccan force of much larger numbers.

272 For once, the reading of SKḤ (*yarthī*) is clearly better than that of ʿASH (*yarā*, "... to see"); cf. al-Ṭabarī, *Tārīkh*, i, 1369: "he began to incite against the Messenger of God (ṣ), reciting poems and weeping over the men thrown into the pit ..."

273 The bodies of Meccans fallen at Badr had been thrown into a pit or well at the Prophet's order.

274 ʿAbd al-Ashhal ibn Jusham is a branch of al-Aws (*ǦN*, i, 179). Muḥammad ibn Maslamah, being one of the "companions" of the Prophet, is found in countless sources, among them Ibn Qutaybah, *Maʿārif*, 269, where he is said to have been of al-Khazraj but allied to ʿAbd al-Ashhal.

275 Other sources (Ibn Hishām, al-Ṭabarī) add "and drinking".

276 Taking *naqūla* (or *nuqawwila*) to be the equivalent (or a corruption) of *nuqāwila*, as the context requires. Guillaume's translation ("We shall have to tell lies") does not make sense. Similarly with the following *qūlū* (or *qawwilū*, or *qāwilū*).

لكم فأنتم في حِلّ. فاجتمع على قتْله محمّد بن مَسْلَمة، وسِلْكان بن سَلامة بن وَقْش، وهو
أبو نائلة، أحد بني عبد الأشهل، وكان أخاه من الرَّضاعة، وعَبّاد بن بِشْر بن [وَقْش، والحارث
بن أوْس بن مُعاذ، وعبد الرحمن بن][١] جَبْر أخو بني حارثة، فاستأذنوا رسول اللّٰه صلّى اللّٰه | ١٤٥
عليه وسلّم فأَذِن لهم، فمضوْا حتّى انتهوْا إلى أُطُمِهِ[٢] فتَقدَّمهم أبو نائلة فهتف بكعب، وكان
حديثَ عهدٍ بعُرْس، فوثب في مِلْحَفته، فأخذَتِ امرأتُه بناحيتها وقالت: مُحارب، وإنّ صاحب
الحرب لا ينزل في مثل هذه الساعة! فقال: إنّه أبو نائلة، لو وجدني نائماً ما أَيْقَظَني. فقالت:
واللّٰهِ إنّي لَأَعْرِف في صوته الشَّرّ! فقال كعب: لو يُدْعى الفتى لطعنة أجاب! فنزل فتحدّث معه
ساعةً وقال له: هل لك يا ابن الأشرف في أن نتماشى إلى شِعْب العَجوز فنتحدّث به بقيّةَ ليلتنا؟
فمشى وهو يُنْشِد كلمته:

رُبَّ خالٍ لِيَ لو أبصرتَه   سَبِط المِشْيةِ أبّاءٍ أَنِفْ

وقد استخفى أصحابُه بظِلّ النخْل، ثمّ قال له أبو نائلة: ويْحك يا ابن الأشرف، إنّي جئتُك لحاجةٍ أذكُرها لك، فاكتُمْ عليّ. قال: أفعلُ. فقال: كان قدومُ هذا الرجل علينا بَلاءً من البلاء، عادَتْنا العربُ ورمَوْنا عن قَوْسٍ واحدة، وقُطعتْ عنّا السُّبُل، حتى ذهب العِيال، وجُهدت الأنفُس! فقال كعب: أما واللّٰهِ لقد كنتُ أُخبرك يا ابن سَلامة أنّ الأمرَ سيصير إلى ما كنتُ

١ الزيادة من المحبّر لابن حبيب والسيرة النبويّة لابن هشام وغيرهما.

٢ هـ، ك: (أَطَمة).

277 *ǦN*, i, 179.

278 An obvious lacuna in the text has been supplied from Ibn Ḥabīb, *Muḥabbar*, 282; Ibn Hishām, *Sīrah*, ii, 55; al-Ṭabarī, *Tārīkh*, i, 1370; and similar sources. For the lineages of ʿAbbād and al-Ḥārith, see *ǦN*, i, 179; on Abū ʿAbs ʿAbd al-Raḥmān ibn Jabr, of al-Khazraj, see *ǦN*, i, 180 and Ibn Qutaybah, *Maʿārif*, 326.

279 Reading *uṭumihī* (literally, "his fortified place") instead of *aṭamatin* [*sic*, for *uṭumatin*], "a fortified place" as in ʿASH, followed by SKḤ. Other sources (Ibn Hishām, al-Wāqidī, al-Ṭabarī) have *ḥiṣnihī*, "his fortress". Remnants of what is alleged to be Kaʿb's fortress can still be seen (pictures may be found on the Internet).

280 For a similar response, see above, § 5.

As a result the following men agreed to carry out the killing, apart from Muḥammad ibn Maslamah: Silkān ibn Salāmah ibn Waqsh Abū Nā'ilah, one of the Banū ʿAbd al-Ashhal,[277] who was his foster-brother; ʿAbbād ibn Bishr [ibn Waqsh; al-Ḥārith ibn Aws ibn Muʿādh; and ʿAbd al-Raḥmān] ibn Jabr,[278] of the
Banū Ḥārithah. They asked permission from the Messenger of God (ṣ), | which 145
he granted. They went off and reached Kaʿb's fortified place.[279] Abū Nā'ilah approached first and called out to Kaʿb, who had recently married. He jumped up in his bedcover, while his wife grabbed the end of it. "You are a warrior," she said, "and someone at war does not go out at this hour!" "It is Abū Nā'ilah," he replied, "Had he found me asleep he would not have woken me up." His wife said, "By God, I hear evil in his voice!". But Kaʿb said, "If a man is called for a stabbing he responds."[280] He went down and talked with Abū Nā'ilah for a while. "Ibn al-Ashraf,", said Abū Nā'ilah, "would you like to walk with me to the Old Woman's Gorge?[281] Then we can talk the rest of the evening." Kaʿb went along with this, reciting his poem that opens with:[282]

Many a maternal uncle of mine—would that you saw him,
walking straight of posture, proudly, with disdain ...

Abū Nā'ilah's companions had hidden themselves in the shade of some palm trees. He said to Kaʿb, "I say, Ibn al-Ashraf, I have come to you to discuss something, but please keep it confidential!" "I will", said Kaʿb. "This man's arrival",[283] continued Abū Nā'ilah, "has caused us much trouble. The Arabs are hostile to us, they are united against us, all roads are blocked to us, and our families are deprived of sustenance. We are all distressed." Kaʿb said, "But, by God, didn't I tell you, Ibn Salāmah, that this would happen! I always said it would!"

---

281 Yāqūt, *Muʿjam al-buldān* only mentions what is obvious from this story: "A place outside Medina, where Kaʿb ibn al-Ashraf the Jew was killed at the order of the Messenger of God (ṣ)."

282 The following line, with four more lines, is in Ibn Sallām, *Ṭabaqāt*, 238–239 and Qudāmah ibn Jaʿfar, *Naqd al-shiʿr*, 13; with three lines in al-Marzubānī, *Muʿjam*, 231. Three lines, but not the opening one, in al-Iṣfahānī, *Aghānī*, xxii, 131. Qudāmah praises the lines for their fine prosody; they were set to music by several famous singers of the 2nd/8th and 3rd/9th centuries. A poem by Ḥassān ibn Thābit, a Muslim and the most prominent among the poets supporting the Prophet, contains a very similar line also in praise of his maternal relations (*Dīwān*, 192: "Many a maternal uncle of mine—would that you saw him, | walking straight of posture, proudly, on a cold day"); since this poem deals with Ḥassān's private affairs and does not allude to Kaʿb ibn al-Ashraf it is possible that the latter stole the line, in order to annoy his rival.

283 He alludes to the Prophet's arrival in Medina in the year of the Hijra (AD 622).

أقول لك! فقال سِلْكان: إنّي أردتُ أن تبيعَنا طعاماً ونُرْهِنَك ونوثِّق لك ونُحْسِن في ذلك. فقال:
تُرْهِنوني أبناءكم؟ فقال له سلكان: لقد أردتَ أن تفضحنا، إنّ معي أصحاباً لي على مِثل رأْيي،
وقد أردتُ أنْ آتِيَك بهم فتبيعَهم وتُحْسِن إليهم | في ذلك، ونُرْهِنَك من الحَلْقة ما لك فيه وَفاء. ١٤٦
فقال كعب: إنّ في الحلقة لَوَفاءً. ثمّ إنّ سلكان شامَ يَدَه في فَوْد رأسه ثمّ شَمَّ يدَه وقال: ما رأيت
كالليلة طِيبَ عِطْرٍ قَطُّ! ثمّ مشى ساعةً ثمّ عاد لمِثْلها حتّى إذا اطْمأنّ عاد لمثلها، فأخذ بفَوْدَي
رأسه ثمّ قال: اضرِبوا عَدُوَّ اللّٰه! فاختلفتْ عليه أسيافُهم فلم تُغْنِ شيئاً. فأخذ محمد بن مسلمة
مِغْوَلاً كان معه فوضعه في ثُنَّته وتحامَل عليه حتّى بلغ عانَتَه.

[§٢٣] **ومنهم** أبو رافع سَلّام بن أبي الحُقَيْق، وهو ممّن حزّب الأحزاب على رسول اللّٰه صلّى اللّٰه عليه وسلّم. فلمّا قتلت الأوسُ كعباً أرادت الخزرج أن تفعل مثلَ فِعْل الأوس، لأنّهم كانوا يتبارَوْن بأفعالهم في الجاهليّة والإسلام. فاستأذن رسولَ اللّٰه صلّى اللّٰه عليه وسلّم منهم خمسةُ نَفَر لقتْل أبي رافع، فخرج عبد اللّٰه بن عَتيك، ومسعود بن سِنان، وعبد اللّٰه بن أُنَيْس، وأبو قَتادة الحارث بن رِبْعيّ، وخُزاعيّ بن أَسْوَد حليف لهم من أَسْلَم. فخرجوا[1] وأمَّر النبيُّ[2] صلّى اللّٰه عليه وسلّم عبدَ اللّٰه بن عتيك عليهم، ونهاهم أن يقتلوا وليداً أو امرأة.

١ الكلمة ناقصة في كـ
٢ كـ: (رسول اللّٰه).

284 Other sources say that Kaʿb perfumed his hair with musk and ambergris.

285 *Mighwal*, of the same root (*GhWL*) as *mughtāl*, "murdered".

286 More details may be found in Ibn Hishām, *Sīrah*. Al-Ḥārith had been wounded in the struggle, by one of their own swords; but the Prophet spat on the wound and cured him.

287 Among the numerous parallels, some of them with many more details, are Ibn Hishām, *Sīrah*, ii, 273–275 (tr. Guillaume, 482–483); Maʿmar ibn Rāshid, *Maghāzī / The Expeditions*, 144–147 (with English translation); Ibn Saʿd, *Ṭabaqāt*, ii, 87–88; al-Bukhārī, *Ṣaḥīḥ* (*K. al-Maghāzī*), 991–992; ʿUmar ibn Shabbah, *Tārīkh al-Madīnah al-Munawwarah*, 462–467; al-Ṭabarī, *Tārīkh*, i, 1375–1380, tr. *The History*, viii, 482–483. For modern studies, see Mattock, "History and Fiction" (with translations of versions from al-Ṭabarī, *Tārīkh*; Ibn Hishām, *Sīrah*; and al-Wāqidī, *Maghāzī*) and, very thoroughly, Motzki, "The Murder of Ibn Abī l-Ḥuqayq", with translations of several major versions of the story (pp. 182–183, from *al-Ṣaḥīḥ* by al-Bukhārī; 191–192, from *al-Muṣannaf* by ʿAbd al-Razzāq; 207–211, from

Silkān replied, "I should like you to sell us some food. We'll give you a pledge as security and you will be good to us!" "Will you give your sons as security?" asked Kaʿb. Silkān replied, "Do you want to make a mockery of us? I've got some friends with me who think as I do. I wanted to take them with me to you so that you could sell something to them, dealing favourably with them. | We'll give 146
you some armour, to the full value of the goods!" "Armour, that is good value", said Kaʿb. Then Silkān ran his hand through the hair on Kaʿb's temple; he smelt his hand and said, "I have never smelt anything as fragrant before tonight!"[284] They walked on a bit and he repeated the same, until Kaʿb felt wholly at ease. Then he grabbed Kaʿb by the hair on his temples and said, "Strike the enemy of God!" The swords came down together on him, but with little effect. Then Muḥammad ibn Maslamah took a dagger[285] he had on him and thrust it into the lower part of his belly, bearing it down to his pubes.[286]

[§ 23 Abū Rāfiʿ Sallām ibn Abī l-Ḥuqayq[287]]

Another is Abū Rāfiʿ Sallām ibn Abī l-Ḥuqayq,[288] who is one of those who had rallied the confederated tribes against the Messenger of God (ṣ).[289] When al-Aws had killed Kaʿb,[290] al-Khazraj wanted to do something similar, for the two tribes were always competing, both in pre-Islamic and Islamic times. Five men of al-Khazraj asked the permission of the Messenger of God (ṣ) to kill Abū Rāfiʿ: ʿAbd Allāh ibn ʿAtīk, Masʿūd ibn Sinān, ʿAbd Allāh ibn Unays, Abū Qatādah al-Ḥārith ibn Ribʿī, and Khuzāʿī ibn Aswad, who was their ally from Aslam.[291] They left, after the Prophet (ṣ) had appointed ʿAbd Allāh ibn ʿAtīk as their commander. He forbade them to kill any young children or women. They left and

---

al-Ṭabarī, *Tārīkh*). Ibn Ḥabīb's *Asmāʾ al-mughtālīn* is not mentioned by either Mattock or Motzki.

288 He was a Jewish merchant and leader of the tribe of Naḍīr, one of the two main Jewish tribes of Medina; he lived at Khaybar, a Jewish settlement some 150 km from Medina.

289 This refers to the "fight at the trench" (*khandaq*) in the year 5/627, when the Muslims thwarted an attack on Medina by the Meccans aided by various tribes, by the simple expedient of digging a trench at a vulnerable spot.

290 Kaʿb ibn al-Ashraf, see the preceding section (§ 22).

291 In other versions the first four are said to be from Salimah, a branch of al-Khazraj (*ČN*, i, 190), but ʿAbd Allāh ibn Unays is mostly said to belong to Juhaynah (not part of al-Khazraj) but allied with Salimah (*ČN*, i, 279 and ii, 120). On their lineages, see also Ibn Ḥabīb, *Muḥabbar*, 282–283. The other versions also mention explicitly that the Prophet gave permission for the killing, which is omitted here.

فخرجوا حتّى أتوْا دار أبي رافع ليلاً، فلم يَدَعوا فيها | بيتاً إلّا أغلقوه على أهله، وكان في عِلِّيّةٍ ١٤٧
فصَعِدوا إليه حتّى قاموا على بابه فاستأذنوا، فخرجت إليهم امرأته فقالت: من أنتم؟ قالوا: نفر
من العرب نلتمس المِيرة. قالت: ذاك صاحبُكم فادْخُلوا عليه. فلمّا دخلوا أغلقوا الباب عليها
وعليهم، تخوُّفاً من أن يكون دونَه مُحاوَلة[1] تحول بينهم وبينه، فصاحت امرأتُهُ فنوَّهتْ بهم،
وابتدروه وهو على فِراشه بأسيافهم، فما دلّهم عليه في سَواد البيت إلّا بَياضُه، كأنّه قُبْطيّة مُلْقاة،
فضربوه بأسيافهم، وتحامل عليه[2] عبد اللّٰه بن أُنيس في بطنه بسيفه حتّى أنفذه وهو يقول قَطْني
قَطْني! ثمّ رجعوا أدراجَهم وقد قتلوه.

[§ ٢٤] **ومنهم** سيّد وَلَدِ آدَم صلّى اللّٰه عليه وسلّم، وبِشْر بن البَراء ابن معْرور الأنصاريّ. وكانت زَيْنَب بنت الحارث اليهوديّة، امرأة سلّام بن مِشْكَم، أهدتْ لرسول اللّٰه صلّى اللّٰه عليه وسلّم يومَ خَيْبَر شاةً مَصْلِيّة، وقد سألتْ قبل ذلك: أيُّ عُضْوٍ في الشاة أَحَبُّ إلى محمّد؟ فقيل لها: الذِّراع. فأكثرتْ فيه من السمّ، ثمّ سمَّتْ سائرَ الشاة، ثمّ جاءت بها حتّى وضعتْها بين يديْ رسول اللّٰه صلّى اللّٰه عليه وسلّم. فتناول عليه الصلاة والسلام الذِّراعَ فلاكَ منها مُضْغةً فلم يُسِغْها، ومعه بِشْر بن البَراء، وقد أخذ منها كما أخذ رسولُ اللّٰه صلّى اللّٰه عليه وسلّم، [فأمّا

١ كذا في النسختين؛ وفي هـ:(مجاولة) اتّباعاً لما في السيرة والطبريّ.

٢ هـ:(على).

292 ʿASH reads *mujāwalah*, following the texts of Ibn Hishām and al-Ṭabarī; I prefer to keep the text of the manuscripts (*muḥāwalah*), like the following verb (*taḥūlu*) derived from the root ḤWL with a basic sense of "coming between".

293 Thus all sources (*qaṭnī, qaṭnī!*), except Maʿmar, *Maghāzi*, which has "My belly! My belly" (*baṭnī! baṭnī!*), which, even though appropriate, looks as if a copyist was ignorant of the idiom *qaṭnī*.

294 Afterwards, when each proudly claimed to have done the deed, the prophet identified ʿAbd Allāh ibn Unays as the killer, because he could see traces of food on his sword (Ibn Hishām, *Sīrah*, ii, 275, tr. Guillaume, 483; al-Ṭabarī, *Tārīkh*, i, 1375–1380, tr. *The History*, vii, 99–103).

295 The main parallels are Ibn Hishām, *Sīrah*, ii, 337–338 (tr. Guillaume, 516); al-Bukhārī, *Ṣaḥīḥ* (*K. al-Maghāzī*), 782–783, 1041; Ibn Saʿd, *Ṭabaqāt*, i, 145, iii, 528; al-Wāqidī, *Maghāzī* (ed. Kremer), 394; al-Ṭabarī, *Tārīkh*, i, 1583–1584, tr. *The History*, viii, 123–124; al-Masʿūdī, *Tanbīh*, 257. On the siege of Khaybar in the year 7/628, see *EI2*, "Khaybar" (L. Vecca

reached the settlement of Abū Rāfiʿ in the evening. They locked every | room 147
from the outside with its people inside. Abū Rāfiʿ was in an upper chamber; they went up to him; standing at the door they asked permission to enter. His wife came out and asked, "Who are you?" "We are Arab men," they answered, "and we are seeking provisions." She said, "There's the man you want, come inside!" When they were inside they locked the door on him and themselves, fearing that others might intervene[292] between him and them. His wife cried out and alerted the others, but they rushed at him with their swords while he was lying on his bed. The room was dark and it was only his white body, like Egyptian linen cloth, that pointed them to him. They struck him with their swords, ʿAbd Allāh ibn Unays bore down on him plunging his sword into his belly until he pierced him right through, while Abū Rāfiʿ was saying, "Enough! Enough!"[293] Then they returned, having killed him.[294]

[§ 24 The Prophet Muḥammad and Bishr ibn al-Barāʾ ibn Maʿrūr al-Anṣārī[295]]

Among them are also the Lord of all Adam's children (ṣ) and Bishr ibn al-Barāʾ ibn Maʿrūr al-Anṣārī.[296] Zaynab bint al-Ḥārith, a Jewish woman, the wife of Sallām ibn Mishkam,[297] presented the Messenger of God (ṣ) with a roast sheep. She had asked, before that, which part of a sheep Muḥammad would like best and she had been told it was the shoulder. She put a lot of poison in it and also poisoned the rest of the sheep. Then she brought it and put it down in front of the Messenger of God (ṣ). He (ṣ) took the shoulder and chewed a mouthful but he did not swallow it. Bishr ibn al-Barāʾ was with him and he too had taken some of it, just as the Messenger of God (ṣ) had done. [But Bishr swallowed

---

Vaglieri). Although it is by no means unanimously agreed that the Prophet's death was caused by poisoning, the fact that his name appears in the heading of this section, together with the quotation of the Prophet's words on his death-bed, implies that Ibn Ḥabīb includes him among the murder victims.

296 For his lineage see *ǦN*, i, 191; he belonged to Ghanm ibn Kaʿb ibn Salimah, of al-Khazraj. See also *EI2*, "Bishr b. al-Barāʾ" (W. ʿArafat), *EI3*, "Bishr b. al-Barāʾ" (Isaac Hasson). The *Anṣār* ("Supporters" or "Helpers") are those members of al-Aws and al-Khazraj in Medina who supported the Prophet and his Meccan followers, the "Emigrants" (*muhājirūn*).

297 In Ibn Saʿd, *Ṭabaqāt*, i, 145, iii, 528 and al-Wāqidī, *Maghāzī*, 394 she is merely called "a Jewish woman". Sallām ibn Mishkam was a leader of the Jewish tribe of Naḍīr (he appears as Salām in the *EI3* entry "Bishr b. al-Barāʾ", but see the editorial note in Ibn Hishām, *Sīrah*, ii, 46, where Abū Dharr is quoted to the effect that Sallām is correct, and that the form Salām found in a poem is a poetic licence required by the metre). He and Zaynab's father were killed by the Muslims at the siege of Khaybar.

بشر فأساغها وأمّا رسولُ اللّٰه صلّى اللّٰه عليه وسلّم]١ فلَفَظَها. | ثمّ قال: إنّ هذا العَظْمَ يُخْبِرني أنّه ١٤٨
مسموم. ثمّ دعا بها فاعترفتْ، فقال: ما حَمَلَكِ على ذلك؟ فقالت: بَلَغْتَ من قوْمي ما لم يَخْفَ عليك فقلتُ: إنْ كان مَلِكاً استرحْتُ منه، وإنْ كان نبيًّا فسيُخْبَر. فتَجاوزَ عنها صلّى اللّٰه عليه وسلّم، ومات بِشْر من أُكْلته التي أَكَل.

وقد كان رسول اللّٰه صلّى اللّٰه عليه وسلّم قال في مَرَضه الذي تُوُفِّيَ فيه: هذا أَوانُ وجدتُ انقطاعَ أَبْهَري من الأُكْلة التي أكلْتُها مع أخيك. يقول ذلك لأمّ بِشر٢ أخت بِشر بن البراء، ودخلت عليه تَعُوده. فإنْ كان المسلمون لَيَرَوْن أنّ اللّٰه جمع لنبيِّه الشهادةَ، مع ما أكرمه به من النبوّة، صلّى اللّٰه عليه وسلّم.

[§٢٥] **ومنهم** رِفاعة بن قيْس الجُشَميّ، وكان يجمع قيساً لحرب رسول اللّٰه صلّى اللّٰه عليه وسلّم، فوجّه عليه السلام٣ إليه عبدَ اللّٰه بن أبي حَدْرَد، ورجلَيْن معه، فكمنوا له، ورماه ابن أبي حدرد فقتله وجاء برأسه إلى النبيّ صلّى اللّٰه عليه وسلّم.

[§٢٦] **ومنهم** أبو أُزَيْهِر بن أُنَيْس بن الخَيْسَق٤ بن مالك بن سعد بن كعب بن الحارث ١٤٩
الأَزْديّ، وكان أخواله من دَوْس فنُسب إليهم، وكان حليفاً لأبي سُفْيان بن حَرْب. وكان يقعُد

١ ما بين القوسين ناقص في هـ، ك؛ والتكملة من السيرة لابن هشام، والسياق يقتضيها.

٢ ك: (مبشر).

٣ الكلمتان ناقصتان في ك.

٤ هـ، ك: (الحبسي) والتصحيح من المنمّق لابن حبيب وغيره من المراجع.

298 The added words, not in ʿASH or SKḤ, are taken from Ibn Hishām *Sīrah*, ii, 338, as the context requires.

299 In other versions (Ibn Saʿd, *Ṭabaqāt*, al-Masʿūdī, *Tanbīh*) she is killed.

300 This was in 11/632, several years after the siege of Khaybar.

301 The syntax looks incomplete and perhaps the implied apodosis is e.g. "they would do well". The same is found in Ibn Hishām; Guillaume does not translate it as a conditional clause ("The Muslims considered that the apostle died as a martyr in addition to the prophetic office with which God had honoured him").

302 For parallels with considerably more detail, see Ibn Hishām, *Sīrah*, ii, 629–631 (tr. Guillaume, 671–672) and al-Ṭabarī, *Tārīkh*, i, 1607–1608, tr. *The History*, viii, 149–150; briefly also Ibn Ḥabīb, *Muḥabbar*, 123.

it, whereas the Messenger of God (ṣ)][298] spat it out. | He said, "This bone tells me it is poisoned." He called for the woman and she confessed. "What brought you to do this?" he asked her. She replied, "You have done all these things to my people, as you know very well. So I thought, if he is merely a king I'll get rid of him, but if he is a prophet he will be told." He (ṣ) let her go,[299] but Bishr died of what he had eaten. 148

The Messenger of God (ṣ) said during the illness of which he died,[300] "This is the time I find that my aorta is being cut off, from that mouthful I had with your brother!"; he was speaking to Umm Bishr, the sister of Bishr ibn al-Barā'. She had come to visit him. If the Muslims would consider that God has given to His prophet martyrdom, in addition to all the other things with which He has honoured him, including prophethood—God bless and preserve him![301]

[§ 25 Rifāʿah ibn Qays al-Jushamī[302]]

Another was Rifāʿah ibn Qays al-Jushamī.[303] He had rallied Qays to fight the Messenger of God (ṣ), who sent ʿAbd Allāh ibn Abī Ḥadrad[304] with two other men to him. They lay in ambush and Ibn Abī Ḥadrad shot him, killing him. They took his head to the Prophet (ṣ).

[§ 26 Abū Uzayhir[305]]

Another is Abū Uzayhir ibn Unays ibn al-Khaysaq[306] ibn Mālik ibn Saʿd ibn Kaʿb 149
ibn al-Ḥārith al-Azdī.[307] His maternal family were of the tribe of Daws, which is why he was called al-Dawsī.[308] He was an ally of Abū Sufyān ibn Ḥarb[309]

303 He is sometimes called Qays ibn Rifāʿah. His lineage is not known; Jusham ibn Muʿāwiyah is a branch of Hawāzin, part of the large group of North Arabs called Qays (*ĞN*, i, 92, 116).

304 ʿAbd Allāh ibn Salāmah Abī Ḥadrad, of Aslam—Khuzāʿah (*ĞN*, i, 210).

305 For parallels, see Ibn Hishām, *Sīrah*, i, 410–415 (tr. Guillaume, 187–190); Ibn Ḥabīb, *Munammaq*, 199–204; al-Balādhurī, *Ansāb*, i, 152–153; Ḥassān ibn Thābit, *Dīwān*, 353–359.

306 Wrongly *al-Ḥ.b.sī* in ʿASH and SKḤ.

307 For his lineage see *ĞN*, i, 217 and ii, 580–581.

308 Thus in Ibn Hishām, *Sīrah*, and Ibn Ḥabīb, *Munammaq*. For Daws ibn ʿUdhthān, of al-Azd, see *ĞN*, i, 210. Caskel (*ĞN*, ii, 580–581) does not believe Abū Uzayhir belonged to al-Azd; rather, he was of Daws.

309 Abū Sufyān Ṣakhr ibn Ḥarb ibn Umayyah (d. c. 32/653), of Quraysh, leader of the Meccan opposition against the prophet Muḥammad; submitted to Islam shortly before the conquest of Mecca in 8/630; father of Muʿāwiyah who later became the first caliph of the Umayyad Dynasty.

هو وأبو سفيان في أيّامهما فيُصْلِحان بين مَن حضر ذلك المكان الذي هُما به، وكانت ابنته تحت أبي سفيان. ثمّ تزوَّجَ ابنةً له أخرى الوليدُ بن المُغِيرة بن عبد اللّٰه بن عُمَر بن مخزوم، وأخذ أبو أُزَيْهِر من الوليد المَهْر، فبلغه بعدُ أنّه غليظٌ على النساء، فأمسكها ولم يرُدَّ المهرَ. وقال بعض: إنّها أُهْدِيَتْ إليه فقال الوليد لها ليلةَ أن دخل عليها: أنا أشرف أو أبوكِ؟ فقالت له: إنّ أبي سيّدُ قومه، وفي قومك مَن يساويك ويفوقك. فغَضِب ولطمها على خدّها فهربتْ ورجعتْ إلى أبيها، فأمسكها ولم يرُدّها عليه.

فلما حضرت الوليدَ الوفاةُ أوصى بَنِيه بأشياءَ قد كتبناه في أخبار قُريش، منها دَمُه في خُزاعة، وعُقْره عند أبي أزيهر. فلمّا مات الوليدُ وحضر الناسُ سُوقَ ذي المَجاز تَغفَّل هِشامُ بن الوليد أبا أزيهر فقتله. وبلغ ذلك أهلَ مكّة فهاج المطيَّبون والأحلافُ[1] من قُريش وكادوا يقتتلون. وبلغ ذلك أبا سفيان، وهو | بذي المَجاز، وكان داهياً يحبّ قومه، فقعد على فَرَسه حتّى أتى مكّةَ ١٥٠
والناس متواقفون للحرب، ولِواءُ المطيَّبين بِيَد يَزيد بن أبي سفيان، فأخذ اللِّواء من يَزيدَ فضرب به البَيْضة ضَرْبةً هدَّه منها، وفرَّق الناس، وقال: إذا فرغْنا من عَدوِّنا، يعني رسولَ اللّٰه صلى اللّٰه عليه وسلّم، نظرْنا في أمر أبي أزيهر ووَدَيْناه. فوَدَوْه مائتيْ ناقة.

١ ك: (والأخلاف).

310 They held sessions in a pavilion (*qubbah*), according to Ibn Ḥabīb, *Munammaq*.

311 Al-Walīd ibn al-Mughīrah (d. 1/622), a prominent member of Makhzūm, a powerful branch of Quraysh (see *EI2*, "Makhzūm" [M. Hinds]), and an opponent of the Prophet. See *EI2*, "al-Walīd b. Mughīra" (K.V. Zettersteén).

and they used to sit together in their days, making peace between those who came to attend there.[310] His daughter was married to Abū Sufyān; later another daughter of his was married to al-Walīd ibn al-Mughīrah ibn ʿAbd Allāh ibn ʿUmar ibn Makhzūm.[311] Abū Uzayhir took the bride price from al-Walīd, but some time afterwards he heard that al-Walīd was rough to women, so he took his daughter back but did not return the bride price.[312] Some say that she was handed over to al-Walīd, who said to her on the wedding night, “Who is nobler, I or your father?” “My father is the chief of his clan,” she answered, “whereas in your clan some are equal to you and some are superior to you.” Angered, he slapped her cheek. She fled and went back to her father, who took her back without returning the bride price.

On his deathbed, al-Walīd instructed his sons with various things, which we have written in *The Reports on Quraysh*,[313] among them his blood feud with Khuzāʿah and the matter of the bride-price with Abū Uzayhir. After al-Walīd had died and people attended the market of Dhū l-Majāz,[314] al-Walīd’s son Hishām caught Abū Uzayhir unawares and killed him. When the Meccans heard about this, the Scented Ones[315] and the Confederates[316] of Quraysh
became agitated and almost came to blows. Abū Sufyān heard about this while | 150
at Dhū l-Majāz. He was a shrewd man who loved his clan. He mounted his horse and rode to Mecca, where the people were already about to give battle, the standard of the Scented Ones being held by Abū Sufyān’s son Yazīd.[317] He took the standard away from Yazīd, struck his helmet with it so forcefully that Yazīd was all but crushed by it, and made the people disperse. “When we have finished with our enemy”, he said, meaning the Messenger of God (ṣ), “we shall look into the matter of Abū Uzayhir and pay blood money for his death.” They paid two hundred she-camels in compensation.

---

312 The *mahr*, in Islamic times becoming the property of the bride, was handed to her father or guardian in pre-Islamic times. See *EI2*, “mahr” (O. Spies); in the next paragraph the word *ʿuqr* is used.

313 *Akhbār Quraysh*, also known as *al-Munammaq*; see Ibn Ḥabīb, *Munammaq*, 191–192.

314 Like ʿUkāẓ (see above, § 20 note 239), a location near Mecca where a market was held during the sacred months.

315 *Al-Muṭayyabūn*, who dipped their hands in perfume (*ṭīb*) to seal their covenant in Mecca in pre-Islamic times (Ibn Hishām, *Sīrah*, i, 131–132, tr. Guillaume, 56–57).

316 *Al-Aḥlāf*; also called “the Blood-lickers”, see above, § 11 note 149 and Ibn Ḥabīb, *Muḥabbar*, 166–167; *EI2*, “Laʿaḳat al-dam” (Ch. Pellat) and “ḥilf” (E. Tyan).

317 He became governor of Syria during the caliphates of Abū Bakr and ʿUmar; he died in 18/639.

[§٢٧] **ومنهم** المجذَّر بن ذِياد[١] البَلَويّ حليف بني عَوْف بن الخزرج وقيس بن زيد أخو بني
ضُبَيْعة بن زيد، اغتالهما الحارث بن [سُوَيْد، أخو][٢] الجُلاس | الأنصاريّ، وكان مُنافِقاً، وكان ١٥١
يومَ أُحُد مع رسول اللّٰه صلّى اللّٰه عليه وسلّم، فرأى منهما في الحرب غِرّةً فقتلهما، ولَحِق بمكّة
كافراً.

[§٢٨] **ومنهم** الأَسْوَد الكذّاب بن كعب العَنْسيّ، وهو ذو الحِمار، وكان استنكح بصَنْعاءَ امرأةً من الأبناء، وهُم أبناء الفُرْس الذين قدموا اليمن مع وَهْرِز فقتلوا الحَبَشة. وإنّ الأسود تَوعّدَ الأبناءَ بأن يُجْلِيَهم من اليمن أو يَتْرُكهم له بها خَوَلاً. فتحرّز له فَيْرُوز بن الدَّيْلَميّ، وقيس بن هُبَيْرة

---

١ كـ: (ذيار).

٢ كما في هـ، التكملة من المحبّر.

---

318 Parallels: Ibn Hishām, *Sīrah*, i, 288, 520, ii, 89 (tr. Guillaume, 242, 384, 755–756); al-Wāqidī, *Maghāzī* (ed. Kremer), 295–297; Ibn Saʿd, *Ṭabaqāt*, iii, 512; Ḥassān ibn Thābit, *Dīwān*, 301–302.

319 See *ǦN*, i, 329 and ii, 418; of the tribe of Balī. He had killed Suwayd ibn al-Ṣāmit, of al-Aws, and was killed by the latter's son al-Ḥārith.

320 See *ǦN*, i, 178 and ii, 464 (of ʿAwf, a branch of al-Aws). It is not clear why al-Ḥārith murdered him. Ibn Hishām records the view that Qays was not murdered by al-Ḥārith (*Sīrah*, ii, 89, tr. Guillaume, 755–756).

321 The addition is from other sources including Ibn Ḥabīb, *Muḥabbar*, 467 and Ibn Hishām, *Sīrah*, ii. 89; see also *ǦN*, i, 177 and ii, 312. He belonged to al-Aws and is therefore one of the *Anṣār*, "Helpers" or "Supporters", even though he is called a "hypocrite".

322 The "hypocrites" (*munāfiqūn*) are often mentioned in the Qur'an in general terms, referring to those who are either apostates, dissenters, obstructors, etc. within the *ummah*, the community of believers. In subsequent sources many individuals are mentioned as being *munāfiq*; see *EI2*, "Munāfiḳūn" (A. Brockett). Ibn Ḥabīb lists some of them in his *Muḥabbar* (467–470), including al-Ḥārith ibn Suwayd and his brother al-Julās. In exegetical literature al-Ḥārith ibn Suwayd is mentioned in connection with Q Āl ʿImrān 3:86: «How can God guide people who became unbelievers after having believed and having witnessed that the messenger is true and after clear signs had come to them? God does not guide people who do wrong.»

323 At Uḥud, a mountain near Medina, the Muslims suffered a setback in 3/625 when they were defeated by the Meccans led by Abū Sufyān. See *EI2*, "Uḥud" (C.F. Robinson).

324 Other sources (see e.g. al-Wāqidī, *Maghāzī*, 295–297, Ḥassān, *Dīwān*, 301, on a poem alluding to the event), mention that al-Mujadhdhar's body was found on the battlefield at a place where the Meccans could not have been. The Muslims were at a loss until the Prophet was told who was responsible by no less an authority than the angel Gabriel. In this version al-Ḥārith returns to Medina, where the Prophet asks him, "Have you killed al-Mujadhdhar?" Al-Ḥārith confesses but adds that he was overcome by feelings of revenge

[§ 27 al-Mujadhdhar ibn Dhiyād al-Balawī and Qays ibn Zayd[318]]

Among them are also al-Mujadhdhar ibn Dhiyād al-Balawī,[319] the ally of the Banū ʿAwf ibn al-Khazraj, and Qays ibn Zayd,[320] of the Banū Ḍubayʿah ibn Zayd. Both were murdered by al-Ḥārith ibn [Suwayd, the brother of] al-Julās | 151
al-Anṣārī.[321] He was a "hypocrite".[322] He was at the battle of Uḥud[323] with the Messenger of God (ṣ). In the course of the battle he caught them unawares and killed them. He joined the Meccans as an unbeliever.[324]

[§ 28 al-Aswad the Liar ibn Kaʿb al-ʿAnsī[325]]

Another is al-Aswad al-Kadhdhāb (the liar) ibn Kaʿb al-ʿAnsī, Dhū l-Ḥimār (the man with the donkey).[326] He had married, in Sanaa, a woman of the Descendants (al-Abnāʾ), i.e., the descendants of the Persians who had arrived in Yemen with Wahriz and who had killed the Abyssinians.[327] Al-Aswad had threatened to expel the Descendants from Yemen unless they consented to be left as his ser-

---

for his father's death and that he is still a good Muslim and will fast for four months, perform other pious acts, and pay blood money. The Prophet says nothing but orders someone to cut off his head, which is done.

325 For parallel versions see al-Ṭabarī, *Tārīkh*, i, 1795–1798, 1855–1868, tr. *The History*, ix, 164–167, x, 24–38; Ibn Saʿd, *Ṭabaqāt*, vi, 264, viii, 94; al-Balādhurī, *Futūḥ*, 146–148; Ibn Ḥubaysh, *Ghazawāt*, 196–200; al-Yaʿqūbī, *Tārīkh*, ii, 145–146 (tr. *The Works*, 752); al-Masʿūdī, *Tanbīh*, 276–277. See also EI2, "al-Aswad b. Kaʿb al-ʿAnsī" (Ch. Pellat). His movement against the Muslims is considered to be the beginning of the period of the *Riddah* (11–13/632–634) immediately after the death of the Prophet, the "Secession" or "Defection", traditionally taken as "Apostasy from Islam", even though such secession often had little to do with religion; see EI2, *Suppl.*, "Ridda" (M. Lecker). Apart from calling him al-Kadhdhāb ("the Liar"), Ibn Ḥabīb does not mention explicitly, as do other sources, that al-Aswad was a soothsayer and would-be prophet (*takahhana wa-ddaʿā l-nubuwwah*), who called himself Raḥmān al-Yaman ("the Merciful [= God?] of Yemen")—thus al-Balādhurī, *Futūḥ*, 146—and performed tricks (*kāna kāhinan shaʿbādhan wa-kāna yurīhim al-aʿājīb*), al-Ṭabarī, *Tārīkh*, i, 1796.

326 See ǦN, i, 272 and ii, 199. Al-Aswad (the Black One) is a nickname, his proper name is said to be ʿAbhalah or ʿAyhalah. The tribe of ʿAns is a branch of the Yemeni tribe of Madhḥij, on which see EI2, "Ma<u>dh</u>ḥi<u>dj</u>" (G.R. Smith—C.E. Bosworth). He got his nickname Dhū l-Ḥimār ("the man with the donkey") because he is said to have trained his donkey to kneel on command. It is said (EI2, "al-Aswad" and *Suppl.*, "Ridda") that he was also known as Dhū l-Khimār ("the man with the veil", with a difference of only one dot in Arabic); thus in al-Ṭabarī, *Tārīkh*; al-Balādhurī, *Futūḥ*, gives both versions.

327 On the invasion of Yemen by the Abyssinians (al-Ḥabashah) see above, § 17; their power had been broken by a Persian invasion, c. AD 575, led by Wahriz (or Vahrez), on whom see EI2, "Wahriz" (C.E. Bosworth).

المكشوح[١] المُرادي، وداذَوَيْهِ رجل من الأبناء، وكان فيروز يخبر أنّه أتاهم رسولٌ من رسول اللّٰه
صلّى اللّٰه عليه وسلّم يُقال له يُحَنِّس بن وَبَرة الأَزْديّ، فأسلموا معه. وكانت المرأة التي استنكح
العنسيُّ قد أسلمت. قال فيروز: فجئتُها فكلّمتُها في أمر الأسود وقلتُ لها: إنّه قد أراد بقومك من
الشرّ ما تَرَيْنَ:[٢] إمّا إجلاءَهم عن بلادهم، وإمّا استعبادَهم، فهل عندكِ إلى قتله حِيلة أو سبيل؟
قالت: سأحتال له.

فجاء الأسودُ، وفيروز عندها، فضربه ووجأ في عُنقه وأخرجه. فبكَتِ المرأة وقالت: أنتم يا
مَعْشَرَ العرب تَزْعُمون أنكم تُحْسِنون إلى أصهاركم، وأنت تضرب أخي وتُخْرِجه من بيتي. قال:
وإنّه لَأخوكِ؟ قالت: نعم. قال: ما دريْتُ، فابْعَثي له فلَيَأْتِنا. فبعثت إليه: إنّه قد | رضِيَ، وإنّي ١٥٢
سأحفِر لكم في البستان سَرَباً إلى البيت الذي يكون فيه. فحفرتُ سرباً[٣] وجاء فيروزُ وداذويْه
وقيس بن المكشوح، فلمّا قاموا إلى السرب قال بعضهم: أيُّكم يدخل عليه؟ فقال داذويه: أنا
شيخ كبير وأخاف أن أضرِبَه فلا أُغْني فيه شيئاً، ولكنْ يا قيسُ ادْخُلْ أنت! فقال قيس: إنّي رجل
تأخذني رِعْدةٌ عند الحرب، وأخاف إنْ ضربتُه أن لا تُغْنِيَ ضَرْبتي شيئا. فدخل فيروز، وكان أشبَّ
القوم، فإذا هو نائم على حشايا من رِيش، والمرأةُ عند رأسه. فأشار إليها: أين رأسه؟[٤] فأشارت إليه.
ولم يكن مع فيروز سيف فأراد الرجوع إلى أصحابه ليأخذ سيفاً، فكأنّما أتاه شيطانٌ فأيقظه وإنّ
عيناه[٥] تَبِصّان. فعالجه فيروز فأخذ برأسه ولِحْيته فدقّ عنقه وخرج. واتّبعتْه المرأة فقالت: أَنْشُدكم
باللّٰه كلَّكم وعَوْرَتَكم! فقال لها: لا بأسَ قد فتلتُه. وخرج فأخبر أصحابَه. فدخل قيس فاحتزَّ رأسه
وألقاه إلى الناس، وخرج فأذّن بالصلاة.

---

١ هو كـ (هُبَيرة بن المكشوح)، والتصحيح من طبقات ابن سعد ومراجع كثيرة غيرها.

٢ كـ (تريد).

٣ كـ (شربًا).

٤ (فأشار ... رأسه؟): ناقصة في كـ

٥ كذا في النسختين.

---

328 As his name Fayrūz/Pērōz indicates, he is a Persian, son of someone born or originating from Daylam, a region south of the Caspian Sea; he had converted to Islam and is said to have died during the caliphate of ʿUthmān (23–35/644–656). See e.g. Ibn Saʿd, *Ṭabaqāt*, viii, 93; Ibn Qutaybah, *Maʿārif*, 335; al-Ṣafadī, *Wāfī*, xxiv, 98.

329 See *ĞN*, i, 271 and ii, 459. He was a chief of Murād, like ʿAns a branch of Madhḥij; see *EI2*, "Murād" (G. Levi Della Vida). On Qays, see also e.g. Ibn Saʿd, *Ṭabaqāt*, viii, 263–264,

vants. Fayrūz ibn al-Daylamī,[328] Qays ibn Hubayrah al-Makshūḥ al-Murādī,[329] and Dādawayh, a man of the Descendants,[330] sought to protect themselves against al-Aswad. Fayrūz had been informed that a messenger of the Messenger of God (ṣ) called Yuḥannis ibn Wabarah[331] had arrived and that the people had converted to Islam. The woman whom al-ʿAnsī had married had also converted. "I went to her," said Fayrūz, "and I talked to her about the matter of al-Aswad. I said to her, 'He has evil plans with your people, as you can see. He intends either to expel them from their lands or to enslave them. Have you any means or way to kill him?' She replied, 'I'll find a way.'"

Al-Aswad came when Fayrūz was with her. He struck Fayrūz, stabbing him in the neck, and threw him out. The woman cried and said, "You Arabs! You claim that you are good to your in-laws; but you strike my brother and throw him out of my house!" Al-Aswad asked, "Is he your brother then?" "Yes", she said.[332] "I didn't know," said al-Aswad, "Send for him, let him come to us!" She sent a message to Fayrūz, saying, "He is | appeased now. I shall dig a tunnel for you from 152
the garden to the room that he will be in." She dug a tunnel. Fayrūz, Dādaway, and Qays ibn al-Makshūḥ came, and while they were standing by the tunnel, one of them said, "Which of us will go in to him?" Dādawayh said, "I am an old man and I am afraid that if I strike him I would not do him in properly. But you, Qays, why don't you go in!" Qays replied, "I am a man who gets shaky when fighting. I am afraid that if I strike him it would have little effect on him." So Fayrūz went in; he was the youngest. He found al-Aswad sleeping on cushions filled with down, with the woman at his head. He gestured to her, "Where is his head?" She indicated the place. But Fayrūz did not have his sword with him, so he wanted to go back to his friends and get a sword. But it was as if a devil had come to al-Aswad and woke him up. His eyes were gleaming in the dark. Then Fayrūz fought him, grabbing his head and his beard and breaking his neck. He went outside and the woman followed him, saying, "I beg you all, by God and what is dear to you!"[333] But he said to her, "Don't worry, I have killed him". He went outside and told his friends. Qays went in, cut off al-Aswad's head, and threw it down for the people to see. Then he went out and called people to prayer.

---

al-Ṣafadī, *Wāfī*, xxiv, 289–290. Al-Makshūḥ ("branded on his flank", see Ibn Ḥabīb, *Alqāb al-shuʿārāʾ*, 325) was the nickname of Hubayrah, not his son as wrongly in ʿASH and SKḤ.

330 His name is more often spelled Dādhawayh. On him see e.g. Ibn Saʿd, *Ṭabaqāt*, viii, 94.

331 Wrongly Wabrah in ʿASH. He is sometimes called Wabarah ibn Yuḥannis (e.g., al-Ṣafadī, *Wāfī*, xxvii, 430) or Wabar ibn Yuḥannis (Ibn Saʿd, *Ṭabaqāt*, viii, 92, al-Ṭabarī, *Tārīkh*).

332 In al-Ṭabarī (*Tārīkh*, i, 1855) she is said to be a paternal niece of Fayrūz.

333 The precise sense of *wa-ʿawratikum* is not clear.

ثمّ إنّ قيساً خاف على نفسه عَنْساً فأراد أن يُرْضِيَهم بقتْل فيروز ودادويه، فصنع لهما طعاماً ثمّ أرسل إليهما فأتياه، فخرج فيروز يسقي فرسه وتقدّم دادويه إلى منزل قيس فاغتاله على الطعام وقتله. وخرجت امرأةٌ فلقيت فيروزاً[١] وهو مقبِلٌ إلى منزل قيس وقد رأت فتل دادويه، فقالت: ويْحَكَ قد واللّٰهِ قُتل صاحبك! فركب فرسه وانطلق. فقال عمرو بن مَعْدِيكَرِب يعنّف قيساً بقتله دادويه غَدْراً:

ما إنْ دادَوَيْ لكُمُ بفَخْرٍ ولكنْ دادويْ فَضَح الذِّمارا ١٥٣

[§ ٢٩] **ومنهم** الحُطَم وهو شُرَيح بن ضُبَيْعة [بن شُرَحْبِيل][٢] أخو بني قيس بن ثَعْلبة. وكانت بنو ربيعة بن نِزار اجتمعت بالبَحْرَين في الرِّدّة فارْتدّوا وملّكوا عليهم الغَرور وهو المُنْذر بن النُّعمان، فسار إليهم العَلاء بن الحَضْرَميّ، وكان عاملَ رسول اللّٰه صلّى اللّٰه عليه وسلّم على عُمان. فخاض العلاء إليهم خليجاً من البحر، وسارت ربيعة إليهم بجُواثا حتّى كاد يَهلِك المسلمون

١ كذا في النسختين، وهو خطأ كما قال هـ في تعليقه والتصحيح (فيروز) كما في هـ، كـ

٢ في هـ، كـ: (شُريح [بن سُرَحبِيل] بن ضُبَيعة)، نقلاً عمّا في المحبّر لابن حبيب، وهو خطأ.

334 ʿAmr ibn Maʿdīkarib, famous warrior and tribal leader of Zubayd, a branch of Madhḥij, and a poet, see *ǦN*, i, 270 and ii, 178; Sezgin, *Geschichte*, ii, 306–307; *EI3*, "ʿAmr b. Maʿdīkarib" (Thomas Bauer). He converted to Islam c. 9/630, was part of the Riddah but later fought as a Muslim again during the conquests and died at an advanced age, perhaps in 21/642. He is said to be the maternal uncle of Qays ibn al-Makshūḥ (al-Iṣfahānī, *Aghānī*, xv, 209). The verse is found in a piece of four lines in his *Dīwān*, 115–116; also, with one other line, al-Ṭabarī, *Tārīkh*, i, 1996, tr. *The History*, x, 172.

335 The name is spelled twice without the final *h*, apparently for the sake of the metre.

336 See al-Ṭabarī, *Tārīkh*, i, 1961–1962, 1968–1970, 1973, tr. *The History*, x, 138, 143–145, 149–150; al-Iṣfahānī, *Aghānī*, xv, 257–260; al-Balādhurī, *Futūḥ*, 114–116; Ibn Aʿtham, *Futūḥ*, i, 44; Ibn Ḥubaysh, *Ghazawāt*, 182–184.

337 See *ǦN*, i, 155 and ii, 533. The words "ibn Shuraḥbīl" are missing in the manuscripts; ʿASH and SKḤ supply them, but in the wrong place, before "ibn Ḍubayʿah", following ibn Ḥabīb, *Muḥabbar*, 463. On al-Ḥuṭam, see also al-Ṣafadī, *Wāfī*, xvi, 143–144. His nickname, al-Ḥuṭam ("Breakbones" or "pitiless camel driver", see Lane, *Lexicon*, ḤṬM), he got from a

Subsequently Qays feared for his life, afraid of the tribe of ʿAns, and he wanted to appease them by killing Fayrūz and Dādawayh. He prepared a meal for them and invited them. They came. Fayrūz went outside to give water to his horse, and when Dādawayh went inside, Qays murdered him while he was having his meal. A woman went outside and met Fayrūz who was just coming back to Qays's house; she had seen that Dādawayh had been killed. She said, "O dear! Your friend has been killed, by God!" Fayrūz mounted his horse and ran off. ʿAmr ibn Maʿdīkarib[334] said, scolding Qays for treacherously killing Dādawayh:

Dādawayh[335] is no reason for you to boast; 153
but Dādawayh dishonoured his kin.

[§ 29 al-Ḥuṭam[336]]

Another is al-Ḥuṭam, who is Shurayḥ ibn Ḍubayʿah [ibn Shuraḥbīl] ibn ʿAmr ibn Marthad, of the Banū Qays ibn Thaʿlabah.[337] Rabīʿah ibn Nizār assembled in al-Baḥrayn during the Secession;[338] they seceded and made al-Gharūr (the Deluded One) their king; he is al-Mundhir ibn al-Nuʿmān.[339] Al-ʿAlāʾ ibn al-Ḥaḍramī[340] moved towards them; he was the Messenger of God's (ṣ) governor of Oman. To get to them he crossed a bay of the sea. Rabīʿah moved towards him and his men in Juwāthā.[341] In the end the Muslims were almost dying,

poem by Rushayd ibn Rumayḍ al-ʿAnazī made about him after a punishing campaign (al-Jāḥiẓ, *Burṣān*, 275–276; al-Iṣfahānī, *Aghānī*, xv, 254–255; al-Balādhurī, *Futūḥ*, 114).

338 Rabīʿah ibn Nizār (see above, § 5) can refer to a large group of North Arab tribes, but in practice often has a narrower sense. "When in the same year [11/633] the 'Rabīʿah' in Baḥrayn proclaimed a king of their own, this can only refer to the tribes of Ḳays b. Tha̱ʿlaba and ʿAbd al-Ḳays" (*EI2*, "Rabīʿa and Muḍar" [H. Kindermann], see p. 353b). Al-Baḥrayn here does not mean the small present-day island state of that name but a much larger coastal area of eastern Arabia. On the Riddah, see above, § 23.

339 Not to be confused with al-Mundhir ibn al-Nuʿmān of Lakhm mentioned above. Elsewhere (al-Ṭabarī, *Tārīkh*, i, 1961, al-Iṣfahānī, *Aghānī*, xv, 256–257) he is called "al-Gharūr ibn Suwayd, the brother of al-Nuʿman ibn al-Mundhir".

340 Al-ʿAlāʾ ibn al-Ḥaḍramī (d. 14/635 or 21/642), commander of an army sent to restore Muslim rule in eastern Arabia and subsequently made governor of al-Baḥrayn; his proper name is said to be ʿAbd Allāh ibn ʿAmmār, or ibn Ḍammār. See al-Ṣafadī, *Wāfī*, xx, 262–264 (with many other references).

341 Juwāthā is a fortified place belonging to the tribe of ʿAbd al-Qays (Yāqūt, *Muʿjam al-buldān*, Abū ʿUbayd al-Bakrī, *Muʿjam*, 401–402).

جَهْداً. فلمّا اشتدّ ذلك عليهم قال عبد الله بن حَذَف العامريّ، حليف بني عامر بن لُؤَيّ، وكانت أمّه من بني عِجْل:[1]

[ألا أَبْلِغْ أبا بَكْرٍ رَسولاً وفِتْيانَ المدينة أجمعِينا
فهل لكُمُ إلى قومٍ كِرامٍ قُعودٍ في جُواثا مُحْصَرينا
كأنّ دِماءَهمْ في كلِّ فَجٍّ شُعاعُ الشمسِ يُغْشي[2] الناظرينا
توكَّلْنا على الرحمٰن إنّا وجدْنا النَّصْرَ للمتوكّلينا]

١٥٤ وسمع المسلمون أصواتاً[3] بالليل فهالتْهم، فقال [العلاء: من يأتينا بخبر القوم؟ فقال عبد الله بن حَذَف]:[4] أنا آتيكم بالخبر. ونزل من الحِصن فأخذوه فسألوه، فانتسب لهم وجعل ينادي: يا أَبْجَراه! وكان في القوم، فجاء أَبْجَر[5] فعرفه فقال: وَيْلك، ما شأنك؟ أظُنّك بئْسَ ابنُ أختِ القومِ الليلةَ لأخوالك! قال: فقد هلكتُ من الجُوع. فأطعمه وسقاه وحمله على بَعير وخلّى سبيله. فرجع ابن حذف إلى أصحابه فأخبرهم أن القوم سُكارى. فبيّتهم العلاء فيمن معه من المسلمين من العرب والعجم، فقتلوهم قتلاً ذريعاً وانهزموا، وقام الحُطَم إلى فرسه ليركَبه فلمّا وضع رِجله في الرِّكاب انقطع سَيْرُ ركابِه فقال: ألا أحد من قيس يَعقِلني؟ فمرّ به رجل من

١ الأبيات ساقطة من النسختين والتكملة من تاريخ الطبريّ والأغاني للإصفهانيّ، كما في هـ، كـ
٢ كـ: (تغشى).
٣ كـ: (وسمع المسلمين ـ في عسكر المشركين ـ أصواتًا).
٤ كذا في هـ، كـ؛ والتكملة من تاريخ الطبريّ والأغاني للإصفهانيّ.
٥ كـ: (وكان في القوم أبجر فعرفه).

342 On him see *ĞN*, i, 70 and ii, 111. He belonged to the tribe of ʿĀmir ibn Ṣaʿṣaʿah, not to be confused with ʿĀmir ibn Luʾayy, which is a branch of Quraysh (*ĞN*, i, 4 and 27).
343 Either Rome (more usually Rūmiyah) or, more plausibly but still a fiction, the lands of the Byzantines (al-Rūm).

exhausted. In their distress ʿAbd Allāh ibn Ḥadhaf al-ʿĀmirī,[342] the ally of the Banū ʿĀmir ibn Lu'ayy—his mother being of the Banū ʿIjl—said:[343]

[Tell Abū Bakr,[344] being a messenger,
  and the men of Medina, all of them:
Will you not come to assist noble men
  sitting in Juwāthā, besieged?
Their blood in every mountain road
  is like the rays of the sun, blinding the onlookers.
We trust in the Merciful: we
  have found that victory comes to those who trust.]

During the night the Muslims heard sounds that frightened them. [Al-ʿAlā'] said: ["Who will bring me intelligence about those people?" ʿAbd Allāh ibn Ḥadhaf answered,][345] "I'll bring it." He left the fortress; he was taken prisoner and questioned. He made himself known and began to shout, "Hey, Abjar!"[346] Abjar, who was among them, came and recognised him. "I say, what do you want?", he said, "It seems to me that you are a bad cousin to your mother's family tonight!" ʿAbd Allāh replied, "I am dying of hunger!" Abjar gave him food and drink, mounted him on a camel, and let him go. Ibn Ḥadhaf returned to his own side and told them that the men were all drunk. Then al-ʿAlā' and his fellow Muslims, both Arabs and non-Arabs, attacked the enemy by night and killed them with great slaughter; they were routed. Al-Ḥuṭam stood by his horse, wanting to mount it, but when he put his foot into the stirrup its leather strap broke. "Is there anyone of Qays to help me into the saddle?" he shouted. While he was crying for help a man[347] of the Muslims came past and asked, 154

---

344 The first caliph (r. 11–13/632–634), in charge of dealing with the Riddah; see on him below, § 30.

345 Following ʿASH and SKḤ the words between brackets have been supplied from al-Ṭabarī and al-Iṣfahānī.

346 He is Abjar ibn Bujayr according to al-Ṭabarī and al-Iṣfahānī. He is probably identical with Abjar ibn Jābir ibn Bujayr (*ǦN*, i, 159, ii, 134), who was a chief of ʿIjl, the tribe of ʿAbd Allāh ibn Ḥadhaf's mother and therefore known to him.

347 He is identified in *al-Aghānī* (xv, 259–260) and al-Ṭabarī's *Tārīkh* (i, 1969) as ʿAfīf ibn al-Mundhir, of the Banū ʿAmr ibn Tamīm. In another account the famous warrior and tribal leader Qays ibn ʿĀṣim is said to have killed al-Ḥuṭam (al-Ṭabarī, *Tārīkh*, i, 1970, al-Iṣfahānī, *Aghānī*, xv, 260). On Qays ibn ʿĀṣim, see at the end of this section.

المسلمين وهو يستغيث فقال: أبو ضُبيعة؟ قال: نعم. قال: أَعْطِني رِجلَك[١] أعقلْك. فلمّا أعطاه رجله أخذها، ثمّ ضربه بالسيف حتّى قتله.

وقال قيس بن عاصم السَّعْديّ: [...][٢]

لا تُوعِدَنَّا بمفروقٍ وأُسْرتِهِ إِنْ[٣] تأتِنا[٤] تَلْقَ منّا سُنّةَ الحُطَمِ ١٥٥

[§ ٣٠] **ومنهم** عُمَر بن الخطّاب رضي الله عنه. كان عمر رأى كأنّ دِيكاً نَقَره أسفلَ من سُرّته نَقْرتَيْن، فسأل عن رؤْياه أسماءَ بنت عُمَيْس، فقالت: هذا رجل أعجميّ يُصيبك. فمضت أيّام لذلك. ثمّ إنّ أبا لؤلؤة، وهو فيْرُوز عبدُ المُغِيرة بن شُعْبة، لَقِيَه وهو يمشي فقال: يا أمير المؤمنين، إنّ المغيرة قد جعل عليّ خَراجاً كثيراً. قال عمر: وكم هو؟ قال: درهميْن في اليوم. قال: وما تعمَل؟ قال: أجوِّف الأرحاء. قال: ما ذاك بكثير، ما في بلادنا أحدٌ يعملها غيرك. فقال: المستعان اللّٰه! ثمّ

١ الكلمة ناقصة في ك.

٢ قال هـ في الهامش: (كذا، وفي الكلام تحريف ونقص) وزاد تكملة نقلاً عن الطبريّ وفيها البيت التالي منسوب إلى عبد الله بن حذف.

٣ هـ: (وإن) وهو مختلّ الوزن.

٤ ك: (تأتينا).

348 Apparently al-Ḥuṭam had a son called Ḍubayʿah, like his father (unless "Abū Ḍubayʿah", also found in the other sources, is an error for "Ibn Ḍubayʿah").

349 As ʿAbd al-Salām Hārūn says, the text is corrupt at this point and something is missing, for the following line of verse is not by Qays ibn ʿĀṣim. He supplies the text of al-Ṭabarī (*Tārīkh*, i, 1973), where the line is attributed to ʿAbd Allāh ibn Ḥadhaf. He utters it after al-ʿAlāʾ has re-established Muslim domination, but rumours are spreading about Mafrūq (see the next note), who is said to have rallied the tribes of Shaybān, Taghlib, and al-Namir. On Qays ibn ʿĀṣim see *ĞN*, i, 76 and ii, 457–458, *EI2*, "Ḳays b. ʿĀṣim" (M.J. Kister).

350 Mafrūq (al-Nuʿmān) ibn ʿAmr al-Aṣamm, of Dhuhl—Shaybān—Bakr ibn Wāʾil, see *ĞN*, Tab 149 and ii, 451.

351 Al-Ṭabarī: "If he comes to us he ..."

352 Of the four "rightly guided" caliphs reigning after Muḥammad's death, only the first, Abū Bakr, was not murdered. The reign of his successor, ʿUmar (13–23/634–644) was an extraordinarily important one because it was during his time and under his firm rule from Medina that the first and greatest wave of conquests took place. Accounts of his life and death are naturally numerous; on his murder see, among many other sources, Maʿmar ibn Rashīd, *Maghāzī*, 252–261; Ibn Qutaybah, *Imāmah*, i, 39–44; al-Ṭabarī, *Tārīkh*, i, 2722–2725,

"Is it Abū Ḍubayʿah?"[348] "Yes!" "Give me your foot and I'll help you up!" When al-Ḥuṭam gave his foot, the man held on to it, struck him with his sword and killed him.

Qays ibn ʿĀṣim al-Saʿdī said: […][349]

> Do not threaten us with Mafrūq and his kin![350] 155
> If you come to us you[351] will find from us the custom of al-Ḥuṭam.

[§ 30 ʿUmar ibn al-Khaṭṭāb[352]]

Another is ʿUmar ibn al-Khaṭṭāb (may God the Exalted be pleased with him).[353] Once ʿUmar had a dream in which a cock pecked him twice below the navel. He asked Asmāʾ bint ʿUmays[354] what this dream could signify. She said, "A non-Arab[355] man will attack you." A few days went by. Then Abū Luʾluʾah, whose proper name was Fayrūz, a slave of al-Mughīrah ibn Shuʿbah,[356] met ʿUmar when he was walking. "Commander of the believers!",[357] Abū Luʾlaʾah said, "Al-Mughīrah has imposed a heavy tax[358] on me!" ʿUmar asked, "How much is it?" "Two dirhams[359] per day," said Abū Luʾluʾah. "What do you do?" asked ʿUmar. "I make holes in millstones." ʿUmar said, "It is not too much. There is no one in our lands who makes them except you." Abū Luʾluʾah said, "God is the one to

tr. *The History*, xiv, 89–93; Ibn Saʿd, *Ṭabaqāt*, iii, 310–325; al-Balādhurī, *Ansāb*, iii, 249–266; ʿUmar ibn Shabbah, *Tārīkh al-Madīnah*, 868–945; al-Yaʿqūbī, *Tārīkh*, ii, 183, tr. *The Works*, 793; Ibn ʿAbd Rabbih, *ʿIqd*, iv, 272–273; al-Masʿūdī, *Murūj*, iii, 64–65, 125.

353 For his lineage, from a minor branch of Quraysh, see *ǦN*, i, 26 and ii, 571. The pious formula after his name is customary for the early caliphs and prominent early Muslims. On subsequent occurrences the formula (*raḍiya llāhu ʿan* + pronoun) has been replaced by "(*r*)".

354 See *EI2*, *Suppl.*, "Asmāʾ bint ʿUmays" (Ch. Pellat). For her lineage, from the tribe of Khathʿam, see *ǦN*, i, 226 and ii, 198. She was one of the wives of ʿUmar's predecessor, Abū Bakr; before that, she had been married to Jaʿfar ibn Abī Ṭālib, the brother of the caliph ʿAlī ibn Abī Ṭālib. After Abū Bakr's death she married ʿAlī; she had sons from all these marriages. She died in 39/659–660.

355 The word *ʿajamī* often refers to Persians; Abū Luʾluʾah's proper name, Fayrūz, is Persian. He was a Christian (al-Ṭabarī, *Tārīkh*, i, 2722) or, according to some, a Zoroastrian (*majūsī*, al-Masʿūdi, *Murūj*, iii, 64).

356 A prominent Companion of the Prophet, of the tribe of Thaqīf. He died between 48/668 and 51/671. See *EI2*, "al-Mughīra b. Shuʿba" (H. Lammens), *ǦN*, i, 118 and ii, 419–420.

357 *Amīr al-muʾminīn*, the customary address of caliphs.

358 *Kharāj* became the technical term for land tax but was originally a more general term for taxation. See *EI2*, "Kharādj. I. In the central and western Islamic lands" (Cl. Cahen).

359 A dirham (a word ultimately derived from the Greek *drachmē*) was a silver coin.

وَلّى وهو يهَمْهِم. فقال عمر: ما يقول؟ قال: يزعُم أنّه يعمل لك رَحًى يتحدّث بها العرب والعجم. قال عمر: ما يقول العبد، أتهدَّد، أم وَعَدَ، أم خوّف؟ ثمّ مضى.

فلم يلبَثْ بعد ذلك إلّا أيّاماً حتّى وثب على عمر وهو يُسوّي الصفوف لصلاة الفَجْر، وكان يتلفّتُ يميناً وشِمالاً فإذا استوى الصَّفُّ كبّر، فطعنه بسِكّين له طَرَفانِ نِصابُه في وسطه، فوقَ العانة ودُون السُّرّة، طعْنتيْن أو ثلاثاً. وكان على عمر مُلاءة صفراء، فجمعها على بطنه وقال: حَسّ! ﴿وَكَانَ أَمْرُ ٱللَّهِ قَدَراً مَقْدُوراً﴾. وقدّم عبدَ الرحمن بن عوْف فصلّى بالناس الفجْر.

١٥٦ وحُكي عن عائشة رضي الله عنها، أنّها قالت: إنّي لَأسِيرُ بين مكّة والمدينة في سَحَرِ ليلةٍ
مُقْمِرة، إذ سمعتُ قائلاً يقول:

لِيَبْكِ على الإسلام مَن كان باكياً　　فقد أَوْشَكوا هُلْكاً وما قَدُمَ العَهْدُ
وقد ولَّتِ الدنيا وأَدبر خيْرُها　　وقد ملَّها مَن كان يؤْمِن بالوعْدِ[١]

وطُلب الرجل فلم يُوجَد. فقلت: إنّي لخائفةٌ أن يكون هذا لِحَدَث! فلم يكن إلّا أيّاماً حتى قُتل عمر رضي الله عنه.

١ في البيتين إقواء.

360 In the version in al-Ṭabarī's *Tārīkh* Abū Lu'lu'ah says he is a carpenter, a stone mason, and a blacksmith and that he is able to make a windmill ("a millstone that grinds by means of the wind"). Evidence of windmills in Persia is said to go back to 1000 BC. As El-Hibri says (*Parable and Politics*, 121) Abū Lu'lu'ah is speaking with an insinuating metaphor: *raḥā*, "millstone" is a common metaphor for war and fate.

361 The Arabic is "*ḥass!*"; "the Arabs say *ḥass!* when burned by fire or sharp pain" (Ibn Manẓūr, *Lisān al-ʿArab*, ḤSS).

362 Q al-Aḥzāb 33:38. ʿUmar died a few days later of his wounds (26 Dhū l-Ḥijjah 23/3 November 644). A conspiracy was surmised by some, either a Persian one (Abū Lu'lu'ah had been seen in the company of other Persians, see e.g. al-Ṭabarī, *Tārīkh*, i, 2795–2797) or a plot of some prominent Companions of the Prophet, but such suspicions may have been unfounded; see e.g. *EI2*, "al-Hurmuzān" (L. Veccia Vaglieri) and "ʿUmar (I) b. al-Khaṭṭāb" (G. Levi Della Vida and M. Bonner).

be asked for help!" He turned away, muttering. ʿUmar asked, "What is he saying?" Someone answered, "He claims that he can make you a millstone that will be the talk of the Arabs and the non-Arabs".[360] "What is that slave saying," wondered ʿUmar, "Is he threatening or promising or scaring me?" Then he left.

Merely a few days later he sprang upon ʿUmar, who was putting people in straight rows for the morning prayer. Looking right and left, he called out "God is Great!" whenever a row was straight. Abū Luʾluʾah stabbed him twice or three times above the pubic region, below the navel, with a knife that had two blades, with the handle in the middle. ʿUmar was wearing a yellow robe; he clutched it over his belly, saying "Ouch!"[361] «And God's command is destination decreed».[362] He made ʿAbd al-Raḥmān ibn ʿAwf[363] come to the fore to lead the people in the morning prayer.[364]

It is told that ʿĀʾishah (*r*)[365] said, "When I was travelling between Mecca and 156
Medina at dawn after a moonlit night, I heard someone say:

> Let all those who weep weep for Islam,
> for they are all but lost even when the time is still young!
> The world has turned its back, the best of it is gone;
> those who once believed its promise are weary of it."

They looked for the man who said this but he was not found.[366] ʿĀʾishah said, "I was afraid that this would be a portent of some event. Only a few days later ʿUmar (*r*) was killed!"

---

363 A prominent early convert to Islam of the Banū Zuhrah, a branch of Quraysh and one of the ten to whom the Prophet promised Paradise. He played an important role in securing the succession of ʿUmar for ʿUthmān ibn ʿAffān as the third caliph. See *EI3*, "ʿAbd al-Raḥmān b. ʿAwf" (W. Madelung). He died 32/652–653.

364 Other sources (e.g. Maʿmar ibn Rashīd, *Maghāzī*) add that Abū Luʾluʾah, having mortally wounded the caliph and wounded some bystanders, slits his own throat and kills himself.

365 The daughter of Abū Bakr, the first caliph, and the favourite wife of the Prophet, whom she survived until she died in 58/678 at the age of c. 64, having played a prominent role in a few decisive events and as a transmitter of many reports about the Prophet. See *EI3*, "ʿĀʾisha bt. Abī Bakr" (Asma Afsaruddin).

366 The verses are attributed to a jinnee or a disembodied voice (*hātif*); see e.g. al-Jāḥiẓ, *Bayān*, iii, 364, Ibn Dāwūd al-Iṣbahānī, *Zahrah*, 843.

[§ ٣١] **ومنهم** سالم بن دارة، أحد بني عبد الله بن غَطَفان، وكان هجا رجلاً من بني فَزارة يقال له زُمَيل بن وُبَير،١ وهو ابن أمّ دِينار، فقال في قصيدة له طويلة:

آلي ابنُ دارةَ جَهْداً لا يُصالحُكمْ   حتّى يَنيكَ زُميلٌ أمَّ دينارِ

ثمّ إنّ ابن دارة لقي بعد ذلك زُميلاً بالداءة٢ فقال: يا زُميل، ألا تفعل بأمّك حتّى أصالحَ قومي!
فقال له زُميل: مَعْذِرةً إلى الله ثمّ إليك، إنّه ليس معي ولا في رَحْلي إلّا مِخْيَط أشُدُّ به على
وِكائي. ثمّ لقيه مرّةً أخرى بشَراف، فقال له | أيضاً مثل قوْلته الأولى: حتّى أصالح عَشيرتي. فقال ١٥٧
له: معذرةً إلى الله ثمّ إليك، إنّه ليس معي إلّا سِكّين أُصلِح به حِذائي. ثمّ إنّ زُميلاً قَدِم المدينةَ
بعد ذلك بزمان فقضى حوائجه، حتّى إذا صدر عن الشُّقْرة سمع رجلاً يتغنّى بقوله:

---

١ في النسختين (زبير) وفي ك: (دبير) والتصحيح من هـ، نقلاً عن المراجع المعتادة.

٢ في النسختين (الدامة) والتصحيح من هـ، ك، نقلاً عن المراجع المعتادة.

---

367 Sālim ibn Dārah's murder is in the correct place chronologically, because it took place at some time during the caliphate of ʿUmar's successor, ʿUthmān (r. 23–35/644–656). He cannot be counted, however, among the "nobles" (*ashrāf*) and he is primarily known as a poet. He is in fact listed below in the section on murdered poets (§ 111) with the brief remark "One of the Banū ʿAbd Allāh ibn Ghaṭafān; his story went before, among the murdered (*al-mughtālīn*)". Yet stranger than Sālim's appearance here is the absence of one of the most prominent murder victims in Islamic history, one with dire consequences, for the killing of the caliph ʿUthmān in 35/644, with its subsequent recriminations and civil strife, ultimately caused the split between Shi'ites and Sunnites. Perhaps Ibn Ḥabīb did not consider his death, in a small-scale rebellion, a proper *ightiyāl*, "assasination". On Sālim ibn Dārah, see Sezgin, *Geschichte*, ii, 238–239; Ibn Qutaybah, *Shiʿr*, 401–402; al-Mubarrad, *Taʿāzī*, 255–256; ʿUmar ibn Shabbah, *Tārīkh al-Madīnah al-Munawwarah*, 1058–1060; al-Iṣfahānī, *Aghānī*, xxi, 229–248; al-ʿAskarī, *Jamharah*, i, 229–230; al-Maydānī, *Majmaʿ*, ii, 329–330; al-Baghdādī, *Khizānah*, ii, 144–150, xi, 390. The story even made it into dictionaries (Ibn Manẓūr, *Lisān al-ʿArab* and al-Zabīdī, *Tāj al-ʿarūs*, DWR).

368 On ʿAbd Allāh ibn Ghaṭafān, see *ǦN*, i, 92, 136 (where Sālim appears as Sālim ibn Ru'aybah Dārat al-Qamar) and ii, 110. Dārah, short for Dārat al-Qamar ("Moon's Halo"), was the name of his mother (see also Ibn Ḥabīb's *Man nusiba ilā ummih*, 92); his father was Musāfiʿ ibn Yarbūʿ (other names are also mentioned).

[§ 31 Sālim ibn Dārah[367]]

Another is Sālim ibn Dārah, of the Banū ʿAbd Allāh ibn Ghaṭafān.[368] He had lampooned a man of the Banū Fazārah called Zumayl ibn Wubayr, who is the son of Umm Dīnār.[369] He said, in the course of a long poem:[370]

> Ibn Dārah has sworn a solemn oath: he shall not make peace with you
> until Zumayl fucks Umm Dīnār.

Afterwards, when Ibn Dārah met Zumayl in al-Dāʾah,[371] he said to him, "Zumayl, why don't you do it to your mother so that I can make peace with my people?" Zumayl replied, "I ask God's forgiveness and yours, but in my saddlebag I have only a needle for sewing on the strap of my waterskin." Then they met a second
time, in Sharāf.[372] Ibn Dārah asked | the same question again: "… so that I can 157
make peace with my kinsmen!" Zumayl said, "I have only a knife on me to mend my shoes with." Some time afterwards Zumayl went to Medina and did some business there. Upon leaving al-Shuqrah[373] he heard a man sing the following verses:[374]

---

369 Fazārah (see *EI2*, "Fazāra" [W. Montgomery Watt]) was part of Dhubyān, itself part of Ghaṭafān (on which see "Ghaṭafān" [J.W. Fück]). Zumayl was also known among "those traced to their mother" (Ibn Ḥabīb, *Man nusiba ilā ummih*, 92, al-Āmidī, *Muʾtalif*, 129). The name of his father is given as Wubayr or Ubayr. Ibn Qutaybah, *Shiʿr*, 401 mentions Thābit ibn Rāfiʿ as Ibn Dārah's killer, only to say thereafter, "The one who took it upon him to kill him (viz., Ibn Dārah) was Zumayl ibn ʿAbd Manāf". Perhaps Thābit ibn Rāfiʿ (not found elsewhere) is the name of the Christian physician who actually kills Sālim in the version in the present book. Zumayl may have considered himself the killer, judging by lines attributed to him: "I am Zumayl of the Banū Fazārah; | I am Zumayl, the killer of Ibn Dārah" (Ibn Qutaybah, *Shiʿr*, 402, Abū ʿUbayd al-Bakrī, *Faṣl al-maqāl*, 25, etc.).

370 In ʿUmar ibn Shabbah, *Tārīkh al-Madīnah*, 1058 it is the first line of a poem of eight lines, the third of which (in which he accuses the women of Fazārah of being overly fond of male camels) is often quoted; e.g. Ibn Qutaybah, *Shiʿr*, 401 and many other sources. The first line has a variant (e.g. al-Baghdādī, *Khizānah*, ii, 148): "Tell Fazārah I shall not make peace with them until …"

371 A place or a mountain near Mecca (Yāqūt, *Muʿjam al-buldān*, Abū ʿUbayd al-Bakrī, *Muʿjam*, 530–531).

372 A watering place not far from Medina (Yāqūt, *Muʿjam al-buldān*, Abū ʿUbayd al-Bakrī, *Muʿjam*, 788–789).

373 "The first village upon leaving Medina" (Abū ʿUbayd al-Bakrī, *Muʿjam*, 749, 805).

374 The second verse is in ʿUmar ibn Shabbah, *Tārīkh al-Madīnah*, 1060. The first has not been found elsewhere.

مَلَكْتُ بها الإدلاجَ حتّى بدا لها   مع الصُّبح من أشباع[١] رُكْنُ يَلَمْلَمِ
وقد أوغلتْ في السَّيْر حتّى كأنّما   يُكسَّر قَيْضٌ بينهنَّ وحَنْتَمُ[٢]

فعرف زُميل صوتَ سالم، فأقبل إليه فضربه ضَرْبتين، ثمّ عقر بَعيرَه، فحمل سالم إلى عُثْمان بن عَفّان، فدفعه إلى طبيب نَصْرانيّ حتّى إذا برأ ووَعَتْ كُلومُه دخل النصرانيُّ، وإذا سالم يُشامع امرأتَه، فاحتقنها[٣] عليه، فقال له النصرانيّ: إنّي لَأرى عَظْماً ناتئاً، فهل لك أن أجعل عليه دواءً حتّى يسقُط؟ قال: نَعَمْ فافْعَلْ. فسَمَّه فمات.

ويُقال إنّ أمَّ البَنِينَ بنت عُيَيْنة بن حِصْن الفَزاريّ، وكانت عند عثمان بن عفّان رضي الله عنه، جعلت للطبيب جُعْلاً حتّى سمّه فمات. فذلك قول الكُمَيْت بن ثَعْلبة:

فلا تُكْثِروا فيها الضَّجاجَ فإنّه   مَحا السيفُ ما قال ابنُ دارةَ أجْمَعا

١ كذا في النسختين.
٢ في البيتين إقواء.
٣ كذا في النسختين وفي هـ، ك؛ ولعلّ الصواب إمّا (فاحتقدها) كما جعلها الشنقيطيّ وإمّا (فاحتنقها) كما في خزانة الأدب لعبد القادر البغداديّ.

375 The context suggests that the pronoun refers to his she-camel. For the sense of *malaka* here cf. Ibn Manẓūr, *Lisān* (MLK): *malaktu bihā kaffī* (…) *yaʿnī shadadtu bi-l-ṭaʿnah*. The phrase *malaktu bihā l-idlāja* is also found in a poem by Hudbah ibn Khashram (Ibn Maymūn, *Muntahā*, iii, 228, Hudbah ibn Khashram, *Shiʿr*, 132).

376 Not identified.

377 A mountain two nights' travelling from Mecca (Yāqūt, *Muʿjam al-buldān*, Abū ʿUbayd al-Bakrī, *Muʿjam*, 1398–1399).

I exerted her[375] during the night until there appeared to her
in the morning, from Ashbāʿ,[376] the side of Mount Yalamlam.[377]
She had paced so fast that it was as if
ostrich shells and wine-jars were broken between them.[378]

Zumayl recognised Sālim's voice. He turned to him and struck him twice; then he hamstrung his camel. Sālim was carried to ʿUthmān ibn ʿAffān, who handed him over to a physician, a Christian. When he was cured and his wounds had healed the Christian went in to Sālim, finding him fooling around with his wife. Resenting this, he said to Sālim, "I see a bone jutting out through your skin. Would you like me to put some medicine on it to make it come out?" "Yes," said Sālim, "Please do!" The man poisoned him and he died.

It is also said that Umm al-Banīn,[379] the daughter of ʿUyaynah ibn Ḥiṣn al-Fazārī, who was the wife of ʿUthmān ibn ʿAffān (*r*), made a payment to the doctor, who poisoned Sālim, so he died. To this refers the verse by al-Kumayt ibn Thaʿlabah:[380]

Don't make a great to-do about it:
the sword effaced all Ibn Dārah's words.

---

378 Meaning "between the camel's hooves"; cf. an anonymous line quoted in Ibn Manẓūr, *Lisān al-ʿArab* (NHY): "Their hooves crush the pebbles as if | ostrich shells and flasks were broken between them."

379 Mulaykah, known as Umm al-Banīn ("Mother of Sons"), daughter of ʿUyaynah ibn Ḥiṣn al-Fazārī, was one of the wives of the caliph ʿUthmān and the mother of one of his sons, ʿAbd al-Malik (al-Balādhurī, *Ansāb*, vi, 231).

380 Al-Kumayt al-Akbar ("the older", to distinguish him from two other and more famous poets called al-Kumayt) ibn Thaʿlabah, of the tribe of Faqʿas—Asad (*ĞN*, i, 50 and ii, 373, Sezgin, *Geschichte*, ii, 227). The line is quoted in al-Jāḥiẓ, *Bayān*, i, 389; al-Buḥturī, *Ḥamāsah*, 24; al-Āmidī, *Muʾtalif*, 170; al-Marzubānī, *Muʿjam*, 237–238; and, in a poem of 13 lines, al-Baghdādī, *Khizānah*, xi, 389–390. The second half of the quoted line became a proverb (Abū ʿUbayd al-Bakrī, *Faṣl al-maqāl*, 26; al-ʿAskarī, *Jamharah*, i, 229–230; al-Maydānī, *Majmaʿ*, ii, 329–330).

١٥٨ [§ ٣٢] **ومنهم** الزُّبَيْر بن العَوّام رضي اللّٰه عنه. وسبب ذلك أنّه لمّا انصرف عن حرب الجَمَل عندما ذكّره عليّ بن أبي طالب رضي اللّٰه عنه، استجار النَّعِر بن الزَّمّام المُجاشِعيّ، فأتى آتٍ الأحنفَ بن قيْس فقال: هذا الزُّبير قد مرَّ آنفاً! قال الأحنف: ما أصنع به، جمع فِئَتيْن من المسلمين فقتل بعضُهم بعضاً، ثمّ لحق بقومه. فنهض عَمْرو[١] بن جُرْموز، وفَضالة بن حابس، ونُفَيْع بن كعب بن عُمَير، فلحقوه بوادي السِّباع، فكرّ عليهم الزبير حين رآهم، فانهزموا عنه، ولحق الزبيرُ ابنَ جرموز فلمّا رَهِقَه قال: اللّٰهَ اللّٰهَ أبا عبد اللّٰه! فرجع عنه، ومضى الزبير وانصرف عنه فَضالة ونُفيع، ولزمه عمرو بن حرموز، فسايَرَه في ليلة مُقْمِرة، فعطف عليه الزبير فقال: أَنْشُدك اللّٰهَ يا أبا عبد اللّٰه! فكفّ عنه وسايَرَه، وأغفى الزبير على فرسه فطعنه فأذْراه عنه، فقال الزبير: قاتَلَه اللّٰه، يذكِّر باللّٰه وينساه! ومات.

فقالت عاتكة أخت سعيد بن زيد بن عمرو بن نُفَيْل العَدَويّ:

---

١ كـ: (عمر).

---

381 Al-Zubayr ibn al-ʿAwwām opposed ʿAlī ibn Abī Ṭālib and fought him after the latter had become the fourth caliph in the famous "Battle of the Camel" (36/656), near Basra. He was supported by Ṭalḥah ibn ʿUbayd Allāh and the Prophet's widow, ʿĀʾishah, a fierce opponent of ʿAlī; she attended the battle seated on a camel in an armoured palanquin. They were defeated and al-Zubayr was killed soon afterwards. The story is told in numerous sources; see e.g. *EI2*, "Djamal" (L. Veccia Vaglieri), and "al-Zubayr b. al-ʿAwwām" (I. Hasson). The Battle of the Camel is described in detail in al-Ṭabarī, *Tārīkh*, i, 3091–3233, tr. *The History*, xvi, 32–172; on al-Zubayr's death ibid., i, 3218–3219; also al-Iṣfahānī, *Aghānī*, xviii, 53–63.

382 He belonged to Quraysh; for his lineage, see *ǦN*, i, 19 and ii, 608–609. An early convert and, with ʿAbd al-Raḥmān ibn ʿAwf (see above, § 30) and ʿAlī, among those promised Paradise by the Prophet, he distinguished himself in the early conquests. He and others accused ʿAlī of being implicated in the rebellion that ended with ʿUthmān's death, or at least of not dealing firmly with the perpetrators.

383 Al-Ṭabarī, *Tārīkh*, i, 3185–3186; al-Yaʿqūbī, *Tārīkh*, ii, 182; al-Masʿūdī, *Murūj*, iii, 107–108; al-Iṣfahanī, *Aghānī*, xviii, 54.

384 Abū ʿUbaydah, *Naqāʾiḍ*, 80, 222 mentions this name in his commentary on lines by the poet Jarīr (d. 111/729) attacking Mujāshiʿ (the tribe of his rival al-Farazdaq) for failing to protect al-Zubayr. But Ibn Durayd (*Ishtiqāq*, 327) apparently believes there was no person of this name: "Al-Naʿir ibn al-Zammām al-Mujāshiʿī, who gave protection to al-Zubayr as they allege; but this is a false claim, for it is something that [the poet] Jarīr derided them [viz., the tribe of Mujāshiʿ] with; it is derived from the expression *ḥimār naʿir*, i.e., a fly-bitten donkey." In support of this one notes that this al-Naʿir cannot be found elsewhere except in the context of this story and that Naʿir ("fly-bitten") is not known as a personal name.

385 Al-Aḥnaf Ṣakhr ibn Qays (d. 67/686–687), prominent leader of Tamīm, neutral at the time of the Battle of the Camel; on him, see *EI2*, "al-Aḥnaf b. Ḳays" (Ch. Pellat); *ǦN*, i, 76; Ibn Qutaybah, *Maʿārif*, 423–425.

[§ 32 al-Zubayr ibn al-ʿAwwām[381]]

Another is al-Zubayr ibn al-ʿAwwām (*r*).[382] The cause of his death was as follows. When he had withdrawn from the fighting at the Battle of the Camel, after ʿAlī (*r*) had reminded him of past events,[383] he sought protection with al-Naʿir ibn al-Zammām al-Mujāshiʿī.[384] Someone came to al-Aḥnaf ibn Qays[385] and said, "This al-Zubayr has just come past." Al-Aḥnaf said, "What should I do with him? He has made two parties of Muslims meet and kill one another, and then he left to join his own people." Then ʿAmr ibn Jurmūz,[386] Faḍālah ibn Ḥābis, and Nufayʿ ibn Kaʿb ibn ʿUmayr[387] went in pursuit and caught up with al-Zubayr in Wādī l-Sibāʿ.[388] Al-Zubayr attacked them when he saw them and they fled. Al-Zubayr pursued Ibn Jurmūz and when he caught up with him, Ibn Jurmūz said, "By God, by God, please, servant of God!"[389] Al-Zubayr let him go and went his way. Faḍālah and Nufayʿ left, but ʿAmr ibn Jurmūz stuck to al-Zubayr and rode along with him. It was a moonlit night. Al-Zubayr turned to him and Ibn Jurmūz said, "I implore you by God, servant of God!" so al-Zubayr let him off again. They rode on together. Al-Zubayr nodded off, seated on his horse; then Ibn Jurmūz stabbed him, throwing him from the saddle. Al-Zubayr cried out, "God curse him! He mentions God to me and then forgets Him!" Then he died. 158

ʿĀtikah, the sister of Saʿīd ibn Zayd ibn ʿAmr ibn Nufayl al-ʿAdawī,[390] said:

---

386 On ʿAmr ibn al-Jurmūz see *ǦN*, i, 75 and ii, 173. He is often mentioned or referred to (sometimes as Ibn al-Dhayyāl) in Jarīr's invective poems on al-Farazdaq, see Abū ʿUbaydah, *Naqāʾiḍ*, 81–82, 179–180, 318, 592, 833.

387 Faḍālah ibn Ḥābis and Nufayʿ ibn Kaʿb are found only in connection with this event. Instead of Faḍalāh, the editors of *Aghānī*, xviii, 56 have Fuḍālah, probably incorrectly.

388 A place five miles from Basra on the road to Mecca (Yāqūt, *Muʿjam al-buldān*, Abū ʿUbayd al-Bakrī, *Muʿjam*, 715–716). Its name ("Valley of Lions, or predatory animals") is said to be derived from a woman named Asmāʾ bint Duraym who dwelt there and who was nicknamed Umm al-Asbuʿ (Mother of Lions); but the editor of al-Bakrī's *Muʿjam* thinks that real animals are meant, quoting verses by Suḥaym ibn Wathīl in support.

389 He uses *ʿabd Allāh* not as a name but in its literal sense.

390 ʿĀtikah bint Zayd ibn ʿAmr was a wife of al-Zubayr's. She is listed by Ibn Ḥabīb (*Muḥabbar*, 437) among women who married three or more times, having earlier been the wife of ʿUbaydah ibn al-Ḥārith ibn al-Muṭṭalib and then ʿAbd Allāh ibn Abī Bakr, and afterwards of Muḥammad ibn Abī Bakr and finally, it seems, ʿAmr ibn al-ʿĀṣ. That her last husband was al-Ḥusayn ibn ʿAlī (thus al-Iṣfahānī, *Aghānī*, xviii, 62) or al-Ḥasan ibn ʿAlī (thus al-Ṣafadī, *Wāfī*, xvi, 560) is not corroborated by the main sources. See also al-Madāʾinī, *Murdifāt*, 61–64; Ibn Saʿd, *Ṭabaqāt*, x, 252–253; *EI2*, "ʿĀtika" (J.W. Fück); Sezgin, *Geschichte*, ii, 314–315. The following verses are from a poem, lines of which are quoted in many sources, including al-Madāʾinī, *Murdifāt*, 64; Abū Tammām, *Ḥamāsah* (al-Marzūqī, *Sharḥ*, 1106–1107); al-Washshāʾ, *Muwashshā*, 80–81; al-Iṣfahānī, *Aghānī*, xviii, 58; al-Baghdādī, *Khizānah*, x, 373–378 (with a discussion of the syntax of the third line).

غَدَر ابنُ جرموزٍ بفارسِ بُهْمةٍ   يومَ اللِّقاء وكان غيرَ معرِّدِ
يا عَمْرُو لو نبَّهته لَوَجدتَه   لا طائشاً رَعِشَ الجَنانِ ولا اليَدِ
هَبِلَتْكَ أُمُّك إنْ قتلتَ لَمُسْلِماً   حلَّت عليك عقوبةُ المتعمِّدِ

وجاء ابن جرموز بسيف الزبير إلى عليّ بن أبي طالب رضي الله عنه، وقال: أَخَبِروه أنّي قاتل ١٥٩
الزبير. فقال عليّ: بَشِّرْ قاتلَ ابنِ صَفِيّةَ بالنار! وأخذ السيف منه وقال: سيفٌ طالَما فَرَجَ الغَمامةَ عن وجه رسول الله صلّى الله عليه وسلّم.

قال: فكان ابن جرموز يدعو لأمر الدنيا، فقيل له: لو دعوْتَ لأمر آخِرتك. فقال: قد يَئِستُ من الجنّة منذ قتلتُ الزبير.

[§ ٣٣] **ومنهم** مالك بن الحارث الأشتر. وكان أتى عليًّا رضي الله لمّا ولّى عبدَ الله بن عبّاس البصرةَ، وعُبَيدَ الله اليَمَنَ، وقُثَمَ مكّةَ، فقال له: ولَّيْتَ بني عمِّك فلِمَ قتلْنا الشيخَ، يعني عثمانَ رضي الله عنه، إنّما قتلناه حين آثَرَ أهلَ بيتِه بالوِلاية! فتقاولا فأغلظ كلٌّ واحد منهما لصاحبه، فدخل بينهما عبد الله بن جعفر، وكان عليٌّ له مكرِماً، فانصرف الأشتر مغاضِباً، فترك إتْيانَ عليّ رضي الله عنه حتّى قتل أهلُ مصرَ محمّدَ بن أبي بكر رضي الله عنه، وكان عامِلَ عليّ عليها. فلمّا بلغه قتْلُه قال لعبد الله بن جعفر: من ترى لمصر؟ فقال: الأشتر، همْ قومه، وَجِّهْه، فإن هَلَك

---

391 For the literal and figurative meanings of *buhmah*, see Lane, *Lexicon* (BHM); it often has the force of "courageous man".

392 Al-Zubayr's mother was Ṣafiyyah bint ʿAbd al-Muṭṭalib, the Prophet Muḥammad's aunt. ʿAlī's ironic use of *bashshir*, "bring good tidings", may have been inspired by the Qur'an (e.g. Q al-Nisāʾ 4:138: «Bring good tidings to the hypocrites that they will receive a painful punishment!»).

393 For parallels see e.g. al-Yaʿqūbī, ii, 227, tr. *The Works*, 849–850; al-Ṭabarī, *Tārīkh*, i, 3392–3395, tr. *The History*, xvii, 144–146; al-Masʿūdī, *Murūj*, iii, 161.

394 Mālik ibn al-Ḥārith al-Nakhaʿī, called al-Ashtar ("with inverted eyelid") after a wound received at the Battle of the Yarmūk (15/636), belonged to the tribe of al-Nakhaʿ, part of Madhḥij (*ǦN*, i, 264 and ii, 389). He was a leading opponent of ʿUthmān and involved in the rebellion that led to ʿUthmān's violent death. He supported ʿAlī during the Battle of the Camel (see above, § 32) and the Battle of Ṣiffīn (37/657) between the forces of ʿAlī and Muʿāwiyah, but he opposed the truce between the two. His death may have occurred in 37/657–658 or the following year. See on him also *EI3*, "al-Ashtar, Mālik b. al-Ḥārith al-Nakhaʿī" (Harry Munt), al-Ṣafadī, *Wāfī*, xxv, 35–37.

395 ʿAbd Allāh ibn (al-)ʿAbbās ibn Abī Ṭālib (d. c. 68/687–688) was a paternal cousin of the

Ibn Jurmūz betrayed a valiant knight, a rock,[391]
on the day of battle, one who does not flee from the fight.
ʿAmr, if you had awakened him you would have found him
not mindless, trembling of neither heart nor hand.
May your mother be bereft of you! Since you killed a Muslim
the punishment for intentional homicide applies to you!

Ibn Jurmūz took the sword of al-Zubayr to ʿAlī (*r*), saying, "Tell him that I am the one who killed al-Zubayr!" But ʿAlī replied, "Bring good tidings to Ibn Ṣafiyyah's killer: he'll go to Hell!"[392] He took the sword from him, saying, "So often has this sword lifted a cloud from the face of the Messenger of God (*ṣ*)!" 159

Ibn Jurmūz used to pray for his life in this world; they said to him, "Wouldn't you pray for your life in the hereafter?" He replied, "I have lost all hope of Paradise since I killed al-Zubayr."

[§ 33 Mālik ibn al-Ḥārith al-Ashtar[393]]

Another was Mālik ibn al-Ḥārith al-Ashtar.[394] He went to ʿAlī (*r*) when he had appointed ʿAbd Allāh ibn ʿAbbās[395] as governor of Basra, ʿUbayd Allāh[396] as governor of Yemen, and Qutham[397] as governor of Mecca. "You have appointed your cousins," he said, "so why was it that we killed the old man?"—he referred to ʿUthmān—"We only killed him when he began to appoint his own kin as governors!"[398] They started to argue, both using rude words. ʿAbd Allāh ibn Jaʿfar[399] intervened; he was someone ʿAlī respected. But al-Ashtar left angry and stopped seeing ʿAlī (*r*) until the Egyptians killed Muḥammad ibn Abī Bakr (*r*), who was ʿAlī's governor there.[400] When ʿAlī heard about his death he asked ʿAbd Allāh ibn Jaʿfar, "Who do you think should be governor of Egypt?"

Prophet as well as of ʿAlī, who appointed him as governor of Basra in 36/657. His status as a great scholar grew after the founding of the Abbasid dynasty, called after his father. See *EI3*, "ʿAbdallāh b. ʿAbbās" (Claude Gilliot).

396 He is the brother of ʿAbd Allāh ibn ʿAbbās; see *EI2*, "ʿUbayd Allāh b. al-ʿAbbās" (C.E. Bosworth).

397 Qutham is another brother of Ibn ʿAbbās; see *EI2*, "Ḳuth̲am b. al-ʿAbbās" (C.E. Bosworth).

398 ʿUthmān was accused of nepotism, which contributed to the discontent about his rule but was not the direct cause of the rebellion that cost him his life.

399 Another cousin of ʿAlī; see *EI3*, "ʿAbdallāh b. Jaʿfar b. Abī Ṭālib" (Mohammad Ali Amir-Moezzi).

400 He was a son of the caliph Abū Bakr and a half-brother of ʿAbd Allāh ibn Jaʿfar, who had advised ʿAlī to appoint him as governor of Egypt, where he was soon killed by supporters of Muʿāwiyah. See *EI2*, "Muḥammad b. Abī Bakr" (G.R. Hawting).

هَلَك، وإن مَلَك مَلَك. فبعث إلى الأشتر فولّاه مصرَ. فأخذ على طريق الحِجاز إليها، وبلغ ذلك مُعاويةَ، فكتب إلى الجايسْتار،[١] دِهْقان القُلْزُم، يأمره باغتيال الأشتر ويَضَع عنه[٢] خَراجَه. فلمّا نزل به الأشتر أكرمه، وكان الأشتر يحبّ السمك فأمْجَده منه، وجعل الأشتر يأكل السمك أكْلَ مُتَّقٍ، وكان الغالب عليه البَلْغَم. فقال له: أيّها الرجل، لا تَهَبِ السمك، فإنّ | عندي دواءَه، قال: وما هو؟ قال: العَسَل. فأكل ثمّ قال له: هاتِ العسل. فجَدَح له فيه سُمًّا فقتله. فلمّا بلغ معاويةَ قتْلُه قام خطيباً فقال: يا أهلَ الشام، إنّ عليًّا كانت له يَدانِ، إحداهما عمّار بن ياسر، والأخرى الأشتر، فقطعهما الله تعالى.

[§ ٣٤] **ومنهم** عليّ بن أبي طالب رضي الله تعالى عنه. كان سبب ذلك أنّ عبد الرحمن بن مُلْجَم التَّجُوبيّ، وعِدادُه في مُراد، والبُرَك بن عبد الله التَّميميّ وهو صاحب معاوية، وعمرو

١ هـ، ك: (الجانسار)، والتصحيح من تاريخ الطبريّ.

٢ الكلمة ناقصة في ك.

401 The tribe of Madhḥij, to which al-Ashtar belonged, participated in the conquest of Egypt and some of its members were among those rebels coming from Egypt to confront ʿUthmān (*EI2*, "Madhḥidj" [G.R. Smith—C.E. Bosworth]).

402 Muʿāwiyah, son of the Meccan Qurayshite leader Abū Sufyān (see above, §26) was ʿAlī's adversary in the undecided Battle of Ṣiffīn and became the founder of the Umayyad dynasty after ʿAlī's death, reigning as caliph from 41/661 to 60/680.

403 This word, thus in al-Ṭabarī, *Tārīkh*, i, 3393 (with several other corrupt spellings in the critical apparatus) would have been unintelligible to contemporary readers; in ʿASH and SKḤ it appears as *jānsār*. Apparently a Byzantine administrative rank, it has been said to be the Latin word *logistarius* (*EI2*, "al-Ashtar" [L. Veccia Vaglieri]) but other words have also been suggested (see Hawting's translation of al-Ṭabarī, *The History*, xvii, 145, note 598), among them *quaestor* (see al-Ṭabarī, *Tārīkh*, *Glossarium*, clvii) and *augustalis*, which is supported by the form *jasṭāl* found in administrative papyri.

404 *Dihqān* (originally a Persian word), village head or local feudal ruler.

405 Ancient Klysma, on the Egyptian Red Sea coast, at the site of modern Suez.

406 Fish, in the Galenic-Arab medical and nutritional theory, counts as cold and moist (unsurprisingly), and should therefore not be eaten in quantity by people predominantly phlegmatic (also characterised by coldness and moisture). Honey, classified as hot and dry, would be counteractive.

407 ʿAmmār ibn Yāsir, also of Madhḥij (*ĞN*, i, 272 and ii, 167), was an early convert who fought at the Battle of Badr and was killed fighting for ʿAlī at the Battle of Ṣiffīn. See e.g. al-Ṣafadī, *Wāfī*, xxii, 376–378.

408 Among all murder victims in the book ʿAlī and ʿUmar (and the Prophet Muḥammad if he really died of the much earlier poisoning) are the most prominent. ʿAlī was the Prophet's

"Al-Ashtar", he replied, "They are his kin;[401] send him! If he dies, he dies; if he rules, he rules." ʿAlī summoned al-Ashtar and appointed him governor of Egypt. He set off on the Hijaz road towards Egypt. Muʿawiyah,[402] hearing of this, wrote to the *jāyastār*,[403] the local chief[404] of al-Qulzum,[405] ordering him to have al-Ashtar murdered, after which he would relieve him of paying taxes. When al-Ashtar arrived at him, he received him hospitably. Al-Ashtar was fond of fish and the local dignitary served him a lot of it. Al-Ashtar began to eat the fish, but being circumspect, because his was a predominantly phlegmatic nature.[406] His host said to him, "Man, don't be afraid of the fish! For | I have a remedy for it." 160
"What is it?" asked al-Ashtar. "Honey", he answered. And al-Ashtar ate. Then he said, "Give me the honey!" The man had mixed some poison in it, and this killed him. When Muʿāwiyah learned of his death he stood up to give a speech, saying, "Syrians! ʿAlī once had two hands. One was ʿAmmār ibn Yāsir,[407] the other was al-Ashtar. God the exalted has cut off both of them!"

[§ 34 ʿAlī ibn Abī Ṭālib[408]]

Another was ʿAlī ibn Abī Ṭālib (*r*). The cause was as follows. ʿAbd al-Raḥmān ibn Muljam al-Tajūbī,[409] who belonged to Murād, met in Mecca with al-Burak ibn ʿAbd Allāh al-Tamīmī,[410] who was a companion of Muʿāwiyah, and ʿAmr ibn

---

cousin; the husband of his daughter Fāṭimah; the fourth and last of the so-called "Rightly Guided" caliphs (*al-Rāshidūn*), whose troubled reign was characterised by setbacks and recriminations but who should have been the first caliph according to those who later became the Shi'ites (from *shīʿat ʿAlī*, "ʿAlī's party"); and he was the father or forefather of those collectively called the ʿAlids, many of whom were involved in revolts, movements, or sects (for a survey of the ʿAlids, see e.g. *EI2*, "ʿAlids" [B. Lewis] and *EI3*, "ʿAlids" [Farhad Daftary]). On ʿAlī, see e.g. *EI3*, "ʿAlī b. Abī Ṭālib" (Robert M. Gleave). Naturally, ʿAlī's death is described in countless sources. See e.g. al-Ṭabarī, *Tārīkh*, i, 3456–3469, tr. *The History*, xvii, 213–226; al-Dīnawarī, *al-Akhbār al-ṭiwāl*, 227–230; Ibn Saʿd, *Ṭabaqāt*, iii, 31–38; al-Mubarrad, *Kāmil*, iii, 36–39; Ibn ʿAbd Rabbih, *ʿIqd*, iv, 359–361; al-Masʿūdī, *Murūj*, iii, 164–169; al-Iṣfahānī, *Maqātil al-Ṭālibiyyīn*, 43–57. When the Battle of Ṣiffīn between ʿAlī and Muʿāwiyah ended without a clear result and ʿAlī had agreed to arbitration, some of his fiercest supporters, mainly from the tribe of Tamīm, were so disgusted by what they perceived as an unpardonable weakness that they became his fiercest opponents, known as Khārijites (al-Khawārij, "the Leavers"). ʿAlī defeated them at the Battle of al-Nahrawān in 38/658. Ibn Muljam, who assassinated ʿAlī in 40/661, was a Khārijite.

409 For his lineage, on which there is considerable confusion, see *ǦN*, i, 271 and ii, 129. Tajūb is not found in his line, but he belonged to Tadūl, a branch of Murād. One wonders if al-Tajūbī is a corruption of al-Tadūlī. On him and the story of ʿAlī's murder in detail, see e.g. *EI2*, "Ibn Muldjam" (L. Veccia Vaglieri).

410 See *ǦN*, ii, 229; there is some confusion about the name and lineage of Muʿāwiyah's would-be assassin.

بن بُكَيْر التميميّ، وهو صاحب عمرو بن العاص، اجتمعوا جميعاً بمكّة فتذاكروا أهلَ النَّهْرَوان فترحّموا عليهم وقالوا: واللّهِ ما نَعْبأ بالبَقاء في الدنيا شيئاً بعد إخواننا الذين كانوا لا يَخافون في اللّه لَوْمةَ لائم، وكانوا مَصابيحَ الهُدى. ثمّ ذكروا الناسَ فعابوا عليهم أفعالَهم، وقالوا: [لو]١ أنّا شرَيْنا أنفسَنا للّه والْتمَسْنا غِرّةَ هؤلاء الأَئِمّة الضُّلّال فثأرْنا بهم إخوانَنا، وأَرَحْنا منهم العِباد. فقال عبد الرحمن: أنا لكم لعليّ، وقال البُرَك: أنا لكم لمعاوية، وقال عمرو بن بُكير: أنا لكم لعمرو بن العاص. فتعاهَدوا على ذلك وتواثَقوا لا يَنْكُص رجلٌ منهم عن صاحبه الذي سمّاه حتّى يقتلَه
١٦١ أو يموتَ دونه. فاتّعدوا في شهر رمضان ليلة سبْعَ عَشْرةَ ثمّ افترقوا على | ذلك، وتوجّه كلُّ رجل منهم إلى المِصر الذي فيه صاحُبه، وكان عليٌّ رضي اللّه عنه قد ضَجِرَ من أهل الكوفة، وكان كثيراً ما يدعو عليهم، وكان كثيراً ما يُنْشِد إذا آذَوْه:

خَلُّوا سبيلَ العَيْر يأْتِ أهْلَه   سوفَ تَرَوْن فِعْلَكم وفِعْلَه

وكان كثيراً ما يقول:

لا شيءَ إلّا اللّه فارفَعْ ظَنَّكا   يَكْفيك رَبُّ الناس ما أهمَّكا

---

١ كذا في هـ، ك؛ والتكملة من تاريخ الطبريّ، ويقتضيها السياق.

---

411 On this ʿAmr ibn Bukayr there is again some confusion as to his name and identity. In some sources he is a Persian called Zādawayh (or Zādhawayh). On the conspirators see the above-mentioned entry "Ibn Muldjam" in *EI2*.

412 ʿAmr ibn al-ʿĀṣ (d. 42/662 or 43/664), of Sahm, a branch of Quraysh, was a companion of the Prophet and one of the leading generals during the first wave of conquests; he conquered Egypt during ʿUmar's reign and became a strong and shrewd supporter of Muʿāwiyah in his conflict with ʿAlī.

Bukayr al-Tamīmī,[411] who was a companion of ʿAmr ibn al-ʿĀṣ.[412] They talked about those who had died at al-Nahrawān,[413] imploring God for mercy on them. "By God", they said, "We do not care about staying alive in this world now that our brothers have died, who «did not fear» for the sake of God «the blame of any blamer»![414] They were the lamps of the Right Guidance!" They talked about people, denouncing their actions. They said, "What if we give our lives to God, seeking to get at those errant leaders unawares, avenge our brothers, and rid God's servants of them!" ʿAbd al-Raḥmān said, "I'll deal with ʿAlī for you", al-Burak said, "I'll deal with Muʿāwiyah for you", and ʿAmr ibn Bukayr said, "I'll deal with ʿAmr ibn al-ʿĀṣ for you." They made pledges to that effect, affirming that none of them would let the others down, each one either killing his assigned victim or dying in the attempt. They agreed on carrying out their plans on the eve of the seventeenth of the month of Ramadan.[415] Then they dispersed. | Each 161
man went to the town where his intended victim was. ʿAlī (*r*) was annoyed with the Kufans, often cursing them.[416] Often, when they thwarted him, he would recite:[417]

> Let the wild ass run free and it will go to its kin;
> You will see what you do and what it does!

He would also often say,[418]

> There is nothing but God. Leave your assumptions!
> The Lord of People will protect you from your worries.

---

413 A town east of the Tigris in Iraq, where ʿAlī defeated the Khārijites.

414 Q al-Māʾidah 4:54.

415 This corresponds to January 24, AD 661; other dates are also mentioned.

416 Kufa, in Iraq, had been ʿAlī's main residence after he left Medina to fight al-Zubayr ibn al-ʿAwwām (above, § 32), but he had great trouble in keeping his coalition together after the Battle of Ṣiffīn.

417 This couplet in *rajaz* metre, the interpretation of which is not wholly obvious, has not been found elsewhere except in a later anthology, al-Afṭasī (d. 515/1121), *al-Majmūʿ al-lafīf*, 242. It is not found in ʿAlī's *Dīwān* (collected verse); the verb *anshada* ("to recite") suggests that he is quoting an unknown poet. The wild ass or onager (*ʿayr*) is apparently a metaphor for the unruly Kufans.

418 Another *rajaz* couplet, found in ʿAlī's *Dīwān*, 139.

وكان يقول أيضاً:

خَلُّوا سبيل الجاهدِ المُجاهدِ أَبَيْتُ أنْ أعبُدَ غيرَ الواحدِ

وكان يقول:

فأيَّ يومَيَّ من الموتِ أَفِرّْ أيومَ لم يُقْدَرَ أمْ يومَ قُدِرْ

وكان يقول: ما يَحبِس أشقاها، أما واللّٰهِ لَعَهِدَ إلى النبيّ الأُمّيّ صلّى الله عليه وسلّم أنّ هذه تُخْضَب من هذه، يعْني لِحْيته من هامته؛ وكان يقول:

اشْدُدْ ...

... حَيازيمَكَ للموْتِ فإنَّ الموتَ آتيكا
ولا تَجْزَعْ من الموتِ إذا حلَّ بِوادِيكا

فلمّا كانت الليلةُ التي اتَّعدوا لها، وكانت ليلةَ الجُمعة، بات ابن مُلْجَم في مسجد الجامعة بجنْب الأشْعَث بن قيْس الكِنْديّ.

وكان عليّ رضي الله عنه رأى في تلك الليلة[١] رؤيا فخبَّر بها أبا عبد الرحمن السُّلَميّ وهو مجروح، فذكر أبو عبد الرحمن وكان مؤدِّبَ الحَسَن والحُسين رضي الله عنهما، قال: دخلتُ

١ ك: (الليل).

419 The couplet is found in ʿAlī's *Dīwān*, 60.

420 *Al-jāhid al-mujāhid.*

421 A couplet found in ʿAlī's *Dīwān*, 79; al-Buḥturī, *Ḥamāsah*, 51; Ibn ʿAbd Rabbih, *ʿIqd*, i, 105, v, 274, 287; al-Masʿūdī, *Murūj*, iii, 133. It was discussed by grammarians (e.g. Abū Zayd, *Nawādir*, 164; Ibn Jinnī, *Khaṣāʾiṣ*, iii, 94, Ibn Manẓūr, *Lisān al-ʿArab* [QDR]) because of the irregular *yuqdara*, required by the metre, instead of *yuqdar*.

422 An echo of Q al-Shams 91:12, «Then the most wretched of them rose up», on the pre-Islamic people of Thamūd, who slaughtered the God-given camel.

And he would say,[419]

> Let him who struggles strenuously[420] run free!
> I refuse to worship any but the One.

And he would say,[421]

> On which of two days can I flee from death,
> A day that is not predestined or a day that is predestined?

He also used to say, "What can hold back the most wretched man of them?[422] By God, the Prophet who did not read or write[423] (ṣ) has pledged that this …" (meaning his beard) "… would be dyed by that!" (meaning his head).[424] He also used to say,[425]

> Strengthen
> Your breast for death,
> for death will come to you.
> Be not afraid of death
> when it lodges in your valley.

On the evening they had agreed upon, which was the eve of Friday, Ibn Muljam spent the night in the congregational mosque at the side of al-Ashʿath ibn Qays al-Kindī.[426]

In that night ʿAlī (*r*) had a dream, which he told to Abū ʿAbd al-Raḥmān al-Sulamī[427] when he was lying wounded. Abū ʿAbd al-Raḥmān, who was the

---

423 On the somewhat ambiguous term *ummī*, see *EI2*, "ummī" (E. Geoffroy). It could mean "illiterate" in the sense that Muḥammad did not know, or did not have to know, earlier scriptures. It has also been interpreted as "sent to the Gentiles" (cf. *ummah*, "nation").

424 i.e., his beard will be soaked with blood streaming from his head.

425 These lines in *hazaj* metre are quoted in many sources (al-Mubarrad, *Kāmil*, iii, 39; Ibn Saʿd, *Ṭabaqāt*, iii, 31; al-Iṣfahānī, *Aghānī*, xv, 229, idem, *Maqātil*, 45, ʿAlī ibn Abī Ṭālib, *Dīwān*, 140; etc.); the opening word *ushdud* is extra-metrical, a rare occurrence.

426 Maʿdīkarib ibn Qays, nicknamed al-Ashʿath ("Rumple-hair") or al-Ashajj ("Scarface"), a chief of the tribe of Kindah and leading figure in Kufa, a supporter of ʿAlī though preferring peace rather than the latter's supremacy. He died in 40/661, a few weeks after ʿAlī. See *ĞN*, i, and ii, 381, *EI3*, "al-Ashʿath b. Qays" (Khalid Yahya Blankinship).

427 Abū ʿAbd al-Raḥmān ʿAbd Allāh ibn Ḥabīb al-Sulamī (d. in the 80s/between 699 and 707), noted for his knowledge of the Qurʾan; see Ibn Qutaybah, *Maʿārif*, 528, al-Ṣafadī, *Wāfī*, xvii, 121.

عليه وهو مجروح فقال: ادْنُ مِنّي يا أبا عبد الرحمن، والنساءُ يَبْكِينَ، فدنَوْتَ منه فقال لي:
بِتُّ الليلةَ أُوقِظ أهلي، فمَلَكَتْني عَيْني وأنا جالس، فسنح لي رسولُ اللّٰه صلّى اللّٰه عليه وسلّم | ١٦٢
فقلتُ: يا رسولَ اللّٰه، ما لقِيتُ من أُمَّتِك من الأَوَد واللَّدَد! فقال: ادْعُ عليهم.[١] فقلت: اللّٰهُمَّ
أَبْدِلْني بهم مَن هو خيرٌ لي منهم، وأبدلْهم بي مَن هو شرٌّ منّي! ودخل ابن التَّيّاح المؤذِّن على
ذلك، فقال: الصلاة. فأخذتُ بيده، فمشى ابن التيّاح بين يديَّ وأنا خّلْفَه.

(ورجع الحديث) قال: فقال الأشعث لابن مُلْجَم: فَضَحَك الصُّبْحُ! فانطلق ابن ملجم،
وشَبيب بن بَجَرة الأَشْجَعيّ وخرج عليٌّ من منزله وهو يقول: أيُّها الناس الصلاةَ، أيّها الناس
الصلاة! فضربه ابن ملجم ضربةً من جَبْهته إلى قَرْنه، وأصاب السيفُ الحائطَ فثلم فيه، ثمّ
ألقى السيفَ وأقبلَ الناسُ فجعل يقول: أيُّها الناس، إيّاكم والسيفَ فإنّه مسموم! فذكروا أنّه سمّه
شهراً. فأُدْخِلَ عليٌّ رضي اللّٰه عنه، وأُدْخِل ابنُ ملجم عليه فقالت أمُّ كُلْثوم بنت عليّ: أقَتَلت
يا عدُوَّ اللّٰه أميرَ المؤمنين؟! قال: لم أقتُلْ إلّا أباكِ. فقالت واللّٰهِ إنّي لَأرجو أن لا يكون على أمير
المؤمنين بأس. قال: فلِمَ تَبْكين إذاً، واللّٰهِ لقد سممْتُه شهراً، فإنْ أخْلفني فأبعدَه اللّٰه وأسْحَقَه!
ثمّ إنّ عليًّا رحمه اللّٰه قال: أَطِيبوا طعامَه، وأَلينوا فِراشَه، فإنْ أَعِشْ فعَفْوٌ أو قِصاص، وإن أَمُتْ
فألْحِقوه بي أُخاصِمْه عند ربِّ العالَمِين.

وذكروا أنّ ابنَ ملجم خطب امرأةً من الرِّباب يقال لها قَطامِ وكانت من أجملِ الناس،
وكانت خارجيّةً، وكان عليٌّ قتل أهلَ بيتِها بالنهْروان، فقالت: لا أتزوّجك إلّا على ثلاثةِ

١ ك: (ادع اللّٰه عليهم).

428 ʿAlī's two sons; on al-Ḥasan, see below, § 37.

429 First name and lineage unknown.

430 Shabīb ibn Bajarah was another Khārijite, who in other versions (see e.g. Ibn Saʿd, *Ṭabaqāt*, iii, 35; al-Yaʿqūbī, *Tārīkh*, ii, 262; al-Ṭabarī, *Tārīkh*, i, 3458, al-Iṣfahānī, *Maqātil*, 46) had been approached by Ibn Muljam to assist him in the assassination attempt. Instead of Bajarah (thus explicitly e.g. in al-Zabīdī, *Tāj al-ʿarūs* [BJR]) one also finds Bujrah (thus e.g. in ʿASH) or Najdah (thus according to Veccia Vaglieri in *EI2*, "Ibn Muldjam", 889a).

431 She was Zaynab, daughter of ʿAlī and the Prophet's daughter Fāṭimah and not to be confused with her aunt also called Umm Kulthūm, daughter of the Prophet and his first wife, Khadījah. Zaynab had been married to the second caliph ʿUmar.

432 *Qiṣāṣ*, "retaliation", in Islam is applied to cases of killing or wounding; it may be replaced by forgiveness with or without compensation. See e.g. *EI2*, "Ḳiṣāṣ" (J. Schacht).

tutor of al-Ḥasan and al-Ḥusayn (*r*),[428] said, "I went in to him while he was lying wounded. He said to me, 'Come closer to me, Abū 'Abd al-Raḥmān!' The women were all crying. I went closer to him and he said to me, 'I spent the night keeping my family awake, but my eyes got the better of me and I fell asleep, sitting up. Then the Messenger of God (*ṣ*) appeared to me. | I said, 'O Messenger 162
of God! I have encountered such deviousness and obstinacy from your community!' 'Then curse them!' So I said, 'O God, give me instead of them someone who is better to me than they are, and give them instead of me someone who is worse to them than I am!' Ibn al-Tayyāḥ the muezzin[429] then entered, saying, 'Prayer time!' I took him by the hand and we left, Ibn al-Tayyāḥ in front of me and I behind him.'"

To continue the story: al-Ash'ath said to Ibn Muljam, "Shame on you! It is light already!" And Ibn Muljam got up and was off, together with Shabīb ibn Bajarah al-Ashjā'ī.[430] 'Alī came out of his house, shouting, "People, Prayer! People, Prayer!" Then Ibn Muljam struck him one blow, from his forehead to the top of his head. The sword also hit the wall, making an indentation. Then he threw down the sword. People approached. He began to shout, "People! Beware the sword, it is poisoned!". They say that he had poisoned it for a whole month. 'Alī (*r*) was taken inside, together with Ibn Muljam. Umm Kulthūm, 'Alī's daughter[431] cried out, "Enemy of God! Have you killed the Commander of the Believers?" Ibn Muljam replied, "I have merely killed your father." She said, "I do hope, by God, that the Commander of the Believers will be all right!" "Why are you crying then?" he said, "By God, I have poisoned it for a month. If it fails me, may God remove it and destroy it!" 'Alī—God have mercy on him—said, "Feed him well, give him a comfortable place to sleep. If I live, then either forgive him or exact retaliation;[432] if I die, make him join me so that I may sue him in the presence of the Lord of All Beings."[433]

They say that Ibn Muljam had proposed to a woman of al-Ribāb in marriage; she was called Qaṭām,[434] one of the most beautiful women. She was a Khārijite; her nearest kin had been killed at al-Nahrawān. "I shall only marry you,"

433 The text omits to add that 'Alī died of his wound two or three days after the attack and that Ibn Muljam was duly executed, possibly after being mutilated and tortured as some sources tell (al-Mubarrad, *Kāmil*, iii, 39; al-Dīnawarī, *Akhbār*, 229; al-Mas'ūdī, *Murūj*, iii, 168, etc.).

434 Al-Ribāb were a confederation of five tribes of Taym, see *ǦN*, i, 85 and ii, 468 and 486. Qaṭām's brother, father, and paternal uncle had been killed at al-Nahrawān. In other versions Qaṭām asks, in addition, for a male and a female slave (see the following poem).

آلاف، وقتْلِ عليّ بن أبي طالب بعد ذلك. فتزوَّجها وبَنَى بها، فلمّا فَرَغ منها قالت: يا هذا، إنك قد فرغْت فاقْرَع! فخرج فضرب عليًّا.

وقال بعض الشعراء: ١٦٣

فلم أَرَ مَهْراً ساقَهُ ذو سَماحةٍ　　كمَهْرِ قَطامٍ من فَصيحٍ وأعجَمِ
ثلاثةُ آلافٍ وعبدٌ وقَــيْنةٌ　　وضرْبُ عليٍّ بالحُسام المصمِّمِ
فلا مَهْرَ أغْلى من عليٍّ وإنْ غَلا　　ولا قتْلَ إلّا دونَ قتْلِ ابنِ مُلْجَمِ

وأمّا صاحب معاوية فطعن معاويةَ وقد خرج لصلاة الفجْر في تلك الليلة في أَلْيَته، فلم يُولَدْ لمعاوية بعدَها حتّى مات. وبذلك السبب جُعلت المقصورةُ في المسجد الجامع.

[§ ٣٥] **ومنهم** خارجة بن حُذافة العَدَويّ، وكان قاضِيَ مصر، وكان له صلاحٌ وصُحْبة، فخرج صاحب عمرو بن العاص فوجد خارجةَ في مجلس عمرٍو يعشّي الناس، وقد كان عمرو شُغِل تلك الليلة، فدنا منه وهو يظُنّه عَمْراً، وهو على سرير عمرو جالساً، فضربه من ورائه بالسيف على عاتقه. فأُخِذ الرجل، وخرج عمرو، وحُمل خارجةُ إلى منزله مُثْخَناً، فأتاه عمرو فقال له خارجة: واللّهِ ما أراد غيرَك. فقال عمرو بن العاص: ولكنّ اللّه أراد خارجة.

435 In al-Ṭabarī, *Tārīkh*, i, 3467 the lines are attributed to Ibn Abī Mayyās al-Murādī (see also ʿAbbās, *Shiʿr al-Khawārij*, 35–36).

436 *Faṣīḥ aw aʿjam*, meaning probably "either Arab or non-Arab".

437 Instead of *al-muṣammim* ("piercing"), some sources have *al-musammam* ("poisoned"), e.g. al-Maqdīsī, *Badʾ*, v, 233; al-Ṣafadī, *Wāfī*, vii, 89, xviii, 288.

she said, "if you give a bride-price of three thousand dirhams and afterwards kill ʿAlī ibn Abī Ṭālib." He married her and consummated the marriage. Having done so, she said, "I say, man, you have done your business, now strike!" So he left and struck ʿAlī.

A poet said,[435] 163

I never saw a bride-price paid by a generous man,
either eloquent or inarticulate,[436] like that of Qaṭām:
Three thousand, a slave, a slave-girl,
and slaying ʿAlī with piercing sword.[437]
No bride-price, no matter how dear, was dearer than ʿAlī,
and no murder was lower than Ibn Muljam's.

As for Muʿāwiyah's would-be assassin, he stabbed Muʿāwiyah in the buttocks when he was going out to perform the morning prayer that night. After that, no more children were born to Muʿāwiyah before he died. This was why the reserved box in the mosque was introduced.[438]

[§ 35 Khārijah ibn Ḥudhāfah al-ʿAdawī[439]]

Another was Khārijah ibn Ḥudhāfah al-ʿAdawī,[440] who was Chief Judge of Egypt. He was pious and a Companion of the Prophet. The would-be assassin of ʿAmr ibn al-ʿĀṣ went out and found Khārijah in ʿAmr's court, where he was providing supper to the people. ʿAmr was elsewhere occupied that evening.[441] The man approached him, thinking that he was ʿAmr, for he was sitting on ʿAmr's seat. He struck him from behind with his sword on his shoulder. The man was apprehended. ʿAmr came; Khārijah was carried to his house, mortally wounded. ʿAmr visited him and Khārijah said to him, "He only wanted you!" ʿAmr replied, "But God wanted Khārijah."

---

438 On the *maqṣūrah* and the various reports on its introduction see *EI2*, "Masdjid" (J. Pedersen), vi, 661b–662b.

439 For parallels see e.g. al-Mubarrad, *Kāmil*, iii, 40; al-Masʿūdī, *Murūj*, iii, 170; al-Iṣfahānī, *Maqātil*, 44–45.

440 Khārijah ibn Ḥudhāfah (d. 40/661) was of the tribe of ʿAdī, a branch of Quraysh, see *ĞN*, Tab 26 and ii, 344. As he was a Companion of the Prophet, his biography is found in numerous sources (see e.g. al-Ṣafadī, *Wāfī*, xiii, 239). He took part in the conquest of Egypt. His bungling murderer was ʿAmr ibn Bukayr, see § 34.

441 According to al-Mubarrad, *Kāmil*, iii, 40, he had a bellyache.

[§٣٦] **ومنهم** خالد بن المعمَّر السَّدُوسيّ. وكان معاوية دسَّ إليه بالعراق أن يدعُوَ ربيعةَ إلى ١٦٤
الوثوب بعَليّ بن أبي طالب رضي الله عنه، وأن ينقُض عليه أمره، فإنْ هو فَعَل ولّاه خُراسانَ.
ففعل ذلك خالد بن المعمّر حتّى آذتْ ربيعة عليًّا وشنّعوا عليه. وبلغ ذلك معاويةَ، فلمّا قُتِل عليّ
رضي الله عنه أحبّ معاوية الوَفاء لخالد بن المعمّر. وقال بعض شعراء بني سَدوس:

مُعاوِيَ أَكْرِمْ خالدَ بن المعمَّرِ فإنَّك لولا خالدٌ لم تؤمَّرِ

فكتب إليه معاوية بعهده على خُراسان، ودسّ إليه رجلاً فسقاه شَرْبة بظهر الكوفة بقصْر بني
مُقاتِل، فقتلتْه وقد أجمع الناس على معاوية.

[§٣٧] **ومنهم** الحسن بن عليّ رضي الله تعالى عنهما. ذكره يعقوب بن الدَّوْرقيّ. قال: أخبرنا
أسعد بن إبراهيم، قال: حدّثنا ابن عوْن، عن عُمَير بن إسحاق قال: دخلت على الحسن بن
عليّ رضي الله عنهما، أنا ورجل، فقال لصاحبي: أيْ فُلان، سَلْني. قال: ما أنا بسائلك شيئاً. ثمّ
قام من عندنا فدخل كَنيفاً له ثمّ خرج فقال: أيْ فلان، سلْني قبل أن لا تسألني؛ فإنّي واللهِ لقد

442 See Ibn al-ʿAdīm, *Bughyat al-ṭalab*, 3117–3119, and briefly Ibn ʿAsākir, *Tārīkh Dimashq*, xvi, 206.

443 Khālid ibn al-Muʿammar, of the tribe of Sadūs, part of Shayban—Bakr ibn Wāʾil—Rabīʿah. See *ǦN*, i, 153 and ii, 342, al-Ṣafadī, *Wāfī*, xiii, 264. He fought with ʿAlī at the Battle of Ṣiffīn but after ʿAlī's death pledged allegiance to Muʿāwiyah instead of ʿAlī's son al-Ḥasan (on whom see below, §37).

444 Quoted anonymously in Ibn al-Kalbī, *Nasab Maʿadd wa-l-Yaman*, 55, al-Jāḥiẓ, *Bayān*, iii, 108. Ibn al-ʿAdīm, *Bughyat al-ṭalab*, 3118–3119 and Ibn ʿAsākir, *Tārīkh Madīnat Dimashq*, xvi, 206, name the poet as al-Aʿwar al-Shannī (Abū Munqidh Bishr ibn Munqidh, see Sezgin, *Geschichte*, ii, 196).

445 Called Qaṣr Muqātil by Yāqūt (*Muʿjam al-buldān*), said to lie between ʿAyn al-Tamr (N.-W. of Kufa) and Syria, near al-Quṭquṭānah (on which see above, §1, note 9). It was called after Muqātil ibn Ḥassān, one of the ʿIbād of al-Ḥīrah (§19, note 226), see *ǦN*, i, 80 and ii, 431. After its destruction in the 8th century another castle was built there, in modern times called al-Ukhayḍir (*EI2*, "al-Ukhayḍir" [A. Northedge]).

446 This sentence succinctly provides a transition to the following section about ʿAlī's son Ḥasan, who is said to have renounced the caliphate, and who abdicated having reached a settlement with Muʿāwiyah.

[§ 36 Khālid ibn al-Muʿammar al-Sadūsī[442]]

Another was Khālid ibn al-Muʿammar al-Sadūsī.[443] Muʿāwiyah had sent a secret message to him in Iraq, asking him to rally Rabīʿah against ʿAlī ibn Abī Ṭālib (*r*) and to obstruct his cause. If he were to do this, he would appoint him as governor of Khorasan. Khālid ibn al-Muʿammar did so and as a result Rabīʿah harmed ʿAlī's cause and calumniated him. Muʿāwiyah heard of this, and when ʿAlī (*r*) was killed he wanted to be true to his pledge to Khālid ibn al-Muʿammar. But one of the poets of the tribe of Sadūs said,[444] 164

> Muʿāwiyah, honour Khālid ibn al-Muʿammar!
> For but for Khālid you would not have been made to rule!

Thereupon Muʿāwiyah wrote to him, appointing him a governor of Khorasan; but he secretly sent a man to him who gave him a potion to drink outside Kufa, at the castle of the Banū Muqātil,[445] which killed him. People agreed to acknowledge Muʿāwiyah.[446]

[§ 37 al-Ḥasan ibn ʿAlī[447]]

Another was al-Ḥasan ibn ʿAlī (*r*). He is mentioned by Yaʿqūb al-Dawraqī,[448] who said: I was told by Asʿad ibn Ibrāhīm,[449] who said: Ibn ʿAwn[450] told us, on the authority of ʿUmayr ibn Isḥāq,[451] who said:

I visited al-Ḥasan ibn ʿAlī (*r*), together with another man. Al-Ḥasan said to my companion, "Sir, ask me for something!" The man replied, "I am not asking you for anything." Al-Ḥasan stood up, leaving us and entering a closet. He came out again and asked, "Sir, ask from me, before you can no longer ask from me!

---

447 Since he was a son of ʿAlī ibn Abī Ṭālib and Fāṭimah and a grandson of the Prophet, sources about him and his death are very numerous. He is said to have died as the result of an illness or from poisoning, perhaps by one of his many wives (his wives in successive marriages are reckoned in scores and his concubines in hundreds). Jaʿdah bint al-Ashʿath is sometimes named as having been bribed by Muʿāwiyah to do the deed; see e.g. al-Iṣfahānī, *Maqātil*, 60, 80–81. The date of his death is also disputed (49/669–670, or several years later). See e.g. *EI2*, "(al-)Ḥasan b. ʿAlī b. Abī Ṭalib" (L. Veccia Vaglieri).

448 This section and the one about ʿAbd al-Raḥmān ibn Khālid (below, § 39) are exceptional in explicitly naming sources. For Yaʿqūb ibn Ibrāhīm ibn Kathīr al-Dawraqī (d. 252/866) see al-Ṣafadī, *Wāfī*, xxviii, 468–469.

449 Not identified.

450 Identified by ʿASH as ʿAbd Allāh ibn ʿAwn (d. 232/846–847); al-Ṣafadī, *Wāfī*, xvii, 389.

451 See Ibn Saʿd, *Ṭabaqāt*, ix, 219, al-Bustī, *Thiqāt*, v, 254.

١٦٥ لفظْتُ طائفة | من كَبِدي، قلّبْتُها بعُودٍ كان معي، وإنّي قد سُقِيت السمَّ مراراً فلم أُسْقَ مثلَ هذا قطّ، فسلْني! قال: ما أنا بسائلك شيئاً، يعافيك اللّٰهُ إن شاء اللّٰه! ثمّ خرجْنا فأتيتُه الغدَ وهو يسوق، وجاء الحسينُ فقعد عند رأسه فقال: أيْ أخي، نبِّئْني مَن سقاك؟ فقال: لِمَ؟ لِتقتله؟ قال: نعم. قال: ما أنا بمحدِّثك شيئاً. إن يكنْ صاحبي الذي أظُنُّ، فاللّٰهُ أشدُّ نِقْمةً، وإلّا فواللّٰهِ لا يُقتَل بي بريء!

[§٣٨] **ومنهم** سعيد بن عثمان بن عفّان. وكان بلغ معاويةَ أن أهل المدينة يقولون، إماؤهم وعَبيدهم، مقالةً قد شاعت على أفواههم:

إنّ الأمير بعدهُ سعيدُ   حتّى يعَضَّ هامَهُ الحديدُ   واللّٰهِ لا ينالُها يزيدُ

وكانت أمّ سعيد أمّ عبد اللّٰه بنت الوليد بن الوليد بن المُغيرة، وكانت قاتلت عن عثمان يوم قُتل، وأصابتها جراحة؛ وأعانتها نائلةُ بنت الفُرافصة على المدافعة عنه، فجُرِحَتا جميعاً. فلمّا بلغ معاويةَ هذا القول عن سَرَعان أهل المدينة، كتب إلى سعيد بن عثمان فقدم عليه، فلمّا دخل
١٦٦ عليه قال: ما شيءٌ بلغني أنّ أهل المدينة يقولون: | واللّٰهِ لا ينالُها يزيدُ؟ وأنشد الأبيات الثلاثة. فقال سعيد: وما تُنكِر هذا يا معاوية؟ واللّٰهِ إنّ أبي لَخيرٌ من أبي يزيد، وأمّي خير من أمّ يزيد، ولَأنا خير من يزيد. ومع هذا أنّا ولّيناك فما عزلْناك، ورفعناك فما وضعناك، ثمّ صارت هذه الأشياءُ في يدك فحلّأتنا عن جميع ذلك.

452 "The Shīʿīs further maintain that Muʿāwiya tried to poison al-Ḥasan 70 times" (*EI2*, "al-Ḥasan b. ʿAlī b. Abī Ṭālib").

453 His younger brother, who was to become the Shi'ites' greatest martyr when he was killed in a revolt against Umayyad rule at Karbala in Iraq in 61/680, an event still widely commemorated by Shi'ites.

454 This son of the caliph ʿUthmān campaigned in Transoxania in 56/676 and died in Medina shortly after the death of Muʿāwiyah in 60/680. On him see al-Balādhurī, *Ansāb*, vi, 245–248; Ibn Aʿtham, *Futūḥ*, iii, 306–314; al-Ṭabarī, *Tārīkh*, ii, 177–180, tr. *The History*, xviii, 187–190; Ibn Manẓūr, *Mukhtaṣar Tārīkh Dimashq*, ix, 334–336; al-Ṣafadī, *Wāfī*, xv, 241–242.

For, by God! I have just spat out a part | of my liver. I stirred it with a stick: I 165
have been given poison more than once[452] but I have never been given to drink anything like this. So ask!" The man repeated, "I am not asking you for anything. May God restore your health, if He wills!"

We left. The following morning I came to him while he was about to give up the ghost. Al-Ḥusayn[453] also came and sat down at his head. "Brother," he said, "Let me know who gave you poison!" But al-Ḥasan replied, "Why? So that you can kill him?" "Yes!" "I am not going to to tell you," said al-Ḥasan, "For if it is the fellow I suspect, then God will wreak a stronger vengeance. And if it is otherwise, then, by God! no innocent person shall be killed because of me."

[§ 38 Saʿīd ibn ʿUthmān ibn ʿAffān[454]]

Another is Saʿīd ibn ʿUthmān ibn ʿAffān. It had reached Muʿāwiyah that the people of Medina, their slaves female and male, were repeating the following verses publicly and widely:

> By God, Yazīd will not get it[455]
> Until a blade bites his skull!
> The Commander after him is Saʿīd.

Saʿīd's mother was Umm ʿAbd Allāh bint al-Walīd ibn al-Walīd ibn al-Mughīrah.[456] She had tried to defend ʿUthmān the day he was killed and she had been wounded. Nāʾilah bint al-Furāfiṣah[457] had assisted her in defending him and both were wounded. When Muʿāwiyah heard what had been said from some people of Medina, he wrote to Saʿīd ibn ʿUthmān, who came to him. When he had entered the caliph's presence the latter asked. "What's this I hear the people of Medina are saying, | 'By God, Yazīd will not get it …'?"—he recited 166
the three lines. Saʿīd answered, "Why don't you like it, Muʿāwiyah? By God, my father was better than Yazīd's father, my mother was better than Yazīd's mother, and I am better than Yazīd! Nevertheless, we have appointed you and we have not deposed you. We have raised you and not lowered you. And now, when you hold all the power, you keep us away from all of it!"

---

455 Yazīd is Muʿāwiyah's son, who reigned after him, 60–64/680–683 and who died a natural death despite the verses. "It" apparently refers to the succession as caliph.

456 On al-Walīd ibn al-Mughīrah see above, § 26. In al-Ṭabarī, *Tārīkh*, Saʿīd's mother is called Fāṭimah ibnat al-Walīd ibn ʿAbd Shams ibn al-Mughīrah.

457 ʿUthmān's wife.

قال معاوية: أمّا قولك يا ابن أخي إنّ أبي خير من أبي يزيد فقد صدقتَ رحم اللّٰه أميرَ المؤمنين عثمان، هو واللّٰهِ كان خيراً منّي. وأمّا قولك إنّ أمّي خير من أمّ يزيد فصدقتَ، لَعَمْري لَامرأةٌ من قُريش خير من امرأة من كلب، وبحَسْب امرأةٍ أن تكون من صالحي نساء قومها. وأمّا قولك إنّي خير من يزيد فواللّٰهِ يا ابن أخي ما يسُرّني أنّ حَبْلاً[1] مُدَّ فيما بين العراق فنُظِم لي فيه أمثالك بيزيد! ولكنِ انطلقْ فقد ولّيتُك خراسان.

وكتب إلى زياد أنْ وَلِّه ثغْرَها وأقِمْ معه على الخراج رجلاً حازماً يُحصنه ويحفظه على أمير المؤمنين. فضرب زياد البعثَ على أهل السجون والشُطّار وكلّ من يلوذ من أهل المصر من داعر وما أشبهه، فصاروا أربعة آلاف، وولّى أسلم بن زُرْعة الكلابيّ على الخراج. ومضى سعيدٌ حتّى | ١٦٧
نزل مَرْو، وفوّز منها يريد سمرقند، فلمّا انتهى إلى نهر بَلْخ دعا بالعامات ليعبُر عليها. فلمّا تَحمّلوا وجازوا كان أوّل ما سمعه من النداء نداء منادٍ من غلمان العسكر: يا ظَفَر! فتفاءل بالظفر. ثمّ نادى آخر: يا عَلْوان! فقال: علا أمركُم إن شاء اللّٰه. وبدر الناسَ رُفيْع أبو العالية الرِّياحيّ الفقيه، فصلّى ركعتيْن، فكان أوّلَ مَن صلّى ركعتين من وراء النهر.

ونفذ[2] الناسُ حتى انتهى إلى بُخارى، والملكة يومئذ ببخارى يقال لها خُتُك خاتون، فصالَحها صُلْحاً معلوماً على أن تُخليَ له الطريق إلى سمرقند، وأخذ منها رُهُناً على الوفاء ثلاثين غلاماً من أبناء الملوك مُرْداً كأنّ وجوههم السيوف، وسهّلت له الطريق، والتقى هو وخاتون فقرفهما أهلُ خراسان، وغنَّوْا عليهما أُغنيّةً بالخراسانيّة، وهي:

١ كذا في هـ، ك، ولعلّ الصواب (خَيْلاً).

٢ ك: (ونفد).

458 Both Muʿāwiyah and Saʿīd were descendants of Umayyah, great-great-grandfather of ʿUthmān and great-grandfather of Muʿāwiyah.

459 The image is not quite clear and the text is likely to be corrupt. Instead of a rope (*ḥabl*) a manuscript has a mountain (*jabal*) and *Tahdhīb Tārīkh Dimashq* has horsemen (*khayl*), all three differing only by their dots. It seems that *khayl* is the original reading and that Muʿawiyah means: "I would be pleased if horsemen were lined up over Iraq with people like you together with Yazīd!" Compare the variants of this dialogue in Ibn Qutaybah, *al-Imāmah wa-l-siyāsah*, i, 214, where Muʿāwiyah laughs and says, "By God! How I would love (*mā aḥabba*) my house to be filled with men like you instead of Yazīd!", and in al-Ṭabarī, *Tārīkh*, ii, 178: "How I would love the Ghūṭah (a region near Damascus) to be stuffed with men like you for Yazīd!"

Muʿāwiyah replied, "Nephew,[458] when you say, 'My father was better than Yazīd's father', you are right, may God have mercy on ʿUthmān, the Commander of Believers, for, by God, he was better than me. When you say, 'My mother was better than Yazīd's mother', you are right, for upon my life! a woman from Quraysh is better than a woman from Kalb. It is enough for a woman to be one of the good women of her tribe. But when you say, 'I am better than Yazīd', by God, I would not like it if a rope would be extended over all Iraq and those like you strung upon it for me with Yazīd.[459] But leave; I appoint you as governor over Khorasan."

He wrote on his behalf to Ziyād:[460] "Appoint him as governor of the border territory and send with him a judicious man in charge of the land tax (*kharāj*), someone who will keep it safe and preserve it for the Commander of Believers." Ziyād enlisted for the expedition prisoners, villains (*shuṭṭār*), every scoundrel from the city[461] who sought refuge with him, and the like. They amounted to four thousand. He appointed Aslam ibn Zurʿah al-Kilābī in charge of the land
tax. Saʿīd left and | reached Marw. He set out to travel through the desert to 167
Samarqand. When he reached the river of Balkh he called for rafts to cross the river. When they had boarded and crossed, the first thing that he heard was the call of some of the slaves in the army, "Ẓafar!"[462] He took this as a favourable omen. Then another shouted, "ʿAlwān!" Saʿid said, "Your fortune will rise (*ʿalā*), if God wills!" Rufayʿ Abū l-ʿĀliyah al-Riyāḥī,[463] the jurist, took the initiative and performed two *rakʿah*s of ritual prayer;[464] he was the first to do this in Transoxania.

They continued their journey and reached Bukhara. At the time the queen of Bukhara was called Khunuk[465] Khātūn. Saʿīd made a pact with her, which allowed him to proceed to Samarqand. To ensure loyalty he took as hostages from her thirty young men of royal blood, beardless, their faces white like swords. The queen gave him an easy passage. He met the Khātūn, but the Khorasanis had misgivings about their behaviour and sang a song about them in the language of Khorasan, as follows:

---

460 Ziyād ibn Abīh, (d. 53/673), Muʿāwiyah's governor over Iraq and the eastern provinces.

461 *Al-miṣr*, apparently meaning Basra.

462 *Ẓafar*, here apparently a man's name but meaning "victory".

463 Rufayʿ ibn Mihrān Abū l-ʿĀliyah al-Riyāḥī al-Baṣrī (d. 90/708–709), a *mawlā*. See al-Ṣafadī, *Wāfī*, xiv, 138–139.

464 A *rakʿah* is a sequence of movements as part of a *ṣalāt* or ritual prayer. The regular morning prayer consists of two *rakʿahs*, as do some prayers for special occasions, such as being on a journey.

465 *Kh.y.l* in Ibn Aʿtham, *Futūḥ*, iii, 310.

كور[١] خمير آمذ خاتون دروغ كنده

فمضى إلى سمرقند فظَفِر وقتل وسبى ثلاثين ألف رأس، ثمّ رجع فلمّا انتهى إلى بُخارى قالت له الملكة خنك خاتون: اردُدْ عليَّ الرهون فقد سلّمك اللّٰه. فقال: إنّي أخاف غدْرك حتّى أقطعَ النهر. فلمّا قطع النهر بعثت إليه اردُدْهم. قال: حتى أنزلَ مَرْو. فمضى بهم ولم يردُدْهم
عليها. ومضى قافلاً إلى المدينة، | فجعل أولئك الرُّهُنَ فلّاحين في نخلٍ له وحَرْثٍ بالمدينة، ١٦٨
فأتاهم يوماً يتعهّد مالَه فاغتالوه فقتلوه،[٢] وَجَؤوه بخناجرهم.

وبلغ الخبرُ أهلَ المدينة فساروا إليهم فحصروهم في جبلٍ هناك، ولم يُقْدِموا على حرْبهم حتّى ماتوا في ذلك الجبل عَطَشاً. فجعلت ابنةُ سعيد جاريةً لها يُقال لها مَردانة في رِحالة فقالت: مَن يبكي أبي ببيْتين شِعْرُهما في نفسي فله هذه الجاريةُ بما عليها. فقال في ذلك الشعراءُ فلم يصنعوا شيئاً، فقال خُليْد عَيْنَيْن العبْديّ:

يا عينُ أَذْري دَمعةً وابْكي الشَّهيدَ ابنَ الشَّهيدِ
فلقد قُتلتَ بغِرّةٍ وجلبتَ حَتْفَك من بعيدِ

فلمّا قالهما قالت: إن هذانِ[٣] اللّذان كانا في نفسي. وأعطتْه الجاريةَ برِحالتها.

١ ك: (كورع).

٢ الكلمة ناقصة في ك.

٣ كذا.

466 As the editor's note says, *kūr* means "blind"; if read *gawr* it means "unbeliever". Since Saʿīd was one-eyed, *aʿwar* (al-Haytham ibn ʿAdī, *ʿUmyān*, in al-Jāḥiẓ, *Burṣān*, 567; al-Jāḥiẓ, *Burṣān*, 90–91; Ibn Ḥabīb, *Muḥabbar*, 302), *kūr* seems the better reading. But the line is likely to be corrupt and its interpretation unknown. Even the language is uncertain: it has been argued that it is Sogdian rather than Persian or Khorasanian. See the discussions (in Persian) at https://parsianjoman.org/?p=2604 and http://www.bbc.com/persian/arts/story/2004/08/printable/040826_mj-taj-bukhara-oldpoem.shtml (I thank Dr Anna Livia Beelaert, Leiden, for summarising the discussion for me).

Kūr khamīr āmad durūgh kandah.[466]

Saʿīd went on to Samarqand, which he conquered, killing or taking captive thirty thousand people;[467] then he went back. When he reached Bukhara, Queen Khunuk Khātūn said to him, "Give me my hostages back! God has preserved you." Saʿid replied, "I fear that you may betray me before I cross the river." When he had crossed the river she sent him a message saying "Give them back!" He answered, "Let me reach Marw first." He went on with them without returning them to her and travelled back to Medina. | He turned those hostages into 168
farmers on a date palm plantation of his and on farmland in Medina. One day he came to them to look after his property. They murdered him, stabbing him with their daggers.

When the people of Medina learned this they went to them and surrounded them on a mountain in the neighbourhood. They did not attack them but let them die of thirst on that mountain. Saʿīd's daughter mounted a slave-girl of hers called Mardānah on a camel saddle and said, "Whoever will lament my father in two lines of verse that are in my mind will have this girl and what she is wearing!" Several poets came up with something but without success. Then Khulayd ʿAynayn al-ʿAbdī said:[468]

Shed a tear, my eye
  and weep for the martyr, son of a martyr!
You were killed unawares,
  having brought your death from afar.

When he had uttered the lines she said, "These verses were in my mind!" She gave him the slave-girl with the saddle and all.

---

467 Saʿīd's conquest is somewhat doubtful. "The Muslim Arabs do not appear for certain in the affairs of Samarḳand until the time of the governor of K͟hurāsān, Ḳutayba b. Muslim", *EI2*, "Samarḳand" (H.H. Schaeder & C.E. Bosworth). Qutaybah's siege of Samarqand took place in 93/712.

468 On him, a poet from Hajar, see Ibn Sallām, *Ṭabaqāt*, 345, 385; al-Jāḥiẓ, *Ḥayawān*, i, 266; Ibn Qutaybah, *Shiʿr*, 463. ʿAynayn ("Two Wells") refers to a locality. In *al-Aghānī*, ii, 253 these verses, with a third, are said by Ibn Sayḥān, better known as Ibn Arṭāh, and it is Saʿīd's mother, not his daughter, who asks for an elegy. In al-Zawzanī, *Ḥamāsat al-ẓurafāʾ*, 80, the two lines by Khulayd ʿAynayn are said to be not on Saʿīd but on ʿAmr, another son of ʿUthmān.

[§ ٣٩] **ومنهم** عبد الرحمن بن خالد بن الوليد بن المُغِيرة المخزوميّ. ذكر الكَلْبيّ عن خالد بن سعيد[1] عن أبيه [أنّ][2] معاوية قال لأهل الشام لمّا أراد البَيْعة ليَزيدَ: إنّ أمير المؤمنين قد كَبِرتْ سِنُّه، ودنا من أَجَله، وقد أراد أن يولّي الأمر رجلاً من بعدِه فماذا تَرَوْن؟ فقالوا: عليك بعبد الرحمن بن خالد بن الوليد. وكان فاضلاً؛ فسكت معاوية وأضمرها في نفسه. ثمّ إنّ | عبد الرحمن ١٦٩
اشتكى، فدعا معاويةُ ابنَ أُثال الطبيب، وكان من عُظماء الروم، فقال: ائتِ عبدَ الرحمن فانعَتْ له. فأتاه فسقاه شربة انحرف منها عبد الرحمن ومات. فقال معاوية حين بلغه موتُه: لا جَدَّ إلّا ما أنفض عنك ما تَكْرَه. ثمّ إنّ كعب بن جُعَيل التَّغْلِبيّ وكان صديقاً لعبد الرحمن بن خالد دخل على معاوية فقال له: قد كنتَ صديقاً لعبد الرحمن بن خالد فما الذي قلتَ فيه؟ قال: قلت:

ألا تبكي وما ظلمتْ قُريشٌ   بإعوال البُكاء على فتاها
ولو سُئلتْ دمشقُ وأهلُ حِمْصٍ   وبُصْرى مَن أتاح لكمْ[3] قُراها

١ هـ، ك: (يزيد)، والتصحيح من المنمّق لابن حبيب ومصادر غيره.
٢ الكلمة ليست في النسختين.
٣ ك: (لكن).

469 On him see *EI2*, "ʿAbd al-Raḥmān b. Khālid" (H.A.R. Gibb) and *EI3*, "ʿAbd al-Raḥmān b. Khālid b. al-Walīd" (Eric J. Hanne). He was the son of the famous general Khālid ibn al-Walīd (d. 21/642). Under Muʿāwiyah he became governor of Homs but his popularity caused his death in 46/666 as described below. He belonged to Makhzūm, a prominent clan of Quraysh (for his lineage see *ǦN*, i, 23). For parallel texts see e.g. Ibn Ḥabīb, *Munammaq*, 360–362; Muṣʿab ibn al-Zubayr, *Nasab Quraysh*, 324–326; al-Balādhurī, *Ansāb*, x, 210–211; al-Ṭabarī, *Tārīkh*, ii, 82–83, tr. *The History*, xviii, 88–89; al-Iṣfahānī, *Aghānī*, xvii, 197–198; al-ʿAskarī, *Awāʾil*, 159–160; idem, *Jamharah*, ii, 301; al-Maydānī, *Majmaʿ*, ii, 255; Ibn Abī Uṣaybiʿah, *ʿUyūn al-anbāʾ*, ed. Savage-Smith, ii, 326, tr. iii, 322, ed. Müller, i, 118; al-Ṣafadī, *Wāfī*, xviii, 143–144.

470 The historian and genealogist Hishām ibn Muḥammad al-Kalbī (d. 204/819).

471 ʿASH and SKḤ: Khālid ibn Yazīd (suggesting that this is Muʿāwiyah's grandson, son of his successor Yazīd, which is obviously incorrect). It is Khālid ibn Saʿīd ibn ʿAmr ibn Saʿīd ibn al-ʿĀṣ, as in Ibn Ḥabīb's *Munammaq*, 360, al-ʿAskarī, *Jamharah*, ii, 301, and other sources.

[§ 39 ʿAbd al-Raḥmān ibn Khālid ibn al-Walīd[469]]

Another is ʿAbd al-Raḥmān ibn Khālid ibn al-Walīd ibn al-Mughīrah al-Makhzūmī. Ibn al-Kalbī[470] mentions on the authority of Khālid ibn Saʿīd,[471] on the authority of his father, that when Muʿāwiyah wanted the Syrians to pledge allegiance to Yazīd he said to them, "The Commander of Believers is old and his end is nigh. Now he wants to appoint a man to rule after him. What do you think?" They said, "You should appoint ʿAbd al-Raḥmān ibn Khālid ibn al-Walīd!" He was an excellent candidate. Muʿāwiyah said nothing but kept a grudge in his heart. Then it happened | that ʿAbd al-Raḥmān suffered from some complaint. 169
Muʿāwiyah summoned Ibn Uthāl the physician,[472] one of the important Byzantines,[473] and said to him, "Go to ʿAbd al-Raḥmān and prescribe a medicine for him." Ibn Uthāl went to him and gave him a potion that upset ʿAbd al-Raḥmān's constitution, and he died. When Muʿāwiyah heard of his death he said, "There is good fortune to compare with one that removes what you dislike."[474]

Kaʿb ibn Juʿayl al-Taghlibī,[475] who was a friend of ʿAbd al-Raḥmān ibn Khālid, visited Muʿāwiyah, who said to him, "You were a friend of ʿAbd al-Raḥmān ibn Khālid. What have you composed on him?" He replied, "I said:

> Ah, the Quraysh weep—and they do not do wrong—
> bewailing their hero.
> If Damascus were asked, or the people of Homs
> or Buṣrā:[476] 'Who has granted you its villages?'

---

472 He was a Christian physician in Damascus, a favourite of Muʿāwiyah because, as Ibn Abī Uṣaybiʿah explains (*ʿUyūn al-anbāʾ*, ed. Savage-Smith, ii, 322, tr. iii, 317; ed. Müller, i, 116–117), he "possessed extensive knowledge of the properties of simples and compound medicines, including highly toxic ones. Many prominent Muslims and persons of rank died of poisoning in Muʿāwiyah's time." In Sezgin, *Geschichte*, iii, 204–205 his name is given as Ibn Athāl. Al-Ṭabarī mentions that Ibn Uthāl was killed in retaliation by ʿAbd al-Raḥmān's son Khālid.

473 *Min ʿuẓamāʾ al-Rūm*; but his father's name seems to be Arabic.

474 This saying is found in collections of proverbs (al-ʿAskarī, *Jamharah*, ii, 301; al-Maydānī, *Majmaʿ*, ii, 255; al-Zamakhsharī, *Mustaqṣā*, ii, 261). Instead of *anfaḍa ... mā takrahu* "removes ... what you dislike", all other versions (including Ibn Ḥabīb's *Munammaq*) have *aqʿaṣa ... man takrahu* "kills on the spot ... whom you dislike", which is no doubt the original version.

475 A poet, born before Islam, close to Muʿāwiyah. He is said to have died at a good age during the caliphate of ʿAbd al-Malik (reg. 86–96/705–715). See Sezgin, *Geschichte*, ii, 162–163; for his genealogy see *ǦN*, i, 165.

476 Ancient Bostra, in southern Syria.

فسيفُ اللّٰه أدخلَها المنايا وهدَّم حِصنها وحَمَى حِماها
وأسكنها معاويةَ بن حربٍ وكانت أرضُه أرضاً سِواها

[§ ٤٠] **ومنهم** شَيْبان بن عبد شمس بن شِهاب، أحد بني ربيعة بن كعب بن سعد، وكان صاحبَ شُرطة عُبيد اللّٰه بن زياد بن أبيه، وكان عُبيد اللّٰه يُكثر القتل في الخوارج، فأقبل شيبان منصرفاً إلى منزله معه ثمانية بنين له، فعرض له ناس من الخوارج فقالوا: لنا حاجة. فقال: أضع ثيابي وأخرج لكم. فدخل وألقى ثيابه وألقى بنوه سلاحهم، ثمّ خرج فناوله بعضهم كتاباً فجعل
ينظر فيه، ووثبوا عليه فقتلوه، وخرج بنوه حُسَّراً | فقتلوهم، فخرج إليهم بِشْر بن عُتبة أخو بني ١٧٠
ربيعة بن كعب، فقتلهم جميعاً. فقال الفرزدق:

لعمركَ ما ليْثٌ بخَفّانَ خادرٌ بأشجعَ من بِشر بن عُتْبةَ مُقْدِما
أباءَ بِشَيْبانَ الثُّؤورَ وقد رأى بني فاتكٍ هابوا الوشيجَ المقوَّما

[§ ٤١] **ومنهم** عَبّاد بن عَلْقَمة، المعروف بابن أخضر المازنيّ. وهو الذي قتل أبا بِلال مِرْداس بن أُدَيّة بالأهواز. فأقبل عبّاد من الجمعة يريد منزله، حتّى إذا كان في بني كُليب خرج عليه أحدَ عشر رجلاً من السِّكّة التي تَنْحَر مسجدهم، فقام تسعة منهم في السكّة ودنا منه رجلان فقالا:

477 Sayf Allāh was the honorific name given to ʿAbd al-Raḥmān's father Khālid ibn al-Walīd, conqueror of Syria.
478 See al-Balādhurī, *Ansāb*, xii, 378, Ibn Durayd, *Ishtiqāq*, 155.
479 For this tribe see *ĞN*, i, 75; Shaybān is not shown.
480 *Shurṭah*; see *EI2*, "Shurṭa" (J.S. Nielsen).
481 Like his father Ziyād he was Umayyad governor of Iraq and the East, d. 67/686, see *EI2*, "ʿUbayd Allāh b. Ziyād" (C.F. Robinson).
482 According to al-Balādhurī and Ibn Durayd seven sons were killed.
483 Hammām ibn Ghālib, commonly known as al-Farazdaq (d. 110/728), was one of the leading poets of the Umayyad period. The lines are in his *Dīwān*, ii, 811. Bishr ibn ʿUtbah has not been found in other contexts.
484 A place near Kufa said to be roamed by lions (Yāqūt, *Muʿjam al-buldān*).
485 Fātik ibn al-Dīl is a clan of Rabīʿah ibn Kaʿb ibn Saʿd (*ĞN*, i, 75), to which Shaybān apparently belonged.
486 For parallels see al-Mubarrad, *Kāmil*, iii, 80–84; Ibn Abī l-Ḥadīd, *Sharḥ Nahj al-balāghah*, ii, 45.

Well, 'God's Sword'[477] brought death's doom to them,
he destroyed its fortress, protected its territory,
And made Muʿāwiyah ibn Ḥarb dwell there,
whose land had been another land."

[§ 40 Shaybān ibn ʿAbd Shams ibn Shihāb[478]]

Another was Shaybān ibn ʿAbd Shams ibn Shihāb, one of the Banū Rabīʿah ibn Kaʿb ibn Saʿd.[479] He was the commander of the police[480] under ʿUbayd Allāh ibn Ziyād ibn Abīh,[481] who had killed a large number of Khārijites. When Shaybān was on his way home with eight of his sons some Khārijites came up to him and said, "We want a word." "Let me take off my robes", he said, "and I'll see you then." He went in and took off his robes. His sons laid down their weapons. He went out and one of the men handed him a letter. When he started looking at
it they jumped at him and killed him. His sons came out, unarmed, | and they 170
killed them too.[482] Bishr ibn ʿUtbah, allied with the Banū Rabīʿah ibn Kaʿb, went out and killed them all.

Al-Farazdaq composed the following lines:[483]

Upon my life, a lion in his lair at Khaffān[484]
is not more courageous than Bishr ibn ʿUtbah when he advances.
He killed in retaliation for Shaybān, having seen
that the Banū Fātik were afraid of the entangled erect spears.[485]

[§ 41 ʿAbbād ibn ʿAlqamah[486]]

Another is ʿAbbād ibn ʿAlqamah, who is known as Ibn Akhḍar al-Māzinī.[487] He is the one who killed Abū Bilāl ibn Udayyah in al-Ahwāz.[488] ʿAbbād was on his way home from the Friday communal prayer.[489] When he was among the Banū Kulayb[490] eleven men came to him from the alley opposite the mosque. Nine

---

487 For his lineage see *ǦN*, i, 82; he is called Ibn Akhḍar after the second husband of his mother. Māzin is a tribe belonging to Tamīm.

488 Abū Bilāl Mirdās ibn Udayyah was a Khārijite leader who was defeated and killed in al-Ahwāz in 61/680–681; see *EI2*, "Mirdās b. Udayya" (G. Levi Della Vida), where Ibn al-Akhḍar is misspelled as "b. Akhdār".

489 Abū Bilāl's troops had been attacked in spite of an agreement between both camps not to resume fighting until after the end of the Friday prayer. The Khārijites obviously chose a Friday for their revenge.

490 Al-Mubarrad says the incident took place near "the mosque of the Banū Kulayb"; they are Kulayb ibn Yarbūʿ (*ǦN*, i, 68).

قف أيّها الشيخ نكلّمْك. فوقف لهما فدنَوَا منه فقال أحدهما: إنّ هذا أخي قد ظلمني حقّي وغصبني مالي فليس يدفعه إليّ. فقال عبّاد: استعْدِ عليه. فقال: إنّه أَوْجَهُ عند السلطان منّي. فقال عبّاد: خُذ حقّك منه إن قدرْتَ عليه. فقالا جميعاً: الله أكبر، قضيتَ على نفسك. ثمّ ابتدراه بسيفيْهما، وخرج عليه التسعة الذين كانوا في السكّة وأخذوا بلِجامه فقتلوه وحكّموا، وتنادى الناس، وبلغ الخبر بني مازن، فأقبل مَعْبَدٌ أخوه، فلمّا انتهى إلى الخوارج وهم في السكّة وعليهم السلاح وعلى جميع من معه من بني مازن قال للشرطة: خَلُّوا عنّا وعن ثأرنا. وقال لأصحابه: انزِلوا إليهم فاقتلوهم رَجّالةً في مثل حالهم. فنزلوا فاقتتلوا، فقتلوا الخوارجَ إلّا رجلاً أفْلَتَ في الزِّحام. فقال الفرزدق:

١٧١ لقد طَلَبَتْ بالذَّحْلِ غيرَ ذميمةٍ   إذا ذُمَّ طُلّابُ الذُّحول الأَخاضرُ
لقد جرَّدوا الأسيافَ يومَ ابنِ أخضرٍ   فنالوا التي لا فوقَها نالَ ثائرُ
أقادوا[١] به أُسْداً لها في اقتحامها   على الغَمَرات في الحروب بَصائرُ

[§٤٢] **ومنهم** مسعود بن عَمرو العَتَكيّ الذي يقال له قمر العراق. وكان سبب قتْله أنّ عامل البصرة كان استشاره في نافع بن الأزرق وعَطيّة بن الأسْود الخارجِيَّيْن، وكان بالبصرة،

١ كـ: (أفادوا).

491 Al-Mubarrad states that ʿAbbād was riding a mule, with a son sitting behind him (not mentioned in the present account). His father threw him down and he escaped.

492 This slogan of the Khārijites derives from an incident at the Battle of Ṣiffīn, the beginning of the Khārijī movement and (later) sect.

493 He was a son of Akhḍar.

494 *Al-shurṭah.*

495 Al-Mubarrad identifies him as ʿUbaydah ibn Hilāl.

496 Al-Farazdaq, *Dīwān*, 391 (in a poem of ten lines); al-Mubarrad, *Kāmil*, iii, 83; Ibn Abī l-Ḥadīd, *Sharḥ Nahj al-balāghah*, ii, 45. In the lines not quoted here, the poet lampoons the Banū Kulayb who had failed to come to the rescue.

497 For this sense of *baṣīrah* (here in the plural *baṣāʾir*) see al-Ṭabarī, *Tārīkh, Glossarium*, cxxxv: "[*baṣīrah*] *est ardor, inflammatio animi* (enthousiasme)".

498 He was a leader of al-Azd in Basra and was killed in 64/684. See al-Ṭabarī, *Tārīkh*, ii, 450–456, Abū ʿUbaydah, *Naqāʾiḍ*, 113, 117, and index, p. 219.

of them positioned themselves in the alley and two approached him. "Stop, Sir," they said, "We want to have a word." He stopped and they came nearer. One of them said, "This is my brother. He has wronged me, he took my money and will not give it back!" ʿAbbād said, "You must raise a formal complaint." The man replied, "But he has more influence with the authorities than I have!" ʿAbbād said, "Take from him what he owes you if you can!" Then they both cried out, "*Allāhu akbar*! You have killed yourself!" They sprang upon him with their swords, and the nine others who were in the alley came, took his reins,[491] and killed him. They shouted, "Judgement belongs only to God!"[492] People called out to one another and the news reached the Banū Māzin. ʿAbbād's brother Maʿbad[493] came to the scene. When he reached the Khārijites in the alley, who were still carrying their weapons, as were all the Māzinīs who were with him, he said to the police,[494] "Leave us, let us deal with our revenge!" To his companions he said, "Dismount, kill them on foot, just as they are!" They dismounted and fought, and they killed all the Khārijites except one, who escaped into the crowd.[495]

Al-Farazdaq said:[496]

> The sons of Akhḍar sought revenge, they cannot be faulted, 171
> if ever those seeking revenge can be faulted.
> They unsheathed their swords on the Day of Ibn Akhḍar
> and attained what no avenger can surpass.
> They killed in revenge for him, as lions full of fervour,[497]
> when they attacked, submerged in fights.

[§ 42 Masʿūd ibn ʿAmr al-ʿAtakī[498]]

Another is Masʿūd ibn ʿAmr al-ʿAtakī, called "the Moon of Iraq".[499] He was killed because the governor of Basra had consulted him about Nāfiʿ ibn al-Azraq and ʿAṭiyyah ibn al-Aswad, the Khārijites.[500] He was in Basra.[501] Masʿūd had pointed

---

499 See *ǦN*, i, 213, ii, 402, where his lineage in al-Azd does not go back to al-ʿAtīk, so that his *nisbah* al-ʿAtakī is apparently incorrect; it is al-Maʿnī in some sources. In Abū ʿUbaydah, *Naqāʾiḍ*, 720 he is Masʿūd ibn ʿAmr ibn ʿAdī with a line going back to Maʿn ibn Malik ibn Fahm. His owed his nickname to being handsome (al-Samʿānī, *Ansāb*, iv, 24).

500 On Nāfiʿ (d. 65/685), see *EI2*, "Nāfiʿ b. al-Azraḳ" (A.J. Wensinck). He was a leading Khārijite whose followers became known as the Azāriqah, see *EI3*, "Azāriqa" (Keith Lewinstein). ʿAṭiyyah also gave his name to another, less famous, sub-sect of the Khārijites, the ʿAṭawiyyah (al-Ashʿarī, *Maqālāt*, i, 176).

501 It is not clear who "he" is; perhaps instead of *kāna* ("he was") one should read *kānā* ("the two [Khārijites] were").

فأشار عليهما فحبسهما وكانا من رؤوس الأزارقة، فحقدت الأزارقةُ ذلك عليه فدسُّوا له مَن قتله، ولا يُعْرَف قاتله. ويقال: إنّه لمّا مات يزيد بن معاوية، وفُتِن أهل البصرة، وهرب عُبيد الله بن زياد، رأّست اليمنُ وربيعةُ عليها مسعوداً، فأقبل مسعود وعليه قَباء ديباجٍ أصفر، مولَّع بسواد في الأزْد وربيعة، ورأّست تميم عليها عَبْساً أخا كَهْمَس[1] السَّعْديّ، فأقبل مسعود قاصداً إلى المسجد الجامع، فصَعِد المنبر فجعل يأمر بالسُّنّة وينهى عن الفتنة، وغفل الناسُ عن السجن وفيه الخوارج الذين حبسهم ابن زياد، فجاءهم[2] أولياؤهم حتّى أخرجوهم من السجن، وكان أكثرُهم من بني تميم، فدخلوا المسجد فاغتالوه وهو غافل، فقتلوه ومضوْا من وجههم إلى الأهواز، فقال سوّار بن حَيّان المِنْقَريّ:

ألم يكنْ في قتلِ مسعودٍ غِيَرْ   جاءَ يُريد إمرَةً[3] فما أَمَرْ ١٧٢
نحن ضربْنا رأسَ مسعودٍ فخَرّْ   ولم يوسَّدْ خَدُّه حيث انقعَرْ
فأصبح العبدُ المَزُونيُّ عَثَـرْ   حتّى رأى الموتَ قريباً قد حَضَرْ
فطمَّهمْ[4] بحرُ تميمٍ إذ زَخرْ   وقيْسِ عيلانَ ببحرٍ فانفجَرْ
من حوْلِهم فما درَوْا[5] أين المَفَرّْ   حتّى علا السيْلُ عليهمْ فغمَرْ

١ كـ: (لهمس).
٢ كـ: (فجاء).
٣ كذا في نقائض جرير والفرزدق، وفي هـ، كـ: (يزيد أمرَه).
٤ كـ: (فأطعمهم).
٥ كـ: (دورا).

502 In 64/683.

503 Two important tribal groupings. Many Khārijites were of Tamīm.

504 cf. al-Mubarrad, *Kāmil*, i, 201: "'Abs ibn Ṭalq al-Ṭiʿān, known as the brother of Kahmas, of the tribe of Ṣarīm ibn Yarbūʿ"; Abū ʿUbaydah, *Naqāʾiḍ*, 732: ʿAbd ibn Ṭalq ibn Rabīʿah (with a long lineage via Ṣarīm to Kaʿb ibn Saʿd).

505 The awkward repetition of *fa-aqbala Masʿūd* ("Masʿūd came") suggests that its first occurrence, with the description of his arrival in his finery, was misplaced by a copyist, since it fits better here.

them out to him and he had imprisoned them. They were among the leaders of the Azāriqah. The Azāriqah resented this and sent someone to kill him; the killer was not identified.

It is said that when Yazīd ibn Muʿāwiyah died[502] and there were riots in Basra and ʿUbayd Allāh ibn Ziyād fled, al-Yaman and Rabīʿah[503] made Masʿūd their leader. Masʿūd, wearing a yellow robe brocaded with black stripes, came with men from al-Azd and Rabīʿah. Tamīm made ʿAbs, the brother of Kahmas al-Saʿdī, their leader.[504] Masʿūd came[505] towards the Friday mosque, ascended the pulpit, and began to command people to follow the Sunnah and to abstain from rioting.[506] The people failed to keep an eye on the jail in which the Khārijites had been imprisoned by Ibn Ziyād. Then their followers came and freed them. Most of them belonged to Tamīm. They entered the mosque and murdered him before he was aware of what was happening. Having killed him they went their way to al-Ahwāz. Sawwār ibn Ḥayyān al-Minqarī said:[507]

> The killing of Masʿūd, now wasn't there a change of fortune![508] 172
> He came, wanting to command—but he did not command.
> We struck Masʿūd's head and he fell
> And his cheek was not laid on a pillow where he bit the dust.
> The slave from al-Mazūn stumbled[509]
> And finally saw death had come close.
> A sea of Tamīm inundated them, overflowing,
> And Qays ʿAylān were at sea and it burst
> Around them. They knew not where to flee
> Until the flood rose over them, submerging them.

---

506 *Sunnah* here does not refer to the Sunnites as opposed to the Shi'ites but to proper behaviour in general; the word here rendered as "riot" is *fitnah*, originally "temptation" but often meaning "test, trial, disturbance, civil war".

507 Minqar is a branch of Tamīm (ĞN, i, 76). The lines (in *rajaz* metre) are also in Abū ʿUbaydah, *Naqāʾiḍ*, 117.

508 Instead of *ghiyar*, *Naqāʾiḍ* has *ʿibar*: "Wasn't there a lesson to be learned from the killing of Masʿūd!"

509 Although the context suggests this is still about Masʿūd, it appears to be a reference to al-Muhallab ibn Abī Ṣufrah (d. 82/702 or 83/703), a general who fought the Azāriqah. See EI2, "al-Muhallab b. Abī Ṣufra" (P. Crone). Although he is given a lineage in al-Azd with the *nisbah* al-ʿAtakī (ĞN, i, 204), he may have been of humble origin, from Oman, and was mockingly called al-Mazūnī, al-Mazūn being another name for Oman (Yāqūt, *Muʿjam al-buldān*).

وقال نافع بن الأزرق:

فتكْنا بمسعودِ بن عمرو لِقِيلهِ   لِبَبّـةَ[1] لا تُخْرِجْ من السجن نافعا
ولا تُخْرِجَنْ منه عطيّةَ وابنَه   فخُضْنا له شَوْباً من السّمِّ ناقعا
وكانت له في الأزدِ حالٌ عظيمة   وكان لِما يهوى من الأمر صانعا[2]
فقالت تميمٌ نحن أصحابُ ثأره   ولن ينتهوا حتّى يعَضُّوا الأصابعا
ويَصْلَوْا بحرب الأزد والأزدُ جَمْرةٌ   متى يصطلوها يُصبح الأمر جاشعا
فقُلْ لتميمٍ ما أردتمْ بكِذْبة   تكون لها الأوطانُ منكمْ بَلاقعا

[§٤٣] **ومنهم** محمّد بن عبد اللّٰه بن خازم السُّلَميّ. وكان عبد اللّٰه بن خازم ولّى ابنَه محمداً هَراةَ، وجعل معه شمّاس بن دِثار[3] العُطارديّ على أمره وقَفّانِ[4] حالِه وقال لابنه: لا تقطع أمراً دون شمّاس. | وقد كان ابنُ عمّ لشمّاس قُتل في الحرب النبي كانت بين ابن خازم وبين بني تميم، ١٧٣
فشرب يوماً شمّاس، فلمّا أخذتْ[5] فيه الشرابُ ذكر ابنَ عمّه ذلك فقال: لا أرى ابن السَّوداء

١ هـ، كـ: (لِبَيْبةَ) غلطاً.
٢ كذا في كـ، وأظنّها الصواب. وفي هـ: (مانعا).
٣ هـ، كـ: (زيادٍ) والتصحيح من أنساب الأشراف للبلاذريّ وتاريخ الطبريّ.
٤ كـ: (قَفَّان) بدون واو العطف.
٥ كـ: (أخذ)، مع تعليقة: "والتاء زائدة فحذفتها". وتعليقة هـ: "والتأنيث لتضمين معنى الخمر".

510 The poem is in ʿAbbās, *Shiʿr al-Khawārij*, 68–69, Ibn Ḥabīb's text being its only source.

511 Thus instead of Baybah as in ʿASH, SKḤ. Babbah was the nickname of ʿAbd Allāh ibn al-Ḥārith ibn Nawfal, a descendant of ʿAbd al-Muṭṭalib (the Prophet's grandfather). He was appointed *amīr* in Basra in 65/684. See *ĞN*, i, 7, ii, 111, al-Ṣafadī, *Wāfī*, xvii, 114–115. His nickname derives from an often-quoted song his mother used to sing to him when he was young ("I'll marry Babbah / to a buxom girl …").

Nāfiʿ ibn al-Azraq said:[510]

We murdered Masʿūd ibn ʿAmr because he said
To Babbah,[511] "Don't let Nāfiʿ get out of jail!
And don't let ʿAṭiyya get out nor his son!"
Then we mixed for him a deadly brew of poison.
He had among the Azd a mighty position
And he did whatever he liked.[512]
Tamīm said, "We shall take revenge on him!"
They will not stop until they bite their fingers in regret,
And they warm themselves with war with al-Azd: al-Azd is a glowing ember;
when they warm themselves at them, the affair will be … (?)[513]
Say to Tamīm, "What do you want with a lie
that will leave your homelands wastelands?"

[§ 43 Muḥammad ibn ʿAbd Allāh ibn Khāzim al-Sulamī[514]]

Another is Muḥammad ibn ʿAbd Allāh ibn Khāzim al-Sulamī. ʿAbd Allāh ibn Khāzim[515] had appointed his son Muḥammad as governor of Herat and sent with him Shammās ibn Dithār al-ʿUṭāridī[516] as his associate in command and to look after his affairs. He told his son, "Don't make any decision without consulting Shammās." | A cousin of Shammās had been killed in the war between 173
Ibn Khāzim and the Banū Tamīm. One day, Shammās was drinking. Under the influence of the wine he mentioned his cousin, saying, "I don't think it is right

512 Instead of *māniʿā*, as in ʿASH and ʿAbbās, *Shiʿr al-khawārij*, which I do not understand, I prefer reading *ṣāniʿā*, as in SKḤ.

513 The sense of *jāshiʿā* ("eager, desirous" or "terrified") is uncertain here. ʿASH suggests reading *khāshiʿā*, "submissive, humble", which is not much clearer.

514 See al-Ṭabarī, *Tārīkh*, ii, 593, tr. *The History*, xx, 177.

515 ʿAbd Allāh ibn Khāzim took part in an expedition to Khorasan in 31/651–652 and was its governor intermittently. He was killed c. 73/692–693 by a deputy of his. See *EI2*, "ʿAbd Allāh b. Khāzim" (H.A.R. Gibb), *EI3*, "ʿAbd Allāh b. Khāzim" (Abdulhadi Alajmi).

516 He was a leading member of Tamīm, ʿUṭārid being a branch of it. ʿASH and SKḤ incorrectly have Ziyād instead of Dithār.

قتل ابن عمّي وهو حيّ يتنعّم بيننا. فاغتال محمّد بن عبد الله بن خازم فقتله، ثمّ خرج بمن تابَعه من بني تميم، حتى انتهى إلى مَرْو، وبها عبدُ الله بن خازم.

[§ ٤٤] **ومنهم** عبد الله بن بشّار بن أبي عَقِب الشاعر. وكان رضيعَ الحسين بن عليّ بن أبي طالب، وكان يجالس عُبيدَ الله بن الحُرّ الجُعْفيّ فيخبر بما خبَّره عن عليّ رضي الله عنه، وهو صاحب أشعار المَلاحم. وكان يقول: إنّ الحسين رضي الله عنه قال لي: إنك تُقْتَل، يقتلك عُبيد الله بن زياد بالجازر.

وقال ابن الحرّ: إنّ ابن أبي عقب كان يخبرني عن الحسين رضي الله عنه أشياءَ يكذِبها عليه، ويزعُم أنّ ابن زياد يقتله. فأتاه عُبيد الله بن الحرّ ليلاً مشتملاً على السيف، فناداه فخرج إليه، فقال: ابلُغْ معي إلى حاجة لي. فخرج معه ابن أبي عقب، فلمّا برز إلى السَّبَخة ضربه بالسيف حتّى مات.

[§ ٤٥] **ومنهم** مَرْوان بن الحَكَم بن أبي العاص. وكان خطب حَبّةَ[١] بنت أبي هاشم بن ١٧٤
عُتْبة بن ربيعة بن عبد شمس، وهي أمّ خالد بن يزيد بن معاوية. فقال لها خالد: لا تَزَوَّجيه

١ هـ، ك: (حَيَّةَ) غلطاً؛ وحبّة لَقَبُها كما في أنساب الأشراف للبلاذريّ، واسمها فاختة.

517 Ibn Ḥabīb (*Muḥabbar*, 308) lists ʿAbd Allāh ibn Khāzim among "the sons of Abyssinian (or Ethiopian) women (*abnāʾ al-Ḥabashiyyāt*)"; his mother was called ʿAjlā. He is called "Ibn Khāzim, son of ʿAjlā" by a black poet in a poem boasting of eminent black people (al-Jāḥiẓ, *Fakhr al-sūdān*, 191).

518 The account ends rather abruptly.

519 He is not often found in other sources. Lines by Ibn Abī ʿAqib, usually without *ism* or *nasab*, are quoted by al-Balādhurī (*Ansāb*, iii, 406), al-Ṭabarī (*Tārīkh*, ii, 360, 678, with *nisbah* al-Laythī) and al-Iṣfahānī (*Aghānī*, vii, 71–72). In *Ansāb*, xi, 105 he is called ʿAbd Allāh ibn Yasār ibn Abī ʿAqib, a member of Banū Layth, a branch of Kinānah. Bashshār and Yasār differ only in their diacritical dots and could easily be confused.

520 See below, § 114.

521 *Malāḥim*, pl. of *malḥamah*, "epic battle, bloody fight", could refer to apocalyptic and eschatological accounts. Whatever it means here, no such poems by him are known.

522 A place near al-Madāʾin, the site of a battle between ʿUbayd Allāh ibn Ziyād and Ibrāhīm ibn Mālik al-Ashtar in 67/686; see e.g. Yāqūt, *Muʿjam al-buldān*. There is some confusion with another place, al-Khāzir (also in Yāqūt).

that that son of a black woman[517] who killed my cousin is living a life of ease among us!" and he murdered Muḥammad ibn ʿAbd Allāh ibn Khāzim. Then he and those of the Banū Tamīm that followed him left and went to Marw, where ʿAbd Allāh ibn Khāzim was.[518]

[§ 44 ʿAbd Allāh ibn Bashshār ibn Abī ʿAqib[519]]

Another was ʿAbd Allāh ibn Bashshār ibn Abī ʿAqib, the poet. He was a foster-brother of al-Ḥusayn ibn ʿAlī ibn Abī Ṭālib and he was a companion of ʿUbayd Allāh ibn al-Ḥurr al-Juʿfī,[520] who would pass on information about what ʿAlī (*r*) had told him. He composed poems about battle days.[521] He used to say, "Al-Ḥusayn (*r*) said to me, 'You will be killed. ʿUbayd Allāh ibn Ziyād will kill you at al-Jāzir'"[522]

Ibn al-Ḥurr said, "Ibn Abī ʿAqib told many lies in what he told me about al-Ḥusayn (*r*), and he asserted that Ibn Ziyād would kill him." ʿUbayd Allāh ibn al-Ḥurr went to him one evening, carrying a sword under his robe. He called him and when Ibn Abī ʿAqib came out he said to him, "Come with me, I've got something to do!" Ibn Abī ʿAqib went along with him. When they reached al-Sabakhah[523] he struck him with the sword and killed him.

[§ 45 Marwān ibn al-Ḥakam ibn Abī l-ʿĀṣ[524]]

Another was Marwān ibn al-Ḥakam ibn Abī l-ʿĀṣ. He proposed to Ḥabbah bint Abī Hāshim ibn ʿUtbah ibn Rabīʿah ibn ʿAbd Shams,[525] who was the mother of Khālid ibn Yazīd ibn Muʿāwiyah.[526] Khālid said to her, "Don't get married to 174

523 "The Swamp", a place near Basra.

524 He was the first caliph of the Marwānid branch of the Umayyads. He reigned only briefly in 64–65/684–685, at the age of at least 63, possibly over 70; al-Damīrī (*Ḥayāt al-ḥawawān*, i, 62) has 83. See e.g. *EI2*, "Marwān I b. al-Ḥakam" (C.E. Bosworth). For the story of his death see e.g. al-Balādhurī, *Ansāb*, v, 389, vi, 299–300 (followed by a different account involving poisoned milk); al-Ṭabarī, *Tārīkh*, ii, 576–578, tr. *The History*, xx, 161; Ibn ʿAbd Rabbih, *ʿIqd*, iv, 398.

525 In ʿASH and SKḤ she is called Ḥayyah, which is a corruption of Ḥabbah, her nickname, whereas her proper name was Fākhitah (al-Balādhurī, *Ansāb*, vi, 299: *ismuhā Fākhitah wa-laqabuhā li-qiṣarihā Ḥabbah*). On her father, Abū Hāshim al-Walīd ibn ʿUtbah, see *ǦN*, i, 8; al-Ṣafadī, *Wāfī*, xxvii, 473.

526 He was one of the sons of the caliph Yazīd, Muʿāwiyah's son. At the death of his brother Muʿāwiyah (II) in 64/683, he was a potential candidate for the caliphate but on account of Khālid's youth (he was still in his teens) the elderly Marwān was elected instead.

فإنّه إنّما يريد أن يَضَعَ منّي. فأَبَتْ وتزوّجتْه،[١] فتكلّم يوماً خالدٌ ومروانُ حاضر، فقال له مروان: اسْكُتْ يا ابن الرحيبة! فأُرْتِجَ عليه وخَجِل. وبلغ الخبر أمَّ خالد، فلمّا انصرف إليها قالت: قد بلغني ما كلَّمك به الفاسق. قال خالد: قد قال لي شيئاً هو أعلم به منّي. قالت: أما واللّٰهِ ليعلمنّ، فأُحِبّ أن لا يرى في وجهك غَضَباً. قال: نَعَم. فلمّا انصرف مروان إليها سكتت عنه حتّى إذا صار إلى فراشه قامت إلى مِرْفَقة فألقَتْها على وجهه، ثمّ اضطجعتْ عليها، فلم تفارقْه حتّى لَفَظَ عصْبه.

[§٤٦] **ومنهم** قَبيصة بن القَيْن الهِلاليّ. وكان سبب [قتلـ]ـه[٢] أنّ المُغِيرة بن شُعبة أُتي برجلَيْن من الخوارج فحبسهما، وكتب إلى معاوية في أمرهما، وكان المغيرة يتّقي الدماء، وكان أحدُ الرجلين من بني تميم والآخر من مُحارب، فكتب معاوية إلى المغيرة: إنْ شهِدا أنّي أمير المؤمنين فخلِّ سبيلهما، وإنْ أبَيا ذلك فاقتلْهما. فجاء بنو تميم فشهدوا على صاحبهم بالجُنون فخَلّى سبيله. ثمّ دعا بالمُحاربيّ، وكان يقال له مُعَيْن، وقبيصة بن القين جالسٌ عند المغيرة فقال لمُعَيْن: أتشهَد أنّ معاوية أمير المؤمنين؟ قال: أشهد أنّ بني تميم أكثرُ من محارب! فقام قبيصة بن القين فقال: أصلح اللّٰه الأمير، | أَسْقِني دمَه. قال: اضرِبْ عنقَه. فضرب قبيصة عنق مُعَين ١٧٥
الخارجيّ.

فمضى المغيرة، ووُلِّيَ بعده زيادُ بن أبيه، وبعده عُبيد اللّٰه بن زياد، ثمّ خالد بن أَسِيد، ثمّ الضحّاك بن قيس الفِهْريّ، ثمّ عبد الرحمن بن أمّ الحَكَم، ثمّ النُّعمان بن بَشير، إلى أن ولّي بِشر

١ (فإنّه إنّما يريد أن يَضَعَ منّي. فأَبَتْ وتزوّجتْه): ناقصة في ك.

٢ هـ، ك: (سببه)، والزيادة يقتضيها السياق.

527 "Wide one", a literal translation of *al-raḥībah*, is a shortening of "wide-cunted one". In al-Ṭabarī and Ibn ʿAbd Rabbih it is *yā bna l-raṭbat al-ist* ("You son of a wet-arsed woman").

528 *Lafaẓa ʿaṣbahu*, a somewhat unusual idiom; literally, "he spat out his dried-up saliva". In al-Balādhurī's account she is assisted by her female servants.

529 See on him al-Balādhurī, *Ansāb*, v, 173, Ibn al-Athīr, *Kāmil*, iii, 277 (year 41/661–662).

530 See above, §30.

531 On Muḥārib ibn Khaṣafah (*ĞN*, i, 92), see *EI2*, "Muḥārib" (G. Levi Della Vida).

him, for he wants to humble me!" But she refused to listen and got married to Marwān. One day Khālid was speaking when Marwān was present. Then Marwān said, "Shut up, you son of the wide one!"[527] Khālid fell silent, embarrassed. His mother heard what happened. When Khālid saw his mother she said to him, "I have heard what that wicked man said to you." Khālid replied, "He said something that he would know better than me." "O yes, by God!" she said, "He surely knows! But I would prefer it if he did not see you with an angry face." "All right!", he said.

When Marwān came home to her she did not say a thing. When he went to bed she got a pillow, put it on his face, and lay down on it, not stopping until he gave up the ghost.[528]

[§ 46 Qabīṣah ibn al-Qayn al-Hilālī[529]]

Another is Qabīṣah ibn al-Qayn al-Hilālī. He was killed on account of the following. Al-Mughīrah ibn Shuʿbah[530] was sent two men of the Khārijites and he detained them. He wrote to Muʿāwiyah about them; al-Mughīrah was averse to shedding blood. One of the two men was of the Banū Tamīm and the other belonged to Muḥārib.[531] Muʿāwiyah wrote back to al-Mughīrah, "If they testify that I am the Commander of the Believers, you must let them go. But if they refuse, kill them." The Banū Tamīm came and testified that their man was insane, and al-Mughīrah let him go. Then he summoned the Muḥāribī, who was called Muʿayn.[532] Qabīṣah ibn al-Qayn was seated with al-Mughīrah, who asked Muʿayn, "Do you testify that Muʿāwiyah is the Commander of the Believers?" The man replied, "I testify that the Banū Tamīm are larger in number than Muḥārib."[533] Qabīṣah ibn al-Qayn stood up and said, "God make the emir prosper! | Give me his blood!" Al-Mughīrah said, "Cut off his head!" Then 175
Qabīṣah cut off the head of Muʿayn, the Khārijite.

Al-Mughīrah was succeeded by Ziyād ibn Abīh, then ʿUbayd Allāh ibn Ziyād was appointed governor, then Khālid ibn Asīd, then al-Ḍaḥḥāk ibn Qays al-Fihrī, then ʿAbd al-Raḥmān ibn Umm al-Ḥakam, then al-Nuʿmān ibn Bashir;

---

532 Al-Balādhurī identifies him as Muʿayn (specifying that this is a diminutive of Maʿn) ibn ʿAbd al-Muḥāribī (it is Muʿayn ibn ʿAbd Allāh in Ibn al-Athīr).

533 Instead of this non-sequitur, in Ibn al-Athīr, *Kāmil*, he says, "I testify that God, Almighty and Glorious, is the Truth; that the Hour is coming, no doubt about it; and that God will resurrect those that are in the graves." In al-Balādhurī's account he begins with a pious sentence, adding that he hopes to be one of the pious jinnees, and ending with saying that Tamīm is nobler (*akram*) than Muḥārib. Although al-Mughīrah calls him a madman (*majnūn*), too, the outcome is the same as in the present story.

بن مروان بن الحكم، فأكرم هذا الحيَّ من قيس، وكانوا أخوالَه، ثمّ بني عامر خاصّةً، وأكرم قبيصة بن القين الهلالي، فتقدّم رجل من عُمان يرى رأي الخوارج فدخل مسجد الكوفة، فأتى حلقةً فيها قبيصة بن القين في صدر المجلس، فقال العُمانيّ ليفهم: مَن هذا؟ فقال: قبيصة بن القين خالُ الأمير. قال: ما أعرفه. فقال الرجل المسئول: هذا قاتل معينٍ الخارجيّ المحاربيّ! فأقبل على الذي يليه فسأله كما سأل الأوّل، فقال له مثلَ قول صاحبه، حتّى سأل أربعةَ نفر، فاتّفقوا على قولٍ واحد. فلمّا اجتمعوا على مَنْطق واحد انطلق إلى الصياقلة، وفي كُمّه نُفَيْقة له، فطلب سيفاً صارماً، فأُتِي بسيف من البِيض، فهزّه فإذا هو شديد المتن فاشتراه. وكانت الأُمَراء تعشّي عند العصر فلا تفرُغ إلّا عند احمرار الشمس. فخرج قبيصة بن القين من عند بِشر، فعرض له العُمانيّ فقال: أصلحك اللّٰه، إنّي رجل غريب ظَلَمني عاملي ولا أحَد لي، وقد أُخبرتُ بمكانك من الأمير. فقال: هي! وطوّلها وهو يسير رُوَيْداً، والعُمانيّ يتلفّت يريد الخَلْوة من الطريق، وقبيصة يسير رُوَيداً حتّى انتهى إلى دار السِّمْط بن مُسلم، إلى زُقاق يأخذ إلى بني دُهْن من بَجيلة، فخلا له الطريق فطرح بَتَّه وقال: لا حُكْمَ
إلّا لِلّٰه[1]، يا ثارات مُعَين! ثمّ ضربه | ضربةً أطنَّ منها فَخِذَه، ثمّ ولّى العمانيّ وأقبل الناس ١٧٦
إليه، فنادى قبيصة: إنّه لا بأس عليّ، أَدْرِكوا الرجل! فلمّا سمع العمانيّ قوله: لا بأس عليّ رجع على الناس فصاح بهم: افْرِجوا! ففرجوا له وضربه حتّى قتله، ومضى العمانيّ فطُلب فلم يُوجَد.

١ هـ: (لا حَكَم إلا اللّه).

534 On Khālid ibn Asīd, a descendant of Umayyah, see al-Ṣafadī, *Wāfī*, xiii, 246; on al-Ḍaḥḥāk ibn Qays see *EI2*, "al-Ḍaḥḥāk b. Ḳays al-Fihrī" (A. Dietrich); ʿAbd al-Raḥmān ibn Umm al-Ḥakam is identified as ʿAbd al-Raḥmān ibn ʿAbd Allāh ibn Rabīʿah by Ibn Ḥabīb (*Muḥabbar*, 380), who lists him under "the stupid people (*ḥamqā*) of Thaqīf". On al-Nuʿmān ibn Bashīr see *EI2*, "al-Nuʿmān b. Bas̲h̲īr" (K.V. Zettersteén), and on Bishr ibn Marwān, a son of Marwān ibn al-Ḥakam, see *EI2*, "Bishr b. Marwān" (L. Veccia Vaglieri). He was made governor of Kufa in 73/692–693 and died soon afterwards of an illness.

and then Bishr ibn Marwān was appointed.[534] He honoured this tribe of Qays, who were his in-laws, and the Banū ʿĀmir in particular,[535] and he honoured Qabīṣah ibn al-Qayn al-Hilālī. There came a man from Oman who was of the Khārijite persuasion. He entered the mosque in Kufa and came upon a circle of people, in which Qabīṣah ibn al-Qayn was seated in the place of honour. The Omani asked, to find out, "Who is that?" Someone answered, "Qabīṣah ibn al-Qayn, the maternal uncle of the emir." "I don't know him", said the Omani. "He is the man who killed Muʿayn, the Khārijite of Muḥārib," said the other. The Omani turned to the next man and asked the same question and received the same answer as before. In the end he had asked four people, who all said the same. When all their answers agreed he went to a sword-seller.[536] He had a small sum in his sleeve[537] and he asked for a sharp sword. He was shown a shining one. He swung it, it proved to be a strong blade, and he bought it.

The commanders had gone to have their dinner and did not finish until the sun was red. Then Qabīṣah ibn al-Qayn left Bishr. The Omani walked up to him and said, "God make you prosper! I am a stranger here. My governor has wronged me and I have no one to help me. I was told about your status with the emir." Qabīṣah said, "Yeeeaaah!",[538] lengthening it, and walked on slowly. The Omani looked about, seeking a lonely spot on the way, while Qabīṣah walked on slowly. When they reached the house of al-Simṭ ibn Muslim,[539] at an alley leading to the Banū Duhn, of Bajīlah, they were alone together. The Omani threw off his coarse robe and said, "Judgement belongs only to God![540] Revenge for Muʿayn!" Then he struck him | with a blow that cut off his thigh. The Omani 176
ran away, while people went to Qabīṣah, who called out, "I am all right! Get that man!" When the Omani heard Qabīṣah's "I am all right" he turned back to the crowd, shouting, "Make way!" They made way for him and he struck Qabīṣah until he had killed him. Then he ran off. They looked for him but he was not found.

---

535 Hilāl is a branch of ʿĀmir ibn Ṣaʿṣaʿah, part of Qays (*ǦN*, i, 92, 110).

536 A *ṣayqal* is strictly someone who polishes, burnishes, or sharpens swords.

537 Sleeves served as pockets.

538 The Arabic has *hy*, probably pronounced *hī*, or *hīī* when lengthened. It is not among the common interjections. It could be a variation of *ī* which means "yes".

539 A commander, associate of the governor Khālid al-Qasrī (*ǦN*, i, 222, ii, 513).

540 See above, § 41. ʿASH has *lā ḥakama* (instead of *ḥukma*) *illā llāh* (instead of *li-llāh*), which is likely to be an error.

فذكروا أنّه خرج بعد ذلك مع شَبيب بن يزيد الشيْبانيّ، وكان بْشر أخذ بالعمانيّ يومئذ البريءَ والسقيمَ. فلمّا دخل شبيب الكوفة والحجّاجُ أمير العراق جعل العُمانيّ يصيح: يا أهل الكوفة، يا فَسَقة، تأخذون البريء بالسقيم، أنا قاتلُ قبيصةَ بن القين!

[§٤٧] **ومنهم** بَحير بن وَرْقاء[١] السَّعْديّ. وكان عبد الملك استعمل أُمَيّة بن عبد اللّٰه بن خالد بن أَسِيد بن أبي العِيص على خراسان حيث اجتمع الناسُ عليه. فولّى أُميّةُ بَحيراً شُرَطَه،[٢] وولّى بُكَير بن وِشاح[٣] السَّعْديّ أيضاً ساقتَه، فغدر بُكير بن وِشاح بأُميّة بن عبد اللّٰه وقد عبر أميّة نهرَ بَلْخ يريد سمرقند، فعمد بكير فحرّق المَعابر ورجع إلى مَرْو فغلب عليها وجعل يَجْبيها، فرجع أميّةُ فلم يجدْ ما يعبُر عليه، فمضى إلى التِّرْمِذ ليعبر من هناك، وحاصر بُكيراً، ثمّ أعطاه الأمان، ففتح له مدينة مرو.

١٧٧ وإنّ بَحيراً وشى ببُكير وقال له: إنّه على الوثوب بك. فقال له أميّة: أنا أُوَلّيك من أمره ما تولّيت فكنْ أنت قاتِلَه. فقال له بُكير: يا بَحير دعْ أميّة يولّي قتلي غيرك، فإنّي أخاف إن فعلتَ أفسدتَ بين قومنا. فقدّمه بَحير فضرب عنقه.

وبلغ بَحيراً أنّ عشرةً من بني سعد يطلبونه بدم بُكير، فكان لا يفارق الدِّرع. وإنّ رجلاً من قومه أتى عاملَ سجستان فانتمى له إلى بني حنيفة وسأله أن يكتب له كتاباً إلى بَحير

١ هـ: (بجير بن الورقاء) وفي كـ: (بجير بن الوفاء)، والتصحيح من تاريخ الطبريّ والكامل لابن الأثير وغيرهما من المراجع.

٢ كـ: (شرطته)، كما في نسخة الشنقيطيّ.

٣ كـ: (وسّاج).

541 On Shabīb ibn Yazīd, a Khārijite leader who led a rebellion from 76/695 until 77/697, see *EI2*, "Shabīb b. Yazīd" (K.V. Zettersteén & C.F. Robinson).

542 Al-Ḥajjāj ibn Yūsuf (d. 95/714) was the most powerful, ruthless, and loyal governor of the Umayyads. See *EI2*, "al-Ḥadjdjādj b. Yūsuf" (A. Dietrich).

543 In ʿASH his name is spelled Bujayr ibn al-Warqāʾ and in SKḤ it is Bujayr ibn al-Wafāʾ; it has been corrected here following al-Ṭabarī, *Tārīkh*, ii, 1047–1051, tr. al-Ṭabarī, *History*, xxii, 197–200; Ibn al-Athīr, *Kāmil*, iv, 195–197; and other sources. His *nisbah* is also given as al-Ṣarīmī (Ṣarīm being a branch of Saʿd/Tamīm see *ǦN*, i, 76). The murder of Baḥīr took place in 81/700–701.

544 On him see *ǦN*, Tab, 11, ii, 569; he was governor of Khorasan between 74/693 and 78/697.

545 *Shuraṭ.*

They say that he rebelled afterwards, together with Shabīb ibn Yazīd al-Shaybānī.[541] At that time Bishr had apprehended every Omani, the innocent and the bad alike. When Shabīb entered Kufa, while al-Ḥajjāj[542] was the ruler of Iraq, the Omani cried out, "People of Kufa! You evil ones! You arrest the innocent instead of the bad! I am the one who killed Qabīṣah ibn al-Qayn!"

[§ 47 Baḥīr ibn Warqāʾ al-Saʿdī[543]]

When ʿAbd al-Malik had been generally acknowledged as caliph by the people he had appointed Umayyah ibn ʿAbd Allāh ibn Khālid ibn Asīd ibn Abī l-ʿĪṣ as governor of Khorasan.[544] Umayyah appointed Baḥīr as head of his police forces[545] and he appointed Bukayr ibn Wishāḥ al-Saʿdī[546] as commander of his rearguard.[547] Bukayr ibn Wishāḥ betrayed Umayyah ibn ʿAbd Allāh. Umayyah had crossed the river at Balkh on his way to Samarqand but Bukayr went there, burnt the ferries, and returned to Marw. He took the town and imposed taxes on it. When Umayyah returned he did not find a place to cross the river, so he went to Tirmidh[548] in order to cross there, and he laid siege to Bukayr. But then he pardoned him and Bukayr opened the city of Marw to him.

Baḥīr denounced Bukayr, saying to Umayyah, "He will attack you!" Umayyah 177[549]
said, "I will let you deal with him as you wish; be the one who kills him!" Then Bukayr said to him, "Let Umayyah assign my killing to someone else, for I fear that if you do it you will stir up trouble within our tribe." But Baḥīr had him brought up and cut off his head.

When Baḥīr heard that ten people of the Banū Saʿd[550] were after him seeking to revenge Bukayr's blood, he never took off his coat of mail. One man of his tribe[551] went to the governor of Sijistān[552] saying that he belonged to the Banū Ḥanīfah. He asked him to write a letter for him to Baḥīr with advice.[553] The

546 On him see *EI2*, "Bukayr b. Wis͟hāḥ" (J. Sourdel-Thomine) and *EI3*, "Bukayr b. Wishāḥ" (Elton L. Daniel). His father's name is sometimes given as Wassāj.

547 *Sāqah*.

548 Tirmidh, in present-day Uzbekistan, lies on the river Oxus, some 100 km NE of Balkh (in modern Afghanistan).

549 The page in ʿASH is wrongly numbered 178.

550 In al-Ṭabarī they are seventeen men.

551 In al-Ṭabarī he is identified as Ṣaʿṣaʿah ibn Ḥarb al-ʿAwfī (ʿAwf ibn Kaʿb being a branch of Saʿd).

552 Sijistān, or Sīstān, now in Iran and Afghanistan, is the region south of Khorasan.

553 According to al-Ṭabarī the man says he hopes the letter will help him to claim an inheritance he is entitled to.

بالوَصاة. فكتب له ولا يظُنّه إلّا حَنَقيّاً. فلمّا قدم على بَحير أدناه، فجعل الجُشَميّ[1] من بَحير غِرّةً فلا يجدها، فلبث كذلك حتّى عزل عبد الملك أُميّةَ وولّى الحجّاجَ العراقَ. فولّى الحجّاجُ المهلَّبَ بن أبي صُفْرة خراسان. فقال[2] بَحير عند رواق المهلَّب وهم في عسكر وقد أتى بَحير والناس يطلبون الإذْنَ على المهلّب إذ جاء العَوْفيّ من خلفه، الذي ذكر أنّه حنفيّ، كأنّه يُسارّه، فأصغى إليه بَحير فطعنه بخنجر كان معه فنحره به. ونادى الناسُ: الحَروريّ! الحروريّ! فرمى بالخنجر ونادى: واللّٰهِ ما أنا بحَروريّ ولكنّي اخز يالثارات[3] بُكير بن وشاح! وأُخذ الرجل وكان عيّره رجلٌ بالبادية بأن قال له: إنك لَنَؤوم عن طلب وِتْرك في بُكير بن وشاح! فجعل على نفسه أن لا يأكل لحماً ولا يدهُن رأسَه حتّى يقتل قاتلَ بُكير.

١٧٨ [§٤٨] **ومنهم** يزيد بن الحُصين بن نُمير السَّكُونيّ.[4] وكان سبب ذلك أنّ الحجّاج أُخبر عن راهبٍ بطريق الشام بعلم بارع، فوفد الحجّاجُ إلى عبد الملك فأتى الراهبَ فقال له: يا راهب، أنا الحجّاج وإنّي لَأعلم أنّي بين موت وعزل فمَن تُرى يلي مكاني؟ فنظر الراهب فقال: يلي

---

١ كذا، وهو ظاهر الغلط، والصحيح إمّا أن يكون (العَوْفيّ) أو (الحَنَفيّ).

٢ كذا ولعلّ الصحيح (فكان).

٣ كذا في هـ؛ وفي ك: (ولكني آخذ بالثاراث [كذا] بكير). ولعلّ الصحيح (ولكنّي آخذ بثأْرات بكير).

٤ هـ، ك: (السَّكْسَكي)؛ والصحيح (السَّكُونيّ) كما في المراجع.

---

554 Thus in ʿASH and SKḤ, which is clearly an error, as SKḤ points out in a note, for al-ʿAwfī or al-Ḥanafī.

555 Reading, tentatively, *fa-kāna Baḥīr* instead of *fa-qāla Baḥīr* ("and Baḥīr said") as in ʿASH and SKḤ, which does not fit the context—unless *qāla* means "he had a midday nap" here, which sounds unlikely.

556 *Fa-naḥarahū*. In al-Ṭabarī he stabs him in his side (*fa-waja'ahī bi-khanjarihī fī khāṣiratihī fa-ghayyabahū fī jawfihī*).

governor wrote it, believing the man to belong to Ḥanīfah. When he reached Baḥir the latter received him among his close associates, but although the man of Jusham[554] sought an opportunity to take Baḥīr by surprise, he did not find it. This lasted a while until ʿAbd al-Malik dismissed Umayyah and al-Ḥajjāj became governor of Iraq, and al-Ḥajjāj appointed al-Muhallab ibn Abī Ṣufrah as governor of Khorasan. Baḥīr was[555] in the pavilion of al-Muhallab, for they were in the same army camp. Baḥīr had come when people were asking permission to see al-Muhallab. Then the man of ʿAwf, who had said he was from Ḥanīfah, came up behind him, as if he wanted to say something in private. Baḥīr listened to him; then the man stabbed him with a dagger that he was carrying and cut his throat.[556] People cried, "A Ḥarūrī! A Ḥarūrī!"[557] He threw down his dagger and shouted, "By God, I am not a Ḥarūrī! Shame! Revenge for[558] Bukayr ibn Wishāḥ!" The man was apprehended. Someone in the desert had upbraided him, saying, "You are shirking from seeking revenge for Bukayr ibn Wishāḥ!" Then he pledged not to eat meat or anoint his head until he killed Bukayr's killer.[559]

[§ 48 Yazīd ibn al-Ḥuṣayn ibn Numayr al-Sakūnī[560]]

Another is Yazīd ibn al-Ḥuṣayn ibn Numayr al-Sakūnī. The story is as follows. 178[562]
Al-Ḥajjāj had been informed that on the road to Syria[561] there was a monk who possessed surpassing knowledge. When he was on his way to see ʿAbd al-Malik he visited the monk and said to him, "Monk! I am al-Ḥajjāj and I am aware that I am hanging between death and dismissal. Who do you think will take my place?" The monk reflected and replied, "Yazīd will take your place."

557 i.e., a Khārijite, after Ḥarūrāʾ, a place near Kufa, where the Khārijite movement originated in 37/658 as a protest against ʿAlī ibn Abī Ṭālib's decision to submit to arbitration between him and Muʿāwiyah.

558 ʿASH's text could be read as *wa-lākinnī ikhza yā la-thaʾrāt Bukayr*; SKḤ has *wa-lākinnī ākhidhun* (or *ākhudhu*) *bi-l-thārāth* [*sic*, with article and final *th*] *Bukayr*.

559 The murderer, Ṣaʿṣaʿah, is executed.

560 Both editions give the *nisbah* as al-Saksakī (after al-Saksak ibn Ashras, or al-Sakāsik, a South Arab tribe, see *ĞN*, i, 243); however, Yazīd ibn al-Ḥuṣayn ibn Numayr's proper *nisbah* is al-Sakūnī (see e.g. *ĞN*, i, 241, ii, 594, al-Ṣafadī, *Wāfī*, xxviii, 385). The confusion may have arisen because another Yazīd who figures in this story, Yazīd ibn Abī Kabshah, belonged to the Sakāsik. Yazīd ibn al-Ḥuṣayn was governor of Homs and died in 103/721–722. No parallels of Ibn Ḥabīb's account have been found.

562 The page in ʿASH is misnumbered 177.

561 *Al-Shām* could also refer to Damascus.

مكانك يزيد. فسأل الحجّاج سُفيانَ منجّمه عمّا قال الراهب فقال له: صدقك. فقال الحجّاج: أمّا يزيد بن أبي مسلم فليس العبدُ هناك، وأمّا يزيد بن المهلّب فخليق أن يكون، أو يزيد بن الحُصين بن نُمير فإنّه سيّد الشام.

فلم يزل يحمل عبدَ الملك والوليدَ بعده على آل المهلّب حتّى أمكن فيهم فعذّبهم وأغرمهم ستّةّ آلاف.[١] ودسّ سفيانَ منجّمه إلى يزيد بن الحُصين فقال: اكْفِنيه.[٢] فأتاه سفيانُ فلاطَفه حتّى أنِسَ به واطمأنّ إليه واختلط به، ثمّ سقاه سمًّا فقتله. فولّى العراقَ بعده الوليدُ بن عبد الملك يزيدَ بن أبي كَبْشة ثمّ وَلِيَه لسليمان بن عبد الملك يزيدُ بن المهلّب.

[§٤٩] **ومنهم** نَجْدة بن عامر الحَنَفيّ، وكان رئيس الخوارج، فوجدوا عليه بأنّه ظفر ببنت ١٧٩
عمرو بن عثمان بن عفّان فردّها إلى قُريش. وفي أنّه أمر لمالك بن مِسْمَع، وكان هرب إليه من مُصْعَب، بمائة ناقة. وأعطى عُبيد اللّٰه بن زياد بن ظَبْيان، أحد بني تيْم اللّٰه بن ثَعْلَبة بن عُكابة، وكان هرب إليه أيضاً، مثلَ ذلك. فرأّسوا عليهم أبا فُدَيك، وخلعوا نجدة، فجلس في منزله وخلّاهم.

---

١ كذا في هـ، ك، ولا شكّ أن الصحيح (ستّة آلاف ألف) كما في تاريخ الطبريّ.

٢ ك: (اكفينيه).

---

563 No such person has been found in other sources.

564 Yazīd ibn Abī Muslim Dīnār, secretary of state and governor (d. 102/720–721), was a *mawlā* (freedman) of Thaqīf, al-Ḥajjāj's tribe. See *EI2*, "Yazīd b. Abī Muslim" (Patricia Crone).

565 A son of al-Muhallab ibn Abī Ṣufrah (see above, §§42 and 47); after a chequered career he was killed in 102/720. See *EI2*, "Muhallabids" (P. Crone).

566 Walīd succeeded his father ʿAbd al-Malik in 86/705 as caliph.

567 Dirhams are meant. This paltry sum is no doubt an error and instead of *sittat ālāf* it should be *sittat ālāf alf*, "six million", as in al-Ṭabarī, *Tārīkh*, ii, 1209.

568 Yazīd ibn Ḥaywīl Abī Kabshah al-Saksakī, see *ĞN*, i, 243, ii, 594.

569 Sulaymān, an enemy of al-Ḥajjāj, succeeded his brother al-Walīd as caliph in 96/715.

570 He was a Khārijite leader in Yamāmah (eastern Arabian Peninsula). On him see *ĞN*, i, 156 and ii, 441–442; al-Balādhurī, *Ansāb*, vii, 173–187; al-Ṣafadī, *Wāfī*, xxvi, 720–721. His death occurred in 72/691.

Al-Ḥajjāj then asked his Sufyān, his astrologer[563] about the monk's words. "He spoke the truth" said Sufyān. Then al-Ḥajjāj said, "Now Yazīd ibn Abī Muslim, that slave, he can't be it.[564] As for Yazīd ibn al-Muhallab,[565] he would be eligible, or else Yazīd ibn al-Ḥuṣayn ibn Numayr, for he is the lord of Syria."

Then he kept on inciting ʿAbd al-Malik and after him al-Walīd[566] against the Muhallabids. In the end he was given power over them; he put them to torture and imposed fines on them of six thousand.[567] He sent his astrologer, Sufyān, to Yazīd ibn al-Ḥuṣayn with the words, "Deal with him for me!" Sufyān went to him and fawned upon him so that he got on intimate terms with him; Yazīd trusted him and let him into his company. Then Sufyān put poison in his drink, killing him. Upon his death, Al-Walīd ibn ʿAbd al-Malik appointed Yazīd ibn Abū Kabshah[568] as governor of Iraq. Subsequently, Yazīd ibn al-Muhallab became its governor under Sulaymān ibn ʿAbd al-Malik.[569]

[§ 49 Najdah ibn ʿĀmir al-Ḥanafī[570]]

Another is Najdah ibn ʿĀmir al-Ḥanafī, a leader of the Khārijites. They were 179
angry with him because he had captured the daughter or ʿAmr ibn ʿUthmān ibn ʿAffān[571] but had returned her to Quraysh. Also, because he had given orders for one hundred she-camels to be given to Mālik ibn Misma', who had fled to him from Muṣʿab,[572] and because he had given the same to ʿUbayd Allāh ibn Ziyād ibn Ẓabyān,[573] one of the Banū Taym Allāh ibn Thaʿlabah ibn ʿUkābah, who had also fled to him. So they made Abū Fudayk[574] their leader and deposed Najdah, who stayed at home and let them go.

---

571 ʿAmr (d. 73/692) was a son of the caliph ʿUthmān.

572 Mālik ibn Misma' (d. 72/691 or shortly afterwards) was a leading figure in Basra, of the Banū Shaybān. In 69/688–689 or 70/689–690 he fled to Yamāmah after an unsuccessful attempt to expel Muṣʿab ibn al-Zubayr from Basra; he returned after Najdah's death. See *EI2*, "Masāmiʿah" (P. Crone), *ĞN*, i, 155, ii, 391. Muṣʿab (d. 72/691), son of al-Zubayr ibn al-ʿAwwām and brother of the "anti-caliph" ʿAbd Allāh ibn al-Zubayr, was a prominent leader who had taken Basra from the rebel al-Mukhtār in 67/687. See on him *ĞN*, i, 19 and ii, 437, *EI2*, "Muṣʿab b. al-Zubayr" (H. Lammens & Ch. Pellat).

573 ʿUbayd Allāh ibn Ziyād ibn Ẓabyān killed Muṣʿab ibn al-Zubayr in the latter's battle with ʿAbd al-Malik's troops and took his head to ʿAbd al-Malik. See e.g. al-Ṭabarī, *Tārīkh*, ii, 809; al-Masʿūdī, *Murūj*, iii, 311–312; *ĞN*, i, 151, ii, 563.

574 Abū Fudayk ʿAbd Allāh ibn Thawr left Nāfiʿ ibn al-Azraq (see above, § 42), to join Najdah, after whose murder he was able to resist the caliphal troops until he was defeated and killed in 73/693. See *EI2*, "Abū Fudayk" (M.Th. Houtsma), *EI3*, "Abū Fudayk" (Keith Lewinstein).

ثمّ إنّ أصحاب أبي فُديك تذامروا بينهم قالوا: لا نأمن أصحابَ نجدةَ أن يغاوِروه، لقَدْر نجدةَ كان فيهم. فاغتالوه حتّى قتلوه في منزله.

[§ ٥٠] **ومنهم** أبو هاشم عبد اللّٰه بن محمّد بن عليّ بن أبي طالب، وكان من رجال قُريش،
وإنّه وفد إلى سليمان بن عبد الملك، ومعه عدّة من الشيعة، وكان من أشدّ أهل زمانه عارضةً
وأبْيَنهم بياناً، فلمّا كلّمه سليمان عَجِب منه وقال: ما كلّمتُ قُرَشيًّا قطّ يُشْبه هذا، ما أظُنّه إلّا
الذي كنّا نحدَّث عنه! وأحسنَ جائزتَه وجوائزَ مَن معه، وقضى حوائجه وحوائجهم، ثمّ شخَصَ
يريد فلسطين، فبعث سليمان قوماً إلى بلاد لَخْم وجُذام، فضربوا أبنيةً، بين كلّ بِناءيْن مِيلٌ وأكثرُ
من ميل، ومعهم اللَّبَن المسموم، فلمّا مرّ بهم أبو هاشم وهو على بَغْلة له قالوا: يا عبد اللّٰه[١]، هل
لك في الشراب؟ فقال: جُزيتم خيراً. | ثمّ مرّ بآخَرين فعزموا عليه أيضاً، ففعل ذلك مِراراً حتّى ١٨٠
مرّ بقوم أيضاً فعزموا عليه فقال: هَلُمّوا. فلمّا شرب واستقرّ في جوفه اللبنُ قال: يا هؤلاء، أنا واللّٰهِ
ميّت فانْظروا هؤلاء القوم مَن هُم. فنظروا فإذا القوم قد قوّضوا أبنيتَهم وذهبوا، فقال: مِيلوا بي إلى
ابن عمّي محمّد بن عليّ بن عبد اللّٰه بن العبّاس، وما أظُنّني مُدْرِكَه. فأغذُّوا به السيْر حتّى أتوْا
كُداداً من الشَّراة وبها محمّد بن عليّ بالحُمَيمة، فنزل عنده ومات بها.

١ هـ، كـ: (يا أبا عبد اللّٰه) وهو واضح الغلط.

575 Abū Hāshim, great-grandson of the Prophet, son of Muḥammad ibn al-Ḥanafiyyah, succeeded his father as leader of a Shi'ite branch. His death occurred c. 98/716. See *EI2*, "Abū Hāshim" (S. Moscati), EI3, "Abū Hāshim" (Tamima Bayhom Daou). An often discussed, and contested, account (not part of Ibn Ḥabīb's) tells that on his death (leaving no sons) he designated Muḥammad ibn ʿAlī ibn ʿAlī ibn ʿAbd Allāh ibn (al-)ʿAbbās (al-ʿAbbās being the Prophet's uncle), who is mentioned in the present story, as successor, thus legitimising the claims of the Abbasids who came to power some decades afterwards. For parallel texts on his murder, see e.g. al-Yaʿqūbī, *Tārīkh*, ii, 356–358, tr. *The Works*, 1008–1010; Ibn ʿAbd Rabbih, *ʿIqd*, iv, 475–476; al-Iṣfahānī, *Maqātil*, 123–124.

Subsequently the followers of Abū Fudayk were grumbling among themselves and said, "We cannot be sure that Najdah's supporters will pressure him into action"—because of Najdah's status with them. So they murdered him in his house.

[§ 50 Abū Hāshim ʿAbd Allāh ibn Muḥammad ibn ʿAlī ibn Abī Ṭālib[575]]

Another was Abū Hāshim ʿAbd Allāh ibn Muḥammad ibn ʿAlī ibn Abī Ṭālib, of Quraysh. He visited Sulaymān ibn ʿAbd al-Malik[576] in the company of some Shiʾites. He was one of the sturdiest men of his time and the most eloquent. When Sulaymān conversed with him he was amazed and said, "I have never spoken with anyone from Quraysh like him. I think he must be the one we have been told about!" He gave him and those who were with him handsome gifts and fulfilled his and their needs. Then Abū Hāshim went towards Palestine. Sulaymān sent some men to the land of Lakhm and Judhām[577] who erected a series of buildings,[578] each one mile or more apart. They had with them some poisoned milk. When Abū Hāshim came along, riding his mule, they said, "ʿAbd
Allāh,[579] would you like a drink?" "May God reward you well!", he replied. | He 180
came past some others who also invited him. This happened several times until he came past yet other men who invited him, and he said, "Out with it!" When he had drunk and the milk had settled in his stomach he said, "Men, I am dying, by God! Find out who these people are!" They went back to look and, behold! they had taken down their buildings and had gone. Abū Hāshim said, "Take me to my cousin Muḥammad ibn ʿAlī ibn ʿAbd Allāh ibn al-ʿAbbās; but I think I may not make it to him!" So they increased their speed until they reached Kudād in al-Sharāh, where Muḥammad ibn ʿAlī dwelled in al-Ḥumaymah.[580] There, with him, he stayed and there he died.

---

576 Umayyad caliph, reg. 96–99/715–717.

577 Lakhm and Judhām are two South Arab tribes settled in Palestine and Syria.

578 *Abniyah*; al-Yaʿqūbī has *akhbiyah nazalū fīhā*, "tents in which they camped". *Akhbiyah* could easily be misread as *abniyah*.

579 In ʿASH and SKḤ he is, clearly incorrectly, addressed as Abū ʿAbd Allāh. It is *yā ʿAbd Allāh* in al-Yaʿqūbī, even though one might have expected the somewhat more polite *yā Abā Hāshim*. One can also address any stranger as *ʿabd allāh*, "servant of God", which may be intended here.

580 Kudād, though not found in geographical dictionaries, is apparently a place-name, as in al-Balādhurī, *Ansāb*, iv, 164. Al-Sharāh, according to Yāqūt, is a region between Damascus and Medina and, as said in his entry on al-Ḥumaymah, "part of the district of Amman". The ruins of al-Ḥumaymah are in the south of present-day Jordan, see *EI2*, "al-Ḥumayma" (D. Sourdel).

[§ ٥١] **ومنهم** عمر بن عبد العزيز بن مروان رضي اللّٰه تعالى عنه. وكان أراد أن يجعل الخلافةَ
في بني هاشم، فكتب إلى الآفاق ليأتيه فقهاؤهم فيشاوروه، وجعل يرُدّ المَظالم ويُنْصف من
بني أميّة، حتّى أسرع ذلك في ضَياعهم.١ وكان بنو مروان يعظِّمون أمّ البَنين بنت الحَكَم بن أبي
العاص. ذكر محمّدُ بن الحسين قال: أخبرنا نَوْفَل بن الفُرات قال: كانت أمّ البنين إذا دخلتْ
على خلفاء بني أميّة نزلت على أبواب مجالسهم، فلمّا ولي عمرُ بن عبد العزيز دخلت عليه
فتلقّاها وأنزلها، فلمّا جلست جعل يكلّمها ويقول: يا عمّة، أما رأيتِ الحَرَس بالباب، مازحاً أيْ
إنّه لا حَرَس لي. فلمّا رأى أنّها لا تكلِّمه قال: يا عمّة، إنّ رسول اللّٰه صلّى اللّٰه عليه وسلّم قُبِض
والناس على نهرٍ مورود، فولِيَ بعدَه رجلٌ قُبض ولم يستقْضِ منه شيئاً، ثمّ ولي رجلٌ آخَرُ قُبض
ولم | يستقضِ منه شيئاً، ثمّ ولي رجل آخَر كرى فيه ساقيةً، ثمّ كُرِيَت السَّواقي حتّى جفَّ ماؤه ١٨١
وذهب، وإنْ قدرتُ لأُعيدنّ ذلك النهر إلى مجراه. قال: فقالت: فلا يسُبّوا عندك أهلَ بيته. قال:
ومَن يسبّهم؟ إنّما هو الرجل يَرفع المظلمة، فآمُر بردّها.

١ ك: (ضَياعِيهم).

581 ʿUmar ibn ʿAbd al-ʿAzīz (reg. 99–101/717–720) is the only Umayyad caliph with a wholly favourable reputation of piety and fairness among Arabic historiographers (who wrote in Abbasid times); hence the pious blessing after his name. See e.g. *EI2*, "ʿUmar (II) b. ʿAbd al-ʿAzīz" (P.M. Cobb). For al-Ṭabarī's account of his death see his *Tārīkh*, ii, 1361–1362, tr. *The History*, xxiv, 91; there is no mention of poisoning, but al-Yaʿqūbī (*Tārīkh*, ii, 370, tr. *The Works*, 1023) says it was rumoured that ʿUmar was poisoned by members of his family. See also e.g. Ibn ʿAbd Rabbih, *ʿIqd*, iv, 439 (where Yazīd ibn ʿAbd al-Malik is mentioned as the culprit), al-Suyūṭī, *Tārīkh al-khulafāʾ*, 292–293.

582 The Banū Hāshim are the descendants of Hāshim, the great-grandfather of the Prophet Muḥammad. These would include the ʿAlīds ("Shiʾites") and the Abbasids but not the Umayyads. The designation al-Hāshimiyyah, used by the Abbasids during their early days, was said to be derived from this Hāsim, but it is thought that the movement of Abū Hāshim (see the preceding story) may originally have been behind this name.

583 *Fuqahāʾ*, "specialists in Islamic Law"; but in ʿUmar's time the word probably had a more general sense.

[§ 51 ʿUmar ibn ʿAbd al-ʿAzīz ibn Marwān[581]]

Another is ʿUmar ibn ʿAbd al-ʿAzīz ibn Marwān (*r*). He intended to let the Banū Hāshim have the caliphate.[582] He wrote to all regions telling their learned men[583] to come to him for consultation. He redressed wrongs[584] and dealt without discrimination with the Umayyads, which hastened their ruin.

The descendants of Marwān[585] greatly respected Umm al-Banīn, the daughter of al-Ḥakam ibn al-ʿĀṣ. Muḥammad ibn al-Ḥusayn reports: Nawfal ibn al-Furāt[586] told us: When Umm al-Banīn came to visit the caliphs she would take up quarters near the doors of their audience rooms. When ʿUmar ibn ʿAbd al-ʿAzīz became caliph she visited him and he received her and made her stay with him. When she sat down he began to converse with her. "Aunt," he asked, "Haven't you seen the guard at the door?" He was joking, for he meant "I don't have a guard." When he saw that she did not speak he said, "Aunt, the Messenger of God (God bless and preserve him) passed away when people were all drinking from the same river. After him a man ruled who did not | appropriate 181
anything of it.[587] Then another man ruled who dug an irrigation channel.[588] Then more irrigation channels were dug and in the end the water dried up and disappeared. If I could, I would make the river run its course again."

Nawfal continued: Then she said, "And let them not curse his family in your presence!"[589] The caliph asked, "And who is cursing them?! If a man raises a complaint about being wronged, I shall give orders to redress it."

---

584 *Radda l-maẓālim*. The institution known as *al-maẓālim*, for the dispensation of justice directly by the ruler, is sometimes attributed to ʿAbd al-Malik, but it was under the early Abbasids that it became regular. See *EI2*, "Maẓālim" (J.S. Nielsen).

585 See above, § 45. Umm al-Banīn was Marwān's sister and a great-aunt of ʿUmar (who had a daughter also called Umm al-Banīn, which literally means "Mother of Sons").

586 Another of the few *isnād*s in this work. Nawfal ibn al-Furāt (or ibn Abī l-Furāt) ibn Muslim (or Sālim) Abū l-Jarrāḥ, a *mawlā*, has an entry in Ibn Manẓūr, *Mukhtaṣar Tārīkh Dimashq*, xxvi, 219. For parallels to the following, see ibid., xx, 265–266, Ibn Abī l-Ḥadīd, *Sharḥ Nahj al-balāghah*, v, 49–50.

587 Translation of *lam yastaqḍi minhu shay'an* uncertain. Other readings are *lam yastakhiṣṣa* (Ibn Manẓūr, *Mukhtaṣar Tārīkh Dimashq*, xx, 366) and *lam yustanqaṣ* (ibidem).

588 *Karā minhu sāqiyah*. A *sāqiyah* often means "water wheel" but here seems to be "channel for irrigation" (cf. Lane, *Lexicon*) and *karā* could mean "he let, farmed out", but here it probably means "to dig a bed for a river, to regulate a river" (thus *WKAS*, *Kāf*, 159a).

589 The Prophet's family are primarily the ʿAlids, many of whom opposed the Umayyads believing that the caliph (or imam) should be a direct descendant of Muḥammad through his daughter Fāṭimah and her spouse ʿAlī. ʿUmar is credited with abolishing the formal cursing of ʿAlī during Friday sermons (e.g. al-Suyūṭī, *Tārīkh al-khulafā'*, 290).

ومن غير حديث ابن معين قال: فلمّا رأى ذلك بنو مروان دسّوا حاضنه وأعطوْه ألف دينار على أن يسُمّه، ففعل. فلمّا أحسَّ[١] عمر من نفسه دعا الخادمَ فسأله فأقرّ، فقال له: كم أُعْطِيتَ؟ قال: ألف دينار. فأخذها عمر منه فطرحها في بيت المال وقال للخادم: انْجُ لا تُقْتَل. فمضى الخادم، ومات عمر.

وذكر ابن أبي شيخ أنّ مُجاهداً دخل على عمر في مرضه، فقال له: ما يقول الناس يا مُجاهد؟ قال: يقولون إنك مسحور. فقال: لستُ مسحوراً ولكنّي مسموم، سمَّني غلامي هذا. ثمّ قال له: ما حملك على ما فعلتَ؟ قال: جُعل لي عِتْقي وألف دينار. قال: هاتِ الألف. فأخذها فجعلها في بيت المال، وقال اذهَبْ فأنت حرّ.

[§ ٥٢] **ومنهم** عمر بن يزيد بن عُمَير الأُسيِّديّ. وكان يلي البصرة مرّةً، ويليها مالك بن المُنْذِر ١٨٢
بن الجارود مرّة، وكان صديقاً لمالك، فدخل بينهما رجل من بني كُرَيز فأفسد ذلك، فوَلِيَ مالك بن المنذر فحبس الفرزدق وادّعى عليه أنّه هجا نهر المُبارك، وكتب إلى خالد بن عبد الله القَسْري وهو عامل العراق يحمله على عمر بن يزيد، فكتب إليه خالد يأمره بحبسه، فبعث إليه في داره. ثمّ دسّ إليه مَن لَوى عنقَه فقتله. فلمّا كان الغد حُمل على دابّة، ورَكِب وراءه

١ كذا في هـ، ك؛ ولعلّ الصحيح (أَيِسَ).

590 Or Mu'ayn, Muʿīn. As noted in ʿASH, he has not been mentioned before.

591 The word *ḥāḍin* is more often found as a feminine noun, *ḥāḍinah*, "nurse". One would not expect a grown-up man such as ʿUmar to have a male nurse and perhaps the text is corrupt. Below, the man is called *khādim* and *ghulām*, "servant" or "slave".

592 The text has *aḥassa ... min nafsihī*, which seems to miss an object and I suspect it is a corruption of the common idiom *ayisa min nafsihī*.

593 Mujāhid ibn Jabr (d. between 100/718 and 104/722) was a famous early Qur'anic exegete. See *EI2*, "Mudjāhid b. Djabr al-Makkī" (A. Rippin).

594 viz., the servant. This is obviously a slightly different account of what went before and a proper transition is missing.

595 Abū Ḥafṣ ʿUmar ibn Yazīd ibn ʿUmayr al-Usayyidī al-Tamīmī was head of police in Basra under al-Ḥajjāj. He was killed in 109/727. See al-Ṭabarī, *Tārīkh*, ii, 1495–1496, tr. *The His-*

In a tradition not from Ibn Maʿīn[590] he said: When the Marwānids saw this they schemed with ʿUmar's personal servant.[591] They gave him one thousand dinars to poison ʿUmar. When ʿUmar was aware he would die[592] he summoned the servant and questioned him. The man confessed. ʿUmar asked, "How much did they give you?" "One thousand dinars." Then ʿUmar took them away from him and put them in the treasury. He said to the servant, "Get away or you will be killed!" The man got away and ʿUmar died.

Ibn Abī l-Shaykh mentions that Mujāhid[593] visited ʿUmar during his illness. ʿUmar asked him, "What are people saying, Mujāhid?" He answered, "They say you have been bewitched." "I have not been bewitched, I have been poisoned! That servant of mine gave me poison." Then he asked him,[594] "What brought you to what you did?" The man replied, "I was given my freedom and one thousand dinars." "Give me the thousand", said ʿUmar. He took them and put them in the treasury. Then he said, "Go, you are free!"

[§ 52 ʿUmar ibn Yazīd ibn ʿUmayr al-Usayyidī[595]]

Another is ʿUmar ibn Yazīd ibn ʿUmayr al-Usayyidī. He was governor of Basra 182
alternating with Mālik ibn al-Mundhir ibn al-Jārūd,[596] who was a friend of his. A man of the Banū Kurayz came between them and sowed enmity. When Mālik ibn al-Mundhir came to power again he imprisoned al-Farazdaq, claiming that he had made a lampoon on the Mubārak canal.[597] He wrote to Khālid al-Qasrī, who was the governor of Iraq, inciting him against ʿUmar ibn Yazīd, upon which Khālid wrote to him, ordering him to imprison ʿUmar. So Mālik sent for him and detained him in his house. Then he secretly sent someone who twisted his neck,[598] killing him. The following morning he was carried on a mule,[599] with

---

tory, xxv, 33–34; al-Iṣfahānī, *Aghānī*, xxi, 379–380; Ibn Manẓūr, *Mukhtaṣar Tārīkh Dimashq*, xix, 166–167; Ibn al-Athīr, *Kāmil*, iv, 370, where the vowelling al-Usayyidī is given explicitly as being favoured by Hadith specialists (*muḥaddithūn*), whereas grammarians (*nuḥāh*) prefer al-Asīdī, both groups deriving the *nisbah* from Usayyid/Asīd ibn ʿAmr ibn Tamīm (see *ǦN*, i, 83, where he appears as ʿUmar ibn Yazīd ibn ʿUmar, of Usayyid ibn ʿAmr).

596 Ibn Manẓūr, *Mukhtaṣar Tārīkh Dimashq*, xxiv, 68–71.

597 Nahr al-Mubārak ("the Blessed Canal") had been a project of the famous governor Khālid al-Qasrī. For al-Farazdaq's poem, see his *Dīwān*, 600–601 (2 lines), Ibn Sallām, *Ṭabaqāt*, 294 (3 lines), where it begins: "You have wasted God's money unjustifiedly | on your Wretched, not Blessed, canal." See also al-Iṣfahānī, *Aghānī*, xxi, 313–314, 331, xxii, 20.

598 *Lawā ʿunuqahu*, an unusual but effective method of killing.

599 *Dābbah*, which could be any riding animal but most likely a mule here.

رجل يُمسِك ظهره، فجعل رأس عمر يتذبذب، فجاء١ الذي وراءه عنقه ويقول: أَقِمْ رأسك فإنك نجّاث! وأدخل فلما أصبحوا من غد قالوا: مصَّ خاتَمَه وفيه سمٌّ ومات.

وكان الفرزدق محبوساً في غير السجن الذي كان فيه عمر فأتى الفرزدقَ ابنُه لَبَطة فقال: أما
علمتَ أنّ عمر بن يزيد مصَّ خاتمه فوجدوه ميتاً؟ فقال له | الفرزدق: وأعلم أن ذلك معمول وأنّه ١٨٣
قُتل، وأبوك، واللّهِ، إن لم يَلحق واسط سيمصُّ خاتمه!

[§٥٣] **ومنهم** قَتادة بن سابة بن ثابت بن مَعْبَد أخو بني أبي ربيعة بن ذُهْل بن شيْبان، وكان أصاب دماً في بني شَريك، فمشت السُّفَراء حتّى صَلح الأمر، فمشوْا بذلك ما شاء اللّه. ثمّ إنّ حُرَيث بن أَسْود بن شريك وموْلى له يقال له يَقْظان لقيا قتادة بالبصرة وقد أسلم خُفَّيْن له إلى إسكاف، فجعلا للإسكاف جُعْلاً على أن يَحبِس خفَّيْه إلى الليل، ففعل ذلك، وقال لقتادة: ائتِني صلاةَ المغرب حتّى أُعْطِيَك خفَّيك: فلمّا جاء ليأخذها وقد كَمَنا له شدّا عليه فقتلاه، وهاج بينهما الناس فصاحا: إنّما نحن ثائران! فأحجم الناسُ عنهما فنُجِّيا.

وقال حُريث في قتله:

فقلتُ له صبْراً حُريثُ فإنّنا   كذلك نجزى قرْضَكم آلَ مَرْثَدِ
قتادةُ يعلو رهطَه وعلوْتُه   بأبيضَ من ماءِ الحديد مهنَّدِ

١ كذا في هـ، وقال المصحّح: "ولعلها (فحتأ). حتأه: ضربه." وفي كـ: (فجاء الذي وراءه [فضرب]).

600 A guess, for *fa-jāʾa … ʿunuqahū*, as in ʿASH, is strange; Hārūn suggests (without convincing me) reading *fa-ḥataʾa*, explained as *fa-ḍaraba* ("he struck"), as in SKḤ.

601 ʿASH and SKḤ have *fa-innaka najjāth*, which they explain as "someone who investigates (*baḥḥāth*) reports", which strikes me as unlikely. I am unable to suggest a translation or emendation. In *Aghānī*, xxi, 379 the corpse is taken to prison. The gaoler refuses to admit a dead body but they take the keys from him and bring the body inside. The following morning they spread the rumour that ʿUmar ibn Yazīd had killed himself with poison from his signet ring.

602 This somewhat cryptic statement appears in *Aghānī*, xxi, 379 as *la-in lam talḥaq bi-Wāsiṭ la-yamaṣṣu abūka khātamahū*. Wāsiṭ is a town in Iraq roughly between Kufa and Basra.

603 He is not found in other sources. Sābah is not known as a personal name; as Hārūn mentions in a note, Sayābah is found (but no Qatādah ibn Sayābah is known). On the possibility of identifying him as Qatādah ibn Jandal, see below, note 607.

a man riding behind who held his back. ʿUmar's head was dangling; the man behind him struck[600] his neck and said, "Keep your head up! You are a … (?)"[601] He was brought inside again. The following morning they said, "He sucked his signet ring, which contained poison, and he died."

Al-Farazdaq was detained in another prison, not that of ʿUmar. Labaṭah, al-Farazdaq's son, came to see him and said, "Did you know that ʿUmar ibn Yazīd
sucked his signet ring and they found him dead?" Al-Farazdaq replied, | "I know 183
that was done and that he was killed. Your father, by God! unless he reaches Wāsiṭ, will also suck his signet ring!"[602]

[§ 53 Qatādah ibn Sābah ibn Thābit ibn Maʿbad[603]]

Another is Qatādah ibn Sābah ibn Thābit ibn Maʿbad, a member of the Banū Rabīʿah ibn Dhuhl ibn Shaybān.[604] He had incurred a blood-guilt among the Banū Sharīk.[605] Emissaries moved between the parties and a reconciliation was reached; they spent much effort in this. Subsequently Ḥurayth ibn Aswad ibn Sharīk and a *mawlā* ("client") of his called Yaqẓān met Qatādah in Basra. He had given a pair of shoes to a cobbler. The two paid some money to the cobbler on condition that he would keep the shoes until the evening. This he did. He said to Qatādah, "Come at the time of the sunset prayer and I'll give you your shoes." When Qatādah came to pick them up, the two were hiding in ambush. They sprang upon him and killed him. There was a commotion among the people, but the two cried, "We are only taking revenge!" Then the people let them go and they escaped. Ḥurayth said about the killing:

I said to him, Patience, Ḥurayth![606]
 Thus we requite your loan to the clan of Marthad.[607]
Qatādah overcame his kinsmen but I overcame him,
 with a white Indian sword of lustrous steel.[608]

---

604 On this tribe see *ǦN*, i, 149.

605 This is probably Sharīk ibn ʿAmr, of Murrah ibn Dhuhl ibn Shaybān, see *ǦN*, i, 146, where Aswad ibn Sharīk (but not his son Ḥurayth mentioned below) is found.

606 Poets often address themselves, but if Ḥurayth is the poet it is strange to find "I said to him" meaning himself. Hārūn suggests *Ḥuraythu* may be an error for *Qatāda* (short for *Qatādatu*).

607 Not identified with certainty. One notes that Marthad ibn ʿĀmir belongs to Abū Rabīʿah ibn Dhuhl, and that this Marthad has a great-grandson called Qatādah ibn Jandal (*ǦN*, i, 149), so one wonders if he is the Qatādah of the present story.

608 This hemistich is a near-quotation of al-Shanfarā, see *Aghānī*, xxi, 190. High-quality swords are often said to be of Indian make (*muhannad*).

[§ ٥٤] **ومنهم** عمرو بن محمّد الثَّقَفيّ. وكان عاملاً على السِّنْد، فوجّه إليه منصورُ بن جمهور ١٨٤
الكلبيّ، وكان منصور بن جمهور افتعل عهداً فوَلِيَ العراق، وهو الذي يقول له الناس: منصور بن جمهور، أمير غير مأمور، وذلك في فتنة مروان بن محمد؛ فوجّه إلى عمرو بن محمد بن القاسم الثقفيّ، وكان عامل مروان، رجلاً من أهل الشام يقال [له] فُلان بن عِمْران يأخذ عَمراً بالحِساب، فحبسه ودسّ إليه مَن قتله فأصبح ميّتاً وأشاع أنّه قتل نفسه من خوف المُحاسَبة.

[§ ٥٥] **ومنهم** منظور بن جمهور، أخو منصور. وكان منصور ضمَّ إلى أخيه منظور رجلاً من أهل الشام من الأهل اليَمَن يقال له رِفاعة بن ثابت بن نُعَيم، فكان الغالبَ على أمر منظور، وكان يسامره وينادمه. فلمّا ضبط أبو مُسْلِم خراسانَ وجّه على السند رجلاً من بكر بن وائل، يقال له مغلِّس،[١] فبلغ ذلك رفاعة بن ثابت. وأنّ مغلّساً قد دنا من السند، فقعد هو ومنظور ووصيفٌ لمنظور يشربون، فلمّا أخذ فيهم الشراب نام منظور ووصيفه، وخرج رفاعة فأتى منزله وجاء بسيفه وبمولى له معه، وأخذ سِكّة فرسه، وأتى حائطاً يُفْضي إلى درجة الغرفة
التي منظور ووصيفه فيها، فنقبه هو ومولاه حتّى أفضيا | إلى الدرجة، فصَعِدا إلى السطح ١٨٥
فإذا منظور ووصيفه نائمان، فقتل منظوراً وجاء إلى الوصيف ليقتله فانتبه الوصيفُ حين وجد مسَّ الحديد، فقال: يا منظور، تُسامرني من أوّل الليل وتقتلني من آخره؟! وهو يظُنّه منظوراً،

---

١ في هـ، كـ: (معلّس) والتصحيح من تاريخ خليفة بن خيّاط وغيره.

---

609 ʿAmr ibn Muḥammad ibn al-Qāsim founded the city called al-Manṣūrah, allegedly called after the governor al-Manṣūr ibn Jumhūr. ʿAmr was the son of Muḥammad ibn al-Qāsim al-Thaqafī, conqueror of Sind (roughly modern Pakistan). See *EI2*, "al-Manṣūra" (Y. Friedmann), "Muḥammad b. al-Ḳāsim" (Y. Friedmann). No parallel texts on his murder have been found.

610 The awkward construction of this sentence in the Arabic has been followed in the translation.

611 *Amīr ghayr maʾmūr.*

612 Marwān ibn Muḥammad ibn Marwān (reg. 127–132/744–750) was the last Umayyad caliph. He was killed in the course of the revolution that brought the Abbasids to power.

613 The Arabic for "So-and-so" is Fulān. Possibly it is here corruption of the name given in al-Ṭabarī, *Tārīkh*, ii, 1839, tr. *The History*, xxvi, 199–200, as Muḥammad ibn Ghazzān, or ʿAzzān, al-Kalbī.

[§ 54 ʿAmr ibn Muḥammad al-Thaqafī[609]]

Another is ʿAmr ibn Muḥammad al-Thaqafī. He was governor of Sind. Manṣūr 184
ibn Jumhūr al-Kalbī[610]—this Manṣūr ibn Jumhūr had forged a covenant and had become governor of Iraq; he is the one people called "Manṣūr ibn Jumhūr, the non-commissioned emir"[611] (and this was during the civil war in Marwān ibn Muḥammad's time)[612]—he sent to ʿAmr ibn Muḥammad ibn al-Qāsim al-Thaqafī, Marwān's governor, a man from Syria called So-and-so ibn ʿImrān,[613] to audit ʿAmr. He arrested ʿAmr and secretly sent someone to kill him. He was found dead the following morning but the rumour was spread that he had killed himself for fear of the audit.

[§ 55 Manẓūr ibn Jumhūr[614]]

Another is Manẓūr ibn Jumhūr, the brother of Manṣūr. Manṣūr had sent a man from Syria belonging to Yaman called Rifāʿah ibn Thābit ibn Nuʿaym,[615] to join his brother Manẓūr. Rifāʿah came to dominate Manẓūr. He would spend the evenings with him and be his drinking companion. When Abū Muslim[616] had secured Khorasan he sent a man of the Bakr ibn Wāʾil called Mughallis[617] to take control of Sind. Rifāʿah heard about this and learned that Mughallis was approaching Sind. He, together with Manẓūr and a servant of Manẓūr, were drinking together. Overcome by the wine, Manẓūr and his servant fell asleep. Rifāʿah left and went home, picked up a sword and took a *mawlā* of his with him. He took the road of his horse[618] and came to a wall that was level with the steps leading to the room in which Manẓūr and his servant were. He and
his *mawlā* made a hole in the wall and reached | the staircase. They went up 185
and found Manẓūr and his servant, fast asleep. Rifāʿah killed Manẓūr and went to the servant to kill him too, but the man awoke when he felt the steel. "Manẓūr!", he cried, "You spend the evening with me early in the evening and you kill me later?", thinking that it was Manẓūr. Rifāʿah finished him off. He said to

614 No parallel texts on his murder have been found. According to al-Balādhuri, *Ansāb*, iv, 233, Manẓūr was killed after being defeated by Abū Muslim.

615 Not found in other sources. *Min ahl al-Yaman* could also mean "(originally) from Yemen", but it is more likely that al-Yaman here stands for the South Arabs collectively.

616 On him see also below, § 63. Probably of Persian descent, he was the effective leader of the Abbasid revolution that ended the Umayyad dynasty.

617 ʿASH and SKḤ: Muʿallis (or Muʿallas). It is an error for Mughallis, as e.g. in Khalīfah ibn Khayyāṭ, *Tārīkh*, 413.

618 I am not sure what this means.

فأجهز عليه. وقال لوصيفٍ[١] لمنظور: افعلْ ما آمُرك به وإلّا قتلتُك. فقال: مُرْني بما شئت. فقال: ادْعُ لي صاحب الحَرَس على لسان مَوْلاك! وكان رجلاً من بني أسد، فأشرف الغلام وقال: الأمير يدعوك! فلمّا أطلع رأسَه قام رفاعة ومولاه فقتلاه، وجعل يقتل الرجلَ من الوجوه هكذا، حتّى قتل ثمانيةَ نفر. قال الشاعر:

يا رِفاعَ بن ثابت بن نُعَيم ما جزيْتَ الإحسانَ بالإحسانِ
ولقد أتلفَتْ يَمينُك خِرْقاً أَرْيَحِيًّا وفارسَ الفُرسانِ
فأدال المليكُ منك فقد أَصْـ ـبحتَ في كَفّ ثائرٍ حَرّانِ

وظفر منصورٌ برفاعة فقتله.

[§ ٥٦] **ومنهم** عبد اللّٰه بن عمر بن عبد العزيز. وكان عاملَ مروان على العراق قبل ابن هُبَيرة، فغلبت الخوارجُ على الكوفة، ثمّ مضوْا إلى واسط فحصروه بها، وكان رئيس الخوارج الضحّاك بن قيس الشيْبانيّ، فلمّا طال حِصاره بعث إليه عبد اللّٰه بن عمر: إنّي عاملك فامْضِ إلى مروان فقاتِلْه فإنْ ظفرتَ به أو قتلتَه فأنا عاملُك وداعٍ لك. فمضى الضحّاك فقتله مروان. وولّى يزيدَ بن عمر بن هُبيرة على العراق. فقتل الخوارجَ. وبعث إليه بعبد اللّٰه بن عمر فحبسه بحَرّان. ثمّ دسَّ إليه قوماً فوضعوا على وجهه مِرْفقته فأصبح في السجن ميّتاً.

١ ك: (الوصيف).

619 He is the son of the caliph ʿUmar ibn ʿAbd al-ʿAzīz (see above, § 51). See *EI2*, "ʿAbd Allāh b. ʿUmar b. ʿAbd al-ʿAzīz" (K.V. Zetterstéen), *EI3*, "ʿAbdallāh b. ʿUmar b. ʿAbd al-ʿAzīz" (Steven C. Judd). He died in 132/749–750. According to some accounts he was not murdered but died in prison of the plague (see e.g. Ibn Manẓūr, *Mukhtaṣar Tārīkh Dimashq*, xiii, 188).

another servant of Manẓūr, "Do what I tell you or I'll kill you!" "Tell me whatever you want!" said the man. Rifāʿah said, "Call the head of the guard in the name of your master!". He was a man of the Banū Asad. The servant called out, "The commander calls you!". When the man showed his face Rifāʿah and his servant got up and killed him. In the same manner he killed one after the other of the leaders, until he had killed eight of them. A poet said,

Rifāʿah ibn Thābit ibn Nuʿaym,
  You did not requite a good deed with another!
Your right hand destroyed a generous man,
  a munificent man, the most eminent knight!
May God overthrow your fortune! You are now
  in the hand of an avenger thirsty for revenge!

Manṣūr seized Rifāʿah and killed him.

[§ 56 ʿAbd Allāh ibn ʿUmar ibn ʿAbd al-ʿAzīz[619]]

Another is ʿAbd Allāh ibn ʿUmar ibn ʿAbd al-ʿAzīz. He was the governor of Iraq under Marwān[620] before Ibn Hubayrah.[621] The Khārijites took Kufa. Then they went to Wāsiṭ and laid siege to it, where Allāh ibn ʿUmar resided. The leader of the Khārijites was al-Ḍaḥḥāk ibn Qays al-Shaybānī.[622] When the siege was protracted ʿAbd Allāh ibn ʿUmar sent him a message saying, "I am your governor. Go to Marwān and fight him! If you are victorious or kill him, I will be your governor and support your case."[623] Al-Ḍaḥḥāk marched off but Marwān killed him. He appointed Yazīd ibn ʿUmar ibn Hubayrah as governor of Iraq, who killed the Khārijites. ʿAbd Allāh ibn ʿUmar was sent to him and he imprisoned him in Ḥarrān.[624] He secretly sent some men to him, who smothered him with his pillow. The following morning he was found dead in the prison.

---

620 The caliph Marwān ibn Muḥammad, see above § 54.

621 Yūsuf ibn ʿUmar ibn Hubayrah, governor of Iraq 129–132/741–749. See on him and his father *EI2*, "Ibn Hubayra" (J.-C. Vadet); his son Yazīd (mentioned below and § 60) was the last Umayyad governor of Iraq (see on him e.g. al-Ṣafadī, *Wāfī*, xxviii, 415–418).

622 On him see *EI2*, "al-Ḍaḥḥāk b. Ḳays al-Shaybānī" (L. Veccia Vaglieri). He fell in battle against Marwān in 128/746.

623 As Judd states (*EI3*), the fact that an Umayyad prince was prepared to give allegiance to the Khārijites (and he was not the only one) is an indication of the desperate state of Umayyad rule.

624 Ḥarrān, ancient Carrhae, a town in northern Mesopotamia, now in Turkey.

١٨٦ [§٥٧] **ومنهم** الإمام إبراهيم بن محمّد بن عليّ بن عبد الله بن عبّاس. وكان نَصْر بن سيّار
كتب إلى مروان يُعْلِمه بخروج أبي مُسْلِم وكثرةِ تَبَعِه وأنّه يخاف أن يستوليَ على خراسان،
وأنّ الدعوة لإبراهيم بن محمّد بن عليّ بن عبد الله. فأُلقِيَ الكتاب إلى مروان، وقد أتى إبراهيمَ
رسولُ أبي مسلم بكتاب. فسأل إبراهيمُ الرسولَ: ممّن هو؟ قال: من العرب. فردّ جوابَ كتاب
أبي مسلم يلعَنه فيه أن ترك[١] المواثَبة لجُدَيع الكِرْمانيّ ونصر بن سيّار ويأمره فيه ألّا يدع بخراسان
عربياً إلّا قتله.

فانطلق الرجل إلى مروان بالكتاب فوضعه في يده، فكتب مروان إلى معاوية بن الوليد بن عبد الملك، وهو عامله على دمشق، أن اُكْتُبْ إلى عامل البَلْقاء فلْيَسْرِ إلى كُداد والحُمَيمة، فلْيأخذْ إبراهيم بن محمّد فلْيَشُدَّه وِثاقاً[٢] ولْيبعَثْ به إليه مع خيل كثيفة، ثمّ وجِّهْ به إلى أمير المؤمنين.

قال: فأُتِيَ وهو جالس في مسجد القرية، فأُخذ فلُفَّ رأسُه وحُمل فأُدخل على مروان، فأنّبه
وشتمه، فاشتدّ لسان إبراهيم عليه وقال: يا أمير المؤمنين، ما أظُنّ ما يروى الناس عليك إلّا حقًّا،
١٨٧ في بغْض بني هاشم، وما لي وما تَصِف؟ | فقال له مروان: أَدْرَكك اللّهُ بأعمالك الخبيثة، فانّ اللّه

١ كذا في هـ، ولعلّ الصواب (يترك) أو (اترك) كما في كـ.

٢ كـ: (فليشده وثاقه).

625 He was the brother of the first two Abbasid caliphs, al-Saffāḥ and al-Manṣūr, and the son of Muḥammad ibn ʿAlī mentioned before (§ 50). At his orders the rising against the Umayyads was begun in 129/747. While the revolution was in full swing he was captured and died in 132/749. He is often called Ibrāhīm al-Imām, as here. See e.g. *EI2*, "Ibrāhīm b. Muḥammad" (F. Omar). For a parallel text see Anon., *Akhbār al-Dawlah al-ʿAbbāsiyyah*, 391–393 (quoting Ibn Ḥabīb), al-Ṭabarī, *Tārīkh*, ii, 1974–1975.

626 Naṣr ibn Sayyār al-Laythī was the last governor of Khorasan under the Umayyads and vainly tried to resist the uprising. While Umayyad power was crumbling in the East he died a natural death at an advanced age in 131/748. See *EI2*, "Naṣr b. Sayyār" (C.E. Bosworth).

[§ 57 Ibrāhīm ibn Muḥammad ibn ʿAlī ibn ʿAbd Allāh ibn ʿAbbās[625]]

Another is the Imam Ibrāhīm ibn Muḥammad ibn ʿAlī ibn ʿAbd Allāh ibn 186
ʿAbbās. Naṣr ibn Sayyār[626] had written to Marwān, informing him of the rebellion of Abū Muslim and the multitude of his followers, adding that he feared Abū Muslim would take control of Khorasan and that the revolt was carried out in the name of Ibrāhīm ibn Muḥammad ibn ʿAlī ibn ʿAbd Allāh. The letter was conveyed to Marwān after a messenger of Abū Muslim had brought Ibrāhīm another letter. Ibrāhīm asked the messenger, "Who sent it?" He answered, "The Arabs." Ibrāhīm sent a reply to Abū Muslim's letter, cursing him, telling him to leave off attacking Judayʿ al-Kirmānī[627] and Naṣr ibn Sayyār, and ordering him to leave no Arab alive in Khorasan.

But the messenger went to Marwān with that letter and handed it to him. Then Marwān wrote to Muʿāwiyah ibn al-Walīd ibn ʿAbd al-Malik,[628] who was his governor in Damascus saying, "Write to the governor of al-Balqāʾ and tell him to go to Kudād and al-Ḥumaymah.[629] Let him apprehend Ibrāhīm ibn Muḥammad and put him in chains. He should have him sent to him[630] with a large cavalry escort, then have him sent to the Commander of the Believers."

They came for Ibrāhīm while he was sitting in the mosque of the village. He was apprehended, his head was wrapped up and he was carried and brought in to Marwān, who scolded and reviled him. Then Ibrāhīm spoke harshly to him, saying, "Commander of the Believers, I think everything people say about you is true, about hating the descendants of Hāshim![631] What have I to do with how you describe them?" | Marwān replied, "May God requite you for your evil 187

---

627 Judayʿ ibn ʿAlī, a chief of the Azd tribe, of the "Yamanite" faction, was involved in another rebellion against the Umayyads. On his sons ʿAlī and ʿUthmān see below, § 61. The *nisbah* al-Kirmanī refers to Kirmān, a region in southern Persia to the east of Fārs. The "vulgar" from Kirmān is generally used (cf. *EI2*, "Kirmān" [A.S. Lambton]) even though the Arab lexicographers and Yāqūt in *Muʿjam al-buldān* say the correct form is Karmān (which is supported by its ancient Greek and Latin name, Carmania).

628 He was a son of caliph al-Walīd (reg. 86–96/705–715). As Hārūn notes, other sources mention al-Walīd ibn Muʿāwiyah ibn ʿAbd al-Malik (al-Ṭabarī, *Tārīkh*) or al-Walīd ibn Muʿāwiyah ibn Marwān ibn al-Ḥakam (al-Masʿūdī, *Tanbīh*, Anon., *Akhbār al-Dawlah al-ʿAbbāsiyyah*).

629 Al-Balqāʾ is a region roughly corresponding to modern Jordan. For Kudād and al-Ḥumaymah see above, § 50.

630 viz., the governor of Damascus.

631 See above, § 51 note 582.

لا يأخذ على أوّلِ ذنْب؛ اذْهَبا به إلى السجن. فحبسه أيّاماً، ثمّ أمر قوماً فدخلوا إلى السجن بعد ما مر صدرٌ من الليل، فغُمَّ إبراهيم في جِرابِ نُورة، وغُمَّ عبد اللّٰه بن عمر بن عبد العزيز بمِرْفقةٍ، فأصبحا ميّتيْن في غداة واحدة. رحمهما اللّٰه تعالى.

[§٥٨] **ومنهم** أبو سَلَمة حَفْص بن سليمان مولى بني مُسْلِيَة، وكان يقال له وزير آل محمّد. وكان أبو سلمة لمّا استتبّ الأمر واستقامت خراسان والجبال وفارس وجّه أبو سلمة للعُمّال في السهل والجبل، ثمّ أقام[١] أبو سلمة نحواً من أربعين يوماً لا يُظهر أمر أبي العبّاس، وأبو جعفر وعبد اللّٰه وإسماعيل وعيسى وداود بنو عليّ قد قدموا من الشام، فأنزلهم أبو سلمة دارَ الوليد بن سعيد في بني أَوْد.

وكان القُوّاد الذين قدموا من خراسان يقولون لأبي سلمة: أين الإمام؟ فيقول: لا تعجَلوا. وكان أبو سلمة يدبّرها لبني فاطمة رضي اللّٰه عنها، فجعل يريّثهم[٢] ويقول: نِعْمَ اليوم غداً! حتّى خرج أبو حُمَيد، وهو يريد الكُناسة، فلقي مولًى لهم أسْود قد كان يعرفه حيث كان يأتي إبراهيم بالشام.
فلمّا رآه احتضنه وقال: ويْلك، ما فعل الإمامُ ومَواليك؟ قال: هم ها هنا واللّٰهِ مذْ أكثر من شهريْن. | ١٨٨
قال: وأين هم؟ قال: في دار الوليد بن سعيد في بني أود. قال: فانطلقْ فأَرِنيهم.[٣] فخرج الأسود

١ ک: (قام).

٢ ک: (يرثيهم).

٣ ک: (فأرينيهم).

632 For no apparent reason the text uses a dual form for the imperative; *Akhbār al-Dawlah al-ʿAbbāsiyyah* has a plural.

633 He was a freed slave from Kufa, one of the emissaries of the Abbasid cause and the first to be called vizier (*wazīr*). He died in 132/750. See *EI2*, "Abū Salama" (S. Moscati) and *EI3*, "Abū Salama Ḥafṣ b. Sulaymān al-Khallāl" (Elton L. Daniel). On his death see e.g. al-Ṭabarī, *Tārīkh*, iii, 58–61, tr. *The History*, 182–184; al-Balādhurī, *Ansāb*, iv, 203–205; al-Yaʿqūbī, *Tārīkh*, ii, 422, tr. *The Works*, 1079; Ibn Qutaybah, *Imāmah*, ii, 165–166; al-Tanūkhī, *Faraj*, iv, 272–277.

634 Al-Jibāl, "the Mountains", i.e., the Zagros Mountains, a region in western Iran, ancient Media; Fārs or Fāris (the Arabicised form of Pārs) is south-western Iran.

deeds! God does not punish a first offender! Take him to jail!"[632] He imprisoned him for a few days. Then he told some men to enter the prison early at night. Ibrāhīm was put in a sack with quicklime and 'Abd Allāh ibn 'Umar ibn 'Abd al-'Azīz was smothered with a pillow. Both were found dead the same morning, God the Exalted have mercy on them.

[§ 58 Abū Salamah Ḥafṣ ibn Sulaymān[633]]

Another is Abū Salamah Ḥafṣ ibn Sulaymān, the *mawlā* of the Banū Musliyah; he was called "the Vizier of the Family of Muḥammad". When matters were settled and Khorasan, al-Jibāl, and Fārs[634] were secured, Abū Salamah sent messages to all governors in the lowlands and highlands. Then he stayed put for some forty days without declaring openly for Abū l-'Abbās.[635] Abū Ja'far, 'Abd Allāh, Ismā'īl, 'Īsā, and Dāwūd, all sons of 'Alī,[636] had arrived from Syria and Abū Salamah let them lodge in the house of al-Walīd ibn Sa'īd among the Banū Awd.[637] The army commanders who had come from Khorasan would ask Abū Salamah, "Where is the Imam?"[638] and Abū Salamah would say, "There's no hurry!" He was arranging the imamate for the descendants of Fāṭimah (*r*). He began to delay matters and would say, "Tomorrow is a good day!" This lasted until Abū Ḥumayd[639] went on his way to al-Kunāsah.[640] He met a black *mawlā* of theirs[641] whom he used to know when he visited Ibrāhīm[642] in Syria. When he saw him he embraced him and asked, "I say, what are the Imam and your masters doing?" "They have been here, by God, for more than two months!" | 188
"Where are they?" asked Abū Ḥumayd. The man answered, "In the house of al-Walīd ibn Sa'īd, among the Banū Awd." "Come on," said Abū Ḥumayd, "Show

635 Abū l-'Abbās 'Abd Allāh ibn Muḥammad ibn 'Alī, also known as al-Saffāḥ, was the first Abbasid caliph.

636 They are the sons of 'Alī ibn 'Abd Allāh ibn al-'Abbās (as explicitly said e.g. in al-Dīnawarī, *al-Akhbār al-ṭiwāl*, 357), the grandfather of the first two Abbasid caliphs and the ancestor of all subsequent Abbasids. He died in 117/735 or the following year.

637 Al-Ṭabarī, *Tārīkh*, iii, 34 calls him al-Walīd ibn Sa'd, a *mawlā* of the Banū Hāshim. The Banū Awd were a branch of Madhḥij; they had settled in Kufa (*ĞN*, i, 270 and ii, 206).

638 *Imām*, literally "leader" (e.g. in ritual prayer) is often used (especially by Shi'ites) for the leader of the Muslim community generally, as a synonym of *khalīfah*, caliph.

639 Abū Ḥumayd Muḥammad ibn Ibrāhīm al-Ḥimyarī was one of the "missionaries" or propagandists (*du'āh*) of the Abbasid movement, see e.g. Anon., *Akhbār*, 321.

640 A famous market and meeting place in Kufa.

641 He is named as Sābiq al-Khwārazmī in al-Ṭabarī, *Tārīkh*, iii, 34.

642 i.e., the Imam Ibrāhīm ibn Muḥammad (§ 57).

بين يديه وأبو حُميد يتبعه في موْكِبه حتّى دخل فقال: السلام عليك أميرَ المؤمنين ورحمة الله. ثمّ أرسل عينيه بالبُكاء وقال: ما لكم هاهنا؟ قالوا: تركَنا أبو سلمة ها هنا منذ شهرين. فقال: يا أمير المؤمنين، منذ شهرين أركب. فحمله وأهل بيته ثمّ أقبل بهم إلى المسجد، وعَلِم أبو سلمة ما وقع فيه[١] فقال: إنّما أخَّرتُ أمركم لإحكام ما أُريد منه.

ثمّ إن أبا العبّاس تنكَّر لأبي سلمة، فلمّا همّوا به كرِهوا الإقدام عليه دون مشاوَرة أبي مسلم، فكتب إليه يُعْلمه بغِشّه وما أراد من صَرْف الأمر إلى غيره وما يتخوّف منه. فكتب أبو مسلم إلى أبي العبّاس: فلْيقتلْه أمير المؤمنين. فقال له داود بن عليّ: لا تفعلْ يا أمير المؤمنين فيحتجَّ عليك أبو مسلم وأهل خراسان الذين معك، وحاله عندهم حاله، ولكنْ اكتُبْ إلى أبي مسلم أن يبعث إليه مَن يقتله. فكتب إليه بذلك، فوجّه[٢] أبو مسلم مَرّار بن أَنَس الضَّبّيّ، فقدم على أبي العبّاس فأعلمه قدومه. وكان أبو سلمة يسمُر عند أبي العبّاس، فجاء مرّار الضبّيُّ فجلس على باب أبي العبّاس، فلمّا خرج أبو سلمة وتنحّى عن الباب شدَّ عليه فقتله. فلمّا أصبح لُعِن على باب الخليفة، وذكروا فِسْقَه وغِشّه وغَدْره، فقال سليمان بن المُهاجر البَجَليّ:

إنّ الوزيرَ وزيرَ آلِ محمّدٍ أَوْدى فمَنْ يَشْناك كان وزيرا

١٨٩ [§ ٥٩] **ومنهم** عبد الله بن معاوية بن عبد الله بن جعفر بن أبي طالب. وكان عبد الله خرج بالكوفة[٣] في ولاية عبد الله بن عمر بن عبد العزيز على العراق فقاتَلَه فهزمه، فسار إلى المدائن

١ ك: (وعَلمِ أبو سهل فيه).
٢ (أن يبعث ... فوجّه أبو مسلم): ناقصة في ك.
٣ ك: (في الكوفة).

643 Dāwūd ibn ʿAlī ibn ʿAbd Allāh (d. 133/750–751), a paternal uncle of Abū l-ʿAbbās, see e.g. al-Ṣafadī, *Wāfī*, xiii, 478–479.

644 Marrār ibn Anas, of the tribe of Ḍabbah, is listed among the seventy missionaries (*duʿāh*), Anon, *Akhbār*, 221.

645 See Sezgin, *Geschichte*, ii, 454. The line is quoted in e.g. al-Ṭabarī, *Tārīkh*, iii, 60; anonymously in al-Dīnawarī, *Akhbār*, 368; al-Masʿūdī, *Murūj*, iv, 116; Ibn al-Ṭiqṭaqā, *Fakhrī*, 156.

me!" The black *mawlā* went before, with Abū Ḥumayd following him with his escort. Upon entering he said, "Peace upon you, Commander of the Believers, and God's mercy!" He burst into tears. "What are you doing here?" he asked. They replied, "Abū Salamah has left us here for two months." "But, Commander of the Believers," said Abū Ḥumayd, "I have been riding for two months!" He took him and the members of his family and brought them to the mosque. Abū Salamah learned what had happened and said, "I have delayed your cause in order to strengthen what I wanted for it."

Abū l-ʿAbbās had become hostile to Abū Salamah. When they were about to act they did not want to proceed against him without consulting Abū Muslim. Abū l-ʿAbbās wrote to him, telling him of his duplicity, that Abū Salamah wanted to change his allegiance to another, and that he was afraid of him. Abū Muslim wrote in reply to Abū l-ʿAbbās: "The Commander of the Believers must kill him!" But Dāwūd ibn ʿAlī[643] said, "Don't do it, Commander of the Believers, or else Abū Muslim and the Khorasanis with you will use it against you, for they are in a similar situation as Abū Salamah. But write to Abū Muslim, telling him to send someone to kill him!" Abū l-ʿAbbās wrote accordingly. Then Abū Muslim sent Marrār ibn Anas al-Ḍabbī,[644] who went to Abū l-ʿAbbās and informed him of his arrival. Abū Salamah used to spend the evenings in the company of Abū l-ʿAbbās. Marrār al-Ḍabbī came and sat at the door of Abū l-ʿAbbās's place. When Abū Salamah left and had turned away from the door he attacked him and killed him. The following morning he was publicly cursed at the caliph's door; they mentioned his depravity, his disloyalty, and his treachery. Sulaymān ibn al-Muhājir al-Bajalī said,[645]

> The Vizier, the vizier of Muḥammad's Family,
> has perished! He who hates you has become vizier.

[§ 59 ʿAbd Allāh ibn Muʿāwiyah ibn ʿAbd Allāh ibn Jaʿfar in Abī Ṭālib[646]]

Another is ʿAbd Allāh ibn Muʿāwiyah ibn ʿAbd Allāh ibn Jaʿfar ibn Abī Ṭālib. He 189
rose in revolt in Kufa when the governor of Iraq was ʿAbd Allāh ibn ʿUmar ibn ʿAbd al-ʿAzīz,[647] who fought him and defeated him. ʿAbd Allāh ibn Muʿāwiyah

646 On this ʿAlid, a great-grandson of ʿAlī's brother Jaʿfar, and his uprising see *EI2*, "ʿAbd Allāh b. Muʿāwiya" (K.V. Zettersteen), *EI3*, "ʿAbdallāh b. Muʿāwiya" (Antoine Borrut). On his revolt and death see also e.g. al-Iṣfahānī, *Maqātil*, 155–159. He was killed probably in 131/148–149.

647 See above, § 56.

فتبعه بها قومٌ فساروا إلى حُلْوان فأخذ الجِبال ودعا لنفسه، ثمّ مضى إلى أصبهان فأقام بها، ثمّ
سار إلى إصطخر فجبى كُوَر فارس، وضرب دراهم عليها: ﴿قُلْ لَا أَسْأَلُكُمْ عَلَيْهِ أَجْرًا إِلَّا ٱلْمَوَدَّةَ
فِي ٱلْقُرْبَىٰ﴾. فلمّا قدم يزيد بن عمر بن هُبيرة عاملاً على العراق بعد عبد الله بن عمر وجّه إليه
ابن ضُبارة فهزمه إلى سِجِسْتان، ثمّ صار إلى هَراة وقد استتبّ أمر خراسان لأبي مسلم، وأخذوا
أخويْه الحسن ويزيد ابنَيْ معاوية، فاعتُقِل في الحبس ثمّ وُجِد ميّتاً فيه.

[§ ٦٠] **ومنهم** يزيد بن عمر بن هُبَيرة الفَزاريّ، أمير العراق لمروان بن محمّد. وكان أبو جعفر
المنصور حاصَره بِواسط، ومعه حُمَيد والحسن ابنا قَحْطَبة، ومالك بن الهيْثَم الخُزاعيّ، فطلب
الأمانَ، فكتب إلى أبي العبّاس بذلك فأعطاه الأمان على نفسه وقراباته[١] وحاشيته وقُوّاده،
فمكث كتاب الأمان يُقرأ على الفقهاء أكثرَ من أربعين يوماً حتّى أُكّد، وأراد | أبو جعفر الوفاء ١٩٠
به،[٢] وإنّ داود بن عليّ ولي الحجاز وصاحب مقدّمته أبو حمّاد. فأخذ أبو حمّاد رجلاً فقال له:
أين تريد؟ قال: العراق. قال: ممّن أنت؟ قال: من موالي بني هاشم. ففتّشه فلم يجد معه كتاباً،
فقدّمه ليضرب عنقه، فقال: لا تَعجلْ، وفتق قَباءً محشوًّا، فأخرج منه حريرةً فيها كتاب من

١ ك: (وأقربائه).

٢ ك: (الوقاية).

648 Al-Madāʾin ("the Cities"), on the site of ancient Ctesiphon, lies some 20 miles southeast of Baghdad. Ḥulwān is a town on a pass through the Zagros Mountains (al-Jibāl).

649 A town near ancient Persepolis in Fārs.

650 Q al-Shūrā 42:23. Although the Qur'anic text is not explicit about the sense of *fī l-qurbā*, exegetes, especially of pro-ʿAlid leanings, would naturally see a reference to the Prophet's kin.

651 See below, § 60.

652 See above, § 56.

653 ʿĀmir ibn Ḍubārah al-Murrī.

654 Other sources explicitly say that he was killed at the order of Abū Muslim; he may have been poisoned (al-Iṣfahānī, *Maqātil*, 158).

655 On his father see above, § 56. On Yazīd, whose death occurred in 132/750, see e.g. Ibn Khallikān, *Wafayāt*, vi, 313–321; al-Ṣafadī, *Wāfī*, xxviii, 415–418; al-Balādhurī, *Ansāb*, iv, 191–202; al-Ṭabarī, *Tārīkh*, iii, 68–71, tr. *The History*, xxvii, 191–194.

656 Abū Jaʿfar, brother of Abū l-ʿAbbās al-Saffāḥ, was to become the second Abbasid caliph (reg. 136–158/754–775).

went to al-Madā'in[648] where some people followed him. They went to Ḥulwān, and he took the al-Jibāl region and proclaimed himself imam. Then he went to Isfahan and stayed there a while; then he went to Iṣṭakhr,[649] levied taxes on the rural districts of Fārs, and had dirhams struck with the inscription «Say: I do not ask you a fee for it except love for kinship».[650]

When Yazīd ibn 'Umar ibn Hubayrah[651] arrived as governor of Iraq, succeeding 'Abd Allāh ibn 'Umar,[652] he sent Ibn Ḍubārah[653] who defeated 'Abd Allāh ibn Mu'āwiyah, who fled to Sijistān and then to Herat, after Khorasan was under the control of Abū Muslim. They apprehended his two brothers al-Ḥasan and Yazīd, sons of Mu'āwiyah. and he himself was detained in prison. Subsequently he was found dead there.[654]

[§ 60 Yazīd ibn 'Umar ibn Hubayrah[655]]

Another is Yazīd ibn 'Umar ibn Hubayrah al-Fazārī, commander in Iraq under Marwān ibn Muḥammad. Abū Ja'far al-Manṣūr[656] besieged him in Wāsiṭ, together with the two sons of Qaḥṭabah, Ḥumayd and al-Ḥasan,[657] and Mālik ibn al-Haytham al-Khuzā'ī.[658] Yazīd asked for an assurance of protection, so Abū Ja'far wrote about this to Abū l-'Abbās, who granted protection to Yazīd himself, his kinsfolk, his retinue, and his commanders. The letter of protection remained in the hands of the legal scholars who studied it for more than forty days before it was finally confirmed. Abū Ja'far | intended to be loyal to 190
the promise.

Dāwūd ibn 'Alī was governor of the Hijaz;[659] the commander of his vanguard was Abū Ḥammād.[660] This Abū Ḥammād apprehended a man and asked him, "Where are you going?" The man replied, "To Iraq." "To whom do you belong?" "To the *mawālī* (clients) of Abū Hāshim." He was searched but they did not find a letter on him. He was brought to be beheaded, but he said, "Don't be hasty!" and he tore open a lined robe, extricating a silk purse containing a letter from

657 Qaḥṭabah ibn Shabīb al-Ṭā'ī (d. 132/749) was a leading commander of the Abbasid revolt. See *EI2*, "Ḳaḥṭaba" (M. Sharon). His son Ḥumayd (d. 159/775–776) became governor of northern Mesopotamia (al-Jazīrah), then Egypt, then Khorasan (al-Ṣafadī, *Wāfī*, xiii, 199); al-Ḥasan ibn Qaḥṭabah (d. 181/797–798) became a general of Hārūn al-Rashīd (al-Ṣafadī, *Wāfī*, xii, 208).

658 Mālik ibn al-Haytham ibn 'Awf al-Salūlī was another Abbasid missionary and commander.

659 Dāwūd ibn 'Alī ibn 'Abd Allāh ibn 'Abbās (d. 133/750–751) was a paternal uncle of Abū l-'Abbās al-Saffāḥ and Abū Ja'far al-Manṣūr; see e.g. al-Ṣafadī, *Wāfī*, xiii, 478–479.

660 He is Abū Ḥammād al-Abraṣ Ibrāhīm ibn Ḥassān al-Sulamī (al-Ṭabarī, *Tārīkh*, iii, 73).

محمّد بن عبد الله بن الحسن، جوابُ كتاب ابن هُبيرة، كتب إليه: لا تعجلْ بالخروج، وماطِلْهم حتّى يستتبّ أمرُنا؛ فقد ذكرتَ أنّ قِبَلك من فُرسان العرب ثلاثين ألفاً. فدافِعِ القومَ بتأكيد الأمان.

فرفع الرجلَ والحريرة إلى داود، فقتل الرجلَ وبعث بالحريرة إلى أبي العبّاس، فكتب أبو العبّاس إلى أبي جعفر يأمره بقتله، فراجَعه أبو جعفر وأراد الوفاء له فكتب إليه: إنْ أنت فعلتَ، وإلّا أمّرتُ على عسكرك الحسنَ بن قحطبة. وقد كان أبو جعفر أحرز الخزائنَ والأموال، وجعل ابن هُبيرة يركب غِبًّا إلى أبي جعفر في قُوّاد أهل الشام، فلمّا همّ بذلك بعث خازم بن خُزَيمة النَّهْشَليّ، والهيثم بن شُعْبة، والأغلب بن سالم، وكلٌّ من بني تميم، في جماعة أصحابهم، فدخلوا رحبة القصر وأرسلوا إلى أبي هبيرة: إنّا نريد أن ننظر إلى الخزائن ونحمل ما فيها. فأَذِن لهم فدخلوا وطافوا ساعةً وجعلوا يخلّفون عند كلِّ بابٍ جماعةً من أصحابهم، ثمّ انصرفوا إليه فقالوا: أرسِلْ
معنا مَن يدُلّنا على المواضع التي فيها الخزائن وبيت الأموال. فقال: أَوَلَيْس قد ختمتم | عليها ١٩١
وأحرزتموها؟ يا أبا عثمان، يريد كاتِبَه، اذهبْ معهم فادْلُلْهم على الذي يريدون، أو أرسلْ معهم. فأرسلَ معهم، فطاف خازمٌ وأصحابه في القصر، ثمّ أقبل على ابن هبيرة وعليه قميص مصريّ، ومُلاءة مؤزَّرة، وهو مُسْنِدٌ ظهرَه إلى حائط المسجد، وبُنَيُّه صُبْحٌ غُلامٌ صغير في حِجره، فقتلوا داودَ ابنه وكاتبَه وحاجبَه وأربعة من مواليه، ثمّ مشوْا نحوه فخرّ ساجداً وقال: نَحُّوا عنّي هذا الصبيّ. فقتلوه وهو ساجدٌ.

وبعث أبو جعفر إلى قُوّاده وهم لا يعلمون[١] بأمر ابن هبيرة، فلمّا أُدخلوا الرِّواق كُتِّفوا ودُفعوا إلى القوّاد فقتلوهم في منازلهم.

١ ك: (وهم يعلمون).

661 Muḥammad ibn ʿAbd Allāh ibn al-Ḥasan ibn al-Ḥasan ibn ʿAlī ibn Abī Ṭālib. But cf. Ibn Khallikān, *Wafayāt*, vi, 318 and al-Ṣafadī, *Wāfī*, xxviii, 417, where it is said that Ibn Hubayrah corresponded with ʿAbd Allāh ibn al-Ḥasan ibn al-Ḥasan, the leader of the ʿAlids.

662 Abbasid commanders, Khāzim ibn Khuzaymah being the most prominent of the three.

Muḥammad ibn ʿAbd Allāh ibn al-Ḥasan,[661] in response to a letter from Ibn Hubayrah, which read as follows: "Do not rashly leave but put them off until our cause is settled. You mentioned that you have thirty thousand Arab horsemen with you. Resist the men, while confirming the promise of protection."

The man and the purse were taken to Dāwūd, who had the man killed and the purse sent to Abū l-ʿAbbās, who wrote to Abū Jaʿfar, ordering him to kill Ibn Hubayrah. Abū Jaʿfar wrote to him again, because he wanted to be true to his promise. But Abū l-ʿAbbās answered, "You either do it or I shall make al-Ḥasan ibn Qaḥṭabah the commander of your army." Abū Jaʿfar had put all coffers and money in a secure place. Ibn Hubayrah rode to Abū Jaʿfar every other day together with the commanders of the Syrians. When Abū Jaʿfar was about to act, he sent Khāzim ibn Khuzaymah al-Nahshalī, al-Haytham ibn Shuʿbah, al-Aghlab ibn Sālim,[662] all of them of the Banū Tamīm, with all their followers. They entered the courtyard of the castle and sent a message to Ibn Hubayrah, saying, "We want to have a look at the treasury and take away the contents." He gave permission and they entered. They moved around for a while, leaving some of their men behind at every gate. Then they went to Ibn Hubayrah and said, "Send someone with us who can lead us to the places where the coffers are stored and where the treasure rooms are!" Ibn Hubayrah replied, "But you
have sealed | them and you have put them in a secure place, haven't you! Abū 191
ʿUthmān!"—meaning his secretary—"Go with them and take them where they want, or send someone with them." He sent someone with them. Khāzim and his men went around in the castle. Then he came to Ibn Hubayrah, who was wearing an Egyptian shirt[663] and a wrap round his loins.[664] He was sitting, his back leaning against the wall of the mosque, with his little son, Ṣubḥ, on his lap. They killed his son Dāwūd, his secretary,[665] his chamberlain, and four of his *mawlā*s. Then they went for him. He prostrated himself as for prayer and said, "Take this boy away from me!" Then they killed him while prostrated.

Abū Jaʿfar sent for Ibn Hubayrah's commanders, who were not aware of what had happened to Ibn Hubayrah. When they were brought into the portico their hands were tied behind their backs. They were handed over to the commanders, who killed them in their several dwellings.

---

663 Egyptian textiles were noted for quality.

664 I am not certain about the precise nature of this piece of clothing (*mulāʾah muʾazzarah*). A *mulāʾah* is not only worn by women, as wrongly suggested in *EI2* (entry "Libās" and Index volume); see also Dozy, *Supplément*, s.v.

665 He is identified as ʿAmr ibn Ayyūb in al-Ṭabarī, *Tārīkh*, iii, 69.

[§ ٦١] **ومنهم** عليّ وعثمان، ابنا جُدَيع الكِرْمانيّ الأزديّ. وكانا سارا إلى أبي مسلم بعد قتل
نصر بن سيّار أباهما غِيلةً وغدراً، فناصحا أبا مسلم وأحْسنا مَعُونته، حتّى إذا استقامت خراسان
دعا أبو مسلم عليًّا فقال له: سَمِّ لي[١] أصحابك فقد نصحتَ وأحسنتَ وقضيتَ ما عليك،
وبقِيَ ما علينا. فسمّاهم له، فولّى عثمانَ أخاه طُخارستان، ففرّق عنه فُرسانه. ثمّ قال له: أحضِرْ
لي أصحابَك لأُجيزَهم. فقال لهم عليّ: اغْدوا على جوائز أبي مسلم. فغدَوْا وغدا، فأُدْخِلوا داراً
فأُعْطُوا فيها الجوائزَ، ثمّ قيل: ادْخلوا[٢] فتشكَّروا لأبي مسلم. فلمّا خرجوا أُدخلوا داراً أخرى قُمطوا
وأُخِذت الجوائز منهم فقُتلوا، وكتب إلى أبي داود الذُّهْليّ، | وهو خالد بن إبراهيم: لا يغلِبَنّك ١٩٢
عثمانُ بن الكِرْمانيّ. فاتّخذ له[٣] طعاماً، وبعث إليه فأتاه في قُوّاده ووجوه فُرسانه، وكان أبو داود
عاملاً على ما وراء النهر. فلمّا أتوْه وحضر الطعام أُخذوا فضُربت أعناقهم، ثمّ ركب إلى عسكرهم
فقتل فيه تسعمائة رجل، وتتبّع من كان أبو مسلم ولّاه منهم فقتله.

[§ ٦٢] **ومنهم** عبد اللّٰه بن عليّ بن عبد اللّٰه بن العبّاس. وكان عبد اللّٰه لمّا بلغه موت أبي العبّاس خلع أبا جعفر ودعا إلى نفسه وكان أبو جعفر حاجًّا، وثار عيسى بن موسى بن محمّد بن عليّ، فأحرز الخزائن وضبط الأمر حتّى قدم أبو جعفر، فوجّه أبا مسلم لحربه، فحاربه فهزمه، فلجأ إلى أخيه سليمان بن عليّ، وهو عامل على البصرة، فأخذ له الأمان المؤكّد.

---

١ ك: (لك).

٢ كذا.

٣ ك: (لهم).

---

666 On their father Juday' see above, § 57; see also *ĞN*, i, 213, ii, 263. 'Alī and 'Uthmān were killed in 130/747–748; see e.g. al-Ṭabarī, *Tārīkh*, ii, 1997–2000, tr. *The History*, xxvii, 104–107. Ibn Ḥabīb does not give a motive for the murder. It appears that Abū Muslim is merely consolidating his position by removing potential rivals after having used them to his advantage; see Hawting, *The First Dynasty of Islam*, 115–116.

667 On him see above, § 57.

668 The region of Balkh, ancient Bactria.

669 The context seems to require "Go outside".

670 'ASH suggests that instead *qumiṭū* one could read *fa-muṭū*, "they were thrown on their backs".

671 Abū Dāwūd Khālid ibn Ibrāhīm (d. 140/757) was the governor of Balkh and Transoxania. See *ĞN*, i, 152, ii, 341.

672 Abd Allāh ibn 'Alī (d. 147/764) was a paternal uncle of Abū l-'Abbās al-Saffāḥ and Abū

[§ 61 ʿAlī and ʿUthmān, sons of Judayʿ al-Kirmānī al-Azdī[666]]

Among them are ʿAlī and ʿUthmān, the two sons of Judayʿ al-Kirmānī al-Azdī. They had gone over to Abū Muslim after Naṣr ibn Sayyār[667] had betrayed their father and had him assassinated. They acted as advisers to Abū Muslim and supported him. When Khorasan was under control, Abū Muslim summoned ʿAlī and said, "Give me the names of your followers! You have given me good advice and you have done what you had to do. Now it remains for me to do what I have to." ʿAlī gave him their names. Then Abū Muslim appointed ʿAlī's brother ʿUthmān as governor of Tokharistan.[668] He separated ʿAlī's cavalry from him, then he said to him, "Bring your followers, so that I can reward them!" ʿAlī told them, "Tomorrow you'll get rewards from Abū Muslim." He and they came the following day. They were led into a house and given presents. Then they were told, "Go inside[669] and give thanks to Abū Muslim!" When they went outside they were made to enter another house, where their hands and feet were tied up together,[670] their presents were taken away from them, and they were killed. He wrote to Abū Dāwūd al-Dhuhlī, | i.e., Khālid ibn Ibrāhīm:[671] "Don't let ʿUth- 192
mān, al-Kirmānī's son, get the better of you!" Abū Dāwūd prepared a dish for him and had it sent to him. He visited him amidst his commanders and cavalry leaders; Abū Dāwūd was governor of Transoxania. When they got to him and the food was served, they were apprehended and they were beheaded. Then he rode to their army camp and killed nine hundred men. He traced all those that Abū Muslim had appointed and killed them.

[§ 62 ʿAbd Allāh ibn ʿAlī ibn ʿAbd Allāh ibn al-ʿAbbās[672]]

When ʿAbd Allāh heard that Abū l-ʿAbbās had died, he refused allegiance to Abū Jaʿfar and proclaimed himself as successor. Abū Jaʿfar was on pilgirimage. ʿĪsā ibn Mūsā ibn Muḥammad ibn ʿAlī[673] rose into action; he secured the treasury and took control until Abū Jaʿfar returned. The latter sent Abū Muslim to fight ʿAbd Allāh. Abū Muslim gave battle and defeated him. ʿAbd Allāh sought refuge with his brother Sulaymān ibn ʿAlī, who was governor of Basra, and he

---

Jaʿfar al-Manṣūr. See *EI2*, "ʿAbd Allāh b. ʿAlī" (K.V. Zetterstéen & S. Moscati), *EI3*, "ʿAbdallāh b. ʿAlī" (J. Lassner). He played a major part in the Abbasid revolt and claimed the caliphate after al-Saffāḥ's death, having a better military record than al-Manṣūr.

673 ʿĪsā's father Mūsā was a brother of al-Saffāḥ and al-Manṣūr. On ʿĪsā (d. 167/783–784) see *EI2*, "ʿĪsā b. Mūsā" (D. Sourdel).

ثمّ إنّ أبا جعفر دفعه عيسى بن موسى فكان محبوساً عنده، فجعل يرفّهُ عنه ويشتري له الجارية بعد الجارية. ولمّا خرج محمّد بن عبد الله بن الحسن بالمدينة أمر عيسى بن موسى بالخروج إليه، وأن يدفعه إلى أبي الأزهر عبد الملك[١] بن عُبَيْثِر المَهْرِيّ، فجاء به حتّى أدخله بيتاً في قصر أبي جعفر، وخرج أبو جعفر إلى أَوانا، وسقط البيت على عبد الله بن عليّ، رحمه الله.

١٩٣ [§٦٣] **ومنهم** أبو مُسْلِم صاحب الدولة. وكان أبو جعفر وجّهه أبو العبّاس في ثلاثين من وجوه قُريش والعرب إلى خراسان زائراً أبا مسلم، فرأى منهم استخفافاً احتقنها[٢] أبو جعفر عليه، وكان إذا كتب إليه بدأ بنفسه قبله. فكان أبو جعفر يقول لأبي العبّاس كثيراً: إنّه لا مُلْك لك وأبو مسلم حيّ، فتغدَّه قبل أن يتعشّى بك! وكان أبو العبّاس يأبى ذلك لقَدْره في أهل خراسان.

فلمّا أفضى الأمرُ إلى أبي جعفر وكان أبو مسلم حاجًّا فقدِم ووجّهه[٣] أبو جعفر فحاربَ عبد الله بن عليّ واستباح عسكرَه. ثمّ وجّه أبو جعفر إلى أبي مسلم يَقْطينَ بن موسى لقبْض ما صار في يد أبي مسلم من عسكر عبد الله، فغَضِب أبو مسلم وقال: لا يُوثَق بي في هذا القدر! وشتم

١ كذا في هـ، كـ؛ ويظهر أنّ الصحيح (أبي الأزهر المهلّب) كما في المراجع.

٢ لعلّ الصحيح، كما قال هـ، (فرأى منه استخفافا وأشياء احتقنها).

٣ كـ: (وَوَجَّه).

674 Muḥammad ibn ʿAbd Allāh ibn (al-)Ḥasan ibn (al-)Ḥasan ibn ʿAlī, called al-Nafs al-Zakiyyah ("the Pure Soul"), led an ʿAlid revolt in Medina and was killed in 145/762–763. See al-Iṣfahānī, *Maqātil*, 206–262; al-Ṣafadī, *Wāfī*, iii, 297–300; *EI2*, "Muḥammad b. ʿAbd Allāh (…) al-Nafs al-Zakiyya" (F. Buhl).

675 As often, the use of pronouns is confusing and potentially misleading. In this sentence the first "him" seems to refer to al-Nafs al-Zakiyyah and the second to ʿAbd Allāh ibn ʿAlī.

676 This seems to be an error for Abū l-Azhar al-Muhallab ibn ʿUbaythir al-Mahrī, who is mentioned in al-Jāḥiẓ, *Bayān*, ii, 111, iii, 372 and *ĞN*, i, 328, ii, 421.

677 ʿAbd Allāh's imprisonment seems to have lasted for several years. His death, here described as an "accident", was clearly considered as intended (or else he would not have been included in the book). Other accounts say that he was strangled together with a concubine, after which the room was made to collapse (e.g. al-Masʿūdī, *Murūj*, iv, 160–161). Al-Manṣūr is said to have denied responsibility: "It is not my fault if a room has collapsed on him!" (al-Ṣafadī, *Wāfī*, xvii, 322).

678 ʿAbd al-Raḥmān ibn Muslim, usually called Abū Muslim (d. 137/755), has already appeared above on many occasions. He was probably Persian (see the discussion of his descent

was guaranteed protection. Abū Jaʿfar had him sent to ʿĪsā ibn Mūsā and he was detained at his place. ʿĪsā made his life comfortable and provided him with one concubine after another.

When Muḥammad ibn ʿAbd Allāh ibn al-Ḥasan[674] rebelled in Medina, Abū Jaʿfar ordered ʿĪsā ibn Mūsā to march to him and to deliver him[675] unto Abū l-Azhar ʿAbd al-Malik ibn ʿUbaythir al-Mahrī.[676] He brought him to a room in Abū Jaʿfar's castle. The room collapsed on ʿAbd Allāh ibn ʿAlī, God have mercy on him.[677]

[§ 63 Abū Muslim[678]]

Another is Abū Muslim, "Master of the Dynasty".[679] Abū Jaʿfar had been sent 193
by Abū l-ʿAbbās, together with thirty prominent members of Quraysh and the Arabs, to Khorasan to visit Abū Muslim. Abū Jaʿfar then noticed a disdain in Abū Muslim[680] and saw things he resented. When Abū Muslim wrote to him he began with his own name before Abū Jaʿfar's. Abū Jaʿfar would often say to Abū l-ʿAbbās, "You do not reign as long Abū Muslim is alive. Have him for breakfast before he has you for dinner!" But Abū l-ʿAbbās turned down this advice because of Abū Muslīm's status among the Khorasanians.

When Abū Jaʿfar came to power Abū Muslim was away on pilgrimage. When he returned, Abū Jaʿfar sent him to fight ʿAbd Allāh ibn ʿAlī,[681] whose army camp he plundered as booty. Then Abū Jaʿfar sent Yaqṭīn ibn Mūsā[682] to confiscate the goods Abū Muslim had taken from ʿAbd Allāh's army. This incensed Abū Muslim, who said, "Am I not to be trusted to that extent?!" and he uttered vile

in e.g. al-Masʿūdī, *Murūj*, iv, 78 and the Persian lineage given to him in Ibn Khallikān, *Wafayāt*, iii, 145 that goes back to the Sassanid minister Buzurgmihr). He was the effective leader of the Abbasid movement that began in Khorasan and ended with the overthrow of the Umayyads. On him see *EI3*, "Abū Muslim al-Khurasānī" (Salah Said Agha). Among the many parallel texts about his death see al-Ṭabarī, *Tārīkh*, iii, 99–117, tr. *The History*, xxviii, 18–41; al-Balādhurī, *Ansāb*, iv, 270–276; al-Masʿūdī, *Murūj*, iv, 138–143; al-Dīnawarī, *al-Akhbār al-ṭiwāl*, 373–378; Ibn Qutaybah, *al-Imāmah wa-l-siyāsah*, ii, 183–185; al-Maqdisī, *al-Badʾ wa-l-tārīkh*, vi, 76–82.

679 The word *dawlah* often means "dynasty" (and, in modern Arabic, "state"), but its original meaning is "alternation, rotation, change of fortune" and *ṣāḥib al-dawlah* could therefore also be interpreted as "Master of the Revolution".

680 As ʿASH suggests, one ought to read *minhu* ("from him", viz. Abū Muslim) instead of *minhum* ("from them").

681 See § 62.

682 Yaqṭīn ibn Mūsā (d. 186/802) was one of the "missionaries" of the Abbasid movement. See e.g. al-Ṣafadī, *Wāfī*, xxix, 40–41.

شَتْماً قبيحاً. ومضى من الأنبار يريد خراسان مُخالِفاً، ومضى أبو جعفر إلى المدائن فنزل الروميّة. وقد كان قيل لأبي مسلم: إنك تُقتل بالروم. فوجّه أبو جعفر إلى أبي مسلم جريرَ بن يزيد بن جرير بن عبد الله البَجَليّ، وكان أرجلَ[1] أهل زمانه. وكتب معه فلم يلتفت إلى كتابه. فلم يزل جريرٌ يفتِل[2] أبا مسلم في الذِّرْوة والغارب حتّى أقبل إلى أبي جعفر، فلمّا قدِم أمَرَ القوّادَ والناسَ أن يتلقَّوْه، ثمّ أَذِن له فدخل على دابّته وعانَقَه وأكرمه وقال: كدتَ تخرج قبل أن أفضِيَ إليك ما[3]
أريد. قال: | يا أمير المؤمنين، قد أتيتُك فمُرْ بأمرك. قال: انصرفْ إلى منزلك فضعْ ثيابك، وادخلِ ١٩٤
الحمّام يذهبْ عنك كَلالُ السفر. فجعل أبو جعفر ينتظر به الفُرَص، فمكث به أيّاماً يأتي أبا جعفر كلَّ يوم فيُريه من الإكرام أكثرَ ممّا أراه قبل ذلك، ويتزيّد في القُرب واللُّطف، حتّى إذا مضت له أيامٌ أقبل على التجنّي عليه. فأتى أبو مسلم عيسى بن موسى فقال: اركَبْ معي إلى أمير المؤمنين، فإنّي أريد عِتابه بحضرتك. فقال له: تقدّمْ حتّى آتِيَك. فقال: إنّي أخافه. فقال له عيسى: أنت في ذِمّتي. وأقبل أبو مسلم فقيل له: ادخلْ. فدخل حتّى إذا صار إلى الرواق قيل: أمير المؤمنين يتوضّأ، فلو جلست. فجلس وأبطأ عيسى عليه، وقد هيّأ أبو جعفر عثمانَ بن نَهيك العَكّيّ، وهو على حرسه، في عِدّةٍ فيهم شَبيب بن واج وأبو حنيفة، وتقدّم إلى عثمان فقال: إذا عاتبتُه فعَلا صوْتي فلا تحرَّكوا، فإذا صفّقتُ بِيَدي فدونَك يا عثمان!

وقد صيَّر عثمان وأصحابه في رِواقٍ خلف أبي جعفر، ثمّ قيل لأبي مسلم: قد جلس أمير المؤمنين فقُمْ. فقام ليدخل فقيل له: انزَعْ سيفك. فقال: ما كان يُصنَع هذا بي. قالوا: وما عليك؟ فنزع سيفه وعليه قَباءٌ أسود على جُبّة خَزٍّ بَنَفسجيّة، فدخل فسلّم وجلس على وِسادةٍ ليس في

١ لعلّ الصحيح (أوحد).

٢ كـ (يقتل).

٣ لعلّ الصحيح (بما).

683 See §1 note 4.

684 A location near al-Madāʾin, see e.g. al-Dīnawārī, *Akhbār*, 70, 379. Al-Masʿūdī, *Murūj*, i, 307 says it was built by the Sassanid emperor Anūsharwān with spoils taken from the Romans.

685 The text has *arjal*, whatever this means. Probably it is a misreading of *awḥad*. Al-Maqdisī, *Badʾ*, vi, 79, calls Jarīr ibn Yazīd "unmatched in his time in cunning, deceit, shrewdnes, duplicity, and eloquence" (*awḥad zamānihī fī l-makr wa-l-khidāʿ wa-l-dahāʾ wa-l-talbīs wa-l-lisān*): the right man to lure Abū Muslim back.

insults. He left al-Anbār,[683] intending to go to Khorasan, disobeying orders. Abū Jaʿfar went to al-Madāʾin and stayed in al-Rūmiyyah.[684] Abū Muslim had been told, "You will be killed in Rūm".

Abū Jaʿfar sent Jarīr ibn Yazīd ibn Jarīr ibn ʿAbd Allāh al-Bajalī, the most fleet-footed man of his time,[685] to Abū Muslim, and he sent letters with him, but Abū Muslim did not pay any attention to the writing. Jarīr kept coaxing Abū Muslim high and low[686] until in the end he went to Abū Jaʿfar. When he arrived, Abū Jaʿfar told the commanders and the other people to receive him; then he gave him permission to enter. He came in on his mount. Abū Jaʿfar embraced him and honoured him, saying, "You were almost gone before I could let you know what I want." Abū Muslim replied, | "Commander of the Believers, I have come 194
to you. Tell me your command." "Go home, take off your robes, go and have a bath, to recover from the fatigue of travelling!"

Abū Jaʿfar kept waiting for an opportunity. Abū Muslim stayed for days, seeing Abū Jaʿfar every day, while being paid more respect than he had ever been paid before. Abū Jaʿfar showed ever more intimacy and friendliness, until, after several days, Abū Muslim even dared to accuse him. He went to ʿĪsā ibn Mūsā[687] and said, "Ride with me to the Commander of the Believers, for I want to reproach him in your presence." ʿĪsā said, "You go ahead, I'll come." "I am afraid of him", said Abū Muslim. ʿĪsā replied, "I'll protect you." Abū Muslim arrived and they said to him, "Enter!" He entered, and when he got to the portico they said, "The Commander of the Believers is performing the minor ablution. Wouldn't you sit down?" So he sat down, waiting for ʿĪsā's arrival. Abū Jaʿfar had instructed ʿUthmān ibn Nahīk al-ʿAkkī, the commander of his guard, with a number of others, including Shabīb ibn Wāj[688] and Abū Ḥanīfah.[689] He told ʿUthmān, "When I reproach him in a loud voice, don't move, but when I clap my hands, it's your turn, ʿUthmān!"

ʿUthmān and his men had been posted in the portico, behind Abū Jaʿfar. They told Abū Muslim, "The Commander of Believers has sat down; stand up!" He stood up in order to enter. "Take off your sword!", they told him. He said, "They never did this to me!" But they said, "Don't you worry!" So he took off his sword. He was wearing a black robe over a violet silk mantle. He entered,

---

686 Literally, "kept twisting Abū Muslim from the top of the camel's hump to the bottom".

687 See above, § 62.

688 Al-Ṭabarī calls him Shabīb ibn Wāj al-Marwarrūdhī, i.e., from Marwarrūdh (or Marw al-Rūdh), a town in Khorasan.

689 In al-Ṭabarī's *Tārīkh* he is called Abū Ḥanīfah Ḥarb ibn Qays.

المجلس غيرها، وخلْف ظهره القوم، فقال: يا أمير المؤمنين صُنع بي ما لم يُصنع بأحد، نُزع
سيفي من عنقي. قال: ومن فعل ذلك بك قَبَحه اللّٰه؟ ثمّ أقبل يعاتبه: فعلتَ وفعلتَ. فقال أبو
١٩٥ مسلم: ليس يقال هذا لي بعد بَلائي وما كان منّي! فقال: يا ابنَ الخبيثة، | لو كانت أَمَةٌ مكانَك
لأجزأتْ ناحِيَتَها. إنّما عمِلتَ ما عملتَ في دولتنا، ألستَ الكاتبَ إليَّ تبدأ بنفسك، والكاتب
إليَّ تخطب أمينةَ بنت عليّ بن عبد اللّٰه بن العبّاس، وتزعُم أنّك ابن سَليط بن عبد اللّٰه بن
العبّاس؟ لقد ارتقيتَ لا أُمَّ لك مرتقًى صعباً! وهو يفرك بيديه. فلمّا رأى أبو مسلم عينيه قال: يا
أمير المؤمنين لا تُدْخِلْ على نفسك؛ فإنّ قدْري أصغر من أن يبلُغ هذا منك.

ثمّ صفّق بيديه، فيضربه عثمان ضربة خفيفة، فأخذ برجْل أبي جعفر وقال: أنشُدك اللّٰهَ يا أمير المؤمنين! فدفعه برجله وضربه شبيب بن واجٍ ضربةً على حبل العاتق، فأسرعتْ فيه، فصاح: وانفْساه! ألا قُوّة، ألا مُغيث! وخرج القوم فاعتَوَروه بأسيافهم، ولحِق بأُمّه الهاوية.

[§ ٦٤] **ومنهم** مَعْن بن زائدة الشَّيبانيّ، وكان أبو جعفر ولّاه اليمن، فلمّا صار إلى الكوفة بعث إلى محمّد بن سهل، راوية شعر الكُمَيت بن زيد، فأتاه فقال: أنْشِدْني قصيدة الكميت التي يدعو فيها ربيعةَ إلى قطْع حِلْفها مع اليمن. وهي: ألَمْ تُلْمِمْ على الطَّلَل[١] المُحِيلِ؛ فأنشده

---

١ ك: (الطّلّ).

---

690 *Qabaḥahu llāh*, literally "God make him ugly"; on this idiom see Ullmann, *Flüche*, 94–99.

691 In al-Maqdisī, *Bad'*, he claims to be Salīṭ himself. No such son of al-ʿAbbās is found in other sources.

692 *Lā umm laka*, literally "you have no mother!" (i.e., no known mother), or, alternatively, "may you have no mother!"; see e.g. Lane, *Lexicon* (*'MM*).

693 Al-Ṭabarī has: "Abū Muslim began to rub the caliph's fingers and kiss them, apologising".

694 *Lā tudkhil ʿalā nafsika*; cf. e.g. al-Dīnawarī, *Akhbār*: *lā tudkhil ʿalā nafsika al-ghamm wa-l-ghayẓ bi-sababī*.

695 *Laḥiqa bi-ummihi al-hāwiyah*, a reference to Q al-Qāriʿah 101:9, *fa-ummuhū hāwiyah*, a much-debated expression. Arberry: «shall plunge in the womb of the Pit»; Abdel Halim: «will have the Bottomless Pit for his home»; Jones: «His mother will take possession» or «… will be childless» (arguing that *hāwiyah* cannot be "the bottomless pit", being indefinite). This is the only occasion that Ibn Ḥabīb makes a clear and unmistakably negative comment on the afterlife to be expected for the victim.

696 Abū l-Walīd Maʿn ibn Zā'idah (d. 152/759–760), of Shaybān (for his lineage see *ǦN*, i, 146), general and governor under the last Umayyads and the early Abbasids. See *EI2*, "Maʿn b. Zā'ida" (H. Kennedy). He was famous for his generosity and patronage of poets. On his murder see e.g. al-Yaʿqūbī, *Tārīkh*, ii, 462–463, tr. *The Works*, 1119–1120; Ibn Khallikān,

greeted (the caliph), and sat down on a pillow, the only one in the audience hall. The men were standing behind him. "Commander of the Believers," he said, "They did to me what has never been done to anyone! My sword has been taken from me!" The caliph replied, "And who did this? Damn him!"[690] But then he began to reproach him: "You did this, you did that …!" Abū Muslim replied, "One cannot say this to me, after all the trouble I have endured and what I have achieved!" The caliph said, "You son of a bad woman! | If a slave woman had 195
been in your place she would have done the same. You did all these things to our reign; haven't you written letters to me mentioning yourself first? And didn't you write to me asking for the hand in marriage of Amīnah, the daughter of ʿAlī ibn ʿAbd Allāh ibn al-ʿAbbās, claiming that you are the son of Salīṭ ibn ʿAbd Allāh ibn ʿAbbās?[691] You have climbed too high, damn you!"[692] Abū Muslim was rubbing the caliph's fingers all the while.[693] When he looked into the caliph's eyes, he said, "Commander of the Believers, don't let it affect you![694] I am too unimportant for the matter to come to this!"

Then the caliph clapped his hands. ʿUthmān struck Abū Muslim lightly. He grabbed Abū Jaʿfar's foot and said, "I implore you, by God, Commander of the Believers!" But the caliph pushed him away with his foot and then Shabīb ibn Wāj struck him between his neck and his shoulder, which made for a quick end. He shouted "O my soul! Is there no power, no helper …?" The men came and took turns to strike him with their swords, and he went to "his mother the Bottomless Pit".[695]

[§ 64 Maʿn ibn Zāʾidah al-Shaybānī[696]]

Another is Maʿn ibn Zāʾidah al-Shaybānī. Abū Jaʿfar had appointed him as governor of Yemen. When he arrived in Kufa he sent for Muḥammad ibn Sahl, the transmitter of al-Kumayt.[697] When he had come Maʿn asked him, "Recite to me al-Kumayt's poem in which he calls upon the Rabīʿah to cut off their alliance with the Yaman!"[698] It begins with "Have you not visited the campsite's remains

---

Wafayāt, v, 249. His murderers were Khārijites, whom he had fought and defeated. The would-be workmen had hidden their swords in bundles of reeds left in the house, as told in al-Yaʿqūbī's *Tārīkh*.

697 Al-Kumayt ibn Zayd (d. 126/743 or 127/744) was a poet noted for his pro-Shiʿite poems; on him see Sezgin, *Geschichte*, ii, 347–349, *EI2*, "al-Kumayt b. Zayd al-Asadī" (J. Horovitz & Ch. Pellat). Major poets often had a "transmitter" (*rāwī* or, as here, *rāwiyah*), who memorised their poems.

698 Rabiʿah and al-Yaman stand for the North and South Arab tribal federations, respectively. It should not be thought that the tribes belonging to al-Yaman actually lived in Yemen.

إيّاها حتّى أتى عليها، وأمر بعِمامةٍ فلُوِيَت ومُدّت بين رَجُلين، ثمّ قام معنٌ فضربها بالسيف
فقطعها، وقال: اشهَدوا أنّي قد قطعت حِلْف اليمن وربيعة كما قطعتُ هذه العمامة. | ثمّ سار ١٩٦
إلى اليمن فأوعث فيها، فلمّا وليَ سجستان ابتنى بها داراً، فدخل عليه قومٌ متشبّهة بالفَعَلة وهو
مُغْتَرٌّ قد احتجم، فمالوا عليه فقتلوه.

[§ ٦٥] **ومنهم** عُقْبة بن سَلْم الهُنائيّ. وكان أبو جعفر ولّاه البحريْن، فجعل يباري مَعْناً بالقتل حتّى أثخن في ربيعة، فلمّا كان زمان المَهْديّ تَبِعه رجل فاغتاله وهو راكب، فوجأه وَجْأةً بخنجر مسموم فوقع في مِنْطقته حتى وصل إلى جوفه، فأُخِذ فأُتِيَ به المهديّ فسأله ممّن هو، فلم يُجبْه مَن هو ولا من أيّ البلدان هو. فسأله: أين كان يأوي وأين كان يَطْعَم فقال: كنتُ آوي المَساجد، وأطعم في سُوق البقّالين. فقتله المهديّ. فيه تضرِب العامّة المَثَل: أجسر[١] من قاتل عقبة.

[§ ٦٦] **ومنهم** الربيع بن يونس الحاجب. وكان هو أهدى إلى موسى الهادي أَمَةَ العزيز، فوقعت
منه بالموقع الذي لم يقع أحد عنده مثله، فبلغه أنّ الربيع يقول: ما خلوتُ بامرأةٍ أطْيبَ خَلْوةً من | ١٩٧
أمة العزيز. فدعاه فتغدّى معه وقال له: اشربْ على غَذائك أقداحاً. وأمر صاحبَ شرابه فجدح
له في قَدَحه سمًّا، فلما صار في جوفه انصرف فمات من تحت ليلته.

١ هـ، كـ (أخسَرُ)، والتصحيح من مجمع الأمثال للميدانيّ.

699 In al-Kumayt's *Dīwān*, 350 only the two opening verses are given and no more verses are known. A long poem (71 verses) beginning with an identical hemistich is by ʿUmar ibn Lajaʾ (contemporary of Jarīr and al-Farazdaq), found in Ibn Maymūn, *Muntahā*, iii, 83–87, but it does not refer to Rabīʿah or Yaman and is therefore not the poem requested by Maʿn.

700 For his lineage, of Hunāʾah, a branch of al-Azd (belonging to al-Yaman), see *ǦN*, i, 211 and ii, 573. He was murdered in ʿĪsābādh near Baghdad in 167/783–784. See al-Ṭabarī, *Tārīkh*, iii, 520–521, tr. *The History*, xxix, 238. In al-Masʿūdī, *Murūj*, iv, 70 he is called ʿUqbah ibn Sālim (but Salm is confirmed by several eulogies, notably one by Bashshār ibn Burd, where Sālim would not fit the metre).

701 Not the present-day island-state called Bahrein but the nearby eastern coastal area of the Arabian Peninsula.

702 Maʿn ibn Zāʾidah, see above, § 64.

703 Al-Mahdī (reg. 158–169/775–786) succeeded his father Abū Jaʿfar al-Manṣūr as caliph.

704 ʿASH and SKḤ have *akhsar* ("a greater loser"), evidently a misreading of *ajsar*, as in al-Maydānī, *Majmaʿ al-amthāl*, i, 241–242, al-Zamakhsharī, *Mustaqṣā*, i, 49; compare al-ʿAskarī, *Jamharah*, i, 274–275, which has *ajraʾ* ("bolder").

705 Al-Rabīʿ ibn Yūnus, of obscure origin was born a slave in Medina, was appointed as *ḥājib* (chamberlain) by al-Manṣūr and also served his successors al-Mahdī and al-Hādī (reg. 169–

of yesteryear …?"[699] The transmitter recited it until the end. Maʿn asked for a turban to be brought. It was wound and stretched taut by two men. Then Maʿn stood up and cut it into two with his sword and said, "Be witness that I cut off the alliance of al-Yaman and Rabīʿah just as I have cut this turban!" | Then he 196
went off to Yemen, where he acted harshly. When he was appointed governor in Sijistān he built a house for himself. Some men, dressed as workmen, entered when he was off-guard, having just been bled. They went for him and killed him.

[§ 65 ʿUqbah ibn Salm al-Hunāʾī[700]]

Another is ʿUqbah ibn Salm al-Hunāʾī. Abū Jaʿfar had appointed him governor of al-Baḥrayn.[701] There he vied with Maʿn[702] in killing, making great slaughter among the Rabīʿah. In the time of al-Mahdī[703] a man followed him while he was riding, and he murdered him by stabbing him with a poisoned dagger. It hit his belt but then entered his body. The man was apprehended and taken to al-Mahdī, who asked to whom he belonged. The man did not answer saying who he was or where he was from. Then he asked where he had been staying the night and taking his meals. The man answered, "I've been staying in mosques and eating at the greengrocers' market." Al-Mahdī had him executed. The common people coined a saying, "More daring than ʿUqbah's killer".[704]

[§ 66 al-Rabīʿ ibn Yūnus[705]]

Another is al-Rabīʿ ibn Yūnus, the chamberlain. He had presented Mūsā al-Hādī with Amat al-ʿAzīz,[706] who pleased al-Hādī like nobody else. Then al-Hādī heard that al-Rabīʿ used to say, "I have never been intimate with a nicer woman than | Amat al-ʿAzīz." The caliph invited him and had breakfast with him. "You 197
must drink some cups with you breakfast!" he said. He told his wine steward to mix poison in his cup.[707] When it reached his stomach al-Rabīʿ left. He died that night.

170/785–786). He died in 169 or 170. Some sources say he died of an illness (Ibn Khallikān, *Wafayāt*, ii, 299). See *EI2*, "al-Rabīʿ b, Yūnus" (A.S. Atiyah). On his death see also al-Ṭabarī, *Tārīkh*, iii, 520–521, tr. *The History*, xxx, 85–87.

706 Amat al-ʿAzīz was a slave-girl owned by al-Rabīʿ ibn Yūnus. Al-Ṭabarī, *Tārīkh*, iii, 597–598 says that she was first offered to al-Mahdī, who thought she was more fit to be al-Hādī's. After the latter's death she became Hārūn al-Rashīd's and was the mother of Hārūn's son ʿAlī.

707 The word *sharāb*, "drink", often means "wine", as is also suggested by the word *ka's* in al-Ṭabarī's version, where the drink is called *sharāb ʿasal*, a "honey drink", perhaps a kind of mead.

[§٦٧] **ومنهم** إدريس بن عبد الله بن حسن بن الحسن بن عليّ بن أبي طالب. وكان خرج
على موسى الهادي [هو][١] والحسن والحسين ابنا عليّ بن الحسن بن الحسن، فقُتلا بفَخّ،
وانضمّ[٢] إدريس إلى أهل المغرب، فحملوه إلى بلادهم واشتملوا عليه وأعظموه وأمّروه عليهم.
فلمّا ولي هارونُ الرشيد وولّى هرثمةَ إفريقيةَ دسَّ هرثمةُ رجلاً من أهل المدينة لإدريس، وجعل له
بقتله مائة ألف درهم، فقدم المَدَنيّ عليه فأَنِس به إدريس وجعل يسأله عن أهله فيخبره بمعرفة
حتّى غلب عليه ووَثِق به، وجعل يهتبل الفُرصة ويضع الخَيْل في القُرى فيما بينه وبين إفريقية.

وإنّ إدريس اشتهى سمكاً طريًّا فقال له المدنيّ: أنا حَسَن العِلاج له. فعالجه وسمّه. ثمّ خرج
يريد حاجة، ودعا إدريس بالسمك، فلمّا أكله واستقرّ في جوفه رَكِب، فجعل يركب من قرية
إلى قرية ويحلف ما تحته[٣] حتّى وصل | إلى إفريقية، وكانت جاريته حاملاً فولدت غلاماً فسُمّي ١٩٨
إدريس بن إدريس.

١ كذا في هـ، ك، والزيادة لمقتضى السياق.

٢ ك: (وانظم).

٣ كذا في النسختين والعبارة غير واضحة. ولعلّ الصواب (ويخلّف ما تحته)، يعني الفرس الذي كان يركبه.

708 The name may appear with or, as here, without the article.

709 Idrīs ibn ʿAbd Allāh (d. 175/791), another ʿAlid, the brother of al-Nafs al-Zakiyyah (see above, §62), is the founder of the dynasty that ruled in Morocco for some two centuries, called after him the Idrīsids, see Bosworth, *New Islamic Dynasties*, 25–26; *EI2*, "Idrīs I" (D. Eustache) and "Idrīsids" (D. Eustache); *EI3*, "Idrīsids" (Chafik T. Benchekroun). On his death see e.g. al-Ṭabarī, *Tārīkh*, iii, 561–562, tr. *The History*, xxx, 28–30, al-Iṣfahānī, *Maqātil*, 407–408.

710 A place near Mecca, the site of a battle in 169/786; see *EI2*, "Fakhkh" (L. Veccia Vaglieri), *EI3*, "Fakhkh" (John P. Turner).

711 *Al-maghrib*, "the place where the sun sets" or "the West", usually refers to North Africa with the exception of Egypt; here it is Morocco (which today is called al-Maghrib).

712 In 170/786.

713 Harthamah ibn Aʿyan (d. 200/816), prominent general and governor especially under Hārūn al-Rashīd. See *EI2*, "Harthamah b. Aʿyan" (Ch. Pellat), *EI3*, "Harthamah b. Aʿyan" (John P. Turner).

714 Ifrīqiyah (also spelled Ifrīqiyyah) is the eastern part of al-Maghrib, more or less modern Tunisia.

[§ 67 Idrīs ibn ʿAbd Allāh ibn Ḥasan[708] ibn al-Ḥasan ibn ʿAlī ibn Abī Ṭālib[709]]

Another is Idrīs ibn ʿAbd Allāh ibn Ḥasan ibn al-Ḥasan ibn ʿAlī ibn Abī Ṭālib. He had led a revolt against Mūsā al-Hādī, together with al-Ḥasan and al-Ḥusayn the sons of ʿAlī ibn al-Ḥasan ibn al-Ḥasan. These two were killed at Fakhkh.[710] Idrīs joined people from the Maghrib,[711] who took him to their land. They rallied around him, honoured him, and made him their leader. When Hārūn al-Rashīd had come to rule[712] and had appointed Harthamah[713] as governor of Ifrīqiyah,[714] the latter secretly sent a man from Medina[715] to Idrīs, giving him 100,000 dirhams if he would kill him. The man from Medina went to him and received a friendly reception from Idrīs, who asked him about his family. The man told him, and in the end Idrīs trusted him. The man was scheming to find an opportunity, while posting horses[716] in the villages between him and Ifrīqiyah.

Idrīs wanted some fresh fish. The man from Medina said to him, "I am good at preparing it". So he did, and he put poison in it.[717] Then he left on some business. Idrīs called for the fish and when it was inside him he rode off, riding on,
while leaving a horse behind in every village(?),[718] until he reached | Ifrīqiyah. 198
His concubine was pregnant and gave birth to a boy, who was called Idrīs ibn Idrīs.[719]

---

715 He is called al-Shammākh al-Yamāmī in al-Ṭabarī, al-Shammākh al-Yamānī in al-Ṣafadī, *Wāfī*, viii, 318, and Sulaymān ibn Jarīr al-Jazarī, a Zaydī-Shiʿite theologian, in al-Iṣfahānī, *Maqātil*, 407–408, where also a physician called al-Shammākh is mentioned.

716 ʿAbd al-Salām Hārūn suggests that *wa-yaḍaʿu l-khayl*, could be a corruption of *wa-yaṣnaʿu l-ḥiyal*, but I believe the emendation may not be needed.

717 In al-Ṭabarī he is given poisoned tooth powder (*sanūn*), after he had complained of toothache, in al-Yaʿqūbī, *Tārīkh*, ii, 488–489 (tr. *The Works*, 1150–1151) it is a poisoned toothbrush (*miswāk*), and in one version in al-Iṣfahānī, *Maqātil*, 407–408 it is a poisoned perfume (*ghāliyah*, misspelled *ghāniyah* on p. 407).

718 The editions have *wa-y.ḥ.l.f mā taḥtahū*, which is unclear to me. SKḤ, taking Idrīs to be the subject of *rakiba* and *fa-jaʿala yarkabu*, suggests it means he "made people swear", i.e., allegiance, or else that Idrīs's flesh or limbs gradually disintegrated. Perhaps one should read *wa-yukhlifu* (for the verb *akhlafa* in the sense of "relieve oneself", also after been poisoned, see below, § 70) but I do not know *mā taḥtahū* as a euphemism and I have translated as if it were *wa-yukhallifu mā taḥtahū*. It would be tempting to assume that it is the poisoner who makes a fast escape using the post-horses (and this is what *Maqātil* says), but here the syntax and what follows show that it can only be Idrīs who travels west. He died in Walīlā, ancient Volubilis, near Meknes (also called Walīlī, see *EI2*, "Walīlī" [Mohamed El Mansour]).

719 The concubine was a Berber woman called Kanzah; she gave birth in Walīlā in 175/791 to Idrīs ibn Idrīs who, after a period of regency, reigned 187–213/803–828.

[§٦٨] **ومنهم** الفضل بن سهل وزير عبد الله المأمون. وكان قد ضيَّق على المأمون، وحال بينه وبين كثير من لَذّاته، وكان أخذ عليه ألّا ينظر في قِصّة أحدٍ حتّى صار كالوصيِّ[١] الحاجر عليه، فدسَّ المأمون غالباً الروميَّ موْلاه فدخل عليه الحمّام فقتله فيه ومضي، فأُتِيَ به المأمون فقتله. وقُتل بسبب الفضل عليُّ بن أبي سعد، وعبد العزيز بن عِمران الطائيّ، وخَلَف المصريّ، ومؤْنِس البصريّ.

[§٦٩] **ومنهم** إسحاق بن موسى الهادي. وقد كانت الحربيّة اشتملت عليه وأمّرتْه، والمأمون
بخراسان، حين خرج | إبراهيم بن المَهْديّ، فاستولى على الأمر، فدسّ إليه المأمون ابنَه وخادماً ١٩٩
له فقتلاه، ثمّ أقاد به ابنه وقتل الخادمّ بالسِّياط.

١ كـ: (كالوحي).

720 Al-Faḍl ibn Sahl ibn Zadhānfarrūkh, of Iranian origin as his grandfather's name shows, had supported al-Ma'mūn during and after the conflict and civil war (193–198/809–813) between the latter and his brother al-Amīn, both sons of Hārūn al-Rashīd. He became head of the administrative as well as military affairs, earning him the title of Dhū l-Riʾāsatayn ("He with the two leaderships"). That al-Ma'mūn was behind al-Faḍl's assassination in 202/818, as told here, is uncertain. He was succeeded by his brother al-Ḥasan ibn Sahl. On al-Faḍl see *EI2*, "al-Faḍl b. Sahl b. Zadhānfarūkh" (D. Sourdel), *EI3*, "al-Faḍl b. Sahl b. Zadhānfarrūkh" (Hayrettin Yücesoy). On his death see e.g. al-Yaʿqūbī, *Tārīkh*, ii, 451–452 (tr. *The Works*, 1215); al-Masʿūdī, *Murūj*, iv, 299; al-Ṭabarī, *Tārīkh*, iii, 1027, tr. *The History*, xxxii, 80–81; Ibn Khallikān, *Wafayāt*, iv, 44; al-Ṣafadī, *Wāfī*, xxiv, 43–45.

721 Al-Masʿūdī, *Murūj*, iv, 299, for instance, speaks of a concubine whom al-Ma'mūn wanted to buy, but who was killed by al-Faḍl.

722 Al-Ṭabarī mentions four men: Ghālib al-Masʿūdī al-Aswad, Qusṭanṭīn al-Rūmī, Faraj al-Daylamī, and Muwaffaq al-Ṣaqlabī, an interesting ethnic combination of African, Byzantine, Iranian, and Slavic, with at least one Arab to follow.

723 In al-Ṭabarī's account all four men mentioned there are beheaded, as well as those others suspected of being implicated. Their heads were presented to al-Faḍl's brother al-Ḥasan.

[§ 68 al-Faḍl ibn Sahl[720]]

Another is al-Faḍl ibn Sahl, the vizier of ʿAbd Allāh al-Maʾmūn. He had annoyed al-Maʾmūn by often hindering him from enjoying his pleasures.[721] He also resented that he could not look at anybody's petition without al-Faḍl acting like his guardian who denied him access. So al-Maʾmūn secretly sent his *mawlā* Ghālib al-Rūmī,[722] who entered the hammam, killed al-Faḍl, and left. He was taken to al-Maʾmūn, who had him executed.[723] Also killed on account of al-Faḍl's murder were ʿAlī ibn Abī Saʿd,[724] ʿAbd al-ʿAzīz ibn ʿImrān al-Ṭāʾī,[725] Khalaf al-Miṣrī, and Muʾnis al-Baṣrī.[726]

[§ 69 Isḥāq ibn Mūsā al-Hādī[727]]

Another is Isḥāq ibn Mūsā al-Hādī. The troops of al-Ḥarbiyyah[728] had rallied around him and made him their leader when al-Maʾmūn was still in Khorasan and when | Ibrāhīm ibn al-Mahdī revolted.[729] Isḥāq took control, but al- 199
Maʾmūn secretly sent his[730] son and a servant who killed him. Then he had the son executed by way of retaliation and the servant killed with whips.

724 In al-Ṭabarī it is ʿAlī ibn Abī Saʿīd, said to be a son of al-Faḍl's sister.

725 ʿAbd al-ʿAzīz ibn ʿImrān ibn ʿAmr al-Ṭāʾī was the son of one of al-Manṣūr's generals.

726 Instead of the two last-mentioned, al-Ṭabarī has "ʿAlī, Mūsā, and Khalaf", without further clues as to their identities.

727 He was a son of caliph al-Hādī. See e.g. Ibn al-Athīr, *Kāmil*, v, 425 on the mutiny of the army in Baghdad, and the appointment of Isḥāq. The account of his murder has not been found in other sources. Isḥāq is mentioned among the eight sons of al-Hādī listed in al-Yaʿqūbī, *The Works*, 1153 (he is not mentioned in the Leiden edition).

728 Al-Ḥarbiyyah was a location in Baghdad, called after a general of al-Manṣūr called Ḥarb ibn ʿAbd Allāh al-Balkhī (Yāqūt, *Muʿjam al-buldān*).

729 Ibrāhīm ibn al-Mahdī (d. 224/839), son of caliph al-Mahdī, a gifted musician, poet, and cook, was proclaimed caliph in Baghdad in 201/817. Isḥāq ibn Mūsā was designated as his successor (al-Ṭabarī, *Tārīkh*, iii, 1014, 1024), but as al-Maʾmūn approached Baghdad Ibrāhīm lost support and went into hiding in 104/819. When he was apprehended he was forgiven by his nephew al-Maʾmūn. See *EI2*, "Ibrāhīm b. al-Mahdī" (D. Sourdel), *EI3*, "Ibrāhīm b. al-Mahdī" (John P. Turner).

730 Clearly, a son of Isḥāq is meant.

[§ ٧٠] **ومنهم** حُمَيد بن عبد الحَميد الطُّوسيّ. وكان حُميد كثيراً ما يقول: ما للمأمون عندي يدٌ، إنّما الأيادي عندي لأبي محمّد الحسن بن سهل. فيُرْفَع إليه.

وإنّه دعاه المأمونُ يوماً فأتاه وعنده أحمد بن أبي خالد الأحْول. وكان الذي بين حميد وبين أحمد بن أبي خالد سيّئاً.[١] فلما قُرّبت المائدة أجلس المأمونُ ابنَ أبي خالد معه على المائدة، فساء ذلك حميداً فقال له: يا أمير المؤمنين، لا أماتني اللّٰه حتّى يُرِيَني الدنيا عليك سهْلةً حتّى نَرى[٢] أيُّنا أنفع لك. فقال له ابن أبي خالد: يا أمير المؤمنين، إنّما يتمنّى فَسادَ مُلكك والفتنة. فقام المأمون عن المائدة ولم يتمَّ غَداءه واحتقنها عليه. وإنّه لمّا أراد المأمون الخروج للبِناء ببُوران ابنة الحسن بن سهل قال لحميد: يا أبا غانم، قد أَذِنْتُ لك في الحجّ. فانصرف حميد مسروراً، فدعا قهارِمتَه فأمرهم بآلات السفر، ثمّ أتاه جِبريل بن بخْتِيشُوع فقال: يا أبا غانم طَرِّ بدنك فإنّي أرجو أن تأتي[٣] بكلّ جارية معك حاملاً. وكان حميد مُغْرَماً بالنكاح، حلالاً وغيره، فسقاه شربة، وكان عنده متطبّب يقال له عبد اللّٰه الطَّيْفوريّ، فلمّا رأى الشَّربة قال لجبريل: أبو غانم اليومَ قد ضَعُف عن هذه. فقال له جبريل: قد نسيتَ اليوم! وعرف الطّيفوريُّ قصّة الشربة فلم يكشف له

١ ك: (شيئًا).
٢ كذا في هـ، ك، ولعلّ الصحيح (تَرى).
٣ ك: (تأتيني).

731 Abū Ghānim Ḥumayd ibn ʿAbd al-Ḥamīd al-Ṭūsī (d. 220/835) was al-Maʾmūn's general who ended Ibrāhīm ibn al-Mahdī's rebellion. His generosity was praised by poets. See *EI2*, "Ḥumayd b. ʿAbd al-Ḥamīd" (Ed.). He belonged to the Arab tribe of Ṭayyiʾ and was from Marw, rather than Ṭūs (see Ibn Abī Uṣaybiʿah, *ʿUyūn al-anbāʾ*, ed. Savage-Smith, ii, 404–406, tr. iii, 413–416, ed. Müller, i, 155–156), where his relationship with the physician ʿAbd Allāh al-Ṭayfūrī is described. No parallel texts on his death from poison have been found. Although Ibn Ḥabīb's text suggests that the caliph was behind the murder, he does not say this explicitly.

732 Al-Ḥasan ibn Sahl (d. 236/850–851), the brother of al-Faḍl ibn Sahl (above, § 68) was secretary and governor under al-Maʾmūn, See *EI2*, "al-Ḥasan b. Sahl" (D. Sourdel).

733 Aḥmad ibn Abī Khālid (d. 210/825–826), a *mawlā*, was vizier under al-Maʾmūn after al-Ḥasan ibn Sahl; see Ibn al-Ṭiqṭaqā, *Fakhrī*, 224–225.

734 Interpretation and translation of *ḥattā yuriyanī l-dunyā sahlatan ʿalayka ḥattā narā* uncertain; I have translated as if the text had *tarā* instead of *narā*.

735 The betrothal of the caliph and Būrān (also called Khadījah), born in 192/807, took place when she was some ten years old, but the consummation was celebrated in 210/825–826,

[§ 70 Ḥumayd ibn ʿAbd al-Ḥamīd al-Ṭūsī[731]]

Another is Ḥumayd ibn ʿAbd al-Ḥamīd al-Ṭūsī. He often said, "I owe no favours to al-Maʾmūn. Rather, I owe favours to Abū Muḥammad al-Ḥasan ibn Sahl!"[732] This was reported to al-Maʾmūn.

Al-Maʾmūn invited him one day; Aḥmad ibn Abī Khālid al-Aḥwal[733] was also present. Ḥumayd and Aḥmad ibn Abī Khālid were on bad terms. When the food was served al-Maʾmūn told Ibn Abī Khālid to sit with him at the table, which annoyed Ḥumayd. "Commander of the Believers," he said, "May God not let me die before He shows me that it is easy for you to see[734] which one of us is more useful to you!" Ibn Abī Khālid said, "Commander of the Believers, he only wishes to destroy your rule and to make trouble!" Al-Maʾmūn stood up and left the table without finishing his meal, keeping a grudge against Ḥumayd.

When al-Maʾmūn wanted to leave for the feast for the consummation of his wedding with Būrān, the daughter of al-Ḥasan ibn Sahl,[735] he said to Ḥumayd, "Abū Ghānim, I give you permission to go on the Hajj." Ḥumayd, pleased, left and told his stewards to make preparations for the journey. Then Jibrīl ibn Bukhtīshūʿ[736] came to him and said, "You should refresh your body, Abū Ghānim! For I should like you to come back with every concubine being pregnant!" Ḥumayd was fond of sex, whether legitimate or otherwise. Jibrīl gave him a potion. Ḥumayd had his own physician, called ʿAbd Allāh al-Ṭayfūrī.[737] When the latter saw the potion he said to Jibrīl, "Abū Ghānim is too weak today to take this!" But Jibrīl replied, "You have forgotten today!"[738] Al-Ṭayfūrī understood what the matter was with the potion but he did not tell Ḥumayd about it. When Ḥumayd had taken it, it made him have to relieve himself two

---

on such a lavish scale that it became proverbial as "the First Feast of Islam" (*daʿwat al-Islām al-ūlā*), see e.g. al-Thaʿālibī, *Thimār*, 165–166, idem, *Laṭāʾif al-maʿārif*, 73–74, tr. *The Book of Curious and Entertaining Information*, 99–100. Būrān died in 271/884. See *EI2*, "Būrān" (D. Sourdel), *EI3*, "Būrān" (Katherine H. Lang). Her name survives in several dishes, as *būrāniyyah, boronía, borani*, etc. (see Perry, "*Būrān*: The History of a Dish"), as does that of her husband (see Rodinson, "*Maʾmūniyya* East and West").

736 Jibrīl ibn Bukhtīshūʿ (d. 212/827) was a member of a family of famous Christian court physicians. See *EI2*, "Bukhtīshūʿ" (D. Sourdel), Ibn Abī Uṣaybiʿah, *ʿUyūn al-Anbāʾ*, ed. Savage-Smith, ii, 345–367, tr. iii, 344–370, ed. Müller, i, 127–138.

737 On this physician of Iranian origin see Ibn Abī Uṣaybiʿah, *ʿUyūn al-anbāʾ*, ed. Savage-Smith, ii, 400–406, tr. iii, 406–416, ed. Müller, i, 153–156.

738 The sense is not entirely clear; perhaps "You've forgotten to tell him this today (and now it is too late)." There is some inconsistency in the story, for at the end one is told that al-Ṭayfūrī had told Ḥumayd not to take the potion.

٢٠٠ أمرها، فلمّا شربها أخلفَتْه مائتي مَرّة، وجعل | الطَّيفوريُّ يُطْفئها حتّى تماثل قليلاً. ثمّ أقام بعد ذلك فشكا إليه ما أصابه من الشربة، فقال له: ادخُلِ الساعةَ الحمّام. فدخل من ساعته الحمّام فانتقضت به. فمكث مبطوناً شهرَ رمضان كلّه، ومات ليلة الفِطر سنة عشرين[١] ومائتين.

فخبّرني أبو عِصام، وكان صديقاً، أنّ الطَّيفوريَّ كان يُطيف بقبر حميد ويقول: يا حميد، قد نهيتُك عن الشربة فعصيتَني!

[§ ٧١] **ومنهم** عبد الله بن موسى الهادي. وكان قد عضَّل بالمأمون ممّا يعربد عليه إذا شرب معه، فأمر به فجعل حَبْسَه في منزله، وأقعد على بابه حَرَساً. ثمّ إنّه تذمَّم من ذلك فأظهر له الرِّضاء وصرف الحرس عن بابه، وكان عبد الله مُغرَماً بالصيْد، فدسّ إلى خادم من خدمه يقال له حسين فسقاه سمًّا في دُرّاج وهو بموسى باد، فدعا عبد الله بالعشاء فأتاه حسين بذلك الدُّرّاج، فلمّا أحسّ به ركب في الليل وقال لأصحابه: هو آخِرُ ما ترَوْني: وقد أكل معه من الدُّرّاج خادمان: فأمّا أحدهما فمات، وأمّا الآخر فضَنِيَ حتّى مات، ومات عبد الله بعد أيّام.

٢٠١ [§ ٧٢] **ومنهم** أحمد بن عليّ بن هارون الرشيد. وكان له غلام يقال له نَفيس وكان قد غلب عليه، وإنّ نفيساً وأربعة[٢] من غِلمانه أجمعوا على قتل أحمد، وكان بين أحمد وبين عياله ثلاثةُ

---

١ في هـ، ك: (عشر) والتصحيح من تاريخ الطبريّ وغيره من المراجع.

٢ ك: (وأربعًا).

---

739 *Fa-ntaqaḍat bihi*: this could also mean "it (the hammam, *ḥammām* being sometimes feminine) collapsed with him", but the following shows that the subject is *al-sharbah*, the potion.

740 ʿASH and SKḤ have wrongly 210.

741 Not identified.

742 A brother of Isḥāq (see above, § 69), he was another son of caliph al-Hādī. His mother was Amat al-ʿAzīz (see above, § 66). He was erudite and some poetry of his is quoted (al-Ṣūlī, *Awrāq*, iii, 84–87; al-Iṣfahānī, *Aghānī*, x, 193–195; al-Ṣafadī, *Wāfī*, xvii, 646). The year of his death is unknown. For parallels see al-Iṣfahānī, *Aghānī*, x, 197 (with the following *isnād*: *akhbaranī ʿAlī ibn Sulaymān al-Akhfash fī kitāb al-mughtālīn qāla ḥaddathanā Abū Saʿīd al-Sukkarī ʿan Muḥammad ibn Ḥabīb qāla*), al-Ṣafadī, *Wāfī*, xvii, 645–646.

hundred times. Al-Ṭayfūrī proceeded | to assuage its force, so that he recovered a little. After that he kept complaining of the effect of the potion. Al-Ṭayfūrī said, "You should enter the hammam now." He went into the hammam but there he collapsed.[739] During all of Ramadan he suffered from bellyache and he died on the eve of the Eid al-Fitr feast of the year 220.[740] 200

Abū ʿIṣām,[741] a trustworthy source, informed me that al-Ṭayfūrī used to visit Ḥumayd's grave, saying, "O Ḥumayd! I told you not to take the potion, but you disobeyed me!"

[§ 71 ʿAbd Allāh ibn Mūsā al-Hādī[742]]

Another is ʿAbd Allāh ibn Mūsā al-Hādī. He had annoyed al-Maʾmūn by his quarrelsome behaviour when he was drinking with him. He put him under house arrest and put a guard at his door. When ʿAbd Allāh appeared to have abandoned his bad habits the caliph made it appear that he was pleased with him and had the guard removed from his door. ʿAbd Allāh was fond of hunting. The caliph secretly sent one of his servants called Ḥusayn, who prepared a francolin for him that contained poison, when he was in Mūsābād.[743] When ʿAbd Allāh called for his dinner, Ḥusayn served the francolin. When he felt its effect he rode away that evening and said to his companions, "This is the last you see of me!" Two servants had eaten from the francolin with him; one of them died and the other pined away until he, too, died. ʿAbd Allāh died after a few days.

[§ 72 Aḥmad ibn ʿAlī ibn Hārūn al-Rashīd[744]]

201 Another is Aḥmad ibn ʿAlī ibn Hārūn al-Rashīd. He had a servant called Nafīs, to whom he had been overbearing. Nafīs and four others among his servants agreed to kill Aḥmad. Between Aḥmad and his dependents there were three

743 A place near al-Rayy (near modern Tehran), named after Mūsā al-Hādī, according to Yāqūt, *Muʿjam al-buldān*, where the place is called Mūsayābādh, and where a place with the same name, apparently another, is said to have been called after a certain Mūsā from Hamadhān.

744 This grandson of Hārūn al-Rashīd is not mentioned in any other source and no parallels to the story have been found.

أبواب كلّها تُغْلَق دونهم، وإنّ أحمد أمر بإغلاق الأبواب عند القيْلولة كما كان يفعل، فدخل عليه نفيس بمِشْمَلٍ وهو نائم. فضربه ضربتين إحداهما على رأسه والأخرى على فمه، وإنّ أحمد تناول المشمل من يد نفيس فخرطه نفيسٌ من يده، فقطع أصابعه غير أنّها لم تَبِنْ. ثمّ عاد نفيس فأجهز له بسكّين، وأخذ خاتَمه فبعث به إلى أهله وقال لهم: هذا خاتم الأمير يأمركم أن تبعثوا إليه بصندوق المال ليُعْطِيَ الحَشَمَ أرزاقَهم. فدفعوا إليه الصندوق، فاقتسموا ما فيه من الدنانير ومضوْا.

[§ ٧٣] **ومنهم** عليّ بن موسى بن جعفر بن محمّد بن عليّ بن الحسين بن عليّ. وكان المأمون قد بايع له بالعهد بعده، وضُربت الدراهم باسمه، وجعل على شُرَطِه العبّاسَ بن جعفر بن محمّد بن الأشعث، وكان ابنُه خليفته، وعلى حَرَسه سعيد بن صيلم، وعلى حِجابته يحيى بن مُعاذ بن مُسْلِم، وإنّه سقط عند المأمون بكلام في الفضل بن سهل فأخبر به المأمونُ الفضلَ؛ للمَوْثِق الذي كان الفضلُ أخذه على المأمون. | وذكر رَوْح بن السَّكَن عن عُبيد الله بن الحسن العَلَويّ ٢٠٢
ثمّ العبّاسيّ، أنّ الفضل قال يوماً وعنده الناس: ما تقولون في بقرة جعلتُ لها قَرْنَيْن من ذهب وكنتُ أوّلَ مَن نطحَتْه بهما؟ فلم يمض بعد ذلك إلّا قليل حتّى اعتلّ فمات.

745 He is known as ʿAlī al-Riḍā, the eighth imam of the Twelver Shia. See *EI2*, "ʿAlī al-Riḍā" (B. Lewis); *EI3*, "ʿAlī al-Riḍā" (Tamima Bayhom Daou). In 201/816 al-Maʾmūn appointed him as his heir. His motives are not entirely clear, and it does not seem to have meant that it was a general recognition of the ʿAlids as rightful heirs to the caliphate. The appointment caused great consternation among the Abbasids and their followers. The murder of al-Faḍl ibn Sahl, who may or may not have been behind the appointment, took place in 202/818 (above, § 68), and ʿAlī al-Riḍā died a few months later, in 203/818 after a short illness. On his death see e.g. al-Ṭabarī, *Tārīkh*, iii, 1030, tr. *The History*, xxxii, 84–85, al-Iṣfahānī, *Maqātil*, 457–458. According to al-Yaʿqūbī (*Tārīkh*, ii, 551, tr. *The Works*, 1217) he died of a poisoned pomegranate. Al-Maʾmūn showed distress at his death but his involvement in it (as in al-Ḥasan ibn Faḍl's death) has been suspected. It was certainly convenient to him. In some sources al-Maʾmūn's involvement is explicitly mentioned, but Ibn Ḥabīb merely suggests it.

doors, each of them with a lock. Aḥmad gave orders for the doors to be locked when he had a siesta, as was his wont.[745] Nafīs went in, holding a poniard,[746] while Aḥmad was sleeping. He hit him twice, on his head and his mouth. Aḥmad took the poniard from Nafīs's hand but Nafīs pulled it back, cutting but not severing his fingers. Then Nafīs killed him off with a knife. He took away his signet ring and brought it to Aḥmad's family, saying, "This is the prince's signet ring. He tells you to send his treasure chest, so that he can pay his servants their wages." They gave him the chest. He and his comrades divided the dinars it contained and absconded.

[§ 73 ʿAlī ibn Mūsā ibn Jaʿfar[747]]

Another is ʿAlī ibn Mūsā ibn Jaʿfar ibn Muḥammad ibn ʿAlī ibn al-Ḥusayn ibn ʿAlī. Al-Maʾmūn had people take the pledge of allegiance to him as his heir. Dirhams with ʿAlī's name were minted, al-ʿAbbās ibn Jaʿfar ibn Muḥammad ibn al-Ashʿath[748] was made his head of police, and his son was his second-in-command. Saʿīd ibn Ṣaylam[749] was head of the guard, Yaḥyā ibn Muʿādh ibn Muslim[750] was his chamberlain. But his status with al-Maʾmūn fell because of what was said about al-Faḍl ibn Sahl. Al-Maʾmūn informed al-Faḍl of it, in accordance with the agreement that al-Faḍl had attained from al-Maʾmūn. Rawḥ ibn al-Sakan[751] mentions, on the authority of ʿUbayd Allāh ibn al-Ḥasan 202
al-ʿAlawī al-ʿAbbāsī,[752] that al-Faḍl once said, publicly, "What would you say of a cow I had given two horns of gold, and me being the first she would gore with them!" Only a few days afterwards ʿAlī fell ill and died.

745 Despite the repeated mention of doors with locks, they do not seem to play a part in the story, for the murderous servant enters without problem. Perhaps a moral point is made: multiple locked doors cannot save a man from Fate.

746 *Mishmal*, a rather uncommon word for a small dagger; the knife mentioned hereafter is *sikkīn*.

748 Not found elsewhere.

749 Not found elsewhere. Ṣaylam is not known as a personal name and may be a corruption.

750 On Yaḥyā ibn Muʿādh see al-Ṣafadī, *Wāfī*, xxviii, 325.

751 He is mentioned in an *isnād* in al-Iṣfahānī, *Aghānī*, xxi (Brünnow), 22. but nothing else is known about him.

752 Not identified.

[§ ٧٤] **ومنهم** العبّاس بن محمّد بن عليّ بن عبد اللّٰه بن العبّاس. وكان قدم على هارون الرَّقّةَ فحباه حِباءً كثيراً، وعظّمه أشدَّ تعظيم. وإنّ العبّاس اعتلّ فدسّ له شَرْبة، فلمّا استودعه إيّاها أَذِن له في الانحدار إلى مدينة السلام، وكانت سببَ موته.

[§ ٧٥] **ومنهم** إسماعيل بن هَبّار بن الأسود بن المطَّلِب بن أسد. دخل الحمّام بالمدينة وفيه مُصْعَب بن عبد الرحمن بن عوْف الزُّهْريّ وكان جميلاً بارعاً، فأمَرَّ يدَه على ظَهره وعجيزته، وتكلّم بكلام فيه بعضُ ما فيه، فضحك مُصْعَب في وجهه ليؤنِسَه، حتّى إذا كان الليلُ جمع مصعب رجالاً فيهم القَتّال الكِلابيّ، وبعث مولًى له أسْودَ، يُكنى أبا عَجْوة، إلى ابن هبّار، فدعاه فلمّا خرج إليه تنحّى به إليهم، فوثب عليه القتّال فضربه حتّى قتله. وهو قول[١] ابن قيْس الرُّقَيّات:

فلن أُجيبَ بليلٍ داعياً أبداً   أخْشى الغُرورَ كما غُرَّ ابنُ هبّارِ ٢٠٣
باتوا يجُرّونه في الحُشِّ منجدِلاً   بئسَ الهَدِيّةُ لابن العمِّ والجارِ

١ ك: (يقول:).

753 A younger brother of the first two Abbasid caliphs al-Saffāḥ and al-Manṣūr, al-ʿAbbās died in 186/802, after a career in which he distinguished himself particularly in campaigns against the Byzantines. See *EI2*, "al-ʿAbbās b. Muḥammad" (E. Lévi-Provençal), *EI3*, "al-ʿAbbās b. Muḥammad b. ʿAlī" (Teresa Bernheimer). There seems to be nothing in other sources about his being a murder victim. Ibn Ḥabīb does not give a motive. One notes that Ibn Ḥabīb is described as being a *mawlā* of his sons, so he may have had some inside information or picked up a family rumour.

754 Hārūn al-Rashīd spent much of his time in al-Raqqah in Syria, his base for campaigns against the Byzantines.

755 Madīnat al-Salām, the official name of Baghdad.

756 He belonged to the Asad ibn ʿAbd al-ʿUzzā branch of Quraysh, see *ĞN*, i, 19 for his lineage. He is described in Muṣʿab al-Zubayrī, *Nasab Quraysh*, 219, as "one of the men of Medina known for toughness and manliness (*al-jalad wa-l-futuwwah*)". For the story of his death see ibid., 220, 267, 288–289, 372, al-Iṣfahānī, *Aghānī*, xxiv, 178–182; the incident in the hammam is not mentioned in these sources.

757 He belonged to the Banū Zuhrah, another branch of Quraysh, see *ĞN*, i, 20. He was head of police under Marwān ibn al-Ḥakam in Medina during the caliphate of Muʿāwiyah and was killed in 64/683 during the siege of Medina, having taken the side of ʿAbd Allāh ibn al-Zubayr.

758 *Takallama bi-kalām fīhi baʿḍ mā fīh*, "he spoke words in which there was some of what there was in it", an interesting euphemistic phrase.

[§ 74 al-ʿAbbās ibn Muḥammad ibn ʿAlī ibn Muḥammad ibn al-ʿAbbās[753]]

Another is al-ʿAbbās ibn Muḥammad ibn ʿAlī ibn Muḥammad ibn al-ʿAbbās. He had come to Hārūn in al-Raqqah.[754] Hārūn bestowed many favours upon him and paid him great respect. Al-ʿAbbās fell ill, and Hārūn schemed to send him a potion. When he had given it him for safekeeping, he gave him permission to go down to the City of Peace.[755] This was the cause of his death.

[§ 75 Ismāʿīl ibn Habbār ibn al-Aswad ibn al-Muṭṭalib ibn Asad[756]]

Another is Ismāʿīl ibn Habbār ibn al-Aswad ibn al-Muṭṭalib ibn Asad. Once he entered the hammam. Muṣʿab ibn ʿAbd al-Raḥmān ibn ʿAwf al-Zuhrī was there too; he was strikingly handsome.[757] Ismāʿīl stroked his back and buttocks and addressed him with certain words.[758] Muṣʿab laughed to his face in a friendly manner. But that night Muṣʿab gathered some men, among them al-Qattāl al-Kilābī.[759] He sent a black *mawlā* of his, called Abū ʿAjwah, to Ibn Habbār asking him to come. When Ibn Habbār came out, Abū ʿAjwah took him towards the men. Then al-Qattāl sprang upon him and struck, killing him. Ibn Qays al-Ruqayyāt mentions this:[760]

I will never answer someone's call at night: 203
I am afraid of being deceived, just as Ibn Habbār was deceived.
They dragged him, struck down, during the night to the latrines.[761]
What a bad present to a cousin and neighbour!

---

759 He has an entry in Muḥammad ibn Ḥabīb, *Muḥabbar*, 226–229 as one of the *futtāk al-Jāhiliyyah*, "the killers (or reckless men) of the pre-Islamic period", even though he lived most of his life in the Islamic era. Al-Qattāl (another word for "killer") is a nickname, his real name as given at the end of the entry is ʿUbādah ibn Mujīb al-Maḍrahī (?); see also Ibn Ḥabīb, *Kunā l-shuʿarā'*, 295, idem, *Alqāb al-shuʿarā'*, 312. Instead of Mujīb, ʿASH and SKḤ have M.ḥ.b.b (Muḥabbab?) as also in *Muḥabbar*, 226 and al-Āmidī, *Mu'talif*, 167, and instead of ʿUbādah one finds ʿAbd Allāh, ʿUbayd Allāh, and ʿAbbād. He was a poet; see Sezgin, *Geschichte*, ii, 143–144. There is a long entry on him in al-Iṣfahānī, *Aghānī*, xxiv, 167–195. He died in or soon after 64/683. His *nisbah*, given in ʿASH as al-Maḍraḥi, is al-Muḍarriḥī in *Aghānī*, xxiv, 168.

760 On the poet ʿUbayd Allāh ibn Qays al-Ruqayyāt (d. 80/699), see Sezgin, *Geschichte*, ii, 418–419. He was famous mostly for love poetry. On the several explanations of his nickname, "Ibn Qays of the Ruqayyahs" see al-Baghdādī, *Khizānah*, vii, 278–284. The verses are also in Ibn Qays al-Ruqayyāt, *Dīwān*, 183; Muṣʿab al-Zubayrī, *Nasab Quraysh*, 220; al-Balādhurī, *Ansāb*, ix, 463.

761 *Fī l-ḥushsh*, referring to a deserted place of the Banū Zuhrah called Ḥushsh Banī Zuhrah (*Nasab Quraysh*, 220). *Ḥushsh*, originally "garden", came to mean "privy", "because they used to ease themselves in the gardens" (Lane, *Lexicon*, *ḤShSh*).

وطُلب القتّال فهرب وقال:

تركتُ ابنَ هبّارٍ يُصدَّع رأسُهُ   وأصبح دوني شابةٌ وأَرومُ
بسيفِ أمرئٍ لن أُخبرَ الدهرَ باسْمِهِ   ولو حفزتْ نفسي إليَّ هُمومُ
ودوني من الدّْهنا بَساطٌ كأنّها   إذا انجاب ضوءُ الصبح عنه أديمُ

القتّال: عُبادة بن مُجيب[١] بن المَضْرَحيّ، وعبد الرحمن بن صبحان المُحاربيّ.

[§٧٦] أسماء من قتل حميمَه من الملوك ٢٠٤

[§٧٦ا] عمرو بن تُبَّع قتل أخاه حسّان بن تُبَّع.

[§٧٦ ب] وسَلَمة بن الحارث الملك بن عمرو المقصور بن حُجْر آكل المَرار الكِنْديّ قتل أخاه شُرَحْبِيل بن الحارث، وكان الحارث ملَّك ولدَه سلمة على حَنْظَلة وتَغْلِب، وشرحبيل على الرِّباب وبَكْر بن وائل، وحُجراً على كِنانة وأَسَد ابنيْ خُزَيمة، ومَعْديكَرِب على قيْس عَيْلان. فوثبتْ بنو أسد فقتلوا حجراً، وسعى المُفْسِدون بين سلمة وشرحبيل حتّى احتربا، فقتل سلمةُ شرحبيلَ.

١ هـ، كـ: (مَحبب)، والتصحيح من كنى الشعراء لابن حبيب وألقاب الشعراء له.

762 The first two verses, but with some differences including a different rhyme (*-ūmuhā* instead of *-ūmū*), are also in Ibn Ḥabīb, *Muḥabbar*, 228; al-Iṣfahānī, *Aghānī*, xxiv, 180, 182; Yāqūt, *Muʿjam al-buldān* (entry Shābah).

763 Shābah is a mountain in Nejd or the Hijaz, Arūm is a mountain in the territory of the Banū Sulaym (both according Yāqūt, *Muʿjam al-buldān*).

764 The verb varies in the several sources: *ḥafazat* (ʿASH, SKḤ), *ḥaḍarat* (*Muḥabbar*), *ḥaqarat* (*Aghānī*, xxiv, 180), *ajhashat* (*Aghānī*, xxiv, 182).

765 Al-Dahnāʾ is a very long, narrow sandy desert in Arabia.

766 This person has not been found elsewhere and the reading and vowelling Ṣabḥān are uncertain.

They sought al-Qattāl but he fled and said,[762]

> I left Ibn Habbār, his head smashed,
> —and Shābah and Arūm are now between me and him—[763]
> With the sword of a man whose name I shall never divulge,
> even if my soul should beset me with worries.[764]
> Between us is a stretch of the Dahnā'[765]
> when the light of dawn reveals the earth.

Al-Qattāl is ʿUbādah ibn Mujīb ibn al-Maḍraḥī and (also the name of) ʿAbd al-Raḥmān ibn Ṣabḥān al-Muḥāribī.[766]

[§ 76] | The Names of Rulers who Killed Their Kinsman[767] 204

[§ 76a]
ʿAmr ibn Tubbaʿ: he killed his brother Ḥassān ibn Tubbaʿ.[768]

[§ 76b][769]
Salamah ibn al-Ḥārith al-Malik ibn ʿAmr al-Maqṣūr ibn Ḥujr Ākil al-Murār al-Kindī: he killed his brother Shuraḥbīl ibn al-Ḥārith. Al-Ḥārith had made his son Salamah the ruler of of Ḥanẓalah and Taghlib; Shuraḥbīl the ruler of al-Ribāb and Bakr ibn Wā'il; Ḥujr the ruler of Kinānah ibn Khuzaymah and Asad ibn Khuzaymah; and Maʿdīkarib the ruler of Qays ʿAylān. The Banū Qays attacked and killed Ḥujr. Some people stirred up dissension between Salamah and Shuraḥbīl and as a result they fought each other, and Salamah killed Shuraḥbīl.

767 This section differs from all others because it lists people who killed, not murder victims. Some of them have been mentioned in preceding section. The word *ḥamīm* can mean "kinsman", "brother", and "friend".

768 See above, § 2.

769 Al-Ḥārith ibn ʿAmr al-Maqṣūr was the last ruler of the Kingdom of Kindah, a tribe that came to dominate much of the Arabian Peninsula in the 5th and 6th centuries AD. See *EI2*, "Kindah" (I. Shahîd), and for the lineages *ĞN*, i, 238. He was killed c. 529 by the Lakhmid king al-Mundhir of al-Ḥīrah. Al-Ḥārith had divided the main tribes of the North Arabs among his four sons, Ḥujr (the father of the celebrated poet Imru' al-Qays), Shuraḥbīl, Salamah, and Maʿdīkarib; their discord led to the end of the kingdom of Kindah. The killing of Shuraḥbīl is part of the narratives of *Yawm Kulāb al-Awwal*, The First Battle-Day of Kulāb, see e.g. Abū ʿUbaydah, *Naqā'iḍ Jarīr wa-l-Farazdaq*, 448, 452–461, 1072–1079, al-Iṣfahānī, *Aghānī*, xii, 208–214.

[§٧٦ ج] **ومنهم** عبد اللّٰه بن الزبير، قتل أخاه عمرو بن الزُّبير، وكان عاملُ المدينة وجّهه لمحارَبة أخيه ففضَّ جيشَه وأَسَرَه، وكان عمروٌ بَدَنا، فأقامه عبد اللّٰه للناس وقال: مَن كان له عنده حقٌّ فلْيقتصَّ منه. فضُرب[1] حتّى مات.

[§٧٦ د] **ومنهم** عبد الملك، قتل عمرو بن سعيد بن العاص. وأمُّه أمُّ البَنِين بنت الحَكَم بن ٢٠٥
أبي العاص بن أُميّة. وكان نازَع عبد الملك وحارَبه حتّى جرتْ بينهما السُّفَراء على أن يجعل عمروٌ مع كلّ عاملٍ لعبد الملك عاملاً له، ففعل، فلم يزل عبد الملك يلطُف له حتّى قتله. وله حديث طويل.

[§٧٦ هـ] **ومنهم** يزيد بن الوليد بن عبد الملك، ويزيد الناقص، وثب على ابن عمه الوليد بن يزيد بن عبد الملك فقتله واستولى على مُلكه.

[§٧٦ و] **ومنهم** أبو جعفر المنصور، وهو عبد اللّٰه بن محمّد بن عليّ بن عبد اللّٰه بن العبّاس، وثب عليه عمُّه عبد اللّٰه بن عليّ، وخلعه ودعا إلى نفسه، فظَفِر به فحبسه في بيتٍ فسقط عليه البيت.

١ ك: (فضربه).

770 ʿAbd Allāh ibn al-Zubayr, son of the prominent Companion al-Zubayr ibn al-ʿAwwām, played a major role as caliph (or anti-caliph) in Medina during the civil war for several years until he was killed in 73/692, when ʿAbd al-Malik ibn Marwān was victorious. See *EI3*, "ʿAbdallāh b. al-Zubayr" (Sandra Campbell). For his and his brother ʿAmr's lineage see *ĞN*, i, 19. See also Muṣʿab al-Zubayrī, *Nasab Quraysh*, 178, 214–215 (where it is said that ʿAmr died in ʿAbd Allāh's prison), Ibn Ḥabīb, *Muḥabbar*, 481 (where ʿAbd Allāh is said to have crucified his brother).

771 ʿAmr al-Ashdaq ibn Saʿīd ibn al-ʿĀṣ, see *ĞN*, i, 9, ii, 183; *EI2*, "ʿAmr b. Saʿīd" (K.V. Zettersteén). On his death see the next paragraph.

[§ 76c][770]
Another is ʿAbd Allāh ibn al-Zubayr, who killed his brother ʿAmr ibn al-Zubayr. The governor of Medina[771] had sent ʿAmr to fight his brother, but ʿAbd Allāh routed his army and took him captive. ʿAmr was an old man. ʿAbd Allāh made him stand up in front of his people and said, "Whoever has a claim on him, let him retaliate!" He was beaten until he died.

[§ 76d][772]
Another is ʿAbd al-Malik. He killed ʿAmr ibn Saʿīd ibn al-ʿĀṣ, whose mother 205
was Umm al-Banīn, the daughter of al-Ḥakam.[773] He challenged ʿAbd al-Malik's authority and fought him. Then emissaries moved between and it was agreed that ʿAmr would appoint a governor for every governor appointed by ʿAbd al-Malik. This was done. ʿAbd al-Malik was friendly towards him, but in the end he killed him; it is a long story.[774]

[§ 76e][775]
Another is Yazīd ibn al-Walīd ibn ʿAbd al-Malik. Yazīd "the Reducer" revolted against his paternal nephew al-Walīd ibn Yazīd ibn ʿAbd al-Malik; he killed him and took over his reign.

[§ 76f][776]
Another is Abū Jaʿfar al-Manṣūr, who is ʿAbd Allāh ibn Muḥammad ibn ʿAlī ibn ʿAbd Allāh ibn al-ʿAbbās. His paternal uncle ʿAbd Allāh ibn ʿAlī revolted against him, declared him deposed, and proclaimed himself caliph. But al-Manṣūr defeated him and imprisoned him in a house, which collapsed on him.

---

772 On the events see e.g. al-Ṭabarī, *Tārīkh*, ii, 783–791 (yr AH 69), tr. *The History*, xxi, 154–163, al-Masʿūdī, *Murūj*, iii, 303–305.

773 See above, § 51.

774 Many details are given by al-Ṭabarī, al-Masʿūdī and others. ʿAbd al-Malik personally initiated the killing by smashing ʿAmr's front teeth.

775 Yazīd ibn al-Walīd reigned as caliph for only six months in 126/744. He got his nickname al-Nāqiṣ (the reducer, or diminisher), it is said, because he reduced the salaries of the troops. Al-Nāqiṣ could also mean "the deficient", but al-Masʿūdī (*Murūj*, iv, 58) says he was deficient in neither body nor intellect. He came to power after a revolt against al-Walīd ibn Yazīd, whose notoriously bad behaviour and good poetry is found in many sources. See *EI2*, "Yazīd (III) b. al-Walīd" (G.R. Hawting), "al-Walīd" (H. Kennedy and, on the poetry, Renate Jacobi).

776 The story has been told above, § 62.

[§ ٧٦ ز] **ومنهم** هارون الرشيد، حبس عمَّه جعفر بن المنصور المعروف بابن الكُرْديّة، فذكروا أنّه أصابه زحير فمات منه.

[§ ٧٦ ح] **ومنهم** عبد الله المأمون، قتل أخاه محمداً الأمين واستولى على ملكه. ٢٠٦

[§ ٧٦ ط] **ومنهم** أبو إسحاق المعتصم، كان بلغه أنّ العبّاس بن المأمون قد مالأَ ملكَ الروم على أهل الإسلام عامَ فَتَحَ المعتصمُ عَمّورِيَةَ، وأنّه أراد الوثوب على المعتصم، فحبسه وأثقله بالحديد فمات في حديده.

[§ ٧٧] **وممن قُتل غِيلةً** زياد بن عُبيد الله بن عبد الله بن عبد المَدان الحارثيّ من بني الحارث ٢٠٧
بن كعب، وكان خالَ أبي العبّاس أمير المؤمنين، وإنّه ولاّه مكّة والمدينة فلم يزل عليهما حتّى

---

777 On Jaʿfar, a son of caliph al-Manṣūr, called Jaʿfar al-Aṣghar (the Younger), to distinguish him from another son called Jaʿfar al-Akbar; also called "the son of the Kurdish woman", see e.g. al-Ṣafadī, *Wāfī*, xi, 107–109. He is said to have died in 151/768 in al-Baghdādī, *Tārīkh Madīnat al-Salām*, viii, 26 (in the entry on Jaʿfar al-Akbar), but al-Ṣafadī reports that he led the Hajj in 188/804, which is during Hārūn's reign and thus makes more sense. It is not clear, however, why Hārūn is said to have killed him, nor have I found other sources that assert this.

778 *Zaḥīr*.

779 Hārūn al-Rashīd had divided his realm between two sons, Muḥammad al-Amīn (son of an Abbasid prinses, Zubaydah), who was to reign over the western part in Baghdad, and ʿAbd Allāh al-Maʾmūn (son of a concubine), who was to rule over the east. Soon after Hārūn's death in 193/809 a civil war broke out and after a protracted siege Baghdad was taken by al-Maʾmūn's forces in 198/813 and al-Amīn was killed, not in fact by al-Maʾmūn, who regretted, it is said, his brother's execution by his general Ṭāhir ibn al-Ḥusayn.

780 Al-Muʿtaṣim, another son of Hārūn al-Rashīd, ruled as caliph from 218/833 until 227/842, succeeding al-Maʾmūn who had designated him on his deathbed. The army supported al-Maʾmūn's son al-ʿAbbās but the latter was unwilling to press his case.

781 ʿAmmūriy(y)ah or Amorium was a Byzantine city, S.-W. of Ankara. It was besieged and temporarily captured by al-Muʿtaṣim in 223/838. Abū Tammām composed a celebrated ode on the occasion (*Dīwān*, i, 40–74; for a translation and analysis see Bray, "Al-Muʿtaṣim's 'bridge of toil'"). See *EI3*, "ʿAmmūriyya" (Nadia M. El Cheikh). After the capture of Amorium a plot was discovered: disgruntled generals wanted to kill the caliph and, after all, put

[§ 76g][777]
Another is Hārūn al-Rashīd. He imprisoned his paternal uncle Jaʿfar ibn al-Manṣūr, known as Ibn al-Kurdiyyah. They say that he was struck by a griping bellyache,[778] of which he died.

[§ 76h][779]
Another is ʿAbd Allāh al-Maʾmūn, who killed his brother al-Amīn and took over 206
his reign.

[§ 76i][780]
Another is Abū Isḥāq al-Muʿtaṣim. It had reached him that al-ʿAbbās ibn al-Maʾmūn had conspired with the king of the Byzantines against the people of Islam in the year al-Muʿtaṣim conquered ʿAmmūriyah,[781] and that he intended to revolt against al-Muʿtaṣim. So he imprisoned him and had him clapped in irons. He died in chains.[782]

[§ 77]
And among those who were killed murderously[783] is Ziyād ibn ʿUbayd Allāh 207
ibn ʿAbd Allāh ibn ʿAbd al-Madān al-Ḥārithī,[784] of the Banū l-Ḥārith ibn Kaʿb. He was a paternal uncle of Abū l-ʿAbbās, the Commander of Believers,[785] who made him governor of Mecca and Medina,[786] which he remained until

---

his nephew al-ʿAbbās in his place. A purge ensued and many leading persons including al-ʿAbbās perished. See e.g. al-Ṭabarī, *Tārīkh*, iii, 1249–1250, 1256–1258, 1263–1265, (tr. *The History*, xxxiii, 112–113, 121–123, 128–130), al-Yaʿqūbī, *Tārīkh*, ii, 581, tr. *The Works*, 1247. On al-ʿAbbās, see *EI2*, "al-ʿAbbās b. al-Maʾmūn" (K.V. Zettersteén), *EI3*, "al-ʿAbbās b. al-Maʾmūn" (John P. Turner).

782 It is reported that al-Afshīn, one of al-Muʿtaṣim's generals (soon to be executed himself), killed al-ʿAbbās by giving him salty food but no water.

783 *Wa-mimman qutila ghīlatan.* This paragraph is presented in ʿASH as a separate section of the book, and in SKḤ as *Tatimmat al-Bāb al-Awwal*, "the Complement of the First Chapter". With Ziyād ibn ʿUbayd Allāh it moves back in time somewhat; the end is missing and after a gap the second part of the book begins. This was originally a separate work, it appears, and deals with poets who were killed, beginning with an entry on one of the earliest known poets.

784 He was a maternal uncle of Abū Jaʿfar al-Saffāḥ, the first Abbasid caliph. On his lineage see *ǦN*, i, 259, where he appears as Ziyād ibn ʿUbayd Allāh ibn ʿAbd al-Ḥijr ibn ʿAbd al-Madān, of al-Ḥārith ibn Kaʿb, a branch of Madhḥij. See also al-Ṣafadī, *Wāfī*, xv, 14–15, who says that he died in the 150s (between 767 and 776). His death is not recorded in other sources.

785 Al-Saffāḥ, the first Abbasid caliph.

786 This was in 133/750–751, see e.g. al-Ṭabarī, *Tārīkh*, iii, 73.

مات، فأقرّه أبو جعفر على عمله، ثمّ كتب إليه أن يقتُلَ أبا محمّد بن عبد الله بن يزيد بن معاوية، وكان شيخَ بني أُميّة، فقتله.

فلمّا تغيَّب محمّد وإبراهيم ابنا عبد الله بن الحسن بن الحسن بن عليّ بن أبي طالب، رضي الله عنهم، كتب إليه أبو جعفر أن يُوثِق عبدَ الله بن الحسن حديداً، ويضيِّقَ عليه. فكان زيادٌ يرفِّه عن عبد الله ويُحْسِن إليه في حبْسه. ثمّ إنّ أبا جعفر كتب إليه يأمره بقتله، فلم يفعل، فعزله وأغرمه ثمانين ألف دينار، وكَرِه أن يكشف قتْلَه، لموْضعه كان من أبي العبّاس. فلمّا أخرج أبو جعفر ابنَه المَهْديّ إلى الرَّيّ قال لزياد: سِرْ مع ابن أخيك. فسار ثلاث مراحل.

وإنّ زياداً تغدّى مع المهديّ ثمّ انصرف إلى فُسطاط، ثمّ أتى بقَدَح فشَرِبه ولم يعلم المهديُّ بذلك. فلمّا ترحل الناس قام المهديّ على باب سُرادقه[١] فقال: ويْلك يا غلام [...][٢]

[...]

[أسماء من قُتل من الشعراء]

[§٧٨] [مهلْهِل بن رَبيعة] ٢٠٨

[...] وإنّ فتياناً من بني قيس بن ثعلبة اتّخذوا طعاماً وابتاعوا خمراً، ثمّ أتوْا عَوْفاً فقالوا: إنّا نحبّ أن تأذَنَ لمهلهل يأتينا فيتحدّث معنا اليوم. ففعل عوفٌ ذلك، فأتاهم مهلهل،

١ ك: (سراقه).

٢ انقطع النصّ هنا وبينه وبين ما يليه سقط.

787 Al-Manṣūr.

788 *Shaykh Banī Umayyah*; Yazīd ibn ʿAbd Allāh ibn Yazīd ibn Muʿāwiyah ibn Abī Sufyān, called Abū Muḥammad al-Sufyānī, who rebelled and was killed in 133/750–751, see e.g. al-Yaʿqūbī, *Tārīkh*, ii, 425 (tr. *The Works*, 1081–1082).

789 On Muḥammad, called al-Nafs al-Zakiyyah, see above, § 62; on his brother Ibrāhīm, who rebelled together with him, see *EI2*, "Ibrāhīm b. ʿAbd Allāh" (L. Veccia Vaglieri). He was killed in 154/762.

790 Al-Manṣūr sent his son al-Mahdī, still in his teens, to al-Rayy (near present-day Tehran) in 141/758–759, to be governor of Khorasan.

791 *Fusṭāṭ*, described in al-Zabīdī, *Tāj al-ʿarūs* as "a structure built when travelling, smaller than a *surādiq*" (on which see next note).

792 *Surādiq*, a structure (tent or awning) made of cotton; or an enclosure without a roof surrounding a tent (see Lane, *Lexicon*).

793 Here the text breaks off. One can make an informed guess as to what follows: the drink

Abū l-ʿAbbās died. Abū Jaʿfar[787] confirmed him in his governorship. Then he wrote to him, telling him to kill Abū Muḥammad ibn ʿAbd Allāh ibn Yazīd ibn Muʿāwiyah, who was the senior member of the Umayyads,[788] and he killed him.

When Muḥammad and Ibrāhīm the sons of ʿAbd Allāh ibn al-Ḥasan ibn al-Ḥasan ibn ʿAlī ibn Abī Ṭālib (*r*) disappeared,[789] Abū Jaʿfar wrote to him, telling him to put ʿAbd Allāh ibn al-Ḥasan in chains and treat him harshly. But Ziyād made his life comfortable and treated him well. Then Abū Jaʿfar wrote to him again, telling him to kill ʿAbd Allāh, but Ziyād did not do this. So the caliph deposed him and fined him eighty thousand dinars, but was reluctant to have him killed openly, on account of Ziyād's standing with Abū l-ʿAbbās. When Abū Jaʿfar sent his son al-Mahdī to al-Rayy,[790] he said to Ziyād, "Travel together with your nephew!" They travelled for three day-marches.

Ziyād was having breakfast with al-Mahdī and then went off to a marquee.[791] He was brought a cup, which he drank. Al-Mahdī was not aware of this. When the people were departing al-Mahdī went to the door of his pavilion[792] and said, "Dammit, hey servant! ..."[793]

[...]

[THE NAMES OF POETS WHO WERE KILLED][794]

[...]

[§ 78 Muhalhil ibn Rabīʿah[795]]

[...] | Some men of the Banū Qays ibn Thaʿlabah[796] prepared a meal and bought wine. They went to ʿAwf[797] and said, "We would like you to allow Muhalhil to come to us so that he can talk with us today." ʿAwf agreed and Muhalhil came to 208

---

was poisoned, and al-Mahdī finds Ziyād dead or dying in his tent. It is strongly suggested that al-Manṣūr was behind the murder, but no other accounts of the event survive.

794 After the lacuna the manuscript continues with an entry of which the beginning is missing, but which may well have been the first entry of the section on poets who were killed (*Asmāʾ man qutila min al-shuʿarāʾ*), originally perhaps a separate monograph by Ibn Ḥabīb, but amalgamated with the book on prominent murder victims.

795 ʿAdī (or Imruʾ al-Qays) ibn Rabīʿah, nicknamed Muhalhil, of the tribe of Taghlib ibn Wāʾil (see *ǦN*, i, 164), is said to have been one of the earliest known poets, the first to compose a longer poem (*qaṣīdah*), and a major player in the legendary "War of Basūs". He was the maternal uncle of the famous poet Imruʾ al-Qays and his death is said to have occurred around AD 525. See Sezgin, *Geschichte*, ii, 148–149. For parallels see e.g. al-Iṣfahānī, *Aghānī*, v, 51–52; Ibn al-Athīr, *Kāmil*, i, 423; al-Baghdādī, *Khizānah*, ii, 173.

796 Qays Ibn Thaʿlabah is a branch of Bakr, see *ǦN*, i, 141, 155.

797 ʿAwf ibn Mālik ibn Ḍubayʿah, nicknamed al-Burak, of Qays ibn Thaʿlabah, hero of the War of Basūs. See *ǦN*, i, 155. Muhalhil is his captive in this account.

فلمّا أخذت فيه الخمرُ جعل يُنشد ما قال في بكر بن وائل وما ذكرهم به، فبلغ ذلك عوفاً فغَضِب، فحلف لا يذوقُ عنده قَطرةَ شرابٍ ولا ماء حتّى يَرِدَ دنيب[١]، وكان دنيب جملاً لعوف لا يرد إلّا خِمْساً، وشدّ عليه القُدود، ثمّ تركه، فمات مهلهل قبل أن يَرِدَ دنيب. وفي ذلك قال مهلهل:

جَلَّلوني جِلْدَ حَوْبٍ بازلٍ يرتـقي النفس مَوْهِناً للتراقي
عند عوفِ بن مالكٍ لستُ أرجو لذَّةَ العيْش ما عُصِبْتُ بِساقي
وإليكِ ابنةَ[٢] المجلّل عنّي لا يواتي العِناقُ مَن في الوَثاقِ ٢٠٩

[§ ٧٩] **ومنهم** عامر بن جُوَين بن عبد رُضا بن قَمْران الطائيّ، أحد بني جَرْم بن عمرو بن الغَوْث، وكان سيّداً شاعراً فارساً شريفاً، وهو الذي نزل به امرؤ القيس بن حُجْر. وكان سبب قتله أنّ كلباً غزت بني جرم، فأَسَر بِشْرُ بن حارثة وهُبيرة بن صَخْر الكلبيُّ عامرَ بن جُوين، وهو شيخ كبير، فجعلوا يتدافعونه لكِبَره، فقال عامر بن جوين: لا يكنْ لعامر بن جوين الهَوان! فقالوا له: وإنك لَهُو؟ قال: نعم. فذبحوه ومضوْا. وأقبل الأسود بن عامر، فلمّا رأى أباه قتيلاً بينهم أخذ منهم ثمانية نفر، وكانوا قتلوا عامراً وقد هبَّت الصَّبا، فكَعَمهم ووضع أيدِيَهم في جِفانٍ فيها

١ كذا في هـ، كـ: (دنيب)، وكما قال هارون في التعليق لعلّ الصحيح ما جاء في الأغاني وهو (رَبيب الهِضاب).

٢ كـ: (وإليكِ يا ابنةَ).

798 The camel is called Danīb or Dunayb (not found elsewhere as a name or a noun) in ʿASH and SKḤ. As Hārūn says in his note, the name appears as Rabīb al-Hiḍāb in al-Iṣfahānī, *Aghānī*, v, 52, as Zabīb in Ibn al-Athīr, *Kāmil*, i, 423, and as al-Khuḍayr in al-Baghdādī, *Khizānah*, ii, 173; there are other variants.

799 For a somewhat different version of vss. 1–2 see *Aghānī*, v, 56; a variant of vs. 3 in *Aghānī*, v, 54, Ibn al-Athīr, *Kāmil*, i, 423. The metre of the first hemistich of vs. 1 is irregular. See also Muhalhil, *Dīwān*, 58–59.

them. Under the influence of the wine he began to recite poems he had composed on Bakr ibn Wā'il and what he had said on them. When ʿAwf heard about this he was angry and swore that Muhalhil would not drink one drop of wine or water until Danīb[798] had had a drink (Danīb was a camel of ʿAwf that drank only once in four days). He tightened Muhalhil's leather straps and left him. Muhalhil died before Danīb drank. Muhalhil says on this:[799]

They covered me in leather from a young camel stallion;
  my soul rises, in the middle of the night, to my collar-bones.[800]
With ʿAwf ibn Mālik I do not expect
  a pleasant life when my legs are tied.
Leave me, daughter of al-Mujallil![801] 209
  Embracing is not easy for a man in fetters.

[§ 79 ʿĀmir ibn Juwayn ibn ʿAbd Ruḍā ibn Qamrān al-Ṭāʾī[802]]

Another is ʿĀmir ibn Juwayn ibn ʿAbd Ruḍā ibn Qamrān al-Ṭāʾī, one of the Banū Jarm ibn ʿAmr ibn al-Ghawth.[803] He was a tribal leader, a poet, a horseman, and a nobleman. It was with him that Imruʾ al-Qays stayed.[804] He was killed because of the following. The tribe of Kalb raided the Banū Jarm. Bishr ibn Ḥārithah[805] and Hubayrah ibn Ṣakhr al-Kalbī[806] took ʿĀmir ibn Juwayn prisoner; he was an old man. They started to quarrel, each one pushing him to the other, because ʿĀmir was so old. ʿĀmir said, "ʿĀmir ibn Juwayn will not be humiliated!" They asked him, "Are you really him?" ʿĀmir said, "Yes!" Then they cut his throat and left. Then al-Aswad, ʿĀmir's son, arrived. When he saw that his father had been killed he took eight men of Kalb. They had killed ʿĀmir when the east wind was blowing. Al-Aswad gagged their mouths and put their hands in large bowls

---

800 An idiom for being on the point of death.

801 In al-Mubarrad, *Taʿāzī*, 301, *Aghānī*, v, 51, 54 it is al-Muḥallil. Mujallil/Muḥallil ibn Thaʿlabah ibn Jusham ibn Ghubar is the maternal uncle of Muhalhil's mother according to *Aghānī*, v, 51. The last hemistich is also in a poem by ʿAdī ibn Zayd (*Aghānī*, ii, 116).

802 See Sezgin, *Geschichte*, ii, 209. For a parallel see al-Baghdādī, *Khizānah*, i, 53 (quoting *Asmāʾ al-mughtālīn*).

803 On his lineage see *ǦN*, i, 252 (which has Qamarān instead of Qamrān; in Abū Ḥātim al-Sijistānī, *Muʿammarūn*, 43 it is Qumrān).

804 See Ibn Qutaybah, *Shiʿr*, 117, al-Iṣfahānī, *Aghānī*, ix, 95–96.

805 Not found elsewhere.

806 Hubayrah ibn Ṣakhr ibn Rabīʿah, of ʿĀmir al-Akbar, a branch of Kalb; see *ǦN*, i, 288.

ماء، وجعل كُلّما هبّت الصَّبا ذبح واحداً | حتّى أتى عليهم. وكان الذي وَلِيَ قتلَ عامرٍ مسعودَ ٢١٠
بن شَدّاد، فقالت أخته عَمْرة بنت شدّاد:

يا عينُ بَكّي لمسعودِ بن شَدّادِ   بُكاءَ ذي عَبَراتٍ حُزْنُهُ بادِ
من لا يُمارُ له لحْم الجَزورِ ولا   يَجفُو الضيوفَ إذا ما ضُنَّ بالزادِ
ولا يحُلُّ إذا ما حلَّ منتبذاً   خوفَ الرزيَّة بين الحَضْر والبادِ
ألّا سقيتمْ بني جَرْمٍ أسيرَكُمُ   نفسي فِداُؤك مِن ذي كُربةٍ صادِ
يا فارساً ما قتلتمْ غيرَ جِعْثِنةٍ   ولا بَخيلٍ على ذي الحاجة الجادي
قد يطْعن الطَّعْنةَ النَّجْلاء يَتْبعها   مضرّج بعدها تَغْلي بإزبادِ
ويترُك القِرْنَ مصْفَرّا أنامِلُهُ   كأنَّ أثوابَه مُجَّت بفِرْصادِ

[§ ٨٠] **ومنهم** عَنْتَرة بن معاوية العَبْسيّ. وكان أغار على بني نَبْهان فأطرد طريدة[١] وهو شيخ كبير، فجعل يطرُدها ويقول:

حَظُّ بني نبهانَ منها الأثلَبْ   كأنَّما آثارها لا تُحْجَبْ   آثارُ ظِلْمانٍ بقاعٍ مُجْدِبْ

١ ك: (طريده).

807 *Waliya qatla ʿĀmir*; the sense is not clear, because one is told that ʿĀmir was killed by Bishr and Hubayrah.

808 There is much confusion about these verses. Lines 1–4, 6 are found in a poem attributed to Fāriʿah bint Shaddād on her brother (al-Qālī, *Amālī*, ii, 323–324). Lines 4 and 6 are also attributed to the sister of ʿAmr ibn ʿĀṣiyah al-Sulamī in *Aghānī*, xii, 106–107, where it is said that they are also attributed to al-Fāriʿah, sister of Masʿūd ibn Shaddād. See also *Aghānī*, xii, 109–111, al-Qālī, *Amālī*, ii, 323–324. Line 7 is part of a poem by ʿAbīd ibn al-Abraṣ (*Dīwān*, 71, see also al-Baghdādī, *Khizānah*, xi, 253–258).

809 Translation and interpretation of *lā yumāru lahū* uncertain. *Amālī* has *lā yudhābu lahū shaḥmu l-sadīfi* ("the fat of a camel's hump was not melted for him").

810 *Jiʿthinah*, literally "tree trunk"; cf. an anonymous hemistich quoted in Ibn Manẓūr, *Lisān al-ʿArab* (*JʿThN*): *fa-yā fatan mā qataltum ghayra jiʿthinatin*, glossed as *jabān thaqīl*.

811 The son of a black slave woman, he won his freedom by his bravery in battle. He is the poet of one of the celebrated pre-Islamic *Muʿallaqāt* and he is more commonly called ʿAntarah ibn Shaddād, Muʿāwiyah being his grandfather or great-grandfather; for his genealogy see al-Iṣfahānī, viii, 237, *ĞN*, i, 257, ii, 190. In later times he became the hero, now called ʿAntar,

filled with water. Then, whenever the east wind blew, he cut the throat of one of them | until he had finished them off. The man who had been in charge of 210
ʿĀmir's killing[807] was Masʿūd ibn Shaddād. His sister ʿAmrah said:[808]

Weep, my eye, for Masʿūd ibn Shaddād,
  weep with tears of manifest sorrow!
The flesh of a slaughtered camel was never brought to him(?),[809]
  nor was he unkind to guests whenever people were sparing with food.
Whenever he alighted in a remote place he would not do so
  fearing a misfortune among sedentary or nomad folk.
Would you, Banū Jarm, not let your captives drink?
  My soul be your ransom, you tormented, parched one!
You horseman! You have killed someone who was no sluggish coward[810]
  nor a miser towards a needy one begging a gift.
He would stab opening a large wound, followed by
  a stream of blood, bubbling and foaming
And leave his adversary with pale fingers,
  his clothes as if dyed with mulberries.

[§ 80 ʿAntarah ibn Muʿāwiyah al-ʿAbsī[811]]

Another is ʿAntarah ibn Muʿāwiyah al-ʿAbsī. He had raided the Banū Nabhān[812] and was driving away some cattle. He was an old man. While driving them, he said,[813]

The Banū Nabhān will only have pebbles and dust!
Their traces cannot be concealed,
Traces of ostriches in a barren plain.

---

of a lengthy and very popular epic (*Sīrat ʿAntar*). On ʿAntarah see Sezgin, *Geschichte*, ii, 113–115; *EI2*, "ʿAntara" (R. Blachère); *EI3*, "ʿAntar, Sīrat" (Peter Heath) and "ʿAntara" (Alan Jones). His *Dīwān* was recently edited and translated by James Montgomery (ʿAntarah ibn Shaddād, *War Songs*). For the account of his death see *Aghānī*, viii, 244–245 (with other versions), translated in *War Songs*, 281–282.

812 See *ǦN*, i, 252 and 257; Nabhān is a branch of Ṭayyiʾ.

813 Of the following three lines in *rajaz* metre, *Aghānī* has only the last. Montgomery (*War Songs*) translates the other two in a note on p. 316. I take the pronominal suffix *-hā* to refer to the cattle, whereas Montgomery takes it to refer to Nabhān ("Pebbles, that's what Nabhān are worth. Their exploits can never be concealed—they are the exploits of ostriches in a barren plain.").

وكان وَزَر بن جابر بن سُدوس بن أصمع النبْهاني في مَنْزَه، فرماه وقال: خُذها وأنا ابن سلمى ٢١١
فقطع مَطاه، فتحامل بالرَّمْية حتّى أتى أهلَه فمات. فقال وهو مجروح:

فإنَّ ابن سَلْمى عنده فاطْلبوا دمي وهيْهات لا يُرْجى ابنُ سَلْمى ولا دَمي
يظلُّ يمشّي بين أجبالِ طيّءٍ مكانَ الثُّريّا ليس بالمتهضَّمِ

[§ ٨١] **ومنهم** عَبيد بن الأبرص، وكان المُنْذِر بن امرئ القيْس اللَّخْميّ، ابنُ ماء السماء، وهو الذي يُسمَّى ذا القَرْنَين، له يومٌ يخرج فيه فيقتل أوّلَ مَن يلقى في ذلك اليوم. فخرج فلقِيَ عبيدَ بن الأبرص. فأُتي به، فلمّا رآه قال: ويْلك ما أتاني بك؟ قال: المنايا على الحوايا. فذهبت مَثَلاً. فقال أَنْشِدْني: أقفرَ مِن أهله مَلحوبُ. فقال: أقفر من أهله عبيدُ. فقال: أنشدْني: أقفر من أهله ملحوبُ! فقال: حالَ الجريضُ دون القريض. فذهب قوله مثلاً، وقتله.

814 *Aghānī* has Zirr, Montgomery has Wizr, but see *ĞN*, i, 257, ii, 588.

815 *Fī manzah*; *Aghānī* has *fī futuwwah*, "among some men".

816 Al-Baṭalyawsī, *Sharḥ al-ashʿār al-sittah*, ii, 297–298 (followed by a third line); in the commentary the killer is called ʿAmr ibn Salmā (cf. also al-Āmidī, *Muʾtalif*, 99).

817 Another famous pre-Islamic poet. On his lineage (of Saʿd ibn Thaʿlabah, a branch of Asad) see *ĞN*, i, 54. His poems have been edited and translated by Charles Lyall (see ʿAbīd ibn al-Abraṣ, *Dīwān*). See Sezgin, *Geschichte*, ii, 169–171; *EI2*, "ʿAbīd b. al-Abraṣ" (F. Gabrieli); *EI3*, "ʿAbīd b. al-Abraṣ" (Reinhard Weipert). For parallels of the account of his death, which must have taken place before the king's death in AD 554, see Lyall's commentary, *The Dīwāns*, 2–4; Ibn Qutaybah, *Shiʿr*, 267–268; al-Iṣfahānī, *Aghānī*, xxii, 87–88; al-Qālī, *Dhayl al-Amālī wa-l-nawādir*, 195–196; al-Baghdādī, *Khizānah*, ii, 217–219.

Wazar[814] ibn Jābir ibn Sudūs ibn Aṣmaʿ al-Nabhānī was in a place remote 211
from the water.[815] He shot an arrow at ʿAntarah and said, "Take that! I am Ibn Salmā!" The arrow penetrated ʿAntarah's back but he kept himself going despite the injury until he reached his people; then he died. While wounded, he said:[816]

My blood is upon Ibn Salmā—get him!
But how can one hope to get at him and avenge my blood?
He moves between the mountains of Ṭayyiʾ
as remote as the Pleiades. He'll not give himself up.

[§ 81 ʿAbīd ibn al-Abraṣ[817]]

Another is ʿAbīd ibn al-Abraṣ. Al-Mundhir ibn Imriʾ al-Qays al-Lakhmī ibn Māʾ al-Samāʾ—he is the one called Dhū l-Qarnayn (the Two-Horned)[818]—used to keep a day on which he would go out and kill the first person he would meet that day. He went out and met ʿAbīd ibn al-Abraṣ, who was taken to him. When he saw him he said, "Damn you! What brought you to me?" ʿAbīd replied, "Fate! On a plate!" which became a proverbial saying.[819] The king said, "Recite to me 'Malḥūb is desolate, without its people'!"[820] ʿAbīd replied, "'ʿAbīd is desolate, without his people!" The king repeated, "Recite to me 'Malḥūb is desolate, without its people'!" But ʿAbīd said, "A choking throat prevents a quote." This became a proverbial saying.[821] The king had him killed.

818 On him see above, §§ 13 and 21. Of the "two days" observed by the king (a Day of Woe and a Day of Bliss, as told in § 13) only the former is mentioned here.

819 A free rhyming translation of *al-manāyā ʿalā l-ḥawāyā*, literally "the Fates (come) on clothes wound around the hump of a camel" (see Lane, *Lexicon*, ḤWY, with a different interpretation of *manāyā*). It is found in collections of proverbs, with the sense of "one's fate cannot be avoided", e.g. al-ʿAskarī, *Jamharah*, i, 290, ii, 220–221; also with *balāyā* ("afflictions") instead of *manāya*, as e.g. in al-Maydānī, *Majmaʿ*, i, 152.

820 This is the opening of ʿAbīd's most famous poem, sometimes counted as one of the *Muʿallaqāt*. See his *Dīwān*, 5–17 (Arabic), 17–20 (Lyall's translation), Jones, *Early Arabic Poetry*, ii, 25–51 (with translation and extensive commentary). Malḥūb is said to be a place in the territory of Asad.

821 Another saying in rhymed prose, *ḥāla l-jarīḍ dūna l-qarīḍ*, literally "a choking throat stands in the way of versifying". It is found in proverb collections, e.g. Abū ʿUbayd al-Bakrī, *Faṣl al-maqāl*, 444; al-ʿAskarī, *Jamharah*, i, 290; al-Maydānī, *Majmaʿ*, i, 251. For a similar excuse at death's door see below, § 97.

[§ ٨٢] **ومنهم** طَرَفة بن العبد أخو بني قيس بن ثَعْلَبة. وكان عمرو بن هِند مضرِّطُ الحِجارة ٢١٢
اللَّخْميّ جعل طرفةَ والمتلمِّس في صحابة قابوسَ أخيه، فكان قابوس يتصيّد يوماً ويشرب يوماً.
فكان إذا خرج إلى الصيْد خرجا معه، فنَصِبا وركضا يومَهما، فإذا كان يومُ لَهْوِهِ وقفا على بابه
يومَهما كلَّه، فلمّا طال عليهما ذَكَرَه طرفةُ فقال:

فليْتَ لنا مكانَ المَلْك عمرٍو   رَغوثاً حول قُبَّتنا تَخورُ
يشاركنا لنا رَخِلانِ فيها   وتعْلوها الكِباشُ فما تثورُ
لَعَمْرِك إنَّ قابوسَ بن هندٍ   لَيجمع مُلكَهُ نوكٌ كثيرُ
قسمتَ العيشَ في زمنٍ رخيٍّ   كذاك الحُكمُ يَعدِل[١] أو يجورُ
لنا يومٌ وللكِرْوانِ يومٌ   تَطيرُ البائسات وما نَطيرُ
فأمّا يومُهنّ فيومُ سوءٍ   يطاردهنّ بالحَدَب الصُّقورُ
وأمّا يومُنا فنظلُّ رَكْباً   وُقوفاً ما نحُلُّ وما نَسيرُ

وقد كان طرفة هجا ابن عمٍّ له وصِهراً يقال له عبد عمرو بن بِشْر بن عمرو بن مَرْثَد، فقال:

١ ك: (يَعدك).

822 Ṭarafah is another of the poets of the *Muʿallaqāt*. On him see *EI2*, "Ṭarafa" (J.E. Montgomery), Sezgin, *Geschichte*, ii, 115–118. On his death and the escape of his companion, al-Mutalammis, see e.g. al-Mufaḍḍal, *Fākhir*, 110–111; Ibn Qutaybah, *Shiʿr*, 186, 188–189; al-Anbārī, *Sharḥ al-qaṣāʾid al-sabʿ al-ṭiwāl*, 122–128; al-Qurashī, *Jamharat ashʿār al-ʿArab* (ed. Dār Ṣādir) 74–78, (ed. al-Bijāwī), 89–97; al-Yaʿqūbī, *Tārīkh*, i, 239–240, tr. *The Works*, 519–521; al-Iṣfahānī, *Aghānī*, xxi (Brünnow), 192–195; al-ʿAskarī, *Jamharat al-amthāl*, i, 476–478; al-Maydānī, *Majmaʿ al-amthāl*, i, 501–504; al-Baghdādī, *Khizānah*, ii, 415–423.

823 On his lineage see *ĞN*, i, 155, ii, 556. Qays ibn Thaʿlabah is a branch of Bakr ibn Wāʾil.

824 This king of al-Ḥīrah (reg. c. AD 554–569 or 570) earned his nickname by "the severity of his character", see *EI2*, "ʿAmr b. Hind" (A.J. Wensinck, who renders the nickname prudishly as "he who makes the stone emit sounds"), *EI3*, "ʿAmr b. Hind" (Irfan Shahîd). He was killed, it is said, by the poet ʿAmr ibn Kulthūm (also a poet of one of the *Muʿallaqāt*).

825 Another poet, see Sezgin, *Geschichte*, ii, 163–175, *EI2*, "al-Mutalammis" (Ch. Pellat).

826 Qābūs succeeded his brother and died in AD 573.

827 See Ṭarafah's *Dīwān* in al-Baṭalyawsī, *Sharḥ al-ashʿār al-sittah*, ii, 435–441; al-Mufaḍḍal, *Fākhir*, 110; al-Baghdādī, *Khizānah*, ii, 415–418.

[§ 82 Ṭarafah ibn al-ʿAbd[822]]

Another is Ṭarafah ibn al-ʿAbd, of the Banū Qays ibn Thaʿlabah.[823] ʿAmr ibn Hind Muḍarriṭ al-Ḥijārah ("Who Makes Stones Fart") al-Lakhmī[824] had included Ṭarafah and al-Mutalammis[825] in the company of his brother Qābūs.[826] Qābūs would hunt and drink on alternate days. When he went hunting the other two would go with him; they would run and ride all day. When it was his day of entertainment the other two would sit at his gate all day. When they had waited a long time, Ṭarafah mentioned this and said,[827] 212

I wish we had, instead of king ʿAmr,
  a ewe suckling her young, bleating around our tent!
We would have to share her milk with two lambs,
  while rams are mounting her, and she not rising.[828]
Upon your life, the reign of Qābūs ibn Hind,
  comprises much foolishness.
You[829] have distributed the good life in a time of ease—
  thus a judgement[830] is either just or unjust.
One day is for us, another for the curlews;[831]
  the wretched creatures fly up but we do not.
Their day is a bad day,
  saker falcons hunt them in the hills.
And as for our day, we are still mounted,
  standing still, neither dismounting nor going!

Ṭarafah had lampooned a nephew of his, a relation by marriage called ʿAbd ʿAmr ibn Bishr ibn ʿAmr ibn Marthad,[832] saying,[833]

---

828 Instead of *fa-mā tathūru* the *Dīwān* has *fa-mā tanūrū*, "and she not avoiding (them)", which may be the better reading. Al-Baṭalyawsī explains the sense of vss. 1–2 as if the poet says, We would be satisfied with such a sheep, even though it would be little good to us, since she would not have left much milk for us. But it would be better than having ʿAmr.

829 He addresses Qābūs. Al-Baṭalyawsī paraphrases the sense of lines 3–5 as "You divide your time into two, one part for hurting animals and one for hurting people. You are helped in this by a time in which your bad qualities are ignored."

830 *Dīwān*: *al-dahru*, "Fate" or "Time".

831 *Karawān* (here the plural, *kirwān*) is a bird translated as "partridge", "plover", "stone curlew", or "curlew".

832 For his lineage see *ǦN*, i, 155. Marthad was a brother of Ṭarafah's paternal grandfather.

833 The verse is often quoted, see e.g. al-Baṭalyawsī, *Sharḥ*, ii, 432; al-Mufaḍḍal, *Fākhir*, 110; al-Baghdādī, *Khizānah*, ii, 419, 421. In the *Dīwān* it is the second of a piece of six lines.

لا عيْبَ فيه غير أنْ قِيلَ واجدٌ وأنَّ له كَشْحاً إذا قام أهضما

٢١٣ وكان عبد عمرو نديماً لعمرو بن هند وجليساً وإنساً، فدخل معه الحمّام، فلمّا تجرّد نظر إليه عمرٌو فقال: كأنّ[١] ابنَ عمّك كان يراك حين يقول:

لا عيْبَ فيه غير أنْ قيل واجدٌ وأنَّ له كَشْحاً إذا قام أهضما

حتّى أتى على الشعر. فقال: ما قال فيك أيّها الملك أشدُّ! قال: وما قال؟ قال: فأنشده: فليْتَ لنا مكانَ المَلْك عمروٍ، إلى آخرها. فقال: لا أصدِّقك عليه لِما بينك وبينه. واحتملها في قلبه على طرفة.

فلمّا كان بعد ذلك بيسير قال لطرفة وللمتلمِّس: أظُنّكما قد اشتَقْتما أهلَكما، فهل لكما في أن أكتب لكما إلى عامل البحْرَين بصِلةٍ وجائزة؟ قالا: نعم. فكتب إليه بقتْلهما. فأخذا كتابَهما ومضَيا، وأحسَّ المتلمّسُ بالشرّ وخاف الداهية، فقال لطرفة: إنّ حمْلَنا هذين الكتابين ولا ندري ما فيهما عَجْز، فهل لك أن ننظر فيهما؟ فقال طرفة: لم يكن لِيُقْدِمَ عليَّ ولا على قومي، وما بينهما إلّا خير! فمرّا بنهر الحِيرة فإذا بغِلْمان يلعبون، ففكَّ المتلمّس صحيفتَه ودفعها إلى غلامٍ منهم فقرأها فإذا الشرُّ، فألقاها في الماء وقال لطرفة: اعلمْ أنَّ في كتابك ما في كتابي. فقال: لم يكن لِيفعل ولا يجترئ على قومي. فقال المتلمّس:

قذفتُ بها بالثِّنْي[٢] من جَنْبِ كافرٍ كذلك أقنو كلَّ قِطٍّ مضلِّلِ
رَضِيتُ لها بالماء لمّا رأيتُها يجول بها التيّارُ في كلِّ جَدْوَلِ

١ من (كأنّ ابن عمّك ...) إلى (... على الشعر فقال:) ساقط في كـ.
٢ كـ: (الثني).

834 The commentators say that Ṭarafah describes ʿAbd ʿAmr with terms suitable for women rather than men.

835 See §29 note 338.

No blame is attached to him, except that he is rich
and has a slim waist when he stands up.[834]

ʿAbd ʿAmr was a boon companion of ʿAmr ibn Hind. He would sit with him 213
as one would with a familiar friend and he bathed together with him in the hammam. When ʿAbd ʿAmr took off his clothes, ʿAmr looked at him and said, "It is as if your nephew saw you when he said, 'No blame is attached to him, except that he is rich / and has a slim waist when he stands up.'" He recited the whole poem. Then ʿAbd ʿAmr said, "What he said about you, Sire, is worse!" "What did he say?" asked ʿAmr. Then ʿAbd ʿAmr recited "I wish we had, instead of king ʿAmr …", until the end. The king said, "I don't believe you, because of your bad relationship with him!" But secretly he harboured a grudge against Ṭarafah.

A short time after this he said to Ṭarafah and al-Mutalammis, "I think you must be longing for your family. Would you like me to write a letter on your behalf to the governor of al-Baḥrayn,[835] together with a present and a gift?" They assented, and he wrote letters to him ordering their execution. They took their letters and left. Al-Mutalammis had a feeling that something was amiss. He feared the worst and said to Ṭarafah, "It cannot be right that we carry these letters without knowing what is in them. Shall we see what they say?" But Ṭarafah replied, "He would not do anything to me or my people! We are on good terms with him." When they came along the river of al-Ḥīrah[836] they came upon some boys who were playing. Al-Mutalammis opened his letter, handed it to one of the boys, who read it to him.[837] It turned out to be the worst. He threw it into the water and said to Ṭarafah, "Surely your letter contains the same as mine!" But Ṭarafah said, "He wouldn't dare to do that to my people!" Al-Mutalammis said,

I threw it in the bend of the river Kāfir:
that is how I reward a misleading gift.
I was pleased to let the water have it when I saw
how the current ran away with it in every stream.

---

836 Al-Ḥīrah, located near present-day Najaf and not far from Kufah, lies on the Euphrates, but the river (or canal) meant here is called Kāfir, as in the following. See e.g. Yāqūt, *Muʿjam al-buldān*, entry "Kāfir".

837 Pellat says (*EI2*, "al-Mutalammis") that this shows that al-Mutalammis was illiterate, rather than that he may have been able to read the South Semitic script but could not read the early form of Arabic writing used in al-Ḥīrah, as Beeston suggested.

ومضى المتلمّس إلى الشام، ومضى طرفة بكتابه إلى عامل البحريْن، وهو عبد هِنْد بن جرد[1] ٢١٤
بن جُرَيّ بن جُرْوة بن عُمَير التَّغْلبيّ، فلمّا قرأ الكتاب قال: أترى ما في كتابك؟ قال: لا. قال:
فإنّ فيه قَتْلَك، وأنت رجلٌ شريف، وبيني وبين أهلك إخاءٌ قديم فانْجُ قبل أن يُعْلَم بمكانك؛
فإنّي إنْ قرأتُ كتابك لم أجدْ بُدًّا من قتلك! فخرج ولقيه شَباب من عبد القيس، فجعلوا يَسْقونه
ويقول الشعر، فلمّا علم بمكانه قدّمه فضرب عنقه. وهو قول المتلمّس:

وطُرَيفةُ بن العبدِ كان هديَّهمْ   ضربوا صميمَ قَذاله بمهنَّدِ

[§ ٨٣] **ومنهم** بِشْر بن أبي خازم الأَسَديّ. وكان أغار في مِقْنَبٍ من قومه على الأبناء من بني
صَعْصَعة بن معاوية وكان بنو صعصعة إلّا عامر بن صعصعة يُدْعَون الأبناء، وهم وائلة ومازن
وسَلول. فلمّا جالت الخيل بموضع يقال له الرَّدْه مرَّ بشر بغلام من بني وائلة، فقال له بشر: أعْطِ
بيَدِك. فقال له الوائلي: لتتنَحَّيَنَّ[2] أو لَأُشْعِرنّك سهماً من كِنانتي! فأبى بشرٌ إلّا أسْرَه، فرماه بسهم
على | ثُنْدُوَته، فاعتنق بشرٌ فَرَسَه، وأخذ الغلامَ فأوثقه، فلمّا كان الليل أطلقه بشر من وَثاقه ٢١٥
وخلّى سبيلَه، وقال: أَعْلِمْ قومَك أنّك قد قتلتَ بشراً. وهو قوله:

١ كذا في هـ، ك؛ ولعلّ الصحيح (جُرَذ).

٢ ك: (لتتنحنَّ).

838 Not found in *ǦN*; instead of J.r.d in ʿASH and SKḤ, I read Juradh, as in al-Baghdādī, *Khizānah*, ii, 422. Al-Anbārī, *Sharḥ al-qaṣāʾid al-sabʿ al-ṭiwāl*, 127 has Jurad with a variant Jarad, but Juradh, despite meaning "rat", is attested as a man's name.

839 The details about Ṭarafah's end and the manner of his execution differ in the various sources, but they all end with his death. The expression *ṣaḥīfat al-Mutalammis* ("al-Mutalammis's letter") became proverbial. It may seem odd that it mentions al-Mutalammis, for one would expect it to be *ṣaḥīfat Ṭarafah*, but *ṣaḥīfat al-Mutalammis* offers a better metrical fit for poets, see e.g. the line by al-Farazdaq, *Dīwān*, 483, also in al-Iṣfahānī, *Aghānī*, xvi, 167, xxi, 383, with two more examples of the phrase in verse cited in al-Thaʿālibī, *Thimār*, 217–218.

840 Instead of Ṭarafah (which would not fit the metre) the poet uses the diminutive form, Ṭurayfah, which could convey the sense of "dear Ṭarafah" or "young Ṭarafah". He is said to have been in his twenties when he died (Ibn Qutaybah, *Shiʿr*, 188 calls his *ibn al-ʿishrīn*).

841 Al-Jāḥiẓ, *Burṣān*, 77, quoting this verse, says that *hadiyy* means "bride" (*ʿarūs*). I prefer to take it as a masculine form of *hadiyyah*, the sacrificial animal led to the Kaaba in Mecca. Alternatively, it means "prisoner" (*asīr*), see Ibn Manẓūr, *Lisān al-ʿArab* (HDY), quoting this verse.

842 On "Indian", see above, § 53.

Al-Mutalammis went to Syria and Ṭarafah took his letter to the governor 214
of al-Baḥrayn, ʿAbd Hind ibn Juradh ibn Jurayy ibn Jurwah ibn ʿUmayr al-Taghlibī.[838] When the latter read the letter he said, "What do you think is in your letter?" "I don't know", answered Ṭarafah. "It says you are to be killed", said the governor. "You are a man of nobility and there is an old friendship between me and your family. Now save yourself before it gets known where you are, for I have read your letter and I would be bound to have you killed." Ṭarafah left. He met some young men of the tribe of ʿAbd al-Qays, who gave him some wine to drink. He composed some poetry, and when his whereabouts became known he was taken and beheaded.[839] Al-Mutalammis refers to this in his verse:

> Young Ṭarafah[840] ibn al-ʿAbd was their sacrificial victim:[841]
> they struck the nape of his neck with an Indian sword.[842]

[§ 83 Bishr ibn Abī Khāzim al-Asadī[843]]

Another is Bishr ibn Abī Khāzim al-Asadī. He was on a raid, in a troop of horsemen of his kinsmen, against the Abnāʾ of the Banū Ṣaʿṣaʿah ibn Muʿāwiyah. The Banū Ṣaʿṣaʿah, with the exception of the branch of ʿĀmir ibn Ṣaʿṣaʿah, were called al-Abnāʾ ("the sons"); they are Wāʾilah, Māzin, and Salūl.[844] When the horses arrived at a place called al-Radʾh,[845] Bishr came past a boy of the Banū Wāʾilah.[846] "Give me your hand!" said Bishr.[847] The Wāʾilī replied, "Move aside or I'll make you feel an arrow from my quiver!" But Bishr insisted on taking him
prisoner. The boy shot an arrow that hit | his chest. Bishr clung to the neck of his 215
horse, he grabbed the boy and tied him up. But when night fell Bishr released him and let him go. "Tell your people", he said, "that you have killed Bishr." To this he refers in his verse:[848]

---

843 See Sezgin, *Geschichte*, ii, 211–212, *EI2*, "Bishr b. Abī Khāzim" (J.W. Fück). He lived in the second half of the 6th century. For his lineage see *ǦN*, i, 55. For a parallel see al-Baghdādī, *Khizānah*, iv, 441–442 (quoting Ibn Ḥabīb), Ibn al-Shajarī, *Mukhtārāt*, 302, and see Bishr's *Dīwān*, 25.

844 See *ǦN*, i, 92. The term Abnāʾ ("Sons") is used for collectives of brother tribes when younger brothers ally themselves against older brothers (*ǦN*, ii, 135).

845 See Yāqūt, *Muʿjam al-buldān*: "A place in the territory of Qays, where the poet Bishr ibn Abī Khāzim is buried", quoting a line by Bishr that mentions it, taken from the same poem mentioned below. See Ibn al-Shajarī, *Mukhtārāt*, 305, Ibn Maymūn, *Muntahā l-ṭalab*, i, 155.

846 He is identified as ʿAmr ibn Ḥudhār in al-Marzubānī, *Muʿjam al-shuʿarāʾ*, 37 and as ʿAbs ibn Ḥudhār in al-Anbārī's commentary on the *Mufaḍḍaliyyāt*, 31.

847 Meaning, "Surrender to me as a captive!" (*Khizānah* has *istaʾsir*).

848 It is line 4 of a poem of twenty lines, found in Ibn al-Shajarī, *Mukhtārāt*, 302–313 (with commentary), Ibn Maymūn, *Muntahā l-ṭalab*, i, 155–156, and Bishr's *Dīwān*, 35–36.

وإنَّ الوائليَّ أصابَ قلبي بسهمٍ لم يكن نِكْساً لُغابا

في شعر طويل.

[§ ٨٤] **ومنهم** عَديّ بن زيد العِباديّ وقد مرّ حديثه في المغتالين.

[§ ٨٥] **ومنهم** تأبّط شرًّا الفَهْميّ وهو ثابت بن جابر بن سُفيان، وكان من شعراء العرب وفُتّاكهم
وإنّه خرج غازياً في نفر من قومه إذ عرض لهم بيتٌ من هُذيل[١] بين صَدَّيْ جبل فقال: اغْنَموا
هذا البيت. فقالوا: واللّهِ ما لنا فيه أَرَب، ولئن كانت فيه غنيمةٌ فما نستطيع أن نَسوقها، فقال:
إنّي أتفاءل أن تكون غنيمةٌ! ووقف وأتت له ضَبُعٌ عن يساره، فكرهها وعاف على غير الذي
رأى، وقال: أبْشِري أُشْبِعْك من القوم غداً. فقال له أصحابه: ويْلك انطلقْ، واللّهِ ما نرى[٢] أن نقيم
عليها! فقال: | واللّهِ لا أَريمُ! وأتت له الضبع فقال لها: أبشِري أشبعْك من القوم غداً! فقال أحد ٢١٦
القوم: واللّهِ إنّي لَأَراها تأتي لك.

١ ك: (هزيل).

٢ ك: (ترى).

849 Above, §19.

850 On this famous brigand-poet see e.g. Sezgin, *Geschichte*, ii, 137–139; *EI2*, x, 2–3 "Ta'abbaṭa Sharran" (A. Arazi); Toumi, "Ta'abbaṭa Šarran—ein Räuberdichter der vorislamischer Zeit". Arabic sources include Ibn Ḥabīb, *Muḥabbar*, 196–198; al-Balādhurī, *Ansāb*, xiii, 278–284; Ibn Qutaybah, *Shiʿr*, 312–314, 672–674; al-Iṣfahānī, *Aghānī*, xxi, 126–173; al-Maqrīzī, *Luṣūṣ* (in Webb, *Arab Thieves*, 192–237, with translation). For the story of his death see *Ansāb*, xiii, 282, *Aghānī*, xxi, 166–168, identical with the present text apart from some slight variations; al-Maqrīzī offers a shortened version (*Luṣūṣ*, 216–219). In *Aghānī* it is followed (169–170) by a different account of his death, also by the hand of a boy who shot him. This account is attributed to Abū ʿAmr al-Shaybānī; it is also found in al-Sukkarī, *Sharḥ ashʿār al-Hudhaliyyīn*, 845–846.

851 For his genealogy see *ǦN*, i, 140; Fahm ibn ʿAmr is a branch of Qays ʿAylān. Their territory was adjacent to that of Hudhayl. His nickname, which translates as "He took evil under

The Wāʾilī hit my heart
with an arrow that was no badly fletched dud.

It is part of a longer poem.

[§ 84 ʿAdī ibn Zayd al-ʿIbādī]

Another is ʿAdī ibn Zayd al-ʿIbādī. His story has been told above, among the murder victims.[849]

[§ 85 Taʾabbaṭa Sharrā[850]]

Another is Taʾabbaṭa Sharrā al-Fahmī, Thābit ibn Jābir ibn Sufyān,[851] one of the poets and killers (*futtāk*) of the Arabs. When on a raid with some others of his tribe he came upon a tent of the tribe Hudayl, between the two sides of a mountain.[852] He said, "Plunder it!" But the others said, "By God, there is nothing for us there. If there are camels to take we will not be able to drive them away!" Taʾabbaṭa Sharrā replied, "But I predict success, there will be booty!"[853] He stopped and a hyena appeared on his left side. He did not like this but gave a prediction[854] contrary to what he had seen. "Good tidings to you," he said to the animal, "I'll fill your belly with the men tomorrow!" His companions said to him, "Damn you, move on! By God, we are not going to stay here!" But he said, | "By God, I won't budge!" The hyena[855] appeared (again) and he said to 216
it, "Good tidings to you, I'll fill your belly with the men tomorrow!" One of his companions said, "By God, I think it is coming for you, rather!"

---

his arm", is explained variously: as a young boy he was seen carrying a sword under his arm, or a ram that turned out to be a ghoul, or a bag with snakes (thus in Ibn Ḥabīb, *Alqāb al-shuʿarāʾ*, 307). Sometimes his name is shortened to Taʾabbaṭa. I follow Lyall in giving his name in correct pausal form, with Sharrā; most modern studies write it as Taʾabbaṭa Sharran.

852 *Bayna ṣadday jabal*; Instead of *ṣadday*, *Aghānī* has *ṣuwā* "hillocks" or "marking stones".

853 He uses the verb *tafāʾala*, "to see a favourable omen". The appearance of animals is often part of taking omens: coming from the right, this is a good sign (*sāniḥ*). The hyena that appears from the left (*bāriḥ*), however, is an inauspicious sign.

854 The verb *ʿāfa* strictly refers to augury involving the flight of birds but is here used in a more general sense.

855 *Aghānī* has "a hyena (i.e., another one) appeared on his left".

فبات حتّى إذا كان في وجه الصبح وقد عدَّهم على النار وأبصر سوادَهم غلامٌ مع القوم دُوَين المحتلِم، فذهب في الجبل، وعدَوْا على القوم فقتلوا شيخاً وعجوزاً، وحازوا جاريتين و إبلاً. ثمّ قال تأبّط شرًّا: فأين الغلام الذي كان معكم؟ وأبصروا أثره، فاتّبعه، فقال له أصحابه: ويلك، دعْه فإنك لا تريد إليه شيئاً. فاتّبعه واستذرى الغلامُ بوقفةٍ[١] إلى صخرة، وأقبل تأبّط شرًّا يقُصّه، وأوفق[٢] الغلام سهماً حين رأى ألّا يُنجِيَه شيء، وأمهله حتّى إذا دنا منه قفز قفزةً فوثب على الصخرة وأرسل السهم، فلم يسمع تأبّط شرًّا الحَبْضة،[٣] فرفع رأسه وانتظم السهم قلبَه، وأقبل نحوه وهو يقول: لا بأس! فقال الغلام: لا بأس؟ واللّٰهِ، لقد وضعتُه[٤] حيث تكره. وغَشِيَه تأبّط شرّا بالسيف، وجعل الغلام يلوذ بالدَّرَقة، ويضربها تأبّط شرّا بحُشاشته فيحُذّ[٥] منها ما أصاب منها حتى خلص إليه فقتله، ونزل إلى أصحابه يجُرّ برجله. فلمّا رأوه وثبوا فسألوه: ما أصابك؟ فلم ينطِق ومات في أيديهم، فانطلقوا وتركوه، فجعل لا يأكل منه سبعٌ ولا طائر إلّا مات، فاحتمله هُذيل فطرحوه في غار يقال له غار رَخْمان. فقالت أخته رَيْطة ترثيه:

---

١ لعلّ الصحيح (بِرَنْفة).

٢ كـ: (أوافَقَ).

٣ هـ، كـ: (الحيضة)، والتصحيح من الأغاني.

٤ كذا في الأغاني وأظنّه الصواب. وفي هـ: (وأقبل الغلامُ نحوه وهو يقول: لا بأس! فقال الغلام وهو يقول: أما واللّٰه لقد وضعتُه) وفي كـ: (وأقبل الغلام نحوه، وهو يقول: لا بأس. فأقبل الغلام وهو يقول: أما واللّٰه لقد وضعته).

٥ كـ: (فيخذُّ).

---

856 In *Aghānī* Ta'abbaṭa Sharrā sees the shape (*sawād*) of the boy and the words "left for the mountain" are omitted. The following shows that Ta'abbaṭa Sharrā has indeed seen the boy, so possibly both texts are incomplete.

857 He presumably asks the girls; cf. *Aghānī*: "with them", asking his companions.

858 Possibly *bi-waqfah* is a misreading of *bi-ranfah*, "at a willow tree", see note 860 below.

859 *Aghānī* has "When Ta'abbaṭa heard the twanging of the bowstring he raised his head", which may be the better reading.

860 In *Aghānī* the boy hides behind a thorny bush (*qatādah*) which Ta'abbaṭa Sharrā hacks away. Al-Maqrīzī (*Luṣūṣ*, 218, also al-Zabīdī, *Tāj al-ʿarūs* [RNF]) adds: "it is (also) said that he took refuge behind a willow tree (*ranfah*)"; it seems likely that the rare word *ranfah* was misread again, this time as *daraqah* ("leather shield").

He stayed there that night and when morning dawned he was able to count the men sitting at the fire. A young lad among them, not yet having reached puberty, saw their shapes in the dark and left for the mountain.[856] Then they attacked the people, killing an old man and an old woman. They took two girls and some camels. Ta'abbaṭa Sharrā asked, "Where is that boy who was with you?"[857] They noticed his footprints, so he followed them. His companions said, "Come on, leave him! You don't want anything from him." But he went on tracking the boy, who had taken refuge behind a rock where he stopped.[858] When Ta'abbaṭa Sharrā, following his tracks, approached, the boy put an arrow to his bow, seeing that he would not be able to escape from him. He waited until the other was near, then he jumped up, leapt on top of the rock, and shot his arrow. Ta'abbaṭa Sharrā did not hear the twanging of the bowstring, he raised his head,[859] and the arrow pierced his heart.

The boy approached him. "It's all right!" said Ta'abbaṭa Sharrā. "All right?" said the boy, "By God, I've put it where you don't like it!" Ta'abbaṭa Sharrā struck him with his sword. The boy protected himself with a leather shield.[860] With his last strength Ta'abbaṭa Sharrā hewed upon it, cutting it away until the boy was at his mercy and he killed him. Dragging his feet he went down and returned to his companions. They jumped up and asked him, "What has happened to you?" But he did not speak another word and died in their arms. They departed and left him. Whenever a wild beast or bird started to eat from his body it would die.[861] The men of Hudhayl carried his corpse away and left it in a cave called Rakhmān Cave.[862] His sister Rayṭah lamented him:[863]

---

861 Al-Maqrīzī (*Luṣūṣ*, 218–219) dwells at some length on the bad miasma of the body and its dire effects, adding: "and it was said that whenever the stench of his corpse wafted over any living being, it became ill. Some youths from the Huḏayl went to bury Ta'abbaṭa Šarran, but all of them who smelled his body died. Some others veiled their faces and plugged their noses, and they hurled his corpse into the Cave of Raḫmān, yet when they returned, the bones of every one of them decayed and then they all went blind" (tr. Webb). These details have not been found in older texts.

862 See Abū 'Ubayd al-Bakrī, *Muʿjam*, 646–647, Yāqūt, *Muʿjam al-buldān*, who give no more information than what they know of Ta'abbaṭa Sharrā's story.

863 Nearly identical verses are attributed to his mother in al-Sukkarī, *Sharḥ ashʿār al-Hudhaliyyīn*, 846; the first two lines are anonymous in Ibn Qutaybah, *Shiʿr*, 312. The metre of these lines is called *rajaz* in the index of *Nawādir al-makhṭūṭāt*, ii, 485, whereas in a note in *Aghānī* (xxi, 168) it is called *sarīʿ*. On the similarity of *rajaz* and *sarīʿ* see Ullmann, *Untersuchungen*, 16–17, where it is argued that the rhyme scheme should decide in ambiguous cases. This means it is taken to be *rajaz* here. See also EI2, "sarīʿ" (W. Stoetzer).

نِعْمَ الفتى غادرتُمُ برَخْمانْ   ثابتُ بن جابرِ بن سُفْيانْ ٢١٧
قد يقتل القِرْنَ ويَروي النَّدْمانْ

[§٨٦] **ومنهم** صَخْر بن الشَّريد السُّلَميّ. وكان غزا بني أسد بن خُزيمة وأصاب غنائمَ وسَبْياً، وإنّ أبا ثَوْر بن ربيعة[١] بن ثعلبة بن رِئاب[٢] بن الأشتر الأسديّ طعن صخراً وعليه الدِّرع، فدخلت حَلْقةٌ من حلقات الدرع بطنَ صخر، فتحامل بالطعنة،[٣] وفاتَ بني أسد، فجَوِيَ منها، وكان تمرّض قريباً من سنة حتّى ملّه أهله، فسمع امرأة وهي تسأل سَلْمى امرأته: كيف بَعْلكِ؟ قالت:[٤] لا حيٌّ فيُرْجى ولا ميّت فيُنْعى، لَقِينا منه الأَمَرَّيْن! فلمّا سمع ذلك منها قال:

أرى أمَّ صَخْرٍ ما تمَلُّ عِيادتي   وملَّت سُلَيمى مَضْجَعي ومكاني
فأيُّ امرئٍ ساوى بأمٍّ حليلةً   فلا عاش إلّا في شَقاً وهَوانِ
لَعَمري لقد نبَّهْت مَن كان نائماً   وأسمعْت من كانت له أُذُنانِ
أهُمُّ بأمر الحزم لو أستطيعهُ   وقد حِيلَ بين العَيْر والنَّزَوانِ

١ هـ، كـ: (أبا ثَوْر بن ربيعة).
٢ هـ، كـ: (رباب).
٣ الكلمتان ناقصتان في كـ.
٤ كـ: (فقالت).

864 ʿASH and SKḤ read *Thābitu bnu Jābiri*, which is metrically irregular. In *Aghānī* it is vowelled as *Thābitun-i bnu Jābiri*, correcting the metre but grammatically irregular. In other versions (al-Balādhurī, al-Sukkarī, Ibn Qutaybah) it is *bi-Thābiti bni Jābiri*.

865 Listed here among poets, the fame of Ṣakhr ibn ʿAmr al-Sharīd of Sulaym as a poet is eclipsed by that of his sister al-Khansāʾ ("Snubnose"; her given name being Tumāḍir), who composed numerous elegies on him and his brother Muʿāwiyah, both of whom died shortly before the coming of Islam. She died as a Muslim c. 640 or even some decades later. On their lineage see *ĞN*, i, 122. For parallels see e.g. al-Mubarrad, *Kāmil*, iii, 254–255; idem, *Taʿāzī*, 90–92; Ibn Qutaybah, *Shiʿr*, 344–345; idem, *ʿUyūn*, iv, 118–119; Ibn ʿAbd Rabbih, *ʿIqd*, v, 166–167; al-Iṣfahānī, *Aghānī*, xv, 77–79; al-Shimshāṭī, *Anwār*, i, 110–112; Abū ʿUbayd, *Faṣl al-maqāl*, 71–72; al-ʿAskarī, *Jamharah*, i, 300; al-Maydānī, *Majmaʿ*, ii, 117–118; Ibn Ḥamdūn, *Tadhkirah*, vii, 386–387; al-Nuwayrī, *Nihāyah*, xv, 368; al-Baghdādī, *Khizānah*, i, 436–437.

A splendid man you left at Rakhmān! 217
Thābit, son of Jābir, son of Sufyān,[864]
Who would kill his opponent and quench the thirst of his drinking companions!

[§ 86 Ṣakhr ibn al-Sharīd al-Sulamī[865]]

Another is Ṣakhr ibn al-Sharīd al-Sulamī. He had raided the Banū Asad ibn Khuzaymah and had taken booty and prisoners. Abū l-Thawr Rabīʿah ibn Thaʿlabah ibn Riʾāb ibn al-Ashtar al-Asadī[866] had stabbed Ṣakhr, who was wearing a coat of mail. One of its rings had entered Ṣakhr's belly. He had kept himself going despite the wound and had escaped from the Banū Asad. The wound festered and he was ill for nearly a year, so that in the end his people became weary of it. He heard a woman ask Salmā, his wife, "How is your husband?" She answered, "Neither alive so that one could expect him to live, nor dead so that his death could be announced: we suffer with him the two most bitter things".[867] When he heard this, he said,[868]

I see that Umm Ṣakhr is not tired of coming to my sickbed,
but Sulaymā is weary of lying with me and being with me.[869]
Any man who would equal a wife to a mother,
may he not live except in misery and disgrace!
Upon my life, you[870] have woken up a sleeping man
and you have given it to hear to whoever has two ears.
I am eager to act resolutely, if only I could,
but the wild ass is prevented from mounting.[871]

---

866 See *ĠN*, i, 50. Instead of Abū Thawr Rabīʿah, ʿASH and SKḤ have Abū Thawr ibn Rabīʿah; instead of Riʾāb they have R.bāb.

867 Some versions (such as al-Maydānī, *Majmaʿ*) add that a man, seeing Ṣakhr's wife, asked her, "Are the buttocks for sale?" upon which she replied, "Soon."

868 This is a poem included in the collection of early poetry, *al-Aṣmaʿiyyāt* (146–147), where it has seven lines.

869 Umm Ṣakhr is his mother. In *al-Aṣmaʿiyyāt* it is "I see that Umm Ṣakhr's tears are not drying up". Sulaymā is a common variant of Salmā.

870 For this verb ʿASH offers two readings, *nabbahti* (2nd ps. fem. sing.) and *nabbahtu* (1st ps. sing.); likewise for the following verb. Most parallels favour the former reading.

871 This metaphor became a proverb, found in all major collections of proverbs. As for his resoluteness, Ibn Qutaybah tells that, angry with Salmā, he tied her to a post of the tent until she died. An alternative version has it that he asked for his sword in order to kill her, but he was too weak to carry out his intention.

فلما طال عليه البَلاء والمرض وقد نتأتْ قطعة من جنبه[1] مثل اللِّبد في موضع | الطعنة، قالوا: ٢١٨
لو قطعتَها رجوْنا أن تبرأ منها، فقال: شأْنَكم! وأشفق عليه بعضُهم فنهاه، فقال: الموت أهْوَنُ عليَّ ممّا أنا فيه! فأحْمَوْا له شَفْرة فقطعوها، فيئس من نفسه. وسمع أختَه الخنساء تسأل: كيف كان صبرُه؟ فقال:

أجارتَنا إنَّ الخطوبَ تُريبُ   علينا وكلّ المُخْطئين تُصيبُ
فإنْ تسأليني كيف صبْري فإنّني   صَبورٌ على رَيْب الزمان أريبُ
كأنّي وقد أدْنَوْا لحَزٍّ شِفارَهمْ   من الصبر دامي الصَّفْحتيْن رَكوبُ
أجارتَنا لستُ الغداةَ بظاعنٍ   ولكنْ مقيمٌ ما أقام عسيبُ

فمات فدُفن هناك.

[§ ٨٧] **ومنهم** طَريف بن تميم العَنْبَريّ. وكان قُتل يومَ مُبايِض. وكان طريفٌ قتل شَراحيلَ[2] أخا بني [أبي] ربيعة بن ذُهل بن شَيْبان. وكان[3] الفرسان لا تشهد عُكاظَ إلّا مُبرقَعةً مَخافةَ الثُّؤْرة، وكان طريف لا يتبرقع كما يتبرقعون. فلمّا ورد عكاظ قال حَمَصِيصة بن شَراحيل | الشيبانيّ: ٢١٩

١ الكلمة ناقصة في ك.
٢ هـ، ك: (شرحبيل) والتصحيح من العقد الفريد ومراجع أخرى.
٣ ك: (وكانت).

872 *A-jāratanā*, literally "female neighbour of us!", is ambiguous. A *jārah* is often one's wife, but the context makes it clear that he is addressing his sister.

873 This hemistich is also attributed to Imru' al-Qays, see his *Dīwān*, 357; al-Iṣfahānī, *Aghānī*, ix, 100–101; Yāqūt, *Muʿjam al-buldān*, s.v. ʿAsīb.

874 According to al-ʿAskarī, *Jamharah*, i, 300, "he was buried at the side of ʿAsīb, a mountain near Medina; his grave is marked there."

875 On his lineage see *ǦN*, i, 81. For parallels see Abū ʿUbaydah, *Dībāj*, 149–151; idem, *Ayyām*, 445–451; al-Mufaḍḍal, *Fākhir*, 247–250; al-Jāḥiẓ, *Bayān*, iii, 100–101; Ibn ʿAbd Rabbih, *ʿIqd*, v, 208–210 (on Yawm Mubāyiḍ); al-Shimshāṭī, *Anwār*, i, 96–101 (where the battle day is called Yawm Ubāyiḍ); Ibn al-Athīr, *Kāmil*, i, 477–479; al-Nuwayrī, *Nihāyah*, xv, 394–395. The battle was between Tamīm and Bakr ibn Wāʾil.

His misery and illness lasted a long time. An excrescence protruded from his
side, like a piece of felt, at the place | of the wound. They said to him, "If you cut 218
it off, we expect you may be cured." "As you wish", he said. Someone was concerned for him and told him not to do it, but he said, "I would rather die than stay like this!". They heated a blade and cut it off. As a result he gave up any hope of living. He heard his sister al-Khansā' ask someone, "How did he endure it?" Then he said,

> Sister![872] Mishaps are alarming us
> and they hit unerringly all those who err.
> If you ask me how I endured it, well, I am
> one who bears Time's misfortunes, skilled in it.
> When they took their blade to me, ready to cut, it was as if
> I were, for endurance, a riding camel with bloodied flanks.
> Sister, I shall not be departing this morning
> but I shall remain here, as long as Mount ʿAsīb remains.[873]

Then he died and was buried there.[874]

[§ 87 Ṭarīf ibn Tamīm al-ʿAnbarī[875]]

Another is Ṭarīf ibn Tamīm al-ʿAnbarī. He was killed on the battle day of Mubāyiḍ. Ṭarīf had killed Sharāḥīl, one of the Banū Abū Rabīʿah ibn Dhuhl ibn Shaybān.[876] Knights would come to the market at ʿUkāẓ wearing veils, fearing blood revenge,[877] but Ṭarīf would not wear a veil as the others did. When he
arrived at ʿUkāẓ, Ḥamaṣīṣah, the son of Sharāḥīl | al-Shaybānī,[878] said, "Show 219

---

876 For this branch of Bakr ibn Wā'il see *ĞN*, i, 149. Sharāḥīl is not mentioned there. In ʿASH and SKḤ this name is spelled as Shuraḥbīl; since Ṭarīf's killer is given as Ḥamaṣīṣah ibn Sharāḥīl, I have emended Shuraḥbīl to Sharāḥīl, as it is also in e.g. Ibn ʿAbd Rabbih, *ʿIqd* and al-Shimshāṭī, *Anwār*.

877 During the annual market days at ʿUkāẓ, not far from Mecca (see *EI2*, "ʿUkāẓ" [Irfan Shahîd]) bloodshed was forbidden, but taking precautions was no doubt wise.

878 Ḥamaṣīṣah (also absent from the lineage in *ĞN*) is spelled Ḥimṣiyyah in Abū ʿUbaydah, *Dībāj*, 148; Ḥumayṣīṣah in Abū ʿUbaydah, *Ayyām*, ii, 445 and al-Shimshāṭī, *Anwār*, i, 97; Ḥaṣīṣah in Ibn ʿAbd Rabbih; *ʿIqd*, v, 208; and as Ḥamīṣah (or Ḥumayṣah) in al-Maydānī, *Majmaʿ*, ii, 525 and Ibn al-Athīr, *Kāmil*, i, 477. Ibn Manẓūr, *Lisān al-ʿArab* (ḤMṢ) gives *ḥamaṣīṣ* as the name of a plant.

أَرُوني طريفاً. فأروْه إيّاه فجعل يتأمّله، فقال له طريف: ما لك؟ فقال: أتوسّمك لأعرِفَك، فإنْ لقِيتُك في حرب فلِلّهِ عليَّ أنْ أقتلَك أو تقتلَني! فقال طريف:

أَوَكُلَّما[١] وردتْ عُكاظَ[٢] قَبيلةٌ   بعثوا إليَّ عَريفَهم يتوسَّمُ
فتوَسَّموني إنّني أنا ذاكُمُ   شاكي سِلاحٍ في الحوادث مُعْلَمُ
تَحْتي الأَغرُّ وفوقَ جِلدي نَثْرةٌ   زَغْفٌ تَرُدُّ السيفَ وهْو مثلَّمُ
ولكلِّ بَكْريٍّ عليَّ عَداوةٌ   وأبو ربيعةَ شانئٌ ومحلِّمُ[٣]
حوْلي أُسَيِّدُ والهُجَيم ومازنٌ   وإذا حللْتُ فَحَوْلَ بيْتِيَ خَضَّمُ

فمضى لذلك ما شاء اللّٰه. ثمّ إنّ عائذة، وهم حُلَفاء لبني أبي ربيعة بن ذهل، أغار عليهم طريفٌ في بني العنبر، وفَدَكيّ بن أَعْبَد في بني مِنْقَر، وأبو الجَدْعاء في بني طُهَيّة، فالتقوْا بمُبايض فاقتتلوا قتالاً شديداً، فقُتل أبو الجدعاء، وهرب فَدَكيّ، ولم يكن لحمصيصة همٌّ غير طريف، فلمّا عرفه رماه فقتله. فقال أبو مارد[٤]، أخو بني أبي ربيعة، في قتل حمصيصة طريفاً:

خاضَ الغداةَ إلى طريفٍ في الوَغى   حمصيصةُ المِغْوار في الهيْجاءِ

١ هـ، كـ: (أو كلّما).
٢ كـ: (كعاظ).
٣ هـ، كـ: (ومحرم)، والتصحيح من الأصمعيّات ومصادر كثيرة غيرها.
٤ كـ: (رماد).

879 Apart from being quoted in the sources given above, the poem is also included in *al-Aṣmaʿiyyāt*, 127–128 and al-Akhfash, *al-Ikhtiyārayn*, 189–190.

880 This line is given in the famous grammar by Sībawayh (ii, 215) as an example of the form *faʿīl* (here *ʿarīf*) functioning as *fāʿil* (here *ʿārif*).

881 His horse.

882 ʿASH and SKḤ have *muḥarram* or *muḥarrim*; I have read Muḥallim, as found in all other sources. The context seems to require a name. In *ǦN*, i, 148 one finds two persons called Muḥallim, both belonging to Dhuhl ibn Shaybān: Muḥallim ibn Sayyār ibn Abī ʿAmr ibn al-Ḥārith ibn Dhuhl and Muḥallim ibn Ẓafar ibn Sayyār ibn al-Ḥārith ibn Dhuhl; but it is likely that Muḥallim ibn Dhuhl ibn Shaybān is meant here (*ǦN*, i, 142).

me Ṭarīf!" They pointed Ṭarīf out to him and he looked at him attentively. Ṭarīf asked him, "What do you want?" Ḥamaṣīṣah replied, "I am taking note of your features so that I can recognise you. If I meet you again in battle, I swear to God I will kill you or else you will kill me." Then Ṭarīf said,[879]

> Whenever a tribe arrives at ʿUkāẓ, do they then
> send for an expert of theirs to take note and examine?[880]
> Examine me then! I am that man,
> arms at the ready, distinguished in battle events.
> Beneath me is Bright Blaze,[881] on my skin is a smooth
> coat of mail that leaves a sword blunted.
> Every man of Bakr is hostile to me,
> and the Abū Rabīʿah and Muḥallim hate me.[882]
> Around me are Usayyid, al-Hujaym, and Māzin,
> and when I am at home, then around my tent are Khaḍḍam![883]

Subsequently, the ʿĀʾidhah,[884] who were allied to the Banū Abī Rabīʿah ibn Dhuhl, were raided by Ṭarīf together with Fadakī ibn Aʿbad with men of the Banū Minqar[885] and Abū l-Jadʿāʾ with men of the Banū Ṭuhayyah.[886] They met at Mubāyiḍ[887] where they fought a hard battle. Abū l-Jadʿāʾ was killed, Fadakī fled, but Ḥamaṣīṣah's only concern was Ṭarīf. Upon recognising him he shot an arrow at him and killed him. Abū Mārid, of the Banū Abī Rabīʿah, said,[888]

> That morning there plunged into the fray
> Ḥamaṣīṣah, a man bold in battle.

---

883 Usayyid, al-Hujaym, and Mālīk are branches of Tamīm, see *ǦN*, i, 81. Khaḍḍam is said to be another name for al-ʿAnbar ibn ʿAmr ibn Tamīm, the branch to which Ṭarīf belonged, see e.g. Ibn Manẓūr, *Lisān al-ʿArab* (*KhḌM*), where this verse is quoted.

884 On ʿĀʾidhah, a branch of Quraysh, see *ǦN* i, 4, 30 and ii, 148 (ʿĀʾidhah being a "matriarch", the patriarch being Khuzaymah ibn Luʾayy).

885 For his lineage in Minqar see *ǦN*, i, 76.

886 Ṭuhayyah is the collective name of several branches of Tamīm, see *ǦN*, i, 59. Abū l-Jadʿāʾ cannot be found there.

887 On detailed descriptions of this battle day see the sources quote above, note 875. Mubāyiḍ is mentioned in Yāqūt, *Muʿjam al-buldān*, but its location is not given. It is said to be a waterhole of the Banū Abī Rabīʿah (see e.g. al-Mufaḍḍal, *Fākhir*, 248).

888 Abū Mārid has not been identified. The line is also ascribed to Abū l-Najm al-ʿIjlī (al-Mufaḍḍal, *Fākhir*, 249–250). Abū l-Najm, better known as a poet of *rajaz*, also composed a poem with the same rhyme and metre but the line is not found in the edition of the *Dīwān* by Hämeen-Anttila (1–3).

[§٨٨] **ومنهم** السُّلَيك بن السُّلَكة، وهي أمّه، وأبو[هُ عُمَيْر][١] السَّعْديّ. وكان غزا خَثْعَم فسبى امرأة فأولدَها. ثمّ إنّ المرأة قالت لسُليك: أَزِرْني قومي،[٢] وإنّي لا أغدر بك، وما ولدي منك إلّا كولدي من غيرك. فاحتملها وأتى بها أرض خثعم فقالت له: أقِمْ بهذا الموضع، لموضعٍ أمرتْ به، حتّى آتِيَك بعد يومين أو ثلاثة. فلمّا أتت زوجها قالت له: هذا سُليك بموضعِ كذا. فلم تر عند زوجها خيراً، فقالت لابن عمّه أَنَس بن مُدْرِك، فخرج أنس فقتله،[٣] فوثب زوج المرأة على أنس حتّى عَقَلَه، فقال أنس: ٢٢٠

غَضِبتُ للمرء إذ نيكت[٤] حليلتُهُ وإذ يُشَدُّ على وَجْعائها الثَّفَرُ
أَنَّى تناسِيَّ هاماتٍ بمَجْزرةٍ[٥] لا يزدهيني سَوادُ الليل والجَهَرُ

١ التكملة من الأغاني.
٢ هـ: في النسختين (قومك).
٣ كذا، كما يقتضيه السياق. وفي هـ، كـ:(فقاتله).
٤ كـ: (للمرء نكحت).
٥ كذا في الديباج لأبي عبيدة والأغاني للإصفهانيّ، وفي هـ: (فمحرورة) وفي كـ: (فَمَحْروه).

889 Oddly, there are two somewhat overlapping entries on him, see below, § 93, perhaps through a copyist's error. Rather than merging them they are given here as they are found in the text.

890 On this brigand and poet, whose name is also spelled without articles (Sulayk ibn Sulakah), see e.g. Abū ʿUbaydah, *Dībāj*, 44–46, 71–73; al-Balādhurī, *Ansāb*, xii, 349–351; Ibn Qutaybah, *Shiʿr*, 365–368; al-Iṣfahānī, *Aghānī*, xx, 374–387; Sezgin, *Geschichte*, ii, 139–140; al-Maqrīzī, *Luṣūṣ*, 246–261 and index. Al-Sulakah was the name of his mother, a black woman (Ibn Ḥabīb, *Muḥabbar*, 307–308 lists him among the "sons of Ethiopian women", *abnāʾ al-Ḥabashiyyāt*). He is counted among the "Arab Crows" (*aghribat al-ʿArab*), see e.g. al-Thaʿālibī, *Thimār*, 160 and Webb in al-Maqrīzī, *Luṣūṣ*, 47–51, and like some other

[§ 88 al-Sulayk ibn al-Sulakah[889]]

Another is al-Sulayk ibn al-Sulakah,[890] al-Sulakah being his mother. His father 220
was ʿUmayr al-Saʿdī. On a raid against the tribe of Khathʿam he captured a woman and had a child by her. One day the woman said to Sulayk, "Let me visit my people; I shall not betray your trust, for my child with you is as dear to me as my other children." Sulayk took her to the territory of Khathʿam. She said to him, "Stay in this place"—pointing out some place to him—"until I return to you after two or three days." When she came to her husband she told him, "Sulayk is in such-and-such a place." But she did not find him up to anything, so she went to his paternal cousin, Anas ibn Mudrik.[891] He went out and killed al-Sulayk.[892] Then the woman's husband rushed at Anas and made him pay the blood-price. Then Anas said,[893]

> I was angry on behalf of that man when his spouse was fucked[894]
>   and when on her behind a crupper was tied.
> How could I forget the skulls in a place of carnage,[895]
>   when neither the nights' blackness nor the moon (?)[896] lifted my spirits!

---

brigands such as al-Shanfarā (see § 97) he was famous as a fast runner (al-ʿAskarī, *Jamharah*, ii, 60; al-Maydanī, *Majmaʿ*, ii, 55–56; al-Thaʿālibī, *Thimār*, 134–135; see on this motif Webb in *Luṣūṣ*, 34–47). The name of his father is given as ʿAmr, ʿĀmir, or ʿUmayr ibn Yathribī. See *Ǧn*, i, 76.

891 See *Ǧn*, i, 224. He is also called Anas ibn Mudrikah [thus] al-Khathʿamī (e.g. al-Jāḥiẓ, *Ḥayawān*, iii, 81, *Aghānī*, x, 35).

892 The two editions have *fa-qātalahu* "(Anas) fought with him" but the context makes clear that he killed him and that one ought to read *fa-qatalahu*.

893 Some or all of these lines are also, with several variants, in Abū ʿUbaydah, *Dībāj*, 45–46; al-Jāḥiẓ, *Ḥayawān*, i, 18; Ibn Qutaybah, *Shiʿr*, 368; idem, *Maʿānī*, 928, 1009; Ibn ʿAbd Rabbih, *ʿIqd*, iii, 130; al-Iṣfahānī, *Aghānī*, xx, 387; Abū ʿUbayd al-Bakrī, *Faṣl al-maqāl*, 387–388; al-Maydānī, *Majmaʿ*, ii, 170–171; al-Zabīdī, *Tāj* (*wjʿ*).

894 In SKḤ the word *nīkat* is replaced by the less offensive but unmetrical *nukiḥat*; the same on its reappearance in § 93.

895 Reading, with *Dībāj* and *Aghānī*, *bi-majzaratin* instead of the editions' *fa-maḥrūratan*, which I do not understand. Abū ʿUbayd al-Bakrī, *Faṣl al-maqāl*, 387, has *bi-makhruʾatin*, "in a shitting place" (with the comment, "this is more contemptible").

896 I do not understand *al-jahar* (ʿASH, SKḤ) and have translated the version of *Aghānī* (*al-qamar*); *Dībāj* has al-*khumur* ("the thicket").

أَغْشَى الهِياجَ وسِرْبالي مضاعَفةٌ تغْشى البنانَ وسيفي صارمٌ ذَكَرُ
إنّي وقتْلي سُليكاً ثمّ أَعْقِلَهُ كالثور يُضْرَب لمّا عافتِ البَقَرُ

[§ ٨٩] **ومنهم** عبد عَمْرو بن عمّار الطائيّ. كان[١] الحارث بن أبي شَمِر الغَسّانيّ لمّا قُتل المُنْذِر بن ماء السماء بعث رجلاً من أهل بيته يقال له الأبرد، فنزل بين العراق والشام، وكان يسمّى المُلَيْك،[٢] أي ليس بملكٍ تامٍّ، فأتاه عبد عمرو فامتدحه فوَصَله، فلم يرض صِلَتَه، فهجاه فقال: ٢٢١

كأنَّ ثناياه إذا افترَّ ضاحكاً رؤوسُ جَرادٍ في رؤوسٍ تُحَسْحَسُ

فقال: ويْلكم، ائتوني بجَراد. فأُتي بجراد فأمر به فوُضع على النار، فرآهنّ يتحرّكن، فقال: ويْلكم، إنّ ابن عمّار لم يهجُني ولكنْ سلح عليَّ! وكان ممّا هجاه به أيضاً قوله:

١ ك: (وكان).
٢ هـ، ك: (المَلِيك).

897 For the unusual subjunctive (*aʿqilahū*) see Wright, *Grammar*, ii, 33. The word *thawr*, close to *baqar*, "cows", of course suggests "bull", but several sources (among them *ʿIqd*; *Majmaʿ al-amthāl*; *Lisān al-ʿArab* [*ThWR*]) record that others took *thawr* to mean *ṭuḥlub*, "green moss or algae". Lines by al-Aʿshā (see Ibn Qutaybah, *Maʿānī*, 928) seem to support "bull" (*innī … la-ka-l-thawri wa-l-jinniyyu yaḍribu ẓahrahū | wa-mā dhanbuhū an ʿāfati l-māʾa mashrabā*). The second hemistich became a proverb for someone who feels wronged. See also al-Maqrīzī, *Luṣūṣ*, 258–261.

898 He is ʿAbd ʿAmr ibn ʿAmmār ibn ʿAmr, of Jamr, a branch of Ṭayyiʾ; see *ĞN*, i, 252, ii, 122; Sezgin, *Geschichte*, ii, 175. For a (very brief) parallel see Ibn Durayd, *Ishtiqāq*, 235, where a line by al-Aʿshā mentioning Ibn ʿAmmār is quoted; cf. al-Aʿshā, *Dīwān*, 179.

899 He was the Lakhmid king of al-Ḥīrah, see above, § 21. He was defeated in 554 by al-Ḥārith ibn Jabalah ibn al-Mundhir, Ghassānid king of the Jafnid dynasty (reg. AD 529–569). On him see e.g. *ĞN*, i, 193, ii, 305–306; *EI2*, "al-Ḥāri͟th b. D͟jabala" (Irfan Shahîd).

900 For al-Ḥārith ibn Abī Shamir Jabalah ibn al-Ḥārith, also of Ghassān, see *ĞN*, i, 193, ii, 312–313. There is some confusion between this al-Ḥārith (who is said to have died in 8/630, much later than the events here described) and al-Ḥārith ibn Jabalah, mentioned in the previous note, who is probably meant here.

I join the fray with a double coat of mail
that covers the fingers, and my sword is sharp, of good steel.
Having killed Sulayk and then to pay the blood-price, I was
like a bull beaten away when the cows are loath to drink.[897]

[§ 89 ʿAbd ʿAmr ibn ʿAmmār al-Ṭāʾī[898]]

Another is ʿAbd ʿAmr ibn ʿAmmār al-Ṭāʾī. When al-Mundhir ibn Māʾ al-Samāʾ[899] was killed, al-Ḥārith ibn Abī Shamir al-Ghassānī[900] sent a man of his family called al-Abrad,[901] who established himself between Iraq and Syria. He was called al-Mulayk[902] ("the Kinglet"), meaning that he was not a full king. ʿAbd ʿAmr came to him and eulogised him. for which he received a reward.[903] He was not satisfied with the reward and lampooned him, saying,[904] 221

When he opens his mouth, laughing, his front teeth
are like the heads of locusts when their heads are roasted.[905]

Al-Mulayk said, "Damn you, bring me some locusts!" When they were brought to him he told them to put them on the fire. He saw them move about and said, "Damn you, Ibn ʿAmmār did not just lampoon me, he shat on me!" Ibn ʿAmmār had also lampooned him with the following:[906]

---

901 His lineage has not been found. In al-Anbārī, *Sharḥ al-qaṣāʾid al-sabʿ*, 131, he is called al-Ubayrid al-Ghassānī.

902 ʿASH and SKḤ vowel this as al-Malīk, but this seems unlikely in view of what follows. *Malīk* is a synonym of *malik*, "king", and is even applied to God in the Qurʾan (al-Qamar 54:55: *ʿinda malīkin muqtadir*), so I prefer to read it as the diminutive form *mulayk*.

903 The only extant poem of any length attributed to ʿAbd ʿAmr is a *qaṣīdah* of 32 lines which is also attributed to ʿĀmir ibn Juwayn; see Ibn Maymūn, *Muntahā l-ṭalab*, iii, 327–329. It is not a panegyric on al-Abrad.

904 This line is found in al-Anbārī, *Sharḥ al-qaṣāʾid al-sabʿ*, 131; it is attributed to Ṭarafah, lampooning ʿAmr ibn Hind, in al-Qurashī, *Jamharah* (ed. Dār Ṣādir), 79, (ed. al-Bijāwī), 96, with rhyme-word *tukhashkhishū* instead of *tuḥashḥasū*.

905 The verb *ḥashḥasa* and its synonym *khashkhasha* imply sound as well as movement. Instead of *fī ruʾūsin*, with its awkward repetition of *ruʾūs*, the version in al-Anbārī, *Sharḥ* and al-Qurashī, *Jamharah* has *fī irīnin* (wrongly *arīnin* in ed. Dār Ṣādir), "in fireplaces", *irīn* being the plural of *irah* (W'R).

906 Lines 2–6, in a different order and with variants, are attributed to Ṭarafah in al-Qurashī, *Jamharah* (Dār Ṣādir), 78–79, (Bijāwī), 95–96, and to al-Mutalammis in al-Anbārī, *Sharḥ al-qaṣāʾid al-sabʿ*, 130–131 and al-Iṣfahānī, *Aghānī*, xxi (Brünnow), 192. A version of line 1 is quoted anonymously in Thaʿlab, *Majālis*, ii, 416. The verses are not in Ṭarafah's *Dīwān* such as edited by Ahlwardt and Nāṣir al-Dīn or in al-Baṭalyawsī, *Sharḥ al-ashʿār*.

قل للّذي خَيْرُهُ دون الصهاقيمِ[1] ومنطني عندنا أحلا من الدبسِ[2]
لو كنتُ كلبَ قنيصٍ كنتَ ذا جُدَدٍ قُــبِّح ذا وجهِ أنفٍ ثَمَّ منتَكِسِ
إنّ المُلَيكَ إذا .....[3] عَثَروا على تَعَرْقُبِه باللّٰه لم يَكُسِ ٢٢٢
تَــعلَّمَنْ أنَّ شرَّ الناسِ كُلِّهِمُ ألْأفقمُ[4] الأنفِ والأضراسُ كالعَدَسِ
كان امْرَأً صالحاً فارتدَّ مُومِسةً[5] حَمْرا يرهّــزُها رامي بني مرسِ
يمشي بَطيناً ولمّا يقْضِ نَهْمتَه ماءُ الرجال على فَخْدَيْه كالقَرَسِ

ثمّ إنّ الأسود بن عامر بن جُوَين الطائيّ انطلق إلى الشام فنزل بالمُليك فنسبه فانتسب له فعرفه، فقال: أيّ رجلٍ ابن عمّار فيكم؟ فأخبره أنّه من أُسرة قليلة ذليلة وأنّه لا خير فيه. فقال: لا جَرَمَ لا تفارقُني حتّى أُوتى به. وكان ابن عمّار قد لجأ إلى أَوْس بن حارثة بن لأْم الطائيّ، فأعطى الأسودُ المليكَ رهينةً من ولده، وأقبل حتّى أخذ ابن عمّار، فذهب أوسٌ يحُول بينه وبينه؛ فقال: أتحُول بيني وبين ابن عمّي؟ فدُونَك؛ أتُراني كنتُ مُسْلِمَه للقتل؟! فانطلق به إلى المليك فضرب عنقه، فقال خَوْليّ بن سَهْلة الطائيّ:

١ كذا في هـ، وفي كـ كأنّها كلمتان: (الصها قيم).
٢ كذا في الأصل والبيت واضح التحريف. والأرجح أنّ العجز: (ومَنطِقي عندنا أحلى من الدِّبِسِ).
٣ في البيت نقص.
٤ أوّل الهمزتين يقتضيها الوزن.
٥ كـ: (مومِـةٌ).

907 The last word, *al-ṣahāqīm*, does not make sense metrically or semantically. In SKḤ it is printed as two words, which does not help much. Perhaps it is to be read as *dūna l-Suhā*, "less than al-Suhā" (a star in Ursa major proverbial for its dimness), but the following word remains obscure.

908 Instead of the unintelligible *wa-m.nṭ.nī* I have translated as if it is *wa-manṭiqī*.

909 Following al-Anbārī's commentary on *judad* (*shabbahahū bi-kalb fīhi buqaʿ wa-in shiʾta baqaʿ*), similar to that of Thaʿlab (*al-ʿalāmāt wa-l-ṭuruq*); Hārūn interprets it as "collars".

910 Translation of the second hemistich tentative; it looks corrupt. In *Aghānī* and *Majālis Thaʿlab* it is *takūnu urbatuhū fī ākhiri l-marasī*, "his collar would be at the end of the rope" (meaning, according to Thaʿlab, that he is no good).

911 There is a lacuna in the text. The line, for which I have not found parallels, is obscure.

912 *Afqam* often means "having unequal jaws, having an over- or an underbite". Other versions have the more plausible *akhnas*, "pugnosed".

Say to him whose good is beneath ...[907]
—and my speech, in our opinion, is sweeter than honey—[908]
If you were a hunting dog you would have spots and stripes;[909]
what an ugly face with that nose is there, turned upside down![910]
Al-Mulayk, when ...[911] they stumble 222
despite being hamstrung, by God, he does not hop.(?)
You should know that the worst of all people
is someone with a crooked nose[912] and teeth like lentils.
He was a decent man but he turned into a red
whore, rogered by the archer of the Banū Maras.[913]
He walks, fat-bellied, not yet having fulfilled his craving,
with men's spunk on his thighs, congealed.

Al-Aswad ibn ʿĀmir ibn Juwayn al-Ṭāʾī[914] went to Syria. He stopped at al-Mulayk and identified himself to him with his lineage. Al-Mulayk recognised him and asked him, "What status has Ibn ʿAmmār among your tribe?" Al-Aswad told him that Ibn ʿAmmār belonged to a humble family of small numbers and that he was no good. Al-Mulayk said, "You must certainly not leave me before he is brought before me!" Ibn ʿAmmār had taken refuge with Aws ibn Ḥārithah ibn Laʾm al-Ṭāʾī.[915] Al-Aswad left one of his sons as a hostage with al-Mulayk and went forth until he had taken Ibn ʿAmmār prisoner. Aws intervened, but al-Aswad said, "Will you come between me and my cousin? Think twice! Do you think I would surrender him to be killed?!" Then he took him to al-Mulayk, who had him beheaded.

Khawlī ibn Sahlah al-Ṭāʾī said,[916]

---

913 Vowelling uncertain; no such tribe or clan has been found. Perhaps Maras is a corruption of Ḍaras. Other versions have "A king by day, you are a whore at night", followed by the last hemistich of the following line. "Red" is obviously pejorative here, probably short for the common obscenity *ḥamrāʾ al-ʿijān*.

914 On him see the entry on his father, ʿĀmir ibn Juwayn above, § 79.

915 See *ǦN*, i, 250, ii, 214 ("der einflussreichste Häuptling der Ǧadīla/Ṭaiyiʾ um die Wende des 6. Jahrhunderts"). Ibn Ḥabīb lists him among the *ajwād al-Jāhiliyyah*, "the generous men of the pre-Islamic period" (*Muḥabbar*, 145).

916 There is some confusion about this name, see *ǦN*, ii, 299 s.v. Ḥaras b. Ǧundab. The poem is found in al-Akhfash, *Ikhtiyārayn*, 129–120, attributed to ʿĀmir ibn Juwayn and in Abū Tammām, *Waḥshiyyāt*, 146. Lines 1–2, 4 are ascribed in al-Jāḥiẓ to Abū Qurdūdah (*Ḥayawān*, iv, 243, v, 332, *Bayān*, i, 222–223, 349; see also al-Marzubānī, *Muʿjam al-shuʿarāʾ*, 59). Al-Jāḥiẓ says that with these lines Ibn ʿAmmār was warned not to be the drinking companion of king al-Nuʿmān (ibn al-Mundhir), and that he was killed by al-Nuʿmān. Line 3 is attributed by Ibn Qutaybah to ʿĀmir ibn Juwayn (*Maʿānī*, 827). The attribution to Abū Qurdūdah is possibly due to the fact that in *Waḥshiyyāt* the preceding piece is by Abū Qurdūdah, who is then mistakenly taken as the subject of the following *wa-qāla*.

لقد نهيْتُ ابنَ عمّارٍ وقلتُ له   لا تأمَنَنْ أحمرَ العينيْن والشَّعَرَهْ
إنّ الملوك إذا حللتَ ساحتَهمْ   طارت بثَـوْبك من نِيرانهمْ شَرَرَهْ
إنْ[١] يقتُلوك فلا نِكْسٌ ولا وَرَعٌ   عند اللِّقاء ولا هَوْهاءةٌ هُمَرَهْ
يا غارةً كانسجال السَّيْل قد قَتَلوا   ومَنْطِقاً مثلَ وَشْي اليَمْنة الحِبَرَهْ
٢٢٣ لقد نصحتُ له والعِيسُ باركةٌ   بين الحُدَيْباء والمرْماة والأَمَرَهْ
لقد نهيتُك عمّنْ لا كِفاءَ له   عند الحِفاظ وعن عَوْفٍ[٢] وعن قَطَرَهْ
ما قتلوه على ذنْبٍ ألمَّ به   إلّا تَواصَوْا وقالوا قومهُ خَسَرَهْ

وقال المُليك للأسود بن عامر:

قتلتَ ابنَ عمِّك مِن خَشْيِنا   وفي أهله يقتُلنَّ الخَشِي

[§ ٩٠] **ومنهم** سُوَيد بن صامت الأَوْسيّ. وكان يُدْعى الكامل، وقد كتبناه في أشراف المغتالين.[٣]

١ كذا في الاختيارين للأخفش والوحشيّات لأبي تمّام، وفي هـ، كـ: (أو).
٢ لعلّ الصحيح (غوث) كما في الاختيارين والوحشيّات.
٣ كذا، ولم يسبق له خبر.

917 I prefer to read *in yaqtulūka* (as in *Waḥshiyyāt* and *Ikhtiyārayn*) instead of *aw yaqtulūka*, as in ʿASH and SKḤ; the parenthesis is my interpretation of the verse.
918 The comparison of Ibn ʿAmmār to a raid (*ghārah*) is a strange metaphor. In the other versions he is compared to a bowl (*jafnah*), image for a generous man.
919 *Waḥshiyyāt* has al-Judaydāʾ, al-Mawmāh, and al-Amarah. The places have not been identified.

I held Ibn ʿAmmār back and said to him,
You cannot trust a man with red eyes and hair!
If you sit in the courtyard of kings
a spark of their fires will fly into your robe.
If[917] they kill you, (you were in any case) not a worthless man, not weak
in battle, no coward or idle talker.
Ah, what a raid like the flow of a torrent they have killed,[918]
what a speech like the brocade of a striped Yemeni cloth!
I gave you good advice when the reddish-white camels were kneeling 223
between al-Ḥudaybāʾ, al-Marmāʾ, and al-Amarah;[919]
I told you to hold back from one who has no match in battle
when honour is to be defended, and from gifts rich or paltry. (?)[920]
They did not kill him for a sin associated with him,
except that they told one another: his people are lowly.[921]

Al-Mulayk said to al-Aswad ibn ʿĀmir,

You have killed your cousin for fear of us,
and in his family the fearful kills.[922]

[§ 90 Suwayd ibn Ṣāmit al-Awsī]

Another is Suwayd ibn Ṣāmit al-Awsī. He was called al-Kāmil ("the Perfect"). We have written about him in *Prominent Murder Victims*.[923]

---

920 Translation tentative. I cannot make sense of *wa-ʿan ʿawfin wa-ʿan q.ṭarah* (ʿASH, SKḤ). *Waḥshiyyāt* and *Ikhtiyārayn* have *wa-ʿan ghawthin wa-ʿan quṭurah*. If *ghawth* ("cry for succour") can be taken as if standing for *ghayth* ("abundant rain")—the roots are related—and *quṭ(u)rah* for "a drop, or a paltry thing", then they may refer to al-Mulayk's gift mentioned before.

921 *Khasarah*, literally "losers".

922 The sense is not altogether clear.

923 He does not have a separate entry in *Asmāʾ al-mughtālīn*, but see above, § 27 on al-Mujadhdhar ibn Dhiyād, who had killed him and who was killed in turn by Suwayd's son al-Ḥārith. Suwayd ibn al-Ṣāmit (normally with the article) was a tribal leader and poet from Yathrib (Medina) and was killed, probably before the Hijra, in battle. See Sezgin, *Geschichte*, ii, 285, *ĞN*, i, 177, ii, 521.

[§ ٩١] **ومنهم** دُرَيد بن الصِّمّة الجُشَميّ. وقُتل مُشْرِكاً[١] يوم حُنين. وكان مالك بن عوْف النَّصْريّ جمع لحرب رسول الله صلّى الله عليه وسلّم، فاجتمعت إليه ثَقيفٌ كلُّها ونصْر وجُشَم ابنا معاوية، وسعد بن بكر، وناس قليل من بني هِلال بن عامر، ولم تحضر كعبٌ وكِلاب. فخرج في بني جشم دريدٌ شيخاً كبيراً في شِجار، ليس عنده إلّا التيمُّن برأيه ومعرفته بالحرب، وكان شيخاً مجرَّباً. فعسكر مالكُ بن عوف بأوطاس، ومعهم نساؤهم وأبناؤهم وأموالهم، فأقبل دريد
في شِجار يُقاد | به بَعيره، فقال: أين نزلتم؟ قالوا: بأوطاس. قال: نِعْمَ مَجال الخَيل، لا حَزن شَرْس، ٢٢٤
ولا سَهل دَهْس؛ فما لي أسمعُ رُغاء البعير، ونُهاق الحمير، وبُكاء الصغير، وثُغاء الشاء؟ قالوا: ساق مالكُ بن عوف مع الناس أبناءهم ونساءهم وأموالهم. قال: أين مالك؟ قالوا: هذا مالك قد عنَّ له. فقال: يا مالك، إنك قد أصبحت رئيس قومك، وإنّ هذا يوم كائن له ما بعده من الأيّام، ما لي أسمع رُغاء البعير، ونُهاق الحمير، وبُكاء الصغير، وثُغاء الشاء؟ قال: سُقْتُ مع الناس أبناءهم ونساءهم وأموالهم. قال: ولِمَ؟ قال: أردتُ أن أجعل خلف كلِّ رجل أهلَه وماله ليقاتل عنهم. فأنقض به دريد وقال: راعي ضأنٍ واللّهِ! وهل يردّ المنهزِمَ شيءٌ؟ إنّها إن كانت لك لم ينفَعْك إلّا رجل بسيفه ورُمحه، وإن كانت عليك فُضحتَ في أهلك ومالك!

ثمّ [قال]:[٢] ما فعلتْ كعب وكلاب؟ قالوا: لم يشهَدْها منهم أحد. قال: غاب الجَدّ والحَدّ، لو كان يومَ رِفعة لم يغِبْ عنه كعب وكلاب، وَدِدْتُ أنكم فعلتم مثل ما فعلوا. قال: فمن شهدها

١ ك: (مأسوراً).

٢ التكملة من السيرة، والسياق يقتضيها.

924 On this famous tribal leader and poet see *EI2*, "Durayd b. al-Ṣimma" (K. Petráček), Sezgin, *Geschichte*, ii, 267–268. For his lineage (in Ghaziyyah ibn Jusham, a branch of Hawāzin) see *ĞN*, i, 116, ii, 234. He died at a very advanced age at the Battle of Ḥunayn near Mecca in 8/630, fighting against the Muslims. For parallel passages on his death see Ibn Hishām, *Sīrah*, ii, 437–439, 453 (tr. Guillaume, 566–567, 574); Ibn Qutaybah, *Shiʿr*, 749–750; al-Ṭabarī, *Tārīkh*, i, 1655–1657, 1665–1666, tr. *The History*, x, 3–6, 16–17; al-Iṣfahānī, *Aghānī*, x, 30–32; al-Ṣafadī, *Wāfī*, xiv, 11; al-Baghdādī, *Khizānah*, xi, 119–121.

925 *Mushrik*, literally "polytheist".

926 Mālik ibn ʿAwf, of the Banū Naṣr (Hawāzin), commanded Hawāzin against the Muslims at Ḥunayn. After his defeat he converted to Islam and took part in the Muslim conquests. See *EI2*, "Mālik b. ʿAwf" (H. Lammens), "Ḥunayn" (H. Lammens & Abd al-Hafez Kamal); *ĞN*, i, 115, ii, 387. The battle is related in numerous sources. Hawāzin included several tribes including Naṣr, Jusham, Thaqīf, Kilāb ibn Rabīʿah, and Kaʿb ibn Rabīʿah (see e.g. *ĞN*, i, 92, ii, 281).

[§ 91 Durayd ibn al-Ṣimmah al-Jushamī[924]]

Another is Durayd ibn al-Ṣimmah al-Jushamī. He was killed at the Battle of Ḥunayn, as an unbeliever.[925] Mālik ibn ʿAwf al-Naṣrī had mustered forces to fight the Messenger of God (God bless and preserve him).[926] All Thaqīf, Naṣr ibn Muʿāwiyah, Jusham ibn Muʿāwiya, Saʿd ibn Bakr, and a small number of the Banū Hilāl ibn ʿĀmir. Kaʿb and Kilāb did not show up. Durayd came with the Banū Jusham. He was an old man who travelled in a small camel litter.[927] He was present only because this was taken as a good omen, and on account of his sound views and knowledge of warfare; he was an experienced old man. Mālik ibn ʿAwf encamped in Awṭās.[928] They had brought their women, children, and livestock with them. Durayd arrived in his litter, his camel | being 224
led. "Where have you camped?" he asked. They said, "At Awṭās." Durayd said,[929] "A good place for horses to move around; neither rough, uneven ground nor soft, loose sand. But why is it that I can hear camels grunting, asses braying, children crying, and sheep bleating?" They answered, "Mālik ibn ʿAwf has led with his men their children, wives, and cattle." "Where is Mālik?", Durayd asked. "Here is Mālik, he has just come!" Durayd said, "Mālik, you are now the leader of your tribe. This is a day that will have momentous consequences. Why is it that I hear camels grunting, asses braying, children crying, and sheep bleating?" Mālik replied, "I have led with the men their children, their wives, and their livestock." "But why?", asked Durayd. "I wanted to put behind each man his family and his livestock, so that he would fight defending them." Durayd tut-tutted[930] and said, "You're a shepherd, by God! Will anything make a defeated man turn back? If you win the only useful thing is a man with his sword and lance; if you lose it will be a disgrace for you with your family and your livestock!"

Then he asked, "What have Kaʿb and Kilāb done?" They replied, "Not one of them has shown up." Durayd said, "Gone are good fortune and force![931] If this were a day of high glory, Kaʿb and Kilāb would not have stayed away. I wish you

---

927 *Shijār*, glossed by Ibn Qutaybah (*Shiʿr*, 749) as "a litter, smaller than a *hawdaj*, open on top".

928 Awṭās is said to be a wadi in the territory of Hawāzin (Yāqūt, *Muʿjam al-buldān*, where Durayd's description is quoted).

929 Durayd speaks in rhymed prose.

930 *Anqaḍa*, cf. *Lisān al-ʿArab* (NQḌ): *naqīḍ, ay ṣawt khafiyy kamā yunqiḍu l-rajul li-ḥimārihi idhā sāqahū ... wa-fī ḥadīth Hawāzin: fa-anqaḍa bihī Durayd, ay naqara bi-lisānihī fī fīhi kamā yuzjaru l-ḥimār, faʿalahu istijhālan.*

931 *Al-jadd wa-l-ḥadd. Sīrah* and *Aghānī* have *al-ḥadd wa-l-jidd*, "force and seriousness".

منكم؟ قالوا: عمرو بن | عامر، وعوف بن عامر: قال: ذانِكَ الجَذَعانِ من عامر لا ينفعان ولا ٢٢٥
يضُرّان. يا مالك، إنّكَ لم تصنَع بتقديم بَيْضةِ هَوازن إلى نحور الخيل شيئاً. ارفَعْهم إلى مُمتَنَع
بلادهم[١] وعَلْياء[٢] قومهم، ثمّ الْقَ العِدا على مُتون الخيل. فإن كانت لك لَحِقَ بك مَن وراءك،
وإن كانت عليك أُلْفِيَ[٣] ذلك وقد أحرزتَ مالك وأهلك. قال: واللّهِ لا أفعل، إنك قد كَبِرت
وكَبِر[٤] عِلمُك. وكَرِه أن يكون لدريد فيها يدٌ وذِكر[٥] ورأْي. فقال دريد: هذا يوم لم أشهده ولم أغِبْ
عنه.

يا ليْتَني فيها جَذَعْ   أخُبُّ فيها وأضَعْ
أقودُ وَطْفاءَ الزَّمَعْ   كأنّها شاةٌ صدَعْ

فلمّا هزم اللّه المشركين أدرك دريداً رَبيعةُ بن رُفَيْع، من بني سَمّال[٦] بن عَوْف من سُليم، وكان
يقال له ابن لدغة، فأخذ بخِطام جمله وهو يظُنّه امرأة، فأناخ به، فإذا شيخٌ كبير، وإذا هو دريد،
والغلام لا يعرفه. فقال له دريد: ماذا تريد بي؟ قال: أقتلك. قال: ومن أنت؟ قال: ربيعة بن رُفَيع
السُّلَميّ. فضربه الفتى بسيفه فلم تُغْنِ شيئاً. قال: بئْسَما سلحَتْك أُمُّك! | خُذْ سيفي من مؤخَّرة ٢٢٦
الرحْل في القِراب فاضرِبْ وارفعْ عن العِظام، واخفِضْ[٧] عن الدِّماغ؛ فإنّي كنت أضرب الرجال![٨]

---

١ ك: (إلى ممتجلاتهم).

٢ هـ، ك: (عليا).

٣ ك: (أُلغي).

٤ هـ: (كير).

٥ ك: (يَدٌ تذكر).

٦ هـ، ك: (سِماك).

٧ ك: (واخنض).

٨ كذا في هـ، ك؛ ولعلّ الصحيح (فإنّي كذلك كنت أضرب الرجال) كما في المصادر الأخرى.

had done the same. Who has shown up on your side?" They said, "'Amr ibn | 225
ʿĀmir and ʿAwf ibn ʿĀmir."[932] Durayd said, "Those two lads of ʿĀmir, they will be useless and harmless. Mālik, you've done wrong to advance all of Hawāzin *en masse* to confront the cavalry. Take them to higher, inaccessible ground in their lands, to their heights, and then meet the enemy on horseback. If it goes well for you, those behind you will join you, and if things go against you, you will find that at least you have saved your livestock and your families." But Mālik said, "I won't do that, by God! You have grown old and your knowledge has aged too!" He did not want Durayd to have any say in the matter. Durayd said, "This is a battle-day where I was neither present nor absent.

> Would that I had been a young lad there,
> Ambling there and going at a gentle pace,
> Leading a mare[933] with long hair on the fetlocks,
> Like an antelope, young and strong."

When God had routed the polytheists, Durayd was overtaken by Rabīʿah ibn Rufayʿ, of the Banū Sammāl ibn ʿAwf, of Sulaym;[934] he was also called Ibn Ladghah.[935] He took the nose-rein of Durayd's camel, thinking that he was a woman. When he made the camel kneel he found an old man instead—it was Durayd, but the lad did not recognise him. Durayd said, "What do you want to do with me?" "I'll kill you." "And who are you?" "Rabīʿah ibn Rufayʿ, of Sulaym." The young man struck him with his sword, but to no effect. Durayd said, "Your
mother has excreted you badly![936] | Take my sword that is in its sheath behind 226
the saddle, and strike above the spine and below the brain. That's how I used

---

932 Two clans of ʿĀmir ibn Rabīʿah (Hawāzin), see *ĞN*, i, 92, 107, 108.

933 He describes the Arab custom of going to battle riding a camel while leading a horse, to be mounted when engaging in battle.

934 See *ĞN*, i, 123. Instead of Sammāl ʿASH and SKḤ wrongly have Simāk.

935 Ibn Hishām, *Sīrah* has "he was called Ibn al-Dughunnah, after his mother ... one also says it was Ibn Ladhʿah". Al-Ṣafadī, *Wāfī*, xiv, 88 has Ibn al-Dughunnah.

936 Guillaume translates "What a poor weapon your mother has given you", reading *sallaḥatka*. But the scatological sense of *salaḥatka ummuka* is confirmed e.g. by al-Hamadhānī, *Maqāmāt*, 257 (*qāla Bishr: thakilatka man salaḥatka, fa-qāla: yā Bishr wa-man salaḥatka*).

فإذا أتيتَ أمّكَ فأخبِرْها أنّك قتلتَ دريد بن الصمّة، فرُبَّ واللّٰهِ يومٍ قد منعتُ فيه نساءك. وأخبر أمّه فقالت: قد واللّٰهِ أعتقَ لك أُمّهات ثلاثاً.

[§٩٢] **ومنهم** كعب بن الأشرف اليهوديّ الطائيّ، وقد كتبناه في المغتالين.

[§٩٣] **ومنهم** السُّلَيْك بن السُّلَكة. وكان خرج في تَيْم الرِّباب يتبع الأريافَ حتّى مر بفخّة، فيما بين أرض بني عُقَيل وسعد تميم، فلقي رجلاً من خثعم يقال له مالك بن عُمَير بن أبي وَداع بن جُشَم بن عوْف، فأخذه ومعه امرأة له من خَفاجة تُدعى نَوار. فقال له الجثعميُّ: أنا أفدي نفسي منك. فقال له السُّليك: ذلك لك على أن لا تَخيس بي ولا تُطْلِع عليَّ أحداً من خثعم. فأعطاه ذلك، فرجع إلى قومه، وخَلَف السليك على امرأته فنكحها، وجعلت تقول له: احذَرْ خثعم فإنّي أخافهم عليك! فأنشأ يقول:

تُحذّرني أن أحذَرَ العامَ خثعماً وقد علمتْ أنَّي امرؤٌ غيرُ مُسْلَمِ
وما خثعمٌ إلّا لئامٌ أَدِقّــةٌ إلى الذُّلّ والإسخاف[١] تُنْمَى وتَنْتمي ٢٢٧

فبلغ شُبَيلَ بن قِلادة بن عمرو بن سعد وأَنَسَ بن مُدْرِك الخثعميَّيْن الخبرُ فخالفا الخثعميَّ زوجَ المرأة، فلم يعلم السليك حتّى طرقاه،[٢] فأنشأ يقول:

١ كـ: (والإسفاف).
٢ كـ: (طَرَّه).

937 Al-Ṣafadī, *Wāfī*, xiv, 11 adds: "'… on one morning, and he cut off the forelock of your father.' The boy replied, 'I didn't know.'" There and in other sources the boy also says that when he struck the old man he fell and accidentally uncovered himself. His buttocks and the inside of his thighs were like parchment (*qarāṭīs*, also "papyrus"), a result of frequent horse riding without a saddle.

938 See above, § 22.

939 The second entry on al-Sulayk offers a version that differs somewhat from the preceding (see above, § 88). It follows the account given by al-Sukkarī in al-Iṣfahānī, *Aghānī*, xx, 385–387.

940 i.e., the tribe of Taym ibn ʿAbd Manāf, see *ǦN*, i, 85. Al-Ribāb was an alliance of five tribes (see above, § 34).

to strike men! And then when you go back to your mother, tell her that you have killed Durayd ibn al-Ṣimmah. By God, on many a day I have protected your women!"

He told his mother, who said, "By God, he has set free three of your female forbears!"[937]

[§ 92 Kaʿb ibn al-Ashraf]

Another is Kaʿb ibn al-Ashraf al-Yahūdī al-Ṭāʾī. We have written about him in *Prominent Murder Victims*.[938]

[§ 93 al-Sulayk ibn al-Sulakah[939]]

Another is al-Sulayk ibn al-Sulakah. He had gone out among Taym al-Ribāb[940] on a raid to cultivated lands when he came past Fakhkhah, between the territories of the Banū ʿUqayl and Saʿd Tamīm. There he met a man of Khathʿam called Mālik ibn ʿUmayr ibn Abī Wadāʿ[941] ibn Jusham ibn ʿAwf. He took him prisoner and with him his wife, a woman of Khafājah called Nawār. The man of Khathʿam said to him, "I'll get you a ransom for myself!" Sulayk said, "You may, on condition that you will not betray me and that you will not tell anybody of Khathʿam about me." The man agreed to this and returned to his people. Al-Sulayk remained with the man's wife and had sex with her. "Beware of Khathʿam!" she said to him, "For I fear for you on account of them." He said,

She warns me to be wary, this year, of Khathʿam,
    though she knows I am not a man to be surrendered.
Khathʿam are nothing but base, insignificant people, 227
    linked with and traced to lowliness and poverty.[942]

When Shubayl ibn Qilādah ibn ʿAmr ibn Saʿd[943] and Anas ibn Mudrik, both of Khathʿam, heard this they took the part of the Khathʿamī who was the woman's spouse. Before al-Sulayk knew what happened both men came upon him. Al-Sulayk said,

941 *Aghānī*: Dhirāʿ.

942 For *askhafa* "to be poor" see e.g. Ibn Manẓūr, *Lisān al-ʿArab*. *Iskhāf* could also mean "foolishness".

943 *Aghānī* has Shibl instead of Shubayl. ǦN, i, 224 has an ʿAmr ibn Saʿd, great-grandfather of Anas ibn Mudrik, which could mean that Anas was a nephew of Shubayl. *Aghānī* has ʿUmar instead of ʿAmr.

مَن مبلغٌ حَرْباً بأنّي مقتولْ   يا رُبَّ نَهبٍ[١] قد حويتُ عُثْكولْ
وربَّ خِرْقٍ تركتُ مَجْدولْ   وربَّ زوجٍ قد نكحتُ عُطْبولْ
وربَّ عانٍ قد فككتُ مكبولْ   وربَّ وادٍ قد قطعتُ مشبولْ

فقال أنس لشُبيل: إن شئتَ كفيْتُك القوم وتكفيني[٢] الرجل. فشدّ أنس على السليك فقتله، وقتل شبيلٌ وأصحابُه من كان معه. فقال عوف وهو ابن عمّ مالك بن عُمير: واللّٰهِ لأقتلنّ أنساً في إخفاره[٣] ذِمّةَ ابن عمّي:

مَن مُبْلِغٌ خثعماً عنّي مغلْغَلةً   إنَّ السليكَ لَجاري حين يدْعوني

في شعر طويل. ثمّ إنّ أنساً وَدَى السليك بعد أن كاد يتفاقم الأمرُ بينهم، فقال أنس بن مدرك:

كم من أخٍ لي كريمٍ قد فُجعتُ به   ثمّ بقِيتُ كأنّي بعدَه حَجَرُ
لا أستكين على رَيْب الزّمان ولا   أُغضي على الأمر يأتي دونه القَدَرُ
مِرْدَى حروبٍ أُجيلُ الأمر جائلَهُ[٤]   إذ بعضُهم لأمورٍ تعتري حَذِرُ ٢٢٨
إنّي وعقلي سُلَيكاً بعد مَقتَله   كالثّور يُضْرَب لمّا عافت البقرُ

١ ك: (نهد).
٢ ك: (وتكفني).
٣ هـ، ك: (اختفاره)، والتصحيح من شرح الحماسة للتبريزيّ.
٤ ك: (أجول ... جائلة).

944 According to al-Tibrīzī (*Sharḥ Dīwān al-Ḥamāsah*, 581) Ḥarb is al-Sulayk's son. Since no son called Ḥarb is known from other sources, this may well be guesswork on al-Tibrīzī's part. *Aghānī*, has *jidhmī*, "my kin".

945 One is tempted to read, with *Aghānī*, *qirn* ("adversary") instead of *khirq* ('ASH, SKḤ), but *khirq* reappears in a similar context below in a line by al-Shanfarā (§ 97).

Who will inform Ḥarb[944] that I've been killed!
Many bunches of plunder have I robbed,
Many an excellent young man[945] have I left, struck down,
Many a man's pretty long-necked wife have I had sex with,
Many a captive, put in irons, have I redeemed,
Many a wadi where lion-cubs dwell[946] have I traversed!

Anas said to Shubayl, "If you wish I'll leave the others to you and you'll leave that man to me!" Then Anas attacked al-Sulayk and killed him while Shubayl and his companions killed the others that had come with al-Sulayk.

ʿAwf, the paternal cousin of Mālik ibn ʿUmayr, said, "By God, I'll kill Anas, for he has not respected the protection of my cousin![947]

Who will let Khathʿam know a message from me:
al-Sulayk is my protégé when he calls me ..."

—it is a long poem.[948] Then Anas paid the blood-price for al-Sulayk, after the matter had come to a head between them. Anas ibn Mudrik said,

I have been bereaved of so many noble brothers,
and remained as if I were, after their death, a stone.
I shall not yield to time's uncertainty, nor shall I
close my eyes to a thing when destiny intervenes.
A rock in warfare, I make matters go round 228
when someone else is wary of things that happen.[949]
When I paid the blood-price for Sulayk, after killing him, I felt
like a bull beaten away when the cows are loath to drink.

---

946 Thus also in al-Tibrīzī, *Sharḥ Dīwān al-Ḥamāsah*. Instead of the unusual *mashbūl* the reading of *Aghānī*, *masbūl* ("well-trodden"), may be preferable.

947 ʿASH assumes *thumma qāla* "then he said" or something similar has been lost.

948 The line and the poem are not in *Aghānī* nor found elsewhere. *Aghānī* has: "Matters came to a head between Anas and ʿAbd al-Malik [ibn Muwaylik al-Khathʿamī], because the latter had given protection to al-Sulayk ..." (as is told in a following passage, *Aghānī*, xx, 387).

949 Instead of *ḥadhir* ("wary"), *Aghānī* has *jazar* "slaughtered flesh", as has al-Buḥturī, *Ḥamāsah*, 155, which quotes ll. 1–3. For the following verses, see above.

غَضْبتُ للمرء إذْ نيكت حليلتُه[١]   وإذ يُشَدُّ على وَجْعائها الثَّفَرُ
أنّي تَناسِيّ هاماتٍ بمَجْزرةٍ   لا يزدهيني سَوادُ الليل والجَهَرُ
أَغْشى الهِياج وسِرْبالي مضاعَفةٌ   تَغْشى البنانَ وسيفي صارمٌ ذَكَرُ

[§ ٩٤] **ومنهم** الحارث بن ظالم المُرّيّ. وكان الحارث قتل خالدَ بن جعفر بن كلاب في جِوار الأسود بن المُنذر وهرب إلى مكّة. ثمّ إنّ النعمان بن المنذر كتب للحارث كتابَ أمان، وأشهد عليه شهوداً من مُضَر وربيعة، وكتب إلى الحارث يسأله القدوم عليه، وكفل له الشهود وأن لا يهيجه النعمان لِما كان من قتل خالد أخيه[٢] وقتْله ابنَه، فقدم الحارثُ حتّى أتى النعمان وهو بقصر بني مُقاتل، فقال للحاجب: استأذنْ لي. وذلك حين رأى الناسَ اجتمعوا عنده، فاستأذن له الحاجب فقال: ضعْ سيفك وادخلْ. فقال: ولِمَ أضَعُه؟ قال: ضعْه فإنّه لا بأس عليك. فلمّا ألحّ عليه وضعه ومعه أمانُه[٣] الذي كتب له، فدخل فقال: انْعِمْ صباحاً أبيْتَ اللعْنَ. فقال: لا أنْعَمَ اللّهُ صباحَك! فقال الحارث: هذا كتابك، وأخرجه. فقال النعمان: واللّهِ ما أُنْكِره، أنا كتبتُه لك، وقد غدرتَ وفتكتَ مِراراً، فلا ضَيْر[٤] إن غدرتُ بك مرّة واحدة! ثمّ نادى: من يقتل هذا؟ فقام ابن الخِمْس التغْلبيّ، وكان الحارث فتك بأبيه،[٥] فقال: أنا أقتله. فقال الحارث: | أنت يا ابن [راعي][٦] ٢٢٩

١ أمّا بقيّة الشعر فليست في هـ ولا في كـ. قال هـ: "(الأبيات التى تقدمت قبل)" وقال كـ: "إلى آخر الأبيات التي تقدمت قبل".
٢ الصحيح (جارَه).
٣ كـ: (أمانة).
٤ كـ: (ضر).
٥ كـ: (بابنه).
٦ في النسختين بياض.

950 For the remainder of the poem, ʿASH and SKḤ refer to the earlier section on al-Sulayk, without quoting them.
951 On him see above, §14. For his death, see al-Iṣfahānī, *Aghānī*, xi, 118–120; Ibn ʿAbd Rabbih, *ʿIqd*, v, 146–150; al-Nuwayrī, *Nihāyah*, xv, 353–356; also Oller, "Al-Ḥārith ibn Ẓālim".
952 This murder is told above, §14.
953 Al-Nuʿmān ibn al-Mundhir (reg. AD 580–602) was the last Lakhmid ruler of al-Ḥīrah.

I was angry on behalf of that man when his spouse was fucked[950]
and when on her behind a crupper was tied.
How could I forget the skulls in a place of carnage,
when neither the nights' blackness nor the moon (?) lifted my spirits!
I join the fray with a double coat of mail
that covers the fingers, and my sword is sharp, of good steel.

[§ 94 al-Ḥārith ibn Ẓālim al-Murri[951]]

Another is al-Ḥārith ibn Ẓālim al-Murrī. He had killed Khālid ibn Jaʿfar ibn Kilāb when the latter was a guest of al-Aswad ibn al-Mundhir,[952] and he had fled to Mecca. Al-Nuʿmān ibn al-Mundhir[953] sent him a letter assuring protection, letting witnesses from Muḍar and Rabiʿah testify to it.[954] He wrote to al-Ḥārith asking him to come to him. The witnesses guaranteed him that al-Nuʿmān would not act against him on account of the killing of his brother[955] Khālid and killing his son.[956] Al-Ḥārith came and arrived at al-Nuʿmān in the castle of the Banū Muqātil.[957] When he saw that people had gathered with the king, he said to the chamberlain, "Ask permission for me to enter!" The chamberlain let him enter, saying, "Lay down your sword and enter." "And why should I lay it down?" al-Ḥārith asked. "Lay it down, you will be all right", said the man. He insisted, so al-Ḥārith laid it down, holding the letter with the safeguarding, and entered, saying, "A good morning! May you avoid being cursed!"[958] The king replied, "*Not* a good morning to you!" Al-Ḥārith said, "But this is your letter!", producing it. "By God," said al-Nuʿmān, "I do not deny it, I wrote it to you. But you have been treacherous and you have murdered more than once, so there is nothing wrong if I betray you once." Then he called out, "Who will kill this man?" The son of al-Khims al-Taghlibī stood up—al-Ḥārith had murdered his father[959]—and said, "I'll kill him!" Al-Ḥārith said, | "You, son of a camel-herd, 229

954 Muḍar and Rabīʿah together cover almost all of the North Arab tribes. In *Aghānī*, xi, 120, al-Yaman (the South Arabs) are added.

955 As remarked by ʿASH, this is an error for "his guest" (*jārihi*).

956 Al-Ḥārith had killed a young son of al-Nuʿmān and composed a boastful poem about it, see *Aghānī*, xi, 102–104.

957 See above, § 36.

958 The somewhat enigmatic expression *Abayta l-laʿna*, literally "May you refuse cursing", is the customary greeting of kings in pre-Islamic times. See e.g. Lane, *Lexicon* (ʾBY), WKAS, *Lām*, 859–860.

959 He had killed al-Khims, a soothsayer (*kāhin*), for divining that he had slaughtered a camel belonging to the king in order to satisfy the craving of one of his wives, see *Aghānī*, xi, 118, *ʿIqd*, v, 150.

الإبل تقتلني! أما واللّهِ ما نفسي من أبيك ولا من أشباهه لؤمه. فقتله ابن الخمس. فقال قيس بن زُهير يرثي الحارث بن ظالم:

ما قَصَرتْ من حاصنٍ دونَ سِتْرها أبرَّ وأوْفى منكَ حارِ[١] بن ظالمِ
أعزَّ وأوْفى عند جارٍ وذِمّةٍ وأضربَ في كابٍ من النَّقْع قاتمِ[٢]

فقال رجل من بني ضرس من جُرْهُم، وممّن كان يقوم على رأس النعمان حين رأى الحارثَ مقتولاً:

يا حارِ حِنِّيّا لم تَكُ تِرْعِيّا في البيت ضِجْعِيّا

[§ ٩٥] **ومنهم** عبد اللّه بن رَواحة الأنصاريّ ثمّ الخَزْرَجيّ. وكان رسول اللّه صلّى اللّه عليه وسلّم وجّه جيشاً إلى مؤْتةَ وأمّر عليهم مولاه زيدَ بن حارثة الكلبيّ وقال: إنْ أُصيبَ زيدٌ فالأميرُ

١ ك: (حارث).
٢ ك: (قائم).

960 The sense of *mā nafsī min abīka wa-ashbāhihi luʾmuhu* is not quite clear to me and the translation uncertain. In *Aghānī*, al-Ḥārith calls the son of al-Khims *ibn sharr al-aẓmāʾ*, "son of the worst of thirsts" (*khims* denoting the drinking of camels on the fifth day, not having drunk for four days), upon which the other, dying with a pun, calls al-Ḥārith *ibn sharr al-asmāʾ* ("son of the worst of names"), referring to al-Ḥārith's father, for *ẓālim* means "wrongdoer".

961 On Qays ibn Zuhayr ibn Jadhīmah al-ʿAbsī see Sezgin, *Geschichte*, ii, 216, *ĞN*, i, 132. He played a leading role in the troubles known as the war of Dāḥis and al-Ghabrāʾ. According to *Aghānī* and *ʿIqd* the sequence of killings continued. Ibn al-Khims had picked up al-Ḥārith's sword and offered it for sale at the market of ʿUkāẓ, advertising it as al-Ḥārith's. Qays ibn Zuhayr asked to see it, and with it killed Ibn al-Khims, even though this was during the sacred months in which killing was taboo.

962 A common shortening of Ḥārith, used in addressing.

963 Instead of this repetition, *Aghānī* and *ʿIqd* have *aḥmā* ("a better defender").

964 Not found elsewhere, nor are the Banū Ḍarī (thus *Aghānī* and *ʿIqd*). Jurhum (or Jurham) is a legendary tribe that once had settled in Mecca; see *EI2*, "Djurhum" (W. Montgomery Watt).

965 *Aghānī*, xi, 119 adds three more lines. See Ullmann, *Untersuchungen zur Rağazpoesie*, 13 (without translation).

are you going to kill me? By God, I have nothing to do with your father and those like him in baseness!"[960] Then Ibn al-Khims killed him.

Qays ibn Zuhayr elegised al-Ḥārith ibn Ẓālim:[961]

No chaste woman ever lowered her curtain
to someone more devoted and more loyal than you, Ḥāri[962] son of Ẓālim,
Dearer and more loyal[963] to a protected guest,
or striking better in a rising dark cloud of dust.

A man of the Banū Ḍaras,[964] of Jurhum, one of the attendants of al-Nuʿmān, said upon seeing al-Ḥārith slain:[965]

O Ḥāri, of the Ḥinn,[966]
You were no common camel-herd,[967]
Always lying down at home.

[§ 95 ʿAbd Allāh ibn Rawāḥah al-Anṣārī al-Khazrajī[968]]

Another is ʿAbd Allāh ibn Rawāḥah al-Anṣārī, of al-Khazraj. The Messenger of God sent an army to Mu'tah,[969] appointing his freedman Zayd ibn Ḥārithah al-Kalbī[970] as commander. "If Zayd is struck down," he said, "then Jaʿfar ibn Abī

---

966 Possibly referring to the *ḥinn*, said to be a kind of jinnees. Ullmann has *ğinnīyā*.

967 An editorial note in *Aghānī* explains that camel-herding was a lowly job.

968 ʿAbd Allāh ibn Rawāḥah belonged to al-Khazraj, one of the two tribes in Medina most of whose members supported the Prophet Muḥammad and were therefore called *Anṣār*, "Supporters". In addition to fighting actively for Islam he was a poet who composed poems in support of the Prophet, who esteemed him highly. He was killed in 8/629 during the expedition to Mu'tah. See on him *ĞN*, i, 188; *EI2*, "ʿAbd Allāh b. Rawāḥah" (A. Schaade); *EI3*, "ʿAbdallāh b. Rawāḥa" (Sarah Mirza); Sezgin, *Geschichte*, ii, 292–293. On his death, see e.g. Ibn Hishām, *Sīrah*, ii, 373–379 (tr. Guillaume, 532–535); al-Yaʿqūbī, *Tārīkh*, ii, 66–67, tr. *The Works*, 667; al-Ṭabarī, *Tārīkh*, i, 1610–1616, tr. *The History*, viii, 152–158.

969 The aim of the expedition to Mu'tah, not far south of the Dead Sea, was apparently to secure the route to the North. It brought the Muslims in contact with the Byzantines for the first time and the former were defeated by combined Byzantine and Arab forces. See e.g. *EI2*, "Mu'ta" (F. Buhl); Ibn Hishām, *Sīrah*, ii, 373–389 (tr. Guillaume, 531–540).

970 Zayd ibn Ḥārithah was a freedman (*mawlā*) of the Prophet, who adopted him as a son. He is mentioned in the Qur'an (al-Aḥzāb 33:37), in connection with Muḥammad's marriage to Zaynab, who had earlier been married to Zayd. See *EI2*, "Zayd b. Ḥāritha" (M. Lecker).

جعفر بن أبي طالب، وإنْ أصيب جعفر بن أبي طالب فالأمير عبد الله بن رواحة. فأُصيبوا ثلاثُتهم رحمهم الله وأخذ خالد بن الوليد الراية من غير تأمير من رسول الله صلّى الله عليه وسلّم، فقتل ابن زافلة[١] وبَلْقَيْن المُشْركين، وهزمهم الله تعالى به.

[§٩٦] **ومنهم** جَزْء بن الحارث الأزْديّ ثمّ الشَّعْبيّ. وكان الْتقى ناسٌ من بني خُنَيس وناس ٢٣٠
من بني كِنانة ليلاً ولا يعرف بعضهم بعضاً، فرمى رجلٌ من بني كنانة فأصاب جَزْءاً، فقال جزء: حَسّ حَسّ![٢] وصاح رجل من بني كنانة: يا آلَ واهب، ليُراعوا مَن هم! وهم من خَثْعم. وقال رجل من بني خُنيس: ارجِعي يا مَيْدعان فإنّي أجد ريحَ القارة. فرجعوا عليهم فقتلوهم غيرَ رجليْن. ومات جزءٌ من السهْم الذي أصابه. فقال عمرو بن أبي عُمارة:

١ في النسختين: (داقلة)، وفي هـ، كـ: (راقلة).

٢ كـ: (حَسنٌ حَسنٌ).

971 Older brother of ʿAlī and cousin of Muḥammad; see *EI2*, "Djaʿfar b. Abī Ṭālib" (L. Veccia Vaglieri).

972 The verb *aṣāba* normally means "to strike down, hit, injure", but here it means that all three were killed.

973 Khālid ibn al-Walīd (d. 21/642) was to become one of the great commanders of the early Muslim conquests, earning the honorific Sayf al-Islām (Sword of Islam). See *EI2*, "Khālid b. al-Walīd" (P. Crone).

974 ʿASH and SKḤ have Ibn Rāqilah, a form that has not been found elsewhere and has not been adopted. The name appears as Ibn Rāfilah and Ibn Zāfilah. Ibn Hishām, *Sīrah*, ii, 381 (tr. Guillaume, 536) says that Mālik ibn Zāfilah ibn al-Irāsh was killed by Quṭbah ibn Qatādah al-ʿUdhrī, commander of the right wing, whose boasting epigram is quoted; a variant form Mālik ibn Rāfilah is also given (*Sīrah*, ii, 382, tr. Guillaume, 772). He is called Ibn Zāfilah al-Balawī in Ibn Ḥabīb, *Muḥabbar*, 123, where Khālid is mentioned as the one who killed him.

Ṭālib[971] is to be commander, and if Jaʿfar ibn Abī Ṭālib is struck down, then ʿAbd Allāh ibn Rawāḥah is to be commander." All three were struck down[972]—God have mercy on their souls. Khālid ibn al-Walīd[973] took the banner, without having been appointed commander by the Messenger of God (God bless and preserve him). He killed the polytheists Ibn Zāfilah[974] and Bal-Qayn,[975] and God the Exalted routed them by means of him.

[§ 96 Jazʾ ibn al-Ḥārith al-Azdī[976]]

Another is Jazʾ ibn al-Ḥārith al-Azdī al-Shaʿbī.[977] One evening some men from 230
the Banū Khunays[978] and others from Kinānah[979] met in battle.[980] They did not know one another. A man of the Banū Kinānah shot an arrow and hit Jazʾ, who cried out, "Ouch!"[981] A man of the Banū Kinānah said, "Men of Wāhib![982] Let them find out who they are!" They themselves were of Khathʿam. A man of the Banū Khunays said, "Come back, Maydaʿān,[983] for I think I can smell al-Qārah!"[984] So they returned and killed them all, except for two men. Jazʾ died of the arrow wound. ʿAmr ibn Abī ʿUmārah said:[985]

---

975 The text may be corrupt. It suggests that this is a person, but Balqayn, or Bal-Qayn, short for Banū l-Qayn (al-Qayn ibn Jasr), is in fact a tribe in the region of Muʾtah; see *ǦN*, i, 310, ii, 455, *EI2*, "al-Ḳayn" (W. Montgomery Watt).

976 No parallels of this report have been found.

977 Listed as a poet, he must have been a very obscure one and the only verse by him known to me is the one quoted below, in the section on al-Shanfarā (§ 97), a line attributed to another poet in *Aghānī*. He has not been found elsewhere and even his name is uncertain; the MSS have J.r.w (Jurw?) instead of Jazʾ, as in ʿASH and SKḤ. There are two persons called Jazʾ ibn al-Ḥārith in *ǦN* (i, 132, 270, ii, 261) but neither belongs to al-Azd.

978 Khunays (Mālik) ibn Zahrān, a branch of al-Azd; *ǦN*, i, 210, ii, 349.

979 This is apparently not the important tribe of Kinānah ibn Khuzaymah (see above, § 6), but Kinānah ibn al-Ḥārith ibn Aklub, a branch of Khathʿam (who are mentioned below), see *ǦN*, i, 224, ii, 371.

980 The following suggest that *iltaqā* "to meet" here means "to meet in battle", as it often does.

981 In Arabic: *ḥass ḥass!* In SKḤ it is *ḥasan ḥasan* ("Good, good!"), clearly mistakenly.

982 Probably Wāhib ibn al-Ḥārith ibn Aklub, of Khathʿam, is meant (*ǦN*, i, 224).

983 Maydaʿān ibn Mālik ibn Naṣr, a branch of al-Azd (*ǦN*, i, 210).

984 Translation of *fa-innī ajidu rīḥ al-qārah* uncertain. *Qārah* can mean "basalt plain", but al-Qārah is also the name of a tribe consisting of a few branches of al-Hawn ibn Khuzaymah (*ǦN*, i, 49, ii, 465); they were famous archers (al-Mufaḍḍal, *Amthāl*, 54: *al-Qārah fīmā yadhkurūna armā ḥayy fī l-ʿArab*) and are possibly meant in this context about a shooting.

985 Al-Marzubānī, *Muʿjam*, 55 mentions ʿAmr ibn Abī ʿUmarah al-Khunaysī al-Azdī as a poet in the pre-Islamic era and quotes line 2 of the poem. The other lines have not been found in other sources.

دَعَوْا واهباً مسر[١] عَشِيّا وكُلُّنا رأى واهباً رأْيَ الخليلِ المُواصلِ
وأدعو فناعتْ[٢] من خُنَيسٍ عِصابةٌ إلى الضَّرب مَشْيَ المحْنَقات الروافلِ
فلَيْتَك بالمَعْزاء حين تقسّموا فتنظُرَ بلعا[٣] من قتيلٍ وقاتلِ
وليْتك حيٌّ حين سُلّك فَرُّهُمْ فُغَيّةَ حرب كالسِّهام النواصلِ
فتعلمَ أنّا لم نَدَعْهم بعَمْرنا وأن لم يَؤُبْ مَن آبَ منهمْ بِطائلِ

[§٩٧] **ومنهم** الشَّنْفَرى الأزْديّ، من الأَواس بن الحَجْر بن الهَنْو بن الأزْد وغيرها. وإنّه قتل من ٢٣١
بني سَلامان بن مُفْرِج تسعة وتسعين رجلاً في غاراته عليهم، وإنّ بني سلامان أقعدت له رجالاً من بني الرَّمْد من غامد يرصُدونه، فجاءهم للغارة فطلبوه فأفلتَهم، فأرسلوا عليه كلباً لهم يقال له حُبَيش فقتله، وإنّه مر برجليْن من بني سلامان فأعجله فِرارُه عنهما، فأقعدوا له أُسَيْد بن جابر

١ كذا في هـ، ك، ولعلّ الصحيح (مَسْرَى) أو (مُسْرَى).
٢ ك: (فناعة).
٣ ك: (بلغا).

986 I do not understand *m.s.r ʿashiyyan*; perhaps it should be emended to *masrā* ("night journey") or *musrā* (*maṣdar mīmī* of *asrā*, "to travel by night").
987 The imperfect tense is strange; in al-Marzubānī, *Muʿjam* it is *daʿawtu*, "I called".
988 Al-Marzubānī, *Muʿjam*: *thābat ilā l-ṣawt*, "returned, (responding) to the call".
989 Or "fat": the word has two contrasting senses, see Lane, *Lexicon*. Instead of *rawāfil* ("prancing, strutting"), al-Marzubānī has *rawāqil* ("pacing quickly").
990 *Al-maʿzāʾ*; perhaps a place name here.
991 One word (ʿASH: *b.l.ʿ.*, SKḤ: *b.lgh.*) is unclear and I am unable to think of a suitable emendation.
992 Translation tentative; Hārūn calls the line "evidently corrupt". I read ... *ḥīna sullika farruhum* | *fughayyata ḥarbin*, taking *farr* as the plural of *fārr* "fugitive", and *fughayyah* as the diminutive of *faghā*, "a dust that comes upon unripe dates, spoiling them" (Lane), "refuse" (Hava). For the image of fearful people as arrows without tip, cf. Abū Dhuʾayb: ... *wa-l-ḍulūʿu ka-annahā* | *mina l-khawfi amthālu l-sihāmi l-nawāṣilī* (al-Sukkarī, *Sharḥ ashʿār al-Hudhaliyyīn*, 144).
993 I do not understand *bi-ʿamrinā*.
994 Secondary literature about him is extensive, thanks to his colourful life as a brigand-poet and even more because he is the reputed poet of one of the best and most famous poems, called *Lāmiyyat al-ʿArab* ("the poem of the Arabs rhyming in L"). The attribution has been questioned and many of the stories about him are of uncertain historicity. Like his friend Taʾabbaṭa Sharrā (above, § 85) and some other brigands he carried out raids on foot and was proverbial as a fast runner. See on him e.g. Michael Cooperson, "al-Shanfara"; Sezgin,

They called Wāhib on a nightly campaign (?).[986] All of us
thought of Wāhib as a good and close friend.
And I call,[987] and a band of Khunays pounced
to the fighting,[988] walking like prancing lean[989] camels.
Would that you were at the pebbly ground[990] when they dispersed
so that you could see a …[991] of the slain and the slayer,
Would that you were alive when those that fled of them were sent on
their way
as war's refuse, like arrows without arrowheads.[992]
Then you would know that we have not left them …[993]
and that those of them who returned did not return with any gain.

[§ 97 al-Shanfarā[994]]

Another is al-Shanfarā al-Azdī, one of the clan of al-Awās ibn al-Ḥajr ibn al-Hanw ibn al-Azd, and others.[995] He killed ninety-nine men of the Banū Salāmān ibn Mufrij[996] on his raids on them. The Banū Salāmān made some men of the Banū l-Ramd, of Ghāmid,[997] sit on the lookout for him. He came for a raid and they pursued him, but he escaped. Then they sent after him a dog called Ḥubaysh,[998] but he killed it. He came past two men of Banū Salāmān, but he fled and was too quick for them. Then they set up Usayd[999] ibn Jābir, of 231

Geschichte, ii, 133–137; *EI2*, "al-Shanfarā" (A. Arazi); Jones, *Early Arabic Poetry, I:* Marāthī *and* Ṣuʿlūk *Poems*, 139–204; Stetkevych, *The Mute Immortals Speak*, 119–157; Webb in al-Maqrīzī, *Luṣūṣ*, 107–110, 238–245 (al-Maqrīzī's text and translation) and index. The main Arabic source of his life is al-Iṣfahānī, *Aghānī*, xxi, 177–194, where three accounts of his death are given (181–182, 184–185, 192–194); see also al-Anbārī in *al-Mufaḍḍaliyyāt*, 194–207; al-Baghdādī, *Khizānah*, iii, 340–348. For an English translation of *Aghānī*'s second account see Stetkevych, *Mute Immortals*, 128–129.

995 It is not clear what is meant by *wa-ghayrihā*; possibly it is shorthand to say that there are other accounts of his lineage, as indeed there are; see in particular the articles by Arazi and Cooperson mentioned above, and see *ǦN*, i, 209 (which has al-Aws and al-Hinw instead of al-Awās and al-Hanw). It is said that al-Shanfarā was a nickname ("Biglip") and his proper name was Thābit ibn Jābir, but others give it as Mālik or ʿAmr ibn Mālik.

996 *ǦN*, i, 210. They also belonged to al-Azd. It is said that, having been exchanged, at a young age, for a prisoner and adopted by the Banū Salāmān, he grew up believing himself to be one of them. After a quarrel he learnt the truth and swore he would kill one hundred men of them.

997 On Ghāmid, another branch of al-Azd, see *ǦN*, i, 218.

998 This dog, but not its death, is mentioned in *Aghānī*, xxi, 180.

999 The name is also read as Asīd, see e.g. al-Baghdādī, *Khizānah*, ii, 347, where it is said that al-Shanfarā had killed his brother.

السَّلامانيّ وحازماً البُقْميّ من البُقوم من حَوالة بن الهَنْو بن الأزْد، بالناصف من أَبِيدة وهو وادٍ
فرَصَداه، فأقبل في الليل قد نزع إحدى نَعْليْه فهو يضرِب برجله. فقال حازم: هذا الضَّبُع! فقال
أُسَيد: بل هو الخبيث. فلمّا دنا توجّس ثمّ رجع فمكث قليلاً، ثمّ عاد إلى الماء ليشرب فوثبوا
عليه فأخذوه وربطوه وأصبحوا به في بني سلامان، فربطوه إلى شجرة فقالوا: قِفْ أنْشِدْنا. | فقال: ٢٣٢
إنّما النشيد على المَسَرّة! فذهبت مَثَلاً. وجاء غلام قد كان الشنفرى قتل أباه فضرب يده بالشَّفْرة
فاضطربت فقال:

لا تَبْعَدي إمّا هلكْتِ شامَهْ　　فرُبَّ وادٍ قد قطعْت هامَهْ
وربَّ حيٍّ أهلكتْ سَوامَهْ　　وربَّ خَرْقٍ قَطعَتْ قَتامَهْ
وربَّ خِرْقٍ فَصَلَتْ عِظامَهْ

ثمّ قالوا: أين نقْبُرك؟ فقال:

1000 *Aghānī*, xxi, 181: Khāzim al-Fahmī.

1001 Al-Nāṣif and Abīdah are places in the territory of the Banū Salāmān (Abū ʿUbayd, *Muʿjam*, 102, 1287).

1002 In *Aghānī*, Usayd's nephew is with them.

1003 *Yaḍribu bi-rijlih*. Compare *Aghānī*, xxi, 185: "He had taken off one sandal and put (only) one sandal on, in order to conceal his treading. When the two lads heard his footsteps, they said, 'That's a hyena!' but Usayd said, 'It's not a hyena, it is al-Shanfarā!'" It is not clear to me how walking on only one sandal could be effective in hiding the sounds of one's footsteps.

1004 In *Aghānī*, al-Shanfarā sees a dark shape and shoots at it (as was his wont whenever he saw something in the dark), wounding Usayd's nephew. In the ensuing sword fight he severs two of Ḥāzim's fingers, but he is overmastered after a struggle, described in entertaining detail. At one stage, Usayd gets hold of his nephew's foot and exclaims, "Whose foot is this?". Al-Shanfarā says, "It's mine!" But his ploy fails.

1005 Al-ʿAskarī, *Jamharah*, ii, 241, but not found in other collections of proverbs. Far more popular is a similar excuse made by another famous poet, ʿAbīd ibn al-Abraṣ, about to be executed by king al-Nuʿmān of al-Ḥīrah (cf. above, § 81). Abū ʿUbayd al-Bakrī, *Faṣl al-maqāl*, 444 and numerous other sources.

1006 The hand was severed, as said explicitly in Ibn Durayd, *Jamharah*, 1121; *Aghānī*, xxi, 182, 185, 194; al-Baghdādī, *Khizānah*, iii, 347. The verb for "twitched" in *Aghānī* is *taʿarraḍat*, which is a corruption of *tabaʿraṣat* (as in Ibn Durayd).

Salāmān, and Ḥāzim al-Buqmī,[1000] of the Banū l-Buqūm of Ḥawālah ibn al-Hanw ibn al-Azd, in al-Nāṣif, in Abīdah, a wadi,[1001] to be on the lookout for him.[1002] Al-Shanfarā came in the night. He had taken off one of his sandals and stamped the earth with his foot.[1003] "That's a hyena!" said Ḥāzim. But Usayd said, "No, it's that wicked man!" When al-Shanfarā came nearer he listened apprehensively and he retreated. After a short while he returned to the water to drink. Then they sprang upon him and seized him.[1004] They tied him up and in the morning took him to the Banū Salāmān. They tied him to a tree and said, "Come on, recite us a poem!" | He replied, "One recites only when cheerful!", 232
which became a proverb.[1005] A young man whose father had been killed by al-Shanfarā came and struck his hand with a blade. The hand twitched.[1006] He said,

> Do not go far![1007] Though you are lost, (with) a mole,[1008]
> Many a wadi have I crossed ...,[1009](?)
> Many a tribe's pasturing camels has it destroyed,[1010]
> On many a path in the desert has it cut through dark dust,
> And of many a noble young man has it severed bones!

They asked him, "Where shall we bury you?" But he replied,[1011]

1007 As above, § 9 note 114, it is a formula used in elegies. He is addressing his hand. The poem is found with several variants in *Aghānī*, xxi, 182 and 185; Ibn Durayd, *Jamharah*, 1121; al-Tibrīzī, *Sharḥ*, 351. For a compound version with 14 lines (but not including l. 2), see al-Shanfarā, *Dīwān*, 75–76.

1008 The second account in *Aghānī* (xxi, 185) mentions that there was a black mole on the severed hand. The verb is vowelled in ʿASH as *halaktu* (1st ps. sing.) but possibly it should be *halakti* (2nd ps. sing. fem.), as in Ibn Durayd, *Jamharah*, 1121, like the variant *dhahabti* (*Aghānī*, xxi, 182, 194, al-Tibrīzī, *Sharḥ*, 351). He is addressing the hand, even though in the following the hand is referred to with the 3rd ps. fem. sing. The syntax is somewhat unclear.

1009 *Qaṭaʿtu* (or *qaṭaʿti*) *hāmah*; the sense of the last word is not clear to me. If instead of *wādin* one reads e.g. *qirnin*, it would be "Of many an adversary I/you cut off his head." *Aghānī*, xxi, 182, 194 and Ibn Durayd, *Jamharah*: *fa-rubba wādin naffarat ḥamāmah*, "in many a wadi it (i.e., my hand) has stirred up the pigeons (scil., when I was hunting)".

1010 Instead of "destroyed" (*ahlakat*), *Aghānī*, xxi, 194 has "scattered" (*farraqat*).

1011 The lines are often quoted. They are in Abū Tammām's *Ḥamāsah* (al-Marzūqī, *Sharḥ*, 487–491, al-Tibrīzī, *Sharḥ*, 349–350); al-Jāḥiẓ, *Burṣān*, 253 and 492; idem, *Ḥayawān*, vi, 450 (there attributed to Taʾabbaṭa Sharrā); Ibn Qutaybah, *Shiʿr*, 80; Ibn ʿAbd Rabbih, *ʿIqd*, i, 101–102 and see vi, 183; al-Qālī, *Dhayl al-Amālī*, 36; *Aghānī*, xxi, 182; al-Baghdādī, *Khizānah*, iii, 347–348; al-Shanfarā, *Dīwān*, 48, etc. For English translations see Nicholson, *Literary History*, 81 (rhymed); Stetkevych, *Mute Immortals*, 129; Webb in al-Maqrīzī, *Luṣūṣ*, 241.

لا تقبُروني إنّ قبْري محرَّمٌ   عليكمْ ولكنْ أَبْشِري أُمَّ عامرِ
إذا احتملتْ رأسي وفي الرأس أكثَري   وغودِرَ عند الملتقى ثَمَّ سائري
هنالك لا أرجو حياةً تسُرّني   سَمير الليالي مُبْسَلاً بالجرائرِ

وإنّ رجلاً من بني سلامان رماه بسهْم في عينه فقتله، فقال جَزْء[١] بن الحارث في قتله:

لَعَمْرك لَلسّاعي أُسَيْدُ بن جابرٍ   أحقُّ بها منكمْ بني عَقِب الكلْبِ

وكان الشنفرى حلف لَيقتُلنّ مائةً من بني سلامان، فقتل تسعة وتسعين فبقي عليه تمامُ نَذْره، فمرّ رجل من بني سلامان بجُمْجُمته فضربها فعقرتْ رِجْلَه فمات، فتمَّ نذره بالرجل بعد موته.

[§٩٨] **ومنهم** خالد بن جعفر بن كِلاب. وقتله الحارث بن ظالم في جِوار الأسود بن المنذر، ٢٣٣
وقد كتبتُ سبب قتله في المغتالين.

[§٩٩] **ومنهم** حارثة بن قَيْس الكِنانيّ. وكان مدح الحارثَ بن أبي شَمِر الغَسّانيّ ووفد إليه فأحسن جائزتَه، فلمّا انصرف سُرق ما معه، فظنّ أنّ الحارث دسَّ إليه مَن يسرِقه، فقال يهجوه:

١ في النسختين: (جرو)، والتصحيح من شرح المفضّليّات للأنباريّ.

1012 A nickname of the hyena, who will eat his corpse. Webb opts for another interpretation ("I'm only for the Hyena!"), taking the whole sentence, *ibshirī* (or *khāmirī*, in other versions) *umma ʿĀmirī*, to be a name for the hyena, following commentaries such as Abū ʿUbayd al-Bakrī, *Simṭ al-laʾālī*, 920 or al-Marzūqī, *Sharḥ*, 488–489. This makes for odd syntax, as *lākin* is then not followed by a complete sentence.

1013 *Idhā ḥtamalat*, as in *Aghānī*, xxi, 182; the subject is the tribe but could also be the hyena. Other versions have *idhā ḥtamalū* or *idhā ḥamalū*, "when they pick up", or *idhā ḍarabū* "when they strike".

1014 *Multaqā* could also be "crossroads" or "place of battle".

1015 *Samīra l-layālī*, cf. *Lisān al-ʿArab* (SMR): *lā afʿaluhu samīr al-layālī, ay ākhirahā*, with a quotation of this verse. In Abū Tammām's *Ḥamāsah* it is *sajīsa l-layālī* (al-Marzūqī, *Sharḥ*, 490, al-Tibrīzī, *Sharḥ*, 350), with the same sense.

1016 In *Aghānī*, xxi, 186 this line, preceded by two others, is attributed to Ẓālim al-ʿĀmirī. On Jazʾ ibn al-Ḥārith see above, § 96.

Don't bury me! Burying me is forbidden
to you. But good tidings, Umm ʿĀmir![1012]
When they pick up[1013] my head—and in the head is most of me—
and the rest of me is left there, where people gather:[1014]
There I shall not expect a life to cheer me,
through all nights,[1015] surrendered on account of my crimes.

A man of Salāmān shot an arrow in his eye, killing him. Jazʾ ibn al-Ḥārith said about his death:[1016]

Upon my life, Usayd ibn Jābir, who did the work,
was more entitled to it than you, sons of a dog's heel.[1017]

Al-Shanfarā had sworn an oath that he would kill one hundred men of the Banū Salāmān. He killed ninety-nine of them, so the completion of his vow remained to be fulfilled. A man of the Banū Salāmān came past his skull and kicked it. It wounded his foot and he died of it. Thus his vow was fulfilled after his death.

[§ 98 Khālid ibn Jaʿfar ibn Kilāb]

Another is Khālid ibn Jaʿfar ibn Kilāb, who was killed by al-Ḥārith ibn Ẓālim 233
when he was enjoying the protection of al-Aswad ibn al-Mndhir. I have written the account of why he was killed in *Prominent Murder Victims*.[1018]

[§ 99 Ḥārithah ibn Qays al-Kinānī[1019]]

Another is Ḥārithah ibn Qays al-Kinānī. He had eulogised al-Ḥārith ibn Abī Shamir al-Ghassānī[1020] and paid a visit to him for which he was rewarded handsomely. When he left, all his possessions were stolen. He suspected that al-Ḥārith had sent someone to rob him, so he lampooned him:

1017 He upbraids al-Azd for having been unable to stop al-Shanfarā's raids. The feminine pronoun in *bihā* "it" possibly refers to *rijl Shanfarā* (thus, without the article), "Shanfarā's foot" in one of the lines that precede in *Aghānī*: "Why did you not reach Shanfarā's foot (i.e., overtake him) though you are nimble, like crows' wings"?

1018 See above, § 14.

1019 Like Jazʾ ibn al-Ḥārith (above, § 96), Ḥārithah ibn Qays is listed as a poet but he is not found anywhere else and not one line of his verse is known. Parallels of the present story have not been found.

1020 See above, § 89.

أَدِّ الدنانيرَ إنّ الغَدْرَ مَنْقَصةٌ   وإنّ جَدّك لم يَغدِرِ ولم يُطِقِ

فبلغ هجاؤه الحارثَ فحلف[١] أن لا يمَسَّ رأسَه غِسْلٌ حتّى يقتلَ حارثة بِهجائه إيّاه، وإنّ الحارث بن أبي شمر جعل لابن عُرْوة الكنانيّ جُعْلاً على أن يدُلّه على عَوْرة قومه، فدلّه فغزاهم، وندم ابنُ عروة فقال في الطريق وهو يسير مع الحارث:

بَلِّغْ بني مُدْلجٍ عنّي مغلغَلةً   ....[٢] النُّذُرِ
أنَّ الهُمامَ الذي يَخْشَوْن صَولته   بيني وبينكُمُ يَسْري ويبتكرُ
في مُسْبَطِرٍّ[٣] تَهاب الطيرُ صولتَه   ولا يُحيط به في السَّرْبَخ[٤] البَصَرُ
في كُلِّ مَنْزِلةٍ منه ومعتَرَكٍ   تَلْقى[٥] سلائلَ لم ينبُتْ لها شَعَرُ

٢٣٤ فلم يبلغهم إنذارُه،[٦] وأغار عليهم الحارث بمغبط الجُحْفة فقتل حارثةَ بن قيس، وأوقعَ ببني[٧] كنانة،[٨] فقالت ابنة حارثة ولَبِست السواد وحلفتْ لا تنزِعه حتّى تثأر بأبيها من ابن عمّه الذي دلّ عليه، فقالت:

---

١ كـ: (فخلف).

٢ بياض في الأصل.

٣ كـ: (مُسيطرٍّ).

٤ كـ: (السَّريْخِ).

٥ كـ: (تَبقى).

٦ كـ: (نذاره).

٧ هـ: (بينى).

٨ كـ: (كنة).

Give up my dinars! Treachery is a bad thing!
Your grandfather was not treacherous, he would not stand it!

His lampoon reached al-Ḥārith, who swore he would not wash his head until he had killed Ḥārithah because of his lampoon. Al-Ḥārith agreed with Ibn ʿUrwah al-Kinānī[1021] on a price if he would tell him where the vulnerable spot of Ḥārithah's people was. Ibn ʿUrwah told him, and al-Ḥārith raided them. Ibn ʿUrwah regretted his deed and when he was on his way together with al-Ḥārith, he said:

Convey to the Banū Mudlij[1022] from me a quick message
...... vows,[1023]
That the hero whose force they fear,
among you and me, is coming by night and early morning,
In a far-stretching army, its force held in awe by the birds,[1024]
that the eye cannot encompass on the broad plain.
At every station or battle site on its march
you will find foetuses that have not yet grown any hair.[1025]

But his warning did not reach them and al-Ḥārith raided them at Maghbiṭ 234
al-Juḥfah,[1026] where he killed Ḥārithah and attacked the Banū Kinānah. The daughter of Ḥārithah put on a black dress, swearing that she would not take it off until her father's death had been avenged on his cousin who had betrayed him. She said,

1021 Not identified.

1022 Mudlij is a branch of Kinānah ibn Khuzaymah, see *ǦN*, i, 44, ii, 416.

1023 There is a lacuna of a few words in the manuscript.

1024 The verb *hāba* often means "to fear", which would not fit here, for one would rather expect the birds (i.e., predators and vultures) to rejoice expectantly, in accordance with a common motif found in Arabic and other literatures (cf. Van Gelder, "Birds of Battle").

1025 Female camels or horses have aborted their foetuses: a result of forced marches. On this motif, found in Dhū l-Rummah and several other poets, see Papoutsakis, *Desert Travel*, 146–147.

1026 Al-Juḥfah is a place between Mecca and Medina. It is not clear whether Maghbiṭ (or Mughbaṭ, the vowelling being uncertain) is part of the place name or a noun (perhaps "place with dense herbage"). Alternatively, it is a corruption of *bi-ghabṭin* (see below, note 1028).

جزى اللّٰهُ ابنَ عُروةَ حيث أمسى   عُقوقاً والعقوق له أَثامُ[١]
أتيتَ طليعةً للقوم تَسْري   نعط[٢] لا يجار ولا ينام
فما علمتْ مساكنَنا بَليٌّ   ولا غسّانُ تلك ولا جُذامُ
بأيْدِينا وإنْ لم يقتُلونا   بذي المسروح أصداءٌ وهامُ
فإنَّ مَدافع التوفيق منكمْ   إلى حبنا وإن دفعَتْ حَرامُ[٣]

[§ ١٠٠] **ومنهم** عُتَيْبة بن الحارث بن شِهاب أخو بني جعفر بن ثَعلبة بن يَرْبوع. غزت بنو نَصر بن قُعَين، فسمع عُتيبةُ بمَسيرهم فقال: خَلُّوا بين بني نصر وبين النَّعَم. فبلغ ذلك بني نصر، فعبّوا للنَّعَم خيْلاً وللقِتال خيلاً. فلمّا صبّحوهم ذهبت الفِرقة التي وكّلوها بالنعم، وتأخّرت الأخرى، فقاتلت بنو يربوع منهم نفراً، وكانت تحت عتيبة يومئذٍ فرسٌ فيها مِراح واعتراض، فأصاب غلامٌ | ٢٣٥
من بني أسد يقال له ذؤاب بن رُبَيِّعة أرنبةَ عُتيبة فنُزف حتّى مات، فحمل رَبيعُ بن عتيبة على ذؤاب فأخذه سَلَماً، وقتلوا ثمانية من بني نصر وبني غاضرة،[٤] واستنقذوا النعم، وساروا بذؤاب إلى منزلهم، فقال رُبَيّعة أبو ذؤاب:

١ كـ: (آثام).
٢ كذا في هـ، وفي كـ: (بغيْظٍ).
٣ هـ، في تعليقه: كذا وردت «التوفيق» و «حبنا»، وهما موضعان يظهر أنهما محرّفان.
٤ كـ: (عادرة).

1027 This line is attributed to Balʿāʾ ibn Qays in Abū ʿUbaydah, *Majāz al-Qurʾān*, ii, 81; to Shāfiʿ al-Laythī in Ibn Manẓūr, *Lisān al-ʿArab* (*ʾThM*); anonymously in al-Mubarrad, *Kāmil*, ii, 337.

1028 The word left unpointed in ʿASH is read as *bi-ghayẓin* ("with rage") in SKḤ. Perhaps it could be read as *bi-ghabṭin*, taking *ghabṭ* as a synonym of *ighbāṭ*, "constantly being in the saddle", which would fit the context.

1029 On Balī see *ǦN*, i, 328–329, ii, 223; on Judhām see *ǦN*, i, 176, 245, ii, 264; on Ghassān see *ǦN*, i, 193, ii, 273.

1030 Dhū l-Masrūḥ is a place name according to al-Fīrūzābādī, *Qāmūs* (*SRḤ*), probably the same as Masrūḥ, without the article, a place near Mecca (Yāqūt, *Muʿjam al-buldān* s.v. Masrūḥ, Abū ʿUbayd, *Muʿjam*, 1225, quoting a line by Nuṣayb in which it is Dhū l-Masrūḥ).

1031 This is a free rendering of *aṣdāʾ wa-hām*. The meanings given to the singular *ṣadā* in Hava's *Dictionary* are "thirst; voice; echo; corpse; brain; owl" and *hāmah* can mean "head, skull" as well as "owl". The words refer to the belief that the spirit of someone

God requite Ibn ʿUrwah, wherever he goes,
for being disloyal, for disloyalty will be punished![1027]
You came in the vanguard of the men who came in the evening
…,[1028] without deviating or sleeping.
Balī did not know our abodes,
nor did Ghassān or Judhām.[1029]
Though they have not killed us, we have,
in Dhū l-Masrūḥ,[1030] voices crying and thirsting for vengeance![1031]
The water-courses of al-Tawfīq,
as far as Ḥabnā,[1032] when they are defended (?), are forbidden to you.

[§100 ʿUtaybah ibn al-Ḥārith ibn Shihāb[1033]]

Another is ʿUtaybah ibn al-Ḥārith ibn Shihāb, of the tribe of Jaʿfar ibn Thaʿlabah ibn Yarbūʿ. The Banū Naṣr ibn Quʿayn[1034] went on a raid. When ʿUtaybah heard they were marching he said, "Separate the Banū Naṣr from the camels." The Banū Naṣr were informed of this and they deployed some horse to raid the camels and some horse for the fight. When they attacked them in the morning, the detachment charged with raiding the camels moved but the other detachment was delayed. The Banū Yarbūʿ fought with some of them. That day ʿUtaybah was riding a horse that was fiery and refractory. A young man | of the 235
Banū Asad, called Dhuʾāb ibn Rubayyiʿah[1035] hit ʿUtaybah's nose, and he died from the bleeding.[1036] ʿUtaybah's son Rabīʿ attacked Dhuʾāb, who surrendered to him. They killed eight men of the Banū Naṣr and the Banū Ghāḍirah,[1037] they saved the camels, and took Dhuʾāb to their abode. Rubayyiʿah, Dhuʾāb's father, said,

---

whose death is unavenged appears over his grave in the shape of an owl who screeches for a drink; see Homerin, "Echoes of a Thirsty Owl".

1032 These place-names are apparently corrupt and their reading is uncertain.

1033 ʿUtaybah ibn Ḥārith, here listed as a poet, was more famous as a leader of Thaʿlabah ibn Yarbūʿ (see *ĞN*, i, 69, ii, 577), reckoned one of the "Arab horsemen" (*fursān al-ʿArab*), called Ṣayyād al-Fawāris ("Hunter of Horsemen"), see e.g. Abū ʿUbaydah, *Dībāj*, 15–18; Ibn Qutaybah, *Faḍl al-ʿArab*, 62–63; Ibn ʿAbd Rabbih, *ʿIqd*, i, 117. For parallels of the story of his death on the battle-day of Khaww, see Ibn ʿAbd Rabbih, *ʿIqd*, v, 249–250, al-Nuwayrī, *Nihāyah*, xv, 422–423; Abū ʿUbaydah, *Ayyām*, ii, 486–488 (with wrongly Kharr instead of Khaww).

1034 Naṣr ibn Quʿayn was a branch of Asad, see *ĞN*, i, 50, 51.

1035 See *ĞN*, i, 51.

1036 In Ibn ʿAbd Rabbih, *ʿIqd*, it is said that ʿUtaybah's stallion smelled a mare and went for it, ʿUtaybah being unable to see well in the dark and stumbling upon Dhuʾāb, who stabs him in the throat.

1037 Presumably Ghāḍirah ibn Mālik, a branch of Asad (*ĞN*, i, 55).

إنْ يقتلوك فقد ثللْتَ عروشَهمْ   بعُتيبةَ بن الحارث بن شهابِ
بأشدِّهمْ ضرًّا على أعدائهمْ   وأعزِّهمْ فَقْداً على الأصحابِ

[§ ١٠١] **ومنهم** المنخَّل اليَشْكُريّ. وكانت امرأة النُّعمان بن المُنذر قد شُغفت به، فخرج ٢٣٩
يتصيّد، فعمدت إلى قيْدٍ فجعلت رِجْلَها في إحدى حَلْقتَيْه، ورِجل المنخَّل في الأخرى شَغَفاً
به، وجاء النعمان فألْفاهما على حالهما، فأمر بالمنخّل فقُتل، فضربتْ به العرب المَثَل، فقال
أوْس بن حَجَر:

فجئتُ بِبَيْعي[1] مُولِياً لا أزِيده   عليه بها حتّى يؤوبَ المنخَّلُ

وقال ذو الرُّمّة:

تُقاربُ حتّى يطمَعَ الناوي في الهوى   وليست بأدنى من إيابِ المنخَّلِ

١ هـ، ك: (ربيعى)، والتصحيح من ديوان أوس بن حجر رسالة الغفران للمعرّي.

1038 They did, as is told in the version of *ʿIqd*. When Rabīʿ took Dhuʾāb captive he was not aware that he had taken his father's killer. A ransom was agreed. Rubayyiʿah brought the required number of camels but Rabīʿ was delayed and Rubayyiʿah, thinking his son was dead, unwisely recited his poem (five lines including the two given by Ibn Ḥabīb). When ʿUtaybah's son heard them he killed Dhuʾāb. The poem (five lines) is also in Abū Tammām's *Ḥamāsah* (al-Marzūqī, *Sharḥ*, 843–846, attributed to "a man of the Banū Naṣr ibn Quʿayn") and with ten lines in al-Qālī, *Amālī*, ii, 72–73.

1039 The poet al-Munakhkhal ibn ʿUbayd (or Masʿūd, or ʿAmr, or al-Ḥārith, or Khalīl) ibn ʿĀmir belonged to the tribe of Yashkur (see *ǦN*, i, 162, without mention of al-Munakhkhal) and lived in al-Ḥīrah at the court of al-Nuʿmān ibn al-Mundhir (d. AD 602). There is some confusion about his genealogy and it is not certain that he is the person who became proverbial as someone who will never return; see *ǦN*, ii, 428; Sezgin, *Geschichte*, ii, 183; *EI2*, "al-Munakhkhal al-Yashkurī" (Ch. Pellat). There is

They may kill you[1038] but you overthrew their power,
by killing ʿUtaybah ibn al-Ḥārith ibn Shihāb,
The strongest of them in inflicting harm on their enemies,
the one most sorely missed by his fellows.

[§ 101 al-Munakhkhal al-Yashkurī[1039]]

Another is al-Munakhkhal al-Yashkurī. The wife of al-Nuʿmān ibn al-Mundhir had fallen in love with him. The king went out hunting. She took a pair of shackles and put one of her feet in one of its rings and al-Munakhkhal's foot in the other, being smitten with him. When al-Nuʿmān returned he found the two in that state. Al-Munakhkhal was killed at his orders.[1040] Among the Arabs he became proverbial; Aws ibn Ḥajar said,[1041] 239

Then I came back with what I'd bought; I'll give no more
for it—until al-Munakhkhal comes back!

And Dhū l-Rummah said,[1042]

She approaches (with her words), so that one, remote, would hope for her love,
but she is no nearer than al-Munakhkhal's return.

---

additional confusion about his death and its cause. Ibn Qutaybah (*Shiʿr*, 404–405) says he was killed by king ʿAmr ibn Hind (d. c. AD 568) after he had made love poetry on his sister Hind, and also that he was suspected of having an affair with (and two sons by) al-Mutajarridah, the wife of king al-Nuʿmān ibn al-Mundhir; see also al-Iṣfahānī, *Aghānī*, xxi, 1–7 (esp. 4–5 for a parellel with the present text).

1040 In the version of *Aghānī* he was handed over to ʿIkabb, who was in charge of the prison and who tortured him to death.

1041 Aws ibn Ḥajar died probably shortly before the Hijra. See Sezgin, *Geschichte*, ii, 171–172, *EI3*, "ʿAws b. Ḥajar" (Reinhard Weipert). The verse, corrupt in ʿASH and SKḤ, is in Aws ibn Ḥajar, *Dīwān*, 98 and al-Maʿarrī, *Risālat al-Ghufrān*, i, 280–281 (where the words *ḥattā yaʾūba l-Munakhkhalū*, "until al-Munakhkhal comes back", is Englished as "when pigs will fly"). See also al-ʿAskarī, *Jamharah*, i, 292, al-Zamakhsharī, *Mustaqṣā*, ii, 58. The expression is also found in a verse by al-Namir ibn Tawlab (Ibn Sallām, *Ṭabaqāt*, 155, al-Iṣfahānī, *Aghānī*, xxi, 1).

1042 On Dhū l-Rummah (d. 117/735), see Sezgin, *Geschichte*, ii, 394–397. The verse is in his *Dīwān*, 1473 and *Aghānī*, xxi, 1. The translation follows the commentary in the *Dīwān*.

[§١٠٢] **ومنهم** عَمْرٌو ذو الكَلْب، وكان من رجال[1] هُذَيل، وكان قد عَلِقَ امرأة من فَهْم يقال ٢٤٠
لها أمّ جُلَيحة، فأحبّها وأحبّتْه، وقد كان أهلُها وجدوا عليهما وطلبوا دمَه إلى أن جاءها عاماً
من ذلك، فنذروا به فخرجوا في إثره وخرج هارباً منهم وتَبِعوه، وكان أهدى الناسِ بطريق، فتبعوه
يومَهم ذلك حتّى أمْسَوْا، وهاجت علهم [ريح شديدة في][2] ليلةٍ ظَلْماءَ شديدةِ الظُّلْمة، فبينا هو
يسير وهو على الطريق إذ رأى ناراً عن يمينه فقال: أخطأتُ واللّٰهِ الطريق، وإنّ النار لَعلى الطريق.
وحار وشدَّ فقصد للنار[3] حتّى أتاها وقد كاد يُصْبِح، فإذا رجل قد أوقد ناراً وليس معه أحد. فقال
عمرو ذو الكلب: من أنت؟ قال: أنا رجل من عَدْوان. فقال: ما اسم هذا المكان؟ قال: السدّ.
فعرف أن قد هلك وأخطأ، والسدّ شيء لا يُجاز. فقال: ويْحَك، لِمَ أوقدتَ؟ فواللّٰهِ ما تَشْوي ولا
تصطلي، ويْلي، حَيْن عمرٍو وأمرٌ لأمر، هل عندك شيء تُطْعِمني؟ قال: نعم. فأخرج له تَمَرات
فألقاها في يده، فلمّا رآها قال: تمرات، تتْبَعُها عَبَرات، من نسوة خَفِرات! ثمّ قال: اسْقِني،
قال: ماذا؟ لَبَناً؟ قال: لا ولكنِ اسقني ماءً | قَراحاً، فإنّي مقتول صباحاً. ثمّ انطلق فأسند[4] في ٢٤١
السدّ، ورأى القوم يطلبون أثره حيث أخطأ، فتبعوه حتّى وجدوه قد دخل في غار السدّ. فلمّا

١ كـ: (رجل).
٢ التكملة من الأغاني.
٣ كـ: (النار).
٤ كـ: (فاشتد).

1043 On ʿAmr ibn al-ʿAjlān called Dhū l-Kalb see Sezgin, *Geschichte*, ii, 254; Webb, *The Arab Thieves*, 102–106, 178–191 (al-Maqrīzī's text and translation); al-Iṣfahānī, *Aghānī*, xxii, 351–353; al-Sukkarī, *Sharḥ ashʿār al-Hudhaliyyīn*, 565–586 and 854–856; al-ʿAskarī, *Jamharah*, ii, 53–54; al-Jarīrī, *Jalīs*, i, 545–547. He was called Dhū l-Kalb ("the one with the dog") because he had a dog that accompanied him on his raids (*Aghānī*, xxii, 251, al-Sukkarī, *Sharḥ*, 565). Some called him ʿAmr al-Kalb, ʿAmr the Dog. There are three accounts of his death. In one, he is killed and eaten by two leopards while on a raid (*Aghānī*, xxii, 251; al-Sukkarī, *Sharḥ*, 578). In a bizarre story (found in Kushājim, *Maṣāyid*, 172–173; al-Jarīrī, *Jalīs*, i, 545–547; and al-Maqrīzī, *Luṣūṣ*, 188–191) it is told that he was killed by a snake. The third and longest account is told here, with a close parallel in *Aghānī*, and a less close one in al-Sukkarī, *Sharḥ*, 854–856. The confusion may have originated in the famous elegy on him by his sister Janūb (not in Ibn Ḥabīb's text). In this poem (al-Sukkarī, *Sharḥ*, 583–586, al-Baghdādī, *Khizānah*, x, 382–390, translated and discussed in detail by Jones, *Early Arabic Poetry*, i, 37–50), it is said that ʿAmr was killed by two leopards (vss. 2–10) but subsequently she mentions the report that he was

[§102 ʿAmr Dhū l-Kalb[1043]]

Another was ʿAmr Dhū l-Kalb, one of the men of Hudhayl.[1044] He had fallen in 240
love with a woman of the tribe of Fahm called Umm Julayḥah. He loved her and she loved him, but her family were against it and sought to kill him. After one year he came to her again, but they found out and went out after him. He fled and they followed his tracks. He was an excellent pathfinder. They followed him all day until the evening. A strong wind began to blow in the very dark night. While ʿAmr was on his way he saw a fire on his right. “I must have missed the path, by God!” he said, “for the fire is surely on the road.” He hesitated, then quickened his pace.[1045] He went towards the fire and reached it when it was almost dawn. There he found a man who had lit the fire; he was on his own. ʿAmr Dhū l-Kalb asked him, “Who are you?” The man answered, “I am from the tribe of ʿAdwān.”[1046] “What is this place called?” “The Barrier”[1047] Then ʿAmr knew that he was lost and had missed the path, for a barrier is something that cannot be passed. “I say, why have you lit a fire?” he asked, “for you are not roasting anything or warming yourself! Poor ʿAmr, he’ll be dead! One thing is by another led.[1048] Have you some food for me?” The man said “Yes, I have”. He produced some dates and handed them to ʿAmr. When he saw them he said, “Dates, followed by tears post haste, shed by women chaste!”[1049] Then he said, “Give me something to drink!” The man asked, “What do you want? Milk?” ʿAmr replied, “No, with clear water I’ll be filled, | for this morning I shall be killed.”[1050] 241
Then he left. He went up the Barrier and spotted the men who were following him where he had gone the wrong way. They followed him until they found that he had entered a cave in the Barrier. Coming up to the Barrier they were aware

---

killed by men of Fahm in a cave (*qatalnāhu fī ghārah*), the killers bringing his arrows in evidence (vs. 11). One could even speculate that *qatalnāhu fī ghārah* means “on a raid” and that the story of the cave, told in our text, was fabricated on the basis of a misinterpretation.

1044 Hudhayl was a tribe living in the neighbourhood of Mecca. See ǦN, i, 3, 58, ii, 286; EI2, “Hudhayl” (G. Rentz); EI3, “Hudhayl, Banū” (Kirill Dmitriev). Exceptionally, their “tribal *dīwān*” (their collected poetry) has been preserved, see al-Sukkarī, *Sharḥ ashʿār al-Hudaliyyīn*.

1045 *Shadda*; *Aghānī* has *shakka* “had doubts”.

1046 ʿAdwān is a sister tribe of Fahm, see ǦN, i, 92, 139, 140.

1047 Al-Sudd. For places of that name see e.g. Yāqūt, *Muʿjam al-buldan*.

1048 He uses rhyming prose: *ḥayn ʿAmr, wa-amr li-amr.*

1049 *Tamarāt, tatbaʿuhā ʿabarāt, min niswah khafirāt.*

1050 *Isqini māʾan qarāḥā, fa-innī maqtūl ṣabāḥā.*

ظهروا السدّ علموا أنّه في الغار، فنادَوْه فقالوا: يا عمرو! قال: ما تشاءون؟ قالوا: اخرُجْ! فقال: فلِمَ إذاً دخلتُ؟ قالوا: بَلى فاخرجْ. قال: لا، لا أخرج! قالوا: فأَنْشِدْنا قولك:

ومَقْعَدِ كُربةٍ قد كنتُ فيها مكانَ الإصبعَيْن من القِبالِ

فقال:[١] هاهي هذه أنا فيها. ويَعِنُّ له رجلٌ من القوم فيرميه عمرو فيقتله. قالوا: قتلتَه يا عدوَّ اللّٰه! قال: أَجَلْ. قد[٢] بقيتْ معي أربعة أسْهُم كأنّها أنياب أمّ جُليحة. قالوا: يا أبا بِجاد، ادخلْ عليه وأنت حُرّ! فتهيّأ أبو بجاد ليدخل فقال له عمرو: ويْحك، ما ينفعك أن تكون حرًّا إذا قتلتُك! فنكص عنه. فلمّا رأوْا ذلك صَعِدوا فنقبوا عليه، ثمّ رموْه حتّى قتلوه وأخذوا سَلَبَه فرجعوا به. و إذا أمُّ جُليحة تتشوّف، فلمّا رأوها قالوا: يا أمّ جُليحة، ما رأْيُكِ في عمرو؟ قالت: رأيِي واللّٰهِ أنّكم طلبْتُموه سريعاً،[٣] ولقِيتموه منيعاً، وصِبْتموه مريعاً. قالوا: واللّٰهِ قتلناه. قالت واللّٰهِ ما أُراكم فعلتم، ولئن كنتم فعلتم لرُبَّ ثَدْيٍ | منكم افترشه، وضَبٍّ منكم احترشه، ونَهْبٍ منهبٍ[٤] منكم اخترشه. ٢٤٢
فطرحوا إليها ثيابه وقالوا لها: دونَكِ، خُذيها. فشمَّتْها فقالت: ريحُ عِطْرٍ، وثوْب عمرو، أما واللّٰهِ ما وجدتم حُجْزتَه جافية، ولا عانتَه وافية، ولا ضالتَه كافية. فقالت[٥] أختُه رَيْطة ترثيه:

١ ك: (قال).

٢ الكلمة ناقصة في ك.

٣ ك: (تركتموه صريعا).

٤ الكلمة ناقصة في ك.

٥ ك: (قالت).

1051 From a poem of thirty lines (al-Sukkarī, *Sharḥ*, 565–572). Ibn Qutaybah (*Maʿānī*, 493) explains that the sense is the reverse: he meant "like the sandal-thongs between two toes", but al-Sukkarī denies this (*Sharḥ*, 571–572), saying that the poet means that he was able to extricate himself just as the sandal is carried by the two toes nearest to the thong.

1052 This is meant to be a compliment (al-Sukkarī, *Sharḥ*, 855: "She had the most beautiful teeth"). Umm Julayḥah was ʿAmr's beloved.

1053 Abū Bijād is a slave, as is clear from the context and is made explicit in *Aghānī*, where his name is given as Abū Nijād (the same in al-Maqrīzī, *Luṣūṣ*, 182–183).

that he was inside the cave. They called him, saying, "Hey ʿAmr!" "What do you want?" "Come outside!" "Why do you think I went in then?" "Yes, but come outside!" "No, I won't!" "Then recite us you what you said: 'In many a tight spot I was | like two toes to a sandal-thong'!"[1051] "That is just where I am now!"

One of the men came within his view. ʿAmr shot an arrow and killed him. They said, "You've killed him, you enemy of God!" "Sure! I have four more arrows left, like the eyeteeth of Umm Julayḥah!"[1052] They said, "Abū Bijād, go inside and you will be free!"[1053] Abū Bijād got ready to enter but ʿAmr said, "Hey you! It won't be of much use to you to be free when I kill you!" The man recoiled. When they saw this they climbed up and dug an opening and shot at him until they had killed him. They took his spoils and returned with them. They came upon Umm Julayḥah, who had gone to find out. "Umm Julayḥah!" they said when they saw her, "What do you think of ʿAmr?" "I think, by God, that you pursued him, a fast man; you found him, an unassailable man; you hit him, a noble man!"[1054] They said, "We swear by God, we killed him!" She said, "By God, I don't believe you've done that! On many a breast | of your women has he rested; many a liz- 242
ard of yours has he lured from its hole; many a booty has he taken from you!" They threw down his clothes at her feet. She took them up and smelled them. "A smell of scent, ʿAmr's robe!"[1055] she said, "By God, you have not found his waistband out of place,[1056] or his pubes abundant, or his bow and arrows[1057] broken!"

His sister Rayṭah elegised him:[1058]

1054 Here and in her following utterances she uses rhyming prose. SKḤ reads the first phrase (*ṭalabtumūhu sarīʿā*) as *taraktumūhu ṣarīʿā*, "you left him a slain man". In *Aghānī* the last phrase is "you laid him low, a slain man (*ṣarīʿā*)"; Webb translates the Maqrīzī version (*wadaʿtumūhu marīʿā*) as "you left him well", which would suit the context, as she does not believe at first that ʿAmr is dead. Nevertheless, the wording of the several parallel versions seems to indicate that she believes he has been slain.

1055 This (as "Scent, and the smell of ʿAmr") is given as a proverb in al-ʿAskarī, *Jamharah*, ii, 53–54. It is not found in other collections of proverbs.

1056 This and the following phrase apparently indicate his chasteness.

1057 *Ḍālah* can mean "weapons" in general, or "bow and arrows", or "arrows", made of *ḍāl*, wood of a kind of lotus tree.

1058 The sister is called Janūb in al-Sukkarī, *Sharḥ*, 582–583 (five lines) and Ibn Abī Ṭayfūr, *Balāghāt al-nisāʾ*, 297 (four lines). Line 2 is ascribed to "a Hudhalī" in al-Jāḥiẓ, *Ḥayawān*, i, 388, ii, 72, v, 75. There is some confusion with an elegy with the same metre and rhyme by another Hudhalī woman, Rayṭah, on her brother Ibn ʿĀṣiyah (al-Sukkarī, *Sharḥ*, 864–866), and the second line is also attributed to Hubayrah ibn Abī Wahb (Ibn Hishām, *Sīrah*, ii, 131, 132, Guillaume's translation, 405) and to ʿAmr ibn al-Ahtam (al-Maydānī, *Majmaʿ*, i, 343).

يا لَيْتَ عَمْراً ولَيْتٌ ضَلّةٌ جَزَعٌ   لم يغْزُ فَهْماً ولم يهبِط بِواديها
وليلةٍ يصطلي بالفَرْث جازرُها   يختصُّ بالنَّقَرى المُثْرِين داعيها
أطعمتَ فيها على جُوعٍ ومَسْغَبةٍ   لحْمَ الجَزور إذا ما قام ناعيها

وقالت أيضاً ترثيه:

كلُّ امرئٍ بمِحال الدَّهر مكروبُ   وكلُّ مَن غالَبَ الأيّامَ مغلوبُ
وكلُّ حيٍّ وإن عزُّوا وإن سَلِموا   يوماً طريقُهُمُ في السوء دُعْبوبُ
أبلِغْ هُذيلاً وأبلغْ مَن يبلِّغها   عنّي رسولاً وبعضُ النَّعْي تكذيبُ
بأنّ ذا الكلبِ عَمْراً خيرَهم نَسَباً   ببطنِ شِرْيانَ يَعْوي حوْلَه الذِّيبُ ٢٤٣
الطاعن الطعْنةَ النَّجْلاءَ يَتبَعُها   مُثْعنْجِرٌ من نجيع الجَوْف أُسكوبُ
والتارك القِرْنَ مُصْفَرًّا أناملُهُ   كأنّه من نجيع الجوْف[١] مخضوبُ
تمشي النُّسور إليه وهْي لاهيةٌ   مَشْيَ العَذارى عليهنَّ الجلابيبُ
والمُخْرِج العاتقَ العذراء مُذْعِنةً   في السَّبْي ينفَح من أردانها[٢] الطِّيبُ

١ كذا في هـ، كـ؛ ولعلّ الأصحّ:(من نقيع الوَرْس) كما في الأغاني.
٢ كـ: (بنفح من أرد أنها).

1059 Instead of the somewhat obscure *wa-laytun ḍallatun jazaʿun* the other sources have *wa-mā laytun bi-nāfiʿatin*, "but 'would that' is of no avail". In the poem by Rayṭah bint ʿĀṣiyah it is *wa-laytun ḍallatun safahun* (al-Sukkarī, *Sharḥ*, 866, cf. ibid. *wa-lahfun ḍallatun jazaʿan* in another poem by this Rayṭah).

1060 Other versions (al-Sukkarī, *Sharḥ*, al-Maqrīzī, *Luṣūṣ*, 186) have *idhā mā qāma bāghīhā*, "whenever someone stood up, desiring it".

1061 The poem is also in al-Iṣfahānī, *Aghānī*, xxii, 353; al-Sukkarī, *Sharḥ*, 578–581 (with 13 lines and attributed to ʿAmr's sister, Janūb); al-Buḥturī, *Ḥamāsah*, 319–320 (10 lines, attributed to ʿAmrah, ʿAmr's sister); al-ʿAskarī, *Jamharah*, ii, 54 (9 lines, attributed them to Umm Julayḥah); al-Baghdādī, *Khizānah*, x, 390–391 (8 lines, attributed to Rayṭah, said to be another sister of ʿAmr). For a German translation see Borg, *Mit Poesie vertreibe ich*, 182–183.

1062 Al-Sukkarī, followed by Jones, has (al-)Sharyān; Yāqūt, *Muʿjam al-buldān*, specifies the reading Shiryān and quotes four lines of the poem.

1063 Thus in ʿASH and SKḤ as well as al-Baghdādī, *Khizānah*. The repetition of *min najīʿi l-jawfi* is somewhat suspect and clumsy (the corpse is stained with blood, not "as if stained" with it) and perhaps the better reading is that of *Aghānī* and al-Maqrīzī's

O would that ʿAmr—but "would that" is perplexity, anxiousness—[1059]
had not raided Fahm or descended in that wadi!
On many a night on which a man warms his hands with the stomach contents of the animal he has slaughtered,
when a man invites only wealthy people to partake,
You fed men, in times of hunger and starvation,
with the flesh of a slaughtered camel when its death was announced.[1060]

She also said, elegising him:[1061]

Every man is afflicted by the cunning power of Fate
and each man who tries to overcome Time is himself overcome.
Every tribe, however mighty they are and safe and sound,
will one day walk a well-trodden path to misfortune.
Inform Hudhayl and inform those informing them
for me as a messenger—for some deaths are announced falsely—
That "He with the Dog", ʿAmr, the best of them in lineage, 243
lies in the valley of al-Shiryān,[1062] with the wolves howling round him.
He was one who could, stabbing, cause a gaping wound to flow
unstintingly with a stream of running blood from the body;
One who left his adversary with pale, yellow fingers,
as if dyed with running blood from the body,[1063]
While vultures are walking to him, having a good time,
walking like maidens wearing robes.
And he would take a young virgin from her home, submissive
as a captive, with scent wafting from her sleeves.[1064]

Luṣūṣ, 186: *min naqīʿi l-warsi makhḍūbū*, "dyed with an infusion of turmeric". *Wars* is a plant from which a yellow dye is made (Dozy, *Supplément*: "curcuma, safran d'Inde"; Hava, *Farāʾid*: "*Memecylon tinctorium*, … turmeric, Indian saffron"; Schopen & Kahl (eds.), *Natāʾiǧ al-fikar*, 189–190: "falscher Safran, … Flemingia macrophylla, … liefert einen gelben Farbstoff").

1064 Webb translates "He was one who freed from capture / Maidens …". It may seem strange to a modern reader that a woman would praise her brother for taking women as captives, but it would be a normal "*jāhilī*" attitude. The words *mudhʿinatan* ("submissive") and *fī l-saby* ("into captivity") seem to support this. Poets boast of it, such as Ṭufayl al-Ghanawī: "We slaughtered their nobles openly | and brought back captive women and spoils, || Captive women of Ṭayyiʾ, forcibly taken out, | having their palaces exchanged for mountain roads" (al-Iṣfahānī, *Aghānī*, xvii, 257–258).

[§١٠٣] **ومنهم** حُمْران بن مالك بن عبد ملك الخَثْعَميّ. وكان فارساً شاعراً. وكان سبب قتله أنّ خثعم قتلَتِ الصُّمَيل أخا ذي الجَوْشَن الكِلابيّ، فغزا ذو الجوشن خثعماً، وسانَده عُيَيْنة بن حِصن الفَزاريّ على أنّ لذي الجوشن الدِّماء، ولعُيينة الغنائم. فغزَوْا خثعمَ جميعاً فلقُوها بالفَرْز[1] جَبَل، فقتلا وأثخنا وغنما، وإنّ حُمران توقَّل في الجبل فجعلوا يأمرونه أن يستأسر فأنشأ يقول وهو يقاتل:

٢٤٤ أقسمتُ لا أُقْتَلُ إلّا حُرّا إنّي رأيتُ الموتَ شيئاً مُرّا
أَكْرَه أن أُخدَع أو أُغَرّا

فقُتل، فقالت أخته ترثيه:

ويلَ حُمرانَ أخا مَضِنَّهْ[2] أوْفى على الخير[3] ولم يمُنَّهْ
والطاعن النَّجْلاء مُرْثَعِنَّهْ عانِدُها مثلُ وكيفِ الشَنَّهْ

---

١ كـ: (بالفَرز[ة]).

٢ كذا في هـ، كـ، ولعلّ الصحيح (مَظِنّة).

٣ كـ: (الخبر).

1065 For his lineage see *Ǧn*, i, 224. As a poet he is very obscure and not found in the usual sources. No parallels of the account have been found; the event may have occurred shortly before the coming of Islam.

1066 On al-Ṣumayl ibn al-Aʿwar and his brother Shuraḥbīl Dhū l-Jawshan ("He with the cuirass", a nickname said to have been given to him because of his protruding chest) of the tribe of Kilāb, see *Ǧn*, i, 98; on the latter, see also al-Ṣafadī, *Wāfī*, xvi, 131.

[§103 Ḥumrān ibn Mālik ibn ʿAbd al-Malik al-Khathʿamī[1065]]

Another is Ḥumrān ibn Mālik ibn ʿAbd al-Malik al-Khathʿamī, who was a knight and a poet. He was killed because Khathʿam had killed al-Ṣumayl, the brother of Dhū l-Jawshan al-Kilābī.[1066] Dhū l-Jawshan raided Khathʿam, assisted by ʿUyaynah ibn Ḥiṣn al-Fazārī,[1067] on the understanding that Dhū l-Jawshan should be concerned with the blood feud and that ʿUyaynah should have the spoils. Together they raided Khathʿam and met them at al-Farz, a mountain.[1068] Both fought, inflicting heavy losses and taking spoils. Ḥumrān went up the mountain and they told him to give himself up as a prisoner. Still fighting, he said,[1069]

I swear I will be killed only as a free man; 244
I see that death is a bitter thing.
I hate to be cheated or deceived.

Thereupon he was killed. His sister elegised him:

Woe for Ḥumrān, a man in whom one surmises good qualities,[1070]
Who was beneficent but did not want to be reminded of it,[1071]
Who could stab making large wounds, gushing like rain,
Bleeding like a leaking old basket.

1067 On ʿUyaynah (or Ḥudhayfah) ibn Ḥiṣn, a chief of the tribe of Fazārah and a contemporary of the prophet Muḥammad, see *ĞN*, i, 130, *EI2*, "ʿUyayna ibn Ḥiṣn" (M. Lecker). He is also mentioned in the next entry, §104.

1068 Not found; Yāqūt, *Muʿjam al-buldān*, mentions a mountain called al-Farzah and another called al-Fard.

1069 The three lines are in *rajaz* metre. Lines 1–2 are uttered by Muslim ibn ʿAqīl ibn Abī Ṭālib in a similar situation in the year 60/680, see Ibn Aʿtham, *Futūḥ*, v, 54; al-Ṭabarī, *Tārīkh*, ii, 262, tr. *The History*, xix, 55; al-Masʿūdī, *Murūj*, iii, 254; al-Iṣfahānī, *Maqātil*, 106.

1070 ʿASH has *akhā maḍinnah*, which is probably an error for *akhā maẓinnah* (cf. Lane, *Lexicon*: *fulān maẓinnah li-l-khayr*, "*Such a one is one in whom good, or goodness is thought* [&c.] *to be*").

1071 For this interpretation of *manna*, cf. al-Zabīdī, *Tāj* (MNN); another interpretation is "and did not cut off (his benefices)".

[§ ١٠٤] **ومنهم** مالك بن نُوَيْرة بن جَمْرة اليَرْبوعيّ، وهو فارس ذي الخِمار، وقُتل في الرِّدّة. ذلك أنّ العرب لمّا ارتدّت وجّه أبو بكر خالدَ بن الوليد بن المُغِيرة، فسار في المهاجرين والأنصار حتّى لقي أَسَداً وغَطَفان ببُزاخةَ، واقتتلوا قِتالاً شديداً ففضّ اللّهُ المرتدّين، وأُسر عُيَيْنة بن حِصن بن حُذَيفة بن بدر بن عمرو الفَزاريّ، فوُجّه به مجموعةً يداه إلى عنقه إلى أبي بكر فاستحياه، وأُسِر قُرّة بن هُبَيْرة القُشَيْريّ فاستحياه أيضاً.

ثمّ إنّ خالداً سار إلى البُطاح، نِيران[١] من بني تَميم، فلم يجدْ بها | جمعاً، فبثَّ السرايا في ٢٤٥
نواحيها، فأُتِيَ بمالك بن نُويرة في نفر معه من بني حَنْظلة، فاختلف فيهم الناس، وكان في السَّرِيّة التي أصابتهم أبو قَتادة، فقال أبو قتادة: لا سبيل عليه ولا على أصحابه، لأنّا قد أذَّنّا فأذّنوا، وأقمنا فأقاموا، وصلَّيْنا فصلَّوْا.

وقد كان من عهد أبي بكر إلى خالد: أيّما دارٍ غَشِيتُموها فسمِعتم أذانَ الصلاة فيها فأَمْسِكوا عن أهلها حتّى تسألَهم ما نقموا وما يبْتَغون، وأيّما دارٍ لم تسمعوا فيها أذاناً فشُنُّوا الغارةَ عليها، فاقتُلوا وحَرِّقوا.

١ كذا في النسختين، ولعلّها (قيزان) جمع قوز، وهو الكثيب الصغير، كما قال هارون. أو لعلّ الصحيح (قِيران).

1072 Chief of the Banū Thaʿlabah (Tamīm), hero and poet, brother of the poet Mutammim ibn Nuwayrah, who composed a celebrated elegy on him ("perhaps the most famous elegy in ancient Arabian verse", thus Charles Lyall in his translation of the *Mufaḍḍaliyyāt*, 205). See *EI2*, "Mālik b. Nuwayra" (Ella Landau-Tasseron); Sezgin, *Geschichte*, ii, 203–204; *ĞN*, i, 69, ii, 393. His death in 13/634, controversially ordered by Khālid ibn al-Walīd who allegedly lusted after Mālik's wife, is told in many sources, including al-Yaʿqūbī, *Tārīkh*, ii, 148–149 (tr. *The Works*, 754–755); and in detail al-Ṭabarī, *Tārīkh*, i, 1922–1929, tr. *The History*, x, 98–104; al-Iṣfahānī, *Aghānī*, xv, 298–306.

1073 Dhū l-Khimār ("the one with the veil") was the name of his horse.

1074 At the death of the prophet Muḥammad several tribes in the Arabian Peninsula renounced their (often informal) allegiance to Islam. In a series of campaigns during the caliphate of Abū Bakr (11–13/632–634) these tribes were subdued, as a prelude to the great conquests that followed. This period is known as *al-riddah*, which became the term for religious apostasy.

1075 See above, § 39 note 469 and § 95 note 973.

[§ 104 Mālik ibn Nuwayrah[1072]]

Another is Mālik ibn Nuwayrah ibn Jamrah al-Yarbūʿī, called the horseman of Dhū l-Khimār.[1073] He was killed during the "Apostasy".[1074] When the Arabs defected, Abū Bakr sent Khālid ibn al-Walīd ibn al-Mughīrah,[1075] who marched with the Emigrants and the Helpers[1076] until they met Asad and Ghaṭafān at Buzākhah.[1077] A fierce battle ensued and God routed the apostates, ʿUyaynah ibn Ḥiṣn ibn Ḥudhayfah ibn Badr ibn ʿAmr al-Fazārī[1078] was taken prisoner and he was sent, his hand tied at his neck, to Abū Bakr, who spared his life. Qurrah ibn Hubayrah al-Qushayrī[1079] was also taken prisoner and his life was spared too.

Then Khālid marched to al-Buṭāḥ,[1080] …[1081] of the Banū Tamīm. Not finding there | any troops, he sent detachments to the neighbouring regions. They 245
brought to him Mālik ibn Nuwayrah together with some men from the Banū Ḥanẓalah.[1082] They had different views about what to do with them. Abū Qatādah,[1083] who had been in the detachment that found them, said, "We should not do anything to him or his companions, for we called to prayer and they responded with the same, we performed the salat and prayed, and they performed the salat and prayed."

Abū Bakr had enjoined to Khālid, saying, "Whenever you come upon an abode and you hear the call to prayer, you should leave the people alone until you ask them what resentment they have and what they want. But whenever you come upon an abode where you do not hear the call to prayer, you must attack it, killing and burning."

1076 See above, § 24 note 296.

1077 On the battle at Buzākhah (a place in Nejd, the central plateau of the Peninsula, see Yāqūt, *Muʿjam al-buldān*, s.v., EI2, "Buzākha" [C.E. Bosworth]) in 11/632, see al-Ṭabarī, *Tārīkh*, i, 1886–1891, tr. *The History*, x, 60–67.

1078 See the preceding entry, § 103.

1079 On Qurrah ibn Hubayrah see ǦN, i, 105, ii, 472.

1080 On the battle at al-Buṭāḥ (said to be a well in the territory of Asad, see Yāqūt, *Muʿjam al-buldān*, or a place in the territory of Tamīm, as here and in Abū ʿUbayd al-Bakrī, *Muʿjam*, 256) in 13/634, see al-Ṭabarī, *Tārīkh*, i, 1921–1929, tr. *The History*, x, 98–104.

1081 The text has *nīrān min Banī Tamīm*, "fires, of the Banū Tamīm", which does not seem to make sense. Hārūn suggests reading *qīzān*, "hillocks"; perhaps more likely is *qīrān*, "basalt grounds" or "black hillocks", plural of *qārah*.

1082 Ḥanẓalah ibn Mālik, a branch of Tamīm (ǦN, i, 59, ii, 298) to which Mālik also belonged.

1083 Abū Qatādah al-Ḥārith ibn Ribʿī, one of the Helpers, nicknamed Fāris al-Nabī, "the Prophet's Knight"; see al-Ṣafadī, *Wāfī*, xi, 241–242. He denounced Khālid's action to Abū Bakr.

وقال بعض مَن كان في هذه السريّة: ما سمعناهم أذّنوا ولا صلّوْا ولا كبّروا، فاختلف فيهم الناس، فأمر خالد بمالك وأصحابه فضُربت أعناقهم، وتزوّج أمَّ تميم امرأةَ مالك، فلمّا سمع ذلك عمرُ بالمدينة تكلّم في شأنهم له، فلم يزل عمر واجداً عليه حتّى مات.

[§ ١٠٥] **ومنهم** أبو عَزّة، وهو عَمْرو[1] بن عبد الله بن عُمَير بن وَهْب بن حُذافة بن جُمَح، وأسره رسولُ الله صلّى الله عليه وسلّم يومَ بدر، فشكا إليه بَناتِه وسوءَ حاله، فرقّ له وأطلقه وأخذ عليه صلّى الله عليه وسلّم أن لا يهْجُوَه ولا يكثّر عليه، فأعطاه ذلك. ثمّ إنّ قُريشاً ضَمِنت له القيامَ ببناته وكِفايتَه المَؤونةَ، فلم يزالوا له حتّى خرج وأُسر يومَ أُحُد، فأُتي به رسولُ الله صلّى الله عليه وسلّم فشكا إليه نَحْواً ممّا شكا يومَ بدر، فقال صلّى الله عليه وسلّم: المؤمن لا يُلْدغ من حَجَرٍ مرّتيْن. وضرب صلّى الله عليه وسلّم عُنقه.

[§ ١٠٦] **ومنهم** عبد يَغُوث بن وقّاص بن صَلاءة الحارثيّ. وكان مدح خالد بن نَضْلة بن الأشتر ٢٤٦
بن جَحْوان بن فَقْعَس، فقال: ناهِيك فيها إهاب واحد، يا خالد بن نضلة فقط! فرفع خالد يديْه
فقال: اللّهُمَّ إن كان كاذباً فاقتُلْه على يديْ شَرِّ حيٍّ من مُضَر.

١ هـ، ك: (عمر).

1084 ʿUmar ibn al-Khaṭṭāb had succeeded Abū Bakr in 13/634.

1085 For the story of Abū ʿAzzah, see e.g. Ibn Hishām, *Sīrah*, i, 660, ii, 104, 128 (tr. Guillaume, 317–318, 370, 403); Ibn Sallām, *Ṭabaqāt*, 212–215; and collections of proverbs such as al-Mufaḍḍal, *Fākhir*, 279–280; al-ʿAskarī, *Jamharah*, ii, 302–303; al-Maydānī, *Majmaʿ*, ii, 254; al-Zamakhsharī, *Mustaqṣā*, ii, 276.

1086 ʿUmar (as in ʿASH and SKḤ following the MS) has been emended to ʿAmr, in accordance with all other sources.

1087 For his lineage see *ĞN*, i, 24, ii, 167. Jumaḥ is a branch of Quraysh.

1088 See above, § 22.

1089 Ibn Hishām, *Sīrah*, i, 660 adds a poem of five lines by Abū ʿAzzah in praise of Muḥammad (three lines in Ibn Sallām, *Ṭabaqāt*, 212).

1090 See above § 27.

1091 This is found in the collections of proverbs mentioned above. The verb used (*ladagha*), like that in other versions (*lasaʿa*) is normally reserved for the stinging of insects, spiders, or scorpions, or for the biting of snakes.

But another who had been in this detachment said, "We did not hear them call to prayer, they did not pray, they did not say *Allāhu Akbar*." Thus they had different views about what to do with them. Then Khālid gave orders for Mālik and his companions to be beheaded. He took Mālik's wife, Umm Tamīm, as his own wife. When ʿUmar[1084] heard about this in Medina he talked to him about what he had done to them, and he remained angry with him until he died.

[§ 105 Abū ʿAzzah[1085]]

Another is Abū ʿAzzah, who is ʿAmr[1086] ibn ʿAbd Allāh ibn ʿUmayr ibn Wahb ibn Ḥudhāfah ibn Jumaḥ.[1087] The Messenger of God (God bless and preserve him) had taken him prisoner at the Battle of Badr.[1088] He pleaded with him, mentioning his daughters and his poverty,[1089] and the Prophet (God bless and preserve him) took pity on him and released him, making him pledge not to lampoon him nor to slander him. This he promised. Subsequently Quraysh undertook to support his daughters and provide them with sufficient sustenance. They did this until he rebelled and was again taken prisoner, at the Battle of Uḥud.[1090] When he was taken to the Messenger of God (God bless and preserve him), he pleaded in the same way he had done at the Battle of Badr. But the Prophet (God bless and preserve him) said, "A believer will not be bitten twice from the same snake-hole",[1091] and he cut off his head.

[§ 106 ʿAbd Yaghūth ibn Waqqāṣ[1092]]

Another is ʿAbd Yaghūth ibn Waqqāṣ ibn Ṣalāʾah al-Ḥārithī. He had eulogised 246
Khālid ibn Naḍlah ibn al-Ashtar ibn Jaḥwān ibn Faqʿas,[1093] and he said, "Only one skin is enough for you,[1094] Khālid ibn Naḍlah!" Khālid raised his hands and said, "O God! If he is lying, kill him at the hands of the worst man alive of Muḍar!"[1095]

1092 ʿAbd Yaghūth ibn al-Ḥārith was a chief of the Bal-Ḥārith (or Banū l-Ḥārith), a branch of Madhḥij (see *ǦN*, i, 258, ii, 133) and a poet; see Sezgin, *Geschichte*, ii, 304. On him and the story of his death see Abū ʿUbaydah, *Naqāʾiḍ*, 149–154; Ibn ʿAbd Rabbih, *ʿIqd*, v, 224–231; al-Iṣfahānī, *Aghānī*, xvi, 327–335; and the commentary of his famous poem in the *Mufaḍḍaliyyāt* (ed. Lyall), 315–320, tr. Lyall, 111–114. See also al-Baghdādī, *Khizānah*, ii, 195–203.

1093 A chief of Asad; see *ǦN*, i, 50, ii, 342.

1094 The meaning of this sentence, *nāhīka fīhā ihāb wāḥid* (in prose, not verse, and not found in other sources) is obscure, nor is it clear why Khālid is offended.

1095 For Muḍar see above, § 5 note 75.

فلمّا كان يومِ الكُلاب الثاني قتلتْ بنو الحارث بن كعب النُّعْمانَ بن جِساس صاحبَ راية تَيْم الرِّباب، وأسرت بنو سعد بن زيد مناة بن تميم عبدَ يغوث، فأتت بني سعد فقالوا لهم: إنّه لم يُقْتَل لكم فارس، وقد قُتل فارسُنا ورئيسُنا فادْفعوا إلينا عبدَ يغوث لنقتُله بصاحبنا. فدفعوه إليهم فقال لهم: يا معشر تيم، اللَّبَن اللَّبَن! فقالوا: الدم أحبُّ إلينا. وأوثقوا لسانَه بنِسْعةٍ مَخافةَ أن يهجُوَهم، فقال في شعر له طويل:

أقول وقد شدُّوا لساني بنِسْعةٍ   أمَعْشَرَ تَيْمٍ أَطْلِقوا من لِسانِيا
وتضحَكُ منّي شيخةٌ عَبْشَميّةٌ   كأنْ لم يَرَوْا قبْلي أسيراً يَمانيا
وظلَّ نِساءُ التَّيمِ[١] حوْلِيَ رُكَّداً   تُحاول منّي ما تريد نسائيا

فقدّموه فضُربت عنقه.

[§١٠٧] **ومنهم** يزيد بن الطَّثْريّة، وهو يزيد بن الصِّمّة القُشَيْريّ، فنُسب إلى أخواله. وأمُّه ٢٤٧
من بني طَثْر ثمّ من عَنْز بن وائل. وكان المندلِث بن إدريس الحَنَفيّ في الفِتنة، فأتى بني جَعْدة وبني قُشير وبني عُقيل مصدِّقاً لهم، فعاثَ فيهم، فأرسلُ عبد الله بن جَعْوَنة القُشيريّ

١ ك: (نساء تيم)، والمشهور (نساءُ الحيِّ).

1096 Al-Kulāb was the site of two famous battle-days, on the second of which the tribes of Saʿd ibn Zayd Manāh and al-Ribāb defeated the Madhḥij, some years after AD 620. See e.g. Yāqūt, *Muʿjam al-buldān*; Abū ʿUbaydah, *Naqāʾiḍ*, index (p. 266); Abū ʿUbaydah, *Ayyām*, ii, 66–94; Ibn ʿAbd Rabbih, *ʿIqd*, v, 224–233; al-Shimshāṭī, *Anwār*, i, 209–221.

1097 A tribe considered part of Madhḥij, see *ĞN*, i, 258, ii, 308.

1098 For al-Nuʿmān ibn Jisās (properly al-Nuʿmān ibn Mālik ibn al-Ḥārith) see *ĞN*, i, 85, ii, 452. On Taym and al-Ribāb see above, § 34, note 434.

1099 In another version, he is asked how he prefers to be killed. He asks for wine and is given some; and after they opened a vein he recites, dying, his famous poem (Abū ʿUbaydah, *Naqāʾiḍ*, 153, al-Iṣfahānī, *Aghānī*, xvi, 333).

1100 The text reads as a *non sequitur*; in other versions (e.g. *Mufaḍḍaliyyāt*, 317) he asks for the gag to be removed so that he may reproach his fellow tribesmen and lament his own fate, promising not to lampoon his killers. They let him utter his poem. In the last line of the fragment quoted here he is clearly breaking his pledge; Lyall (*Mufaḍḍalīyāt*, translation, 114) thinks that the line may be spurious.

On the second battle-day of al-Kulāb[1096] the Banū l-Ḥārith ibn Kaʿb[1097] killed al-Nuʿmān ibn Jisās, the standard-bearer of Taym al-Ribāb,[1098] and the Banū Saʿd ibn Zayd Manāh ibn Taym took ʿAbd Yaghūth prisoner. The Taym went to the Banū Saʿd and said, "No knight of yours has been killed, but our knight and our leader was killed. Now hand over ʿAbd Yaghūth to us so that we may kill him in requital for our chief." They handed him over. ʿAbd Yaghūth said to them, "Men of Taym! Milk! Milk!" They replied, "We prefer blood!"[1099] They gagged him with a thong, fearing that he might lampoon them, but[1100] he said, in a long poem:[1101]

I said, when they gagged my tongue with a thong,
"Men of Taym, free my tongue!"
An old woman of ʿAbd Shams[1102] laughs at me
as though they[1103] had never seen a Yemeni captive.
The women of Taym were standing around me all the time,
seeking from me that which my women want!

Then they brought him up and cut off his head.

[§107 Yazīd ibn al-Ṭathriyyah[1104]]

Another is Yazīd ibn al-Ṭathriyyah, who is Yazīd ibn al-Ṣimmah al-Qushayrī, but 247
he came to be named after his mother's family; she belonged to the Banū Ṭathr, a branch of ʿAnz ibn Wāʾil.[1105]

1101 The poem has 20 lines in *al-Mufaḍḍaliyyāt*, lines 8, 12, and 13 are quoted here.

1102 ʿAbd Shams (or ʿAbshams) ibn Saʿd ibn Zayd Manāh, see *ĞN*, i, 78, ii, 136.

1103 This follows the reading of the manuscript, *lam yaraw*. As ʿASH and SKḤ say in their notes, the standard version (*Mufaḍḍaliyyāt* and many other sources) has *lam taray*, "you have never seen" (with a shift, *iltifāt*, to the 2nd person); *Aghānī* has *lam tarā* (with final *alif* instead of *yāʾ*), which is grammatically irregular, clearly an attempt to avoid *lam tara* ("she has never seen"), which would be a very unusual metrical irregularity. The version adopted here has not been found elsewhere.

1104 On Yazīd, who died in 126/744, see Sezgin, *Geschichte*, ii, 336–337. On his death on the battle day of al-Falaj, see al-Balādhurī, *Ansāb*, ix, 208; *Aghānī*, viii, 180–184; Ibn Athīr, *Kāmil*, iv, 491–492; Ibn Khallikān, *Wafayāt*, vi, 372–373.

1105 For his paternal lineage see *ĞN*, i, 105, ii, 538 (mentioning al-Ṣimmah ibn ʿAbd Allāh al-Qushayrī but not Yazīd); some sources mention a different father, Salamah ibn Samurah (al-Iṣfahānī, *Aghānī*, viii, 155; Yāqūt, *Muʿjam al-udabāʾ*, xx, 46; Ibn Khallikān, *Wafayāt*, vi, 367), or al-Muntashir (al-Balādhurī, *Ansāb*, ix, 208). For ʿAnz ibn Wāʾil, the tribe of his mother, see *ĞN*, i, 141, 166, ii, 190.

إلى بني عُقيل وبني قُشير فأتاه أبو لَطيفة العُقيليّ في جماعة، وأتاه يزيد بن الطثريّة في بني قُشير، فقتلوا المندلث وهرب أصحابه وقتلوا فيهم وأسروا. وكان بنو قُشير أرادت أن تنضمّ إلى بني عُقيل وتسير مع أبي [لطيفة][1] فقال يزيد بن الطثريّة:

قُلْ للبوادر والأحلافِ ما لَكُمُ   أمرٌ إذا كان شُورى أمرِكمْ شُعَبا
لا تُنْشِبوا في جَناح القوم رِيشَكُمُ   فيجعَلوكمْ ذُنابى يُنْبِت الزَّغَبا
لا عيْبَ فيّ لكمْ إلّا مُعاتَبتي   إذا تعتَّبتُ من أخلاقكمْ عَتَبا

والبوادر: بنو بادرة بنت حارثة بن عَبْس[2] بن رِفاعة من بني سُلَيم، ولدها عبد الله وعامر وقُرْط وحَزْن[3] ومعاوية، بنو سَلَمة بن قُشير. والأحلاف سائر بني سلمة بن قُشير، وهم لِعَلّات. | وكانت الرياسة ٢٤٨
لعبد الله بن جَعْونة والراية في يد يزيد ين الطثريّة. فجاء القوم حوله حين لَقُوهم، وثبت يزيد بالراية وفرّ[4] عنه أصحابُه، وعليه جُبّة خزٍّ يسحَبها، فنَشِبت في خشبةٍ فعَثَر، فضربه به الحَنَفيّون حتّى قتلوه، فقال القُحَيف بن الحُمَيِّر[5] العُقيليّ يرثيه:

١ ليست في النسختين.
٢ ك: (عدس).
٣ هـ، ك: (وجوز).
٤ ك: (وقرّ).
٥ هـ، ك: (عُمير).

1106 Al-Mundalith ibn Idrīs, of the tribe of Ḥanīfah, was appointed in charge of al-Falaj, a town in al-Yamāmah (eastern Arabia), by al-Nuʿmān ibn ʿAbd Allāh (al-Balādhurī, *Ansāb*, ix, 208, Ibn al-Athīr, *Kāmil*, iv, 491). He is wrongly called al-Mundalif in *Aghānī*.

1107 *Kāna … fī l-fitnah*; apparently referring to the situation after the violent death of caliph al-Walīd ibn Yazīd in 126/744, when the conflict between the North Arab (Qays) and South Arab (Yaman) confederations flared up again. Alternatively, *al-fitnah* is an error for *al-Falaj*.

1108 Jaʿdah and ʿUqayl are sister tribes to Qushayr, see *ĞN*, i, 101.

1109 He has not been found in other sources. The point of the message is apparently to muster troops to fight al-Mundalith.

1110 In *Aghānī*, viii, 181 he is called Abū Laṭīfah ibn Muslim al-ʿUqaylī.

Al-Mundalith ibn Idrīs al-Ḥanafī[1106] was involved in the troubles.[1107] He went to the Banū Jaʿdah, the Banū Qushayr, and the Banū ʿUqayl[1108] to fight them and he wrought havoc among them. ʿAbd Allāh ibn Jaʿwanah al-Qushayrī[1109] sent a message to the Banū ʿUqayl and the Banū Qushayr. Abū Laṭīfah al-ʿUqaylī[1110] came to him with a company, as did Yazīd ibn al-Ṭathriyyah among the Banū Qushayr. They fought with al-Mundalith, whose followers fled; they killed some and took prisoners. The Banū Qushayr wanted to join the Banū ʿUqayl and march with Abū Laṭīfah. Yazīd ibn al-Ṭathriyyah said,[1111]

> Say to the Bādirahs[1112] and their allies: "You have no
> command, when the counsel of your command is split.
> Don't stick your feathers to the wing of the men,
> lest they turn you into a tail that grows downy feathers!
> You cannot blame me for anything except my reproach
> when I reproach you for a defect in your character."

The Bādirahs are the Banū Bādirah bint Ḥārithah ibn ʿAbs ibn Rifāʿah, of the Banū Sulaym; her offspring are ʿAbd Allāh, ʿĀmir, Qurṭ, Ḥazn, and Muʿāwiyah, the Banū Salamah ibn Qushayr.[1113] The allies are the other sons of Salamah ibn Qushayr by other wives. | ʿAbd Allāh ibn Jaʿwanah had the command and Yazīd 248
ibn al-Ṭathriyyah held the standard. The men rallied around him when they joined in battle. Yazīd stood his ground with the standard while his companions fled. He was wearing a silk robe, trailing it. It got stuck on a piece of wood and he tripped. The men of Ḥanīfah struck him and killed him. Al-Quḥayf ibn al-Ḥumayyir al-ʿUqaylī[1114] said, elegising him:[1115]

1111 The lines have not been found elsewhere.

1112 The explanation follows.

1113 ʿAbs ibn Rifāʿah is part of the tribe of Sulaym (*ĞN*, i, 124). "Her offspring" apparently refers to Bādirah, a woman; they are sons of Salamah (also called Salamat al-Khayr) ibn Qushayr (*ĞN*, i, 105); seven more sons are listed, here called "the allies". Instead of Ḥazn, ʿASH and SKḤ have Jawz (or Jūz), clearly a copyist's error.

1114 Al-Quḥayf ibn al-Ḥumayyir (d. after 132/750) was a poet, see e.g. Sezgin, *Geschichte*, ii, 337, al-Iṣfahānī, *Aghānī*, xxiv, 82–90. For his lineage see *ĞN*, ii, 470 (referring to i, 103, where he is not found). His father's name is wrongly given as ʿUmayr in ʿASH and SKḤ; instead of al-Ḥumayyir, *ĞN* has al-Ḫumaiyir (i.e., al-Khumayyir) and Sezgin has al-Ḫumair (al-Khumayr). If al-Ḥumayyir is correct, he is the brother of Tawbah ibn al-Ḥumayyir (on whom see below, §109).

1115 The verses (in *rajaz* metre) are also in *Aghānī*, viii, 182 (quoting Ibn Ḥabīb); lines 1–3 in al-Balādhurī, *Ansāb*, ix, 208.

إنْ تقتُلوا منّا شهيداً صابرا فقد قتلْنا منكُمُ مَجازِرا
عشرين لمّا يدخُلوا المَقابرا قَتْلى أُصِيبت قُعُصاً نحائرا
نعجاً[١] يُرى أرْجُلها شواغرا

وقال أيضاً القُحيف:

يا عينُ بكِّي هَمَلاً على هَمَلْ على يزيدَ ويزيدَ بن حَمَلْ[٢]
قتَّال أبطالٍ وحَوْلَهُ حُلَلْ[٣]

ويزيد بن حَمَل أيضاً قُشيريّ، قُتل معه يومئذ.

[§١٠٨] **ومنهم** الأُقَيْشِر، وهو المُغِيرة بن [...][٤] [قَيس بن] محمّد بن الأشعث بن قيس ٢٤٩
الكِنْديّ، وكان أعمى، فمدحه فأمر له بثلاثمائة درهم فقال: ادفَعْها إلى قَهْرمانك، ومُرْه فلْيُعْطِني بكلّ يوم درهماً للّحم ودرهماً[٥] للبقْل. فكان يشتري خمراً بدرهم، ولحماً بدانَقَيْن،

١ في النسختين: (نفخا) وفي هـ، كـ: (نُفْجاً)، وفي الأغاني: (نعجا)، وقال المحقّق: "ولعله «نعجى» جمع نعج كزمن وزمنى. ونعج الرجل ربا وانتفخ، وذلك ملحوظ في الميت بجلاء."
٢ هـ، كـ: (جَمَلْ).
٣ هـ، كـ: (حِلَل).
٤ سقطت من النسختين بقيّة نسبه وبعض الكلام الذي يليه.
٥ كـ: (درهمًا)، بدون واو العطف.

1116 *Ansāb* has "five hundred".

1117 The MSS have *nafkhan* ("puffed up"?), emended in ʿASH and SKḤ to *nufjan*, glossed in a note as "raised". *Aghānī* has *naʿjan*, with a note suggesting that it might be read as *naʿjā*, a plural of *naʿj*, from *naʿija*, "to be bloated". This has been adopted in the present translation.

1118 *Aghānī*, viii, 182 (adding that Ibn Ḥabīb is the only source quoting these lines).

1119 ʿASH and SKḤ read Jamal; I have followed *Aghānī*, which has Ḥamal. Neither Yazīd ibn Jamal nor Yazīd ibn Ḥamal is found elsewhere; I have preferred the latter because

Though you have killed a steadfast martyr of ours,
We butchered many of you:
Twenty,[1116] not yet buried,
Killed swiftly, slaughtered,
Bloated,[1117] their legs in the air.

Al-Quḥayf also said,[1118]

Weep, mine eye, stream upon stream,
For Yazīd and for Yazīd ibn Ḥamal,[1119]
Killer of heroes, with robes[1120] around him.

Yazīd ibn Ḥamal, also a Qushayrī, was killed together with him that day.

[§ 108 al-Uqayshir[1121]]

Another is al-Uqayshir, who is al-Mughīrah ibn ...[1122] [He went to Qays ibn] 249
Muḥammad ibn al-Ashʿath ibn Qays al-Kindī, who was blind,[1123] and composed a eulogy on him. Qays rewarded him with three hundred dirhams. Al-Uqayshir said, "Hand them to your steward and tell him to give me every day one dirham for meat and one dirham for vegetables!" But he proceeded to buy wine for

---

Ḥamal, unlike Jamal, is found as a personal name, and because a leading Qushayrī is called Abū Ḥamal ibn Sabrah (*ĞN*, i, 105, ii, 296).

1120 ʿASH and SKḤ read *wa-ḥilal*, with ʿASH explaining this as the plural of *ḥillah*, "sedentary people, in multitude", which seems unlikely. I have read *wa-ḥulal*; cf. the version of *Aghānī*: *wa-jarrāra ḥulal*, "one who trails robes".

1121 Al-Uqayshir is the nickname ("the little peeled one", allegedly because of his red face) of the poet al-Mughīrah ibn ʿAbd Allāh, of Asad. He came from Kufa, was famed for his love of wine and invective poetry, and died c. 80/699, apparently at an advanced age because it is said he was born before Islam; see *ĞN*, i, 57, ii. 419; Sezgin, *Geschichte*, ii, 326–327; al-Iṣfahānī, *Aghānī*, xi, 251–276; al-Baghdādī, *Khizānah*, iv, 485–492. Yāqūt (*Muʿjam al-udabāʾ*, xviii, 116) mentions a book by Ibn Ḥabīb entitled *Kitāb shiʿr al-Uqayshir*. The story of al-Uqyashir and Qays ibn Muḥammad ibn al-Ashʿath is told in *Aghānī*, xi, 264–265, but there is nothing about a murder in the bath.

1122 There is a lacuna in the manuscripts.

1123 He has not been found in other sources. For the lineage of his father, Muḥammad ibn al-Ashʿath, see *ĞN*, i, 236. Qays must have been a brother of ʿAbd al-Raḥmān ibn Muḥammad ibn al-Ashʿath, who rebelled against the governor Ibn al-Ḥajjāj in 80–82/699–702, see *EI2*, "Ibn al-Ash̲ʿat̲h̲" (L. Veccia Vaglieri).

ويكتري بغْلاً بأربعة دوانيق، فيمضي إلى الحِيرة فيشرب يومَه ثمّ ينصرف مُمْسِياً. فأَتْلف الدراهمَ، ثمّ أتاه أيضاً فسأله فأعطاه مثلها فأتْلفها. فقيل له: إنّما يشتري بها خمراً يشربه! فلمّا أتاه قال له: يا هذا، إنّه لا يحِلّ لي أن أُعطِيَك ما تشتري به الخمر! ولم يعْطِه شيئاً. فقال الأقيشر:

ألَمْ تر قـيْسَ الأكمَهَ ابنَ[١] محمّدٍ يقول فلا تَلْقاه بالقول يفعَلُ
رأيتكَ أعمى القلبِ والعينِ مُمْسِكاً وما خيرُ أعمى العينِ والقلبِ يبخُلُ[٢]
فلو صَمَّ تمَّتْ لَعْنةُ اللّهِ كلُّها عليه وما فيه من الشَّرّ أفضلُ

فقعد له مَواليه حتّى إذا انصرف سَكْراناً، فأنزلوه في الحمّامات بظهر الكوفة وتركوا البغل فعاد إلى الكوفة ودخّنوا عليه حتّى مات، فوجدوه ميتّاً هناك حين أصبحوا. | ويقال: كان الذي فعل ٢٥٠
بالأقيشر هذا مَوالي إسحاق بن طَلْحة بن عُبيد اللّه، وكان الأقيشر مُولَعاً بهِجائه.

[§١٠٩] **ومنهم** تَوْبة بن الحُمَيِّر أخو بني خَفاجة بن عُقيل. وكان سبب قتله أنّه كان بينه وبين بني عامر بن عَوْف[٣] بن عُقيل، وهم رهط نَصْر بن شَبَث، لِحاءٌ. ثمّ إنّ توبةَ شَهِد بني خفاجة

١ ك: (بن).
٢ هـ: (والقلبُ ينخلُ).
٣ هـ، ك: (عوف بن عامر) والتصحيح من الأغاني ومراجع أخرى.

1124 A *dānaq* (a Persian word) is one-sixth of a dirham.

1125 In *Aghānī* he takes three dirhams each day, for wine, food, and mule.

1126 In *Aghānī*, Qays (who is approached for the fourth time) says, less piously, "Damn you, it is as if you've made it a regular tax for me!"

1127 For Isḥāq ibn Ṭalḥah, of Taym (Quraysh), see *ĞN*, i, 21; son of the more famous Ṭalḥah, companion of the Prophet and "one of the ten" (whom he had promised entry into Paradise). Isḥāq was appointed governor of Khorasan by Muʿāwiyah (Ibn Qutaybah, *Maʿārif*, 232).

1128 Tawbah ibn Ḥumayyir, poet and bandit-warrior, was born shortly before the coming of Islam and died probably at some time between 41/661 and 57/677; the date is much disputed. For a detailed discussion especially on the date of Tawbah's death see Shahin, "Reflections on the Lives and Deaths of Two Umayyad Poets: Laylā al-Akhyaliyyah and

one dirham, meat for two *dānaq*s,[1124] and to hire a mule for the remaining four *dānaq*s.[1125] Then he would go to al-Ḥīrah, drink all day, and return in the evening. When he had squandered all the dirhams he went to Qays again, begging, and was given a like sum. This he squandered again. Qays was told, "He only buys wine with them which he drinks!" When he approached him again, Qays said, "It would not be legal for me to give you money to buy wine", and he did not give him anything.[1126] Then Qays said,

> Have you not seen Qays the blind man, son of Muḥammad?
> He says one thing but you will not find him doing it.
> I have seen you, blind of heart and sight, being niggardly.
> What's the good of someone blind of sight and heart who is stingy?
> If he were deaf as well, God's curse, all of it, would be
> on him; but the evil that is in him is still more.

Qays's clients (*mawālī*) sat in ambush for him. When he returned, being drunk, they put him in the baths beyond Kufa, leaving the mule to find its way back to Kufa. They stoked up the fire and smoke until he died. They found his corpse
there in the morning. | It is said that those who did this to al-Uqayshir were the 250
clients of Isḥāq ibn Ṭalḥah ibn ʿUbayd Allāh;[1127] al-Uqayshir had been fond of lampooning him.

[§109 Tawbah ibn al-Ḥumayyir[1128]]

Another is Tawbah ibn al-Ḥumayyir, a member of the Banū Khafājah ibn ʿUqayl. The cause of his death was as follows. There had been altercations between him and the Banū ʿĀmir ibn ʿAwf[1129] ibn ʿUqayl (they are the clan of Naṣr ibn Shabath[1130]). Tawbah had been involved in a quarrel between the Banū Khafā-

---

Tawba b. al-Ḥumayyir". Tawbah's unrequited love for the poet Laylā l-Akhyaliyyah (on her see Sezgin, *Geschichte*, ii, 399–400, *EI2*, "Laylā al-Akhyaliyya" [F. Gabrieli]) is told in *al-Aghānī* and other sources. See on him *ĞN*, i, 103, ii, 545; Sezgin, *Geschichte*, ii, 398–399; *EI2*, "Tawba b. al-Ḥumayyir" (T. El Achèche). For parallel versions of his death see Ibn Qutaybah, *Shiʿr*, 447, al-Iṣfahānī, *Aghānī*, xi, 210–217 (a close parallel, with Ibn Ḥabīb mentioned as a source) and 217–218 (another version).

1129 ʿASH and SKḤ: ʿAwf ibn ʿĀmir; corrected here following *Aghānī*, *ĞN*, and other sources.

1130 Naṣr ibn Shabath al-ʿUqaylī rebelled in 206–210/821–825 against the caliph al-Maʾmūn. The parenthesis is not in *Aghānī* and is possibly a later addition.

وبني عوف، وهم تختصمون عند هَمّام بم مطرِّف العُقيليّ، وكان مروان بن الحَكَم استعمله على صدقات بني عامر، فضرب ثَوْرُ بن أبي سِمْعان بن كعب بن عامر بن عوف بن عامر بن عقيل توبةَ بن الحُميّر بجُرْز وعلى توبة الدِّرع والبَيْضة، فجرح أنفُ البيضة وجهَه، وأمر همّام بثور بن أبي سمعان فأُقْعِد بين يديْ توبة، فقال: خذْ حقَّك يا توبة. فقال توبة: ما كان هذا الأمر إلّا عن أمرك، وما كان لِيجترئَ عليَّ عند غيرك يا همّام! وذلك أن أمَّ همّام من بني عوف بن عامر بن عُقيل.

فانصرف توبة ولم يقتصَّ، فمكثوا غير كثير. ثمّ إنّ توبة بلغه أنّ ثوراً خرج في نفر من أصحابه على ماء من مياه قومه يقال له هَويّ، يريد ماء لهم | يقال له حَريز، وهو موضع بتثليث، وبينهما ٢٥١
فَلاة من الأرض. فتبعهم توبة في أُناس من أصحابه حتّى ذُكر له أنّه عند رجل من بني عامر بن عُقيل، يقال له سارية بن عُوَيْمر بن أبي عَديّ، وكان صديقاً لتوبة، فقال توبة: واللّٰهِ لا أطرُقهم وهم عند سارية الليلة، حتّى يخرُجوا من عنده. فأرسل توبة رجليْن من أصحابه فقال: ارصُدوا القوم حتّى يخرجوا. وكان القوم أرادوا أن يخرجوا حين يُصْبِحون، فقال سارية: ادَّرِعوا الليل في الفلاة. وغفل صاحبا توبة، فلمّا ذهب الليلُ فزِع توبة وقال: لقد اغتررتُ برجليْن ما صَنَعا شيئاً، وإنّي لَأعلم أن لن يُصْبِحوا بهذه البلدة! فاستضاء لآثارهم، فإذا هو بآثار القوم قد خرجوا، فبعث إلى صاحبيْه فأتياه فقال: دُونكما هذا الجمل فأَوْقِراه من الماء ثمّ اتّبَعوا أثري؛ فإنّه لا يخفى عليكما حتّى تُدْرِكاني، وإنّي سأُوقِد لكما إن أمسيْتُما دوني.

1131 Hammām ibn al-Muṭarrif ibn ʿAbd Allāh, of Rabīʿah ibn ʿUqayl, see *ĞN*, i, 102.

1132 See above, §45.

1133 The context suggests that this is the clan ʿĀmir ibn ʿAwf ibn ʿUqayl just mentioned; alternatively, it is the much larger group ʿĀmir ibn Ṣaʿṣaʿah (see *ĞN*, i, 93), to which ʿUqayl belonged.

1134 See *ĞN*, i, 102, ii, 553, with Samʿān instead of Simʿān, the latter found in ʿASH and *Aghānī*.

1135 According to the old regulations of retaliation (*qiṣāṣ*), partly adopted in Islam, Tawbah would be entitled to inflict a similar injury on Thawr.

1136 The name of the mother, given in *Aghānī*, is Ṣūbānah (with variant Ṭūbānah) bint Jawn (variant Ḥazn) ibn ʿĀmir ibn ʿAwf ibn ʿUqayl.

jah and the Banū ʿAwf in the presence of Hammām ibn Muṭarrif al-ʿUqaylī,[1131] who had been appointed by Marwān ibn al-Ḥakam[1132] to raise the alms tax among the Banū ʿĀmir.[1133] Tawbah ibn al-Ḥumayyir was hit with an iron bar by Thawr ibn Abī Simʿān ibn Kaʿb ibn ʿĀmir ibn ʿAwf ibn ʿĀmir ibn ʿUqayl;[1134] Tawbah was wearing a coat of mail and a helmet. The nasal of his helmet wounded his face. At the order of Hammām, Thawr was made to sit before Tawbah. Hammām said to him, "Do to him what is your right!"[1135] Tawbah said, "This is only your order. He would not have dared to hit me if someone else than you had been here, Hammām!" The point was that Hammām's mother belonged to the Banū ʿAwf ibn ʿĀmir ibn ʿUqayl.[1136] Tawbah left without having retaliated.

A short time afterwards Tawbah learned that Thawr had gone out with some of his men to a waterhole of his tribe called Hawiyy,[1137] intending to go to a waterhole of theirs | called Ḥarīz,[1138] which is a place in Tathlīth.[1139] Between 251
the two lies a wasteland. Tawbah followed them together with some of his own people. It was reported to him that Thawr was staying with a man of the Banū ʿĀmir ibn ʿUqayl called Sāriyah ibn ʿUwaymir ibn Abī ʿAdī,[1140] who was a friend of Tawbah's. "By God," Tawbah said, "I will not attack them tonight, now that they are with Sāriyah, but I'll wait until they leave". Tawbah sent two of his men, saying, "Keep an eye on those men until they leave!" The men intended to leave in the morning, but Sāriyah said, "You should go out into the wasteland in the dark, tonight!"

Tawbah's two men were inattentive and when the night had passed Tawbah said, "I have been deceived by those two men who did nothing! I knew very well that they would not leave in the morning in this terrain." When it was light he looked for their tracks[1141] and indeed he found the tracks of the men after they had left. He sent for his two companions and when they came he said, "Here is a camel. Load it with water, then follow my tracks. They will be clear to you until you overtake me. I'll light a fire for you if you have not yet reached

---

1137 In *Aghānī* it is Qūbāʾ (or Qawbāʾ).

1138 *Aghānī*: "intending to go to their property (*mālahum* instead of *māʾan lahum*) at a place called Jurayr."

1139 Tathlīth lies near Mecca (Yāqūt, *Muʿjam al-Buldān*).

1140 In *Aghānī* he is Sāriyah ibn ʿUmayr ibn Abī ʿAdī; in *ǦN* i, 140, ii, 580 one finds his father as ʿUwaymir ibn Abī ʿAdī ibn ʿĀmir ibn ʿUqayl.

1141 It is possible that *fa-staḍāʾa li-āthārihim* is a corruption of *fa-qtaṣṣa āthārahum* ("he followed their tracks") as in *Aghānī*.

ثمّ خرج توبة في إثر القوم مُسْرِعاً حتّى انتصف النهار وجاوز عَلَماً يقال له أفيح في الغائط،
٢٥٢ فقال لأصحابه: هل تروْن ماءً بين سَمُراتٍ إلى جنب | قرون بَقَر، فإنّ ذلك مَقِيل القوم ولن
يجاوزوه، وليس وراءه ظِلّ. فنظر فقال قائل: نرى رجلاً يقود بعيراً كأنّه يقوده لصيْد. قال: ذلك ابن
الحَبْتَرِيّة، وذلك أَرْمى مَن رمى، فمن له أن يختلجه دون القوم فلا يَنْذَرون بنا؟ فقال عبد الله
بن الحميّر: أنا له. قال: فاحذَرْ أن يَعْقِر بك، وإن استطعتَ أن تَحول بينه وبين أصحابه فافعلْ.
فخلّى طريق فرسه في غَمْض من الأرض ثمّ دنا منه فحمل عليه، فرماه ابن الحَبْتَرِيّة فعقر فرسَ
عبد الله، واختلّ السهمُ ساقَ عبد الله، وانحدر الرجل حتّى أتى أصحابه فأنذرهم، فجمعوا
الرِّكاب وهي متفرّقة، وغَشِيَهم توبة ومن معه، فلمّا رأوْا ذلك صفُّوا رِحالَهم، وجعلوا السَّمُرات
في نحورهم، ثمّ أخذوا سلاحهم وزحف إليهم توبة، فارتمى القوم لا يُغْني أحدٌ منهم في أحد
شيئاً. ثمّ إنّ توبة وكان يُترِّس لأخيه عبد الله قال: يا أخي لا تترّسْ لي؛ فإنّي قد رأيت ثوراً يُكْثِر
٢٥٣ رَفْعَ الرأس، عسى أن أُوافق عند رفعه أناةً منه مَرْمًى فأرْمِيَه. ففعل فرماه توبة فأصابه على | حَلَمة
ثَدْيه، وصرعه، وجال القوم وغَشُوهم فوضعوا فيهم السلاح حتّى تركوهم صَرْعى، وهم تسعة
نفر.

ثمّ إنّ ثوراً قال: انزِعوا هذا السهم عنّي. فقال توبة: ما وضعناه مكانه لننزِعه! وقال أصحاب
توبة لتوبة: انْجُ فخذْ آثارنا لنلقى[١] راويتَنا، فقد متْنا عَطَشاً. فقال توبة: وكيف بأُولى القوم الذين لا
يُمْنَعون ولا يمتنعون؟ قالوا: أبْعَدَهم الله. قال: ما أنا بفاعل، وما هم إلّا عشيرتكم، ولكنْ تأتي

---

١ ك: (نلقى).

1142 Reading uncertain. ʿASH vowels this as Afyaḥ, but it may be that it is either Afīḥ or Ufayḥ, cf. Yāqūt, *Muʿjam al-Buldān* (where some verses are quoted the metre of which does not allow reading Afyaḥ); but Abū ʿUbayd, *Muʿjam*, 177–178 distinguishes between Afīḥ/Ufayḥ and Afyaḥ, which is said to be a land-mark (*ʿalam*) in the territory of the Banū ʿUqayl.

1143 Qurūn Baqar, said by Abū ʿUbayd, *Muʿjam*, 1069, to be a location in the territory of the Banū ʿUqayl, and by Yāqūt, *Muʿjam al-buldān*, a place in the territory of the Banū ʿĀmir adjacent to the Balḥārith ibn Kaʿb.

1144 *Fa-naẓara*, possibly an error for *fa-naẓarū* ("they looked"), as in *Aghānī*.

1145 *Narā*, possibly an error for *arā* ("I see"), as in *Aghānī*.

1146 He has not been found elsewhere. In *Aghānī* it is added that the Banū l-Ḥabtar belong to Madhḥij "among the Banū ʿUqayl"; which I do not understand. Ibn al-Kalbī mentions Ḥabtar ibn ʿAdī, a branch of Khuzāʿah (*ǦN*, i, 198, ii, 290).

me this evening." Then Tawbah set out, quickly following the tracks. At midday, having come past a road-mark called Afyaḥ[1142] in some low-lying ground, he said to his companions, "Do you see a waterhole between some acacia trees, next to | Cows' Horns?[1143] For that is where the men will take a rest. They will 252
not have passed it, for there is no shade to be found beyond it." He looked,[1144] and someone said, "We see[1145] a man leading a camel, as if leading it for a hunt." Tawbah said, "That is Ibn al-Ḥabtariyyah.[1146] He is the best shot of all those who shoot arrows. Who is willing to take him off but without alerting the men?" ʿAbd Allāh ibn al-Ḥumayyir[1147] said, "I'll do it!" Tawbah said, "Take care he won't wound[1148] your horse! If you can, move between him and his fellows!" ʿAbd Allāh made his horse swerve along a hollow patch and then approached the man and attacked him. But Ibn al-Ḥabtariyyah shot an arrow and wounded ʿAbd Allāh's horse; the arrow also pierced ʿAbd Allāh's leg. The man went off to join his fellows and warned them. They assembled their mounts, which had been dispersed. Tawbah and his men attacked them. When they saw that, they aligned their camel saddles in a row, sought shelter behind the acacia trees, and took up their weapons. Tawbah advanced towards them, but when the men threw themselves on their opponents no one was able to achieve anything. Tawbah, who was protecting his brother ʿAbd Allāh with his shield, said, "Brother, don't shield me, for I see that Thawr[1149] often raises his head.[1150] Perhaps when he keeps it raised long enough I have a chance to hit him when I shoot." His brother complied, Tawbah shot at Thawr and hit him in | the nipple on his chest, 253
felling him. The men swerved and they attacked them with their swords until they left them struck down, nine[1151] men in all.

Thawr said, "Pull that arrow from me!" But Tawbah said, "We did not put it there for it to be pulled out!" Tawbah's men said to him, "Save yourself, take your revenge and let us join the camel that carries our water, for we are dying of thirst!" Tawbah replied, "What about these men lying exposed, unable to defend themselves?" "May God remove them!", they answered.[1152] But Tawbah said, "I will not allow that; they are your kinsmen, after all. But let the camel with the

1147 Tawbah's brother.

1148 The verb *ʿaqara* usually means "to hamstring" or "to hock", with a sword or knife. The context requires "wounded" or "struck down".

1149 Thawr ibn Abī Simʿān, mentioned above.

1150 *Aghānī*: "his shield" (*al-turs*), which may be a better reading in view of the following.

1151 *Aghānī*: "seven".

1152 Or, more idiomatically, "May the Devil take them!"

الرواية فأَضَع لهم ماء، وأغسل دِماءهم وأخيِّل عليهم من السِّباع والطير لا تأكلهم حتّى أُوذِن بهم من بعضَ قومهم.

فأقام توبة حتّى أتتهم الرواية قبل الليل، فسقاهم من الماء وغسل عنهم الدماء، وجعل في أساقيهم ماء، ثمّ خيّل عليهم بالثياب على الشجر، ومضى حتّى طرق من الليل ساريةَ فقال: إنّا قد تركنا رهطاً من قومكم بالسمُرات من قرون بقر فأدرِكوهم، فمن كان حيًّا فداوُوه، ومن كان ميِّتاً فادْفنوه. ثمّ انصرف ولحق بقومه. فصبّح ساريةُ القوم فاحتملهم، وقد مات ثورٌ ولم يمتْ غيرُه.

ولم يزل توبة لهم خائفاً، فكان السَّليل بن ثور المقتول رامياً كثير الشرّ والبَغْي، فأُخبِر بغِرّة من توبة، وهو بقُنّة لهم من قِنان السَّرْو سَرْو لُبْن، | يقال لها قُنّة ابن الحُميّر، فركب في نحو من ٢٥٤
ثلاثين فارساً حتّى يطرُقه فتوقّل توبة ورجلٌ من أصحابه في الجبل وأحاطوا بالبيوت، فناداهم توبة: هنا من تبتغون،[١] فاجتنِبوا البيوت. فقال بعضهم لبعض: إنّكم لن تستطيعوه في الجبل، ولكنْ خُذوا ما استطفّ لكم من ماله. فاخذوا أفراساً له ولإخوته، ثمّ انصرفوا. فغزاهم توبة حتّى انتهى إلى مكان يقال له حجْر الراشدة ظليلٍ، أسفلُه كالعَمود وأعلاه منتشر، فاستظلّ فيه وأصحابه، حتّى إذا كان بالهاجرة مرّت به إبل هُبَيرة بن السَّمين، أخي بني عامر بن عوف[٢] بن عُقيل، فأخذها وخلّى طريق راعيها، فلمّا ورد العبد على مولاه أخبره، فنادى في بني عوف فقال: حتّى متى هذا؟ فتعاقد منهم نحوٌ من ثلاثين فارساً فاتّبعوه، ونهضت امرأة من خَثْعَم كانت فيهم، وكانت تؤخِّذ، فقالت: أَروني أَثَرَه، فخرجوا بها وأروْها أثره، فأخذت من تُرابه وقالت: اطلُبوه فإنّه محتبس عليكم. فطلبوه فسبقهم، وخرج توبة حتّى إذا كان بالمَضْجع من أرض بني كِلاب،

١ ك: (يبتغون).

٢ هـ، ك: (عوف بن عامر) والتصحيح من المراجع، كما سبق.

1153 *Ukhayyilu ʿalayhim*, cf. Lane, *Lexicon*: *khayāl*: "A piece of wood with black garments upon it ... in order that the wolf, seeing it, may think it to be a man".

1154 *Sarw* here means "slope of a mountain"; for Sarw Lubn see Abū ʿUbayd, *Muʿjam*, 736.

water come here, then I'll wash their blood away and put a scarecrow[1153] over them so that the wild beasts and birds will not eat them, until we have let some of their people know about them."

Tawbah stayed there until the camel came with the water, before nightfall. He gave the wounded men water, washed the blood off, and put water in their water-skins. Then he draped some clothes over the shrubs by way of scarecrows. He left and in the night he arrived at Sāriyah and told him, "We left some of your men at the acacia trees next to Cows' Horns. Go to them and treat those that are wounded and bury the dead." Then he left and joined his people. Sāriyah went to his men and carried them away; Thawr had died but the others had not.

Tawbah remained living in fear. Al-Salīl, the son of Thawr who was killed, was a good shot and prone to much evil and wrongdoing. He was told that Tawbah could be surprised while at a hillock of theirs, Sarw Lubn, one of the Sarw hillocks[1154] | called "Ibn al-Ḥumayyir's hillock". He rode with some thirty horse- 254
men and reached him at night. Tawbah went up the hill together with one of his men. The others surrounded the tents. Tawbah called out to them, "The one you want is here! Leave the tents alone!" They said to one another, "We won't be able to get at him on the hill, but let's take whatever we can find of his livestock." They took some of the horses belonging to him and his brothers; then they left. Tawbah went after them on a raid, until he came to a place full of shade called Ḥajar al-Rāshidah,[1155] its lower part like a column and spreading wide at the top. He and his companions sat there in the shade until, at midday, the camels of Hubayrah ibn al-Samīn came past, one of the Banū ʿĀmir ibn ʿAwf ibn ʿUqayl.[1156] Tawbah took the camels, letting the camel-herd go free. When the slave reached his master he told him what had happened. Hubayrah called out to the Banū ʿAwf, saying, "How much longer will this go on?" Some thirty horsemen of them agreed to go after Tawbah.

There was a woman of Khathʿam with them who practised magic. She stood up and said, "Show me his tracks!" They took her with them and showed her the tracks. She picked up some of the earth and said, "You must seek him, for he will be held up." They went after him but he outstripped them. Tawbah went on until he reached a resting-place in the territory of the Banū Kilāb, which he

---

1155 Thus Abū ʿUbayd, *Muʿjam*, 626; *Aghānī* has Ḥajr al-Rāshidah, and Yāqūt, *Muʿjam al-buldān*, has Ḥujr al-Rāshidah. Pictures of several toadstool-shaped rocks alleged to be the one mentioned here may be found on the Internet.

1156 As before (note 1129), the text (which has ʿAwf ibn ʿĀmir ibn ʿUqayl) has been emended.

جعل نِذارتَه[١] ويحبس أصحابه، حتّى إذا كان بشِعْب من هَضْبة يقال بنت هَيْدة، | جعل ابنَ ٢٥٥
عمّ له يقال له قابض بن عبد الله على رأس الهضبة، وقال: انظرْ فإنْ شَخَصَ لك شيءٌ فأَعْلِمْناه. فقال عبد الله أخو توبة له: يا توب إنّك حائن أُذكِّرك اللّهَ إلّا نجوتَ، فواللّهِ ما رأيت يوماً أشبه بسَمُرات بني عوف يومَ أدركناهم وساعتَهم التي أتيناهم فيها منه، فانْجُ إن كانت لك[٢] نَجاةٌ!

ثمّ إنّ القوم لَحِقوهم فحمل أوّلهم حتّى غَشُوا توبة، وفَزِع توبة وأخوه فقام إلى فرسه فغلبتْه أن يُلْجِمها،[٣] فخلّى طريقها، وغَشِيَه الرجل فاعتنقه، فصرعه توبة وهو مدهوش قد لَبِس الدِّرْع على السيف، فانتزعه ثمّ أهوى به ليزيد بن رُوَيْبة فاتّقاه بيديْه فقطع منها، وجعل يزيد يناشده الرَّحِم، وغشي القوم توبة من ورائه فضربوه حتّى قتلوه، وعَلِقَهم عبد الله بن الحُميّر يطعنهم بالرمح حتّى انكسر. فلمّا فرغوا من توبة مالوا على عبد الله أخيه فقطعوا رِجله فجعل يقول: هَلُمَّ! ولم يشعُر القومُ أنّهم قطعوا رجله، وانصرف القوم.

[§ ١١٠] **ومنهم** زيادة بن زيد بن مالك وهُدْبة بن خَشْرَم بن كُرْز بن جَحْش العُذْريّان. وكان ٢٥٦
سبب قتلهما أنّهما أقبلا من الشام في ناس من قومهما، فقالوا: من يَسوق بنا؟ فقال زيادة: أنا أسوق بكم. فنزل فساق بهم ساعة، ثمّ ارتجز فقال وعرّض بأختِ هُدبة:

---

١ كذا في الأغاني، وفي هـ، ك: (يُدَاريه).

٢ هـ: (بك)، كما في الأغاني.

٣ كذا في الأغاني، وفي هـ، ك: (يلحقَها).

1157 Instead of *jaʿala yudārīhi* (ʿASH, SKḤ), of which I cannot make sense, I have adopted the reading of *Aghānī*, xi, 215: *jaʿala nidhāratahū*. An editorial note offers an explanation: "If this is the correct reading, then the sense may be: 'He set up someone to warn him about the enemy', i.e., he set him where he would find out about the enemy if they came, so that he could inform him about them."

1158 Bint Haydah; see Abū ʿUbayd al-Bakrī, *Muʿjam*, 1358–1359, calling it Haydah and recording the variants Bint Haydah, Bint Haydhah, and Bint Hind. *Aghānī* has Hind.

1159 *Aghānī*, xi, 216 adds a passage describing how the men, not finding tracks, force a man of Ghanī to admit that he saw their camels on the hill. They send one of theirs, Yazīd ibn Ruwaybah (see below), to explore.

1160 *Aghānī*: "he went".

1161 Adopting the reading of *Aghānī*, *an yuljimahā*, instead of *an yalḥaqahā* (ʿASH, SKḤ).

1162 See on him above, note 1159. In the second account of Tawbah's death in *Aghānī*, xi, 218, he is called a beardless young man (*ghulām amrad*) and identified as Yazīd ibn Ruwaybah ibn Sālim ibn Kaʿb ibn ʿAwf ibn ʿĀmir ibn ʿUqayl.

1163 *Aghānī*, xi, 216 adds that he kept fighting, crouching on his knees.

1164 On Ziyādah, see *ǦN*, i, 330, ii, 608; Sezgin, *Geschichte*, ii, 266. On Hudbah, see *ǦN*, i, 330,

made a vantage post[1157] and where he kept his companions. When he reached a gorge at a hill called "Haydah's Daughter"[1158] | he placed a cousin of his called 255
Qābiḍ ibn ʿAbd Allāh on the summit of the hill. "Keep watch," he said, "and if something appears let us know." Tawbah's brother ʿAbd Allāh said to him, "O Tawbah! You're a goner! I tell you, in God's name, save yourself! For, by God, it looks today very much like the time of the acacia trees of the Banū ʿAwf, on the day we hit upon them, the moment we went at them! Save yourself, if you can still be saved!"

Then the men reached them.[1159] The foremost man of them attacked and they went[1160] for Tawbah. He and his brother were alarmed and Tawbah ran to his horse, but it resisted him and would not be bridled,[1161] so he let it go. The attacker seized him by the neck and Tawbah struck him down. He was at a loss because he had put on his coat of mail on top of his sword. He extricated it and with it hewed down upon Yazīd ibn Ruwaybah,[1162] who warded off the blow with his hands; Tawbah cut off one of them. Yazīd cried out for mercy, but some men attacked Tawbah from behind, striking him until they killed him. ʿAbd Allāh ibn al-Ḥumayyir joined the fray, stabbing them with his lance until it broke. When they had finished off Tawbah they turned on his brother ʿAbd Allah and cut off his foot. He began to shout, "Come on!" and the men were not even aware that they had cut off his foot; then the men left.[1163]

[§ 110 Ziyādah ibn Zayd ibn Mālik and Hudbah ibn Khashram[1164]]

Among them are Ziyād ibn Zayd ibn Mālik and Hudbah ibn Khashram ibn Kurz 256
ibn Jaḥsh, both of ʿUdhrah. They were killed because of the following. They came from Syria[1165] among some men of their tribe. Some said, "Who will urge us on?"[1166] Ziyādah said, "I will." He dismounted and urged them on for a while. Then he said, in *rajaz* verse,[1167] suggestively mentioning Hudbah's sister,

---

ii, 286; Sezgin, *Geschichte*, ii, 265–266. The main sources on Hudbah are Ibn Qutaybah, *Shiʿr*, 691–695; al-Mubarrad, *Kāmil*, iii, 277–279; al-Iṣfahānī, *Aghānī*, xxi, 253–274; al-Tibrīzī, *Sharḥ Dīwān al-ḥamāsah*, 334–340; al-Ṣafadī, *Wāfī*, xxvii, 334–337; al-Baghdādī, *Khizānah*, ix, 329–340. A book on the events, which took place over several years during the 50s/670s, by al-Zubayr ibn Bakkār (d. 256/870), *Akhbār Hudbah ibn Khashram wa-akhbār Ziyādah* is mentioned by Ibn al-Nadīm, *Fihrist* (ed. Sayyid), i, 342. His poetry has been collected by Yaḥyā al-Jubūrī (Hudbah ibn Khashram, *Shiʿr*).

1165 Al-Shām may also be Damascus. The territory of the Banū ʿUdhrah was in the Northern Hijaz.

1166 Referring to driving on the camels with prodding or song.

1167 *Rajaz* was often employed for extemporising and also for urging on camels. Ziyādah's poem, in different versions, is also found in Ibn Qutaybah, *Shiʿr*, 691–692; al-Iṣfahānī, *Aghānī*, xxi, 256–257 with twelve verses, as in al-Baghdādī, *Khizānah*, ix, 335.

عُوجي علينا وارْبَعي يا[1] فاطما ... ما[2] دون أن يُرى البعيرُ قائما
فعوَّجتْ مُطَّرِداً[3] عُراهِما ... رَسْلاً يبُذُّ القُلُصَ الرواسما

في شعر طويل، فغَضِب هدبةُ ونزل وساق بهم، وعرّض بأخت زيادة، فقال في رجز له طويل:

باللّٰهِ لا يَشفي الفؤادَ الهائما ... تَمْساكُكَ اللبَّاتِ[4] والمآكِما
ولا اللِّمامُ دونَ أن تُفاغِما ... ولا الفِغام دون أن تُفاقما ٢٥٧
وتعْلُوَ القوائمُ القوائما

فغضِب[5] زيادة فارتجز بأخت هدبة فقال:

أَنْعُتُ آياتٍ لِكَيْما تَعْلمي ... بالخال بالكَشْح اللطيف الأهضَمِ
والشامةِ السوداءِ بالمخدَّمِ ... أتذكُرين ليلةً بإضَمِ
وليلةً أخرى بخَبْتِ العَلَمِ

فلمّا سمع هدبة هذه الأبيات أتى أختَه فشهر عليها السيف وقال: من أين عَلِمَ هذه العلاماتِ التي وصفك بها؟ فقالت: ويْحك، إنّ النساءَ أخبرنه عنّي. فكفَّ عنها. وقال هدبة يرجُز بأخت زيادة:

---

١ كلمة (يا) ناقصة في هـ، كـ، ويقتضيها السياق والعروض.

٢ كـ: (من).

٣ كـ: (مطّربا).

٤ كـ: (اللّبّابِ).

٥ (فغضِب ... بخَبْتِ العَلَمِ): ناقصة في كـ.

"Turn to us and be nice, Fāṭimah,
While the camels are not seen to rise yet!"
So she turned, going at a fair pace,
Outstripping fleet camels …

It was a long poem. Hudbah got angry. He dismounted and drove them. He suggestively mentioned Ziyādah's sister, in a long poem in *rajaz*:[1168]

By God, the enamoured heart will not be cured
By your holding her breasts and hips,
Nor by touching her without kissing her, 257
Nor by kissing her without screwing her,
With legs on top of legs!

Then Ziyādah got angry and made *rajaz* verse on Hudbah's sister:[1169]

I'll describe some marks, so that you will know:
A mole on the dainty, slender waist,
And a black birthmark on the shin:
Do you remember that night at Iḍam,
And another night in Khabt al-ʿAlam?[1170]

When Hudbah heard these verses he went to his sister with unsheathed sword. "How does he know about those marks he described you with?" he asked. "Shame on you!" she replied, "The women must have told him!"[1171] So he did not do anything to her. Hudbah made the following *rajaz* verses on Ziyādah's sister:[1172]

1168 Nine verses in Ibn Qutaybah, *Shiʿr*, thirteen in *Aghānī*, fourteen in *Khizānah*.

1169 Whereas Hudbah's riposte had used the same rhyme as Ziyādah's poem, here Ziyādah uses another rhyme, as is the case in each of the subsequent poems. This poem is not part of the story as told in the sources mentioned earlier, but it is found, with some variants in another story involving the poets al-Najāshī and ʿAbd al-Raḥmān ibn Ḥassān, who utters the lines (Ibn ʿAsākir, *Tārīkh Madīnat Dimashq*, xiv, 300–301).

1170 Various locations are given for Iḍam in Abū ʿUbayd al-Bakri, *Muʿjam*, 165–166 and Yāqūt, *Muʿjam al-buldān*. Khabt al-ʿAlam has not been found.

1171 Compare the similar motif in the story of Ibn al-Dumaynah (below, § 116).

1172 The verses have not been found elsewhere.

عُوجي علينا وارْبَعي يا طارفا   ما دون أن يُرى البعيرُ واقفا
ما اهتجْتُ حتّى هتكوا الخوالفا   غَدَوْا ورَدّوا جِلّةً مَقاذفا
ألا تَرَيْنَ الأعْيُنَ الذوارفا   حِذارَ دارٍ منكِ أن تساعفا

فغضب زيادة، وكان بين القوم سِبابٌ وشبيةٌ[1] بالقتال، فحُجز بينهم حتّى إذا | رجعوا إلى أهلِيهم ٢٥٨
تَهاجَيا وتفاخرا بأشعار كثيرة، وإنّ هدبة قال:

ناطُوا إلى قمر السماء أُنوفَهمْ   وعن التُّراب خدودُهم لا تُرفَعُ
وَلدتْ أُمَيْمةُ أعبُداً فغَدَتْ بهمْ   ثَجْلا إذا مشَتِ القوائمُ تَظْلَعُ
أَبَني أميْمةَ إنّ طالِعَ لؤْمِكمْ   لونٌ إذا وَضَحَ المراسِنُ أسفُعُ

قال: فغضب زيادة وأصحابه، فجاءوا إلى منزل هدبة ليلاً فأخذوه وأباه، فشجّوا أباه عَشْراً، ووقّفوا
هدبة، فقال زيادة:

شجَجْنا خَشْرَماً في الرأس عَشْراً   ووقَّفْنا هُدَيْبَةَ إذ هَجانا

فقال هدبة:

إنّ[2] الدهرَ مؤتنِفٌ طويلٌ   وشرُّ الخيل أقصَرُها عِنانا
وشرُّ القومِ كلُّ فتىً إذا ما   مَرَتْه الحربُ بعد العَصْب لانا

١ كـ (وشيبةٌ).
٢ كذا، وفي البيت خَرْم. وفي الشعر والشعراء لابن قتيبة (فإنّ الدهر).

1173 The translation of *ḥidhāra dārin minki an tusāʿifā* is uncertain; for the negative "not" (not in the Arabic) see Wright, *Grammar*, ii, 27, Reckendorf, *Arabische Syntax*, 52–53. This line occurs in a poem by Ziyādah in Ibn Qutaybah, *Shiʿr*, 691 and *Khizānah*, ix, 336 as *ḥidhāra dārin minki an tulāʾimā*; and in *Aghānī*, xxi, 256 with *lan tulāʾimā*.

1174 The poem is not found elsewhere. At this stage the two revert to metres other than *rajaz*, with one exception.

Turn to us and be nice, Ṭārifah,
While the camels are not yet seen to stand up!
I did not stir until they broke up the tent-poles;
In the morning they drove back the fast-running adult camels.
Don't you see my tearful eyes?
Beware of your abode, that it be not accessible![1173]

Ziyādah got angry. Insults were exchanged between the men and they almost came to blows but people kept them apart. When they | had returned home 258
they composed many lampoons and vaunting poems. Hudbah said,[1174]

They lifted their noses to the moon in the sky
  But their cheeks are not raised from the dust.
Umaymah gave birth to slaves; she went about with them
  big-bellied, legs limping.
Sons of Umaymah, the ascendant of your baseness
  is black in colour when noses are bright.[1175]

Ziyādah and his kin got angry. They went to Hudbah's dwelling at night, took his father and inflicted ten wounds on his head, and they branded Hudbah's arm.[1176] Ziyādah said,

We gave Khashram's head ten cracks
  and branded Hudaybah,[1177] since he lampooned us.

Then Hudbah said,[1178]

Fate recommences and lasts long.[1179]
  The worst horse is the one with the shortest rein.
The worst of people is a man who, after abstention fed
  with the milk of war, has become soft.

1175 Perhaps meaning "when other people's faces are bright".
1176 *Wa-waqqafū Hudbah*, following ʿASH's explanation, taken from Ibn Manẓūr, *Lisān al-ʿArab* (WQF), where the following verse is quoted.
1177 He uses the diminutive form, to demean and insult him.
1178 The lines are in Ibn Qutaybah, *Shiʿr*, 692 and the first line in al-Buḥturī, *Ḥamāsah*, 47 and al-Tibrīzī, *Sharḥ al-Ḥamāsah*, 336.
1179 Instead of *ṭawīl* ("long"), Ibn Qutaybah, *Shiʿr* has *jadīd* ("new").

فمكث هدبة ما شاء اللّٰه، حتّى إذا بَرئَ جَمَع لهم، فخرج إليهم بأصحابه فوجدوا زيادةَ ورُفَيْعًا وأَدْرَع، ولم يجِدوا من رجال الحيّ غيرَهم، فهرب رُفيع وأدرعُ لمّا رأَيا ما جَمَع القوم، وأخذوا زيادة فجدّعوه بسيوفهم حتّى إذا ظنّوا أنّهم قد قتلوه انصرفوا.

٢٥٩ وقد كان زيادة ذبَّ عن نفسه بالسيف فأصاب هدبةَ فجدّع أنفَه، فلمّا خلّفوا الحيّ وأشرفوا على الثَّنيّة وجد هدبةُ شفيفَ الريح في أنفه، فذهب ينظُر فإذا أنفُه قد جُدّع، فقال لأصحابه: انتظروا حتّى آتِيَكم، فواللّٰهِ لا أعيش أبداً ورجلٌ قد جدع أنفي! فرجع إلى زيادة وهو يقول:

أحْوَسُ في الحيِّ وبالرُّمْحِ خَطِلْ　　ما أحسنَ الموتَ إذا الموتُ نَزَلْ
فقد علِمَتْ أنّي إلى الهيْجا عَجْلْ　　إنّي امرؤٌ لا أقرب الضيْم بِغِلّ

فقتله وأدرك أصحابه. ثمّ إنّ هدبة أخذ أهلَه فجعل يؤامر نفسه، إمّا يأتي القومَ فيضع يدَه في أيديهم أو في يد السلطان. فأقبل حتّى وضع يده في يد سعيد بن العاص، وهو عامل معاوية على المدينة، فأطلق من كان سَجَنه[1] بسببه وسَجَنَه هو، فقال في السجْن أشعاراً كثيرة. ثمّ عُزل سعيدٌ ووُلِّيَ مروانُ بن الحكم مكانَه.

وإنّ بني عمّه قالوا: لو زوّجناه لعلّ اللّٰهَ أن يُبْقِيَ منه خَلَفاً! فزوّجوه وأدخلوا عليه امرأته في السجن، فلمّا رأت ما هو فيه هالَها، فراوَدَها فأبتْ عليه. ثمّ رُدَّ سعيد إلى المدينة فبلغه أنّ امرأة هدبة أبتْ عليه، فأمرها أن تُطِيعه فوقع عليها فحملتْ فولدتْ غلاماً سمّتْه هُدبة. ثمّ إنّ أصحاب هدبة أعطوْا به عَشْر دِيات، وأعطاهم سعيدُ بن العاص، وكان يومئذ على المدينة، مائةَ ألف

١ ك: (في سجنه).

1180 *Aghānī*, xxi, 258–259 lists a number of persons involved in the conflict. Among them is Adraʿ ibn al-Ghassāniyyah but Rufayʿ is not mentioned; there is probably a confusion between Naffāʿ, listed in *Aghānī*, and Rufayʿ.

1181 Hudbah reverts to *rajaz*.

1182 I take the fem. sing. to refer to the tribe.

1183 Interpretation uncertain; perhaps one ought to read *lā aqbalu* "will not accept" instead of *lā aqrabu*.

1184 Saʿīd ibn al-ʿĀṣ ibn Abī Uḥayḥah Saʿīd ibn al-ʿĀṣ ibn Umayyah (d. prob. 59/678–679), prominent member of the Umayyad dynasty, governor of Medina 49–54/669–674. See *ǦN*, i, 9, ii, 500; *EI2*, "Saʿīd b. al-ʿĀṣ" (C.E. Bosworth).

It took Hudbah some time to recover. Then he mustered some men and attacked with them his adversaries. They found Ziyādah, Rufayʿ, and Adraʿ[1180] but no other members of the tribe. When Rufayʿ and Adraʿ saw the multitude coming they fled. The men cut off Ziyādah's nose with their swords and they left, thinking they had killed him.

Ziyādāh had defended himself with his sword and had cut off Hudbah's nose. 259
When the men had left the tribe behind and were about to enter the mountain-pass Hudbah became aware of the wind blowing through his nose. He had a look, and yes! his nose had been cut off. He said to his companions, "By God, I cannot live while there's a man about who has cut off my nose!" He went back to Ziyādah, saying,[1181]

> A bold man in the tribe, quick with the lance—
> How good is death when death descends!
> They[1182] know I am quick to go into battle.
> I am a man who will not approach a wrong with rancour.[1183]

He killed him and joined his companions. He gathered his close kin to consult them about his case, either to deliver himself into the hands of Ziyādah's kinsmen, or to give himself up to the authorities. In the end he went and gave himself up to Saʿīd ibn al-ʿĀṣ, who was Muʿāwiyah's governor of Medina.[1184] Saʿīd imprisoned him and released those he had imprisoned on his account. Hudbah composed many poems in prison.[1185]

Then Saʿīd was deposed and Marwān ibn al-Ḥakam[1186] was appointed in his place. Hudbah's relatives said, "What if we let Hudbah get married! Then God may give him offspring." They arranged a marriage and brought his bride to the prison. When she saw him in his condition she was horrified. He attempted to entice her, but she refused.

Then Saʿid was reinstalled as governor of Medina. When he heard that Hudbah's wife had rejected his advances he ordered her to obey him. Hudbah had intercourse with her and she bore him a son whom she called Hudbah. Hudbah's people offered to pay ten *diyahs*[1187] and Saʿīd ibn al-ʿĀṣ, then governor

---

1185 For five long poems, four of them composed in prison, see Ibn Maymūn, *Muntahā*, iii, 217–231.

1186 See § 45.

1187 On *diyah* "blood money", see above, § 6. It is not clear why it is offered tenfold here; Ibn Qutaybah *Shiʿr*, 693 and *Aghānī*, xxi, 262 mention merely *al-diyah* "the blood money".

٢٦٠ درهم، فأبوْا وكان سعيد لا يألو ما ردّهم، وإنّه سألهم: هل لزيادة وليٌّ سِوى | أختِه؟ فقيل: له ابنٌ
صغير لم يُدْرِك. قال: فليس لنا أن نقتله حتّى يُدرِكَ الغلام.

فحُبس هدبة حتّى أدرك الغلام، فلمّا أدرك جاءت به أمُّه تطلُب قتل هدبة، فدُفع إليها وأُعطِيَ الغلامُ دياتٍ كثيرة فطَمِع، فقالت له أمّه: واللّٰهِ لئن فعلتَ لَأتزوّجنّ رجلاً أَهَبُ له نصيبي من الديات ثمّ يقاسمكها! فجسر على قتل هدبة، فأُخْرِجَ من السجن فأُدْخِل على سعيد، وهو في جُنْبَذة له مُشْرفة، ودخل معه الأخزَر عبد الرحمن [بن] زيد أخو زيادة، فقال له سعيد: يا أخزر، قد أعطاك أميرُ المؤمنين معاوية مائةَ ألف، وعبد اللّٰه بن جعفر مائةَ ألف، والحسن والحسين مائةَ ألف، وأنا أُعطيك مائة ناقة سُود الحَدَق ليس فيها جَدّاء ولا خَدّاء[١] ولا ذاتُ داء. فقال عبد الرحمن: أصلح اللّٰه الأمير، واللّٰهِ لو وهبتَ لي جُنْبَذتك هذه ثمّ سكبتَ فيه الذهب حتّى يخرجَ من ثَقْبها ما كنتُ لِأختارَه على هذا الخلسيّ الأسود عبدِك! فقال له هدبة: يا أُخَيْزِر، أوَبالموت تُخوّفني؟ واللّٰهِ لا أُبالي أَسَقط عليّ أم سقطتُ عليه، فاصنعْ ما أنت صانع! ثمّ رُدّ إلى السجن.

وخرج عبد الرحمن فأتى بكتاب معاوية: أن يُدفع[٢] هدبة إلى أولياء زيادة. فقال سعيد: يومَ
٢٦١ الجُمعة أدفعه إليكم. فلمّا كان يوم الجمعة بعث إليه سعيد | بِلَوْزينَة وخُبْزة. فلمّا انصرف من

---

١ كذا في الأصل ولعلّ الصحيح ما يقترحه هـ: (خذواء) وهي المسترخية الأذن.

٢ ك: (ادفع).

1188 He was called al-Miswar as is made clear below (also *Aghānī*, xxi, 264, 272). Hudbah stayed in prison for three years (xxi, 264).

1189 *Junbadhah*, from Persian *jumbad*, "vault, arch, dome".

1190 ʿAbd Allāh ibn Jaʿfar ibn Abī Ṭālib (d. 80/699 or some years later), nephew of ʿAlī, the fourth caliph.

1191 *Laysa fīhā jaddāʾ wa-lā khaddāʾ wa-lā dhāt dāʾ*. The meaning of *khaddāʾ* is unknown and ʿASH's suggestion, reading *khadhwāʾ*, has been adopted in the translation. In Ibn Qutaybah, *Shiʿr*, 693 the governor offers "one hundred red she-camels, among them none that is dry-uddered or diseased".

1192 The sense of *al-kh.l.sī* is unknown. I have assumed it to be a variant of *al-khilāsī*; cf. al-Jāḥiẓ, *Bighāl*, 298 on mixed breeds of poultry and dogs: *al-dajjāj al-khilāsī min bayn al-Nabaṭī wa-l-Hindī, wa-idhā kāna mithl dhāka bayn al-bayḍāʾ wa-l-Ḥabashī fa-huwa*

of Medina, offered one hundred thousand dirhams, but Ziyādah's kinsmen refused to accept them. Saʿīd spared no efforts in trying to turn them round. He asked them, "Is there someone who can act as Ziyādah's legal executor other than | his sister?" They said, "He has a small son who has not yet reached 260
puberty." Saʿīd said, "Then we cannot let Hudbah be killed until the boy has reached puberty."[1188]

So until that time Hudbah was kept in prison. When the boy had reached puberty his mother took him and demanded that Hudbah be executed. Many *diyah*s were offered to her and the boy. The boy was eager to accept them, but his mother said to him, "I swear by God, if you do that I'll marry a man and give him my share of the *diyah*s and then he will have half your original share!" Then the boy was encouraged to kill Hudbah. He was taken from prison and brought before Saʿīd, who was seated in one of his high, domed pavilions.[1189] Al-Akhraz ʿAbd al-Raḥmān ibn Zayd, Ziyādah's brother, also went in. Saʿīd said to him, "Akhraz! You are given one hundred thousand dirhams by Muʿāwiyah the Commander of the Believers; and one hundred thousand from ʿAbd Allāh ibn Jaʿfar;[1190] and one hundred thousand from al-Ḥasan and al-Ḥusayn. Moreover, I will give you one hundred she-camels with black eyes, among them none that is dry-uddered, slack-eared, or diseased."[1191] Al-Akhraz replied, "May God make the emir prosper! I swear by God, if you were to give this pavilion of yours and gold were poured into it until it spilled from its opening, I would not prefer it to this black half-breed,[1192] your servant!" Hudbah said to him, "Ukhayriz![1193] Are you trying to make me afraid of dying? I swear by God, I don't care whether death befalls me or you. Do what you must do!"

Then he was taken back to prison. ʿAbd al-Raḥmān went and came back with a letter from Muʿāwiyah, saying that Hudbah should be given over to Ziyādah's legal executors. Saʿīd said, "On Friday I shall deliver him to you." On Friday Saʿīd sent Hudbah | a piece of pastry with almond filling[1194] and a piece of bread. 261

---

khilāsī, fa-idhā kāna bayn al-bayḍā' wa-l-Sindī fa-huwa baysarī, wa-ka-dhālika l-khilāsī min al-kilāb alladhī bayn al-Kurdī wa-bayn al-Salūqī. It seems that al-Akhraz literally refers to the governor's slave and not to Hudbah, for there is no indication that Hudbah was of mixed descent; the name of his mother (also a poet) is given as Ḥayyah bint Abī Bakr ibn Abī Ḥayyah (*Aghānī*, xxi, 254).

1193 I follow Hārūn, who adopted al-Shinqīṭī's emendation of *yā khinzīr* ("You swine!") to *yā Ukhayriz*, with the diminutive form of al-Akhraz, here used in order to demean and insult him.

1194 *Lawzīnah*, more often *lawzīnaj*, a much-loved confection (through its use in medical texts this Arabo-Persian word ended up in English as "lozenge").

الصلاة دفعه إليهم، فخرجوا به يسوقونه فمرّ بقومٍ جلوسٍ تحت حائط فقال: يا هؤلاء قُوموا فإنّ هذا الحائط واقعٌ عليكم! فقالوا: ما رأينا مثل هذا، يُساق إلى الموت ويَحذر الحائط! فلم يكن إلّا قليلاً حتى سقط الحائط. ومرّ على بَنّاء يبْني حائطاً فقال: ويْحك عوّجْتَ حائطك! وكان أبواه[١] وامرأته يمشيان على أثره، فنادتْه امرأته: يا هدبة يا هدبة! فالتفتَ، فقطعت قَرْناً من قرون شَعرها، ثمّ نادته ثانية فالتفت، فقطعت قرناً. فناشدوه اللّٰه أن لا يلتفت إليها. ثمّ التفت إلى أبويْه وهما يبكيان فقال:

أَبْلِياني اليومَ صبْراً منكُما   إنّ حُزناً منكما عاجلُ ضَرّْ
لا أرى ذا الموتَ إلّا هيِّناً   إنَّ بعد الموت دارَ المستقَرّ
اصبِرا[٢] اليومَ فإنّي صابرٌ   كلُّ حيٍّ لفَناءٍ وقَدَرْ

ثمّ قال لامرأته:

أقِلِّي عليَّ اللوْمَ يا أمَّ بَوْزَعا   ولا تَجْزَعي ممّا أصابَ فأَوْجَعا
وعِيشي حَبيساً أو تَفَتَّيْ بماجدٍ   إذا القومُ هشُّوا للسَّماح تبرَّعا
ولا تَنْكِحي إنْ فرّق الدهرُ بيننا   أغمَّ القَفا والوجهِ ليسَ بأنزعا
كليلاً سِوى ما كان من حَدِّ ضِرْسهِ   على الزاد مِبْطانَ الضُّحَى غير أروَعا

١ ك: (أبوه).
٢ ك: (اصبر).

1195 Thus ʿASH (*abawāhu*); SKḤ has "his father" (*abūhu*), which may be correct in view of the following dual verb form (but in what follows both parents are said to be present).
1196 Lines 1–2 in al-Mubarrad, *Kāmil*, iii, 279, all three in *Aghānī*, xxi, 270, al-Baghdādī, *Khizānah*, ix, 339.
1197 Instead of *fanāʾ*, "perdition, extinction", *Aghānī* has *qaḍāʾ* "(divine) decree".

Having left the Friday prayer he turned him over to them. They took him out and while they were going with him he came past some people sitting under a wall. "Stand up, you people!" he said, "for that wall is about to fall on you!" They said, "We've never seen anyone being marched to his death who is concerned about a wall!" Shortly afterwards the wall fell down. He also came past a builder building a wall. "Hey you!" he said, "You've not made your wall straight!"

His parents[1195] and his wife were walking behind him. His wife called out to him, "Hudbah! Hudbah!", so he turned to her. She cut off a lock of her hair. Then she called again, Hudbah turned round and she cut off another lock. They implored him not to turn to her again. Then he turned to his parents who were crying, and said,[1196]

Show me your strength today!
 Sorrow is a fleeting harm.
I find this death only a trifling matter.
 After death is the abode of stability.
Be strong today, for I shall be strong.
 Every living being is for extinction and destiny.[1197]

Then he said to his wife,[1198]

Lessen your blame of me, Umm Bawzaʿ,
 and do not grieve about what befalls and gives pain.[1199]
Live a secluded life, or else take yourself an illustrious man
 if the tribesmen are well-disposed to grant it.
But don't get married, if Fate separates us,
 to one with long hair on his neck and face, not keeping them free,
One who is feeble except with the edge of his molars
 on his food, a glutton in the forenoon, unadmired.[1200]

1198 See al-Mubarrad, *Kāmil*, iii, 278 (l. 3 with another line); Ibn Qutaybah, *Shiʿr*, 694 (l. 3 with a different line); al-Buḥturī, *Ḥamāsah*, 152–153 (ll. 2–4 with three more lines); *Aghānī*, xxi, 269 (ll. 1, 3–4 with two more lines), the same *Khizānah*, ix, 338.

1199 I take *fa-awjaʿā* to be a perfect tense (compare Mutammim ibn Nuwayrah's famous *Mufaḍḍaliyyah* no. 67 where the words *mimmā aṣāba fa-awjaʿā* occur in lines 1 and 39) but one is tempted to take it here as a subjunctive: "(do not grieve …) lest I will feel pain".

1200 In the other versions of this line, *arwaʿ* means "frightened, cowardly", but here, with *ghayr*, it must have a positive sense; cf. Lane, *Lexicon* ("who excites admiration and approval …").

فلما قُدّم ليُقتل قال:

إن تقتُلوني في الحديد فإنّني   قتلتُ أخاكمْ مُطْلَقاً لم يُقَيَّدِ ٢٦٢

فحلُّوا[١] قيودَه، فقال: دَعوني أصلّي ركعتيْن، فصلّى ثمّ التفت إلى عبد الرحمن أخي زيادة فقال: قم يا أخزر إلى جَزورك فانحَرْها! فقال عبد الرحمن: بل يقوم إليك من قتلتَ أباه ظالماً متعدّياً عليه [إن] قبِل ذلك منك. قم يا مِسْوَر! فقام إليه غلامٌ[٢] حين احتلم، وأمسك بعضُهم بيده فضربه، فتعلّق رأسُه بجِلدة من حَلْقه، فقال له عمّه: يا ابن أخي أَجهِزْ عليه، إيّاك [أنْ] تدَعَ لهم فَضلة! وإنّ امرأة هدبة أتت جزّاراً فأخذت مُدْية فجدعتْ أنفها وجاءته مجدوعةً ليعلم أنّها لا أَرَبَ لها في الرجال بعد الجَدْع. وذكروا أنّ هدبة قال: علامةُ ما بيني وبينكم إن جَزِعْتُ فإنّي إذا قُطِعَتْ رأسي مددتُ رِجلي وقَبَضتُها. وإنْ أنا بقِيتُ ممدودَ الرِّجلين فإنّي لم أجزَعْ. فلمّا سقط رأسه بقي باسطاً رجليْه.

[§١١١] **ومنهم** سالم بن دارة أخو بني عبد اللّٰه بن غطفان. وقد مرّ حديثه[٣] في المغتالين. ٢٦٣

[§١١٢] **ومنهم** عُقَيْبة بن هُبَيْرة الأسديّ أخو بني نصر بن قُعَيْن. وكان له بنت أو رَبيبة، وكان له ابن عمّ يقال له تميم بن الأخثم، وكانت له بُنَيّة، فلعبت هي وبنت عُقيبة، فكسرتْ بنتُ تميم

١ هـ: (فخلّوا).

٢ كـ: (الغلام) ولعلّها الصواب.

٣ الكلمة ناقصة في كـ.

1201 See above, § 38 and note 464.

1202 Oddly placed in the narrative, this event takes place before Hudbah's execution, as is also told in other sources. In another version she also cuts off her lips (*Aghānī*, xxi, 270).

1203 Compare the versions of, *Kāmil*, iii, 279 and *Aghānī*, xxi, 271–271. In the latter, Hudbah says, "I have heard that when someone is killed, he remains conscious for a short while after his head is cut off. If I'll be conscious I will bend and stretch my leg three times." And he does.

1204 Above, § 31.

1205 On his lineage see *ĞN*, i, 51. As a poet he is a very minor one; Sezgin has no entry for him and only a few fragments of his poetry are known, but he is at least honoured by the

When he was brought forward to be killed he said,

> You may kill me in chains, but I 262
> killed your brother when he was free, unshackled.

Then they released his chains. He said, "Let me pray two *rakʿah*s!"[1201] When he had performed them he turned to ʿAbd al-Raḥmān, Ziyādah's brother, and said, "Come, Akhraz, to your camel to be slaughtered and cut its throat!" But ʿAbd al-Raḥmān replied, "No, the one whose father you killed wrongly and brutally should do it to you, if he accepts. Come on, Miswar!" A young boy, only just having reached puberty, came forward. Someone took his hand and struck Hudbah, holding it. His head was dangling by the skin of his throat. The boy's uncle said to him, "Nephew, finish him off! Take care not to leave them anything of him!"

Hudbah's wife went to a butcher and took a knife. Then she cut off her nose and went to Hudbah,[1202] mutilated, so that he knew that she would have no interest in men, having her nose cut off.

They say that Hudbah said, "I'll make a sign between you people and me: if I am afraid, then, when my head is cut off I'll stretch my leg and fold it again. But if my legs remain stretched it means that I was not afraid." When his head fell his legs remained stretched.[1203]

[§ 111 Sālim ibn Dārah]

Another is Sālim ibn Dārah, of the Banū ʿAbd Allāh ibn Ghaṭafān. His story has 263
been told above, among the murder victims.[1204]

[§ 112 ʿUqaybah ibn Hubayrah al-Asadī[1205]]

Another is ʿUqaybah ibn Hubayrah al-Asadī, a member of the Banū Naṣr ibn Quʿayn. He had a daughter or foster-daughter. A paternal cousin of his was called Tamīm ibn al-Akhtham, who also had a little daughter. When she and ʿUqaybah's girl were playing together, Tamīm's daughter broke a front tooth of

---

inclusion of two of his verses in Sībawayh's *Kitāb* (i, 34, also Ibn Qutaybah, *Shiʿr*, 98–99, al-Baghdādī, *Khizānah*, ii, 260–263). A short poem by him is quoted in al-Iṣfahānī, *Aghānī*, xx, 363. The present sorry tale of excessive *talio* (a life for a milk-tooth) is also found in al-Balādhurī, *Ansāb*, vii, 28 and (virtually identical with the present version) in Ibn Ḥabīb, *Muḥabbar*, 218–221, where ʿUqaybah is listed under the *futtāk al-Islām*, "the murderous, reckless ones or hotheads of the Islamic period". A very brief account (without mention of the tooth and reading ʿUqbah instead of ʿUqaybah) has Ibn Abī Ṭāhir Ṭayfūr, *Balāghāt*, 285–286.

ثَنِيّةَ بنتِ عُقيبة، فذهب تميم فجمع أشرافَ بني أسد، فأتى عُقيبةَ لِما يعلم من فَتْكه، فقال له: يا ابن عمٍّ، إنّه قد كان ما ترى، فدونَك ابنتي فاكسِرْ ثنيّتَها، وإن شئتَ فالعَفْو، وهي جارية بعدُ لم تُثْغِر، وهي تنبُت. فقال القوم: أنصفك الرجلُ. فقال: واللّهِ لأقتلنّه. فأعادوا عليه، فأعاد عليهم مثلَ ذلك، فقالوا لتميم: [قُم].١ وظنّوا أنّ عُقيبة يلعب، وعرف تميم أنّه يفعل، لفتْكه.٢

فمكث تميم سنةً يتحرّز منه، وأمسى ذات يوم وهو صائم فصلّى في مسجد قومه، ثمّ دخل داره وغفل٣ أن يُغْلِق الباب، فدخل عليه عُقيبة بالسيف فضربه حتّى قتله، وتصايح النساء، وأُخذ عُقيبة فرُفع إلى مُصْعَب بن الزُّبير، فسأله فلم يجحَد قتْلَه. ولتميم ابن يقال له عَنْبَسة، فتًى شابٌّ، فأعطى فيه منصورٌ٤ دِيةً، | وأعطى محمّد بن عُمَير دية، وأعطى قومُه دية، فقالت ابنةٌ ٢٦٤
لتميم:

أعُقَيْبُ لا ظَفِرتْ يداك ألم يكنْ　　دَرَكٌ بحقّك غيرَ قتلِ تميمِ
أعُقَيبُ لو نبَّهْتَه لوجدْتَهُ　　كالسيف أهْوَنُ وقْعِه التصميمُ
فَلَتَتْبَعَنَّكَ في العشيرة سُبّةٌ　　ولَتُقْتَلَنّ به وأنت ذميمُ

وقال عُقيبة حين قتله:

خرَّ صريعاً فاغراً تمصُلُ اسْتُه　　بحيث التقينا كالحُوار المخزِّقِ

١ هـ: التكملة من المحبّر.
٢ ك: (لفتكه [وخبثه]) والتكملة من المحبّر.
٣ ك: (وأغفل).
٤ لعلّ الصواب (منظور) كما في المحبّر.

1206 Al-Balādhurī's version drastically shortens the action: when the girl's tooth was broken, "she went to her father, crying. He attacked Tamīm in his home and killed him."

1207 Abū ʿAbd Allāh Muṣʿab ibn al-Zubayr ibn al-ʿAwwām (d. 72/691), son of a famous companion of the Prophet and brother of the "anti-caliph" ʿAbd Allāh ibn al-Zubayr who resisted the Umayyads. Muṣʿab was governor of Iraq in the 60s/680s.

1208 Unidentified. In *Muḥabbar* it is Manẓūr, equally unknown. Hārūn thinks he may be Manẓūr ibn Zabbān ibn Sayyār, a prominent chief of Fazārah, father-in-law to ʿAbd

ʿUqaybah's daughter. Tamīm went and gathered the prominent men of Asad; then he went to ʿUqaybah, well aware of his hotheadedness (*fatk*). "Cousin," he said, "You know what happened. Here is my daughter: break her front tooth! Or if you prefer, my front tooth! Or if you wish, forget about the matter. Your daughter is a young girl who has not yet had her permanent teeth. It will grow again." Those present said, "He is giving you a fair deal!" But ʿUqaybah said, "I swear by God, I'll kill him!" They repeated what they had said, but so did he. They said to Tamīm, "Off you go!" They thought ʿUqaybah was jesting, but Tamīm, aware of his hotheadedness, knew that he would do as he had said.

A year long Tamīm remained on his guard against him. One evening when he was fasting he went to his tribe's mosque to perform the ritual prayer. Then he went home but he forgot to lock the door. ʿUqaybah burst in and struck him with his sword, killing him.[1206] The women started to scream and ʿUqaybah was apprehended and taken to Muṣʿab ibn al-Zubayr.[1207] When he was interrogated he did not deny the killing. Tamīm had a son called ʿAnbasah, a manly youth. Manṣūr[1208] offered to give the blood-money, | as did Muḥammad ibn 264
ʿUmayr.[1209] ʿUqaybah's kinsmen offered blood-money, too. But a daughter of Tamīm said,[1210]

> ʿUqaybah! May you be a loser![1211] Wasn't there
> a way to get your right without killing Tamīm?
> ʿUqaybah, if you had given him warning you would have found him
> like a sword, the least of its blows piercing you!
> Yes, dishonour will follow you among the tribe!
> Yes, you'll be killed in retaliation for him, and you'll be despised!

When he was about to be killed ʿUqaybah said,

> He fell, mouth wide open, his arse dripping
> where we met, like a defecating camel-calf!

Allāh ibn al-Zubayr. Or he could be Manẓūr ibn Qays ibn Nawfal, of Mālik ibn Naṣr ibn Quʿayn—Asad, like ʿUqaybah (*ǦN*, i, 51).

1209 Muḥammad ibn ʿUmayr ibn ʿUṭārid, of Tamīm (*ǦN*, i, 60 ii, 424), held leading positions in various places including Kufa.

1210 The lines are found also in *Muḥabbar* and Ibn Abī Ṭāhir Ṭayfūr, *Balāghāt*, 256. The rhyme of the opening line (*-īmī*) differs from that of the other lines (*-īmū*), a defect called *iqwāʾ*.

1211 Literally, "May your hands be unsuccessful!"

وأعطى أبو سَمّال[١] مائة ألف درهم، فطمِع عنبسةُ في أخذ الدية، فخرجت ابنةٌ لتميم حاسراً، وهي تقول:

إنْ يُـقْتَلْ عُقيبةُ يا لَقومٍ نسرَّ مَعاشراً ونَسُلَّ[٢] داءَ
وإنْ يَسْلَمْ عُقيبةُ يا لَقومٍ نكنْ خَدَماً لعُقْبَةَ[٣] أو إماءَ
لحى اللّٰهُ الذي يجتابُ منّا وعُقبةُ سالمٌ أبداً رِداءَ

فلمّا سمع القوم مَقالها وقد كانوا ركنوا إلى الصُّلح أحفظهم قولُها، ورجعوا عن الصلح، فدفعه إليهم، وجلس مُصْعَب يومئذٍ في المسجد واجتمع الناس، فقال عُقيبة لابنةٍ[٤] تميم حين أيقن بالقتل: أما واللّٰهِ لقد ضربتُ أباكِ ضربةً نظرتُ إلى الثُّرَيّا في سَلْحه! فقالت: أما واللّٰهِ لتُضْرَبَنّ ضربةً أنظرُ إلى بنات نَعْشٍ | في سلْحك! ثمّ التفت عُقيبة إلى الناس فقال: يا معاشرَ[٥] الناس! ٢٦٥ فجلس القائم وأسرع الماشي، فلمّا اجتمعوا قال: اسكُتوا، فواللّٰهِ ما قتلتُ ابن عمّي حين قتلته ألّا يكون قد أعطاني النَّصَفَ وزادني، ولكنْ نظرتُ إلى أمير المؤمنين عليّ، رضوانُ اللّٰه عليه، في هذا المكان الذي فيه الأمير وعَنَّ له تميمٌ من ناحية المسجد ونظر إليه عليٌّ فقال: مَن سرّه أن ينظر إلى جِذْل من أجذال جَهَنّم فلْينظُرْ إلى هذا، وأشار إليه، فرحم اللّٰه قاتلَه! فقتلته. فقال الناس: رحمك اللّٰه! وقُتل.

---

١ هـ، كـ: (سِماك)، والتصحيح من المحبّر وجمهرة النسب لابن الكلبيّ.
٢ كـ: (شرّ معاشرًا وَسُلّ).
٣ كـ: (لعُقيبةَ).
٤ كـ: (لابنه).
٥ كـ: (معشر).

1212 ʿASH, SKḤ: Abū Simāk; *Muḥabbar*: Abū Sammāl. He is clearly Abū Sammāl Simʿān ibn Hubayrah ibn Musāḥiq, of Quʿayn—Asad (*ĞN*, i, 51).

1213 The text ("a daughter") suggests this is another daughter; in *Balāghāt*, where this poem precedes the other, it is the same woman.

1214 She uses ʿUqbah in this and the following line as a variant of ʿUqaybah, for the sake of the metre.

Abū Sammāl[1212] offered to pay one hundred thousand dirhams and ʿAnbasah was tempted to accept the blood-money. Then another daughter[1213] of Tamīm stepped forward, unveiled, and said,

If ʿUqaybah is killed—O kinsmen, help me!—
 we shall gladden people and rid ourselves of a disease!
But if ʿUqaybah lives—O kinsmen, help me!—
 we shall be servants and slave-women to ʿUqbah.[1214]
May God revile those who tear their clothes[1215]
 while ʿUqbah's robe is whole!

The people had been inclined towards reconciliation, but when they heard her words their resentment was stirred and they abandoned thoughts of reconciliation. Muṣʿab delivered him to them. That day he was seated in the mosque and people were gathered there. When ʿUqaybah was certain he would be killed, he said to Tamīm's daughter, "I swear by God, I struck your father and saw his shit rise to the Pleiades!" She replied, "I swear by God, when you are struck I'll see your shit rise | to the Pole Star!"[1216] Then ʿUqaybah turned to the people and 265
said, "You people!" Those who were standing sat down, those going along hurried to be present. When all were gathered he said, "Be quiet! I swear by God, I did not kill my cousin when I killed him because he did not offer me fair compensation and more. But I saw ʿAlī, the Commander of the Believers (*r*), in this very place where the governor is sitting. Then Tamīm appeared to him near the mosque. ʿAlī looked at him and said, 'Whoever would like to look at a tree-trunk of the tree-trunks of Hell, let him look at that one!'—he pointed at Tamīm—'May God have mercy on the one who kills him!' So I killed him."[1217] The people said, "May God have mercy on you!" And he was killed.

1215 A reference to lamenting women rending their clothes. The feminine forms in *Muḥabbar* (*allatī tajtābu*) may be a better reading than the masculine forms (*alladhī yajtābu*) in the present text.

1216 *Banāt naʿsh* may refer to both Ursa Major and Ursa Minor (to which the Pole Star belongs).

1217 It is wholly unclear why the obscure Tamīm ibn al-Akhtham should have been singled out as an evil man by ʿAlī in ʿUqaybah's very unreliable account. ʿAlī died in 40/661, some decades earlier, so ʿUqaybah apparently claims to have seen him in a vision. Lichtenstädter's edition of *Muḥabbar* has a note (p. 221) with a comment by the Indian scholar Muhammad Hamidullah (1908–2002): "Look at ʿUqaybah's cheating, how he murdered Tamīm and then, despairing of his life, he accused him of unbelief! «God's curse be on those who lie!»" (quoting Q Āl ʿImrān 3:1).

[§١١٣] **ومنهم** أعشى هَمْدان وهو عبد الرحمن بن عبد الله[١] بن الحارث بن نِظام. وكان خرج مع عبد الرحمن بن محمّد بن الأشعث بن قيس، وكان له مدّاحاً، وقد كان قال في بعض ما يمدَحه به:

بينَ الأشجِّ وبين قيس باذخٌ   بَخْ بَخْ لوالده وللمولودِ

وقال يهجو الحجّاج: ٢٦٦

شطَّت نَوَى مَن دارُه بالإيوانْ   إيوانِ كِسْرى ذِي القُوَى والرَّيْحانْ
مِن عاشقٍ[٢] أَمسَى بزابُلِسْتانْ   والبَنْدَنيجَيْنِ إلى طَبَرْسِتانْ
إنَّ ثقيفاً منهم الكَذّابانْ   كذّابُها الماضي وكذّابٌ ثانْ

١ هـ، ك: (عبد الله بن عبد الرحمن) كما في الأصل، وهو واضح الغلط.
٢ هـ، ك: (مَن عاش)، والتصحيح من أنساب البلاذريّ وتاريخ الطبريّ وديوان أعشى همدان.

1218 Al-Āmidī, *Muʾtalif*, 12–21 lists 17 poets nicknamed al-Aʿshā ("the night-blind"). The most famous of them is the pre-Islamic Maymūn ibn Qays. Among the others the most prominent poet is without question ʿAbd al-Raḥmān ibn ʿAbd Allāh of the tribe Hamdān, who is therefore usually called "the al-Aʿshā of Hamdān". He was born in Kufa. For his lineage see *ǦN*, i, 228 and al-Iṣfahānī, *Aghānī*, vi, 33. On him, see *Aghānī*, vi, 32–62; Sezgin, *Geschichte*, ii, 345–346; *EAL*, 108 (G.J.H. van Gelder); *EI2*, "Aʿsh̲ā Hamdān" (A.J. Wensinck—G.E. von Grunebaum); *EI3*, "Aʿshā Hamdān" (Tilman Seidensticker). On his execution, which took place in 82/701 or the following year, see also al-Ṭabarī, *Tārīkh*, ii, 1113–1118 (year 81), tr. *The History*, xxiii 59–63; al-Masʿūdī, *Murūj*, iii, 362–363; al-Iṣfahānī, *Aghānī*, vi, 58–62.

1219 ʿASH and SKḤ, following the MS: ʿAbd Allāh ibn ʿAbd al-Raḥmān, which is clearly an error.

1220 He rebelled against the Umayyad governor Ibn al-Ḥajjāj in 80–82/699–702, see *EI2*, "Ibn al-As̲h̲ʿat̲h̲" (L. Veccia Vaglieri).

1221 Aʿshā Hamdān, *Dīwān*, 113 (in a poem of twelve lines); al-Ṭabarī, *Tārīkh*, ii, 1118; *Aghānī*, vi, 46, 61; al-Masʿūdī, *Murūj*, ii, 362.

1222 Al-Ashajj ("Scarface") is the nickname of al-Ashʿath (itself a nickname, "Rumple-hair") Maʿdīkarib ibn Qays, a famous chief of Kindah. See *EI2*, "al-As̲h̲ʿat̲h̲" (H. Reckendorf); *EI3*, "al-Ashʿath b. Qays" (Khalid Yahya Blankinship). The sense of "between" (*bayna*) is not entirely clear to me. Conceivably the word *bādhikhun* ("lofty peak") is a delayed predicate ("is lofty") of the word *al-majdu* ("glory") in the line that precedes.

[§ 113 Aʿshā Hamdān[1218]]

Another is Aʿshā Hamdān, who is ʿAbd al-Raḥmān ibn ʿAbd Allāh[1219] ibn al-Ḥārith ibn Niẓām. He had taken part in the rebellion of ʿAbd al-Raḥmān ibn Muḥammad ibn al-Ashʿath ibn Qays,[1220] on whom he had composed panegyric poems. In one of these he said on him:[1221]

Between al-Ashajj[1222] and Qays is a lofty peak:
Bravo to the father and the son!

Lampooning al-Ḥajjāj, he said,[1223] 266

Far away is he whose dwelling is the Arch,
The Arch of Kisrā,[1224] man of force[1225] and fragrant herbs,
Far from a lover who is now in Zābulistān,
And al-Bandanījayn as far as Ṭabaristān.[1226]
To Thaqīf belong two liars:[1227]
The past liar and the second.

1223 *Dīwān*, 163–164 (in a poem of twenty *rajaz* lines); al-Balādhurī, *Ansāb*, vii, 315; al-Ṭabarī, *Tārīkh*, ii, 1056–1057, tr. *The History*, xxiii, 7; *Aghānī*, vi, 59; al-Masʿūdī, *Murūj*, iii, 362–363. The poem opens with a short *nasīb*, about an absent beloved.

1224 Īwān Kisrā, also called (in Persian) Ṭāq-i Kisrā, the Arch of Khosraw, the famous reception hall of the Sasanid palace at Ctesiphon in Iraq, partially still standing. Kisrā is the Arabic form of Persian Khusraw (Greek Chosroes), name of several Sasanid emperors and in Arabic serving as a generic name of Sasanid rulers.

1225 Instead of *quwā* other versions have *qurā* ("towns, villages").

1226 Zābulistān is a region in what is now eastern Afghanistan. It had been the ruler of Zābulistān that al-Ḥajjāj had ordered Ibn al-Ashʿath to fight, but the latter turned against al-Ḥajjāj on account of his excessive demands in a serious rebellion that was suppressed only with difficulty. Al-Bandanījayn is a place in Iraq north-east of Baghdad (see Yāqūt, *Muʿjam al-buldān*); Ṭabaristān is the region south of the Caspian Sea (the metre requires reading it here as Ṭabarsitān). Instead, al-Balādhurī, *Ansāb* has Ṭ.rāzāstān, which is not only unmetrical but not found anywhere; the editor identifies it as Ṭirāz, somewhere in the land of the Turks (see Yāqūt, *Muʿjam al-buldān*). The *Dīwān* has Ṭardistān, not found elsewhere.

1227 Thaqīf is the tribe of al-Ḥajjāj. They were staunch opponents of the prophet Muḥammad until forced to submit; see *EI2*, "Thaḳīf" (M. Lecker). The "second liar" is clearly al-Ḥajjāj; the earlier one may be another feared Umayyad governor, Ziyād ibn Abīhi. Alternatively, he is the poet Umayyah ibn Abī l-Ṣalt, who seems to have considered himself a rival of the Prophet.

إنّا سَمونْا للكَفُور الفَتّانْ   حين طغَى في الكُفْر بعد الإيمانْ
بالسَّيِّدِ الغِطْريف عبد الرحمٰنْ   سارَ بجمْعٍ كالدَّبا من قَحْطانْ
ومن مَعَدٍّ قد أتى ابن عَدْنانْ   بجَحْفَلٍ جمْعٍ شديد الأركانْ
فقُلْ لحجّاجٍ وليِّ الشَّيطانْ   يثبُتْ لجمعِ مَذْحِجٍ وهَمْدانْ
فَهُمْ مُساقوه بكأس الذَّيْفانْ[1]   أو مُلْحِقوه بِقُرى ابنِ مَرْوانْ

فأسره[2] الحجّاج، وقد كان مدحه، فأنشده مديحه إيّاه، فقال: ألستَ القائل لعَدُوّ الرحمن:

بينَ الأشجِّ وبين قيس باذخٌ   بَخْ بَخْ لوالده وللمولودِ

لا واللّٰهِ لا تُبَخْبِخُ بعدها أبداً! وضُربت عنقه. وقد كان ممّا مدح به الحجّاج فأنشده إيّاه قوله:

سيُغلَب قومٌ غالَبوا اللّٰهَ جَهْرةً   وإن كايَدوه كان أقوى وأكْيَدا
كذاك يُضِلُّ اللّٰهُ من كان قلبُهُ   مريضاً ومَن والى النِّفاقَ وألْحَدا
فقد تركوا الأهْلِينَ والمالَ خلْفَهمْ   وبيضاً[3] عليهنّ الجَلاليبُ خُرَّدا ٢٦٧
ينادينَهمْ مستعبِراتٍ إليهِمُ   وقد دُفْنَ دمْعاً في الخدود وإثْمِدا
فإلّا تدارَكْهنَّ منك برحمةٍ   يكُنَّ سَبايا والبُعولةُ أَعْبُدا
أنَكْثاً[4] وعِصْياناً وجُبْناً وذِلّةً   أهان إلٰهي مَن أهان وأبعَدا

١ ك: (الذّنْفَان).
٢ ك: (فأسرع).
٣ ك: (وحصنًا).
٤ ك: (أنكاثًا).

1228 *Fattān* means "tempter" but is here taken to refer to *fitnah*, not only "temptation" but also "sedition, riot, dissent, civil war".

1229 Qaḥṭān stands for the South Arab tribes, to which Aʿshā Hamdān and Ibn al-Ashʿath belonged, as does the tribe of Madhḥij mentioned below.

1230 ʿAdnān, like Maʿadd, stands for the North Arab tribes. The syntax is odd, for the "son of ʿAdnān" is in fact Maʿadd.

We went up to the unbelieving dissenter[1228]
When he behaved like a tyrant in unbelief, after being a believer,
With the illustrious chief ʿAbd al-Raḥmān.
He marched with a host, like a swarm of locusts, of Qaḥṭān,[1229]
And of Maʿadd, Ibn ʿAdnān had come[1230]
With a large host, strongly composed.
Say to Ḥajjāj, Satan's ally:
Let him stand fast for the host of Madhḥij and Hamdān,
For they will give him to drink a cup of lethal poison
Or drive him back to Ibn Marwān's villages.[1231]

Al-Ḥajjāj took him prisoner. Aʿshā Hamdān had made panegyric poetry on him and recited his eulogy to him, but al-Ḥajjāj said, "Aren't you the one who said to the Merciful God's enemy: 'Between al-Ashajj and Qays is a lofty peak: Bravo to the father and the son!'? I swear by God, you will never do any more bravoing!"[1232] And al-Aʿshā was beheaded. The poem with which he had eulogised al-Ḥajjāj and which he recited to him was the following:[1233]

People who try to overcome God openly will be overcome:
    though they scheme against Him, He is stronger and a better schemer.[1234]
Thus God leads astray those whose hearts
    are sick, who ally themselves to hypocrisy and become heretics.
They have left family and possessions behind them 267
    and white-skinned virgin women wearing robes,
Who call out to them, shedding tears,
    having mingled tears on their cheeks with kohl.
If you do not extend your mercy to them
    they will be captives and their spouses slaves.
Disloyalty, disobedience, cowardice, baseness?
    May my God humble and take away those who humbled!

1231 Ibn Marwān is the caliph ʿAbd al-Malik.

1232 He makes a verb (*tubakhbikhu*) of the interjection *bakh bakh* ("bravo!").

1233 In the *Dīwān*, 101–104 the poem has 38 verses, of which AM quotes ll. 29–34, 37–38, 10, 12, 15–16, 22. Thirty-six lines are in al-Ṭabarī, *Tārīkh*, ii, 1113–1118, twenty-four lines in *Aghānī*, vi, 60–61, three in al-Masʿūdī, *Murūj*, iii, 362.

1234 Compare Q al-Aʿrāf 7:183, where God says *inna kaydī matīn* («my scheming is strong»). Exegetes take pains to explain it as a trope.

لقد شَأمَ المِصْرَيْنِ فَرْخُ محمّدٍ   بحقٍّ وما لاقى من الطَّير أسعَدا
كما شأمَ[١] اللّٰهُ النُّجَيْر وأهلَه   بجَدٍّ له قد كان أشقى وأنكَدا
ولمّا زحفْنا لابن يوسفَ غُدْوةً   وأبرقَ منّا العارضانِ وأرعَدا
فكافَحَنا الحجَّاجُ دونَ صفوفنا   كِفاحاً ولم يضرِبْ لذلك موْعِدا
فما لَبِثَ الحجّاجُ أنْ سَلَّ سيفَهُ   علينا فوَلّى جمعُنا وتبدَّدا
وما زحفَ الحجَّاجُ إلّا رأيتَه   مُعافًى مُلقًّى للحُتوف معوَّدا
إذا قال شُدُّوا شَدّةً حملوا معاً   فأنهل خُرْصانَ الرِّماح وأوردا

فلم ينفعه ذلك عنده حتّى قتله.

[§ ١١٤] **ومنهم** عُبَيد اللّٰه بن الحُرّ الجُعْفيّ. وكانت قيس ......[٢] ٢٦٨
فأتى عبدَ الملك فضَمِن له العراق وقتْل مُصْعَب، فأمر له عبدُ الملك بجائزة، وقال له: أوجِّه معك جيشاً كثيفاً. فقال: أصحابي يَكْفوني. وقد كان هجا قيْساً فقال:

١ ك: (أشأم).
٢ بياض في النسختين.

1235 Ibn al-Ashʿath.
1236 Kufa and Basra.
1237 At al-Nujayr, a fortress in Hadramawt, rebels under al-Ashʿath ibn Qays (Ibn al-Ashʿath's grandfather) were defeated by forces sent by caliph Abū Bakr in 11/633. Al-Ashʿath got a safe-conduct but many of his followers were killed. See *EI2*, "al-Nudjayr" (G.R. Smith), *EI3*, "al-Ashʿath b. Qays" (Khalid Yahya Blankinship).
1238 Al-Ḥajjāj.
1239 The syntax of the Arabic looks faulty (*fa-kāfaḥanā* should not begin with the conjunction), but in the longer versions another verse is the proper apodosis (*qaṭaʿnā ilayhi l-khandaqayni* …, "we crossed the two trenches towards him …").
1240 Following *AM* (*muʿāfan*); *Aghānī* has *ḥusāman* ("as a cutting sword"), al-Ṭabarī and *Dīwān* have *muʿānan* ("supported").
1241 Translation uncertain. Instead of *li-l-ḥutūfi*, *Aghānī* has *li-l-ḥurūbi* ("for battles"), al-Ṭabarī and *Dīwān* have *li-l-futūḥi* ("for victories").
1242 The beginning of the entry is missing. On him see Ibn Ḥabīb, *Muḥabbar*, 230–232 (chapter of *futtāk al-Islām*); al-Balādhurī, *Ansāb*, vii, 29–39; al-Ṭabarī, *Tārīkh*, ii, 765–781, tr. *The History*, xxi, 134–151; Sezgin, *Geschichte*, ii, 355–356; *ǦN*, i, 269; and in detail

Muḥammad's stripling[1235] brought an ill fortune to the two cities[1236]
in truth, and he did not find an auspicious augur,
Just as God brought ill fortune to al-Nujayr[1237] and its people
through a grandfather of his, who was wretched and miserable.
When we marched to Ibn Yūsuf[1238] in the morning
and our faces were full of lightning and thunder,
Al-Ḥajjāj fought us,[1239] confronting our ranks,
a hard battle, without making an appointment for it!
Al-Ḥajjāj lost no time in drawing his sword
against us, and our host fled and scattered.
Wherever al-Ḥajjāj marches, you see him
kept safe,[1240] well-tried in dealing out death,[1241] accustomed to it.
When he says, "Hard at it now!" they attack together
and the tips of the lances drink a first draught of blood and a second.

But it did not avail with al-Ḥajjāj, who had him killed in the end.

[§ 114 ʿUbayd Allāh ibn al-Ḥurr al-Juʿfī[1242]]

... and Qays ... He went to ʿAbd al-Malik and guaranteed that he would secure 268
Iraq for him and kill Muṣʿab.[1243] ʿAbd al-Malik gave orders for provisions to be given to him and said, "I will send a large army with you." But Ibn al-Ḥurr replied, "My own men will suffice me."[1244] He had lampooned Qays:[1245]

Kanazi, "ʿUbaydullāh Ibn al-Ḥurr al-Juʿfī: His Life and Poetry", see pp. 62–63 on the two versions of his death and how Ibn Ḥabīb reconciled them. He counts as a keen warrior and a poet and is sometimes called a "brigand" (*ṣuʿlūk*), which according to Kanazi is unfounded. Kanazi's collection does not contain all the poems by Ibn al-Ḥurr in Ibn Maymūn, *Muntahā l-ṭalab*, i, 257–261. Above (§ 44) it is told that he killed Ibn Abī ʿAqib.

1243 Ibn al-Ḥurr supported Muʿāwiyah against ʿAlī but later allied himself for some time with Muṣʿab ibn al-Zubayr who fought the Umayyads, the brother of ʿAbd Allāh al-Zubayr, the "anti-caliph". After falling out with Muṣʿab, who controlled Iraq, Ibn al-Ḥurr offered his services to the caliph ʿAbd al-Malik.

1244 He had a band of like-minded fighters (whom he calls *aṣḥābī*, "my associates"), perhaps as many as seven hundred (Kanazi, "ʿUbayd Allāh ibn al-Ḥurr", 63).

1245 Qays (or Qays ibn ʿAylān) stands for the federation of North Arab tribes, as opposed to Yaman (the "South Arabs"); they supported Ibn al-Zubayr. For the lines see Kanazi, "ʿUbayd Allāh ibn al-Ḥurr", 122 (with six more lines). In Ibn Maymūn, *Muntahā l-ṭalab*, i, 260–261 the complete poem, of 21 lines, is said to have been composed in prison, but the second line is not found there or in other sources.

ألم تر قيساً قيسَ عيْلانَ برقَعَتْ   لِحاها وباعت نبْلَها بالمَغازِلِ
ولاقَوْا رجالاً يكسُد النَّبلُ عِندهمْ   إذا خَطَرتْ أيْمانُهمْ بالمَناصِلِ

فلم يَدَعْه عبد الملك حتّى بعث معه جيشاً من أهل الشام، فجعل بعضهم يتخلّف عن بعض في كلّ مرتحَل حتّى رقّ من معه، فعرض له عُبيد اللّٰه بن العبّاس السُّلَميّ ثمّ الرِّعْلي فقاتَلَه، ففرّ فتَبِعه حتّى ركب مِعْبرةً بالفُرات، فنادى عُبيد اللّٰه بن العبّاس الملّاحَ صاحب المعبر: لئن عبرتَ به لأقتلنّك! فكرّ به راجعاً فعانقه ابن الحرّ. وكان الملّاح شديدَ البطْش، فغَرِقا جميعاً. فاستخرجت قيسٌ عُبيدَ اللّٰه بن الحرّ، فنصبوه وجعلوا يرمونه ويقولون: أمَغازلاً تَجِدها! حتّى قتلوه.

[§١١٥] **ومنهم** عبد اللّٰه بن بشّار بن أبي عَقِب وقد كتبنا حديثَه في المغتالين، وقتله عُبيد ٢٦٩
اللّٰه الجُعْفيّ.[١]

[§١١٦] [**ومنهم** مُزاحِم بن عمرو السَّلوليّ، وابن الدُّمَيْنة الخَثْعَميّ][٢] وكان رجل من بني

١ هـ، ك: (الخَثْعَميّ) وهو واضح الغلط.
٢ التكملة من هـ، ك؛ قال هـ: والكلام قبلها متّصل بما بعدها في النسختين، وليس بينهما صلة.

1246 Not found in other sources. Riʿl is a branch of the tribe of Sulaym (*ǦN*, i, 123).

1247 Some sources say that Ibn al-Ḥurr drowned (al-Ṭabarī, *Tārīkh*, ii, 777). The ambiguity of *ghariqa*, which can also mean "to become submerged", allows Ibn Ḥabīb to have him rescued, to be killed afterwards.

1248 cf. al-Jāḥiẓ, *Ḥayawān*, i, 134, where Ibn al-Ḥurr's verse about spindles is wrongly attributed to ʿUbayd Allāh ibn al-Ḥārith.

1249 § 44.

1250 ʿASH and SKḤ have "al-Khathʿamī", which is clearly an error.

1251 The poet Ibn al-Dumaynah (ʿAbd Allāh ibn ʿUbayd Allāh ibn ʿAmr, called—like Ibn Ḥabīb—after his mother, al-Dumaynah bint Ḥudhayfah al-Salūliyyah), of Khathʿam (see *ǦN*, i, 226, ii, 119), famous mostly for his love poetry, probably lived in the south-

Have you not seen how Qays ʿAylān have put women's veils
over their beards and sold their arrows for spindles?
They met some men with whom arrows are unsaleable
when their right hands brandished swords.

But ʿAbd al-Malik did not let him go until he sent with him an army of Syrians. Gradually, en route, some of them lagged behind the rest until few were left with him. ʿUbayd Allāh ibn al-ʿAbbās al-Sulamī al-Riʿlī[1246] barred his way and gave battle. Ibn al-Ḥurr fled, followed by his opponent. He boarded a ferry on the Euphrates. ʿUbayd Allāh ibn al-ʿAbbās called out to the ferryman: "If you take him to the other side I'll kill you!" The man turned back, but Ibn al-Ḥurr wrestled with him. The ferryman was a strong fellow. Both fell into the river.[1247] The Qaysites got Ibn al-Ḥurr out, stood him up, and shot at him, saying, "Are they spindles, do you think?" until they killed him.[1248]

[§ 115 ʿAbd Allāh ibn Bashshār ibn Abī ʿAqib]

Another is ʿAbd Allāh ibn Bashshār ibn Abī ʿAqib. We have already written his story above, among the murder victims.[1249] He was killed by ʿUbayd Allāh al-Juʿfī.[1250] 269

[§ 116 Muzāḥim ibn ʿAmr al-Salūlī and Ibn al-Dumaynah al-Khathʿamī[1251]]

[Among them are Muzāḥim ibn ʿAmr al-Salūlī and Ibn al-Dumaynah al-Khathʿamī.][1252] A man of the Banū Salūl called Muzāḥim ibn ʿAmr was suspected of

---

ern Hijaz; others mention al-Yamāmah and Medina. His dates, too, are uncertain; he lived during the Umayyad period but may have died in early Abbasid times. See Sezgin, *Geschichte*, ii, 445–446; *EI2*, "Ibn al-Dumayna" (J.W. Fück); *EAL*, "Ibn al-Dumaynah" (Tilman Seidensticker); and the introduction to his *Dīwān* by the editor, Aḥmad Rātib al-Naffākh. Part of this *Dīwān* is preserved in the redaction of Ibn Ḥabīb. The main sources on him are Ibn Qutaybah, *Shiʿr*, 731–732 (no mention of the tragic events); al-Iṣfahānī, *Aghānī*, xvii, 92–106, whose account is copied in al-ʿAbbāsī, *Maʿāhid*, i, 59–61. The story is also in Ibn al-Dumaynah's *Dīwān*, 6–12. As for Muzāḥim ibn ʿAmr al-Salūlī, he is not known as a poet, apart from the verses in the present story, and he is not found in other contexts. For his tribe, Salūl, see *ǦN*, i, 92, 114, ii, 509.

1252 This sentence, required by the context, is missing in the original, where the following comes immediately, without a break, after the preceding sentence about ʿAbd Allāh ibn Bashshār.

سَلول يقال له مُزاحم بن عمرو يُرْمَى بامرأة[١] ابن الدُّمينة ... عا ...[٢] عليها، فقال مزاحم يذكر امرأة ابن الدُّمينة:

يا ابنَ الدُّمينة[٣] والأخبارُ يرفَعها   وَخْدُ[٤] النَّجائبِ والمحقورُ يَنْمِيها
يا ابنَ الدُّمينة إنْ تغضَبْ لِما فعلتْ   حمَّادُ بالخزْيِ أو تغضَبْ مَواليها
أو تُبْغِضُوني فكم من طعنةٍ نَفَذٍ   [يغذُو خِلالَ اختلاجِ الجَوْف غاذيها][٥]
جاهدتُ فيكمْ بها إنِّي لكمْ أبداً   أَبْغي مخازِيَكمْ عَمْداً فآتيها
لا بُرْءَ عندي لكمْ حتّى تُغَيِّبَني   غَبْراءُ مُظْلِمةٌ هارٍ نَواحيها
أبغي نساءَ بني تَـيْمٍ إذا هجعتْ   عنِّي العيونُ ولا أبغي مَقاريها
وكاعبٍ من بني تيْمٍ قعدتُ لها   أو عانسٍ حينَ ذاق النومَ حاميها

١ هـ، كـ: (يرمي امرأةَ)، والتصحيح من الأغاني.
٢ بياض في الأصل، وفي الأغاني: قال الزُّبير: حدثني موهوب بن رُشَيد الكلابيّ، وإبراهيم بن سعد السُّلميّ، وعُمَر بن إبراهيم السعديّ، عن ميناس بن عبد الصمد، عن مصعب بن عَمْرو السَّلُوليّ، أخي مُزاحم بن عمرو، قالوا جميعا: إنَّ رجلا من سلول يقال له مُزاحم بن عَمْرو كان يُرْمَى بامرأة ابن الدُّمينة، وكان اسمها حَمّاء، قال السكريّ: كان اسمها حَمّادة، فكان يأتيها ويتحدَّث إليها حتى اشتهر ذلك، فمنعه ابن الدُّمَيْنَة من إتيانها، واشتدَّ عليها، فقال مزاحم يَذكرُ ذلك—وهذا من رواية ابن حبيب، وهي أتمُّ وأصحُّ—: يابْنَ الدُّمينةِ والأخبارُ يرفَعُها ... (الأبيات).
٣ كـ: (إن الدُّمَيْنة).
٤ كـ: (وخذ).
٥ كذا في هـ، والتكملة من الأغاني. والبيت كلّه ناقص في كـ.

1253 ʿASH and SKḤ have *yarmī imraʾat Ibn al-Dumaynah* ("accused the wife of Ibn al-Dumaynah") but the context requires *yurmā bi-mraʾat Ibn al-Dumaynah*, as in *Aghānī*, xvii, 94.

1254 There is a lacuna in the original text. See *Aghānī*, xvii, 93–94:
"Al-Zubayr said: I was told by Mawhūb ibn Rushayd al-Kilābī, by Ibrāhīm ibn Saʿd al-Sulamī, and by ʿUmar ibn Ibrāhīm al-Saʿdī, on the authority of Mīnās (or Miʾnās) ibn ʿAbd al-Ṣamad, on the authority of Muṣʿab ibn ʿAmr al-Salūlī, the brother of Muzāḥim

having an affair with the wife of Ibn al-Dumaynah.[1253] […][1254] with her. Then Muzāḥim said, mentioning Ibn al-Dumaynah's wife:[1255]

Ibn al-Dumaynah! The reports are carried
by noble camels making long strides. A despicable man will tell them.[1256]
Ibn al-Dumaynah! If you are angry because of what Ḥammādah did,
shamefully, or if her close kin are angry,
Or if you are angry with me: Well, many a penetrating stab,
[making a seeping wound in the quivering belly (?)[1257]]
I made an effort to perform with her among you. I always
am keen to shame you, on purpose, and visit her!
I have no cure for you, until I am concealed by
dark dust-coloured earth, its sides collapsing.[1258]
I seek[1259] the women of the Banū Taym[1260] when eyes
are slumbering, not seeing me. I do not seek their hospitality with food!
Many a full-breasted woman of the Banū Taym I lay with,
or an unmarried woman, when her protector tasted sleep,

---

ibn ʿAmr—they all said: A man of Salūl called Muzāḥim ibn ʿAmr was suspected of having an affair with the wife of Ibn al-Dumaynah. Her name was Ḥammā' (al-Sukkarī said: her name was Ḥammādah). He used to visit her and talk to her. When this became well-known, Ibn al-Dumaynah told him not to visit her and he was severe with her. Then Muzāḥim said, mentioning this—this is the text transmitted by Ibn Ḥabīb, which is the most complete and most correct one—…"

1255 *Aghānī*, xvii, 94–95 and al-ʿAbbāsī, *Maʿāhid*, i, 59–60 (17 lines, of which *AM* has lines 1–8, 10, 9, 11). Seven lines, with many differences, are quoted in Ibn al-Dumaynah, *Dīwān*, 6–7.

1256 Translation of *wa-l-maḥqūru yanmīhā* uncertain. *Aghānī* has *yukhfīhā*, "will hide them".

1257 Translation uncertain. The hemistich is missing in the original and has been supplied by ʿASH and SKḤ from *Aghānī*. I suspect that instead of *ikhtilāji l-jawfi* ("the quivering of the belly") one ought to read *ikhtilāji l-ḥūqi* ("the quivering of the penis's rim"), see the version of the hemistich in the *Dīwān*, 6: *yaʿwī ntizāʿa khilāfi l-ḥūqi ʿāwīhā*.

1258 He means, until I am dead and buried. I have taken *hār*^{in} (*HRY*) to have the sense of *inhāra* or *munhār*^{un} (*HWR*).

1259 Instead of *abghī*, all other versions have *aghshā*, "I visit" or (plausibly here) "I have sex with".

1260 i.e., Taym Allāh ibn Mubashshir ibn Aklub (*ǦN*, i, 224), a branch of Khathʿam to which Ibn al-Dymaynah belonged.

كقِعْدةٍ الأعسر العُلْفوق مُنْتَحِياً   يَمينَه من متون الترك يُنْحيها[١]
أمارةٌ كيَّةٌ ما بين عانَتِها   وبين سُرَّتِها لا شَلَّ كاويها
وشَهْقةٌ عند حِسِّ الماء تشهَقُها   وقولُ رُكْبتها قِضْ حينَ تَثْنيها
وتَعدِلُ الأيرَ إن زالت قبيعتُه   حتّى تقيم برِفْقٍ صَدْرَهُ فيها[٢]

فلمّا سمع ابن الدُّمينة قول مزاحم أتى امرأته فقال: إنّ مزاحماً قد قال فيك ما قال. قالت: واللّٰهِ ما رأى منّي ذلك الموضع قطّ. قال: فما عِلْمه بالعلامات التي وصف؟ قالت: النساء أخبرْنَه. فلم يصدِّقْها وقال: ابعَثي إلى مزاحم يأتيك في موضع كذا وكذا.

فأرسلت إلى مزاحم: إنك قد سمّعتَ بي، وأنا أحبُّ أن تأتيني. وواعدتْه موضعاً، فقعد ابن الدُّمينة وصاحبٌ له، وأقبل مزاحم وهو يظنّ أنّها في الموضع الذي واعدتْه. فخرج عليه ابنُ الدُّمينة وصاحبه، فأوثقاه وصَرّا صُرّةَ رمْلٍ فضرباه بها حتّى مات، وأتى امرأتَه فقتلها، وقتل ابنةً له منها، وطلبه السَّلوليّون فلم يَجِدوه.

فقالت أمّ مزاحم، وهي أمّ أَبان، خثعميّة، ترثي ابنها مزاحماً، وتحُضّ مُصْعَباً وجَناحاً أَخَوَيْه:

١ كذا في هـ، ك، ولعلّ الصحيح ما في الأغاني: (مُنْتَحِياً متينةً من متون النَّبْلِ يُنْحِيها).

٢ البيت محذوف في ك، وقال المحقّق: "تركته لشدة قبحه فعففت قلمي عن ذكره."

1261 It is not clear to me why he describes himself thus.

1262 I do not understand most of this verse, but I suspect the sense is obscene. *AM* has *muntaḥiyan | yamīnahū min mutūni l-turki yunḥīhā*; *Aghānī* has *muntaḥiyan | matīnatan min mutūni l-nabli yunḥīhā*.

1263 Al-Zabīdī, *Tāj al-ʿArūs* (QḌḌ): "*Qiḍ* is the sound made by a knee" (quoting this hemistich in evidence).

Lying like a heavy, rough left-hander,[1261] applying himself
to a firm one, one of the …, striking with it. (?)[1262]
She has a brand-mark between her pubes
and her navel (may the brander's hand never wither!).
She gasps when she feels the "water";
her knees say "knock!" when she bends them.[1263]
She adjusts my prick when it slips and pursues it
until she puts its forepart gently into herself.[1264]

When Ibn al-Dumaynah heard Muzāḥim's words he went to his wife and said, "Muzāḥim has said these things about you!" She replied, "I swear by God, he has never seen those parts of me!" "But how did he know about the marks he described?" "The women must have told him!"[1265] But he did not believe her. "Send a message to Muzāḥim," he said, "and tell him to come to such-and-such a place!"

She sent a message to Muzāḥim, saying, "You have made me notorious! I want you to come to me!" She arranged a place to meet. Ibn al-Dumaynah and a friend of his lay in waiting. Muzāḥim arrived, thinking she would be at the place she had promised to meet him. Then Ibn al-Dumaynah and his friend attacked him, they bound him, filled a sack with sand and pummelled him with it until he died.[1266] Then he went to his wife and killed her.[1267] He also killed a daughter she had by him.[1268] The men of Salūl sought him but they could not find him.

Muzāḥim's mother, who was called Umm Abān, a woman of Khathʿam, lamented her son Muzāḥim, inciting his two brothers, Muṣʿab and Janāḥ:[1269]

1264 SKḤ replaces this line with a row of dots and explains in a note: "I have omitted a line that is so ugly that my pen shrinks from quoting it. The book contains several similar expressions that I have let pass, as long as the sense is not obvious to the general public, but I have expurgated what was explicit and have replaced it with something alluding to it."

1265 For the same motif see above, in the story of Ziyādah and Hudbah (§110).

1266 *Aghānī*: "He put pebbles in a cloth and struck his liver until he had killed him."

1267 *Aghānī*: "He went to his wife, threw a velvet cloth on her face and sat on it until he had killed her."

1268 Apparently meaning "by Muzāḥim". In *Aghānī* he kills the girl by hitting her against the earth, saying "Never adopt a bad whelp of a dog!" For a nearly identical saying see al-ʿAskarī, *Jamharah*, ii, 298, al-Maydānī, *Majmaʿ*, ii, 266.

1269 See *Aghānī*, xvii, 97; al-ʿAbbāsī, *Maʿāhid*, i, 60; Ibn al-Dumaynah, *Dīwān*, 8; ll. 1–2 in al-Marzubānī, *Ashʿār al-nisāʾ*, 81, where she is called Umm Saʿd al-Salūliyyah.

بأهلي ومالي ثُمّ جُلّ عشيرتي   قتيلُ بني تَيْمٍ بغير سِلاحِ
فهَلّا قتلتمْ بالسِّلاح ابنَ أُختكمْ   فيُصْبحَ فيه للشهود جِراحُ
فلا تطْمَعوا في الصُّلْح ما دمتُ حَيّةً   وما دام حيًّا مُصْعَبٌ وجَناحُ
ألم تعلموا أنَّ الدَّوائر بيننا   تدُور وأنَّ الطالبين شِحاحُ

٢٧١ فخرج مُصعب في طلب ابن الدُّمينة، فأتى العَبْلاء فإذا بنجيبٍ واقفٍ برَحْله في السُّوق، و إذا قوم مجتمعون وابن الدُّمينة يُنْشِدهم. فجاء إلى حانوت قصّاب فوضع عنده رهناً وأخذ منه سِكّيناً، ثمّ أتاه، فلمّا رآه ابن الدُّمينة ولّى، واتّبعه فوجأه بها وجْأتيْن، وأُخذ مصعب وابن الدُّمينة وهو جريح فحُبسا، وأقبل جَناح بن عمرو في ناس من بني سَلول إلى السجن، ولبث ابن الدُّمينة محبوساً، ونظر السلطانُ في أمره فلم يثبُتْ للسَّلوليّ عليه حقٌّ فأطلقه. فبينا ابن الدُّمينة بعد ذلك بسوق العَبْلاء رآه مصعب أخو مزاحم، فشدّ عليه فقتله.

فهذا مقتل مزاحم بن عمرو السلوليّ، ومقتل ابن الدُّمينة الخثعميّ.

[§١١٧] **ومنهم** سُدَيْف بن مَيْمون مولى آل أبي لَهَب، وكان مدّاحاً لأبي العبّاس أمير المؤمنين، وهو الذي حَضَّ على سُليمان بن هِشام بن عبد الملك وعلى ابنيْه أبا العبّاس السفّاح

1270 Apparently being beaten to death with a sandbag is ignominious.

1271 A place in the territory of Khathʿam (Abū ʿUbayd al-Bakrī, *Muʿjam*, 918, Yāqūt, *Muʿjam al-buldān*).

1272 *Aghānī*, xvii, 97–99 has more details and several versions. Ibn al-Dumaynah either died on the spot after the first attack, or the following morning. Ibn al-Dumaynah's friends are said to have tried to break into the prison to get at Muṣʿab and kill him, but the latter's friends came first, broke into the prison and freed him.

1273 The last sentence, which looks superfluous, is perhaps what should have come at the beginning of the section.

1274 On Sudayf ibn Maymūn, a poet and orator born in Mecca, see Sezgin, *Geschichte*, ii, 449–450; *EI2*, "Sudayf b. Maymūn" (Taieb El Acheche). The main sources on him are

With my kin, my wealth, with the main part of my clan
would I ransom the one killed by the Banū Taym without weapons![1270]
Why don't you kill the son of your sister
so that his wounds will be visible to witnesses!
Do not seek reconciliation as long as I am alive
and as long as Muṣʿab and Janāḥ are alive!
Don't you know that calamities happen among us
and that revenge-seekers are niggardly!

Then Muṣʿab went out to seek Ibn al-Dumaynah. When he arrived at al-ʿAblāʾ[1271] 271
he saw a noble camel standing, carrying its saddle, at the market. Some people were gathered and Ibn al-Dumaynah was reciting poetry to them. Muṣʿab went to a butcher's shop and gave him a deposit in exchange for a knife. Then he went for Ibn al-Dumaynah. When the latter saw him he fled but Muṣʿab followed him and stabbed him twice. Both Muṣʿab and Ibn al-Dumaynah, wounded, were apprehended and detained. Janāḥ ibn ʿAmr came to the prison together with some men of Salūl. Ibn al-Dumaynah remained in custody, but when the authorities looked into his case it was decided that the Salūlī had no case against him and he was released.

When, some time later, Ibn al-Dumaynah was at the market of al-ʿAblāʾ, Muzāḥim's brother Muṣʿab saw him. He attacked him and killed him.[1272] This is how Muzāḥim ibn ʿAmr al-Salūlī and Ibn al-Dumaynah al-Khathʿamī were killed.[1273]

[§ 117 Sudayf ibn Maymūn[1274]]

Another is Sudayf ibn Maymūn, the *mawlā* of the clan of Abū Lahab.[1275] He was a panegyrist of the the caliph Abū l-ʿAbbās.[1276] He was the one who incited Abū l-ʿAbbās al-Saffāḥ against Sulaymān ibn Hishām ibn ʿAbd al-Malik and

---

al-Balādhurī, *Ansāb*, iv, 212–213, 297–298; al-Yaʿqūbī, *Tārīkh*, ii, 421–422, 430–431 (tr. *The Works*, 1078–1079, 1087–1088); Ibn Qutaybah, *Shiʿr*, 761–762; Ibn al-Muʿtazz, *Ṭabaqāt*, 37–42; Ibn ʿAbd Rabbih, *ʿIqd*, iv, 485–487, v, 88–89; al-Iṣfahānī, *Aghānī*, iv, 344–346. He was killed in 147/764.

1275 He is called a *mawlā* (client) of the Abbasids (Banū l-ʿAbbās) by Ibn Qutaybah, and by Ibn al-Muʿtazz "a *mawlā* of a woman of (the tribe of) Khuzāʿah, who had a husband belonging to the Lahabīs", i.e., the descendants of Abū Lahab, an uncle of the Prophet.

1276 Abū l-ʿAbbās ʿAbd Allāh al-Saffāḥ, the first Abbasid caliph (reg. 132–136/750–754).

حتّى قتلهم. وإنّه خرج مع محمّد بن عبد الله بن الحسن بن الحسن بن أبي طالب | فمدح ٢٧٢
محمّداً وهجا أبا جعفر، وقُتل محمّد بن عبد الله، ووُلّي عبدُ الصمد بن عليّ مكّة، فكان عبدُ
الصمد الذي وَلِيَ قتله.

[§١١٨] **ومنهم** عبد بني الحَسْحاس، واسمه سُحَيْم، وكان صاحب تغزُّل، فاتّهمه مولاه بابنته، فجلس له في مكان إذا رعى سُحيمٌ قال فيه، فلمّا اضطجع[1] تنفّس الصُّعَداءَ ثمّ قال:

يا ذِكْرةً ما لكَ في الحاضرِ   تذْكُرُها وأنتَ في الصادرِ
من كلِّ بيضاءَ لها كَعْثَبٌ   مِثْلُ سَنام الرُّبَعِ المائرِ

١ هـ: (اضطجعا)، وأظنّها غلطاً.

1277 Sulayman was a son of the Umayyad caliph Hishām (reg. 105–125/724–743). He had resisted Marwān ibn Muḥammad, the last Umayyad caliph (killed 132/750) and had been defeated by him and then pardoned. Sudayf's incendiary poems, not quoted by Ibn Ḥabīb, are found in al-Balādhurī, *Ansāb*, iv, 212–213; al-Yaʿqūbī, *Tārīkh*, ii, 430–431 (tr. *The Works*, 1087–1088); al-Mubarrad, *Kāmil*, iii, 208–209; Ibn Qutaybah, *Shiʿr*, 761; Ibn al-Muʿtazz, *Ṭabaqāt*, 39–40; *Aghānī*, iv, 345; Ibn ʿAbd Rabbih, *ʿIqd*, iv, 486–487; Ibn Rashīq, *ʿUmdah*, i, 62–63. One of these poems (rhyming in *-āsī*) is also attributed to Shibl ibn ʿAbd Allāh (al-Mubarrad, *Kāmil*, iii, 208). That the poems led to the killing of the Umayyad princes (who were clubbed to death according to the accounts of al-Mubarrad, Ibn al-Muʿtazz, *Aghānī*, and others), is confirmed by the sources, *pace* El Acheche in his *EI2* entry, who says that Sudayf "approached the caliph al-Saffāḥ and tried without success to persuade him to slaughter certain remaining Umayyads." Ibn Ḥabīb briefly mentioned the killing of Sulaymān after Sudayf's incitement in his *Muḥabbar*, 486.

1278 He is known as al-Nafs al-Zakiyyah ("the Pure Soul"). He led an ʿAlid revolt in Medina and was killed in 145/762–763; see also above § 62.

1279 Al-Saffāḥ's successor, the caliph al-Manṣūr.

1280 ʿAbd al-Ṣamad ibn ʿAlī ibn ʿAbd Allāh ibn al-ʿAbbās ibn ʿAbd al-Muṭṭalib was an uncle of al-Saffāḥ and al-Manṣūr; see Ibn Khalllikān, *Wafayāt*, iii, 195–196 (who says he died in 175/791) and al-Ṣafadī, *Wāfī*, xviii, 449–450 (who mentions 185/801 as the year of his death, as does al-Ṭabarī, *Tārīkh*, iii, 650).

his two sons, so that he had them killed.[1277] Sudayf joined the rebellion of Muḥammad ibn ʿAbd Allāh ibn al-Ḥasan ibn al-Ḥasan ibn ʿAlī ibn Abī Ṭālib.[1278] He made eulogies on Muḥammad and lampooned Abū Jaʿfar.[1279] Muḥammad 272
ibn ʿAbd Allāh was killed and ʿAbd al-Ṣamad ibn ʿAlī[1280] was appointed governor of Mecca. It was ʿAbd al-Ṣamad who was charged with Sudayf's execution.[1281]

[§ 118 ʿAbd Banī l-Ḥasḥās[1282]]

Another is ʿAbd Banī l-Ḥasḥās ("the slave of the Banū l-Ḥasḥās"), who was called Suḥaym, a poet of love poetry. His master suspected him of having an affair with his daughter, so he lay in wait for him at the place where Suḥaym, while herding the camels, would have a midday nap. When he[1283] lay down, Suḥaym sighed and said,[1284]

> Ah, memory! Why is it now, in the present,
> that you think of her, while you are leaving?
> Leaving every white woman with pudenda
> like the hump of a sprightly young camel.

1281 The text has "his execution" (*qatlahū*), which would seem to suggest the ʿAlid rebel Muḥammad ibn ʿAbd Allāh, but "his" must refer to Sudayf, whose execution took place in 147/764. According to Ibn ʿAbd Rabbih, *ʿIqd*, v, 89 he was buried alive; Ibn al-Muʿtazz (*Ṭabaqāt*, 42) says that he was either buried alive or had his hands and feet and then his head cut off.

1282 Suḥaym, called "the slave of the Banū l-Ḥasḥās" (a branch of Asad), lived in Medina and was famous for his sensual love poetry, some of which led to his death (around 40/660). He was Nubian (*Aghānī*, xxii, 303) or Abyssinian (Ibn Qutaybah, *Shiʿr*, 408)—Suḥaym could be translated as "Blacky"—and his Arabic pronunciation was foreign (*ahshantu* for *aḥsantu*, "I did well!", according to *Aghānī*, xxii, 303; in Ibn Qutaybah it is *aḥsanku*, which points at Ethiopic influence). See Sezgin, *Geschichte*, ii, 288–289; *EI2*, "Suḥaym" (A. Arazi). The main sources are Ibn Sallām, *Ṭabaqāt*, 143, 156–157; Ibn Qutaybah, *Shiʿr*, 408–409; al-Iṣfahānī, *Aghānī*, xxii, 302–311; ʿAbd al-Qādir al-Baghdādī, *Khizānah*, ii, 104–105; and his *Dīwān*, which has been published.

1283 ʿASH has a dual (*iḍṭajaʿā*), "when the two lay down", seemingly meaning the lovers; in view of his master's reaction this is implausible. It is a singular in other sources (Suḥaym ʿAbd Banī l-Ḥasḥās, *Dīwān*, 34, *Aghānī*, xxii, 308, *Khizānah*, ii, 105), as in SKḤ, and in another version (*Aghānī*, xxii, 309) he is resting in the shade of a tree.

1284 The verses are in Suḥaym, *Dīwān*, 34; *Aghānī*, xxii, 308 and (with different second line) 310.

فقال له سيّده، وظهر من موضعه الذي كمن فيه: ما لك؟ فتلجلج في مَنْطِقه. فلمّا رجع
أجمع على قتله. وخرجتْ إليه صاحبتُه فحدّثَتْه وأخبرتْه بما يُراد به، فقام يَنْفُض بُرْدَه ويعفّي
أثَرَه. فلمّا انطُلِق به ليُقْتل ضَحِكَتِ امرأةٌ كان بينها وبينه هوًى، شَماتةً، فقال:

إنْ تضحَكي منّي فيا رُبَّ ليلةٍ   تركتُكِ فيها كالقَبَّاء المفرَّجِ

فلمّا قُدّم ليُقتل قال:

شُدُّوا وَثاقَ العبدِ لا' يُفْلِتْكُمُ   إنّ الحياةَ من المماتِ قريبُ

فلقد تحدَّرَ من جبينٍ فَتاتكمْ   عَرَقٌ على ظهْرِ الفِراشِ وَطِيبُ"

٢٧٣

فقُتل.

[١١٩§] **ومنهم** وضّاح اليَمَن، وهو وضّاح بن إسماعيل بن عبد كُلال، أحد أبناء الفُرْس
الذين قدموا مع وَهْرِز الفارسيّ، فقتلوا الحَبَشة وأقاموا' بصنعاء. وكان شاعراً ظريفاً غَزِلاً جميلاً،

---

١   الكلمة ناقصة في كـ

٢   كـ: (تَخَدَّر).

٣   هـ، كـ: (رطيبُ)، والتصحيح من الديوان وطبقات ابن سلّام والأغاني وغيرها.

٤   كـ: (وسكنوا).

1285   At this stage, according to the *Dīwān* (34–36) and *Aghānī* (xxii, 308–309), Suḥaym recites a poem, mentioning his conversation with the girl and the obliterating of the tracks, which apparently did not prevent him from being apprehended.

1286   The line is in *Dīwān*, 59; Ibn Abī ʿAwn, *Tashbīhāt*, 242; *Aghānī*, xxii, 309; and many later sources.

1287   *Dīwān*, 60; Ibn Sallām, *Ṭabaqāt*, 157 (l. 2); Ibn Qutaybah, *Shiʿr*, 409 (l. 2); *Aghānī*, xxii, 309.

1288   AM has ʿaraqun ... raṭībū ("moist sweat"), a reading that is possible but pleonastic, and I have preferred the reading found in most other sources, wa-ṭībū ("and perfume").

1289   Some reports (*Dīwān*, 64, *Aghānī*, xxii, 309) say that he was thrown into a trench, covered with firewood, and burnt.

His master, having come out of his hiding place, said to him, "What is the matter with you?" Suḥaym stammered, at a loss for words. When his master returned he resolved to kill him. His girlfriend went to him, she talked to him and told him what they intended to do to him. He got up and shook his robe, effacing his traces.[1285]

When he was taken out to be killed, a woman, with whom he had had a love affair, laughed, gloating. He said,[1286]

> You may laugh at me. But on many a night
> I left you like a rent gown!

When he was brought forward to be killed he said,[1287]

> Tightly bind your slave lest he escape!
> Life is close to death.
> From the forehead of your girl dripped 273
> sweat on the bed, and perfume![1288]

Then he was killed.[1289]

[§ 119 Waḍḍāḥ al-Yaman[1290]]

Another is Waḍḍāḥ al-Yaman; he is Waḍḍāḥ ibn Ismāʿīl ibn ʿAbd Kulāl, one of the descendants of the Persians who came with Wahriz the Persian and who killed the Abyssinians and stayed in Sanaa.[1291] He was a fine poet, amorous,

---

1290 Waḍḍāḥ al-Yaman, ʿAbd al-Raḥmān (or ʿAbd Allāh) ibn Ismāʿīl (d. c. 93/712), was a poet famous for his *ghazal*, see Sezgin, *Geschichte*, ii, 433, *EI2*, "Waḍḍāḥ al-Yaman" (A.A. Arazi). Many of the reports about him seem legendary rather than historical. For parallel texts see al-Iṣfahānī, *Aghānī*, vi, 225–226 (said to go back to Ibn al-Kalbī via Muḥammad ibn Ḥabīb); al-Balādhurī, *Ansāb*, viii, 89–90; Ibn Khallikān, *Wafayāt*, ii, 45–46; Ibn Shakir, *Fawāt*, ii, 274–275; Ibn Ḥamdūn, *Tadhkirah*, ix, 232–233; al-Jarīrī, *Jalīs*, i, 581–582 (mentions Yazīd ibn ʿAbd al-Malik instead of al-Walīd); al-Sarrāj, *Maṣāriʿ*, ii, 192–193 (the same); al-Ṣafadī, *Wāfī*, xviii, 118–120 (quoting from *al-Aghānī*). Al-Ṣafadī expresses his doubt about the story: the daughter of ʿAbd al-ʿAzīz b. Marwān could only have been chaste. See also Souissi, "Waḍḍāḥ al-Yaman, le personnage et sa légende", esp. pp. 285–303. For a yet more romanticised and fictionalised version in some redactions of *Miʾat laylah wa-laylah*, the *Hundred-and-One Nights*, see ed. Ṭarshūnah, 398–405. This is not found in the edition and translation by Bruce Fudge in the LAL series (2016).

1291 On the Persian general Wahriz and his expedition to Yemen in c. AD 570, see e.g. *EI2*, "Wahriz" (C.E. Bosworth).

فعَشِقَتْه أُمّ البَنين بنتُ عبد العزيز بن مروان، وكانت تحت الوليد بن عبد الملك، ولها منه عبد العزيز بن الوليد.

وكان يكون عندها في صندوق مخبوءاً. وإنّ الوليد بعث إليها مع خادم له بجوهر، فأتاه وهي غافلة ووضّاح عندها، فلمّا دخل الخادم وأحسّتْ به أدخلتْ وضّاحاً في صندوق، فرآه الخادم وأخبر به الوليد، فأتاها فجلس على الصندوق الذي وصفه له الخادم فقال لها: يا أمّ البنين، لي إليك حاجة. قالت: وما هي يا أمير المؤمنين؟ قال: تَهَبِين لي بعض صناديقك. قالت: كلّها لك. قال: لا أريد إلّا الصندوق الذي تحتي. فقالت: هو لك. فبعث إلى حفّارِين فحفروا بئراً، ثمّ أدْلَوْه فيها وقال: يا هذا، قد بلغَنا عنك شيء، فإنْ كان حقًّا أو باطلاً فسنقطع أثرك. وأُلْقِيَ تُرابها وانصرف. فلم تتبيَّن في وجه الوليد إلى أن مات شيئاً يُذْكَر.

[§ ١٢٠] **ومنهم** قيْس بن الخَطيم، وكان سيّداً شاعراً. فلمّا هدأتْ حرب الأنصار تذاكَرَت ٢٧٤
الخَزْرَجُ قيسَ بن الخطيم ونِكايتَه، فتذامروا وتواعدوا قَتْلَه. فخرج عَشيّةً في مُلاءتيْن مورسَّتين يريد مالاً له بالشَّوْط، حتّى مرّ بأُطُم بني حارثة، فرُمِيَ من الأُطم بثلاثة أَسْهُم فسقط أحدها في صدره فصاح صيْحةً أسمعها رَهْطَه،[1] فجاءوه فحملوه إلى منزله. فلم يروْا له كُفُؤاً إلّا أبا صَعْصَعة بن زيد بن عَوْف بن مبذول النَّجّاريّ،[2] فاندسّ إليه رجل حتّى اغتاله في منزله

١ كـ: (رهطة).

٢ كـ: (البخاري).

1292 Al-Walīd ibn ʿAbd al-Malik reigned 86–96/105–115.

1293 *Aghānī* explains that Waḍḍāḥ used to visit her and that she hid him in a chest whenever she feared anyone might enter her boudoir.

1294 In *Aghānī*, the servant tries to blackmail her, but she refuses and insults him. When the servant tells the caliph, he refuses to believe it. He does not want to find out the truth and possibly cause a scandal, but neither does he want to leave it at that.

1295 According to *Aghānī* the hole was dug in his sitting-room; a carpet was spread over it.

1296 *Aghānī* adds that no trace of Waḍḍāḥ was ever seen again.

1297 Qays ibn al-Khaṭīm, of the tribe al-Aws (*ĞN*, i, 181), was a poet. He died in AD 620, a couple of years before the Hijrah. See on him Sezgin, *Geschichte*, ii, 285–276, *EI2*, "Ḳays b. al-Khaṭīm" (T. Kowalski); al-Iṣfahānī, *Aghānī*, iii, 1–26 (see 10–11 for a close parallel text on his murder, a version said to go back to al-Mufaḍḍal via Muḥammad ibn Ḥabīb).

and handsome. Umm al-Banīn, the daughter of ʿAbd al-ʿAzīz ibn Marwān fell in love with him. She was the wife of al-Walīd ibn ʿAbd al-Malik and he had a son by her, ʿAbd al-ʿAzīz ibn al-Walīd.[1292]

Waḍḍāḥ would hide in a chest when he was with her.[1293] Al-Walīd once sent a servant of his to her with a jewel. He entered upon her unawares, when Waḍḍāḥ was with her. When she noticed the servant was entering she made Waḍḍāḥ go inside a chest. However, the servant saw him and informed al-Walīd,[1294] who went over to her and sat down on the chest that the servant had described to him. "Umm al-Banīn," he said, "I would like to ask you for something." "What it is, Commander of the Believers?" she asked. He replied, "Will you give me one of your chests?" "They are all yours!" "I only want the chest I'm sitting on." "It is yours."

He sent for some men who dug a hole and they let the chest down into it.[1295] Then he said, "You there! We have heard something about you. Now whether it is true or false, we shall cut off any trace of you." The earth was thrown back and he left. She never saw anything about the affair in al-Walīd's face until his death.[1296]

[§ 120 Qays ibn al-Khaṭīm[1297]]

Another is Qays ibn al-Khaṭīm. He was chief and a poet. When the war between the Anṣār abated somewhat,[1298] the tribe of al-Khazraj were discussing Qays ibn al-Khaṭīm and the grievance he was causing.[1299] They uttered complaints and agreed they would kill him. One evening, when Qays was going out, wearing two robes dyed yellow with *wars*,[1300] on his way to some property of his in al-Shawṭ,[1301] he came past a stronghold of the Banū Ḥārithah.[1302] Three arrows were shot from the stronghold, one of which hit his chest. He uttered a cry that was heard by his kinsmen. They came and carried him home. They thought nobody would be his equal in standing except Abū Ṣaʿṣaʿah ibn Zayd ibn ʿAwf 274

1298 The two major tribes in Medina (then called Yathrib), al-Aws and al-Khazraj, had been warring and feuding for many years. The prophet Muḥammad was invited to make peace and migrated from Mecca to Medina in AD 622 (the Hijrah and the beginning of the Muslim calendar). The two tribes are here called, anachronistically, the Anṣār or "Helpers", because they supported the Prophet.

1299 Qays was involved in poetical polemics, especially with Ḥassān ibn Thābit (destined to become the first major poet supporting the Prophet). He had avenged the death of his father and grandfather, who had been murdered.

1300 *Wars* is a yellow dye from a plant variously identified. See e.g. *EI2*, Index, 574.

1301 Al-Shawṭ was a garden or orchard in Medina (Yāqūt, *Muʿjam al-buldān*).

1302 The Banū Ḥārithah belonged to al-Khazraj (*ĞN*, i, 179, 180).

فضرب عُنقَه، واشتمل على رأسه وأتى به قيساً وهو بآخِرِ رَمَقٍ، فألقاه بين يديه وقال: يا قيس لقد أدركتَ ثأرك. فقال: عَضِضتَ بأيْرِ أبيك إنْ كان غيرَ أبي صعصعة! فقال: هو أبو صعصعة. وأراه الرأس فلم يلبَثْ قيس أن مات.

[§ ١٢١] **ومنهم** غَضوب، إحدى بني ربيعة بن مالك بن زيد مَناة بن تميم، وكانت شاعرة، وكانت ناكحاً في بني طُهَيّة ثمّ في بني سُبَيع، فكانت مع زوجها زماناً ثمّ تزوَّج عليها امرأةً منهم، فأُولِعَتْ بهم تَهْجوهم، فقالت:

بنو سُبَيعٍ زَمَعُ الكِلابِ ليسوا إلى سعدٍ ولا الرِّبابِ ٢٧٥
ولا إلى القبائل الرِّغابِ كم فيهمُ من طَفْلةٍ كَعابِ
وكْعاءَ ذاتِ رَكَبٍ قَبْقابِ خبيثة المُشْعَر في الثِّيابِ
تَتْبَعُ كُلَّ عَزَبٍ وثّابِ

فأوعدَها رجالٌ، منهم مَرْبَع وبنو وَقْدان، وبنو سيّار وبنو مجمّع، فقالت:

1303 See *ǦN*, i, 185; Taym Allāh al-Najjār is a branch of al-Khazraj.

1304 On this expression compare the saying attributed in the Hadith to the Prophet Muḥammad: "Whoever practises the pre-Islamic way of asserting one's tribal connections (*taʿazzā bi-ʿazāʾ al-jāhiliyyah*), let him bite his father's 'thing' (*han*), but do not use the euphemism!", quoted e.g. in Ibn Qutaybah, *ʿUyūn*, i, *lām–mīm*, Ibn Manẓūr, *Lisān al-ʿArab* (ʿZW, ʿḌḌ, KNY, HNW/Y).

1305 Ghaḍūb is the only woman among the listed victims in the book. For a parallel text see al-Sukkarī, *Naqāʾiḍ*, 1097–1098 and al-Baghdādī, *Sharḥ Abyāt Mughnī l-labīb*, i, 145–146. Apart from this virtually nothing is known about her. She is mentioned briefly in al-Baghdādī, *Khizānat al-adab*, viii, 520 (cf. al-Zabīdī, *Tāj al-ʿarūs* [ḌBʿ]). Marbaʿ, whom she lampooned, was a contemporary of al-Farazdaq and Jarīr, see al-Sukkarī, *Naqāʾiḍ*, 974–975. Jarīr condemned her killers in a poem (*Naqāʾiḍ*, 1098, Jarīr, *Dīwān*, 458–459).

1306 See *ǦN*, i, 59.

1307 Ṭuhayyah, a branch of Tamīm named after their female ancestor Ṭuhayyah bint ʿAbshams ibn Saʿd ibn Zayd Manāh (*ǦN*, i, 78 ii, 558). It is not clear who the Banū Subayʿ are. It would appear that they are a subdivision of the Banū Ṭuhayyah, but cf. *Naqāʾiḍ*, 415 (*min Banī Subayʿ thumma min Banī Ṭuhayyah*, see also *Naqāʾiḍ*, index, 123).

ibn Mabdhūl al-Najjārī.[1303] So a man was sent who murdered him in his house and cut off his head. He picked up the head and took it to Qays, who was about to breathe his last. He threw it down before him. "Qays," he said, "You have your vengeance!" Qays replied, "May you bite your father's prick[1304] if it isn't Abū Ṣaʿṣaʿah's!" The man said, "It is Abū Ṣaʿṣaʿāh's", showing him the head. Soon after that Qays died.

[§ 121 Ghaḍūb[1305]]

Another is Ghaḍūb, one of the Banū Rabīʿah ibn Mālik ibn Zayd Manāh ibn Tamīm.[1306] She was a poet and had married in the Banū Ṭuhayyah, specifically the Banū Subayʿ.[1307] She lived with her husband for a time. Then he married, in addition, a second wife of her tribe. She became incensed[1308] and lampooned them, saying,

> The Banū Subayʿ are the lowest of dogs,[1309] 275
> They don't belong to Saʿd or al-Ribāb[1310]
> Or to the larger tribes.
> Many a full-breasted soft-bodied girl is there among them,
> Silly,[1311] with a pudendum that makes a plopping sound,[1312]
> Nasty and hairy under her clothes;
> She pursues every dashing unmarried man.

Several men warned her, among them Marbaʿ,[1313] the Banū Waqdān, the Banū Sayyār, and the Banū Mujammiʿ,[1314] but she said, in a lampoon,

---

1308 Understandably, but also true to her name (*ghaḍūb* means "irascible").

1309 *Zamaʿu l-kilāb*. If Marbaʿ, mentioned below, belonged to the tribe Kilāb, it is possible that they are meant, although Kilāb is usually without the definite article.

1310 On al-Ribāb see above, § 34. It is unclear who are meant by Saʿd.

1311 According to the lexicographers *wakʿāʾ*, fem. of *awkaʿ*, can mean "foolish, stupid" (*ḥamqāʾ*) and also "with crooked toes", see the technical description in e.g. Ibn Manẓūr, *Lisān al-ʿArab* (WKʿ), where it is said that this condition "is most common among slave women from hard labour". But this does not go well with "soft-bodied" here.

1312 *Rakab qabqāb*; see *Lisān al-ʿArab* (QBB): a Bedouin calls a girl *dhāt al-ḥir al-qabqāb*; when asked about the meaning of *qabqāb*, he clarifies: "wide and full of water; penetrated by a man's penis, it says *qabqab*, making a sound."

1313 ʿASH and SKḤ read Mirbaʿ, also in Jarīr, *Dīwān*, 459; I follow ǦN, i, 95, ii, 399 where he appears as Marbaʿ ibn Waʿwaʿah, and *Naqāʾiḍ*, 975, where it is said that Marbaʿ is his nickname and his own name Waʿwaʿah. This Marbaʿ belongs to Kilāb, not Tamīm. It seems there is some confusion.

1314 I am unable to identify these groups.

يا مَرْبَعاً يا مَربعَ الضَّلالِ　　يا فاحر مستقبل الشَّمالِ
على بعيرٍ غيرِ ذي جِلالِ　　يا مَربعاً هل حان من إقبالِ

في هجاءٍ لها. فلمّا سمعوا ذلك مشوْا إليها فضربها مَرْبعٌ والفِتْية الآخَرون فقُتلت. فقال مربع:

شفيْتُ الغليلَ من غَضوب فأصبحتْ　　لها إرَمٌ في رأسِ علْياءَ عاقلِ
سأنْــقِم منها جَهْلَها وسَفاهَها　　وإيضاعَها في كلِّ حقٍّ وباطلِ
ألا لا تُراعوا إنّما هي لِصّةٌ　　تَسارَعَ فيها فِــتْيةٌ بمَناصلِ

Marbaʿ, you Marbaʿ who has lost his way,
You who … (?)[1315] facing the north wind,
On a camel without … (?).[1316]
Marbaʿ, is it time to advance?

When they heard this they went to her. Marbaʿ and the other men beat her and she was killed. Then Marbaʿ said,

I have cured my rancour about Ghaḍūb. Now
  she has a gravestone on top of a high hill.
I shall take[1317] vengeance for her brutality, her foolishness,
  and her plain speaking (?)[1318] in everything true or false.
Ah, don't think much of it. She is a thief;[1319]
  the men dealt quickly with her with their blades.

1315 ʿASH and SKḤ have *fāḥir*, which is not found in any dictionary. Possibly one should read either *fājir*, "profligate, shameless", as in the MS and in *Naqāʾiḍ*, 1097, or else *fāghir*, "opening his mouth" (here to the North to cool oneself?).

1316 ʿASH and SKḤ read *jilāl*, which means "roof (of a ship)" or "baskets for dates". Perhaps one should read *jalāl*, "splendour".

1317 The future tense looks incongruous.

1318 ʿASH and SKḤ: *wa-īḍāʿahā* (*awḍaʿa*, "to drive a beast at a gentle pace"). Better may be *wa-inṣāʿahā*, as in *Naqāʾiḍ* (*anṣaʿa: aẓhara mā fī nafsihi*).

1319 It is not clear why she is called a "thief" (*liṣṣah*).

Bibliography

Primary Sources

al-ʿAbbāsī, ʿAbd al-Raḥīm ibn ʿAbd al-Raḥmān ibn Aḥmad, *Maʿāhid al-tanṣīṣ: Sharḥ shawāhid al-Talkhīṣ*, 2 vols. Cairo: al-Maṭbaʿah al-Bahiyyah, AH 1316 [/1899].

ʿAbīd ibn al-Abraṣ, *Dīwān*, in Charles Lyall (ed.), *The Dīwāns of ʿAbīd ibn al-Abraṣ, of Asad, and ʿĀmir ibn aṭ-Ṭufail, of ʿĀmir ibn Ṣaʿṣaʿah*, with a translation and notes, Cambridge: E.J.W. Gibb Memorial Trust, 1913.

Abū Tammām, *al-Waḥshiyyāt, wa-huwa l-Ḥamāsah al-ṣughrā*, ed. by ʿAbd al-ʿAzīz al-Maymanī al-Rājakūtī and Maḥmūd Muḥammad Shākir, Cairo: Dār al-Maʿārif, 1987.

Abū l-Ṭayyib al-Lughawī, *Marātib al-naḥwiyyīn*, ed. by Muḥammad Abū l-Faḍl Ibrāhīm, Cairo: Nahḍat Miṣr, [1974, date of preface].

Abū ʿUbayd al-Bakrī, *Faṣl al-maqāl fī sharḥ al-amthāl, wa-huwa sharḥ li-kitāb al-Amthāl li-Abī ʿUbayd al-Qāsim ibn Sallām*, ed. by Iḥsān ʿAbbās and ʿAbd al-Majīd ʿĀbidīn, Beirut: Dār al-Amānah, 1983.

Abū ʿUbayd al-Bakrī, ʿAbd Allāh ibn ʿAbd al-ʿAzīz ibn Muḥammad, *al-Masālik wa-l-mamālik*, ed. by Jamāl Ṭulbah, 2 vols. Beirut: Dār al-Kutub al-ʿIlmiyyah, 2002.

Abū ʿUbayd al-Bakrī, ʿAbd Allāh ibn ʿAbd al-ʿAzīz, *Muʿjam mā staʿjam min asmāʾ al-bilād wa-l-mawāḍiʿ*, ed. by Muṣṭafā al-Saqqā, al-Qāhirah: Maṭbaʿat Lajnat al-Taʾlīf wa-l-Tarjamah wa-l-Nashr, 1945–1951, repr. Beirut: ʿĀlam al-Kutub, n.d.

Abū ʿUbayd al-Bakrī, *Simṭ al-laʾālī fī sharḥ Amālī al-Qālī*, ed. by ʿAbd al-ʿAzīz al-Maymanī, 2 vols. Cairo: Lajnat al-Taʾlīf wa-Tarjamah wa-l-Nashr, 1936.

Abū ʿUbayd al-Bakrī, *al-Tanbīh see* al-Qālī, *Dhayl al-Amālī*.

Abū ʿUbaydah Maʿmar ibn al-Muthannā, *Ayyām al-ʿArab qabla l-Islām*, ed. by ʿĀdil Jāsim al-Bayātī, 2 vols. Beirut: ʿĀlam al-Kutub, 1987 (I: *Dirāsah muqāranah*; II: *Ayyām al-ʿArab qabla l-Islām*).

Abū ʿUbaydah Maʿmar ibn al-Muthannā, *al-Dībāj*, ed. by ʿAbd Allāh ibn Sulaymān al-Jarbūʿ and ʿAbd al-Raḥmān ibn Sulaymān al-ʿUthaymīn, Cairo: Maktabat al-Khānjī, 1991.

Abū ʿUbaydah, *Majāz al-Qurʾān*, ed. by Fuʾād Sazkīn (Fuat Sezgin), 2 vols. Cairo: Maktabat al-Khānjī, 1955, 1962.

Abū ʿUbaydah, *Naqāʾiḍ Jarīr wa-l-Farazdaq / The Nakāʾid of Jarīr and al-Farazdak*, ed. by Anthony Ashley Bevan, 2 vols. Leiden: Brill, 1905–1912.

ʿAdī ibn Zayd, *Dīwān*, ed. by Muḥammad Jabbār al-Muʿaybid, Baghdad: Dār al-Jumhūriyyah, 1965.

al-Akhfash al-Aṣghar, *al-Ikhtiyārayn*, ed. by Fakhr al-Dīn Qabāwah, Damascus: Majmaʿ al-Lughah al-ʿArabiyyah, 1974.

al-Āmidī, Abū l-Qāsim al-Ḥasan ibn Bishr, *al-Muʾtalif wa-l-mukhtalif fī asmāʾ al-shuʿarāʾ*

wa-kunāhum wa-alqābihim wa-ansābihim wa-baʿḍ shiʿrihim, ed. by F. Krenkow, repr. Beirut: Dār al-Kutub al-ʿIlmiyya, 1982.

al-Anbārī, Abū Bakr Muḥammad ibn al-Qāsim, *Sharḥ al-qaṣāʾid al-sabʿ al-ṭiwāl al-jāhiliyyāt*, ed. by ʿAbd al-Salām Muḥammad Hārūn, Cairo: Dār al-Maʿārif, 1969.

Anon., *Akhbār al-dawlah al-ʿAbbāsiyyah, wa-fīhi akhbār al-ʿAbbās wa-waladihi, li-muʾallif majhūl min al-qarn al-sādis al-hijrī*, ed. by ʿAbd al-ʿAzīz al-Dūrī and ʿAbd al-Jabbār al-Muṭṭalibī, Beirut: Dār al-Ṭalīʿah, 1971.

ʿAntarah ibn Shaddād, *Shiʿr / War Songs*, ed. by James E. Montgomery, transl. by James E. Montgomery with Richard Sieburth (Library of Arabic Literature), New York: New York University Press, 2018.

Aʿshā Hamdān, *Dīwān*, ed. by Ḥasan ʿĪsā Abū Yāsīn, Riyadh: Dār al-ʿUlūm, 1983.

al-Aʿshā l-Kabīr Maymūn ibn Qays, *Dīwān*, ed. by Muḥammad Ḥusayn, Cairo: Maktabat al-Ādāb, [1950, date of preface].

al-Ashʿarī, Abū l-Ḥasan ʿAlī ibn Ismāʿīl, *Maqālāt al-Islāmiyyīn wa-khtilāf al-muṣallīn*, ed. by Muḥammad Muḥyī l-Dīn ʿAbd al-Ḥamīd, 2 vols. Sidon—Beirut: al-Maktabah al-ʿAṣriyyah, 1990.

al-ʿAskarī, Abū Hilāl al-Ḥasan ibn ʿAbd Allāh ibn Sahl, *al-Awāʾil*, Beirut: Dār al-Kutub al-ʿIlmiyyah, 1987.

al-ʿAskarī, Abū Hilāl al-Ḥasan ibn ʿAbd Allāh ibn Sahl, *Jamharat al-amthāl*, ed. by Aḥmad ʿAbd al-Salām and Abū Hājar Muḥammad Saʿīd ibn Basyūnī Zaghlūl, 2 vols. Beirut: Dār al-Kutub al-ʿIlmiyyah, 1988.

al-Aṣmaʿiyyāt, ikhtiyār al-Aṣmaʿī, ed. by Aḥmad Muḥammad Shākir and ʿAbd al-Salām Muḥammad Hārūn, Cairo: Dār al-Maʿārif, 1979.

Aws ibn Ḥajar, *Dīwān*, ed. by Muḥammad Yūsuf Najm, Beirut: Dār Bayrūt, 1980.

al-Baghdādī, ʿAbd al-Qādir, *Khizānat al-adab wa-lubāb lisān al-ʿArab*, ed. by ʿAbd al-Salām Muḥammad Hārūn, 13 vols. Cairo: Dār al-Kātib al-ʿArabī / al-Hayʾah al-Miṣriyyah al-ʿĀmmah, 1967–1986.

al-Baghdādī, ʿAbd al-Qādir, *Sharḥ abyāt Mughnī l-labīb*, ed. by ʿAbd al-ʿAzīz Rabāḥ and Aḥmad Yūsuf al-Daqqāq, 8 vols. Beirut: Dār al-Maʾmūn, 1988.

al-Baghdādī, Abū Bakr Aḥmad ibn ʿAlī ibn Thābit al-Khaṭīb, *Tārīkh Madīnat al-Salām wa-akhbār muḥaddithīhā* (…) [= *Tārīkh Baghdād*], ed. by Bashshār ʿAwwād Maʿrūf, 17 vols. Beirut: Dār al-Gharb al-Islāmī, 2001.

al-Balādhurī, Aḥmad ibn Yaḥyā ibn Jābir, *Jumal min Ansāb al-ashrāf*, ed. by Suhayl Zakkar and Riyāḍ Ziriklī, 13 vols. Beirut: Dār al-Fikr, 1996.

Bashshār ibn Burd, *Dīwān*, ed. by Muḥammad al-Ṭāhir ibn ʿĀshūr, 4 vols. Algiers & Tunis: al-Sharikah al-Waṭaniyyah / al-Sharikah al-Tūnisiyyah, 1976.

al-Baṭalyawsī, Abū Bakr ʿĀṣim ibn Ayyūb, *Sharḥ al-ashʿār al-sittah al-jāhiliyyah*, ed. by Nāṣīf Sulaymān ʿAwwād (Bibliotheca Islamica, 47), 2 vols. Beirut—Berlin: Klaus Schwarz, 2008.

al-Batlūnī, Shākir, *Tasliyat al-khawāṭir fī muntakhabāt al-mulaḥ wa-l-nawādir*, Beirut: al-Maṭbaʿah al-Adabiyyah, 1882.

Bishr ibn Abī Khāzim al-Asadī, *Dīwān*, ed. by Majīd Ṭarād, Beirut: Dār al-Kitāb al-ʿArabī, 1994.

al-Buḥturī, Abū ʿUbādah, *al-Ḥamāsah*, ed. by Maḥmūd Riḍwān Dayyūb, Beirut: Dār al-Kutub al-ʿIlmiyyah, 1999.

al-Bustī, Muḥammad ibn Ḥibbān, *al-Thiqāt*, ed. by Muḥammad ʿAbd al-Muʿīd Khān, 10 vols. Hyderabad: Dāʾirat al-Maʿārif al-ʿUthmāniyyah, 1973.

al-Damīrī, Kamāl al-Dīn, *Ḥayāt al-ḥayawān al-kubrā*, 2 vols. Cairo: al-Maktabah al-Tijāriyyah al-Kubrā, repr. Beirut: Dār al-Fikr, n.d.

Dhū l-Rummah, Ghaylān ibn ʿUqbah al-ʿAdawī, *Dīwān Dhī l-Rummah, sharḥ Abī Naṣr Aḥmad ibn Ḥātim al-Bāhilī ṣāḥib al-Aṣmaʿī, riwāyat Abī l-ʿAbbās Thaʿlab*, ed. by ʿAbd al-Quddūs Abū Ṣāliḥ, 3 vols. Beirut: Muʾassasat al-Īmān, 1982.

al-Dīnawarī, Abū Ḥanīfah, *al-Akhbār al-ṭiwāl*, ed. by V. Guirgass, Leiden: Brill, 1888.

al-Farazdaq, *Dīwān*, ed. and cmt. by ʿAbd Allāh al-Ṣāwī, Cairo: al-Maktabah al-Tijāriyyah al-Kubrā, 1936.

al-Fīrūzābādī, Majd al-Dīn Muḥammad ibn Yaʿqūb, *al-Qāmūs al-muḥīṭ*, 4 vols. Cairo: Maktabat Muṣṭafā al-Bābī al-Ḥalabī, 1952.

Ḥājjī Khalīfah, *Kashf al-ẓunūn ʿan asāmī l-kutub wa-l-funūn*, ed. by Şerefettin Yaltkaya and Rifat Bilge, Istanbul: Maarif Matbaası, 1941–1943.

al-Hamadhānī, Badīʿ al-Zamān, *al-Maqāmāt*, ed. by Muḥammad ʿAbduh, repr. Beirut: Dār al-Mashriq, 1973.

al-Hamdānī, Abū Muḥammad al-Ḥasan ibn Aḥmad ibn Yaʿqūb, *al-Iklīl min akhbār al-Yaman wa-ansāb Ḥimyar*, x (*Fī ansāb maʿārif Hamdān*), ed. by Muḥibb al-Dīn al-Khaṭīb, Cairo: Maktabat al-Salafiyyah, AH1368.

Hudbah ibn Khashram al-ʿUdhrī, *Shiʿr*, ed. by Yaḥyā al-Jubūrī, Kuweit: Dār al-Qalam, 1986.

Ibn ʿAbd Rabbih, Abū ʿUmar Aḥmad ibn Muḥammad, *al-ʿIqd al-farīd*, ed. by Aḥmad Amīn, Aḥmad al-Zayn, and Ibrāhīm al-Abyārī, 7 vols. Cairo, 1948–1953, repr. Beirut: Dār al-Kitāb al-ʿArabī, 1983.

Ibn Abī l-Ḥadīd, ʿIzz al-Dīn Abū Ḥāmid ʿAbd al-Ḥamīd ibn Hibat Allāh al-Madāʾinī, *Sharḥ Nahj al-balāghah, al-jāmiʿ li-khuṭab wa-ḥikam wa-rasāʾil al-Imām Amīr al-Muʾminīn ʿAlī ibn Abī Ṭālib*, ed. by Ḥusayn al-Aʿlamī, 5 vols. Beirut: Muʾassasat al-Aʿlamī, 1995.

Ibn Abī Ṭāhir Ṭayfūr, *Balāghāt al-nisāʾ*, Beirut: Dār al-Ḥadāthah, 1987.

Ibn Abī Uṣaybiʿah, *ʿUyūn al-anbāʾ fī ṭabaqāt al-aṭibbāʾ*, ed. by A. Müller, 2 vols. Cairo—Königsberg: al-Maṭbaʿah al-Wahbiyyah, 1882–1884.

Ibn Abī Uṣaybiʿāh, *A Literary History of Medicine: The* ʿUyūn al-anbāʾ fī ṭabaqāt al-aṭibbāʾ *of Ibn Abī Uṣaybiʿah*, ed. and tr. by Emilie Savage-Smith et al. (Handbook of Oriental Studies, Section One: The Near and Middle East, 134), 3 vols. in 5, Leiden: Brill, 2020.

Ibn al-Anbārī, Abū l-Barakāt Kamāl al-Dīn ʿAbd al-Raḥmān ibn Muḥammad, *Nuzhat al-*

alibbā' fī ṭabaqāt al-udabā', ed. by Ibrāhīm al-Sāmarrā'ī, Beirut: Maktabat al-Manār, 1985.

Ibn al-Athīr, 'Izz al-Dīn, *al-Kāmil fī l-tārīkh*, ed. by Abū l-Fidā' 'Abd Allāh al-Qāḍī and Muḥammad Yūsuf al-Daqqāq, 11 vols. Beirut: Dār al-Kutub al-'Ilmiyyah, 1987–2003.

Ibn Badrūn, *Sharḥ Qaṣīdat Ibn 'Abdūn*, ed. R.P.A. Dozy, Leiden: Luchtmans, 1846.

Ibn al-Dumaynah, *Dīwān, ṣan'at Abī l-'Abbās Tha'lab wa-Muḥammad ibn Ḥabīb*, ed. by Aḥmad Rātib al-Naffākh, Cairo: Maktabat Dār al-'Urūbah, 1959.

Ibn Durayd, Abū Bakr Muḥammad ibn al-Ḥasan, *al-Ishtiqāq*, ed. by Ferdinand Wüstenfeld, Göttingen: Dieterichsche Buchhandlung, 1854.

Ibn Durayd, Abū Bakr Muḥammad ibn al-Ḥasan, *Jamharat al-lughah*, ed. by Ramzī Munīr Ba'labakkī, 3 vols. Beirut: Dār al-'Ilm li-l-Malāyīn, 1987.

Ibn al-Faqīh, Abū Bakr Aḥmad ibn Muḥammad al-Hamadhānī, *Mukhtaṣar kitāb al-buldān* / Ibn al-Fakîh al-Hamadhânî, *Compendium libri Kitâb al-boldân*, ed. by M.J. de Goeje (Bibliotheca Geographorum Arabicorum, 5), Leiden: Brill, 1885.

Ibn Ḥabīb, Muḥammad Abū Ja'far, *Alqāb al-shu'arā' wa-man yu'rafu minhum bi-ummih*, ed. by 'Abd al-Salām Hārūn, in *Nawādir al-makhṭūṭāt* [q.v.], ii, 297–328.

Ibn Ḥabīb, Muḥammad Abū Ja'far, *Asmā' al-mughtālīn min al-ashrāf fī l-jāhiliyyah wa-l-Islām, wa-asmā' man qutila min al-shu'arā'*, ed. by 'Abd al-Salām Hārūn, in *Nawādir al-makhṭūṭāt* [q.v.], ii, 105–278.

Ibn Ḥabīb, Abū Ja'far Muḥammad, *Asmā' al-mughtālīn min al-ashrāf fī l-jāhiliyyah wa-l-Islām, wa-yalīhī Kunā l-shu'arā' wa-man ghalabat kunyatuhu 'alā ismih*, ed. by Sayyid Kasrawī (or Kisrawī) Ḥasan, Beirut: Dār al-Kutub al-'Ilmiyyah, 2001.

Ibn Ḥabīb, Muḥammad Abū Ja'far, *Khalq al-insān* (*fī l-lughah*), ed. by Khalīl Ibrāhīm al-'Aṭiyyah, Basra: Maktabat al-Thaqāfah al-Dīniyyah, 1994.

Ibn Ḥabīb, Muḥammad Abū Ja'far, *Kunā l-shu'arā' wa-man ghalabat kunyatuhu 'alā ismih*, ed. by 'Abd al-Salām Hārūn, in *Nawādir al-makhṭūṭāt* [q.v.], ii, 279–296.

Ibn Ḥabīb, Muḥammad Abū Ja'far, *Man nusiba ilā ummihi min al-shu'arā'*, ed. by 'Abd al-Salām Hārūn, in *Nawādir al-makhṭūṭāt* [q.v.], i, 81–96.

Ibn Ḥabīb, Abū Ja'far Muḥammad, *al-Muḥabbar, riwāyat Sa'īd ibn al-Ḥasan al-Sukkarī*, ed. by Ilse Lichtenstädter, Hyderabad, 1942, repr. Beirut: Dār al-Āfāq al-Jadīdah, n.d.

Ibn Ḥabīb, Muḥammad Abū Ja'far, *al-Munammaq fī akhbār Quraysh*, ed. by Khūrshīd Aḥmad Fāriq, Beirut: 'Ālam al-Kutub, 1985.

Ibn Ḥabīb, Muḥammad, *Ummahāt al-nabī*, ed. by Ḥusayn 'Alī Maḥfūẓ, Baghdād: Sharikat al-Nashr wa-l-Ṭibā'ah al-'Irāqiyyah, 1952 (Nawādir al-makhṭūṭāt al-'Arabiyyah fī Īrān, 1).

Ibn Ḥabīb, Muḥammad, *Ummahāt al-nabī*, ed. by Muḥammad 'Abd al-Qādir Aḥmad, Cairo: Maktabat al-Nahḍah al-Miṣriyyah, 1982.

Ibn Ḥamdūn, Muḥammad ibn al-Ḥasan ibn Muḥammad ibn 'Alī, *al-Tadhkirah al-Ḥamdūniyyah*, ed. by Iḥsān 'Abbās and Bakr 'Abbās, 10 vols. Beirut: Dār Ṣādir, 1996.

Ibn Hishām, *al-Sīrah al-nabawiyyah*, ed. by Muṣṭafā al-Saqqā, Ibrāhīm al-Abyārī. and ʿAbd al-Ḥafīẓ Shalabī, 2 vols. Cairo: Muṣṭafā al-Bābī al-Ḥalabī, 1955.

[Ibn Hishām / Ibn Isḥāq], *The Life of Muhammad, A Translation of Isḥāq's* [*sic*] Sirāt Rasūl Allāh, with introd. and notes by A. Guillaume, Karachi: Oxford University Press, 1978.

Ibn Hishām, *al-Tījān fī mulūk Ḥimyar*, Sanaa: Markaz al-Dirāsāt wa-l-Abḥāth al-Yamaniyyah, [1979].

Ibn Ḥubaysh, Abū l-Qāsim ʿAbd al-Raḥmān ibn Muḥammad, *al-Ghazawāt*, ed. by Muḥammad Ghunaym, Cairo: no publ., 1983.

Ibn al-Kalbī, *Ǧamharat an-nasab / Das genealogische Werk des Hišām ibn Muḥammad al-Kalbī*, ed. by Werner Caskel, 2 vols. (I: Tafeln, II: Register), Leiden: Brill, 1966.

Ibn al-Kalbī, Abū l-Mundhir Hishām ibn Muḥammad ibn al-Sā'ib, *Nasab Maʿadd wa-l-Yaman al-kabīr*, ed. by Nājī Ḥasan, Beirut: ʿĀlam al-Kutub / Maktabat al-Nahḍah al-ʿArabiyyah, 1988.

Ibn Khallikān, Abū l-ʿAbbās Shams al-Dīn Aḥmad ibn Muḥammad ibn Abī Bakr, *Wafayāt al-aʿyān wa-anbā' abnā' al-zamān*, ed. by Iḥsān ʿAbbās, 8 vols. Beirut: Dār al-Thaqāfah, 1968–1972.

Ibn Manẓūr, Jamāl al-Dīn Muḥammad ibn Mukarram al-Anṣārī, *Lisān al-ʿArab*, 20 vols. Cairo: al-Dār al-Miṣriyyah li-l-Ta'līf wa-l-Tarjamah, n.d. (repr. of ed. Būlāq, AH 1300–1308).

Ibn Manẓūr, Muḥammad ibn Mukarram, *Mukhtaṣar Tārīkh Dimashq li-Ibn ʿAsākir*, 31 vols. Damascus: Dār al-Fikr, 1984–1996.

Ibn Maymūn, Abū Ghālib Muḥammad ibn al-Mubārak, *Muntahā l-ṭalab min ashʿār al-ʿarab* (*The Utmost in the Search for Arab Poetry*), facs. ed. 3 vols. Frankfurt am Main: Institute for the History of Arabic-Islamic Science, 1986–1993.

Ibn al-Muʿtazz, *Ṭabaqāt al-shuʿarā' al-muḥdathīn*, ed. by ʿAbd al-Sattār Aḥmad Farrāj, Cairo: Dār al-Maʿārif, 1968.

Ibn al-Nadīm, *al-Fihrist*, ed. by Gustav Flügel, Johannes Roediger, and August Müller, 2 vols. Leipzig: F.C.W. Vogel, 1871–1872.

Ibn al-Nadīm, Abū l-Faraj Muḥammad ibn Isḥāq, *al-Fihrist*, ed. by Ayman Fu'ād Sayyid, 4 vols. London: Mu'assasat al-Furqān, 2009.

Ibn Nubātah, Jamāl al-Dīn—al-Miṣrī, *Sarḥ al-ʿuyūn fī sharḥ risālat Ibn Zaydūn*, ed. by Muḥammad Abū l-Faḍl Ibrāhīm, Cairo: Dār al-Fikr al-ʿArabī, 1964.

Ibn Qays al-Ruqayyāt, ʿUbayd Allāh, *Dīwān*, ed. by Muḥammad Yūsuf Najm, Beirut: Dār Ṣadir, n.d.

Ibn Qayyim al-Jawziyyah, *Akhbār al-nisā'*, ed. by Nizār Riḍā, Beirut: Dār Maktabat al-Ḥayāh, 1982.

Ibn al-Qifṭī, Jamāl al-Dīn Abū l-Ḥasan ʿAlī ibn Yūsuf, *Inbāh al-ruwāh ʿalā anbā' al-nuḥāh*, ed. by Muḥammad Abū l-Faḍl Ibrāhīm, 4 vols. Cairo: Dār al-Fikr al-ʿArabī, 1986.

Ibn Qutaybah, *Faḍl al-ʿArab wa-l-tanbīh ʿalā ʿulūmihā / The Excellence of the Arabs*, ed.

by James E. Montgomery and Peter Webb, tr. by Sarah Bowen Savant and Peter Webb (Library of Arabic Literature), New York: New York University Press, 2017.

Ibn Qutaybah, Abū Muḥammad ʿAbd Allāh ibn Muslim, *al-Imāmah wa-l-siyāsah, al-maʿrūf bi Tārīkh al-khulafāʾ*, ed. by ʿAlī Shīrī, 2 vols. Beirut: Dār al-Aḍwāʾ, 1990.

Ibn Qutaybah al-Dīnawarī, *Kitāb al-Maʿānī l-kabīr fī abyāt al-maʿānī*, 2 vols. Hyderabad: Dāʾirat al-Maʿārif al-ʿUthmāniyyah, 1949.

Ibn Qutaybah, Abū Muḥammad ʿAbd Allāh ibn Muslim, *al-Maʿārif*, ed. by Tharwat ʿUkāshah, Cairo: Dār al-Maʿārif, 1981.

Ibn Qutaybah, Abū Muḥammad ʿAbd Allāh ibn Muslim al-Dīnawarī, *al-Shiʿr wa-l-shuʿarāʾ*, ed. by Aḥmad Muḥammad Shākir, 2 vols. Cairo: Dār al-Maʿārif, 1966–1967.

Ibn Qutaybah, *ʿUyūn al-akhbār*, 4 vols. Cairo: Dār al-Kutub, 1925–1930.

Ibn Rashīq, Abū ʿAlī al-Ḥasan al-Qayrawānī al-Azdī, *al-ʿUmdah fī maḥāsin al-shiʿr wa-ādābihi wa-naqdih*, ed. Muḥammad Muḥyī l-Dīn ʿAbd al-Ḥamīd, 2 vols. repr. Beirut: Dār al-Jīl, 1972.

Ibn Saʿīd al-Andalsusī, *Nashwat al-ṭarab fī tārīkh jāhiliyyat al-ʿArab*, ed. by Nuṣrat ʿAbd al-Raḥmān, Amman: Maktabat al-Aqṣā, 1982.

Ibn Sallām al-Jumaḥī, Muḥammad, *Ṭabaqāt fuḥūl al-shuʿarāʾ*, ed. by Maḥmūd Muḥammad Shākir, Cairo: Dār al-Maʿārif, 1952.

Ibn Sayyār al-Warrāq, *Annals of the Caliphs' Kitchens: Ibn Sayyār al-Warrāq's Tenth-Century Baghdadi Cookbook*, English Translation with Introduction and Glossary by Nawal Nasrallah (Islamic History and Civilization, 70), Leiden: Brill, 2007.

Ibn al-Shajarī, Abū l-Saʿādāt Hibat Allāh ibn ʿAlī, *Mukhtārāt shuʿarāʾ al-ʿArab*, ed. by ʿAlī Muḥammad al-Bijāwī, Cairo: Dār Nahḍat Miṣr, 1975.

Ibn Shākir al-Kutubī, *Fawāt al-Wafayāt*, ed. by Iḥsān ʿAbbās, 5 vols. Beirut: Dār Ṣādir, 1973–1974.

Ibn Shākir al-Kutubī, *ʿUyūn al-tawārīkh* (*AH 219–250*), ed. by ʿAfīf Nāyif Ḥāṭūm, Beirut: Dār al-Thaqāfah, 1996.

Ibn al-Ṭiqṭaqā, Muḥammad ibn ʿAlī ibn Ṭabāṭabā, *al-Fakhrī fī l-ādāb al-sulṭāniyyah wa-l-duwal al-Islāmiyyah*, Beirut: Dār Ṣādir, n.d.

al-Iṣfahānī, Abū l-Faraj, *al-Aghānī*, 24 vols. Cairo: Dār al-Kutub / al-Hayʾah al-Miṣriyyah al-ʿĀmmah, 1927–1974.

al-Iṣfahānī, Abū l-Faraj, *al-Aghānī*, vol. XXI, ed. by Rudolph E. Brünnow, Leiden: Brill, 1888.

al-Jāḥiẓ, *al-Bayān wa-l-tabyīn*, ed. by ʿAbd al-Salām Muḥammad Hārūn, 4 vols. Cairo: Maktabat al-Khānjī, 1968.

al-Jāḥiẓ, *al-Bighāl*, in *Rasāʾil al-Jāḥiẓ*, ed. by ʿAbd al-Salām Muḥammad Hārūn, 4 vols. Cairo: Maktabat al-Khānjī, [1964, date of preface]–1979, ii, 211–378.

al-Jāḥiẓ, Abū ʿUthmān ʿAmr ibn Baḥr, *al-Burṣān wa-l-ʿurjān wa-l-ʿumyān wa-l-ḥūlān*, ed. by ʿAbd al-Salām Muḥammad Hārūn, Beirut: Dār al-Jīl, 1990.

al-Jāḥiẓ, *Fakhr al-sūdān ʿalā l-bīḍān*, in *Rasāʾil al-Jāḥiẓ*, ed. by ʿAbd al-Salām Muḥammad Hārūn, 4 vols. Cairo: Maktabat al-Khānjī, [1964, date of preface]–1979, i, 173–226.

al-Jāḥiẓ, *al-Ḥayawān*, ed. by ʿAbd al-Salām Muḥammad Hārūn, 8 vols. Cairo: Muṣṭafā al-Bābī al-Ḥalabī, 1965–1969.

al-Jāḥiẓ [attrib.], *al-Maḥāsin wa-l-aḍdād / Le livre des beautés et des antitheses*, ed. by G. van Vloten, Leiden: Brill, 1898.

Jarīr, *Dīwān Jarīr bi-sharḥ Muḥammad ibn Ḥabīb*, ed. by Nuʿmān Muḥammad Amīn Ṭāhā, 2 vols. Cairo: Dār al-Maʿārif, 1986.

al-Jarīrī, Abū l-Faraj al-Muʿāfā ibn Zakariyyā al-Nahrawānī, *al-Jalīs al-ṣāliḥ al-kāfī wa-l-anīs al-nāṣiḥ al-shāfī*, ed. by Muḥammad Mursī al-Khawlī and Iḥsān ʿAbbās, 4 vols. Beirut: ʿĀlam al-Kutub, 1993.

al-Khālidiyyān [Abū Bakr Muḥammad and Abū ʿUthmān Saʿīd ibnā Hāshim], *al-Ashbāh wa-l-naẓā'ir min ash'ār al-mutaqaddimīn wa-l-jāhiliyyah wa-l-mukhaḍramīn*, ed. by al-Sayyid Muḥammad Yūsuf, 2 vols. Cairo: Lajnat al-Ta'līf wa-l-Tarjamah wa-l-Nashr, 1958, 1965.

Khalīfah ibn Khayyāṭ, *Tārīkh*, ed. by Akram Ḍiyā' al-ʿUmarī, Riyadh: Dār Ṭaybah, 1985.

al-Kumayt ibn Zayd al-Asadī, *Dīwān*, ed. by Muḥammad Nabīl Ṭarīfī, Beirut: Dār Ṣādir, 2000.

Kushājim, Abū l-Fatḥ Maḥmūd ibn al-Ḥasan, *al-Maṣāyid wa-l-maṭārid*, ed. by Muḥammad Asʿad Ṭalas, Baghdad: Dār al-Yaqaẓah, [1954, date of preface].

al-Maʿarrī, Abū 'l-ʿAlā', *Risālat al-ghufrān / The Epistle of Forgiveness, Vol. One: A Vision of Heaven and Hell, or, A Pardon to enter the Garden; preceded by Ibn al-Qāriḥ's Epistle, Vol. Two: Hypocrites, Heretics, and Other Sinners*, ed. and tr. by Geert Jan van Gelder and Gregor Schoeler (Library of Arabic Literature), 2 vols. New York: New York University Press, 2013–2014.

al-Madā'inī, Abū l-Ḥasan ʿAlī ibn Muḥammad, *al-Murdifāt min Quraysh*, ed. by ʿAbd al-Salām Hārūn, in *Nawādir al-makhṭūṭāt* [q.v.], i, 57–80.

Maʿmar ibn Rāshid, *Kitāb al-Maghāzī / The Expeditions: An Early Biography of Muḥammad*, ed. and tr. by Sean W. Anthony (Library of Arabic Literature), New York: New York University press, 2014.

al-Maqdisī, al-Muṭahhar ibn Ṭāhir, *al-Bad' wa-l-ta'rīkh*, ed. by Clément Huart, 6 vols. Paris: Ernest Leroux, 1899–1919 [attributed by the editor to Abū Zayd Aḥmad ibn Sahl al-Balkhī].

al-Maqrīzī—*al-Maqrīzī's* al-Ḫabar ʿan al-bašar, *Vol. v, Sections 1–2: The Arab Thieves*, critical edition, annotated translation and study by Peter Webb (Bibliotheca Maqriziana, Opera maiora, 6), Leiden: Brill, 2019.

al-Marzubānī, Abū ʿUbayd Allāh Muḥammad ibn ʿImrān, *Ashʿār al-nisā'*, ed. by Sāmī Makkī al-ʿĀnī and Hilāl Nājī, Beirut: ʿĀlam al-Kutub, 1995.

al-Marzubānī, Abū ʿUbayd Allāh Muḥammad ibn ʿImrān, *Muʿjam al-shuʿarā'*, ed. by ʿAbd al-Sattār Aḥmad Farrāj, Cairo: Dār Iḥyā' al-Kutub al-ʿArabiyya, 1960.

al-Marzubānī, Abū ʿUbayd Allāh Muḥammad ibn ʿImrān, *Nūr al-qabas, al-mukhtaṣar min al-Muqtabas fī akhbār al-nuḥāh wa-l-udabā' wa-l-shuʿarā' wa-l-ʿulamā', ikhtiṣār*

Abī l-Maḥāsin Yūsuf ibn Maḥmūd al-Yaghmūrī / Die Gelehrtenbiographien des Abū ʿUbaidallāh al-Marzubānī in der Rezension des Ḥāfiẓ al-Yaġmūrī, Teil I: Text ed. by Rudolf Sellheim (Bibliotheca Islamica, 23a), Wiesbaden: Franz Steiner, 1964.

al-Masʿūdī, *Murūj al-dhahab*, éd. Barbier de Meynard & Pavet de Courteille, 7 vols. revue et corrigée par Charles Pellat, Beirut: al-Jāmiʿah al-Lubnāniyyah, 1966–1979.

al-Masʿūdī, *al-Tanbīh wa-l-ishrāf*, ed. by M.J. de Goeje, Leiden: Brill, 1893 (Arabic title page) / 1894 (Latin title page).

al-Maydānī, Abū l-Faḍl Aḥmad ibn Muḥammad, *Majmaʿ al-amthāl*, ed. by Naʿīm Ḥusayn Zarzūr, 2 vols. Beirut: Dār al-Kutub al-ʿIlmiyya, 1988.

Miʾat laylah wa-laylah, ed. by Maḥmūd Ṭarshūnah, Tunis: al-Majmaʿ al-Tūnisī li-l-ʿUlūm wa-l-Ādāb wa-l-Funūn Bayt al-Ḥikmah, 2013.

Miʾat laylah wa-laylah / A Hundred and One Nights, ed. and tr. by Bruce Fudge (Library of Arabic Literature), New York: New York University Press, 2016.

al-Mufaḍḍal al-Ḍabbī, *Amthāl al-ʿArab*, Constantinople: al-Jawāʾib, AH 1300.

al-Mufaḍḍal ibn Salamah ibn ʿĀṣim al-Ḍabbī, *al-Fākhir fī l-amthāl*, ed. by Muḥammad ʿUthmān, Beirut: Dār al-Kutub al-ʿIlmiyyah, 2011.

[*al-Mufaḍḍaliyyāt*]—*The Mufaḍḍalīyat: An Anthology of Ancient Arabian Odes compiled by al-Mufaḍḍal*, ed. by Charles James Lyall, vol. I: Arabic Text (with cmt. by Abū Muḥammad al-Qāsim ibn Muḥammad al-Anbārī), Oxford: Clarendon Press, 1921, Vol. II: Translation and Notes, Oxford: Clarendon Press, 1918.

Muhalhil ibn Rabīʿah, *Dīwān*, ed. by Ṭalāl Ḥarb, Beirut: al-Dār al-ʿĀlamiyyah, 1993.

Muḥammad ibn Ḥabīb *see* Ibn Ḥabīb, Muḥammad.

Muṣʿab ibn al-Zubayr (Abū ʿAbd Allāh al-Muṣʿab ibn ʿAbd Allāh ibn al-Muṣʿab al-Zubayrī), *Nasab Quraysh*, ed. by E. Levi-Provençal, Cairo: Dār al-Maʿārif, 1982.

al-Nābighah al-Dhubyānī, *Dīwān*, in W. Ahlwardt (ed.), *The Divans of the six ancient Arabic poets*, London: Trübner, 1870.

Nawādir al-makhṭūṭāt, ed. by ʿAbd al-Salām Hārūn, 2 vols. Cairo, Maktabat Muṣṭafā al-Bābī al-Ḥalabī, 1972–1973.

al-Nuwayrī, Shihāb al-Dīn Aḥmad ibn ʿAbd al-Wahhāb, *Nihāyat al-arab fī funūn al-adab*, 33 vols. Cairo: Dār al-Kutub / al-Hayʾah al-Miṣriyyah al-ʿĀmmah li-l-Kitāb, 1923–2007.

al-Qālī, Abū ʿAlī Ismāʿīl ibn al-Qāsim, *al-Amālī*, 2 vols. Cairo: Dār al-Kutub al-Miṣriyyah, 1926.

al-Qālī, Abū ʿAlī Ismāʿīl ibn al-Qāsim, *Dhayl al-Amālī wa-l-Nawādir*, Cairo: Dār al-Kutub al-Miṣriyyah, 1926, repr. Beirut: Dār al-Āfāq al-Jadīdah, n.d., together with Abū ʿUbayd al-Bakrī, *al-Tanbīh ʿalā awhām Abī ʿAlī fī Amālīh*.

Qurʾan—Arthur J. Arberry, *The Koran Interpreted*, London: Oxford University Press, 1964, repr. 1972.

Qurʾan—*The Qurʾan: A new translation* by M.A.S. Abdel Haleem (Oxford World's Classics), Oxford: Oxford University Press, 2005.

Qur'an—*The Qur'ān*, translated into English by Alan Jones, n.pl.: Gibb Memorial Trust, 2007.

al-Qurashī, Abū Zayd Muḥammad ibn Abī l-Khaṭṭāb, *Jamharat ashʿār al-ʿArab*, Beirut: Dār Ṣādir, 1963.

al-Qurashī, Abū Zayd, *Jamharat ashʿār al-ʿArab*, ed. by ʿAlī Muḥammad al-Bijāwī, Cairo: Nahḍat Miṣr, 1981.

al-Rāghib al-Iṣfahānī, *Muḥāḍarāt al-udabāʾ wa-muḥāwarāt al-shuʿarāʾ*, 2 vols. Būlāq: Maṭbaʿat Ibrāhīm al-Muwayliḥī, AH1287 [AD1870].

al-Ṣafadī, Ṣalāḥ al-Dīn Khalīl ibn Aybak, *al-Wāfī bi-l-Wafayāt / Das biographische Lexikon des Ṣalāhaddīn Ḫalīl ibn Aibak aṣ-Ṣafadī* (Bibliotheca Islamica, 6), 30 vols. Beirut—Wiesbaden—Berlin: Franz Steiner—Klaus Schwarz, 1931–2005.

al-Sarrāj, Abū Muḥammad Jaʿfar ibn Aḥmad, *Maṣāriʿ al-ʿushshāq*, 2 vols. Beirut: Dār Ṣādir, n.d.

al-Shanfarā ʿAmr ibn Mālik, *Dīwān*, ed. by Imīl Badīʿ Yaʿqūb, Beirut: Dār al-Kitāb al-ʿArabī, 1996.

al-Shimshāṭī, Abū l-Ḥasan ʿAlī ibn Muḥammad al-Muṭahhar al-ʿAdawī, *al-Anwār wa-maḥāsin al-ashʿār*, ed. by al-Sayyid Muḥammad Yūsuf and ʿAbd al-Sattār Farrāj, 2 vols. Kuwait: Maṭbaʿat Ḥukūmat al-Kuwayt, 1977–1978.

Sībawayh, Abū Bishr ʿAmr, *Kitāb Sībawayh*, 2 vols. Cairo: Dār al-Ṭibāʿah, AH1317–1318 [/1899–1900], repr. Baghdad: Maktabat al-Muthannā, n.d.

al-Sijistānī, Abū Ḥātim, *al-Muʿammarūn*, ed. by Ignaz Goldziher, in his *Abhandlungen zur arabischen Philologie, 2. Theil*, Leiden: Brill, 1899.

Suḥaym ʿAbd Banī l-Ḥasḥās, *Dīwān*, ed. by ʿAbd al-ʿAzīz al-Maymanī, Cairo: Dār al-Kutub, 1950.

al-Sukkarī, Abū Saʿid al-Ḥasan ibn al-Ḥusayn, *Sharḥ ashʿār al-Hudhaliyyīn*, ed. by ʿAbd al-Sattār Aḥmad Farrāj, 3 vols. Cairo: Dār al-ʿUrūbah, 1965.

al-Ṣūlī, Abū Bakr Muḥammad ibn Yaḥyā, *Adab al-kuttāb*, ed. by Muḥammad Bahjah al-Atharī and Maḥmūd Shukrī al-Ālūsī, repr. Beirut: Dār al-Kutub al-ʿIlmiyyah, n.d.

al-Ṣūlī, Abū Bakr Muḥammad ibn Yaḥyā, *al-Awrāq*, ed. J. Heyworth Dunne, 3 vols. London: Luzac, 1936.

al-Suyūṭī, Jalāl al-Dīn ʿAbd al-Raḥmān, *Bughyat al-wuʿāh fī ṭabaqāt al-lughawiyyīn wa-l-nuḥāh*, ed. by Muḥammad Abū l-Faḍl Ibrāhīm, 2 vols. Cairo, repr. Beirut: Dār al-Fikr, 1979.

al-Suyūṭī, Jalāl al-Dīn, *Tārīkh al-khulafāʾ*, ed. by Muḥammad Muḥyī l-Dīn ʿAbd al-Ḥamīd, Beirut: Dār al-Jīl, 1988.

al-Ṭabarī, Muḥammad ibn Jarīr, *Tārīkh al-rusul wa-l-mulūk*, ed. by M.J. de Goeje et al. 3 vols. Leiden: Brill, 1879–1901, with vol. *Introductio, glossarium, addenda et emendanda.*

al-Ṭabarī, *The History*, 40 vols. Albany, NY: State University of New York Press, 1991.

al-Tanūkhī, Abū ʿAlī al-Muḥassin ibn ʿAlī, *al-Faraj baʿd al-shiddah*, ed. by ʿAbbūd al-Shāljī, 5 vols. Beirut, Dār Ṣādir, 1978.

al-Tawḥīdī, Abū Ḥayyān ʿAlī ibn Muḥammad ibn al-ʿAbbās, *al-Baṣāʾir wa-l-dhakhāʾir*, ed. by Wadād al-Qāḍī, 9 vols. Beirut: Dār Ṣādir, 1988.

al-Tawḥīdī, Abū Ḥayyān, *al-Imtāʿ wa-l-muʾānasa*, ed. by Aḥmad Amīn and Aḥmad al-Zayn, 3 vols. Cairo: Lajnat al-Taʾlīf wa-l-Tarjamah wa-l-Nashr, 1939–1953.

al-Thaʿālibī, *The Book of Curious and Entertaining Information* (*The Laṭāʾif al-maʿārif of Thaʿālibī*), tr. with introd. and notes by C.E. Bosworth, Edinburgh: The University Press, 1968.

al-Thaʿālibī, Abū Manṣūr ʿAbd al-Malik ibn Muḥammad ibn Ismāʿīl, *Laṭāʾif al-maʿārif*, ed. by P. de Jong, Leiden: Brill, 1867.

al-Thaʿālibī, Abū Manṣūr ʿAbd al-Malik ibn Muḥammad ibn Ismāʿīl al-Nīsābūrī, *Thimār al-qulūb fī l-muḍāf wa-l-mansūb*, ed. by Muḥammad Abū l-Faḍl Ibrāhīm, Cairo: Dār al-Maʿārif, 1985.

Thaʿlab, Abū l-ʿAbbās Aḥmad ibn Yaḥyā, *Majālis Thaʿlab*, ed. by ʿAbd al-Salām Muḥammad Hārūn, 2 vols. Cairo: Dār al-Maʿārif, (vol. 1: *ṭabʿah* 5) 1987, (vol. 2: *ṭabʿah* 4) 1980.

al-Tibrīzī, Abū Zakariyyā Yaḥyā ibn ʿAlī al-Khaṭīb, *Sharḥ Dīwān al-Ḥamāsah li-Abī Tammām*, ed. by Gharīd al-Shaykh, Beirut: Dār al-Kutub al-ʿIlmiyyah, 2000.

ʿUmar ibn Shabbah, *Tārīkh al-Madīnah al-Munawwarah*, ed. by Fahīm Muḥammad Shaltūt, Beirut: Dār al-Turāth, 1990.

al-Washshāʾ, Abū l-Ṭayyib Muḥammad ibn Isḥāq, *al-Muwashshā*, ed. by Rudolph E. Brünnow, Leiden: Brill, 1886.

al-Yaʿqūbī, Aḥmad ibn Abī Yaʿqūb, *Tārīkh*, ed. by M.Th. Houtsma, 2 vols. Leiden: Brill, 1883.

al-Yaʿqūbī, *The Works of Ibn Wāḍiḥ al-Yaʿqūbī: An English Translation*, ed. by Matthew Gordon, Chase F. Robinson, Everett Rowson and Michael Fishbein (Islamic History and Civilization, Studies and Texts, 152), 3 vols. Leiden: Brill, 2018.

Yāqūt, *Muʿjam al-buldān*, 7 vols. Beirut: Dār Ṣādir, 1995.

Yāqūt, *Muʿjam al-udabāʾ*, ed. by Aḥmad Farīd Rifāʿī, 20 vols. in 10, Cairo, 1936–1938, repr. Beirut: Iḥyāʾ al-Turāth al-ʿArabī, n.d.

al-Zabīdī, Murtaḍā al-Ḥusaynī, *Tāj al-ʿarūs min jawāhir al-Qāmūs*, ed. by ʿAbd al-Sattār Farrāj et al., 40 vols. Kuwait: Maṭbaʿat Ḥukūmat al-Kuwayt, 1965–2001.

al-Zajjājī, *al-Ibdāl wa-l-muʿāqabah wa-l-naẓāʾir*, ed. by ʿIzz al-Dīn al-Tanūkhī, Damascus: al-Majmaʿ al-ʿIlmī al-ʿArabī, 1962.

al-Zamakhsharī, Jār Allāh Abū l-Qāsim Maḥmūd ibn ʿUmar, *Asās al-balāghah*, Beirut: Dār Ṣādir, 1979.

al-Zamakhsharī, Abū l-Qāsīm Jār Allāh Maḥmūd ibn ʿUmar, *al-Mustaqṣā fī amthāl al-ʿArab*, 2 vols. Hyderabad: Dāʾirat al-Maʿārif al-ʿUthmāniyyah, 1962.

al-Zawzanī al-ʿAbdalakānī, Abū Muḥammad ʿAbd Allāh ibn Muḥammad, *Ḥamāsat al-ẓurafāʾ min ashʿār al-muḥdathīn wa-l-qudamāʾ*, ed. by Khalīl ʿImrān al-Manṣūr, Beirut: Dār al-Kutub al-ʿIlmiyyah, 2002.

al-Zubaydī al-Andalusī, Abū Bakr Muḥammad ibn al-Ḥasan, *Ṭabaqāt al-naḥwiyyīn wa-l-lughawiyyīn*, ed. by Muḥammad Abū l-Faḍl Ibrāhīm, Cairo: Dār al-Maʿārif, 1984.

Zuhayr ibn Janāb al-Kalbī, *Dīwān*, ed. by Muḥammad Shafīq al-Bayṭār, Beirut: Dār Ṣādir, 1999.

Modern Studies

Authors of entries in the *Encyclopaedia of Islam* (EI2 and EI3) and *Encyclopedia of Arabic Literature* (EAL) are not listed but are mentioned in the notes.

Baalbaki, Ramzi, *The Arabic Lexicographical Tradition From the 2nd/8th to the 12th/18th Century* (Handbuch der Orientalistik, Section One: The Near and Middle East, 107), Leiden: Brill, 2014.

Biella, Joan Copeland, *Dictionary of Old South Arabic, Sabaean Dialect*, Leiden: Brill, 1982.

Bonebakker, S. A, "Nihil obstat in story-telling?", *Mededelingen der Koninklijke Nederlandse Akademie van Wetenschappen*, 55:8 (1992), 289–307 [also in R.C. Hovannisian & G. Sabagh (eds), *The Thousand and One Nights in Arabic Literature and Society*, Cambridge: Cambridge University Press, 1997, pp. 56–77].

Borg, Gert, *Mit Poesie vertreibe ich den Kummer meines Herzens: Eine Studie zur altarabischen Trauerklage der Frau* (Uitgaven van het Nederlands Historisch-Archaeologisch Instituut te Istanbul, 81), Istanbul/Leiden: Nederlands Historisch-Archaeologisch Instituut, 1997.

Bosworth, Clifford Edmund, *The New Islamic Dynasties: A Chronological and Genealogical Manual*, Edinburgh: Edinburgh University Press, 2004.

Bray, Julia, "Lists and Memory: Ibn Qutayba and Muḥammad b. Ḥabīb", in Farhad Daftary and Joseph W. Meri (eds), *Culture and Memory in Medieval Islam: Essays in Honour of Wilferd Madelung*, London: I.B. Tauris in association with the Institute of Ismaili Studies, 2003, pp. 210–231.

Bray, Julia, "Al-Muʿtaṣim's 'bridge of toil' and Abū Tammām's Amorium *qaṣīda*", in G.C. Hawting et al. (eds), *Studies in Islamic and Middle Eastern Texts and Traditions in Memory of Norman Calder*, Oxford: Oxford University Press, pp. 31–73.

Brockelmann, Carl, *Geschichte der Arabischen Litteratur*, 2. Aufl. 5 vols. Leiden: Brill, 1937–1947.

Brünnow, Rudolf-Ernst, und August Fischer, *Arabische Chrestomathie aus Prosaschriftstellern*, neunte Aufl., unveränderter Nachdruck der fünften, verbesserten Auflage, Leipzig: VEB Verlag Enzyklopädie, 1966.

Caskel, Werner, "*Aijām al-'Arab*: Studien zur altarabischen Epik", *Islamica*, 3 (1927–1930), 1*–99*.

Cooperson Michael, "al-Shanfara", in Michael Cooperson and Shawkat M. Toorawa (eds), *Arabic Literary Culture, 500–925*, (Dictionary of Literary Biography, 311), Detroit: Thomson Gale, 2005, pp. 318–324.

Dozy, R., *Supplément aux dictionnaires arabes*, 2me éd., 2 vols. Leiden: Brill, 1927.

Drory, Rina, "Three Attempts to Legitimize Fiction in Classical Arabic Literature", *Jerusalem Studies in Arabic and Islam*, 18 (1994), 146–164 [also in Rina Drory, *Models and Contacts: Arabic Literature and its Impact on Medieval Jewish Culture*, Leiden: Brill, 2000, pp. 37–47].

EAL = Julie Scott Meisami and Paul Starkey (eds), *Encyclopedia of Arabic Literature*, 2 vols. London: Routledge, 1998.

EI2 = *The Encyclopaedia of Islam, New [= Second] Edition*, 11 vols. with Supplement vol. and Index vol. Leiden: Brill, 1960–2009.

EI3 = *The Encyclopaedia of Islam, Three*, Leiden: Brill, 2007–.

Flanders, Judith, *The Invention of Murder: How the Victorians Revelled in Death and Detection and Created Modern Crime*, London: HarperPress, 2011.

Hava, J.G., *al-Farā'id al-durriyyah / Arabic-English Dictionary*, Beirut, repr. New Delhi: Goodword Books, 2006.

Hawting, G.R., *The First Dynasty of Islam: The Umayyad Caliphate AD 661–750*, 2nd ed. London: Routledge, 2000.

El-Hibri, Tayeb, *Parable and Politics in Early Islamic History: The Rashidun Caliphs*, New York: Columbia University Press, 2010.

Homerin, Th. Emil, "Echoes of a Thirsty Owl: Death and Afterlife in Pre-Islamic Arabic Poetry", *Journal of Near Eastern Studies*, 44 (1985), 165–184.

Jamil, Nadia, *Ethics and Poetry in Sixth-Century Arabia*, n. pl.: E.J.W. Gibb Memorial Trust, 2017.

Jamil, Nadia, "Playing for Time: *Maysir*-gambling in Early Arabic Poetry", in R.G. Hoyland and Ph.F. Kennedy (eds), *Islamic Reflections, Arabic Musings: Studies in Honour of Professor Alan Jones*, Oxford: E.J.W. Gibb Memorial Trust, 2004, pp. 48–90.

Jones, Alan (ed., tr., and cmt.), *Early Arabic Poetry, Volume One:* Marāthī *and* Ṣuʿlūk *Poems*, Reading: Ithaca Press, 1992.

Kanazi, George, "ʿUbaydullāh Ibn al-Ḥurr al-Juʿfī: His Life and Poetry", *Jerusalem Studies in Arabic and Islam*, 3 (1981–1982), 49–71 (English), 72–129 (Arabic, including the poetry).

Kennedy, Philip F. (ed.), *On Fiction and* Adab *in Mediaeval Arabic Literature* (Studies in Arabic Language and Literature, 6), Wiesbaden: Harrassowitz, 2005.

Kilpatrick, Hilary, "The 'Genuine' Ashʿab. The Relativity of Fact and Fiction in Early *adab* Texts", in Stefan Leder (ed.), *Story-telling in the Framework of Non-fictional Arabic Literature* [q.v.], pp. 94–117.

Lane, Edward William, *An Arabic-English Lexicon*, 8 vols. London: Williams and Norgate, 1863–1893.

Lecker, Michael, "Were the Jewish Tribes in Arabia Clients of Arab Tribes?", in Monique Bernards and John Nawas (eds), *Patronate and Patronage in Early and Classical Islam*, Leiden: Brill, 2005, pp. 50–69.

Leder, Stefan, "Conventions of Fictional Narration in Learned Literature", in Stefan Leder (ed.), *Story-telling in the Framework of Non-fictional Arabic Literature* [q.v.], pp. 34–60.

Leder, Stefan (ed.), *Story-telling in the Framework of Non-fictional Arabic Literature*, Wiesbaden: Harrassowitz, 1998.

Leder, Stefan, "The Use of Composite Form in the Making of the Islamic Historical Tradition", in Philip F. Kennedy, (ed.), *On Fiction and* Adab *in Mediaeval Arabic Literature* [q.v.], pp. 125–148.

Levi Della Vida, G., "Muḥammad Ibn Ḥabīb's 'Matronymics of Poets'", *Journal of the American Oriental Society*, 62 (1942), 156–171.

Lichtenstädter, Ilse, "Muḥammad Ibn Ḥabîb and his Kitâb al-Muḥabbar", *Journal of the Royal Asiatic Society*, 1939, pp. 2–5.

Lyons, M.C., *The Arabian Epic: Heroic and Oral Story-Telling* (University of Cambridge Oriental Publications, 49), 3 vols. Cambridge: Cambridge University Press, 1995.

Lyons, M.C., *The Man of Wiles in Popular Arabic Literature*, Edinburgh: Edinburgh University Press, 2012.

Malti-Douglas, Fedwa, "The Classical Arabic Detective", *Journal of Arabic Literature*, 31 (1988), 59–91.

Meyer, Egbert, *Der historische Gehalt der Aiyām al-ʿArab*, Wiesbaden: Harrassowitz, 1970.

Munt, Harry, "The Prophet's City before the Prophet: Ibn Zabāla (d. after 199/814) on Pre-Islamic Medina", in Philip Wood (ed.), *History and Identity in the Late Antique Near East*, Oxford: Oxford University Press, 2013, pp. 103–122.

Muth, Franz-Christoph, "Zopyros bei den Arabern. Streiflichter auf ein Motif Herodots in der arabischen Literatur", *Oriens*, 33 (1992), 230–267.

Nasrallah, *Annals of the Caliphs' Kitchens*, see under *Primary Sources*, Ibn Sayyār.

Nicholson, Reynold A., *A Literary History of the Arabs*, London, 1907, repr. Cambridge: Cambridge University Press, 1966.

Oller, Walter, "Al-Ḥārith ibn Ẓālim and the Trope of *Baghy* in the *Ayyām al-ʿArab*", in Philip F. Kennedy (ed.), *On Fiction and* Adab *in Mediaeval Arabic Literature* [q.v.], pp. 233–259.

Perry, Charles, "*Būrān*: The History of a Dish", in Maxime Rodinson, A.J. Arberry & Charles Perry, *Medieval Arab Cookery: Essays and Translations*, Blackawton, Totnes, Devon: Prospect Books, 2001, pp. 239–250.

al-Qāḍī, Muḥammad, "La composante narrative des «Journées des Arabes» (*Ayyām al-ʿArab*)", *Arabica*, 46 (1999), 358–371.

Reckendorf, H., *Arabische Syntax*, 2. Aufl. Heidelberg: Carl Winter Universitätsverlag, 1977.

Robinson, Chase F., *Islamic Historiography*, Cambridge: Cambridge University Press, 2003.

Rodinson, Maxime, "*Maʾmūniyya* East and West", in Maxime Rodinson, A.J. Arberry, and Charles Perry, *Medieval Arab Cookery: Essays and Translations*, Blackawton, Totnes, Devon: Prospect Books, 2001, pp. 183–197.

Rosenthal, Franz, *A History of Muslim Historiography*, Leiden: Brill, 1968.

Rouayheb, Khaled El-, *Before Homosexuality in the Arab-Islamic World, 1500–1800*, Chicago: The University of Chicago Press, 2005.

Schopen, Armin, & Oliver Kahl, *Die Natāʾiǧ al-fikar des Šaʿbān ibn Sālim aṣ-Ṣanʿānī: Eine jemenitische Gesundheitsfibel aus dem frühen 18. Jahrhundert. Text, Übersetzung und Kommentar*, Wiesbaden: Harrassowsitz, 1993.

Sezgin, Fuat, *Geschichte des arabischen Schrifttums. Band II: Poesie bis ca. 430 H.*, Leiden: Brill, 1975.

Shahin, Aram A., "Reflections on the Lives and Deaths of Two Umayyad Poets: Laylā al-Akhyaliyyah and Tawba b. al-Ḥumayyir", in Maurice A. Pomerantz and Aram Shahin (eds.), *The Heritage of Arabo-Islamic Learning: Studies Presented to Wadad Kadi*, Leiden: Brill: 2016, pp. 398–443.

Souissi, R., "Waḍḍāḥ al-Yaman, le personnage et sa légende", *Arabica*, 17 (1970), 252–308.

Stetkevych, Suzanne Pinckney, *The Mute Immortals Speak: Pre-Islamic Poetry and the Poetics of Ritual*, Ithaca & London: Cornell University Press, 1993.

Stetkevych, Suzanne Pinckney, *The Poetics of Islamic Legitimacy: Myth, Gender, and Ceremony in the Classical Arabic Ode*, Bloomington, Indiana: Indiana University Press, 2002.

Tayyara, Abed El-Rahman, "Ibn Ḥabīb's *Kitāb al-Muḥabbar* and its Place in Early Islamic Historical Writing", *Journal of Islamic Studies*, 29:3 (2018), 392–416.

Toumi, Lotfi, "Ta'abbaṭa Šarran—ein Räuberdichter der vorislamischer Zeit", *Wiener Zeitschrift für die Kunde des Morgenlandes*, 98 (2008), 249–275.

Ullmann, Manfred, *Flüche und unfromme Wünsche in der arabischen Sprache und Literatur*, Wiesbaden: Harrassowitz, 2020.

Ullmann, Manfred, *Untersuchungen zur Raǧazpoesie: Ein Beitrag zur arabischen Sprach- und Literaturwissenschaft*, Wiesbaden: Harrassowitz, 1966.

van Gelder, Geert Jan, "Birds of Battle: Old English and Arabic", *File: A Literary Journal* (Groningen, Dept. of English), 6 (1993), 9–16.

van Gelder, Geert Jan, *Classical Arabic Literature: A Library of Arabic Literature Anthology*, sel. and transl. (Library of Arabic Literature), New York and London: New York University Press, 2013.

van Gelder, Geert Jan, *Close Relationships: Incest and Inbreeding in Classical Arabic Literature*, London: I.B. Tauris, 2005.

van Gelder, Geert Jan, "On Coincidence: The Twenty-Seventh and Twenty-Eighth Nights of al-Tawḥīdī's *al-Imtāʿ wa-l-muʾānasa*. An Annotated Translation", in *Medieval Arabic Thought: Essays in Honour of Fritz Zimmermann*, ed. by Rotraud Hansberger, M. Afifi al-Akiti, and Charles Burnett, London—Turin: The Warburg Institute—Nino Aragno Editore, 2012, pp. 209–220.

Vogt, Matthias, *Figures de califes entre histoire et fiction: al-Walīd b. Yazīd et al-Amīn dans la représentation de l'historiographie arabe de l'époque ʿabbāside* (Beiruter Texte und Studien, 106), Beirut: Ergon Verlag Würzburg, 2006.

Webb, Peter, *Arab Thieves, see under Primary Sources*, al-Maqrīzī.

Winter, Michael, "Historiography in Arabic during the Ottoman Period", in Roger Allen & D.S. Richards (eds), *Arabic Literature in the Post-Classical Period* (The Cambridge History of Arabic Literature), Cambridge: Cambridge University Press, 2006, pp. 171–188.

WKAS = *Wörterbuch der klassischen arabischen Sprache*, ed. by Manfred Ullmann et al., 2 vols. Wiesbaden: Otto Harrassowitz, 1970–.

Wright, W., *A Grammar of the Arabic Language*, translated from the German of Caspari and edited with numerous additions and corrections, 3rd ed. rev. by W. Robertson Smith and M.J. de Goeje, 2 vols. Cambridge: Cambridge University Press, 1896–1898, repr. 1955.

al-Ziriklī, Khayr al-Dīn, *al-Aʿlām*, 8 vols. Beirut: Dār al-ʿIlm li-l-Malāyīn, 2002.

List of Sections

Prominent Murder Victims

§ 1 Jadhīmah al-Abrash
§ 2 Ḥassān ibn Tubbaʿ
§ 3 ʿImlīq
§ 4 al-Aswad ibn ʿAfār
§ 5 ʿĀmir al-Ḍaḥyān
§ 6 ʿAbdah ibn Murārah
§ 7 Zuhayr ibn ʿAbd Shams
§ 8 al-Ḥārith ibn Kaʿb
§ 9 Dāwūd ibn Hubālah
§ 10 Hammām ibn Murrah
§ 11 Jassās ibn Murrah
§ 12 ʿAmr and his brothers, sons of al-Zabbān al-Dhuhlī
§ 13 ʿAmr ibn Masʿūd and Khālid ibn Naḍlah
§ 14 Khālid ibn Jaʿfar ibn Kilāb (*see also* § 98)
§ 15 al-Fiṭyawn
§ 16 Lakhnīʿah Yanūf Dhū l-Shanātir al-Ḥimyarī
§ 17 ʿAlqamah ibn Dhī Qayfān
§ 18 al-Ṣimmah al-Akbar
§ 19 ʿAdī ibn Zayd (*see also* § 84)
§ 20 ʿUrwah al-Raḥḥāl ibn ʿUtbah
§ 21 Kaʿb ibn ʿAbd Allāh al-Namarī
§ 22 Kaʿb ibn al-Ashraf (*see also* § 92)
§ 23 Abū Rāfiʿ Sallām ibn Abī l-Ḥuqayq
§ 24 The Prophet Muḥammad and Bishr ibn al-Barāʾ ibn Maʿrūr al-Anṣārī
§ 25 Rifāʿah ibn Qays al-Jushamī
§ 26 Abū Uzayhir
§ 27 al-Mujadhdhar ibn Dhiyād al-Balawī and Qays ibn Zayd
§ 28 al-Aswad the Liar ibn Kaʿb al-ʿAnsī
§ 29 al-Ḥuṭam
§ 30 ʿUmar ibn al-Khaṭṭāb
§ 31 Sālim ibn Dārah (*see also* § 111)
§ 32 al-Zubayr ibn al-ʿAwwām
§ 33 Mālik ibn al-Ḥārith al-Ashtar
§ 34 ʿAlī ibn Abī Ṭālib
§ 35 Khārijah ibn Ḥudhāfah al-ʿAdawī

§36 Khālid ibn al-Muʿammar al-Sadūsī
§37 al-Ḥasan ibn ʿAlī
§38 Saʿīd ibn ʿUthmān ibn ʿAffān
§39 ʿAbd al-Raḥmān ibn Khālid ibn al-Walīd
§40 Shaybān ibn ʿAbd Shams ibn Shihāb
§41 ʿAbbād ibn ʿAlqamah
§42 Masʿūd ibn ʿAmr al-ʿAtakī
§43 Muḥammad ibn ʿAbd Allāh ibn Khāzim al-Sulamī
§44 ʿAbd Allāh ibn Bashshār ibn Abī ʿAqib (*see also* §115)
§45 Marwān ibn al-Ḥakam ibn Abī l-ʿĀṣ
§46 Qabīṣah ibn al-Qayn al-Hilālī
§47 Baḥīr ibn Warqāʾ al-Saʿdī
§48 Yazīd ibn al-Ḥuṣayn ibn Numayr al-Sakūnī
§49 Najdah ibn ʿĀmir al-Ḥanafī
§50 Abū Hāshim ʿAbd Allāh ibn Muḥammad ibn ʿAlī ibn Abī Ṭālib
§51 ʿUmar ibn ʿAbd al-ʿAzīz ibn Marwān
§52 ʿUmar ibn Yazīd ibn ʿUmayr al-Usayyidī
§53 Qatādah ibn Sābah ibn Thābit ibn Maʿbad
§54 ʿAmr ibn Muḥammad al-Thaqafī
§55 Manẓūr ibn Jumhūr
§56 ʿAbd Allāh ibn ʿUmar ibn ʿAbd al-ʿAzīz
§57 Ibrāhīm ibn Muḥammad ibn ʿAlī ibn ʿAbd Allāh ibn ʿAbbās
§58 Abū Salamah Ḥafṣ ibn Sulaymān
§59 ʿAbd Allāh ibn Muʿāwiyah ibn ʿAbd Allāh ibn Jaʿfar in Abī Ṭālib
§60 Yazīd ibn ʿUmar ibn Hubayrah
§61 ʿAlī and ʿUthmān, sons of Judayʿ al-Kirmānī al-Azdī
§62 ʿAbd Allāh ibn ʿAlī ibn ʿAbd Allāh ibn al-ʿAbbās
§63 Abū Muslim
§64 Maʿn ibn Zāʾidah al-Shaybānī
§65 ʿUqbah ibn Salm al-Hunāʾī
§66 al-Rabīʿ ibn Yūnus
§67 Idrīs ibn ʿAbd Allāh ibn Ḥasan ibn al-Ḥasan ibn ʿAlī ibn Abī Ṭālib
§68 al-Faḍl ibn Sahl
§69 Isḥāq ibn Mūsā al-Hādī
§70 Ḥumayd ibn ʿAbd al-Ḥamīd al-Ṭūsī
§71 ʿAbd Allāh ibn Mūsā al-Hādī
§72 Aḥmad ibn ʿAlī ibn Hārūn al-Rashīd
§73 ʿAlī ibn Mūsā ibn Jaʿfar
§74 al-ʿAbbās ibn Muḥammad ibn ʿAlī ibn Muḥammad ibn al-ʿAbbās
§75 Ismāʿīl ibn Habbār ibn al-Aswad ibn al-Muṭṭalib ibn Asad

§ 76 *Names of Rulers who Killed Their Kinsman:*
§ 76a ʿAmr ibn Tubbaʿ
§ 76b Salamah ibn al-Ḥārith al-Malik ibn ʿAmr ibn Ḥujr Ākil al-Murār al-Kindī
§ 76c ʿAbd Allāh ibn al-Zubayr,
§ 76d ʿAbd al-Malik
§ 76e Yazīd ibn al-Walīd ibn ʿAbd al-Malik.
§ 76f Abū Jaʿfar al-Manṣūr
§ 76g Hārūn al-Rashīd
§ 76h ʿAbd Allāh al-Maʾmūn
§ 76i Abū Isḥāq al-Muʿtaṣim
§ 77 Ziyād ibn ʿUbayd Allāh ibn ʿAbd Allāh ibn ʿAbd al-Madān al-Ḥārithī

Poets Who Were Killed

§ 78 Muhalhil ibn Rabīʿah
§ 79 ʿĀmir ibn Juwayn ibn ʿAbd Ruḍā ibn Qamrān al-Ṭāʾī
§ 80 ʿAntarah ibn Muʿāwiyah al-ʿAbsī
§ 81 ʿAbīd ibn al-Abraṣ
§ 82 Ṭarafah ibn al-ʿAbd
§ 83 Bishr ibn Abī Khāzim al-Asadī
§ 84 ʿAdī ibn Zayd al-ʿIbādī (*see also* § 19)
§ 85 Taʾabbaṭa Sharrā
§ 86 Ṣakhr ibn al-Sharīd al-Sulamī
§ 87 Ṭarīf ibn Tamīm al-ʿAnbarī
§ 88 al-Sulayk ibn al-Sulakah (*see also* § 93)
§ 89 ʿAbd ʿAmr ibn ʿAmmār al-Ṭāʾī
§ 90 Suwayd ibn Ṣāmit al-Awsī
§ 91 Durayd ibn al-Ṣimmah al-Jushamī
§ 92 Kaʿb ibn al-Ashraf (*see also* § 22)
§ 93 al-Sulayk ibn al-Sulakah (*see also* § 88)
§ 94 al-Ḥārith ibn Ẓālim al-Murri
§ 95 ʿAbd Allāh ibn Rawāḥah al-Anṣārī al-Khazrajī
§ 96 Jazʾ ibn al-Ḥārith al-Azdī
§ 97 al-Shanfarā
§ 98 Khālid ibn Jaʿfar ibn Kilāb (*see also* § 14)
§ 99 Ḥārithah ibn Qays al-Kinānī
§ 100 ʿUtaybah ibn al-Ḥārith ibn Shihāb
§ 101 al-Munakhkhal al-Yashkurī

§ 102 ʿAmr Dhū l-Kalb
§ 103 Ḥumrān ibn Mālik ibn ʿAbd al-Malik al-Khathʿamī
§ 104 Mālik ibn Nuwayrah
§ 105 Abū ʿAzzah
§ 106 ʿAbd Yaghūth ibn Waqqāṣ
§ 107 Yazīd ibn al-Ṭathriyyah
§ 108 al-Uqayshir
§ 109 Tawbah ibn al-Ḥumayyir
§ 110 Ziyādah ibn Zayd ibn Mālik and Hudbah ibn Khashram
§ 111 Sālim ibn Dārah (*see also* § 31)
§ 112 ʿUqaybah ibn Hubayrah al-Asadī
§ 113 Aʿshā Hamdān
§ 114 ʿUbayd Allāh ibn al-Ḥurr al-Juʿfī
§ 115 ʿAbd Allāh ibn Bashshār ibn Abī ʿAqib (*see also* § 44)
§ 116 Muzāḥim ibn ʿAmr al-Salūlī and Ibn al-Dumaynah al-Khathʿamī
§ 117 Sudayf ibn Maymūn
§ 118 ʿAbd Banī l-Ḥasḥās
§ 119 Waḍḍāḥ al-Yaman
§ 120 Qays ibn al-Khaṭīm
§ 121 Ghaḍūb

Index of Persons, Tribes, Nations, Groups (translation and annotation only)

The references are to paragraphs. The article (a)l-, in all forms and positions, is ignored for the alphabetical order. Long names have been shortened. Tribes and clans are indicated with "(tr)"; Banū, introducing tribal names, has been omitted. Between names, ibn and bint are abbreviated as b. and bt.

ʿAbbād b. ʿAlqamah 41
ʿAbbād b. Bishr 22
al-ʿAbbās b. ʿAbd al-Muṭṭalib 50n
al-ʿAbbās b. Jaʿfar 73
al-ʿAbbās b. al-Maʾmūn 76i
al-ʿAbbās b. Muḥammad b. ʿAlī 74
ʿAbd b. Ṭalq 42n
ʿAbd Allāh b. (al-)ʿAbbās 33
ʿAbd Allāh b. ʿAbd al-Raḥmān *see* Aʿshā Hamdān
ʿAbd Allāh b. Abī Bakr 32n
ʿAbd Allāh b. Abī Ḥadrad 25
ʿAbd Allāh b. ʿAlī b. ʿAbd Allāh 58, 62, 63, 76f
ʿAbd Allāh b. ʿAmmār 29n
ʿAbd Allāh b. ʿAtīk 23
ʿAbd Allāh b. ʿAwn *see* Ibn ʿAwn
ʿAbd Allāh b. Bādirah (tr) 107
ʿAbd Allāh b. Bashshār 44, 114n, 115
ʿAbd Allāh b. Ḍammār 29n
ʿAbd Allāh b. Ghaṭafān (tr) 31, 111
ʿAbd Allāh b. Ḥabīb *see* Abū ʿAbd al-Raḥmān al-Sulamī
ʿAbd Allāh b. Ḥadhaf 29
ʿAbd Allāh b. al-Ḥārith b. Nawfal 42n
ʿAbd Allāh b. al-Ḥasan b. al-Ḥāsan 60n
ʿAbd Allāh b. al-Ḥumayyir 109
ʿAbd Allāh b. Jaʿfar 33, 110
ʿAbd Allāh b. Jaʿwanah 107
ʿAbd Allāh b. Khāzim 43
ʿAbd Allāh b. Muḥammad b. ʿAlī *see* al-Manṣūr
ʿAbd Allāh b. Muʿāwiyah ibn ʿAbd Allāh 59
ʿAbd Allāh b. Mūsā al-Hādī 71
ʿAbd Allāh b. Rawāḥah 95
ʿAbd Allāh b. Ṣabirah 12n
ʿAbd Allāh b. Thawr *see* Abū Fudayk
ʿAbd Allāh b. ʿUbayd Allāh *see* Ibn al-Dumaynah
ʿAbd Allāh b. ʿUmar b. al-ʿAzīz 56, 57, 59
ʿAbd Allāh b. Unays 23
ʿAbd Allāh b. Yasār 44n
ʿAbd Allāh b. al-Zubayr 49n, 76c, 112n, 114n
ʿAbd Allāh al-Maʾmūn *see* al-Maʾmūn
ʿAbd Allāh al-Ṭayfūrī 70
ʿAbd ʿAmr b. ʿAmmār 89
ʿAbd ʿAmr b. Bishr 82
ʿAbd al-ʿĀṣ b. Thaʿlabah 9
ʿAbd al-Ashhal (tr) 22
ʿAbd al-ʿAzīz b. ʿImrān 68
ʿAbd al-ʿAzīz b. Marwān 119
ʿAbd al-ʿAzīz b. al-Walīd 119
ʿAbd Banī l-Ḥasḥās 118
ʿAbd Hind b. Juradh 82
ʿAbd al-Malik b. Marwān 39n, 47, 48, 49n, 76cn, 76d, 113, 114
ʿAbd al-Malik b. Muwaylik 93n
ʿAbd al-Malik b. ʿUbaythir 62
ʿAbd al-Malik b. ʿUthmān 31n
ʿAbd al-Masīḥ b. ʿAsalah 21n
ʿAbd al-Muṭṭalib 42n
ʿAbd (al-)Qays (tr) 9, 21n, 29n, 82
ʿAbd al-Raḥmān b. ʿAwf 30, 32n
ʿAbd al-Raḥmān b. Ḥassān 110n
ʿAbd al-Raḥmān b. Ismāʿīl *see* Waḍḍāḥ al-Yaman
ʿAbd al-Raḥmān b. Jabr 22
ʿAbd al-Raḥmān b. Khālid b. al-Walīd 39
ʿAbd al-Raḥmān b. Muḥammad b. al-Ashʿath 108n, 113
ʿAbd al-Raḥmān b. Muljam 34
ʿAbd al-Raḥmān b. Muslim *see* Abū Muslim
ʿAbd al-Raḥmān b. Ṣabḥān 75
ʿAbd al-Raḥmān b. Umm al-Ḥakam 46
ʿAbd al-Raḥmān b. Zayd *see* al-Akhraz
ʿAbd al-Ṣamad b. ʿAlī 117
ʿAbd Shams b. Saʿd (tr) 106
ʿAbd al-ʿUzzā (tr) 75n
ʿAbd Yaghūth b. Waqqāṣ 106

ʿAbdah b. Murārah 6
ʿAbhalah 28n
ʿAbīd b. al-Abraṣ 13n, 79n, 81, 97n
Abjar b. (Jābir b.) Bujayr 29
al-Abnāʾ (Yemen) 28
al-Abnāʾ (tr) 83
al-Abrad 89
ʿAbs b. Ḥudhār 83n
ʿAbs b. Rifāʿah (tr) 107n
ʿAbs b. Ṭalq al-Ṭiʿān 42
Abū l-ʿAbbās ʿAbd Allāh *see* al-Saffāḥ
Abū ʿAbd al-Raḥmān al-Sulamī 34
Abū ʿAjwah 75
Abū l-Aswad al-Duʾalī 3n
Abū ʿAzzah 105
Abū Bakr 26n, 29, 30n, 104
Abū Bijād 102
Abū Bilāl b. Udayyah 41
Abū Dāwūd al-Dhuhlī *see* Khālid b. Ibrāhīm
Abū Dhuʾayb 96n
Abū Fudayk 49
Abū Ghānim *see* Ḥumayd b. ʿAbd al-Ḥamīd
Abū Ḥammād 60
Abū Ḥanīfah Ḥarb b. Qays 63
Abū Hāshim ʿAbd Allāh b. Muḥammad 50, 59, 60
Abū Ḥumayd Muḥammad b. Ibrāhīm 58
Abū ʿIṣām 70
Abū l-Jadʿāʾ 87
Abū Jaʿfar *see* al-Manṣūr
Abū Jubaylah 15
Abū Karib Asʿad 2n
Abū Lahab (tr) 117
Abū Laṭīfah al-ʿUqaylī 107
Abū Luʾluʾah 30
Abū Marḥab *see* Thaʿalabah b. Ḥaṣabah
Abū Mārid 87
Abū Muḥammad al-Sufyānī 77
Abū Muslim 55, 57, 58, 59, 61, 62, 63
Abū Nāʾilah *see* Silkān b. Salāmah
Abū l-Najm al-ʿIjlī 87n
Abū Nijād *see* Abū Bijād
Abū Qatādah *see* al-Ḥārith b. Ribʿī
Abū Qurdūdah 89n
Abū Rabīʿah b. Dhuhl (tr) 53, 87
Abū Rāfiʿ *see* Ibn Abī l-Ḥuqayq
Abū Salamah Ḥafṣ b. Sulaymān 58
Abū Sammāl 112
Abū Ṣaʿṣaʿah b. Zayd 120
Abū Simāk *see* Abū Sammāl
Abū Sufyān b. Ḥarb 26, 27n
Abū Thawr Rabīʿah *see* Rabīʿah b. Thaʿlabah
Abū ʿUthmān 60
Abū Uzayhir b. Unays 26
Abyssinians 16, 28, 43n, 118n, 119
ʿĀd (tr) 17n
ʿAdī (tr) 35
ʿAdī b. Marīnā 19
ʿAdī b. Naṣr 1n
ʿAdī b. Rabīʿah *see* Muhalhil b. Rabīʿah
ʿAdī b. Zayd 19, 78n, 84
ʿAdnān (tr) 8, 113
Adraʿ ibn al-Ghassāniyyah 110
ʿAdwān (tr) 102
ʿAfār 3
ʿAfīrah 3n
al-Afshīn 76in
al-Aghlab b. Sālim 60
al-Aḥlāf (tr) 26
Aḥmad b. Abī Khālid al-Aḥwal 70
Aḥmad b. ʿAlī b. Hārūn al-Rashīd 72
al-Aḥnaf b. Qays 32
ʿĀʾidhah (tr) 87
ʿĀʾishah bt Abī Bakr 30, 32n
al-ʿAjam *see* Persians
ʿAjlā 43n
al-Akhraz ʿAbd al-Raḥmān b. Zayd 110
al-ʿAlāʾ b. al-Ḥaḍramī 29
ʿAlī b. ʿAbd Allāh b. al-ʿAbbās 58
ʿAlī b. Abī Saʿd 68
ʿAlī b. Abī Saʿīd 68n
ʿAlī b. Abī Ṭālib 30n, 32, 33, 34, 36, 37n, 47n, 51n, 112, 114n
ʿAlī b. Hārūn al-Rashīd 66n
ʿAlī b. Judayʿ 61
ʿAlī b. Mūsā b. Jaʿfar 73
ʿAlī al-Riḍā *see* ʿAlī b. Mūsā b. Jaʿfar
ʿAlqamah b. Dhī Qayfān 17
al-ʿAmālīq, al-ʿAmāliqah 1, 3n
Amat al-ʿAzīz 66, 71n
al-Amīn 76h
Amīnah bt ʿAlī b. ʿAbd Allāh b. al-ʿAbbās 63
ʿĀmir b. ʿĀmir *see* al-Fiṭyawn
ʿĀmir b. ʿAwf (tr) 109
ʿĀmir b. Bādirah (tr) 107
ʿĀmir b. al-Ḍaḥyān 5
ʿĀmir b. Ḍubārah 59
ʿĀmir b. Juwayn 79, 89n

ʿĀmir b. Luʾayy (tr) 29
ʿĀmir b. Rabīʿah 91n
ʿĀmir b. Ṣaʿṣaʿah 29n, 46, 83, 109n
ʿĀmir al-Akbar (tr) 79n
ʿAmmār b. Yāsir 33
ʿAmr b. ʿAbd Allāh *see* Abū ʿAzzah
ʿAmr b. Abī ʿUmārah 96
ʿAmr b. ʿAdī 1
ʿAmr b. al-Ahtam 102n
ʿAmr b. al-ʿAjlān *see* ʿAmr Dhū l-Kalb
ʿAmr b. ʿĀmir (tr) 91
ʿAmr b. al-ʿĀṣ 32n, 34, 35
ʿAmr b. ʿĀṣiyah 79n, 102n
ʿAmr b. Ayyūb 60n
ʿAmr b. Bukayr 34, 35n
ʿAmr b. Hind 82, 89n, 101n
ʿAmr b. Ḥudhār 83n
ʿAmr b. Jurmūz 32
ʿAmr b. Kulthūm 82n
ʿAmr b. Maʿdī Karib 17n, 28
ʿAmr b. Masʿūd 13
ʿAmr b. Muḥammad al-Thaqafī 54
ʿAmr b. Saʿd 93n
ʿAmr b. Saʿīd 76d
ʿAmr b. Salmā *see* Wazar b. Jābir
ʿAmr b. Tubbaʿ 2, 16, 76a
ʿAmr b. ʿUthmān 38n, 49
ʿAmr b. Yathribī 88n
ʿAmr b. Zabbān al-Dhuhlī 12
ʿAmr b. al-Ẓarib 1
ʿAmr b. al-Zubayr 76c
ʿAmr Dhū l-Adhʿār 7n
ʿAmr Dhū l-Kalb 102
ʿAmrah 79
Amraʿah *see* Imraʿah
Anas b. Mudrik(ah) 88, 93
al-ʿAnbar b. ʿAmr (tr) 87
ʿAnbasah b. Tamīm 112
ʿAns (tr) 28
al-Anṣār 6n, 24n, 27n, 95, 104, 120
ʿAntarah b. Muʿāwiyah 80
ʿAntarah b. Shaddād *see* ʿAntarah b. Muʿāwiyah
Anūsharwān 63n
ʿAnz b. Wāʾil 107
al-ʿArab al-ʿĀribah 1n
al-ʿArab al-Mustaʿribūn 1n
Asad (tr) 6, 13, 31n, 76b, 81n, 86, 100, 104, 106n, 108n, 112, 118n
Asʿad b. Ibrāhīm 37
al-Aʿshā 88n
Aʿshā Hamdān 113
al-Ashajj *see* al-Ashʿath b. Qays
Ashʿarah *see* Ishʿarah
al-Ashʿath b. Qays 34, 113
al-Ashtar *see* Mālik b. al-Ḥārith
Asīd (Usayyid) b. ʿAmr 52n
Asīd b. Jābir *see* Usayd b. Jābir
Aslam (tr) 23, 25n
Aslam b. Zurʿah 38
Asmāʾ bt Duraym 32n
Asmāʾ bt ʿUmays 30
al-Aswad b. ʿAfār 3, 4
al-Aswad b. ʿĀmir 89
al-Aswad b. Kaʿb 28
al-Aswad b. al-Mundhir 14, 94, 97
al-Aswad al-Kadhdhāb *see* al-Aswad b. Kaʿb
Aswad b. Sharīk 53n
ʿĀtikah bt Zayd b. ʿAmr 32
ʿAṭiyyah b. al-Aswad 42
al-Aʿwar al-Shannī 36n
al-Awās b. al-Ḥajr (tr) 97
Awd (tr) 58
ʿAwf 93
ʿAwf b. ʿĀmir (tr) 91, 109n
ʿAwf b. Kaʿb (tr) 47n
ʿAwf b. al-Khazraj (tr) 27
ʿAwf b. Mālik 78
al-Aws (tr) 15, 22n, 23, 27n, 120n
Aws b. Ḥajar 101
Aws b. Ḥārithah 89
ʿAyhalah 28n
al-Azāriqah 42
Azd (tr) 1, 4, 26n, 42, 57n, 65n, 97n

Babbah *see* ʿAbd Allāh b. al-Ḥārith
Bādirah bt Ḥārithah (tr) 107
Baḥīr b. Warqāʾ 47
al-Baʿīth 18
Bakr b. Wāʾil (tr) 9, 10n, 11, 29n, 36n, 55, 76b, 82n, 87
Balʿāʾ b. Qays 99n
Balʿāʾ b. Qays (tr) 20
Balḥārith b. Kaʿb *see* al-Ḥārith b. Kaʿb
Balī (tr) 27n, 99
Bal-Qayn (tr?) 95
al-Barājim (tr) 18
al-Barrāḍ al-Kinānī 20

Bashshār b. Burd 65n
al-Basūs 10n, 11n, 78n
Bilqīṣ b. Ṣayfī 7
Bishr b. Abī Khāzim 83
Bishr b. al-Barāʾ 24
Bishr b. Ḥārithah 79
Bishr b. Marwān 46
Bishr b. ʿUtbah 40
“Blood-lickers” *see* Laʿaqat al-dam
Bukayr b. Wishāḥ (*or* Wassāj) 47
al-Buqūm 97
al-Burak b. ʿAbd Allāh 34
Būrān bt al-Ḥasan b. Sahl 70
Buzurgmihr 63n
Byzantines 39, 74n, 76i (*see also* Romans)

Christians 16, 21n, 30n, 31, 70n
Confederates *see* al-Aḥlāf

al-Ḍaʿājim 9n
Ḍabbah (tr) 58n
Ḍabbah b. Udd 8
Dād(h)awayh 28
al-Ḍaḥḥāk b. Qays 46, 56
al-Ḍaḥyān *see* ʿĀmir al-Ḍaḥyān
al-Ḍajāʿim 9n
Ḍajʿam *see* al-Ḍajāʿim
Ḍaras (tr) 94, 89n
Dārat al-Qamar 31n
Dārim (tr) 18
Daws (tr) 26
Dāwūd b. ʿAlī b. ʿAbd Allāh 58, 60
Dāwūd b. Hubālah (Habālah, Habūlah) 9
Dāwūd b. Yazīd b. ʿUmar 60
the Descendants *see* al-Abnāʾ
Dhū l-Ḥimār *see* al-Aswad b. Kaʿb
Dhū l-Jawshan al-Kilābī 103
Dhū l-Kalb *see* ʿAmr Dhū l-Kalb
Dhū l-Khimār 28n
Dhū Nuwās 16
Dhū l-Qarnayn *see* al-Mundhir b. Imriʾ al-Qays
Dhū Ruʿayn 2
Dhū l-Rummah 101
Dhū l-Shanātir *see* Lakhnīʿah
Dhuʾāb b. Rubayyiʿah 100
Dhubyān (tr) 31n
Dhuhl (tr) 21n, 29n, 87n
Ḍubayʿah b. al-Ḥuṭam 29
Ḍubayʿah b. Zayd (tr) 27
Ḍujʿum *see* al-Ḍajāʿim
al-Dulāmiṣ 21n
al-Dumaynah bt Ḥudhayfah 116n
Durayd b. al-Ṣimmah 18n, 91

the Emigrants *see* al-Muhājirūn
Ethiopians *see* Abyssinians

Fadakī b. Aʿbad 87
Faḍālah b. Ḥābis 32
al-Faḍl b. Sahl 68, 73
Fahm b. ʿAmr (tr) 85, 102
Fākhitah *see* Ḥabbah bt Abī Hāshim
Faqʿas (tr) 13, 31n
Faraj al-Daylamī 68n
al-Farazdaq 7n, 32n, 40, 41, 52, 121n
Fāriʿah bt Shaddād 79n
Fāris al-Nabī *see* al-Ḥārith b. Ribʿī
Fātik b. al-Dīl (tr) 40
Fāṭimah 34n, 37n, 51n, 58n
Fāṭimah bt al-Walīd 38n
Fāṭimah ukht Hudbah 110
Fawzaʿah b. Salamah 9
Fayrūz Abū Luʾluʿah *see* Abū Luʾluʾah
Fayrūz b. al-Daylamī 28
Fazārah (tr) 31, 103n, 112n
al-Fiṭyawn 15
al-Furs *see* Persians

Ghadīrah b. Mālik (tr) 100
Ghaḍūb 121
Ghafār 3n
Ghālib al-Masʿūdī al-Aswad 68n
Ghālib al-Rūmī 68
Ghāmid (tr) 97
Ghanm b. Kaʿb (tr) 24n
al-Gharūr al-Mundhir b. al-Nuʿmān 29
Ghassān, Ghassānids 9n, 15, 21, 89, 99
Ghaṭafān (tr) 13, 14, 31n, 104
al-Ghawth b. Luʾayy 4
Ghaziyyah b. Jusham (tr) 91n
Ghifār 3n
Ghufaylah b. Qāsiṭ 12
Ghufayrah 3n

al-Ḥabash(ah) *see* Abyssinians
Ḥabbah bt Abī Hāshim 45
Ḥabīb (Ḥubayb) b. Khālid 13

al-Ḥabtar (tr) 109n
Haddāj b. Mālik 9
al-Hādī 66, 67, 69n, 71n
al-Ḥajjāj b. Yūsuf 46, 47, 48, 49n, 52n, 108n, 113
Ḥamaṣīṣah b. Sharāḥīl 87
Hamdān (tr) 4, 17, 113
Ḥammādah (or Ḥammā') 116
Hammām b. Murrah 10, 11n
Hammām b. Muṭarrif 109
Ḥanīfah (tr) 47, 107
Ḥanẓalah (tr) 18n, 76b, 104
Ḥarb b. ʿAbd Allāh 69n
Ḥarb (b. Sulayk?) 93
Ḥarb b. Umayyah 18
al-Ḥārith b. Abī Shamir 89, 99
al-Ḥārith b. ʿAmr al-Maqṣūr 76b
al-Ḥārith b. Aws 22
al-Ḥārith b. Baybah 18
al-Ḥārith b. Jabalah 21, 89n
al-Ḥārith b. Kaʿb 6n, 8
al-Ḥārith b. Kaʿb (tr) 77, 106, 109n
al-Ḥarith b. Ribʿī 23, 104
al-Ḥārith b. Suwayd 27, 90n
al-Ḥārith b. Ẓālim 14, 94, 98
Ḥārithah (tr) 22, 120
Ḥārithah b. Qasy 99
Ḥarmalah b. ʿAsalah 21
Ḥarmalah b. al-Ḥukaym 21n
Harthamah b. Aʿyan 67
Hārūn al-Rashīd 66n, 67, 72n, 74, 76g
al-Ḥasan b. ʿAlī b. Abī Ṭālib 32n, 34, 37, 110
al-Ḥasan b. ʿAlī b. al-Ḥasan 67
al-Ḥasan b. Muʿāwiyah b. ʿAbd Allāh 59
al-Ḥasan b. Qaḥṭabah 60
al-Ḥasan b. Sahl 68n, 70, 73n
al-Ḥasḥās (tr) 118
Hāshim (tr) 51, 57
Hāshim b. ʿAbd Manāf 51n
al-Hāshimiyyah 51n
Ḥassān b. Thābit 22n
Ḥassān b. Tubān (Tubbān, Tibān) 2n
Ḥassān b. Tubbaʿ 2, 3n, 4, 76a
Ḥawālah b. al-Hanw (tr) 97
Hawāzin (tr) 25n, 91n
al-Haytham b. Shuʿbah 60
Ḥāzim al-Buqmī 97
Ḥazn b. Bādirah (tr) 107
the Helpers *see* al-Anṣār
al-Hijris 10n, 11
Hilāl (tr) 46n, 91
Hilāl b. Umayyah al-Khuzāʿī 6
Ḥimyar (tr) 2n, 7n, 16
Hind 101
Hind bt Maʿbad b. Naḍlah 13n
Hind bt Muʿāwiyah b. al-Ḥārith 10
Ḥubayb *see* Ḥabīb
Hubayrah b. Abī Wahb 102n
Hubayrah b. Ṣakhr 79
Hubayrah b. al-Samīn 109
Hubayrah al-Makshūḥ 28n
Ḥubayshah 1n
Ḥudād b. Ẓālim 9
Hudbah b. Khashram 31n, 110, 116n
Ḥudhayfah b. Ḥiṣn 103n
Hudhayl (tr) 85, 102
al-Hujaym (tr) 87
Ḥujr b. al-Ḥārith 76bn
Ḥumayd b. ʿAbd al-Ḥamīd al-Ṭūsī 70
Ḥumayd b. Qaḥṭabah 60
Ḥumrān b. Mālik 103
Hunā'ah (tr.) 65n
Ḥurayth b. Aswad 53
Ḥusayn (servant) 71
al-Ḥusayn b. ʿAlī b. Abī Ṭālib 32n, 34, 37, 44, 110
al-Ḥusayn b. ʿAlī b. al-Ḥasan 67
al-Ḥuṭam 29
Huzaylah 3

al-ʿIbād 19n, 21n, 36n
Ibn Abī ʿAqib *see* ʿAbd Allāh b. Bashshār
Ibn Abī l-Ḥuqayq 22n, 23
Ibn Abī l-Shaykh 51
Ibn Akhḍar al-Māzinī *see* ʿAbbād b. ʿAlqamah
Ibn ʿAmmār *see* ʿAbd ʿAmr b. ʿAmmār
Ibn Arṭāh 38n
Ibn al-Ashʿāth *see* ʿAbd al-Raḥmān b. Muḥammad
Ibn Athāl *see* Ibn Uthāl
Ibn ʿAwn 37
Ibn Ḍajʿam 9
Ibn Ḍubārah *see* ʿĀmir ibn Ḍubārah
Ibn al-Dughunnah *see* Rabīʿah b. Rufayʿ
Ibn al-Dumaynah 110n, 116
Ibn Habbār *see* Ismāʿīl b. Habbār
Ibn al-Ḥabtariyyah 109

Ibn Hubayrah *see* Yūsuf b. ʿUmar *and* Yazīd b. ʿUmar
Ibn al-Ḥurr *see* ʿUbayd Allāh b. al-Ḥurr
Ibn ʿImrān 54
Ibn Jurmūz *see* ʿAmr b. Jurmūz
Ibn al-Kalbī 39
Ibn al-Kurdiyyah *see* Jaʿfar b. al-Manṣūr
Ibn Ladghah (*or* Ladhʿah) *see* Rabīʿah b. Rufayʿ
Ibn Maʿīn (Muʿayn, Muʿīn) 51
Ibn Muljam *see* ʿAbd al-Raḥmān b. Muljam
Ibn Qays al-Ruqayyāt 75
Ibn Rāfilah *see* Ibn Zāfilah
Ibn Salmā *see* Wazar ibn Jābir
Ibn Sayḥān *see* Ibn Arṭāh
Ibn al-Tayyāḥ 34
Ibn ʿUrwah al-Kinānī 99
Ibn Uthāl 39
Ibn Zāfilah 95
Ibrāhīm b. ʿAbd Allāh b. al-Ḥasan 77
Ibrāhīm al-Imām *see* Ibrāhīm b. Muḥammad b. ʿAlī
Ibrāhīm b. al-Mahdī 69
Ibrāhīm b. Mālik al-Ashtar 44n
Ibrāhīm b. Muḥammad b. ʿAlī 57
Ibycus 6n
Idrīs b. ʿAbd Allāh b. Ḥasan 67
Idrīs b. Idrīs 67
ʿIjl (tr) 29
ʿIkabb 101n
ʿImlāq 1n
ʿImlīq 1n, 3, 4
Imraʿah bt Dāwūd b. Hubālah 9
Imruʾ al-Qays b. Ḥujr 14n, 76bn, 79
Imruʾ al-Qays b. Zayd Manāh (tr) 19
ʿĪsā b. ʿAlī b. ʿAbd Allāh 58
ʿĪsā b. Mūsā b. Muḥammad 62
Isḥāq b. Mūsā al-Hādī 69
Isḥāq b. Ṭalḥah 108
Ishʿarah bt Dāwūd b. Hubālah 9
Ismāʿīl b. ʿAlī b. ʿAbd Allāh 58
Ismāʿīl b. Habbār 75

al-Jaʿd b. al-Shammākh 18
Jaʿdah (tr) 107
Jaʿdah bt al-Ashʿath 37n
Jadhīmah al-Abrash 1
Jadīs (tr) 3, 4
Jaʿfar b. Abī Ṭālib 30n, 95
Jaʿfar ibn al-Manṣūr 76g
Jaʿfar b. Ṣubḥ al-Tanūkhī 9
Jaʿfar b. Thaʿlabah (tr) 100
Jafnah, Jafnids 9n, 15n, 21n, 89
Jamr (tr) 89n
Janāḥ b. ʿUbayd Allāh 116
Janūb 102n
Jarīr b. ʿAṭiyyah 9n, 32n, 121n
Jarīr b. Yazīd 63
Jarm b. ʿAmr (tr) 79
Jassās b. Murrah 10n, 11
Jazʾ b. al-Ḥārith 96, 97
Jews 22n, 23n, 24
Jibrīl b. Bukhtīshūʿ 70
Judayʿ al-Kirmānī 57, 61
Judhām (tr) 50, 99
Juhaynah (tr) 23n
al-Julās al-Anṣārī 27
Jumaḥ (tr) 105n
Jurhum 94
Jusham b. Muʿāwiyah (tr) 18, 25n, 47, 91

Kaʿb b. ʿAbd Allāh al-Namarī 21
Kaʿb b. al-Ashraf 22, 23, 92
Kaʿb b. al-Ḥārith 5
Kaʿb b. Juʿayl 39
Kaʿb b. Rabīʿah (tr) 91
Kahmas al-Saʿdī 42
Kalb (tr) 38, 79
Kalb b. Wabarah 9
Kanzah 67n
Kathīf (Kuthayf) al-Taghlibī 12
Khaḍḍam (tr) 87
Khadījah 34n
Khafājah (tr) 93, 109
Khalaf al-Miṣrī 68
Khālid b. ʿAbd al-Raḥmān b. Khālid 39n
Khālid b. Asīd 46
Khālid b. Ibrāhim 61
Khālid b. Jaʿfar 14, 94, 98
Khālid b. al-Muʿammar 36
Khālid b. Naḍlah 13, 106
Khālid b. Saʿīd 39
Khālid b. al-Walīd 39n, 95, 104
Khālid b. Yazīd b. Muʿāwiyah 39n, 45
Khālid al-Qasrī 52
al-Khansāʾ 86
Khārijah b. Ḥudhāfah 35

Khārijites 34n, 40, 41, 42, 46, 47n, 49, 56, 64n
Khashram 110
Khath'am (tr) 30n, 88, 93, 103, 109, 116
Khawlī b. Sahlah 89
Khawta'ah 12n
Khāzim b. Khuzaymah 60
Khāzim al-Fahmī 97n
al-Khazraj (tr) 15, 22n, 23, 24n, 95, 120
al-Khims al-Taghlibī 94
Khindif (tr) 20
Khulayd 'Aynayn al-'Abdī 38
Khunays (tr) 96
Khunuk Khātūn 38
Khusraw 113n
Khusraw Parwīz 19n
Khuzā'ah (tr) 6n, 25n, 26, 109n
Khuzā'i b. Aswad 23
Khuzaymah b. Lu'ayy 87n
Kilāb (tr) 14, 91, 103n, 109, 121n
Kinānah b. Khuzaymah (tr) 6, 20n, 44n, 76b, 96n, 99n
Kinānah b. al-Ḥārith (tr) 96
Kindah (tr) 43n, 76b, 113n
Kisrā 19, 113n
Kulayb b. Rabī'ah 10n, 11
Kulayb b. Yarbū' (tr) 41
al-Kumayt b. Tha'labah 31
al-Kumayt b. Zayd 64
Kuntus 6n
Kurayz (tr) 52
Kuthayf *see* Kathīf

La'aqat al-Dam 11n, 26n
Labaṭah b. al-Farazdaq 52
Lakhī'ah *see* Lakhnī'ah
Lakhm, Lakhmids 13, 19n, 21n, 50, 89
Lakhnī'ah Yanūf 2, 16
Lāwudh, Lāwadh 3n
Laylā l-Akhyaliyyah 109n
Layth (tr) 44
Lūdh (Lud) 3n
Lukhay'ah *see* Lakhnī'ah

Mā' al-Samā' 21n
Ma'add (tr) 21n, 113
Ma'bad b. Akhḍar 41
Madhḥij (tr) 8n, 28n, 33n, 58n, 77n, 106n, 109n, 113
Ma'dī Karib 17n
Ma'dīkarib b. al-Ḥārith 76b
Ma'dīkarib b. Qays *see* al-Ash'ath b. Qays
Mafrūq b. 'Amr al-Aṣamm 29
al-Mahdī 65, 66n, 69n, 77
Makhzūm (tr) 26n, 39n
Mālik b. al-'Ajlān 15
Mālik b. 'Awf 91
Mālik b. Bakr *see* al-Ṣimmah al-Akbar
Mālik b. Ḥanẓalah (tr) 18n
Mālik b. al-Ḥārith al-Ashtar 33
Mālik b. al-Haytham 60
Mālik b. Kūmah 12
Mālik b. Misma' 49
Mālik b. al-Mundhir 52
Mālik b. Nuwayrah 104
Mālik b. Rāfilah *see* Ibn Zāfilah
Mālik b. al-Ṣāmit 12n
Mālik b. al-Ṣimmah 18n
Mālik b. Taym Allāh b. Tha'labah 9n
Mālik b. 'Umayr b. Wadā' 93
Mālik b. Zāfilah *see* Ibn Zāfilah
al-Ma'mūn 68, 69, 70, 71, 73, 76h, 109n
Ma'n b. Mālik b. Fahm (tr) 42n
Ma'n b. Zā'idah 64, 65
Manṣūr (?) 112
al-Manṣūr Abū Ja'far 57n, 58, 60, 62, 63, 64, 65, 66n, 69n, 74n, 76f, 77, 117
Manṣūr b. Jumhūr 54, 55
Manẓūr b. Jumhūr 55
Manẓūr b. Zabbān 112n
Maras (tr) 89
Marba' b. Wa'wa'ah 121
Mardānah 38
Marib b. Ma'dī Karib 17n
Marrār b. Anas 58
Marthad b. 'Āmir 53
Marwān b. al-Ḥakam 45, 109, 110
Marwān b. Muḥammad 54, 56, 57, 60, 117
Marwānids 51
Mas'ūd b. 'Amr 42
Mas'ūd b. Shaddād 79
Mas'ūd b. Sinān 23
Māwiyyah bt 'Awf 21n
Mawthabān *see* 'Amr b. Tubba'
Mayda'ān b. Mālik (tr) 96
Māzin (tr) 41, 83, 87
al-Mazūnī *see* al-Muhallab b. Abī Ṣufrah
Minqar (tr) 42n, 87

Mirbaʿ *see* Marbaʿ
Mirdās b. Udayyah *see* Abū Bilāl b. Udayyah
al-Miswar b. Ziyādah 110
Muʿallis (Muʿallas) 55n
Muʿāwiyah b. Abī Sufyān 1n, 15n, 26n, 33, 34, 36, 37n, 38, 39, 47n, 108n, 110, 114n
Muʿāwiyah b. ʿAmr 86n
Muʿāwiyah b. Bādirah (tr) 107
Muʿāwiyah b. Ḥujayr 9
Muʿāwiyah b. Mālik 18n
Muʿāwiyah b. al-Walīd 57
Muʿāwiyah b. Yazīd 45n
Muʿayn al-Muḥāribī 46
Muḍar (tr) 5n, 94, 106
Muḍarriṭ al-Ḥijārah *see* ʿAmr b. Hind
Mudlij (tr) 99
Mughallis 55
al-Mughīrah b. ʿAbd Allāh *see* al-Uqayshir
al-Mughīrah b. Shuʿbah 30, 46
al-Muhājirūn 24n, 104
Muhalhil b. Rabīʿah 78
al-Muhallab b. Abī Ṣufrah 42n, 47, 48n
al-Muhallab b. ʿUbaythir 62n
al-Muḥallil *see* al-Mujallil
Muḥallim (tr) 87
Muḥammad, the Prophet, the Messenger of God 6n, 18n, 22, 23, 24, 25, 27, 28, 20, 30n, 34, 50n, 51, 91, 95, 103n, 105, 113n, 120n
Muḥammad b. ʿAbd Allāh b. al-Ḥasan 59, 60, 62, 67n, 77, 117
Muḥammad b. ʿAbd Allāh b. Khāzim 43
Muḥammad b. Abī Bakr 32n
Muḥammad b. ʿAlī b. ʿAbd Allāh b. al-ʿAbbās 50, 57n
Muḥammad b. al-Ashʿath 108n
Muḥammad b. al-Ḥanafiyyah 50n
Muḥammad b. al-Ḥusayn 51
Muḥammad b. Maslamah 22
Muḥammad b. Sahl 64
Muḥārib (tr) 46
al-Mujadhdhar b. Dhiyād 27, 90n
Mujāhid b. Jabr 51
al-Mujallil b. Thaʿlabah 78
Mujammiʿ (tr) 121
Mujāshiʿ (tr) 32n
al-Mukhtār 49n
al-Mulayk *see* al-Abrad
Mulaykah bt ʿUyaynah *see* Umm al-Banīn
al-Munakhkhal al-Yashkurī 101
al-Mundalith b. Idrīs 107
al-Mundhir b. Imriʾ al-Qays 21n, 81
al-Mundhir b. al-Nuʿmān al-Gharūr 29
al-Mundhir b. al-Nuʿmān Māʾ al-Samāʾ 13, 76b, 89
al-Mundhir Dhū l-Qarnayn 21
Muʾnis al-Baṣrī 69
Muqātil (tr) 36, 94
Muqātil b. Ḥassān 36n
Murād (tr) 4, 28n, 33
Murrah (tr) 21n, 53n
Mūsā al-Hādī *see* al-Hādī
Mūsā b. Muḥammad b. ʿAlī 62n
Muṣʿab b. ʿAbd al-Raḥmān 75
Muṣʿab b. ʿAmr 116n
Muṣʿab b. ʿUbayd Allāh 116
Muṣʿab b. al-Zubayr 49n, 112, 114
Musāfiʿ b. Yarbūʿ 31n
Muslim b. ʿAqīl 103n
Musliyah (tr) 58
al-Mutajarridah 101n
al-Mutalammis 82, 89n
Mutammim b. Nuwayrah 104n, 110n
al-Muʿtaṣim 76i
al-Muṭayyabūn 26
Muwaffaq al-Ṣaqlabī 68n
Muzāḥim b. ʿAmr 116

Nabhān 80
Naḍir (tr) 22n, 23n, 24n
Naffāʿ 110n
Nāfiʿ b. al-Azraq 42, 49n
Nafīs (servant) 72
al-Nafs al-Zakiyyah *see* Muḥammad b. ʿAbd Allāh b. al-Ḥasan
Nāʾilah 1n
al-Naʿir b. al-Zammām 32
al-Najāshī 110n
Najdah b. ʿĀmir 49
al-Nakhaʿ (tr) 33n
al-Namir b. Qāsiṭ (tr) 5n, 29n
Nāshirah b. Aghwāth 10
Naṣr b. Muʿāwiyah (tr) 91
Naṣr b. Quʿayn 100, 112
Naṣr b. Sayyār 57, 61
Naṣr b. Shabath 109
Nawār 93
Nawfal b. al-Furāt 51

Nihm (tr) 17
Nufayʿ b. Kaʿb b. ʿUmayr 32
Nūḥ (Noah) 3n
al-Nuʿmān b. ʿAbd Allāh 107n
al-Nuʿmān b. Bashīr 46
al-Nuʿmān b. Jisās 106
al-Nuʿmān b. Mālik *see* al-Nuʿmān b. Jisās
al-Nuʿmān b. al-Mundhir al-Lakhmī 19, 20, 94, 97n, 101
Nuṣayb 99n

Odenathus 1n

Persians (al-ʿAjam, al-Furs) 2, 28, 30, 119

Qabīṣah b. al-Qayn 46
Qābūs ibn Hind 82
Qadīs (Qiddīs) 3
Qaḥṭabah b. Shabīb 60
Qaḥṭān (tr) 7n, 113
Qaṣīr b. Saʿd 1
Qatādah b. Jandal 53n
Qatādah b. Sābah 53
Qaṭām 34
al-Qattāl al-Kilābī 75
Qawqal (tr) 15
al-Qayn b. Jasr (tr) 95n
Qays b. ʿĀṣim 29
Qays b. Ḥanẓalah (tr) 17, 18n
Qays b. Hubayrah al-Makshūḥ 28
Qays b. al-Khaṭīm 120
Qays b. Muḥammad b. al-Ashʿath 108
Qays b. Thaʿlabah (tr) 29, 78, 82
Qays b. Zayd 27
Qays b. Zuhayr 94
Qays ʿAylān (tr) 20, 25, 46, 76b, 85n, 107n, 114
Qiddīs 3n
Quḍāʿah (tr) 9n
al-Quḥayf b. al-Ḥumayyir 107
Quraysh (tr) 12n, 22, 26, 30n, 32n, 34n, 35n, 38, 39, 49, 50, 63, 75n, 87n, 105, 108n
Qurrah b. Hubayrah 104
Qurṭ b. Bādirah (tr) 107
Qushayr (tr) 107
Qusṭanṭīn al-Rūmī 68n
Quṭbah b. Qatādah 95n
Qutham b. (al-)ʿAbbās 33

al-Rabīʿ b. Yūnus 66
Rabīʿ b. ʿUtaybah 100
Rabīʿah b. Kaʿb b. Saʿd (tr.) 40
Rabīʿah b. Mālik (tr) 121
Rabīʿah b. Nizār (tr) 5, 10n, 13, 29, 36, 42, 64, 65, 94
Rabīʿah b. Rufayʿ 91
Rabīʿah b. Thaʿlabah 86
Rabīʿah b. ʿUqayl (tr) 109n
al-Ramd (tr) 97
al-Rashīd *see* Hārūn al-Rashīd
Rawḥ b. al-Sakan 73
Rayṭah 85, 102
al-Ribāb (tr) 34, 76b, 93, 106n, 121
Rifāʿah b. Qays 25
Rifāʿah b. Thābit 55
Riyāḥ b. Yarbūʿ (tr) 18
Romans (or Byzantines, al-Rūm) 9
Rubayyiʿah b. ʿUbayd 100
Rufayʿ 110
Rufayʿ Abū l-ʿĀliyah al-Riyāḥī 38
al-Rūm 9
Rushayd b. Rumayḍ 29n

Sabaʾ (Sheba) 4n
Sābiq al-Khwārazmī 58n
Sabrah b. ʿUmayr (*or* ʿAmr) 13
Saʿd (tr) 47, 121
Saʿd b. Bakr (tr) 91
Saʿd b. Ḍabbah 8
Saʿd b. Thaʿlabah (tr) 81n
Saʿd b. Zayd Manāh (tr) 106
Saʿd Tamīm (tr) 93
Sadūs (tr) 36
al-Saffāḥ Abū l-ʿAbbās 57n, 58, 60, 62, 63, 74n, 77, 117
Ṣafiyyah bt ʿAbd al-Muṭṭalib 32n
Sahm (tr) 34n
Saʿīd b. al-ʿĀṣ 110
Saʿīd b. Ṣaylam 73
Saʿīd b. ʿUthmān b. ʿAffān 38
Saʿīd b. Zayd b. ʿAmr 32
al-Sakāsik (tr) 48n
Ṣakhr b. ʿAmr *see* Ṣakhr b. al-Sharīd
Ṣakhr b. al-Sharīd 86
Saksak b. Ashras (tr) 48n
Salamah b. al-Ḥārith 76b
Salamah b. Qushayr (tr) 107
Salamah b. Samurah 107n

Salāmān b. Mufrij 97
al-Salīl b. Thawr 109
Sālim b. Dārah 31, 111
Sālim b. Ru'aybah 31n
Salimah (tr) 23n
Salīṭ b. ʿAbd Allāh b. al-ʿAbbās 63
Sallām b. Abī l-Ḥuqayq *see* Ibn Abī l-Ḥuqayq
Sallām b. Mishkam 24
Salmā 86
Salūl (tr) 83, 116
Sām (Shem) 3n
al-Samaw'al 14n
Sammāl b. ʿAwf (tr) 91
Ṣarīm b. Yarbūʿ (tr) 42n, 47n
Sāriyah b. ʿUwaymir 109
Ṣaʿṣaʿah b. Ḥarb 47n
Ṣaʿṣaʿah b. Muʿāwiyah (tr) 83
Sassanids 19n, 113n
Sawwār b. Ḥayyān 42
Ṣayfī b. Saba' al-Aṣghar (tr) 7
Ṣayyād al-Fawāris *see* ʿUtaybah b. al-Ḥārith
Sayyār (tr) 121
"The Scented Ones" *see* al-Muṭayyabūn
Shabīb b. Bajarah (*or* Bujrah) 34
Shabīb b. Wāj 63
Shabīb b. Yazīd al-Shaybānī 46
Shākir (tr) 17
al-Shammākh al-Yamāmī (*or* al-Yamanī) 67n
Shammās b. Dithār 43
al-Shamūs ʿUfayrah *see* ʿUfayrah
al-Shanfarā 1n, 88n, 93n, 97
Sharāḥīl al-Shaybānī 87
Sharīk b. ʿAmr (tr) 53
Shaybān (tr) 21n, 29n, 36n, 49n, 64n
Shaybān b. ʿAbd Shams 40
Shibl b. ʿAbd Allāh 117n
Shibl b. Qilādah *see* Shubayl b. Qilādah
Shihāb b. al-ʿAyyif 21n
Shubayl b. Qilādah 93
Shuraḥbīl 87n
Shuraḥbīl b. al-Ḥārith 76b
Shuraḥbīl Dhū l-Jawsahn *see* Dhū l-Jawshan al-Kilābī
Shurayḥ b. Ḍubayʿah *see* al-Ḥuṭam
Silkān b. Salāmah 22
Simʿān b. Hubayrah *see* Abū Sammāl
al-Ṣimmah al-Akbar 18
al-Ṣimmah b. ʿAbd Allāh 107n
Solomon (Sulaymān) 7n
Suʿayd b. Ḍabbah 8
Subayʿ (tr) 121
Ṣubḥ b. al-Ḥārith b. ʿAmr 9n
Ṣubḥ b. Yazīd b. ʿUmar 60
Sudayf b. Maymūn 117
Ṣudayy b. Mālik b. Ḥanẓalah (tr) 18n
Sufyān the astrologer 48
Suḥaym *see* ʿAbd Banī l-Ḥasḥās
Suḥaym b. Wathīl 32n
al-Sulakah 88
(al-)Sulayk b. (al-)Sulakah 88, 93
Sulaym (tr) 75n, 86n, 91, 107
Sulaymā *see* Salmā
Sulaymah (tr) 21n
Sulaymān *see* Solomon
Sulaymān b. ʿAbd al-Malik 48, 50
Sulaymān b. ʿAlī b. ʿAbd Allāh 62
Sulaymān b. Hishām 117
Sulaymān b. Jarīr 67n
Sulaymān b. al-Muhājir 58
al-Ṣumayl b. al-Aʿwar 103
Suwayd b. (al-)Ṣāmit 27n, 90

Ta'abbaṭa Sharrā (*or* Sharran) 85, 97n
al-Tabābiʿah *see* Tubbaʿs
Taghlib b. Wā'il (tr) 10n, 12, 29n, 76b, 78n
Ṭāhir b. al-Ḥusayn 76hn
Ṭalḥah b. ʿUbayd Allāh 32n
Tamīm (tr) 13, 18, 32n, 34n, 42, 43, 46, 60, 87n, 104, 121n
Tamīm b. al-Akhtam 112
Ṭarafah b. al-ʿAbd 82, 89n
Ṭarīf b. Tammīm 87
Ṭārifah 110
Ṭasm (tr) 3, 4
Ṭathr (tr) 107n
Tawbah b. al-Ḥumayyir 107n, 109
al-Ṭayfūrī *see* ʿAbd Allāh al-Ṭayfūrī
Taym b. ʿAbd Manāf (tr.) 34n, 93, 108n
Taym Allāh b. Mubashshir (tr) 116
Taym Allāh b. Thaʿlabah (tr) 49
Taym Allāh al-Najjār (tr) 120n
Taym al-Ribāb (tr) 106
Ṭayyi' (tr) 3, 4, 22n, 70n, 80, 102n
Thābit b. Jābir *see* Ta'abbaṭa Sharrā
Thābit b. Rāfiʿ 31n
Thaʿlabah al-Fātik 9
Thaʿlabah b. Ḥaṣabah 18

Tha'labah b. Yarbū' (tr) 100n, 104n
Thaqīf (tr) 30n, 91, 113
Thawr b. Abī Sim'ān 109
Tubba's 2
Ṭufayl al-Ghanawī 102n
Ṭuhayyah (tr) 87, 121

'Ubādah b. Mujīb (*or* Muḥabbab) *see* al-Qattāl al-Kilābī
'Ubayd Allāh b. (al-)'Abbās b. Abī Ṭālib 33
'Ubayd Allāh b. al-'Abbās al-Sulamī 114
'Ubayd Allāh b. al-Ḥārith 114n
'Ubayd Allāh b. al-Ḥasan 73
'Ubayd Allāh b. al-Ḥurr al-Ju'fī 44, 114, 115
'Ubayd Allāh b. Qays *see* Ibn Qays al-Ruqayyāt
'Ubayd Allāh b. Ziyād 40, 42, 44, 46
'Ubayd Allāh b. Ziyād b. Ẓabyān 49
'Ubaydah b. al-Ḥārith 32n
'Ubaydah b. Hilāl 41n
al-Ubayrid al-Ghassānī *see* al-Abrad
Ubayy b. Zayd 19n
Udhaynah 1n
'Udhrah (tr) 3n, 110
'Ufayrah 3
Umāmah 5
'Umar b. 'Abd al-'Azīz 51, 55n
'Umar b. al-Khaṭṭāb 26n, 30, 34n, 104
'Umar b. Laja' 64n
'Umar b. Yazīd b. 'Umayr 52
Umaymah 110
'Umayr b. Isḥāq 37
'Umayr b. Yathribī 88n
'Umayr al-Sa'dī 88
Umayyads 45n, 46n, 51, 57n, 77
Umayyah 38n
Umayyah b. 'Abd Allāh b. Khālid 47
Umayyah b. Abī l-Ṣalt 113n
Umm Abān 116
Umm 'Abd Allāh bt al-Walīd 38
Umm al-Banīn bt 'Abd al-'Azīz 119
Umm al-Banīn bt al-Ḥakam 51, 76d
Umm al-Banīn bt 'Uyaynah 31
Umm Bawza' 110
Umm Dīnār 31
Umm Julayḥah 102
Umm Kulthūm bt 'Alī 34
Umm Kulthūm bt Muḥammad 34n
Umm Tamīm 104
'Umlūq 3n
'Uqaybah b. Hubayrah 112
'Uqayl (tr) 93, 107
al-Uqayshir 108
'Uqbah b. Salm 65
'Urwah al-Raḥḥāl b. 'Utbah 20
Usāmah b. Lu'ayy 4
Usayd (Asīd) b. Jābir 97
Usayyid (tr) 87
Usayyid (Asīd) b. 'Amr 52n
'Uṭārid (tr) 43
'Utaybah b. al-Ḥārith 100
'Uthmān b. 'Affān 1n, 18n, 28n, 30n, 31, 32n, 33, 38, 49n
'Uthmān b. Juday' 61
'Uthmān b. Nahīk 63
'Uyaynah b. Ḥiṣn 31, 103

Wabar(ah) b. Yuḥannis 28n
Waḍḍāḥ al-Yaman 119
Wāhib b. al-Ḥārith 96
Wahriz 28n, 119
Wā'ilah (tr) 83
al-Walīd b. 'Abd al-Malik 48, 57n, 119
al-Walīd b. Mu'āwiyah 57n
al-Walīd b. al-Mughīrah 26, 38n
al-Walīd b. Sa'd 58n
al-Walīd b. Sa'īd 58
al-Walīd b. 'Utbah 45n
al-Walīd b. Yazīd 76e, 107n
Waqdān (tr) 121
Wazar b. Jābir 80
Wizr b. Jābir 80n

Yaḥyā b. Mu'ādh 73
Yalammaqah bt Ilīsharaḥ 7n
(al-)Yaman (tr) 42, 55, 64, 65n, 94n, 107n, 114n
Yaqṭīn b. Mūsā 63
Ya'qūb al-Dawraqī 37
Yaqẓān 53
Yarbū' (tr) 100
Yashkur (tr) 10n, 101n
Yazīd b. 'Abd Allāh b. Yazīd *see* Abū Muḥammad al-Sufyānī
Yazīd b. 'Abd al-Malik 51n
Yazīd b. Abī Kabshah 48
Yazīd b. Abī Muslim Dīnār 48
Yazīd b. Abī Sufyān 26

Yazīd b. Ḥamal 107
Yazīd b. al-Ḥuṣayn b. Numayr 48
Yazīd b. Jamal *see* Yazīd b. Ḥamal
Yazīd b. Muʿāwiyah b. ʿAbd Allāh 59
Yazīd b. Muʿāwiyah b. Abī Sufyān 38, 39, 42
Yazīd b. al-Muhallab 48
Yazīd b. Ruwaybah 109
Yazīd b. al-Ṣimmah *see* Yazīd b. al-Ṭathriyyah
Yazīd b. al-Ṭathriyyah 107
Yazīd b. ʿUmar b. Hubayrah 56, 59, 60
Yazīd b. al-Walīd 76e
Yuḥannis b. Wabarah 28
Yūsuf b. ʿUmar b. Hubayrah 56

al-Zabbāʾ 1
al-Zabbān al-Dhuhlī 12
al-Zabībah 1n
Zād(h)awayh 34n
Ẓālim al-ʿĀmirī 97n
Zarqāʾ al-Yamāmah 4n
Zayd b. Ḥārithah 95
Zayd b. Marib 17
Zaynab 1n
Zaynab bt ʿAlī *see* Umm Kulthūm bt ʿAlī
Zaynab bt al-Ḥārith 24
Zenobia 1n
Zirr b. Jābir 80n
Ziyād b. Abīh 38, 46, 113n
Ziyād b. ʿUbayd Allāh 77
Ziyādah b. Zayd b. Mālik 110, 116n
Zopyrus 1n
Zubayd (tr) 28n
al-Zubaybah 1
al-Zubayr b. al-ʿAwwām 32, 49n, 76cn
Zuhayr b. ʿAbd Shams 7
Zuhayr b. Jadhīmah 14
Zuhayr b. Janāb 9
Zuhrah (tr) 30n, 75n
Zumayl b. ʿAnd Manāf 31n
Zumayl b. Wubayr 31
Zurʿah *see* Dhū Nuwās

Geographical Index

Abīdah 97
al-ʿAblāʾ 116
Afīḥ 109n
Afghanistan 47n
Afyaḥ 109
al-Ahwāz 41
Ajaʾ 3n
Aleppo 21n
al-Amarah 89
Amman 50n
ʿAmmūriyah (Amorium) 76i
al-Anbār 1, 63
Ankara 76in
the Arch of Kisrā (Khosraw) 113
ʿArim 4
Arūm 75
Ashbāʿ 31
Awṭās 91
ʿAyn al-Tamr 1, 36n

Badr 105
Baghdad 1n, 59n, 65n, 69n, 113n
al-Baḥrayn 29, 65, 82
Balkh 38, 47, 61n
al-Balqāʾ 57
al-Bandanījayn 113
(al-)Baqqah 1
the Barrier *see* al-Sudd
Basra 32n, 33, 42, 49n, 52n, 62
(al-)Bawn 17
Bint Haydah *see* Haydah's Daughter
Bostra *see* Buṣrā
Bukhara 28
Burqat Ḥārib 9
Buṣrā 39
al-Buṭāḥ 104
Buzākhah 104

Carmania *see* Kirmān
Carrhae *see* Ḥarrān
City of Peace *see* Baghdad
Cows' Horns 109
Ctesiphon 59n, 113n

al-Dāʾah 31
al-Dahnāʾ 75

Damascus 9n, 38n, 39n, 48n, 50n, 57, 110n
Daylam 28n
Dayr Dāwūd 9n
Dhū l-Majāz 26
Dhū l-Masrūḥ 99
Dijlah *see* Tigris
Dimashq *see* Damascus

Egypt 35, 60n
Euphrates 1

Fakhkh 67
Fakhkhah 93
al-Falaj 107n
Fārs 58, 59, 61n
al-Farz 103
al-Farzah 103n
Filasṭīn *see* Palestine
al-Furāt *see* Euphrates
Furḍat Nuʿm *see* Nuʿm's Ford

al-Ghawr 19
al-Ghūṭah 38n

al-Ḥabīl (?) 13
Ḥabnāʾ 99
Hadramawt 113n
Hajar 38n
Ḥajar (Ḥajr, Ḥujr) al-Rāshidah 109
Hamadhān 71n
Harāt *see* Herat
al-Ḥarbiyyah 69
Ḥārib 9n
Ḥarīz 109
Ḥarrān 56
Ḥarūrāʾ 47n
Hawiyy 109
Ḥawrān 9n
Haydah's Daughter 109
Herat 43, 59
Hijaz 3, 33, 60, 75n, 110n, 116n
Ḥimṣ *see* Homs
al-Ḥīrah 1, 13n, 19, 21n, 36n, 76b, 82, 89n, 94n, 97n, 101n, 108
Hīt 1
Homs 39, 48n

al-Ḥubayl 13n
al-Ḥudaybāʾ 89
Ḥulwān 59
al-Ḥumaymah 50, 57
Ḥunayn 91n
Ḥushsh Banī Zuhrah 75n

Iḍam 110
Ifrīqiy(y)ah 67
Iram 3n
Iraq 1, 38, 48, 51, 56, 59, 60, 113n
ʿĪsābādh 65n
Isfahan 59
Iṣṭakhr 59
Īwān Kisrā *see* Arch of Kisrā

al-Jarīb 20
al-Jawf 4
Jaww 4
al-Jāzir 44
al-Jazīrah 1, 60n
al-Jibāl 58, 59
Jordan 50n, 57
al-Jubayl 13n
al-Juḥfah 99
Jurayr 109n
Juwāthā 29

Kāfir 82
Karbala 37n
Karmān *see* Kirmān
Khabt al-ʿAlam 110
Khaffān 40
Khafiyyah 1
Khaww 100n
Khaybar 23n, 24n
al-Khāzir 44n
Khorasan 2n, 36, 38, 43n, 47, 55, 57, 58, 59, 60n, 61, 63, 69, 77n, 108n
Khurāsān *see* Khorasan
Kirmān 57n
Klysma *see* al-Qulzum
Kudād 50, 57
Kufa 1n, 13n, 19n, 34, 36, 40n, 46, 52n, 56, 58n, 59, 64, 108
al-Kulāb 106
al-Kunāsah 58

Liwāʾ Ṭufayl 6n

Mā Warāʾ al-Nahr *see* Transoxania
al-Madāʾin 44n, 59, 63
al-Madīnah *see* Medina
Madīnat al-Salām *see* Baghdad
Maghbiṭ al-Juḥfah 99
al-Maghrib 67
Makkah *see* Mecca
Malḥūb 81
Maʾrib 4n
al-Marmāʾ 89
Marj al-Ṣuffar 9n
Marw 38, 43, 47, 70n
Marwarrūdh 63n
Masrūḥ 99n
Mazūn 42n
Mecca 18n, 22, 26, 30, 31n, 34n, 67, 77, 87n, 91n, 94, 99n, 109n, 117n, 120n
Medina 22n, 23n, 27n, 29, 30, 31, 38, 50n, 62, 66n, 76c, 77, 95n, 99n, 110, 116n, 118n, 120 (*see also* Yathrib)
Meknes 67n
Miṣr *see* Egypt
Morocco 67n
Mubārak Canal 52
Mughbaṭ al-Juḥfah *see* Maghbiṭ al-Juḥfah
Mūsābād 71
Mūsayābādh 71n
Muʾtah 95

Nahr al-Mubārak *see* Mubārak Canal
Najaf 1n
Najd *see* Nejd
Najrān 16
al-Nahrawān 34
al-Nāṣif 97
Nejd 20n, 75n
al-Nujayr 113
Nuʿm's Ford (Furḍat Nuʿm) 2

Oman 29, 42n

Palestine 50
Persepolis 59n

Qaṣr (Banī) Muqātil 36
Qinnasrīn 21n
Qūbāʾ (Qawbāʾ) 109n
al-Qulzum 33
Qurūn Baqar *see* Cows' Horns

al-Quṣaybāt 10n
Quṭquṭānah 1, 36n

al-Rad'h 83
Rakhmān 85
al-Raqam 9
al-Raqqah 74
al-Rayy 77
Rūm 63
Rūmah (Rome or Byzantium?) 2
al-Rūmiyyah 63

al-Sabakhah 44
Salmā 3n
Samarqand 38, 47
Sanaa 28, 119
Sarw Lubn 109
Shābah 75
al-Shām *see* Syria *and* Damascus
Sharāf 31
al-Sharāh 50
al-Shawṭ 120
al-Shiryān 102
al-Shuqrah 31
Ṣiffīn 36n, 41n
Sijistān 47n, 59, 64
Sind 54
al-Ṣinnayn 19
Sīstān *see* Sijistān
al-Sudd 102
Suez 33n
Syria 9, 15, 36n, 48, 50n, 55, 58, 74n, 82, 89, 110

Ṭabaristān 113
Ṭāq-i Kisrā *see* Arch of Kisrā
Tathlīth 109
al-Tawfīq 99
Tehran 77n
al-Thuwayyah 13n
Tigris 1n, 34n
Tihāmah 19n
Tokharistan 61
Transoxania 39, 61
Ṭufayl *see* Wādī Ṭufayl
Ṭukhāristān *see* Tokharistan
Tunisia 67n
Ṭūs 70n

ʿUdhrah 3
Ufayḥ 109n
Uḥud 27, 105
ʿUkāẓ 18n, 20n, 26n, 87
al-Ukhayḍir 36n
ʿUmān *see* Oman
Uwārah 20

Volubilis *see* Walīlā

Wādī l-Sibāʿ 32
Wādī Ṭufayl 6
Walīlā *or* Walīlī 67n
Wāridāt 10
Wāsiṭ 52, 56, 60

Yalamlam 31
(al-)Yamāmah 3, 4n, 49, 107n, 116n
al-Yaman *see* Yemen
Yathrib (Medina) 15, 90n
Yemen 2n, 4, 16, 17n, 19n, 28, 55n, 64, 119n

Zābulistān 113
Ẓarīb 4
Zagros Mountains 58n, 59n

فهرست القوافي Index of Rhymes

أسماء الشعراء الغير المذكورين في النصّ مكتوبة بين قوسين []

القافية	البحر	عدد الأبيات	الشاعر	الفصل
ءَ				
داءَ	وافر	٣	ابنة تميم بن الأخثم	١١٢
ءِ				
الهيْجاءِ	كامل	١	أبو مارد	٨٧
بْ				
الأثلَبْ	رجز	٣	عَنْتَرة بن معاوية العَبْسيّ	٨٠
بَ				
شُعَبا	بسيط	٣	يزيد بن الطَّثْريّة	١٠٧
لُغابا	وافر	١	بِشْر بن أبي خازم الأَسَديّ	٨٣
كَسوبا	متقارب	٣ (٦)	حَرْمَلة بن عَسَلة الشَّيْبانيّ	٢١
بُ				
تُصيبُ	طويل	٤	صَخْر بن الشَّريد السُّلَميّ	٨٦
قريبُ	كامل	٢	سُحَيْم عبد بني الحَسْحاس	١١٨
مغلوبُ	بسيط	٨	رَيْطة (أو جَنوب) أخت عَمْرو ذي الكَلْب	١٠٢
ملحوبُ	بسيط	مصراع	عَبيد بن الأبرص	٨١
بِ				
الكلْبِ	طويل	١	جَزْء بن الحارث	٩٧
فارْكَبي	رجز	٤	–	٣
العَجَبِ	بسيط	٤	الأسود بن عفار	٣
حاربِ	طويل	٤	عبد العاص بن ثعلبة التَّنوخيّ	٩
فحاربِ	طويل	٣	ثعلبة الفاتك	٩

(*cont.*)

القافية	البحر	عدد الأبيات	الشاعر	الفصل
شهابِ	كامل	٢	رُبَيِّعة أبو ذؤاب	١٠٠
الكِلابِ	رجز	٧	غَضوب	١٢١
جِ				
المفرَّجِ	طويل	٨	سُحَيْم عبد بني الحَسْحاس	١١٨
حِ				
سِلاحِ	طويل	٤	أمّ مُزاحِم بن عمرو السَّلوليّ	١١٦
دْ				
الصَّمَدْ	طويل	٢	–	١٣
دَ				
وأكْيَدا	طويل	١٣	أعشى هَمْدان	١١٣
دُ				
العَهْدُ	طويل	٢	–	٣٠
يزيدُ	رجز	٣	–	٣٨
دِ				
مَرْثَدِ	طويل	٢	حُرَيث بن أَسْود بن شريك	٥٣
يُقَيَّدِ	طويل	١	هُدْبة بن خَشْرَم	١١٠
معرِّدِ	كامل	٣	عاتكة بنت زيد بن عمرو	٣٢
بمهنَّدِ	كامل	١	المتلمّس	٨٢
المُجاهدِ	رجز	٢	عليّ بن أبي طالب (؟)	٣٤
بادِ	بسيط	٧	عَمْرة بنت شدّاد	٧٩
وللمولودِ	كامل	١	أعشى هَمْدان	١١٣
الشَّهيدِ	كامل مجزوء	٢	خُلَيْد عَيْنَيْن العبْديّ	٢

(*cont.*)

القافية	البحر	عدد الأبيات	الشاعر	الفصل
رْ				
ضَرّْ	رمل	٣	هُدْبة بن خَشْرَم	١١٠
أَفِرّْ	رجز	٢	عليّ بن أبي طالب	٣٤
غِيَرْ	رجز	١٠	سوّار بن حَيّان المِنْقَريّ	٤٢
رَ				
حُرّا	رجز	٣	حُمْران بن مالك بن عبد ملك الخَثْعَميّ	١٠٣
ٱشْعَرَهْ	رجز	٦	عبد العاص بن ثعلبة التَّنوخيّ	٩
والشَّعَرَهْ	بسيط	٧	خَوْليّ بن سَهْلة الطائيّ	٨٩
آشِرَهْ	طويل	١	أمّ ناشرة بن أغواث	١٠
مُرارَهْ	كامل	٢	وهِلال بن أُمَيّة الخُزاعيّ	٦
وياسرا	طويل	٣	حُداد بن ظالم بن ذُهل بن عِجْل العَبْديّ	٩
صابرا	رجز	٥	القُحَيف بن الحُمَيِّر العُقيليّ	١٠٧
الذِّمارا	وافر	١	عمرو بن مَعْدِيكَرِب	٢٨
وزيرا		١	سليمان بن المُهاجر البَجَليّ	٥٨
رُ				
الثَّفَرُ	بسيط	٤	أَنَس بن مُدْرِك	٨٨
حَجَرُ	بسيط	٧	أَنَس بن مُدْرِك الخثعميّ	٩٣
الأَخاضرُ	طويل	٣	الفرزدق	٤١
تَخورُ	وافر	٧	طَرَفة بن العبد	٨٢
رِ				
النُّذُرِ	طويل	٤	ابن عُرْوة الكِنانيّ	٩٩
تؤمَّرِ	طويل	١	شاعر من بني سَدوس	٣٦
عامرِ	طويل	٣	الشَّنْفَرى الأَزْديّ	٩٧
الصادرِ	سريع	٢	سُحَيْم عبد بني الحَسْحاس	١١٨

(*cont.*)

القافية	البحر	عدد الأبيات	الشاعر	الفصل
هبّارِ	بسيط	٢	ابن قيْس الرُّقَيّات	٧٥
دينارِ	بسيط	٢	سالم بن دارة	٣١
سَ				
يُنْسَى	رجز	٢	أسامة بن لؤيّ	٤
سُ				
تُحَسْحَسُ	طويل	١	عبد عَمْرو بن عمّار الطائيّ	٨٩
سِ				
الدَّبِسِ	بسيط	٦	عبد عَمْرو بن عمّار الطائيّ	٨٩
جديسِ	رجز مزدوج	٣	الشَّموس عُفيرة	٣
شِ				
الخَشِي	متقارب	١	المُلَيك	٨٩
عْ				
الضَّبُع	متقارب	٢	–	٥
جَذَعْ	رجز	٤	دُرَيد بن الصِّمّة الجُشَميّ	٩١
عَ				
فأَوْجَعا	طويل	٤	هُدْبة بن خَشْرَم	١١٠
أجْمَعا	طويل	١	الكُمَيْت بن ثَعْلبة	٣١
أَمْرَعَهْ	رجز	٨	عبد العاص بن ثعلبة التَّنوخيّ	٩
نافعا	طويل	٦	نافع بن الأزرق	٤٢
عُ				
تُرفَعُ	كامل	٣	هُدْبة بن خَشْرَم	١١٠

(*cont.*)

القافية	البحر	عدد الأبيات	الشاعر	الفصل
فْ				
أَنِفْ	رمل	١	كعب بن الأشرف	٢٢
فَ				
طارفا	رجز	٦	هُدْبة بن خَشْرَم	١١٠
قِ				
المخزِّقِ	طويل	١	عُقَيْبة بن هُبَيْرة الأسديّ	١١٢
يُطِقِ	بسيط	١	حارثة بن قَيْس الكِنانيّ	٩٩
للتراقي	خفيف	٣	مهلْهِل بن رَبيعة	٧٨
كَ				
ظَنَّكا	رجز	٢	عليّ بن أبي طالب (؟)	٣٤
آتيكا	هزج	٢	عليّ بن أبي طالب	٣٤
لْ				
هَمَلْ	رجز	٣	القُحَيف بن الحُمَيِّر العُقيليّ	١٠٧
خَطِلْ	رجز	٤	هُدْبة بن خَشْرَم	١١٠
مقتولْ	رجز	٤	السُّلَيْك بن السُّلَكة	٩٣
لَ				
أهْلَه	رجز	٢	–	٣٤
جَبَلَهْ	رجز	٥	شِهاب بن العَيِّف	٢١هـ
لُ				
المنخَّلُ	طويل	١	أوْس بن حَجَر	١٠١
يفعَلُ	طويل	٣	لأُقَيْشِر	١٠٨
باطِلُهْ	طويل	٣	–	١٧

(*cont.*)

القافية	البحر	عدد الأبيات	الشاعر	الفصل
لِ				
النَّمْلِ	وافر	٧	الشَّموس عُفيرة	٣
مضلِّلِ	طويل	٢	المتلمّس	٨٢
الأوّلِ	كامل	١	زُهير بن جَناب	٩
المنخَّلِ	طويل	١	ذو الرُّمّة	١٠١
المُواصلِ	طويل	٥	عمرو بن أبي عُمارة	٩٦
بالمَغازلِ	طويل	٢	عُبَيد الله بن الحُرّ الجُعْفيّ	١١٤
عاقلِ	طويل	٣	مَرْبَع	١٢١
القِبالِ	وافر	١	عَمْرٌو ذو الكَلْب	١٠٢
الضَّلالِ	رجز	٤	غَضوب	١٢١
المُحيلِ	وافر	مصراع	الكُميت بن زيد	٦٤
مَ				
مُقْدِما	طويل	٢	الفرزدق	٤٠
أهضما	طويل	١	طَرَفة بن العبد	٨٢
ظالما	طويل	٣	هُزيلة	٣
فاطما	رجز	٤	زيادة بن زيد بن مالك	١١٠
الهائما	رجز	٥	هُدْبة بن خَشْرَم	١١٠
شامَهْ	رجز	٥	الشَّنْفَرى الأزْديّ	٩٧
مُ				
يتوسَّمُ	كامل	٥	طَريف بن تميم العَنْبَريّ	٨٧
أثامُ	وافر	٥	ابنة حارثة بن قَيْس	٩٩
وأرومُ	طويل	٣	القَتّال الكِلابيّ	٧٥
مِ				
حِلْمِ	كامل	٣	حَرْمَلة بن عَسَلة الشَّيْبانيّ	٢١هـ
يَلَمْلَمِ	طويل	٢	سالم بن دارة (؟)	٣١

(cont.)

القافية	البحر	عدد الأبيات	الشاعر	الفصل
مُسْلَمِ	طويل	٢	السُّلَيْك بن السُّلَكة	٩٣
وأعجَمِ	طويل	٣	[ابن أبي ميّاس المُراديّ]	٣٤
الأهضَمِ	رجز	٥	زيادة بن زيد بن مالك	١١٠
ولا دَمي	طويل	٢	عَنْتَرة بن معاوية العَبْسيّ	٨٠
الحُطَمِ	بسيط	١	[عبد اللّٰه بن حَذَف]	٢٩
ظالمِ	طويل	٢	قيس بن زُهير بن جَذيمة العبسيّ	٩٤
تميمِ	كامل	٣	ابنة تميم بن الأَخثم	١١٢
نْ				
بالإيوانْ	رجز	١٦	أعشى هَمْدان	١١٣
برَخْمانْ	رجز	٣	رَيْطة أخت تأبّط شرًّا [أو أمّه]	
نَ				
هَجانا	وافر	١	زيادة بن زيد بن مالك	١١٠
عِنانا	وافر	٢	هُدْبة بن خَشْرَم	١١٠
أجمعِينا	وافر	٤	عبد اللّٰه بن حَذَف العامريّ	٢٩
مَضِنَّهْ	رجز	٤	أخت حُمْران بن مالك	١٠٣
نِ				
عيْنِ	وافر	٢	ذو رُعين	٢
ومكاني	طويل	٤	صَخْر بن الشَّريد السُّلَميّ	٨٦
بالإحسانِ	خفيف	٣	–	٥٥
يدْعوني	بسيط	١	عوْف (ابن عمّ مالك بن عُمير)	٩٣
هَـ				
فتاها	وافر	٤	كعب بن جُعَيل التَّغْلِبيّ	٣٩
بِواديها	بسيط	٣	رَيْطة (أو جَنوب) أخت عَمْرو ذي الكَلْب	١٠٢
يَنْمِيها	بسيط	١١	مُزاحِم بن عمرو السَّلوليّ	١١٦

(*cont.*)

القافية	البحر	عدد الأبيات	الشاعر	الفصل
يَ				
حِنِّيّا	رجز	٣	رجل من بني ضَرَس من جُرْهُم	٩٤
لِسانِيا	طويل	٣	عبد يَغُوث بن وقّاص بن صَلاءة الحارثيّ	١٠٦

www.ingramcontent.com/pod-product-compliance
Lightning Source LLC
Chambersburg PA
CBHW071143100726
47908CB00002B/238
9789004759046